Going Places

GOING PLACES

The Guide to Travel Guides

Greg Hayes and Joan Wright

The Harvard Common Press
Harvard and Boston
Massachusetts

Printed in the United States of America.

Library of Congress Cataloging in Publication Data
Hayes, Gregory.
    Going places : the guide to travel guides / Greg Hayes and
Joan Wright.
    p. cm.
    Includes index.
    ISBN 1-558-32007-5 : $26.95. ISBN 1-558-32003-2 (pbk.) :
$17.95
    1. Voyages and travels—1981—Guide-books—Bibliography.
    2. Bibliography—Best books—Voyages and travels—1981—
Guide
-books. I. Wright, Joan. II. Title.
    Z6011.H37 1988
    [G153.4]
    016.910′2′02—dc19   88-21205   CIP

Text design by Joyce C. Weston

10 9 8 7 6 5 4 3 2 1

Acknowledgments

We would like to express our sincere thanks to the following: Dianne Deadrich-Rogers, Librarian of the Alpine County Public Library in Markleeville, California, who proved to us again and again that, in this day and age, the smallest library can locate almost anything; Rochelle Jaffe of Travel Books Unlimited in Bethesda, Maryland, who remained ever cheerful and helpful in fielding endless questions over the many months of this project; Joan Marsden and her helpful staff, Anne Krichner and Steve Smith, of Wide World Books & Maps in Seattle, Washington, for enduring a record number of visits to their fine store; and to Anne Brunsell and Larry Prast of Travel Market in San Francisco, Pat Carrier and his staff at Globe Corner Bookstore in Boston, Harriet Greenberg and Murray Herman of The Complete Traveller in New York City, Candace Olmstead, Jane Grossman, Helen Pounds, and Martin Rapp of The Traveller's Bookstore in New York City, Matthew Elkins of Easy Going in Berkeley, California, and Emily Hexter and Ellen Pierce of Book Passage in Corte Madera, California, for their graciousness in allowing us to use their stores as an information resource and for their helpful comments and assistance during our visits. We would also like to thank Liz Johnson of Cobble & Mickle Books in San Diego, California, for her enthusiastic support since the early days of our first self-published work and for her assistance in assembling our travel bookstore appendix. And another thank you to Greg Renker, whose eagle eye helped us locate dozens of last minute titles. Last but not least, a big thank you to the hundreds of publishers who were kind enough to submit thousands of review copies for our use. Their cooperation was almost always beyond our expectations and proved invaluable in helping us complete this project in a reasonable amount of time. We would like to acknowledge several individuals working in various publisher's promotion or publicity departments for their exceptional cooperation and helpfulness: Katy O'Malley of The Globe Pequot Press, Roslyn Bullas of Wilderness Press, Gail Cassel of Passport Books/ National Textbook Co., and Melanie Wilson of Salem House. It is only with the continued cooperation of many individuals that an effort such as ours comes to fruition. All have played a vital part and for this we say again, "thank you!"

To librarians and travel bookstore personnel—some of the nicest, most helpful people in the world.

GH

To travelers through life and around the world.

JW

Contents

Note: The Contents generally includes only those nations and other political entities for which there are specific travel titles. There are a few exceptions to this rule, which have been included for clarity. Otherwise, nations and other political entities that are included only in books covering larger geographical areas are listed alphabetically in the Geographical Index.

World Map x

Introduction xiii

How to Use This Book xvii

Series Reviews 1
(Reviews of Travel Guide
  Series)

General Travel Books 71

The World 83

Africa 96
Africa as a Whole 96
Regions of Africa 97
  Central Africa 97
  Eastern Africa 98
  Northern Africa 98
  Southern Africa 99
  Western Africa 99
Countries of Africa 100
  Egypt 100
  Islands of the Western Indian
    Ocean 102
  Kenya 103
  Morocco 104

South Africa 105
Sudan 106
Tunisia 106

Antarctica 107

Asia 108
Asia as a Whole 108
Regions of Asia 110
  The Middle East 111
  Southeast Asia 112
Countries of Asia 113
  Bangladesh 113
  Bahrain 114
  Bhutan 114
  Brunei 114
  Burma 114
  China 115
  Hong Kong 120
  India 123
  Indonesia 126
  Iran 127
  Israel 127
  Japan 131
  Jordan 138
  Macau 139

Malaysia   140
Nepal   141
North Korea   143
Northern Yemen   143
Oman   144
Pakistan   144
Papua New Guinea   144
Philippines   145
Qatar   145
Saudi Arabia   146
Singapore   146
South Korea   147
Southern Yemen   150
Sri Lanka   150
Syria   152
Taiwan   152
Thailand   153
Turkey   156
United Arab Emirates   158

Australia   160

Central America   166
Central America as a
   Whole   166
Countries of Central
   America   167
   Belize   167
   Costa Rica   168
   Guatemala   169
   Honduras   170
   Panama   170

Europe   171
Europe as a Whole   171
Regions of Europe   195
   Eastern Europe   195
   Scandinavia   195
Countries of Europe   197
   Albania   197
   Andorra   197
   Austria   198
   Belgium   201
   Bulgaria   203
   Cyprus   204
   Czechoslovakia   205

Denmark   205
East Germany   206
Finland   207
France   208
Great Britain   230
Greece   279
Hungary   285
Ireland   286
Islands of the Eastern and
   Northern Atlantic
   Ocean   293
Italy   295
Liechtenstein   306
Luxembourg   307
Malta   308
Monaco   309
Netherlands (Holland)   309
Northern Ireland   313
Norway   314
Poland   314
Portugal   315
Romania   319
Soviet Union   319
Spain   326
Sweden   333
Switzerland   334
West Germany   339
Yugoslavia   344

North America   347
North America as a Whole   347
Countries of North
   America   357
   Canada   357
   Mexico   370
   United States   381
      United States as a
         Whole   381
      Regions of the United
         States   393
      States and Federal District of
         the United States   456

Oceania   637
Oceania as a Whole   637

Countries of Oceania   638
  Cook Islands   638
  Fiji   639
  Micronesia   639
  New Zealand   640
  Tahiti and French
    Polynesia   644

South America   645
South America as a Whole   645
Countries of South America   646
  Argentina   646
  Bolivia   647
  Brazil   648
  Chile   649
  Colombia   650
  Ecuador   650
  Islands of South America   651
  Paraguay   652
  Peru   652
  Uruguay   653
  Venezuela   654

**West Indies and Bermuda
(including the Caribbean and
Bahamas)   655**
Regions of the West Indies   655
  The Caribbean   655
  French West Indies   659
  Leeward Islands and
    Windward Islands   660
Countries of the West
  Indies   660
  Aruba   660
  Bahamas   661
  Barbados   663
  Bermuda 664
  Bonaire   665
  Cayman Islands   665
  Cuba   666
  Curacao   666
  Dominican Republic   666
  Haiti   667
  Jamaica   667
  Puerto Rico   668
  St. Martin/Sint Maarten   670

  Trinidad and Tobago   670
  Virgin Islands   670

Appendixes   672
  Phrase Books   672
  Travel Bookstores and Mail
    Order   675
  Travel Book Publishers   683
  Travel Newsletters and
    Magazines   714

Subject Index   737
Geographical Index   767
**Form for Reader's Suggestions
and Comments   773**

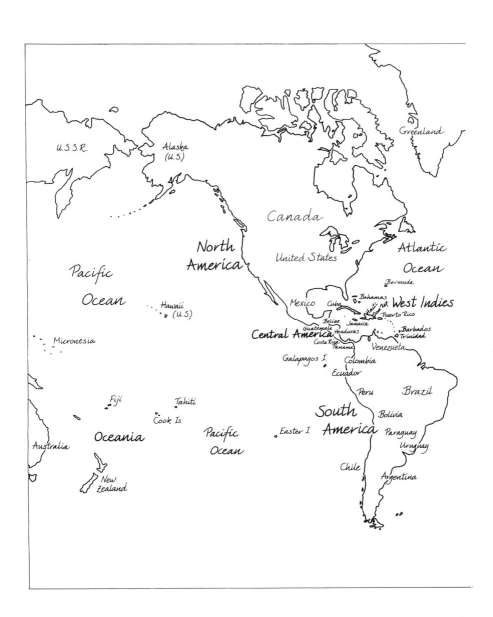

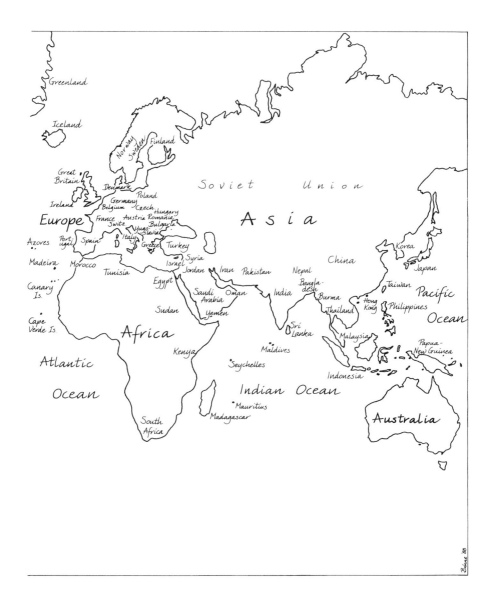

Introduction

The right travel guide can make or break a vacation. Yet only the largest bookstores can afford to stock more than a hopelessly inadequate number of the myriad travel guides available. As a result, few travelers have even a clue as to the existence of the interesting, well-written titles awaiting them. We certainly didn't. Then, somewhere along the way, a friend introduced something entirely unknown to us, the *travel* bookstore.

When we had the opportunity to visit the nearest travel bookstore, we were simply overwhelmed. There were so many books! If only we had known *before* our trip to Europe. That was our first thought. Our second was that we were not alone. Many fellow travelers, people just like ourselves, were missing the boat, or book, out of ignorance.

So we decided to do something about the problem. Our first effort was to self-publish a guide to European travel guides. This small effort, done with limited resources, was well received within its tiny sphere. People found it very helpful. And, from this minor success evolved our current effort—thanks to the encouragement and unwavering support of our publisher, Bruce Shaw, of The Harvard Common Press. He had always wanted to do something like this, he said, but had never had the time. We were able to provide the time and energy needed (family turmoil and strife not withstanding) to complete such a voluminous project.

Our goal has been, and is, to provide a comprehensive, though certainly not exhaustive, summary of the better travel guides available, so that the prospective traveler can become aware of the many options. We have reviewed hundreds of titles not included in the pages that follow, each eliminated because it did not measure up for one reason or another. Others have not been included for lack of a reliable source to the American reader or because current changes within the publishing company left long-term availability uncertain at the time.

While we have eliminated some titles, we have tried not to be too selective in our included choices. Since we acknowledge the truth of the adage that "one man's ceiling is another man's floor," we have included many titles that would not be our personal first choices. The final decision is left to the traveler. To this end, we have included not only the necessary bibliographic information, but a descriptive review as well. Of course, given the large number of titles, we were limited in the space we could dedicate to each book. To mitigate this problem, we have reviewed each series of travel guides collectively, whenever their similar format and content allowed us to do so, while still including specific bibliographic information under the appropriate geographic headings. Where we felt it was particularly important, we have also made additional comments on specific titles within a series. This space-saving format is not ideal; it would certainly be best to review each guidebook separately, but the space needed would be prohibitive and would severely limit the number of books we could include. We have opted instead to make available a broader range of titles while still including useful reviews. Whatever the limitations, the facts provided will substantially increase any traveler's knowledge of the travel literature currently in print.

We should take a moment to point out that we have concentrated on travel *guides*, rather than purely background travel books such as novels or journals. This is not to denigrate the classic travel titles by Twain, James, and Cooper, nor more recent works such as Mary McCarthy's *The Stones of Florence*, Golding's *An Egyptian Journal*, Jan Morris' *Journeys*, Kate Simon's *A Renaissance Tapestry*, and Bill Barich's essays in *Traveling Light*. There is already a fine book available which covers novels, history books, and other background reading—both in print and out-of-print—related to travel. This is Maggy Simony's *The Traveler's Reading Guide* which is reviewed in our General Travel section. While there is a bit of overlap in the materials covered by Simony and ourselves, we think travelers will find the two books complementary.

The word "guide" has been interpreted broadly to include all sorts of specialty books on planning, hiking, cycling, walks, canoeing, boating, health, photography, etc. There are limits, however, on how many topics we could adequately address in a single book. For example, popular subjects such as fishing and hunting have proven simply too large—they deserve a book of their own (a project we leave to some other industrious soul).

We hope our efforts will provide all sorts of wonderful ideas. We also hope they will stimulate many intelligently formed questions, which we encourage travelers to direct to the knowledgeable and helpful people at the nearest travel bookstore or the staff specializing in travel at some of the better general bookstores (see our Travel Bookstore appendix). Visit them. If they are too far away, call them. They are experts in the field and will be able to provide any additional needed details. They are an invaluable resource—use them. Even if they don't have the particular title, they can usually obtain a single copy. Most bookstores and publishers participate in a system that allows them to purchase a single copy of a particular title at their normal discount. If they cannot and the book must be purchased at the full retail cost, they will, of course, ask the traveler to order the book directly. To help with this, we have assembled the names, addresses, and phone numbers of the more than 400 publishers referenced in our book (see the Travel Book Publishers appendix).

This is hardly the kind of book that anyone reads from cover to cover. Nevertheless, we think travelers will find it fun to browse through the sections of interest. However, we do encourage the reading of the "How to Use This Book" section below first. It will make our methodology clearer, allowing travelers to make better use of the resources we have provided.

We have tried to list the most current edition of each travel guide available. Where we have had the information, we have even listed editions not yet released. And we have noted which titles are updated annually or biennially. Each new edition will, of course, probably be a little bit bigger and slightly more expensive. If you find it necessary to order a book on your own, please bear this in mind.

The world of travel guides is a dynamic field. New books are appearing in an ever-increasing stream and frequent updating is crucial for some time-dated travel topics. This means that there will be titles in our book, if not updated, that may no longer be available. Others may appear in a new edition, undoubtedly costing a little more, and some, in their new editions, may even cover additional subjects or geographic areas or entirely change their format. The only thing that is certain is that each guidebook will probably not cost any less. Regardless, the vast majority of the guidebooks listed will remain in print, in one edition or another, for some time to come. Despite inevitable changes, our book will prove useful.

Finally, we would like to ask the help of our readers. If you have comments, criticisms, or suggestions, if you think we have inadvertently left out your favorite travel book, or if you have tried one of our suggestions and been disappointed, please let us know. We have tried to listen carefully to the many travel industry people we have worked with on this project and to the comments they have collected from the travelers who have used these guidebooks. We have also used many of the books ourselves. But, obviously, no one person can use and evaluate so many titles firsthand. If you will offer your comments on the guidebooks you know well (there is a form for this purpose at the back of the book), our future editions will be even more informative.

How to Use This Book

First of all, take a good look at the Contents and the way in which we have arranged the nations (and other political entities) of the world. Occasionally, nations may be listed in a different manner than you might have arranged them. There are some grey zones when it comes to world geography. Familiarity will help. If a particular country still eludes you, turn to the Geographical Index. (Note that, with some exceptions, nations and other political entities for which there are no specific titles, which are covered only in guides to larger regional areas, will be listed *only* in the Geographical Index.)

Secondly, familiarize yourself with the Series Reviews section immediately following these introductory remarks. The many titles in our book that belong to one travel guide series or another will reference this section again and again (for our purposes, a series is defined as three or more titles that are similar in format and content). After each series review, all the titles in that series are summarized. The Series Reviews section is one way to discover particular books of interest.

You need not, however, discover the titles you want through the series reviews. Instead you can concentrate directly on the geographic area of interest. In doing so, be sure to note the additional listings you should also review, which are listed directly under the primary heading. Your place of interest is probably also part of titles covering even broader regions such as Europe, North America, the United States (not to mention the World), so leave no stone unturned.

Some comments on organization: we have struggled with the way in which we could organize this large body of books. Some books do not fit cleanly into one geographic designation or another. Others have titles which do not clearly describe the regions covered by the book. Our decisions on organization have been made with you, the reader, in mind. We have tried to place a reference to each book in each section in which you might look for it. Sometimes this necessitated listing the bibliographic information several times (although the book was actually reviewed in only one location). Here are some of the guidelines we used: If a title was clearly regional (e.g. , *Fodor's Eastern Europe* or *Best Places to Stay in the Southwest*), it was listed under that heading. However, if the title listed individual states or countries (for example, *Webster's Wine Tours: California, Oregon and Washington* or *Collier World Traveler Series: Greece and Yugoslavia*), we listed the bibliographic information under each state or country as well as, where applicable, under the appropriate region (the first example would also be listed under Pacific Northwest; since there is no European region including the countries in the second example, it would only be listed by individual country). Also, if a state or country were included in a regional title which was not part of that region by our definition, the bibliographic reference would again be repeated under that state or country as well (e.g., *Journey to the High Southwest* is listed under the Southwest, but because it includes the states of Utah and Colorado, which are part of our Rocky Mountain/Great Basin States region, the reference is included under the second region as well; if only a single state or country were located outside the region, the reference would be repeated under that specific state or country).

To what degree we needed to employ this system of double listing was a function of the size and complexity of the particular section. Most of the difficulties arose within North America and, most specifically, the United States. How many times the reference was listed was based on two goals: 1) to help you find a title you perhaps dimly remember (for example, if you knew you had seen the title, *Guide to the Recommended Country Inns of Texas*, we wanted to be sure this title was listed under Texas even though the title actually is *Guide to the Recommended Country Inns of Arizona, New Mexico, and Texas* and was listed under the Southwest region; 2) to let you know that a particular title included other geographic regions in addition to what might be inferred from the title (e.g., *The Camper's Companion to Southern Europe* includes Tunisia and Morocco so we listed the reference under these countries as well; *Where to Eat in America* includes both the United States *and* Canada, and it is reviewed under "North America as a Whole," but the reference, because of the nature of the title, is also listed under "United States as a Whole"). We hope these examples will serve to illustrate our rationale. In any case, the only person to truly suffer from the occasional double, triple, or even quadruple listings used to ensure that a title didn't "get lost" has been our poor, long-suffering (and, fortunately, thoroughly supportive) publisher who has had to deal with the fact that our manuscript grew a bit thicker for all these efforts. For you, the reader, these extra listings should only serve to help.

We should also make note of a few definitions that will be repeated throughout the text. We have made a distinction between a primary guide and a companion guide. A *primary guide* usually covers most, if not all, topics of importance to the traveler. It is important for the day-to-day, practical data, including where to eat and sleep. A *companion guide*, is really a supplement to this primary text. Generally, most guides that cover only one or a few travel topics—sightseeing, museums, art, architecture, history, literature—are companion guides. The books we most often refer to as companion guides, however, are those which fill the role of a knowledgeable, traveling companion. They provide the insights and in-depth coverage that is usually lacking in a primary, all-purpose guidebook. Each serves its role; each is important to the success of your vacation.

Another term to be defined is detail map. For our purposes, a *detail map* is a street map or those maps covering small geographic sections that offer travelers the useful detail they need to pinpoint particular locations.

If a particular subject is of interest, use the subject index. The books included in the subject index are those which focus either exclusively or predominantly on one or several subjects such as walks, cycling, museums, nature, recreation, planning, etc. Many subjects overlap. Books that include longer hikes as well as walks may be listed under "Hikes" rather than "Walks" (In European titles, we should note, the word "walks" often means what Americans call a "hike"). Or books listed under "Sightseeing" may have road maps and other information useful to those traveling by car even though they are not specifically listed under "Auto Travel." Books on "Lodging" may include "Hotels," "Inns," and "Bed and Breakfasts," and not be listed under these separate headings. As a consequence, be sure to note the various cross-references. And, as you review these lists, please note that we have not tried to include the many all-purpose titles (except those listed under "Budget Travel") that attempt to include dozens of travel topics under a single cover. Rather, our purpose is to try to assist travelers in finding books on a particular subject that will prove a useful supplement to these more traditional guidebooks.

In addition, there are several helpful appendixes. The first provides a quick summary of the major phrase book series. Of course, there are many other language aids that you will find at most travel bookstores as well as other bookstores, but we have limited our comments to the phrase book, that most helpful traveler's aid. Another appendix lists travel bookstores in the United States and Canada. Yet another is a summary of travel newsletters and magazines that are available by subscription and occasionally on the newsstand.

Once the needed titles are found, a bookstore can, as we have said, usually do the rest. If not, the books can be ordered by following the instructions that precede the Travel Book Publishers appendix. Always be aware, though, that some titles may take a number of weeks to arrive if they are not available to bookstores through local distributors, or if they must be ordered. Last minute purchases mean more restricted choices, and that often proves unfortunate, since there are many lesser-known titles from small, regional publishers that, while they take longer to order and receive, are well worth the time. The bottom line is: plan ahead.

Series Reviews
(Reviews of Travel Guide Series)

The publisher or primary distributor follows the name of each guide-book series. The primary references for each book listed are noted in parentheses. Note that when a title on New York is followed by "New York" in parentheses, this indicates that the book is focused on New York City or another region, rather than the entire state.

AA/Ordnance Survey Leisure Guides
Salem House

Each guide in this large, handsome, illustrated British series addresses its particular area in considerable depth. History and an orientation to the particular region are the first order of business, followed by an A-to-Z listing of places to visit, including Automobile Association-approved locations to stay and eat. The well-done Ordnance Survey maps provide interesting walks and driving tours.

Books currently available: *AA/Ordnance Survey Leisure Guide: Channel Islands* (England); similar titles on: *Cornwall* (England); *Devon and Exmoor* (England); *Ireland; Isle of Wight* (England); *Lake District* (England); *London* (England); *New Forest* (England); *North Yorkshire Moors* (England); *Northumbria* (England); *Peak District* (England); *Scottish Highlands* (Scotland); *South Downs* (England); *The Cotswolds* (England); *Wessex* (England); *Wye Valley and Forest of Dean* (England); *Yorkshire Dales* (England).

AA Town and City Guides
Salem House

A distinct series, but done in a format and size similar to the AA/Ordnance Survey Leisure Guides above. This time the focus is on the major cities of Britain (*sans* London). All the tourist bases are covered in good detail and include walks, sightseeing, shopping, lodging, and eating out. Each book has a full city plan and street index, and driving tours of the nearby areas.

Books currently available: *AA Town and City Guide: Cambridge* (England); similar titles on: *Dublin* (Ireland); *Edinburgh* (Scotland); *Glasgow* (Scotland); *York* (England).

AA Regional Touring Guides
Salem House

The format is simple: tours, tours, and more tours. Two facing pages provide a detail map, driving instructions, several photos, and the sightseeing highlights of the drive. At the back of each of these large-format books are dozens of excellent maps, both road maps and detailed city street maps. This series is a fine collection of driving tours.

Books currently available: *AA Touring Guide: Central England & East Anglia*; similar titles on: *North Country* (England); *Scotland; South & Southeast England; Wales; The West Country* (England).

Access Guides
Prentice Hall Press

The Access series has its ardent fans and those who find it perhaps a little too strange to use. Peruse it yourself and decide if this unique, award-winning design fits your needs. Its developer, Richard Saul Wurman, is a cartographer and graphic designer, as evidenced throughout each book. Wurman uses different colors to represent each particular category of tourist attraction. So, by color alone you can tell at a glance whether the information is on sightseeing, restaurants, or hotels. In addition, the books are designed to be used by the walker/stroller as he or she moves down the avenue. All shops, parks, points of interest, and so forth, show up in a logical color-coded pattern. The descriptions are nicely done, and there are plenty of tips, practical facts, and maps.

Books currently available: *Hawaii/Access*; similar titles on: *Las Vegas* (Nevada); *London* (England); *Los Angeles* (California); *New York* (New York); *Paris* (France); *Rome* (Italy); *San Francisco* (California); *Tokyo* (Japan); *Washington, D.C.* (District of Columbia).

Alive Guides
Alive Publications

After a hiatus of several years, the Alive series is returning in 1988. The series is written by the veteran travel authors Arnold and Harriet Greenberg, who currently pen *Frommer's South America on $30 a Day, Brazil on Your Own,* and *Israel on Your Own.* The new series was released after our deadline, but the authors indicate that, in terms of substance, each title will be a lot like the two On Your Own guides mentioned above, which are reviewed separately. A wide, outer margin will be used to list such things as the times places are open, historical facts, and other notes that might otherwise be difficult to locate as quickly. As opposed to the two On Your Own guides, however, each title in the Alive series will have plenty of maps. Additional titles will be added in 1989. One new title on the drawing board is on Caracas, Venezuela.

Books currently available: *Buenos Aires Alive* (Argentina); *Milan Alive* (Italy); *Rio Alive* (Brazil).

AMC Hiking Guides
Appalachian Mountain Club

As with other non-profit clubs who produce hiking guides, the Appalachian Mountain Club takes their responsibility seriously. The result of their careful work is a series of first-class guides to hikes for all manner of hiking enthusiasts—from the novice testing his or her legs for the first time to the advanced backpacker looking for a bigger challenge. All the information is here: trail descriptions, distances, type of terrain, maps. Each guide is a quality effort.

Books currently available: *AMC Guide to Mt. Washington* (New Hampshire); *AMC Massachusetts/Rhode Island Trail Guide; Hiking the Mountain State* (West Virginia); *Maine Mountain Guide; North Carolina Hiking Trails; The Wildest Country* (Maine).

AMC Walks
Appalachian Mountain Club

The focus is on country walks near major population areas. Each guide is set up in a practical way for the city dweller who likes to get out of the hustle and bustle and just unwind. Each walk is well described with a fine map, and information on distances, type of terrain, and special notes of importance. Directions are very clear and, in keeping with the underlying goal of getting the city folks out to the country, there are plenty of notes on how to get there on public transportation.

Books currently available: *Country Walks Near Baltimore* (Maryland); similar titles on: *Boston* (Massachusetts); *Montreal* (Canada); *New York* (New York). Also in this series: *Country Walks in Connecticut.*

American Express Pocket Guides
Prentice Hall Press

The print is small and, for some, a small reading glass may be in order. Those who read on will be rewarded with an amazing amount of information packed into a small, conveniently sized space. Most titles in this series concentrate on cities or small regions where a small guide can do great justice. Inside are walks, sightseeing (with gallery and museum information in considerable detail), lodging, restaurants, nightlife, and excursions to the areas nearby. As with other books that pack a lot of information in, you will have to get used to a number of hieroglyphic symbols to learn some of the details. The maps, too, are excellent—particularly the fine detail maps.

Books currently available: *The American Express Pocket Guide to Amsterdam* (Netherlands); similar titles on: *Australia; California; England & Wales* (Great Britain); *Florence & Tuscany* (Italy); *Greece; Hong Kong, Singapore & Bangkok* (Southeast Asia); *London* (England); *Mexico; New York* (New York); *Paris* (France); *Rome* (Italy); *South of France; Spain; Tokyo* (Japan); *Venice* (Italy); *Washington, D.C.* (District of Columbia).

American Jewish Landmarks
Fleet Press

A scholarly four-volume set, well suited to the interested traveler. In these books is an immense amount of history and sightseeing material, with thumbnail biographies of over 500 important individuals, details on some 2000 sites and landmarks, and facts on over 800 national and local Jewish institutions. The most extensive, well-researched series of its kind.

Books currently available: *American Jewish Landmarks: A Travel Guide and History, Volume 1: The East* (New England, Mid-Atlantic States); similar titles on: *The South and Southwest; The Middlewest; The West* (Southwest, Pacific Northwest).

Appalachian Trail Guides
Appalachian Trail Conference

The massive Appalachian Trail, stretching from Maine to Georgia, is covered by a series of ten excellent guides that divide the trail into more manageable lengths. Each guide is compact and includes detailed trail notes, distances, etc. The cost of each guide includes one or more separate topographical maps to clearly point the way. Also included are chapters on the history of the trail, and the rules and regulations on camping, parks, shelters, huts, and cabins, as well as practical data on clothing, equipment, and emergencies. Numerous side trails are also described. The two volumes in the Washington, D.C./Virginia area are prepared by the Potomac Appalachian Trail Club. The other eight are the responsibility of The Appalachian Trail Conference. Both groups do a superb job.

Books currently available: *Appalachian Trail Guide: Maine;* similar titles on: *Maryland & Northern Virginia; Massachusetts & Connecticut; New Hampshire & Vermont; New York & New Jersey; North Carolina & Georgia; Pennsylvania; Shenandoah National*

Park (Virginia); *Central and Southern Virginia; Tennessee & North Carolina.*

Appalachian Whitewater Guides
Menasha Ridge Press

Large-format guides for kayaking and canoeing throughout the Appalachian mountain chain. Clear maps mark access points and a detailed narrative describes all the important aspects of each river. In addition, there are suggested United States Geological Survey (U.S.G.S.) topographical maps and a summary chart of each possible trip including the level of skill needed, the months that it is usually runnable, a difficulty rating, the gradient, interesting highlights, average width, hazards, portages, and other particulars. These are very well done, comprehensive guides.

Books currently available: *Appalachian Whitewater, Volume I: The Southern Mountains* (South, U.S.A.); similar titles on: *Volume II: The Central Mountains* (Mid-Atlantic States); *Volume III: The Northern States* (New England).

Arthur's Guides
Aptos Publishing

This series is described under "Hawaii."

Books currently available: *Arthur's Guide to Hawaii;* similar titles on: *Maui, Molokai & Lanai; Waikiki.*

At Its Best Guides
Passport Books/National Textbook Co.

Robert Kane has penned all the titles in this popular series. Previous recipient of the Best Travel Book of the Year Award, Kane is most enjoyable to read. His books begin with a small A-to-Z section on the particular travel essentials of the country in question. The country's principal city (or two) is given a major portion of the book, though 30 to 40 additional cities are also reviewed. For each there are background and orientation notes, and hotel and restaurant listings. Descriptions are informative. And, while price listings vary in range from moderate to luxury, the general tone is for those travelers with a somewhat greater than moderate budget. Sightseeing notes are excellent, but you will have to provide your own maps.

Books currently available: *Britain At Its Best* (Great Britain); similar titles on: *France; Germany* (West and East Germany); *Hawaii; Holland* (Netherlands); *Italy; London* (England); *Paris* (France); *Spain; Switzerland.*

Away for the Weekend Guides
Crown Publishers

Eleanor Berman has collected a large number of possible short holiday or weekend getaways into several very well done books. Each selected destination point is grouped into sections that indicate the best season to go. A good overview is provided, including historical notes. Driving directions are clear and cover public transportation options where they are available. The guides are easy to read, well arranged, and include suggestions for many things to see and do. Several food and lodging choices in different price ranges are described, but notes on each are scant. The strong point of the series is its well-organized ideas for vacation fun.

Books available: *Away for the Weekend: Los Angeles;* similar titles on: *New England* (U.S.A.); *New York* (New York); *Washington, D.C.* (District of Columbia).

Backcountry Bicycle Tours
Backcountry Publications

Each book in the series presents a variety of mostly single- and some multi-day tours through beautiful countryside and charming cities. The maps are clear, the routes are well thought out, and each is accompanied by a detailed mileage log. Plenty of information about the sights along the way, as well as some eating and entertainment ideas, is included. Mention is also made of where the nearest bicycle shop is located. People touring in cars will also enjoy these routes too, but not too many cars please, as these are the scenic routes and the peace and relative quiet are clearly part of their charm. A great series.

Books currently available: *20 Bicycle Tours in and Around New York City* (New York); *20 Bicycle Tours in the Finger Lakes* (New York); *25 Bicycle Tours in Eastern Pennsylvania; 25 Bicycle Tours in Maine; 25 Bicycle Tours in New Hampshire; 25 Bicycle Tours in Vermont.*

Backcountry Canoeing Guides
Backcountry Publications

Authoritative guides to some of the principal rivers of the Northeast. Included are geography notes, suggestions for day and overnight trips, and all the necessary practical data.

Books currently available: *Canoe Camping Vermont and New Hampshire Rivers; Canoeing Central New York; Canoeing Massachusetts, Rhode Island and Connecticut.*

Backcountry Fifty Hikes
Backcountry Publications
  The Fifty Hikes series will transport you all over the New England area with a diverse and well-selected group of suggested hikes in every difficulty range. Each is clearly described, including mileage, vertical rise, time needed to complete, and recommended topographical maps. Each is accompanied by a reproduction of a "topo" with the trail clearly plotted out. In short, quality books with some wonderful hiking ideas whether you are a novice or experienced hiker.
  Books currently available: *Fifty Hikes in the Adirondacks* (New York); similar titles on: *Connecticut; Hudson Valley* (New York); *Maine; Massachusetts; New Hampshire; Central New York; Central Pennsylvania; Eastern Pennsylvania; Western Pennsylvania; Vermont; West Virginia & Western Maryland; White Mountains* (New Hampshire).

Backcountry Ski Tours
Backcountry Publications
  Like other series from Backcountry Publications, their books on ski tours are well conceived, well executed, and clearly written, and contain all the information you will need to find each starting location and follow each planned tour. These excellent books offer some ideas from experienced skiers on where to find the best snow and the most interesting and varied terrain to make your day truly memorable.
  Books currently available: *25 Ski Tours in the Adirondacks* (New York); similar titles on: *Maine; Eastern Massachusetts; Central New York; White Mountains* (New Hampshire).

Baedeker's City Guides
Prentice Hall Press
  Of the several Baedeker's series, the City Guides work best. The reason is the large, foldout map that is keyed to references in the text. The text has practical information on shopping, nightlife, tours, and, briefly, restaurants and hotels. But you don't buy a Baedeker for those kinds of facts; you buy it as a sightseeing guide. The sights, including color photos and public transportation options, are arranged in an A-to-Z format. The format is easy to use because of the large, excellent map that lets you get oriented geographically. There are also numerous color photos, additional detail maps, and museum floor plans to further facilitate your use of vacation time.
  Books currently available: *Baedeker's Amsterdam* (Netherlands); similar titles on: *Athens* (Greece); *Bangkok* (Thailand); *Berlin* (West Germany and East Germany); *Brussels* (Belgium); *Budapest* (Hungary); *Cologne* (West Germany); *Copenhagen* (Denmark); *Florence*

(Italy); *Frankfurt* (West Germany); *Hamburg* (West Germany); *Hong Kong; Istanbul* (Turkey); *Jerusalem* (Israel); *London* (England); *Madrid* (Spain); *Moscow* (Soviet Union); *Munich* (West Germany); *New York* (New York); *Paris* (France); *Prague* (Czechoslovakia); *Rome* (Italy); *San Francisco* (California); *Singapore; Stuttgart* (West Germany); *Tokyo* (Japan); *Venice* (Italy); *Vienna* (Austria).

Baedeker's Country/Regional Guides
Prentice Hall Press

The Baedeker Guides are one of the more popular sightseeing guide series, the oldest travel books of all. They provide good background information, well-done detail maps, usually a large, fold-out roadmap, numerous color photographs, and an A-to-Z listing of cities and points of interest. Some travelers complain that the books can be frustrating to use. Sometimes knowing what next sightseeing point to look for is less than obvious. Nevertheless, the Baedeker Guides are quite comprehensive and, in conjunction with a primary guidebook, will prove useful. (Note: the titles that are listed as "undated" under "General Travel Books" were published during the early 1980s).

Books currently available: *Baedeker's Austria;* similar titles on: *Caribbean* (West Indies); *Denmark; Egypt; France; Germany* (West Germany); *Great Britain; Greece; Greek Islands* (Greece); *Ireland; Israel; Italy; Japan; Loire* (France); *Mediterranean Islands* (Greece, France, Italy, Spain); *Mexico; Netherlands, Belgium & Luxembourg; Portugal; Provence & Cote d'Azur* (France); *Rhine* (West Germany); *Scandinavia; Spain; Switzerland; Turkish Coast* (Turkey); *Tuscany* (Italy); *Yugoslavia.*

Beaches of Hawaii Guides
University of Hawaii Press

This series is reviewed under "Hawaii."

Books currently available: *Beaches of Maui Country;* similar titles on: *The Big Island* (Island of Hawaii); *O'ahu.*

Bed and Breakfast Book Guides
The Globe Pequot Press

This comprehensive series, now owned by Globe Pequot, is beginning to change its name as renewals occur. Nonetheless, we have used the old series name pending such time as the entire series is revised. Each book in the series offers a fine evaluation of selected bed and breakfast inns. Kathy Strong's books are particularly good in this regard (Caribbean and California). Evaluations are detailed and will provide a clear basis upon which to choose the "perfect" inn for you.

Books currently available: *The New England Bed and Breakfast Book* (U.S.A.); *The Mid-Atlantic Bed and Breakfast Book* (Mid-Atlantic States, U.S.A.); *The Southern Bed and Breakfast Book* (South, U.S.A.); *Bed and Breakfast in California; Bed and Breakfast in the Caribbean* (West Indies).

Berlitz Country Guides
Macmillan Publishing

Most of the Country Guides are more recent additions to the Berlitz series. While the Berlitz Guides (below) have focused almost exclusively on a single city or region, the Country Guides have taken on a much larger area, although the number of pages is only double those of the other series. The structure and content are similar. But, the amount of detail is less than the classic Berlitz Guides. The overview provided, however, is practical and helpful. The comments below are applicable to both series.

Books currently available: *Berlitz: Australia;* similar titles on: *Canada; China; France; Hungary; India; Italy; Japan; Switzerland; Turkey; U.S.A.* (United States as a Whole); *Yugoslavia.*

Berlitz Deluxe Guides
Macmillan Publishing

A new series that combines a classic Berlitz Guide (see below), Berlitz phrase book, and an abbreviated dictionary into a single book.

Books currently available: *Berlitz: Amsterdam* (Netherlands); similar titles on: *Barcelona* (Spain); *French Riviera* (France); *Paris* (France); *Rome* (Italy); *Venice* (Italy).

Berlitz Guides
Macmillan Publishing

For tiny, pocket-sized books, these guides are quite informative. If you put a premium on size, and want just a bit of the right essentials, Berlitz can help. These guides are not updated frequently, and make only general comments on lodging and food (although several newer editions now have a separate 16-page supplement at the back specifically on these more time-dated subjects). However, these books provide a good review of the history of the region and a practical facts section, plus much information on where to go, when to go, what to do, sports, and other activities. These are handy little guides and, if the trend toward a hotel-and-restaurant supplement spills over into more titles, they will be all the better. Our listings reflect the price increases of 1988. However, you should be able to find most titles at a lesser price for some time to come.

Books currently available: *Berlitz: Amsterdam* (Netherlands); similar titles on: *Algarve* (Portugal); *Athens* (Greece); *Bahamas* (West

Indies); *Barcelona & Costa Dorada* (Spain); *Berlin* (West Germany); *Brittany* (France); *Brussels* (Belgium); *Budapest* (Hungary); *California; Canary Islands* (Islands of the Eastern and Northern Atlantic Ocean); *Channel Islands* (England); *Copenhagen* (Denmark); *Corfu* (Greece); *Costa Blanca* (Spain); *Costa Brava* (Spain); *Costa del Sol & Andalusia* (Spain); *Crete* (Greece); *Cyprus; Dubrovnik & Southern Dalmatia* (Yugoslavia); *Egypt; Florida; French Riviera* (France); *Florence* (Italy); *French West Indies; Greater Miami* (Florida); *Greek Islands; Hawaii; Helsinki* (Finland); *Hong Kong; Ibiza & Formentera* (Spain); *Istria & Croatian Coast* (Yugoslavia); *Ireland; Istanbul* (Turkey); *Italian Adriatic* (Italy); *Italian Riviera* (Italy); *Jamaica* (West Indies); *Jerusalem; Kenya; Lisbon* (Portugal); *Loire Valley* (France); *London* (England); *Madeira* (Islands of the Eastern and Northern Atlantic Ocean), *Madrid* (Spain); *Majorca* (Spain); *Malta; Mexico City* (Mexico); *Montreal* (Canada); *Morocco; Moscow* (Soviet Union); *Munich* (West Germany); *Nepal; New York* (New York); *New Zealand; Normandy* (France); *Oslo* (Norway); *Oxford & Cambridge* (England); *Paris* (France); *Peloponnese* (Greece); *Prague* (Czechoslovkia); *Puerto Rico* (West Indies); *Rhine Valley* (West Germany); *Rhodes* (Greece); *Rio de Janeiro* (Brazil); *Rome* (Italy); *Salonica & Northern Greece* (Greece); *Saudi Arabia; Scotland; Sicily* (Italy); *Singapore; South Africa; Southern Caribbean* (West Indies); *Split & Dalmatia* (Yugoslavia); *Sri Lanka & Maldives; Stockholm* (Sweden); *Thailand; Toronto* (Canada); *Tunisia; Tyrol* (Austria); *Venice* (Italy); *Vienna* (Austria); *Virgin Islands* (West Indies).

Best Places to Stay Guides
The Harvard Common Press

A particular strength of this series is that it covers the full range of lodging options in each area—hotels, B&Bs, and country inns. The authors have been highly selective in determining what they feel are the very best. In most titles in this series, selections are arranged by type: cabins, family resorts, farms, golf resorts, grand old resorts, guest ranches, romantic getaways, ski lodges, sports lodges—whatever categories are appropriate to the area. The evaluations are enjoyable and provide a good sense of the atmosphere and amenities of each place as well as the practicalities. No fees are accepted for inclusion. A first-class series.

Books currently available: *Best Places to Stay in American Cities* (United States as a Whole); similar titles on: *Asia; Caribbean* (West Indies); *Hawaii; Mexico; New England* (U.S.A.); *Pacific Northwest* (U.S.A.); *Southwest* (U.S.A.).

Bicycling the Backroads
The Mountaineers
   Yet another series written and produced in the classy style typical of The Mountaineers, a group dedicated to preserving, exploring, studying, and, enjoying the beauty of the great outdoors (especially in the Pacific Northwest, where they are located). It's all here—the routes, the descriptions, the mileage logs, the maps. An excellent series.
   Books currently available: *Bicycling the Backroads of Northwest Oregon*; similar titles on: *Northwest Washington*; *Puget Sound* (Washington).

Birnbaum's Guides
Houghton Mifflin
   On our own trips these guides have never let us down. We have arrived in town after town, usually without reservations (not at the height of tourist season, of course), picked an interesting-sounding hotel, and, if there was a room, found it to be exactly as described. What more can you ask? Choices are good and descriptions are accurate. Birnbaum's guides are generally in the moderate-and-up price range, but there are always plenty of moderate choices, as opposed to some of the other guides that purport to appeal to more than the well-heeled traveler. And, what is more, the guides are a pleasure to read. Preparation, history, background information, and sightseeing are excellent, but the "Diversions" are what make these guides special. Depending upon the guide, the diversions may be well-planned driving tours through the French countryside, yachting, tennis or even sports fishing in the Caribbean. In most guides, however, the focus is on the traveler with a car. The amount of information provided is truly staggering. Birnbaum gets top marks. Each guide is thoroughly updated annually. In 1989 Birnbaum's *Great Britain and Ireland* will be split into two, separate titles. During the early 1990s, the massive *United States* guide will be split into six or eight regional titles.
   Books currently available: *Birnbaum's Canada*; similar titles on: *Caribbean, Bermuda & Bahamas* (West Indies); *Europe* (Europe as a Whole); *France*; *Great Britain and Ireland*; *Hawaii*; *Italy*; *Mexico*; *Portugal*; *South America*; *Spain*; *United States* (United States as a Whole).

Blue Guides
W. W. Norton & Co.
   This British series, produced in conjunction with W. W. Norton, provides copious amounts of cultural, historic, and architectural

detail for the sophisticated traveler. The information is often organized by way of driving or walking tours, depending on the location.
Further detail on all points of interest is offered in the tiniest of
print (another guide where some readers will appreciate a small
reading glass)—favorite trips, where the best hotels are located, what
amusements are nearby, other transportation options, where the local post office is located, etc. Detail maps, where provided, are excellent. Floor plans of churches, museums, and other important
buildings are also included. A fine series crafted for more discerning
travelers. Specialty guides in this series are described separately, but
listed below.

Books currently available: *Blue Guide: Athens* (Greece); similar
titles on: *Austria; Belgium & Luxembourg; Boston and Cambridge*
(Massachusetts); *Cathedrals and Abbeys of England and Wales*
(Great Britain); *Channel Islands* (England); *Corsica* (France); *Crete;
Cyprus; Egypt; England; Florence* (Italy); *France; Greece; Holland*
(Netherlands); *Ireland; Istanbul* (Turkey); *Literary Britain and Ire-
land; London* (England); *Malta; Moscow and Leningrad* (Soviet
Union); *Museums and Galleries of London* (England); *Museums and
Galleries of New York* (New York); *New York* (New York); *Northern
Italy; Oxford & Cambridge* (England); *Paris* (France); *Portugal;
Rome* (Italy); *Scotland; Sicily; Southern Italy; Spain; Switzerland;
Venice* (Italy); *Victorian Architecture in England; Wales & The
Marches.*

Boating Almanacs
Western Marine Enterprises

These comprehensive guides to the Pacific Coast area of North
America have been produced annually for more than two decades.
Each well-researched guide tells the boating traveler where to go,
how to get there, where to stop, where to refuel, where to find repairs,
radio weather channels, yacht club flags, and a whole lot more. Also
included are maps appropriate to the waters of the particular area
and detailed tide charts. Everything you could need is found in these
up-to-date guides.

Books currently available: *Pacific Boating Almanac: Northern
California & Nevada*; similar titles on: *Pacific Northwest & Alaska;
Southern California, Arizona & Mexico.*

Born to Shop Guides
Bantam Books

Slick and upmarket, these guides generally appeal to the upper
end of the travel group. But there are bargain shopping tips as well.
As a matter of fact there is a whole, lengthy section devoted to the
"business of bargains." Well researched, these little guides contain

a good deal of the practical details on what to watch out for, how to find fakes, hot merchandise, customs, etc. Selections are arranged by district and cover the gamut: clothing, home furnishing, antiques, collectibles, etc. Well organized and solidly prepared.

Books currently available: *Born to Shop: France;* similar titles on: *Hong Kong; Italy; London* (England); *New York* (New York); *Tokyo* (Japan).

Britain Before the Conquest Guides
Hunter Publishing

The books of this series offer an archaeological tour of the centuries prior to the Middle Ages, before the conquest. Each book is an illustrated history as well as a source of fascinating, recommended sites to visit. These are good books to use in conjunction with a primary guidebook, especially for those intrigued by the ancient past and its archaeological remnants.

Books currently available: *Britain Before the Conquest: Anglo-Saxon England* (England); similar titles on: *Celtic Britain* (Great Britain); *Origins of Britain* (Great Britain).

Cadogan Guides
The Globe Pequot Press

The quality of writing in this British series is exceptional, producing results that are always solid, and usually excellent. Several of the guides are updates of books that were first part of the Island Hopping Guide series (some titles of which are still available and reviewed separately). From practical facts to history, customs, sightseeing, food and lodging, the Cadogan Guides can be counted on for interesting detail and informed recommendations. Aimed at the "discerning traveler," the guides are strongly weighted toward history and cultural information. Each guide is updated biennielly.

Books currently available: *Cadogan Guide: Australia;* similar titles on: *Caribbean* (West Indies); *Greek Islands (Greece); India; Ireland; Italian Islands* (Italy); *Italy; Scotland; South of France; Spain; Thailand and Burma; Turkey.*

Canoeing and Kayaking Guides
Menasha Ridge Press

These solidly done guides to canoeing and kayaking opportunities in Florida, Kentucky, Ohio, and Tennessee provide all the detailed information needed to plan enjoyable, safe day trips or longer camping trips.

Books currently available: *Canoeing and Kayaking Guide to the Streams of Florida* (2 volumes); similar titles on: *Kentucky; Ohio* (2 volumes); *Tennessee.*

Children's Treasure Hunt Guides

Hippocrene Books

These little books are great for kids six and up. Information on local money, a bit of language, and history with the bulk of the text devoted to photos or drawings of landmarks (natural and man-made) is laid out in a manner that encourages children to check off each site as they visit it. Room is provided for taking notes, and comments accompany most of these selections. Following the book, children get more involved in the trip, watching carefully for the next important building, statue, or whatever, and recording their thoughts to take home with them. The unique combination, of both education and fun is probably why these books have stayed in print for so many years.

Books available: *Children's Treasure Hunt Guide: Austria, Germany and Switzerland;* similar titles on: *Belgium and France; Britain* (Great Britain); *Italy.*

Circuit Hikes Guides

Potomac Appalachian Trail Club

An excellent series of well-described and rated circular hikes that conveniently return you to your vehicle after an enjoyable journey of two to eight hours. Hikes range from difficult to easy and for each the necessary facts—elevation gained and lost, total distance, and hiking time expected—are included. Small topographical maps or hand-drawn maps, recommended USGS maps to obtain, and other notes complete each book.

Books currently available: *Circuit Hikes in Northern New Jersey;* similar titles on: *Shenandoah National Park* (Virginia); *Virginia, West Virginia, Maryland, and Pennsylvania.*

Citywalks

Henry Holt & Co.

A series of intimate walking tours of the most historic and enchanting sections of each city. Each book begins with an information and advice section, including tips on local food and drink and other practical details. Each walk is then described with a blend of history, anecdote, and general information. A good map and an occasional photograph round out the format. A fine series for the traveler who likes to stroll through history.

Books currently available: *Florencewalks* (Italy); *Londonwalks* (England); *Jerusalemwalks* (Israel); *Pariswalks* (France); *Romewalks* (Italy); *Viennawalks* (Austria).

Classic Walk Guides
Haynes Publications
   These are large-format books covering primarily long walks or hikes through spectacular country. Included are general maps, recommended additional detailed maps, distances, types of terrain, good descriptions, and plenty of photographs. Some great ideas can be found here.
   Books currently available: *Classic Walks in Europe* (Europe as a Whole); similar titles on: *France; Great Britain; The World.*

Collier World Traveler Guides
Macmillan Publishing
   A series of compact, all-purpose guides, translated from the French, that do a solid job of covering a wide array of travel essentials, including practical tips, sightseeing, lodging, and food. The stress of the series is on budget travel. Notes on sightseeing and transportation are good, but without an update, hotel and restaurant recommendations will have to be carefully verified. These guides are fairly compact and provide an adequate amount of helpful information in a fairly utilitarian fashion.
   Books currently available: *Collier World Traveler Series: Greece and Yugoslavia;* similar titles on: *Great Britain and Ireland; In and Around Paris* (France); *Italy; Mexico, Belize, Guatemala and French Antilles; Northern and Central Europe.*

Companion Guides
Prentice Hall Press
   Several fine titles in this series are no longer in print, but those that are are some of the finest, best-written travel books around. They are much like having a very knowledgeable friend along, explaining the deeper significance of the sights you are seeing, and generally attempting to "conjure up an atmosphere" of the region described. They succeed admirably. Specific topics such as history, architecture, and art are also covered. For the discerning traveler seeking something more than another "what to see and what to do" guide, these efforts make for a much more intimate experience.
   Books currently available: *The Companion Guide to Ireland;* similar titles on: *Jugoslavia* (Yugoslavia); *London* (England); *Madrid and Central Spain; New York* (New York); *Paris* (France); *Rome* (Italy); *Shakespeare Country* (England); *South of France; Venice* (Italy).

Compleat Traveler's Companions
Burt Franklin, Publisher
   This is the official name of the Burt Franklin Country Inns series, another solidly prepared, annually updated series on inns, lodges,

and historic hotels. The evaluations are well done and include up-
to-date details and driving instructions. Each book includes numerous drawings and photographs, which provide visual clues as to the
best choice for your needs. Time-sensitive information on each inn
is conveniently summarized in a chart at the back. No fees are
accepted for inclusion. Personal Preference Note: The two European
titles by the O'Reillys are careful selections of the cream of the crop.

Books currently available: *Country Inns, Lodges and Historic Hotels of California, Oregon and Washington;* similar titles on: *Canada; Great Britain; Ireland; Mid-Atlantic States* (U.S.A.); *Midwest
and Rocky Mountain States* (U.S.A.); *New England States* (U.S.A.);
South (U.S.A.).

Condo Lux Guides
Random House

Each title in this series profiles about 150 condominiums that are
available for your next vacation rental. The profiles provide detailed
information as to the number of guests that can stay, the number of
rooms, whether there is air conditioning, if linens are provided, and
maid service availability. The series, if kept up-to-date, will be a real
help in surveying the vacation rental market. The author also makes
available a newsletter (see "Travel Newsletters and Magazines" appendix).

Books currently available: *The Condo Lux Vacationer's Guide to
Condominium Rentals in the Bahamas and the Caribbean Islands;*
similar titles on: *Mountain Resorts* (Europe as a Whole, United
States as a Whole); *Southeast* (South, U.S.A.); *Southwest and Hawaii*
(U.S.A.).

County Companion Guides
Salem House

This series is reviewed under "England."

Books currently available: *County Companions: Cornwall;* similar titles on: *Cumbria; Devon; Dorset; Kent; Somerset and Avon;
Surrey; Sussex; Yorkshire/Humberside.*

Country Inns and Back Roads
Harper & Row

A delightful and useful series, presenting a wide variety of choices
of country-house hotels, B&Bs, traditional inns, farmhouses, and
castles (depending on the location). One of the most well known of
lodging reviewers, Norman Simpson's reviews are usually friendly
and down to earth. However, it should be noted that Simpson does
require the proprietor of each listing be to a member of his association. While this fact probably does not change what he writes, wri-

teups are rarely critical. Simpson is also a well-known figure to the hotel owner, which makes it harder to know whether the average traveler will receive the same accommodating treatment. Regardless, the books are a pleasure to read and the lodging selections are of obvious quality—in every price range. The series is updated annually.

Books available: *Country Inns and Back Roads: Britain and Ireland*; similar titles on: *Continental Europe* (Europe as a Whole); *North America* (North America as a Whole).

Country Inns of America Guides
Henry Holt & Co.

The two New England and one Mid-Atlantic titles are the only ones in this series even remotely up-to-date. Yet, even these are less than current. Nonetheless, the strong emphasis on color photographs of each establishment's exterior, interior, and some of the surrounding countryside is appealing. The text is informative and the guides make a fine visual supplement to one of the more up-to-date guidebooks on inns.

Books currently available: *Country Inns of America: The Great Lakes* (The Midwest, U.S.A.); similar titles on: *Lower New England* (U.S.A.); *The Mississippi* (The Midwest, U.S.A.); *New York and Mid-Atlantic (Mid-Atlantic States, U.S.A.)*; *Pacific Northwest (U.S.A.)*; *Rocky Mountains* (Rocky Mountain/Great Basin States, U.S.A.); *Southeast* (The South, U.S.A.); *Southwest* (U.S.A.); *Upper New England* (U.S.A.).

Countryman Explorer's Guides
Countryman Press

The first striking thing about the three books of the Explorer's Guide series is their friendly tone—there seems to be a little voice behind the specific information presented that keeps saying, "Come on, let's go." This encouragement to head on out and really explore new parts of each state is infectious. And, once you are there, these guides will help point you in the right direction, while still leaving plenty of room for you to do your own thing. All the possibilities are included: where to swim, or rent a bike, or cross-country ski, the friendly lodging spots in town, where to grab a snack, or sit down to a real dinner, or buy antiques. What is written is informative and even when the description is scant, you can trust that the authors have actually been there and enjoyed it, and that you will too. That seems to be the bottom line: the writers feel like friends.

Books currently available: *Maine: An Explorer's Guide*; similar titles on: *The Other Massachusetts*; *Vermont*.

Countryside Guides
Hunter Publishing

The focus of this series is on car tours, walks, and picnics. Suggestions are made for various one- and two-day tours with picnic sites and optional walks described along the way. The walks are both long and short and are described as to their specific length and difficulty. Included are good color photos and touring maps. A fine series to supplement a primary travel guide.

Books currently available: *Landscapes of Corfu* (Greece); similar titles on: *Cyprus; Eastern Crete* (Greece); *Western Crete* (Greece); *Gran Canaria* (Islands of the Eastern and Northern Atlantic Ocean); *Madeira* (Islands of the Eastern and Northern Atlantic Ocean); *Mallorca* (Spain); *Rhodes* (Greece); *Tenerife* (Islands of the Eastern and Northern Atlantic Ocean).

Covered Bridges Guides
The Village Press

These small, nicely designed guides will take you to the last of the remaining covered bridges, the few vestiges of a bygone day when hundreds dotted the landscape. Each guide includes all the remaining public bridges in that state. For each there is a description, a history, a photograph, an analysis of the type of truss that has supported it all these years, and clear directions on how to find each of them. These helpful guides will enrich your next drive into the country.

Books currently available: *Covered Bridges of Connecticut*; similar titles on: *Maine; Massachusetts.*

Crown Insiders' Guides
Crown Publishers

This fairly new series, edited by Robert Fisher (who also produces his own series as well, Fisher's World Guides, see below), is written by numerous writers who have lived or studied in each area, but who are also Americans and familiar with what interests Americans. They are both insiders and outsiders. As such, they offer a great many inside tips on managing and appreciating the lands you are visiting. This seems to be their strong suit; these writers have really experienced the areas they cover. They also provide planned itineraries coupled with detailed text and a five-star rating system for hotels and restaurants in a wide range of prices (the emphasis is moderate and up.) Comments on hotels and restaurants are fairly brief, but informative. The overall result is a solid, well-produced series that has a growing number of fans. We have our other favorites for some regions, but the Crown series is definitely a good choice for the upper half of spending spectrum.

Books currently available: *Crown Insider's Guide to Britain*; similar titles on: *California; the Caribbean* (West Indies); *France; Italy; Japan; Mexico; New York City and State.*

Cruising Guides

Westcott Cove Publishing

A series of large-format, spiral-bound guides for the boating traveler. Each contains massive amounts of data specific to the boat user, including charts, weather information, chartering information, even a large, separate chart of the waters of that region. However, the books do not overlook what to do once you reach land—where to dock, where to play, and much more. This is a fine series for those who have the pleasure of journeying by boat.

Books currently available: *Cruising Guide to Abacos and the Northern Bahamas;* similar titles on: *Maine* (2 volumes); *Tahiti* (Oceania). Also in series: *Yachtsman's Guide to the Windward Islands* (West Indies).

Discover the Adirondacks Guides

Backcountry Publications

This series is reviewed under "New York."

Books currently available: *Discover the Central Adirondacks;* similar titles on different regions of the Adirondack area: *Eastern; Northeastern; South Central; Southeastern; Southwestern.* Also in series: *Discover the Adirondacks 2.*

Dover Walking Guides

Dover Publications

This series is reviewed under "New York."

Books currently available: *Dover New York Walking Guide: From Battery to Wall Street;* similar titles on: *Wall Street to Chambers Street; Greenwich Village.*

DuMont Guides

Stewart, Tabori & Chang, Publishers

A beautifully produced series on the history, art, and architecture of each region. Each book is arranged in an area-by-area fashion to facilitate its use by tourists and filled with many handsome color and black-and-white photos and reproductions of old engravings and drawings. These books also use fascinating combinations of old and new maps that create an interesting historical perspective. Detailed maps of some of the major cities and floor plans of major buildings are included, and a section of practical tips is found at the back of each book. Interested travelers will appreciate this series most as a guide to history, art, and architecture to supplement their touring guide book.

Books currently available: *DuMont Guide to the French Riviera* (France); similar titles on: *Greek Islands* (Greece); *Ireland; Loire Valley* (France); *Paris* (France).

Earl Steinbicker's Day Trips
Hastings House

The Steinbicker Day Trips guides have been popular for a number of years and the series has recently begun to grow. Each book is a collection of one-day outings from different cities. Information on transportation, whether it be your own or public transport, is provided. Once you arrive at the day's location, Steinbicker details some well-planned walking tours replete with informative comments, fine detail maps, and photographs. Places for food, drink, and other diversions are also suggested. Selected locations include both the well known and those that are still off the beaten path.

Books currently available: *Day Trips in Britain;* similar titles on: *France; Germany; Holland, Belgium and Luxembourg* (Netherlands); *London* (England); *Italy.*

Earl Thollander's Back Roads
Crown Publishers

It is perhaps Earl Thollander's delightful illustrations that have garnered him such a following, but these books contain much more than art. Thollander's large-format books offer some wonderful ideas for slow, meandering vacation days, as he sketches his way down little-known lanes. Bits of local history supplement the artwork and both combined make these books truly enjoyable.

Books currently available: *Back Roads of the Carolinas* (North Carolina, South Carolina); similar titles on: *Oregon; Washington; California* (Lane Publishing).

Earth Treasures
Harper & Row

If you are one of those people who has the urge to look for fossils, rocks, or minerals on those trips into the country, this four-volume series is for you (or at least the volume that includes your quadrant of the country). Each book arranges the states by their counties, plots the interesting locations on a county map, and describes the locations and what types of collectibles can be expected in that area. Via the index, you can sort out all the various areas that might have your favorite type of rock or fossil. These guides are designed for every interested person, not just the devoted rockhound, and can add a whole new measure of fun to your vacation life.

Books currently available: *Earth Treasures, Volume 1: The Northeast Quadrant* (New England, Mid-Atlantic States, Midwest, U.S.A.);

similar titles on: *Volume 2: Southeast Quadrant* (Mid-Atlantic States, The South, U.S.A.); *Volume 3: Northwest Quadrant* (Midwest, Rocky Mountain/Great Basin States, Pacific Northwest, U.S.A.); *Volume 4: Southwest Quadrant* (Rocky Mountain/Great Basin States, Southwest, U.S.A.).

The Economist Business Traveller's Guides
Prentice Hall Press
   This rapidly expanding series of superb business-oriented guides is getting top reviews from those business travelers already using them. You will find information on business practices and local etiquette, some history notes, a rundown of the economic scene by business category in each country or region, and a discussion of the industrial scene (cars, food, drink, etc.), including prospects for the future. Each major business area is covered with hotel and restaurant reviews, which are quite well done and of moderate length. You'll also find specifics on transportation, shopping, sightseeing, and entertainment. The focus is always the businessman or -woman on the go, and some titles provide details on less frequently covered areas like the Arabian Peninsula or Southeast Asia.
   Books currently available: *The Economist Business Traveller's Guides: Arabian Peninsula* (Middle East, Asia); similar titles on: *Britain* (Great Britain); *China; France; Japan; Southeast Asia; United States* (United States as a Whole); *West Germany.*

Eldan Museum Guides
Eldan Press
   These tiny Eldan guides provide a quick reference to essential information on the numerous museums of each area. If you want a compact guide to point you in the right direction rather than a guide with copious detail on each museum, these are just the ticket. You will learn what not to miss without even being aware that you are carrying around another guidebook.
   Books currently available: *Museums of Florence* (Italy); *Museums of Paris* (France); *Small Museums of the French Riviera* (France).

Epicure Guides
Peanut Butter Publishing
   This is a large series of menu guides to major cities of the United States. Updated frequently, they are a good way to select your own restaurants, and judge for yourself rather than reading someone else's opinion. If you feel you can judge a restaurant by the quality of its menu, this is a good series for you. If you wish to use the book as a guide, enough practical information is included.
   Books currently available: *Baltimore Epicure* (Maryland); similar

titles on: *Boston* (Massachusetts); *Chicago* (Illinois); *Dallas* (Texas); *Denver* (Colorado); *Detroit* (Michigan); *Honolulu* (Hawaii); *Houston* (Texas); *Kansas City* (Missouri); *Los Angeles* (California); *Manhattan* (New York); *Miami* (Florida); *Minneapolis/St. Paul* (Minnesota); *New Orleans* (Louisiana); *San Diego* (California); *San Francisco* (California); *Seattle* (Washington); *St. Louis* (Missouri); *Washington, D.C.* (District of Columbia).

Escape Manuals
World Leisure Corp.

These are definitely a change of pace. They are entertainingly written and humorously illustrated, but, at the same time, filled with practical facts on places to go and what to do. The authors make no effort to discuss such basics as hotels and restaurants, but they deliver plenty of advice on ways to make an escape to Europe more memorable and exciting. These guides are a good idea for those who hate to labor through a more traditional guidebook.

Books currently available: *Whole Europe Escape Manual: France/ Holland/Belgium/Luxembourg;* similar titles on: *Germany/Austria/ Switzerland; Italy/Greece; Spain/Portugal; UK/Ireland.*

Everything Under the Sun Guides
Passport Books/National Textbook Co.

This series is reviewed under "Spain."

Books currently available: *Everything Under the Sun: Barcelona;* similar titles on: *Cordoba; Granada; Madrid; Marbella; Palma de Majorca; Salamanca; Seville; Toledo.*

Exploring Rural Europe Guides
Passport Books/National Textbook Co.

This new series, released as we went to press, promises to be a real resource on rural Europe. Each book is a planned tour of rural areas with itineraries ranging from one day to one week. History and a discussion of each region's character and cuisine are followed by sightseeing, reasonably priced hotels and restaurants, and numerous maps.

Books currently available: *Exploring Rural Austria;* similar titles on: *France; Germany* (West Germany); *Greece; Ireland; Italy; Portugal; Scotland; Spain.*

Eyes of Texas Guides
Gulf Publishing

This series is reviewed under "Texas."

Books currently available: *Eyes of Texas Travel Guide: Dallas/ East Texas;* similar titles on: *Fort Worth/Brazos Valley; Hill Coun-*

try/Permian Basin; Houston/Gulf Coast; Panhandle/Plains; San Antonio/Border.

Falcon Press Hiking Guides
Falcon Press
   The Falcon Press series is an excellent hiking series with a wide selection of hikes of varied length. Reproductions of topographical maps are used and each hike is well discussed and rated, its special attractions summarized, and other USGS maps recommended.
   Books currently available: *The Hiker's Guide to Arizona;* similar titles on: *California; Colorado; Idaho; Montana; Utah.*

Famous Restaurants & Recipes
Schildge Publishing
   Each restaurant chosen for these guides is informatively described, clear directions are given, and several recipes, chosen from the many they use, are reproduced. The books are spiral-bound, making them easy to use. For those who can appreciate a fine recipe when they see it, this is a fun way to choose your next dining spot.
   Books currently available: *Famous Adirondack Restaurants & Recipes* (New York); similar titles on: *Albany & Saratoga* (New York); *Minneapolis* (Minnesota); *Vermont.*

Fielding's Historic Trail Guides
William Morrow & Co.
   Fielding now has three titles that structure themselves around one of the famous trails of the western United States: the Lewis and Clark Trail, the Spanish trails of the Southwest, and, most recently, the California Mission Trail—not so much a path as an historic string of Catholic missions. The books should prove of interest to history buffs, as they are laced with many descriptions and quotations from those who were part of the creation of these famous trails. Entwined with the historical pieces is a good deal of detail on what to see, where to go, walking tours, hotels, and restaurants. This is a new focus in travel books for Fielding.
   Books currently available: *Fielding's California: The Mission Trail; Fielding's Lewis and Clark Trail* (Midwest, Rocky Mountain/ Great Basin States, Pacific Northwest, U.S.A.); *Fielding's Spanish Trails in the Southwest* (U.S.A.).

Fielding's Travel Guides
William Morrow & Co.
   Among the titles of this series, only *Fielding's Caribbean* receives high grades, but all are more than adequate travel guides. Plenty of good information on shopping and sightseeing is included, and hotel

and restaurant ratings use a star system of 1 to 5. Selections cover the moderate-to-very-expensive group with a heavy leaning toward the more expensive. A problem we found with these guides is the author's condescending tone of voice. So, while the information may be good, it is difficult to assimilate due to a feeling of being talked down to. However, Fielding plans a "total redesign" with the 1989 editions. If this reflects in form as well as substance, these books may become more palatable. (This review does not include Fielding's many specialized titles, which are reviewed separately, and is not indicative of *Fielding's Caribbean* which, while of similar format, is so outstanding that it, too, is reviewed individually.)

Books currently available: *Fielding's Bermuda and the Bahamas;* similar titles on: *Caribbean* (West Indies); *Europe* (Europe as a Whole); *Far East* (Asia as a Whole); *Mexico; Republic of China.*

Fisher's World Guides
Fisher's World, Inc.

The new version of this series has downplayed the unique annotation system of Robert Fisher, who includes hand-written notes on his special picks in the margins. The annotations are still used, but the series is no longer called Fisher's Annotated Guides, and the annotations, thankfully, are no longer written in red. The guides are produced by some quality, veteran writers, and stress the "best of everything," although selections do dribble down into the moderate range with even an occasional budget item thrown in. Evaluations of hotels and restaurants are short but accurate, particularly at the top end. The new guides (except *U.S.A.*) now have a small, helpful Travel Planner at the back that can be removed and used separately as a quick summary of sightseeing, hotel, restaurant, and practical travel facts when you would prefer to go lightly. Each title contains feature articles on subjects of special interest. The series, which aims "to be the Cadillac" of the industry, is certainly improving, but still does not excite us. Nonetheless, new authors are being brought in for many 1989 editions—a healthy, hopeful sign of Fisher's World's commitment to continued growth. New titles are also planned for 1989, including Atlanta, Brazil, Puerto Rico/Virgin Islands, San Francisco, Washington, D.C., Rocky Mountains South, Rocky Mountains North, Portugal (now separate), California, and Florida, plus entirely new editions of Canada, France, London, Paris, and Los Angeles. Keep an eye on Fisher's World, excellence may be just around the corner.

Books currently available: *Fisher's World: Australia, New Zealand and South Pacific;* similar titles on: *Bahamas* (West Indies); *Bermuda* (West Indies); *Britain* (Great Britain); *Canada; Caribbean* (West Indies); *Europe* (Europe as a Whole); *France; Germany; Greece;*

Hawaii; Ireland; Italy; Japan; London (England); *Los Angeles* (California); *Mexico; Mid-Atlantic* (Mid-Atlantic States, U.S.A.); *Midwest* (U.S.A.); *New England* (U.S.A.); *New York City* (New York); *Northwest* (Pacific Northwest, U.S.A.); *Paris* (France); *Southeast* (South, U.S.A.); *Southwest* (U.S.A.); *Spain/Portugal; U.S.A.* (United States as a Whole); *West* (Rocky Mountain/Great Basin States, Southwest U.S.A.).

Flashmaps
Random House

Here is another series where a premium is placed on space. Each title, perhaps 80 to 100 pages, slips easily into a purse or coat pocket. Yet summarized within is a substantial amount of information on many travel topics: restaurants, theaters, transportation, libraries, etc. The "flashmaps" are single-subject maps that precisely locate each selection. The style is utilitarian, and detailed analysis is nonexistent. These guides certainly give no thought of being comprehensive, but, within their limited format, they are handy and useful. Flashmaps are updated annually so the facts are sure to be as current as possible.

Books currently available: *Flashmaps: Boston* (Massachusetts); similar titles on: *Chicago* (Illinois); *Dallas/Ft. Worth* (Texas); *Los Angeles* (California); *New York* (New York); *San Francisco* (California); *Philadelphia* (Pennsylvania); *Washington* (District of Columbia).

Fodor's City Guides
Fodor's Travel Publications/Random House

Fodor's is showing some distinct signs of improvement (see comments below under Fodor's Country/Regional Guides). For years they have seemed to rest on the laurels earned by Eugene Fodor, even though he sold the company in the late 1960s. The guides follow such a strict formula that they seem to cramp the style of even the most talented of travel writers. Nevertheless, the city guides are solid, with selections in every price range, some good sightseeing information, and other practical facts. In general, these guides are predictable and unexciting.

Books currently available: *Fodor's Amsterdam* (Netherlands); similar titles on: *Atlantic City* (New Jersey); *Beijing, Guangzhou and Shanghai* (China); *Boston* (Massachusetts); *Chicago* (Illinois); *Dallas/Fort Worth* (Texas); *Florence and Venice* (Italy); *Greater Miami* (Florida); *Hong Kong and Macau; London* (England); *Houston and Galveston* (Texas); *Lisbon* (Portugal); *Los Angeles* (California); *Madrid* (Spain); *Mexico City and Acapulco* (Mexico); *Munich* (West Germany); *New Orleans* (Louisiana); *New York City* (New York); *Paris*

(France); *Philadelphia* (Pennsylvania); *Rome* (Italy); *San Diego* (California); *San Francisco* (California); *Singapore; Stockholm, Copenhagen, Oslo, Helsinki and Reykjavik* (Scandinavia); *Sydney* (Australia); *Tokyo* (Japan); *Toronto* (Canada); *Vienna* (Austria); *Washington, D.C.* (District of Columbia); *Williamsburg, Jamestown and Yorktown* (Virginia).

Fodor's Country/Regional Guides
Fodor's Travel Publications/Random House

If you speak with people who make their livelihood selling travel books, you will discover that very few Fodor's titles are strongly recommended. A few specific titles are mentioned as exceptions to the rule and we have noted these accordingly. A few others have been severely criticized. It's certainly not that these guides offer nothing of value. Far from it. They are very popular—partly because of the name Eugene Fodor created for the series. But most knowledgeable travelers find the Fodor titles stodgy and a bit boring. However, there are signs of significant change. Random House now owns Fodor's and recently brought in Michael Spring as the editorial director. Spring has a reputation as a fine travel writer in his own right, which is encouraging (see *Great European Itineraries* and *The Great Weekend Escape Book* for New England and Mid-Atlantic states). Spring has said that he anticipates a significant change in the look and format of this series in 1989. If that happens, these guides will be on their way to the top. For now, Fodor's still covers all the bases more than adequately in most titles. Yearly updates, however, are fairly limited, and major updates have traditionally occurred about every four years. A few titles are updated only occasionally.

Books currently available: *Fodor's Alaska;* similar titles on: *Arizona; Australia, New Zealand and South Pacific; Austria; Bahamas* (West Indies); *Belgium and Luxembourg; Bermuda; Brazil; California; Canada; Canada's Maritime Provinces; Cancun, Cozumel, Merida and Yucatan* (Mexico); *Cape Cod* (Massachusetts); *Caribbean* (West Indies); *Carolinas and Georgia Coast* (South, U.S.A.); *Central America; Chesapeake* (Mid-Atlantic States, U.S.A.); *Colorado; Eastern Europe; Egypt; Europe* (Europe as a Whole); *Far West* (Pacific Northwest, Rocky Mountain/Great Basin States, Southwest, U.S.A.), *Florida; France; Germany* (East Germany, West Germany); *Great Britain; Greece; Hawaii; Holland* (Netherlands); *Hungary; India, Nepal and Sri Lanka; Ireland; Israel; Italy; Japan; Jordan; Kenya; Korea; Loire Valley* (France); *Mexico; Mexico's Baja, Puerto Vallarta and Mazatlan; New England* (U.S.A.); *New Mexico; New York State; New Zealand; North Africa; Pacific North Coast* (Canada; Pacific Northwest, U.S.A.; Canada); *People's Republic of China;*

Portugal; Province of Quebec (Canada); *The Rockies* (Rocky Mountain States, U.S.A; Canada); *Scandinavia; Scotland; South* (U.S.A.); *South America; South Pacific* (Oceania as a Whole); *Southeast Asia; Soviet Union; Spain; Sweden; Switzerland; Texas; Turkey; Virgin Islands* (West Indies); *U.S.A.* (United States as a Whole); *Virginia; Yugoslavia.*

Fodor's Fun Guides
Fodor's Travel Publications/Random House

One of the newer efforts by the Fodor group to break out of the mold has been their Fun Guides to specific city or small area destinations. The format is less rigid and the substance has improved over more traditional Fodor titles. This is a step in the right direction, and with the new energy at Fodor's, a series to watch. One of the positive changes is the increased evaluation space given to selected hotels and restaurants. Fodor has generally been very brief in these areas and it is a pleasure to see more details to help the traveler. Solid information on tours, sporting activities, and sightseeing is also included. While this series appears to be an improvement in the Fodor guides, it isn't perfect and occasionally has been found lacking (e.g., *Fun in Montreal*).

Books currently available: *Fodor's Fun in Acapulco* (Mexico); similar titles on: *Bahamas* (West Indies); *Barbados* (West Indies); *Disney World and Orlando* (Florida); *Jamaica* (West Indies); *Las Vegas, Reno and Lake Tahoe* (Nevada); *London* (England); *Maui* (Hawaii); *Montreal* (Canada); *New Orleans* (Louisiana); *New York City* (New York); *Paris* (France); *Puerto Rico* (West Indies); *Rio* (Brazil); *Riviera* (France, Italy); *St. Martin* (West Indies); *San Francisco* (California); *Waikiki* (Hawaii).

Fodor's Great Travel Values Guides
Fodor's Travel Guides/Random House

This is the new name for Fodor's budget series (*Budget Europe* has retained its old title so far). Although formats on the new guides have changed radically the style is, to date, the style of old: plenty of information on practical issues and sightseeing; cryptic notes on hotels and restaurants. Some good detail maps are included but the overall tone remains lifeless. As with their other traditional guides, updates are minimal on a yearly basis; full updates occur about every four years.

Books currently available: *Fodor's Great Travel Values: American Cities* (United States as a Whole); similar titles on: *Britain; Canada; Caribbean* (West Indies); *France; Germany* (West Germany); *Hawaii; Italy; Japan; London* (England); *Mexico; Spain.* Also in the series: *Fodor's Budget Europe* (Europe as a Whole).

Fodor's Interstate Guides

Fodor's Travel Guides/Random House

These guides focus on some of the major interstate highways. Instead of being arranged regionally, they follow the interstate from one end to the other. The style is dry and utilitarian, but the resources provided—restaurants, hotels, and other services within two miles of the highway—are certainly helpful. There are also ideas for things to do up to ten miles from the freeway. Each page plots the appropriate section of the highway—a handy idea. A helpful, if uninteresting series. However, these are the only guidebooks to follow an entire highway route in a single volume.

Books currently available: *Fodor's I-10* (South, Southwest, U.S.A.); similar titles on: *I-55* (Midwest, South, U.S.A.); *I-75* (Midwest, South, U.S.A.); *I-80* (Mid-Atlantic States, Midwest, Rocky Mountain/Great Basin States, California, U.S.A.); *I-95* (New England, Mid-Atlantic States, South, U.S.A.)

Footsore Guides

This series is reviewed under "Washington."

Books currently available: *Footsore—Seattle to Issaquah Alps;* similar titles on: *Snoqualmie to Skykomish; Everett to Bellingham; Puyallup, Nisqually and Kitsap.*

Francis Chichester Guides

Warner Books

A new series, released after press time, created for the more sophisticated, well-heeled traveler. These pocket guides contain gazetteers for shopping, touring, and fashion. The titles are uniquely split into a male and female editions for each of the three cities currently covered. Plenty of clear maps are included.

Books currently available: *LA Man* (California); *LA Woman* (California); *London Man* (England); *London Woman* (England); *New York Man* (New York); *New York Woman* (New York).

Frommer's City Guides

Prentice Hall Press

The biennially updated city guides from Frommer are enjoyably written titles on shopping, lodging, restaurants, sightseeing, nightlife, and culture. Each selection is given a useful evaluation and description. All price ranges are given thorough coverage, including a number of budget choices. If you need a guide to one particular city, Frommer is a solid, middle-of-the-road choice. Note that while this is a City Guide series, it also includes Hawaii and Ireland.

Books currently available: *Frommer's Guide to Amsterdam and Holland* (Netherlands); similar titles on: *Athens* (Greece); *Atlantic*

City and Cape May (New Jersey); *Boston* (Massachusetts); *Cancun, Cozumel and Yucatan* (Mexico); *Dublin and Ireland; Hawaii; Las Vegas* (Nevada); *Lisbon, Madrid and Costa del Sol* (Spain); *London* (England); *Los Angeles* (California); *Mexico City and Acapulco; Minneapolis/St. Paul* (Minnesota); *Montreal and Quebec City* (Canada); *New Orleans* (Louisiana); *New York* (New York); *Orlando, Disney World and EPCOT* (Florida); *Paris* (France); *Philadelphia* (Pennsylvania); *Rome* (Italy); *San Francisco* (California); *Washington, D.C* (District of Columbia).

Frommer's Dollar-a-Day Guides
Prentice Hall Press

The Dollar-a-Day Guides are one of the better budget guide series. Each receives an extensive biennial update. And, although it is difficult to stay under the daily dollar figure that is part of the title, there are plenty of bargains here. Selections seem to work well consistently. Research for this series is thorough and guarantees, as well as a guidebook can, that you will find their choices meet your approval. Each book provides a good introduction to the area, including history, a discussion of the people, festivals, sports, and foods. Transportation options are covered extensively—there is no assumption that you have your own vehicle. As Frommer guides do, these cover selections of lodging and restaurants fully so you can make an informed choice.

Books currently available: *Frommer's Australia on $30 a Day;* similar titles on: *Eastern Europe; England; Europe* (Europe as a Whole); *Greece; Hawaii; India; Ireland; Israel; Mexico, Belize and Guatemala; New York* (New York); *New Zealand; Scandinavia; Scotland and Wales; South America; Spain, Morocco and Canary Islands; Turkey; Washington D.C. and Historic Virginia* (District of Columbia).

Frommer's Dollarwise Guides
Prentice Hall Press

If your budget is a bit bigger, but you don't want to use one of the guides that may overemphasize the more expensive choices, this is a good series. Emphasis is on moderately priced selections, although all price ranges are included. Each guide has a good orientation section, some fine choices of hotels and restaurants with extensive evaluations, and good sightseeing information. The guides concentrate their effort on major cities and tourist areas. Smaller towns and other, more rural destinations away from the travel mainstream are briefly mentioned. As with every Frommer title, these are significantly updated every other year.

Books currently available: *Frommer's Dollarwise Guide to*

Alaska; similar titles on: *Austria and Hungary; Belgium, Holland and Luxembourg* (Netherlands); *Bermuda and Bahamas* (West Indies); *California and Las Vegas* (Nevada); *Canada; Caribbean* (West Indies); *Egypt; England and Scotland* (Great Britain); *Florida; France; Germany* (West Germany); *Italy; Japan and Hong Kong; Mid-Atlantic* (Mid-Atlantic States, U.S.A.); *New England* (U.S.A.); *New York State and City; Northwest* (Pacific Northwest, U.S.A.); *Portugal, Madeira and Azores; South Pacific* (Oceania); *Southeast and New Orleans* (South, U.S.A.); *Southwest* (U.S.A.); *Switzerland and Liechtenstein; Texas.*

Frommer's Touring Guides
Prentice Hall Press

This newer series offers a different focus from the other Frommer series. Focusing on cultural and historical issues with essays on art, architecture, and culture, these guides provide a good overview to better prepare you to enjoy all the cultural sights. Each book includes photographs, maps, and suggested itineraries in addition to practical information on hotels, restaurants, etc. However, this type of information is not the reason to buy these guides, since other titles, including those from Frommer, would do a much better job. The primary plus of the series is its cultural and historical emphasis. Thus these books make better "companion guides" than primary travel guides.

Books currently available: *Frommer's Touring Guide to Australia;* similar titles on: *Egypt; Florence* (Italy); *London* (England); *Paris* (France); *Thailand; Venice* (Italy).

Gable & Gray Best Choices Guides
Gable & Gray

This series is solid and helpful, but not very exciting. The writeups are informative, but the overuse of bold typeface is somewhat visually distracting and makes the guide difficult to use. Everything stands out yet nothing stands out. As for substance, there is a little bit of everything on myriad subjects: lodging, restaurants, shopping, entertainment, parks, and museums. Directions to different locations are minimal. Hotels and restaurants selected can be in any price range and, although purported to be "the best choices," rarely measure up outside the big cities. A real plus, however, is that a number of the titles cover areas that have relatively few other guides.

Books currently available: *Best Choices in Arizona;* similar titles on: *Central and Eastern Oregon; Colorado; Northern California; Northern California, Bay Area Edition; Orange County* (California); *Oregon Coast; Oregon's Interstates; Portland* (Oregon); *San Diego* (California); *Tampa Bay* (Florida); *Western Washington.*

Gault/Millau 'Best Of' Guides
Crown Publishing, Prentice Hall Press
(Note: The volumes available on American cities are from Prentice Hall Press. They are newer and, unfortunately, no longer being written by the famous pair. Only the name remains the same. The initial comments from those using these guides, particularly the Washington, D.C. title, have been negative.)

The European titles in this series are published by Crown Publishing. The famous 'Best of' Guides from these two respected French critics provide what is often referred to as "opinionated and refreshingly irreverent" ratings of a wide range of night spots, restaurants, hotels, shops, sights, and tourist traps. With most guides steering a somewhat more neutral course, it is always refreshing to read fresh, critical, honest remarks. Henri Gault and Christian Millau are fun to read and show a keen eye for what will please the tourist. Whether their eye matches your own is, of course, the question. You will have to try and see. If you are impressed, their guides will serve you well for a long time. Selections in the restaurant category run the full price and cuisine spectrum; hotels, ranging from moderate to expensive, are a bit more limited.

Books currently available: *The Best of France;* similar titles on: *Italy; London* (England); *Los Angeles* (California); *New York* (New York); *Paris* (France); *San Francisco* (California); *Washington, D.C.* (District of Columbia).

Gibbs M. Smith Architecture Guides
Gibbs M. Smith, Inc.
These comprehensive guides are packed with photographs and maps of the best of architecture. Each book is organized to facilitate architecturally oriented tours. Also included are interesting bits on history, preservation, and trivia.

Books currently available: *Architecture in Los Angeles* (California); *The Guide to Architecture in San Francisco and Northern California; A Guide to the Architecture of Metro Phoenix* (Arizona).

Globe Pequot Bike Rides
The Globe Pequot Press
First-class all the way, with a good overview of each suggested ride, including mileage, terrain, food stops along the route, where to start, a considerable discussion of the highlights of each trip, a detailed mileage log, and a clear map. This series is filled with great route ideas, including many that will take you well off the beaten path, away from the heavy traffic areas. Where traffic can be difficult, there are words of warning of when *not* to contemplate the ride.

Books currently available: *Short Bike Rides on Cape Cod, Nan-*

tucket and the Vineyard (Massachusetts); similar titles on: *Connecticut; Greater Boston and Central Massachusetts; Long Island* (New York); *New Jersey; Rhode Island.*

Globe Pequot Hiking Guides
The Globe Pequot Press

The hiking guides of Globe Pequot are part of their acquisition of East Woods Press. Each is a compact book that will slide into a back pocket or add little weight to a pack. Quality is evidenced throughout the series by careful attention to detail. Hikes of every length are described, and some titles also cover trails for the handicapped. You'll find a bit of history, good trail descriptions, and adequate maps, sometimes hand-drawn.

Books currently available: *Rocky Mountain National Park Hiking Trails* (Colorado); *South Carolina Hiking Trails; Tennessee Trails; Walks in the Catskills* (New York); *Walks in the Great Smokies* (South, U.S.A.)

Globe Pequot Walks
The Globe Pequot Press

A great little series of short, leisurely walks to enjoy and savor. No need to strap on a heavy backpack or any a pack at all unless you would like to take a picnic and share a bottle of wine along the way. Each compact guidebook has dozens of possible walks from a fraction of a mile to several miles in length. Driving directions, good trail notes, maps sufficient for the purpose, and other helpful hints are included.

Books currently available: *Short Walks on Cape Cod and the Vineyard* (Massachusetts); similar titles on: *Connecticut; Long Island* (New York).

Golf Courses of New Zealand
International Specialized Book Services (ISBS)

This series is reviewed under "New Zealand."

Books currently available: *Golf Courses of Auckland*; similar titles on: *Canterbury; Marlborough, Nelson and Wesland; Otago; South Canterbury; Southland and Fiordland; Wellington.*

Great Lakes Guidebooks
The University of Michigan Press

This series is reviewed under "The Midwest" (U.S.A.). Titles include Canadian destinations as well.

Books available: *The Great Lakes Guidebook: Lake Huron and Eastern Lake Michigan;* similar titles on: *Lakes Ontario and Erie; Lake Superior and Western Lake Michigan.*

Great Towns Guides
West Press
   These are guides to out-of-the-way vacation spots, each one a
"great town" in its area. The author, David Vokac, defines a great
town as "an independent, unspoiled community rich in human-scale
charms and scenic splendor." For each town that meets his criteria,
he provides a good overview, including detailed notes on history, and
weather, as well as some well-described possibilities for lodging of
every sort, restaurants, camping, shopping, nightlife, sightseeing,
special events, and just general enjoyment. These are great idea
books/resource guides.
   Books currently available: *Great Towns of California*; similar titles on: *Pacific Northwest* (U.S.A.); *West* (Pacific Northwest, Rocky
Mountain/Great Basin States, Southwest, U.S.A.)

Guides from Russia
Imported Publications
   Each of these titles has been translated and published in the Soviet
Union. Although some are a bit old (there seems to be little concern
for keeping them current) they are fine little hardbacks that show
many Soviet cities as the Soviets themselves see them. Provided first
is a good overview of pertinent history as well as notes on geography
and architecture. Then, various walking excursions are outlined.
Considerable sightseeing information is included for each walk. Additional information on the areas immediately surrounding the city,
numerous interesting photos, and a separate map of the immediate
central area are often included also. These will make great "companion guides," lending a different perspective to more all-purpose
guides prepared by western authors.
   Books currently available: (All titles are listed under the Soviet
Union.) *Alma-Ata: A Guide*; similar titles on: *Ashkhabad; Black
Sea Coast; Burkhara; Dushanbe; Frunze; Greater Yalta; Irkutsk;
Kiev; Kishinev; Minsk; Moldavia; Moscow, Leningrad and Kiev;
Odessa; Petrozavodsk and Kizhi; Pskov; Riga; Smolensk; Suzdal;
Tallinn; Tashkent; Ulyanovsk; Vladimir; Volgograd.*

Guides to Adirondack Trails
Adirondack Mountain Club
   This series is reviewed under "New York."
   Books currently available: *Guide to Adirondack Trails: Volume I:
High Peaks Region*; similar titles on: *Volume II: Northern Region;
Volume III: Central Region; Volume IV: Northville-Placid Trail;
Volume V: West-Central Region; Volume VI: Eastern Region.*

Guides to British Sites
Hunter Publishing
> This series is reviewed under "Great Britain."
> Books currently available: *Guide to Ancient Sites in Great Britain;*
> *Guide to Anglo-Saxon Sites; Guide to Norman Sites in Britain.*

Gulf Camping Guides
Gulf Publishing
> Regionally organized and comprehensive in its coverage, these
> camping guides provide the essential details on hundreds of camping
> sites, as well as maps locating campsites, trails, parking, etc. Special
> features and riding and hiking trails are clearly marked.
> Books currently available: *Camper's Guide to California Parks* (2
> volumes); similar titles on: *Florida; Texas.*

Hachette Guides
Random House
> The Hachette Guides, France's Guides Bleus, are for those who
> want it all in a single volume—maps, tips, details on services, hiking
> and cycling routes, and travel itineraries—with no town too small
> and no subject too obscure. However, this attempt at covering as
> much as possible has its price—small print, numerous symbols and
> very limited descriptions and comments. This vast amount of detail
> can sometimes make these guides difficult to use. Help, though, may
> be on the way as these guides are updated annually and, according
> to the publisher have been "redesigned for easier reading." Mean-
> while, travelers looking for an extremely detailed, all-purpose guide-
> book, will find it here.
> Books currently available: *The Hachette Guide to France;* similar
> titles on: *Great Britain; Italy; London* (England); *Paris* (France).

Hawaiian Hiking Guides
Wilderness Press
> This series is reviewed under "Hawaii."
> Books currently available: *Hiking Hawaii;* similar titles on: *Kauai;*
> *Maui; Oahu;* also in the series: *Hawaii's Best Hiking Trails.*

Hidden Places Guides
Ulysses Press
> Ray Reigert, one of the ex-editors of the infamous *Berkeley Barb*
> of the 1960's, has found his latter-day nitch in writing travel books.
> All but one of this series is his creation. And write he does. His
> *Hidden Hawaii,* now in its 4th edition, recently won the Lowell
> Thomas Travel Journalism Award for Best Guidebook. Perhaps that
> settles for the moment the difficult task of choosing the best guide

to Hawaii. But these guides aren't for everyone. They have a distinct adventurous flare and their hotel and restaurants selections are predominantly moderate and budget in their orientation. The guides are a pleasure to read and will point you toward a vast array of exciting activities. Those hidden, less-known discoveries are marked clearly with a large, black star which allows you to scan the book in search of lodging or vacation playgrounds where you can find some elbow room. Where's the best body surfing, the best snorkeling, the best camping? It's all here in these excellent guidebooks. You need not be young to enjoy them, just ready to get out there and go, go, go. Updated every two years.

Books currently available: *Hidden Coast of California;* similar titles on: *Hawaii; Mexico; San Francisco & Northern California.*

Hildebrand's Guides
Hunter Publishing

A German series, now in somewhat larger new format, that covers most travel topics but is especially good on history and thoughtful travel impressions that will add significantly to your sightseeing pleasure. You will also find a full range of hotel choices, travel maps, lots of practical details, and plenty of color photographs. Food information is more an orientation to local cuisine than specific selections. Compact, useful guides.

Books currently available: *Hildebrand's Travel Guide: Australia;* similar titles on: *China; France; Hispaniola* (Dominican Republic, Haiti); *India & Nepal; Indonesia; Jamaica* (West Indies); *Japan; Kenya; Korea* (South); *Mauritius* (Islands of the Western Indian Ocean); *Mexico; New Zealand; Philippines; Seychelles* (Islands of the Western Indian Ocean); *South Africa; Sri Lanka; Taiwan; Thailand.* Available from Hippocrene Books in the old format: *Hildebrand's Travel Guide: Cuba.*

Historic Restaurants & Recipes
John F. Blair, Publisher

This is a fantastic series of inexpensive, hardback books combining the best recipes of the historic restaurants of each state with informative descriptions and reviews, including the practical details. Of course, the emphasis is on the recipes, so some of the titles are a bit old to be totally reliable on the current state of affairs at any particular restaurant. Nonetheless, they are a good way to start the selection process. For those who like to look over the recipes before they choose their restaurant, this series is just plain great.

Books currently available: *Georgia's Historic Restaurants and Their Recipes;* similar titles on: *Florida; Maryland; North Carolina; Pennsylvania; South Carolina; Virginia.*

Historical Tour Guides
Crossroads Communications

A fine sightseeing series which concentrates on states of the Midwest and Rocky Mountain region that have had little attention from the travel book field except as a chapter in larger, regional titles. Now each state has its own claim to fame. Each guide does a commendable job covering the historical places and the personalities behind them. The format is set up to follow the different major highways that criss-cross each state. You will find them immensely informative and thoroughly enjoyable.

Books currently available: *Iowa Historical Tour Guide;* similar titles on: *Kansas; Nebraska; Wyoming.*

History & Sightseeing Guides
Random House

This is a particularly well written travel series. Its strong suit is sightseeing (including walks), the history behind what you are seeing, and the various activities you might indulge in along the way. Hotels and restaurants are mentioned, but are few in number and are obviously not the primary focus. As title states, these are best seen as more detailed history and touring guides that will admirably supplement a guide which tends more specifically to the issues of sleep and food.

Books currently available: *East Hampton: A History and Guide* (New York); similar titles on: *Florida Keys* (Florida); *Hudson River Valley* (New York); *Northern California; Virginia.*

Holiday Guides
M. Evans & Co.

Finally, after six years, the 10th edition of the long-popular Holiday Guide series has materialized. For those who put a premium on size, these compact guides offer quite a bit of information of a "what to see and what to do" nature on each locale. There are also history notes, a useful planning and preparation chapter, and plenty of selections of hotels and restaurants in various price catagories. Comments on hotels and restaurants, however, are very brief. That aside, the *Holiday Guides* an excellent source of information for their size.

Books currently available: *The New Holiday Guide to Britain* (Great Britain); similar titles on: *Caribbean & Bahamas* (West Indies); *France; Greece & Aegean Islands; Hawaii; Ireland; Israel; Italy; London* (England); *Mexico; Paris* (France); *Rome* (Italy); *Scandinavia; Spain; West Germany.*

Hunter Adventure Guides
Hunter Publishing

A new series, released after press time, which will offer information on numerous possible adventure trips. Anything from hiking, cycling, mountaineering, cross-country skiing, pack trips, whitewater expeditions, canoeing, and horseback riding, depending on the location, with practical details as well.

Books currently available: *The Adventure Guide to American Northwest* (Pacific Northwest, U.S.A.); similar titles on: *Italy; Jamaica* (West Indies).

Hunter Insider's Guides
Hunter Publishing

Slickly produced, this Insider's series from Hunter Publishing has a look a bit like the more famous Insight Guides. With numerous, beautiful color photographs and an informative text, they present a good overview of each area and its many sightseeing options. Other details like hotels, restaurants, and specific activities are merely lists with a price range noted. We much prefer more detail when it comes to hotels and restaurants, but for a good overview and a general, mainstream touring guide, these guides work quite well. Pretty to look at, they also come with a large, fold-out map.

Books currently available: *The Insider's Guide to Australia;* similar titles on: *China; Hawaii; Hong Kong; Japan; Korea.*

Hunter Mountain Walks
Hunter Publishing

A good collection of more mountainous hikes (and some climbs) in the various mountain ranges of Europe, with well-organized preparatory notes, carefully planned routes, and suggested maps. Hikes are rated by distance and difficulty and numerous orientation maps are interspersed throughout the text.

Books currently available: *Mountain Walking in Austria; The Mountains of Greece; Tour of Mont Blanc* (France); *Walks and Climbs in the Engadine* (Switzerland); *Walks and Climbs in The Pyrenees* (Andorra France, Spain).

Hunter Walking/Hiking Guides
Hunter Publishing

This series came to Hunter from the Bradt Enterprises and includes walking, backpacking through countries, as well as hiking in more mountainous terrain. Included are a diverse selection of hiking/walking trails in both Africa and South America. Each book offers fine descriptions of trails, landscape, and people of the area, with information on when and where to go, maps, and more. First-rate guides we are pleased to see are still available.

Books currently available: *Backpacker's Africa: A Walker's Guide to East, Central and Southern Africa; Backpacker's Africa-2: A Guide to West & Central Africa; Backpacking and Trekking in Peru and Bolivia; Backpacking and Walking in Italy; Climbing and Hiking in Ecuador.*

Hunter Walks
Hunter Publishing

In spite of the similarity, this is a distinct series from Hunter Publishing's other series on walks and hikes. The series has a stronger emphasis on short walks, though longer treks are included. The books are well organized and nicely presented. Maps are provided for most hikes and each is rated by time needed, altitude gained, etc. Small photos are sprinkled throughout the text and clear directions are given to the trailheads. Nicely done.

Books currently available: *Walking in the Alps;* similar titles on: *Austria; Northern France; Switzerland.*

I Love Cities Guides
Macmillan Publishing

Marilyn Appleberg's popular guides have been recently updated. They are good, all-purpose travel guides, well organized and enjoyably written with short, no-nonsense writeups on a wide range of important travel topics and good maps. Restaurant and hotel selections are in all price ranges and Appleberg offers tips on just about every conceivable travel concern. Widely acclaimed, they represent a very solid guidebook choice.

Books currently available: *I Love Boston* (Massachusetts); similar titles on: *Chicago* (Illinois); *Los Angeles* (California); *New York* (New York); *Washington, D.C.* (District of Columbia).

In Your Pocket Guides
Barron's Educational Series

If you put a premium on the size of your guide, one series that packs a considerable amount of information into a small space is the Barron's In Your Pocket series. For a mere $3.95 you get a very handy directory to restaurants, hotels, museums, theaters, stores, night life, sightseeing, and important services. Obviously, there isn't as much in one of these small guides as in one ten times its weight, but for the money they have a lot to offer. If small is beautiful to you, take a look at one of these city guides and see if it doesn't meet your needs.

Books currently available: *Boston in Your Pocket;* similar titles on: *Chicago* (Illinois); *Hong Kong*; *London* (England); *Los Angeles* (California); *New York* (New York); *Paris* (France); *San Francisco* (California); *Tokyo* (Japan); *Washington, D.C.* (District of Columbia).

Insight Guides
Prentice Hall Press

The Insight Guides are simply wonderful. Produced by a Singapore company, they weave an interesting text through a potpourri of spectacular photographs. When we first saw the Insight Guides years ago, we though they were simply picture books. Not so. There is a vast amount of information inside as well. They dedicate a good, meaty fifty pages or so to the history, geography, and people of each area. Then they take you on a guided tour of all the major areas—the backcountry, too—as well as providing special features on areas of unusual interest, parks, etc. Their "guide in brief" at the back does a commendable job with practical details, including respectable lists of lodging and accommodations. In general, these guides seem to be updated every two or three years so information is kept quite current.

Books currently available: *Insight Guide: Alaska*; similar titles on: *American Southwest* (Southwest, U.S.A.); *Australia*; *Bahamas* (West Indies); *Bali* (Indonesia); *Barbados* (West Indies); *Burma*; *Canada*; *Continental Europe* (Europe as a Whole); *Crossing America* (United States as a Whole); *Florida*; *France*; *Germany* (West Germany); *Great Britain*; *Hawaii*; *Hong Kong & Macau*; *India*; *Indonesia*; *Ireland*; *Israel*; *Italy*; *Jamaica* (West Indies); *Kenya*; *Korea*; *Malaysia*; *Mexico*; *Nepal*; *New England* (U.S.A.); *New York State*; *New Zealand*; *Northern California*; *Philippines*; *Puerto Rico* (West Indies); *Rockies* (Rocky Mountain/Great Basin States, U.S.A.); *Singapore*; *Southern California*; *Spain*; *Sri Lanka*; *Taiwan*; *Texas*; *Thailand*; *Trinidad & Tobago* (West Indies). *Insight Guide: the Pacific Northwest* (U.S.A., distributed only by Graphic Arts Center Publishing).

The Interstate Gourmet Guides
Summit Books

Have you ever been whizzing down the Interstate when the hunger pangs set in? What to do? It is almost too depressing to deal with—another greasy spoon or fast-food joint. Eating is supposed to be fun. Well, the Interstate Gourmet series is the answer to your prayers. Exit by exit they will tell you what is just down the road that's really worth the time. Directions, hours, and a great, informative review. Sure, a few of these selections may have gone out of business since the book was last revised, but the choices are almost endless. If you're having a problem, hop in the car and drive on down the road a few miles more. There's great food ahead! For the Interstate driver, this series is simply a miracle. The New England volume is currently unavailable. The entire future of the series seems unsure at press time, though such an excellent effort should certainly be continued.

Books currently available: *Interstate Gourmet: California and the Pacific Northwest* (U.S.A.); similar titles on: *Mid-Atlantic* (U.S.A.); *Midwest* (U.S.A.); *New England* (U.S.A.); *Texas & Southwest* (U.S.A.); *Southeast* (South, U.S.A.).

Island Heritage Guides
Island Heritage

This series is reviewed under "Hawaii."

Books currently available: *The Essential Guide to Kaua'i*; similar titles on: *Hawaii, the Big Island; Maui; O'ahu.*

Island Hopping Guides
Hippocrene Books

An aging series on the islands of Europe. There once was a Caribbean title as well, but this and most of the areas covered in the still-available Italian islands volume have since become part of the Cadogan series in updated form (see Cadogan Guides). What is left is still useful for sightseeing, general orientation, and history, but these once-fine guides are otherwise thoroughly out-of-date. Because they cover some interesting island groups, they can be used as a resource, but the series is in need of new, revised editions.

Books currently available: *Canary Island Hopping (The Azores, Madeira): A Handbook for the Independent Traveler* (Islands of the Eastern and Northern Atlantic Ocean); similar titles on: *Channel Islands* (England); *Greek Islands* (Greece); *Mediterranean Islands* (Italy and Spain); *Scottish Islands.*

Itinerary Planners
John Muir Publications

The number of titles in this series is expanding rapidly—all because of the runaway success of Rick Steves's *Europe in 22 Days* (now titled *22 Days in Europe*). Steves is a veteran guide, having lead tours primarily in Europe for almost 15 years. The intent of this series is to help you lead your own tour by providing clear, well-planned itineraries for classic three-week vacations. Optional side trips are included to allow you to expand your trip even further. The itineraries are also designed to let you begin or end a trip at any point in the schedule. Generally, these trips are for energetic souls with some get-up-and-go, although some "R&R" days are planned. And, in spite of the assumption of a vehicle of your own, the orientation is distinctly budget, with good picks for lodging and restaurants. The whole idea is to let the experts lead the way, but not to pay someone to actually be there. It's a great idea for those who want that much direction in their vacation life. Note that the title of each guide in this series was changed in 1988. Be aware that you may find either title on the bookstore shelf for some time to come.

Books currently available: *22 Days in Alaska: The Itinerary Planner;* similar titles on: *American Southwest* (Southwest, U.S.A.); *Australia; China; Europe* (Europe as a Whole); *Germany, Austria and Switzerland; Great Britain; Hawaii; India; Japan; Mexico; New England* (U.S.A.); *New Zealand; Pacific Northwest* (U.S.A.); *Scandinavia; Spain and Portugal; West Indies.*

Karen Brown's Country Inns
Travel Press

The delightful, superbly done Karen Brown series has been consistently adding titles in recent years, updating regularly, and is now distributed by the new Traveler's Bookshelf collection from Warner Books. The series concentrates on quaint, charming places to stay—inns, villas, chalets, castles, chateaux, or paradors. Each book is arranged into travel itineraries with each day ending at the next inn of choice. The itinerary is charted on a map and each day's journey is detailed. In a separate section, every suggested place of lodging is given a full page of coverage, which includes line drawing, the necessary practical facts, and a well-written paragraph on both the building, and, usually, the owners. There is even a helpful section on how to write a letter making reservations in the language of that country as well as other "Inn Discoveries" from users of the series.

Books currently available: *Austrian Country Inns and Castles;* similar titles on: *English, Welsh and Scottish* (Great Britian); *European* (Europe as a Whole); *French; German* (West Germany); *Irish; Italian; Portuguese; Scandinavian; Spanish; Swiss.* Also in the series: *European Country Cuisine: Romantic Inns and Recipes* (Europe as a Whole).

Knopf Guides to Art
Alfred Knopf, Inc.

These excellent art guides contain a helpful gazetteer, critical reviews, and introductions to each region's art centers, as well as specific museum guides and maps. From the famous to the most obscure art treasures of Europe, these well-done books will guide you from region to region. Within each region, each city is listed alphabetically and keyed to a regional map. After a brief background section on the history and art of the city, the key museums and archeological sites are reviewed. Included are the practical details as well as a rating of each museum. These books are full of detail for the museum buff and loaded with color photographs. Unfortunately, rumor has it that these books may soon be phased out. Quality like this, however, will certainly turn up with a new publisher, under a different name. If these guides have indeed disappeared from view, try tracing them by using the author's index of *Books in Print*.

Books currently available: *The Knopf Traveler's Guide to Art: France*; similar titles on: *Great Britain and Ireland; Italy*.

Let's Go Guides
St. Martin's Press

The Let's Go series has been the premier budget guide, especially for the young, for many years. The annual updates are very thorough, generally accomplished by a horde of traveling students and, these days, other somewhat older students-at-heart. Essentially, every selection is reevaluated each year—an uncommon occurence when it comes to annual updates of travel guides. These are guides for the hitchhiker and train rider. Begun in 1960 by a group of Harvard students, the series is still produced by Harvard Student Agencies. Each title covers the big cities as well as many of the nooks and crannies of each region. Even Harvard grads of yesteryear, who have long since given up staying in youth hostels and cheap pensions, buy the series to get at all the well-written travel facts: planning, sights, entertainment, nightlife, and suggested excursions. As opposed to other guides, the heavy emphasis on low, low budget travel means a stronger orientation to the less-expensive rural areas of each country. As a result, the traveler will often find cities covered in Let's Go that are neglected in more mainstream guides. That is not to say that the major cities are neglected. In fact, a tremendous amount of effort goes into reevaluating each large city annually. One researcher is usually assigned to a single city and he or she spends a full month working 18 hour days to cover the territory. The bottom line is that the series is definitely one of the very best, whatever the price range.

Books currently available: *Let's Go: Britain and Ireland*; similar titles on: *California and Hawaii (including Reno, Las Vegas, Lake Tahoe, Baja California); Europe* (Europe as a Whole); *France; Greece, Cyprus, Turkish Coast and Istanbul; Israel, Egypt and Jordan; Italy; Mexico; Pacific Northwest, Western Canada and Alaska; Spain, Portugal and Morocco; U.S.A.* (United States as a Whole.).

Let's Go Somewhere Guides
The Great Outdoors Publishing

This series is reviewed under "Florida."

Books currently available: *Let's Go Somewhere: 150 Day Trips,*

South West Florida; similar titles on: *Tampa and Big Bend; North East Florida.*

Lett's Guides
Prima Publishing

The expressed purpose of these little guides is to give enough information about what to see and do and the people of the area so that travelers can intelligently decide on their destination of choice. The author contends that guidebooks should only point you in the right direction not give detailed accounts of what should be seen and done. Used as preparation, planning, and orientation tools, these guides are quite helpful—and not nearly as outdated as their publication date might indicate.

Books currently available: *Lett's Guide: Costa Brava and Costa Dorada* (Spain); similar titles on: *Costa del Sol and South of Spain; Denmark; France; Greece–Mainland; Greek Islands* (Greece); *Holland* (Netherlands); *Portugal; Spanish Islands* (Spain); *Switzerland.*

Long Stays Guides
Hippocrene Books

The Long Stay Guides are practical guides for those who are planning a longer than usual stay or are perhaps emigrating. Details on visas, packing (a little different than just a vacation), managing in the new country, finding housing, education, family life, communications, and other topics of importance are included. These are definitely helpful planning resources offering a wealth of information not contained in the standard travel guidebook.

Books currently available: *Long Stays in Australia;* similar titles on: *Belgium and Luxembourg; Portugal.*

Lost & Found Guides
Orafa Publishing

The Lost & Found series is a unique set of "companion guides," providing an instructive overview of each town, city, or island. These guides do not contain recommendations for lodging or dining or sightseeing. Rather, they are well-written, entertaining tales of travel experiences. You will be a better tourist for having read them for, unlike many other books written in narrative form, these books seem to be guidebooks as well as stories.

Books currently available: *How to Get Lost & Found in Australia;* similar titles on: *California; Cook Islands* (Oceania); *Fiji* (Oceania); *Hawaii; Japan; London* (England); *New Zealand; Tahiti* (Oceania).

Maine Geographic Canoeing Guides
DeLorme Publishing
This series is reviewed under "Maine."
Books currently available: *Maine Geographic, Volume 1: Coastal and Eastern Rivers;* similar titles on: *Volume 2: Western Rivers; Volume 3: Northern Rivers.*

Maine Geographic Hiking Guides
DeLorme Publishing
This series is reviewed under "Maine."
Books currently available: *Maine Geographic, Hiking Volume 1: Coastal and Eastern Region;* similar titles on: *Western Region; Northern Region.*

Marling Menu-Masters
Altarinda Books
If there is such a thing as a classic in the field of menu guides, the Marling series is first in line. These small, thin, pocket guides, are packed with facts. Each guide is designed with an easy-to-use tab system for the various menu groups. The menus themselves are not just translations of words, but good definitions and explanations of every dish. Not only that, the guides have a sturdy, plasticized cover that means your $5.95 investment will last for a long time.
Books currently available: *The Marling Menu-Master for France;* similar titles on: *Germany; Italy; Spain.*

Marmac Guides
Pelican Publishing
The Marmac Guides offer solid, well-organized views of major cities. These guides include information on how to manage in each city and some of its history and tradition. The hotels and restaurants listed are many, and each is first presented by geographic area, then alphabetically (for hotels) or by type of cuisine. Price ranges run the gamut, but moderate is the most common. The restaurant section is particularly comprehensive and well done. Additional sections cover shopping, sightseeing, museums, sports, nightlife, theater, various excursions, walking tours, and transportation. The format is easy to use and the books are updated every two years.
Books currently available: *A Marmac Guide to Atlanta* (Georgia); similar titles on: *Houston and Galveston* (Texas); *Los Angeles* (California); *New Orleans* (Louisiana); *Philadelphia* (Pennsylvania).

Maverick Guides
Pelican Publishing

Robert Bone's Maverick Guides are nothing short of excellent, and a little time spent reading one of these guides will tell you why. Every hotel, restaurant, and activity is developed fully in an enjoyable style that will leave you feeling well informed about the choices you have to make. Few guidebooks do it better. These guides cover it all and cover it well. From history to outdoor adventures, you will not go wrong with a Maverick Guide in your hand. They are probably best suited to the middle-of-the-road traveler, although you will find selections in all price ranges and activities for almost every need. The Hawaii guide deserves particular notice and is updated annually. The other two guides are updated biennially.

Books currently available: *The Maverick Guide to Australia;* similar titles on: *Hawaii; New Zealand.*

Meed Guides
Routledge & Kegan Paul/Methuen, Inc.

This series of guides to seven Middle Eastern countries offers good, practical information on history, culture, the people, the economy, doing business, and a small number of hotels and restaurants. A few detail maps and photos are included but overall the presentation is a bit dry.

Books currently available: *Bahrain: A Meed Practical Guide;* similar titles on: *Jordan; Oman; Qatar; Saudi Arabia; UAE* (United Arab Emirates).

Michael's Guides
Hunter Publishing

This series, created and written by Michael Shichor, has several strong points. Each guide provides a good orientation to the area covered, delving into all sorts of practical issues that may confront the traveler, and it is a very solid source of sightseeing information, often including well-done walking tours. For these topics the series is particularly good. For other travel issues, the guides are solid but not exceptional. Regarding the primary issues of food and lodging, a number of specific choices are given with brief notes to orient you to the types of foods not to miss as well as realities of accommodations in each area. The guides to Paris and Jerusalem are particularly fine as walking-tour guides.

Books currently available: *Michael's Guide: Amsterdam* (Netherlands); similar titles on: *Argentina, Chile, Paraguay and Uruguay; Bolivia and Peru; Brazil; Brussels and Antwerp; Ecuador, Columbia and Venezuela; Jerusalem* (Israel); *Madrid* (Spain); *New York City*

(New York); *Northern California; Paris* (France); *Scotland; Southern California.*

Michelin Green Guides
Michelin Guides & Maps

This is definitely the best sightseeing series around. The Green Guides concentrate on what they do best and they do so in a manner that facilitates their use. Although they list sights alphabetically, they keep things well organized with suggested tour maps and careful referencing of each point of interest to the famous Michelin maps you can purchase separately. Detailed driving or walking directions are included. Detail maps to help you locate adjacent or nearby sights you might like to see are also included. Before the tour, there are excellently prepared overviews of each area—its economy, history, artistic development, local geography, and vegetation. All the possible things to do are generally broken down into two broad categories: "must do's" and "only if there's time." The directions given are clear and the maps are in the best Michelin tradition. Numerous museum floor plans and those of other important buildings are also included. The Green Guides that try to cover a larger area are, of necessity, less detailed and, with that in mind, the city or small regional guides are the best. Regardless, as a series the Michelin Green Guides are without peer. Note that only those guides available in English are listed below. There is also a Mexico guide available in Spanish and numerous additional regions of France are available in French.

Books currently available in English: *Michelin Green Guide: Austria;* similar titles on: *Brittany* (France); *Burgundy* (France); *Canada; Châteaux of the Loire* (France); *Dordogne* (France); *French Riviera* (France); *Germany* (West Germany); *Greece; Italy; London* (England); *New England* (U.S.A.); *New York City* (New York); *Normandy* (France); *Paris* (France); *Portugal; Provence* (France); *Rome* (Italy); *Scotland; Spain; Switzerland; Washington, D.C.* (District of Columbia); *West Country England.*

Michelin Red Guides
Michelin Guides & Maps

Particularly for the French, the Red Guide is the bible of hotel and restaurant ratings. To receive the highest ranking as a restaurant in France is an honor reserved for a mere handful of the very best (not to mention the most expensive). But the Red Guides go far beyond France, covering most of western Europe in separate editions. Other than the guide to the *Main Cities of Europe,* the guides are not written in English. Instead, there are sections explaining how to use the guide written in various languages. This approach works because the guide is built entirely on a multitude of symbols. The symbols will tell you what class the hotel is, what facilities are available, point out noteworthy amenities, rate the cuisine, describe the prices, and list the credit cards accepted. The amount of information packed into these annually updated guides is amazing. But it all looks like something only an Egyptologist could love and it takes some getting used to—not to mention that the entire guide becomes rather impersonal with this construction. But, if you just want the facts on hotels and restaurants the Red Guide is one of the most up-to-date, comprehensive guides around.

Books currently available: *Michelin Red Guide: Benelux* (Belgium, Luxembourg, Netherlands); similar titles on: *Deutschland* (West Germany); *España and Portugal* (Spain, Portugal); *Europe-Main Cities* (Europe as a Whole); *France; Great Britain and Ireland; Greater London* (England); *Italia* (Italy); *Paris* (France).

Minnesota Walk Books
Nodin Press

This series is reviewed under "Minnesota."

Books currently available: *Minnesota Walk Book, Volume I: A Guide to Backpacking and Hiking in the Arrowhead and Isle Royale;* similar titles on: *Volume II: the Heartland; Volume III: Hiawathaland Area; Volume IV: Metroland Area; Volume V: Pioneer Region; Volume VI: Vikingland Region.*

Mobil Lodging for Less
Prentice Hall Press

New from Mobil in 1988 is a separate guide to inexpensive lodging. Three editions mark the beginning of this new series covering hundreds and hundreds of lodging sites in typical Mobil fashion (see below).

Books currently available: *Mobil Travel Guide: Lodging for Less, Northeast and Midwest* (New England, Mid-Atlantic States, Midwest, U.S.A.); similar titles on: *The South* (U.S.A.); *The West* (Rocky Mountain/Great Basin States, Pacific Northwest, Southwest, U.S.A.)

Mobil Travel Guides
Prentice Hall Press

For many years, Mobil has been the American equivalent of the Michelin Red Guide. Restaurants and hotels take pride in high ratings from Mobil and often publicize it. There is nothing fancy about these large-format guides printed on inexpensive, newsprint-type paper (thus the low cost for their size). And there are no awards for writing style either. Just the facts, in an all-American, meat-and-potatoes fashion, using lots of symbols to save space and allow the editors to cover an incredible number of hotels, motels, and restaurants. If you want to be able to look up whatever diner happens to come along, the Mobil Guide is your best bet. For selectivity and a good, written evaluation of the selected establishments, look elsewhere.

Books currently available: *Mobil Travel Guide: California and the West* (Rocky Mountain/Great Basin States, Southwest, U.S.A.); similar titles on: *Great Lakes Area* (Midwest, U.S.A.); *Major Cities* (United States as a Whole); *Middle Atlantic States* (U.S.A.); *Northeastern States* (New England, U.S.A.); *Northwest and Great Plains States* (Midwest, Pacific Northwest, Rocky Mountain/Great Basin States, U.S.A.); *Southeastern States* (South, U.S.A.); *Southwest and South Central Area* (Midwest, Rocky Mountain/Great Basin States, Southwest, U.S.A.).

Moon Handbooks
Moon Publications

The orientation of this series is on the young and adventurous, but every traveler can glean tremendous value from each, superbly crafted handbook. Most people using the Moon guides will be relying on public transportation, a bicycle, or their thumb, and such is the orientation of these books. However, there is always information for those who wish to rent a car. Remember, though, that these books are certainly not focused on auto travel. Each guide offers an incredible amount of background information on history, natural history, the people, arts and crafts, events, etc. If you read and study this section before you go, you will be a *very* well educated traveler. Sightseeing notes are offered in copious detail and there are always good maps of important areas. Food and lodging recommendations are not neglected, with numerous, well-described choices that generally cover the price ranges of budget to moderate. The occasional guide, such as the *Japan Handbook*, will offer a much wider range. The series is comprehensive and, in a word, superb.

Four exciting announcements have reached us at press time: the long awaited arrival of the *Japan Handbook* update will appear in 1989; the company has now made a commitment to thorough revisions every two years (it will take a while to put this policy into effect), thus solving the only small flaw in the system; new books on Southeast Asia and the Philippines are due out in late 1988; and, finally, the company plans to increase its coverage of the western United States with three titles in 1989: Alaska, New Mexico, and California.

Books currently available: *Alaska-Yukon Handbook*, similar titles on: *Arizona; Hawaii; Indonesia; Japan; Maui* (Hawaii); *Micronesia* (Oceania); *New Zealand; South Korea; South Pacific* (Oceania);

Utah. Other titles in the series: *Finding Fiji; Guide to Catalina Island* (California); *Guide to Jamaica (including Haiti); Guide to Puerto Rico and Virgin Islands (including Dominican Republic).*

Mountaineers Cross-Country Skiing Guides
The Mountaineers

This series contains great selections of cross-country skiing trips of every length and difficulty. Ideas abound, not to mention some helpful descriptions of the terrain, the best time to go, avalanche potential, elevation gain, level of skill required, recommended topographical maps, and driving directions. Inspiring photos and a clean, easy-to-read layout make this series a winner.

Books currently available: *Backcountry Skiing in Washington's Cascades; Colorado High Routes; Cross-Country Ski Routes of Oregon's Cascades; Cross-Country Ski Trails of Washington's Cascades and Olympics.*

Mountaineers Hiking Guides
The Mountaineers

Generally, if a book is published by The Mountaineers, you can count on it to be everything it should be. These hiking guides are no exception. With a clean, crisp layout and nice photos, these guides present all the essentials—distance, time needed, best time of year, tides, obstacles, or other specifics, maps, and recommendation of the best U.S.G.S. map to buy. Also included are clear driving instructions and the many trail details are nicely laid out. Watch for *100 Hikes in the Glacier Peaks Area* (Washington), coming in 1989.

Books currently available: *100 Hikes in the Alpine Lakes* (Washington); similar titles on: *the Alps* (Switzerland); *Inland Northwest* (Washington); *North Cascades* (Washington); *South Cascades and Olympics* (Washington). Other titles in the series: *50 Hikes in Mt. Rainer National Park* (Washington); *55 Ways to the Wilderness in Southcentral Alaska; 94 Hikes in the Canadian Rockies* (Canada); *Northwest Trails* (Pacific Northwest, U.S.A.); *Olympic Mountains Trail Guide* (Washington); *109 Hikes in B.C.'s Lower Mainland* (Canada); *103 Hikes in Southwestern B.C.* (Canada); *Oregon Coast Hikes.*

Mountaineers National Park Guides
The Mountaineers

Each National Park Guide guide gives a rundown on the history behind the park, the essential natural history facts and figures, and practical notes on permits, weather, camping, etc. Following this are suggested short and long trails or canoeing routes, depending on the particular park and its terrain. A good resource for outdoor adventure in our national parks.

Books currently available: *Glacier Bay National Park: A Back-country Guide to the Glaciers and Beyond* (Alaska); similar titles on: *Isle Royale* (Michigan); *Voyageurs* (Minnesota).

Nagel's Guides
Passport Books/National Textbook Co.

This vintage Swiss series is meant for the sophisticated traveler who would like more than the typical amount of detail on history, physical geography, economy, literature, the theater, philosophy, science, art, music, and the cinema. These and similar topics make up the first part of each book. What follows are detailed itineraries through the various regions of each country including copious notes, on history and activities, in each town and point of interest. Detail maps are numerous. The Nagel guides appear unusual compared to the typical American guidebook and are often a thousand pages or more—small, thick, sturdy, hardbound volumes. If the label "sophisticated" sounds correct for you, take the time to evaluate the Nagel Guides for yourself. Though sometimes a little old, they make wonderful companion guides in conjunction with your more practical, primary guidebook.

Books currently available: *Nagel's Encyclopedia Guide: Bolivia*; similar titles on: *Brazil; Bulgaria; Canada; Central America; Ceylon* (Sri Lanka); *China; Czechoslovakia; Denmark and Greenland; Egypt; Finland; France; German Federal Republic* (West Germany); *Great Britain; Gulf Emirates* (The Middle East); *Iceland; India and Nepal; Iran; Ireland; Malta; Mexico; Peru; Philippines; Poland; Rumania* (Romania); *Spain; Sweden; Thailand; Turkey; U.S.S.R.* (Soviet Union).

New Bell's Cathedral Guides
Salem House

This series is reviewed under "England."

Books currently available: *The New Bell's Cathedral Guides: Canterbury Cathedral*; similar titles on: *Coventry Cathedral; St. Paul's Cathedral; Salisbury Cathedral; Wells Cathedral; Westminster Abbey*.

New Visitor's Guides
Hunter Publishing

The New Visitor's Guides, more recent, expanded relatives of the Visitor's Guides series described below, are good guides for general orientation and touring in various countries. They contain a large introduction as well as an extensive practical tips section. Sightseeing notes are extensive and oriented to travelers using a car. Hotel and dining notes are very general, however. Overall, the various titles in this series are solid, helpful guides, but a bit lacking in excitement.

Books currently available: *The Visitor's Guide to Austria*; similar titles on: *Bavaria* (West Germany); *Corsica* (France); *Finland*; *Holland* (Netherlands); *Italian Lakes* (Italy); *Norway*; *Rhine, Mosel and Eifel* (West Germany); *Sweden*; *Turkey*; *Yugoslavia*.

Nicholson Guides
Salem House

The Nicholson Guides are some of the most popular in Britain. Those covered in this series review are specifically touring guides. Each is filled with sightseeing information and good introductions to the history, landscape, architecture and culture of each area. The print is quite small, but the net effect is a lot of information in a small space. Sightseeing spots are tied to good, color maps. You may need a reading glass, but these are fine guides for touring the countryside.

Books currently available: *Nicholson: Guide to Brittany* (France); similar titles on: *Devon* (England); *Greek Islands* (Greece); *Ireland*; *Lake District and Cumbria* (England); *Loire Region* (France); *London* (England); *Normandy* (France); *Visitor's Guide* (London, England).

Off the Beaten Path Guides
The Globe Pequot Press

A great series that does one thing and does it well—it takes you to some of those wonderful, less-discovered spots that most tourists just don't know about. Included are good descriptions, directions, general location maps, and other helpful details.

Books currently available: *Colorado Off the Beaten Path*; similar titles on: *Florida*; *Illinois*; *Indiana*; *Michigan*; *New Jersey*; *New York*; *Ohio*; *Virginia*.

On A Shoestring Guides
Lonely Planet Publications

These are the super budget guides from Lonely Planet—cheap hotels, local food, facts, figures, touring, getting around, and everything on a real financial shoestring. The Southeast Asia guide has long been very popular and part of Lonely Planet's rise to fame. On the other hand, *South America On a Shoestring* is criticized for its inaccuracy. Such difficulties are undoubtedly part of Lonely Planet's decision to focus more on individual countries in their Travel Survival Kit series (a series that covers a broader range of price ranges but is still useful to the budget traveler). The other Shoestring titles are well respected. As a series, the guides are very thorough, touching on all the necessary topics. The detail maps are clear and carefully drawn. Lonely Planet prides itself in its responsiveness to the feedback of those who use their books, so we look for significant improvement in the South America title in its next edition. Traveler feedback is available in Lonely Planet's quarterly updates (see "Travel Survival Kits" below).

Books currently available: *Africa on a Shoestring;* similar titles on: *North-East Asia; South America (including Central America and Mexico); South-East Asia; West Asia.*

On Your Own Guides
Hippocrene Books

These books concentrate on the single topic of getting the most out of the food sources of the country you are visiting. Whether you choose to do all your eating out or cook everything yourself, these books will help you appreciate the best products of every region and make you aware of the specialty shops where you can obtain them. The emphasis is on buying and preparing your own foods, and for this reason, these guides are particularly helpful to those planning longer stays. Quite a few recipes are even included at the back. Even if you don't prepare your own food, the knowledge the books will give you will make restaurant-ordering a breeze, not to mention a delicious experience.

Books currently available: *France On Your Own: Making the Most of Local Food and Drink;* similar titles on: *Greece; Italy; Portugal.*

One-Day Trip Books
EPM Publications

This is a well-done series on trips in and around each title city. Tours include history, sightseeing, shopping, festivals, galleries, music, dance, and just about anything else you could hope to do. There are lots of well-thought-out ideas here. Most titles are kept regularly up-to-date and all the practical facts, including good driving directions, are included.

Books currently available: *Florida One-Day Trip Book;* similar titles on: *Maryland; Philadelphia* (Pennsylvania); *Virginia; Washington* (District of Columbia). Also in the series: *One-Day Trips Through History: 200 Excursions Within 150 Miles of Washington, D.C.* (District of Columbia); *One-Day Trips to Beauty and Bounty: 150 Natural Attractions In and Around Washington, D.C.* (District of Columbia).

Park Explorer's Guides
Homestead Publishing

The Park Explorer's Guides are a series of booklets, filled with many beautiful color photographs, which provide a fine overview of each park, its trails, and particular pleasures. These are clearly just overview material, but they are nicely done and are helpful for vacation planning.

Books currently available: *Grand Teton Explorer's Guide* (Wyoming); similar titles on: *Glacier-Waterton* (Canada, Montana); *Yellowstone* (Wyoming).

Passport Asian Guides
Passport Books/National Textbook, Co.

This new series for 1988, was released after we went to press. The series appears to be a twin of the existent Passport China Guide series (see below).

Books currently available: *Complete Guide to Burma;* similar titles on: *Japan; Korea; Thailand.*

Passport China Guides
Passport Books/National Textbook, Co.

While there are some specific hotel and restaurant choices, the main thrust of these handsome, illustrated guides is on orientation, learning the ropes, cultural topics specific to the region, historical notes, and the important sights. In this they succeed admirably. The color photographs are nothing short of exceptional. Quite a few orientation maps, as well as the occasional detail map of a larger city, are included.

Books currently available: (All titles are listed under China.) *All China; Beijing; Fujian; Guilin, Canton and Guangdong Province; Hangzhou and Zhejiang; Hong Kong; Nanjing and Jiangsu Province; Shanghai; Tibet; Xi'an; Yangzi River; Yunnan.*

Passport Press Guides
Passport Press

These three excellent guides are by Paul Glassman. *Guatemala Guide,* first published in 1977, is the most famous and has been recently updated. All three books are full of well-researched information on hotels, restaurants, sightseeing, history, and culture. The narrative is straightforward and informative. Selections for lodging and food cover a wide range of prices with plenty of inexpensive and moderate choices. Glassman's practical information tips are worth the price of the book alone. He really knows his territory. These books are finely done and definitely recommended. Note: Do not confuse Passport Press with Passport Books.

Books currently available: *Belize Guide; Costa Rica Guide; Guatemala Guide.*

Penguin Travel Guides
Viking Penguin

The first eight titles in this all-new series of tall, thin guides from Viking Penguin are due out in the fall of 1988. Six or so will be released each subsequent year up to a total of 32. Each guide will be revised annually. These guides are planned for well-educated travelers in the 25-to-60-year-old age group. Each will be written primarily by authors living in the areas they explore. The stated purpose is to concentrate on "what's really of value in the country." That sounds a little broad, but Viking Penguin has produced many fine travel titles for the more sophisticated travel audience in the past. The price range will run from $9.95 to $12.95.

Books initially available: *The Penguin Guide to Australia;* similar titles on: *Canada; Caribbean* (West Indies); *England and Wales; France; Italy; Ireland; New York City* (New York).

Phaidon Art and Architecture Guides
Prentice Hall Press

Each of these sturdy hardbacks is arranged to address hundreds of cities and towns, and the many items of cultural significance they possess. The towns are arranged alphabetically for ease of use. The guide contains a great many color photographs and some detail maps to supplement a fine text. Each town is coded to a central map section. The result is a fine assemblage of the best of the cultural "must-sees": paintings, sculpture, icons, and architecture. While these are not primary sightseeing guides, they are an excellent supplement to a primary text.

Books currently available: *Athens and Attica: A Phaidon Art and Architecture Guide;* similar titles on: *Austria; Florence and Tuscany* (Italy); *France; Germany* (West Germany); *Great Britain and Ireland; Greece; Holland* (Netherlands); *Israel; Italy; Loire* (France); *Paris* (France); *Provence and Côte d'Azur* (France); *Rome and Latium* (Italy); *Spain; Switerland.*

Pisces Diving/Snorkeling Guides
PBC International

The Pisces series of guides is marvelously done, containing beautiful photos and information on the best areas, safety tips, and more. Each one will provide the information you need for planning and experiencing the perfect diving and snorkeling vacation.

Books currently available: *Diving and Snorkeling Guide to the Bahamas, Nassau, and New Providence Island* (West Indies); similar titles to: *Bonaire and Curacao* (West Indies); *Cozumel* (Mexico); *Florida's East Coast; Grand Cayman Island, Little Cayman and*

Cayman Brac (West Indies); *Hawaiian Islands* (Hawaii); *Northern California.*

Places to Go With Children Guides
Chronicle Books

These books are filled with ideas on what to do in every category you can think of—art, culture, sports, science, nature, parks, history, to name a few. And the ideas aren't for the children alone. Each resource is briefly described and all the particulars presented. Listed are numerous amusement parks, science stores, culture centers, and special eateries where children are most welcome. With one of these great resource guides, the possibilities are endless.

Books currently available: *Places to Go with Children in Dallas and Fort Worth* (Texas); similar titles on: *Northern California; Puget Sound* (Washington); *Southern California.*

Post Guides
Hunter Publishing

These fairly compact guides emphasize background information, practical survival tips, and sightseeing. The general information section is quite good and runs the gamut (weather, customs, tipping, do's and don'ts, festivals, transportation, etc.). Sightseeing is adequately covered and aimed at the mainstream tourist. There are some eating and sleeping tips in the major cities with brief notes or none at all. Numerous color photos and the occasional map are also included. These books are solid and reasonably thorough, but not particularly exciting.

Books currently available: *Post Guide: Australia;* similar titles on: *Hong Kong; Indonesia; Japan; Malaysia; Singapore; Sri Lanka; Thailand.*

Potomac Hiking Guides
Potomac Appalachian Trail Club

These are great, compact books on hikes in the areas and states surrounding Washington, D.C. Most hikes are in the three- to five-mile range. Each is drawn on a simplified but adequate map, distances are noted, USGS maps are suggested, clear directions to each trailhead are given, and the trail description itself is broken down into very short segments to avoid confusion.

Books currently available: *Hikes in the Washington Area, Part A: Montgomery, Frederick, and Carroll Counties in Maryland;* similar titles on: *Part B: Arlington, Fairfax, Loudoun and Prince William Counties in Virginia; Part C: District of Columbia and Prince George's, Charles and Calvert Counties in Maryland.*

Rainy Day Guides
Chronicle Books

Each Rainy Day Guide is a great collection of ideas on tours, shopping, eating out with kids, exercise, cinema, performing arts, picnics, hikes, etc.—all predicated on the presence of yet another rainy day. These are great resource guides, but they would be even better with a new edition, so keep in mind the publication date.

Books currently available: *Portland Rainy Day Guide;* similar titles on: *Seattle; Vancouver* (Canada).

Rambler Walks
Rambler Books

The Rambler series overlaps and partially coincides with titles produced by the Appalachian Mountain Club on walks near major cities. All are produced in a similar fashion. See review under *AMC Walks.*

Books currently available: *Country Walks Near Chicago* (Illinois); similar titles on: *Philadelphia* (Pennsylvania); *Washington* (District of Columbia); also in the series: *More Country Walks Near Washington* (District of Columbia). In addition, the Rambler Books series includes two titles from the Appalachian Mountain Club (AMC Walks) series: *Country Walks Near Baltimore* (Maryland); *Country Walks Near Boston* (Massachusetts).

Rand McNally Pocket Guides
Rand McNally & Co.

These small, definitely pocket-sized guides provide a good summary of sightseeing ideas, an overview of history and the arts, and brief practical facts on currency, customs, and travel, in addition to some general orientation to food, drink, and lodging. Included are numerous photos, brief descriptions of cities of interest, and some of those well-known Rand McNally maps. Although this series is a good overview in a small package, the print is very small.

Books currently available: *Rand McNally: Amsterdam* (Netherlands); similar titles on: *Austria and Switzerland; Britain* (Great Britain); *California and the Golden West; Eastern Canada; Florida; France; Germany* (West Germany); *Greece; Holland, Belgium and Luxembourg* (Netherlands); *Ireland; Israel; Italy; London* (England); *Mexico; New York City* (New York); *Paris* (France); *Portugal; Rome* (Italy); *Scandinavia; Spain; Venice.*

Recommended Country Inns
The Globe Pequot Press

This is one of the better series to the small inns of America. The reviews are extensive and informative, with each inn represented by an attractive line drawing. The practical details are clearly stated and current, or nearly so, because of the policy of Globe Pequot fully revising each title every 18 to 24 months, and making smaller changes with each printing of the book. Another Globe Pequot policy is that "the authors visit and evaluate each inn personally and accept no payment for the inclusion of any inn." Obviously, there is less money to be made with such a policy, but users of these books can feel confident that the opinions expressed in these books were not affected by monetary exchange.

Books currently available: *Country Inns of Arizona, New Mexico, and Texas;* similar titles on: *Mid-Atlantic States* (U.S.A.); *The Midwest* (U.S.A.); *New England* (U.S.A.); *The Rocky Mountain Region* (Rocky Mountain/Great Basin States, U.S.A.); *The South* (U.S.A.); *The West Coast* (California, Pacific Northwest, U.S.A.)

Roadside Geology Guides
Mountain Press Publishing

Here is a wonderful geology series specifically directed at what can be seen from a car window or at the side of the road. Written for the average person, these guides include a geology primer and avoid using technical, multisyllabic words. Each book is organized by highway and will add a whole level of fascination to your travels. An absolutely superb series—even for those convinced that geology *must* be boring.

Books currently available: *Roadside Geology of Alaska;* similar titles on: *Arizona; Colorado; Idaho; Montana; New Mexico; New York; Northern California; Oregon; Vermont and New Hampshire; Virginia; Washington; Wyoming; Yellowstone Country* (Wyoming).

Robert Silver Art Guides
Robert Silver Associates

This series of thorough, compact resource guides details a wide variety of museums, auction houses, galleries, films, music, libraries, bookshops, etc. Useful information on just about anything in the world of art to be found within the area is covered.

Books currently available: *Amsterdam Art Guide;* similar titles on: *Australia; Berlin* (West Germany); *London* (England); *New York* (New York); *Paris* (France).

Romantic Travel Guides
Beginning Press

The emphasis here is on the most romantic places to visit or stay in. All are rated with, of course, one to four "smacks" or lip imprints (definitely feminine). Romantic places may be a hidden glen, a charming restaurant, or a scenic lodge. The choices are good for those who put a premium on ambiance above all else. Titles may be cute, (*The Best Places to Kiss*), but the idea is sound.

Books currently available: *Best Places to Kiss in Los Angeles* (California); similar titles on: *New York* (New York); *The Northwest* (Pacific Northwest, U.S.A.); *San Francisco* (California).

Rough Guides
Routledge & Kegan Paul/Methuen, Inc.

The Rough Guides are another one of those rare collections of travel guides that seems to be able to maintain top quality across the spectrum of its titles. The guides have a definite budget orientation and, because they are a British series, prices are usually noted in pounds instead of dollars. Oriented toward the traveler using public transportation, they are excellent at pointing in the right direction for sights, lodging or food. There are some hotel suggestions, but restaurant ideas are few and, with a good orientation to the local cuisine, offer a challenge to explore dining options. The maps are excellent, directions clear, and the survival section on "the basics" is very well done. But beware of the publication date. These titles are updated regularly, but the cycle may be as long as three years. As with any other guide that is a few years old or more, be sure to check things out. Independent travelers with a sense of adventure, or even travelers with a larger budget will find much of value in the Rough Guides.

Books currently available: *Rough Guide to Amsterdam and Holland* (Netherlands); similar titles on: *Brittany and Normandy* (France); *China; France; Greece; Kenya; Mexico; Morocco; New York* (New York); *Paris* (France); *Peru; Portugal; Spain; Tunisia; Yugoslavia.*

Serious Shopper's Guides
Prentice Hall Press

A series of four detailed and comprehensive guides to hundreds of area stores (800 in Los Angeles, more than 500 in Paris, London, and Italy). The stores cover a wide range of categories from antiques to wine. The books are organized by category and each store listed is given a good description as well as the practical essentials. In addition, transportation tips, recommendations for tired shoppers to grab a bite to eat, and some practical tips on size conversion, currency exchange, etc, are included. Indices allow you to find your way around either by category, location, or shop name. These books are well done and cover every price range.

Books currently available: *Serious Shopper's Guide to London* (England); similar titles on: *Los Angeles* (California); *Italy; Paris* (France).

Shifra Stein's Day Trips
The Globe Pequot Press
Each book provides a great variety of possible trips into the regions immediately adjacent to the primary city, each within a two-hour drive. The suggested journeys include a clear map, numerous things to do, suggestions of places to eat, and good ideas for just wandering about and enjoying the sights and sounds of the area.
Books currently available: *Shifra Stein's Day Trips from Baltimore* (Maryland); similar titles on: *Cincinnati* (Ohio); *Houston* (Texas); *Phoenix/Tucson/Flagstaff* (Arizona). An additional title, *Shifra Stein's Day Trips: Greater Kansas City* (Missouri), is published by Shifra Stein Productions.

Shopping in Exotic Places
Impact Publications
This is a truly excellent shopping guide series. Each guidebook is replete with information on what to buy and where to buy it as well as specific practical points for each geographic location: when to go, customs, food, lodging, shipping, and how to survive the peculiarities of each location. There are good detail maps of major locations. This comprehensive series is for the serious shopper and is updated every two years.
Books currently available: *Shopping in Exotic Hong Kong*; similar titles on: *Indonesia*; *Korea* (South Korea); *Morocco*; *Singapore and Malaysia*; *South Pacific* (Australia, Oceania as a Whole, Papua New Guinea); *Thailand*. Also in the series: *Shopping in Exotic Places: Your Passport to Exciting Hong Kong, Korea, Thailand, Indonesia, and Singapore* (Southeast Asia).

Shopwalks
Crown Publishers
The Shopwalks series is made up of several two-page map/guides, one for each important shopping district in the city. These provide a large, detail map of the area, on which the recommended shops are plotted. Color coding is used to facilitate quick perusal. Also plotted are "miscellaneous stores," which can be anything from jewelry to antiques. Other things like the Parisian Metro stops and various transportion points are shown as well. The colored dots are numbered and these numbers tie into the brief descriptions offered on the stores selected. These little maps don't have the detailed analysis of other shopping guides, but they are light, convenient, and may be all you need if more specific information is not important.
Books currently available: *Shopwalks: Hong Kong*; similar titles on: *London* (England); *Milan* (Italy); *Montreal* (Canada); *Paris* (France).

Sierra Club Adventure Travel Guides
Sierra Club Books

The Adventure Travel series consistently focuses on the outdoor pleasures each region has to offer. These guides provide a good overview of the natural history of the area, clear directions to any adventure site, the facilities available, camping spots or other lodging tips, and good, well-written sections on the practical points important to planning an adventure in that particular locale (e.g., climate, special precautions, permits, or other local requirements). Plenty of hikes and walks are presented, but the adventure options run the gamut. Whatever is appropriate to the area will be there. These Adventure Travel Guides demonstrate quality, excellence, and attention to detail.

Books currently available: *Adventuring in Alaska: The Sierra Club Travel Guide to the Great Land;* similar titles on: *The Alps* (Switzerland); *The Andes* (Bolivia, Ecuador, Peru); *California Desert; Gulf of Mexico* (Mexico, South, U.S.A.); *The Pacific* (Oceania as a Whole); *The Rockies* (Rocky Mountain/Great Basin States, U.S.A.); *San Francisco Bay Area* (California).

Sierra Club Hiking Totebooks
Sierra Club Books

A series of small, pocket-sized guides for the hiker and the walker. Each describes myriad trails of every length and contains a good, well-organized planning and preparation section. Each hike is carefully detailed, topographical maps are referenced, and important points are summarized. Good notes on natural history topics are a part of every Sierra Club hiking guide. This series is uniformly excellent, although the occasional trail may have been altered since the guide was written (they are not updated with any frequency).

Books currently available: *Bitterroot to Beartooth* (Montana); *Climbing and Hiking the Wind River Mountains* (Wyoming); *Footloose in the Swiss Alps* (Switzerland); *Hiker's Guide to the Smokies* (South, U.S.A.); *Hiking the Bigfoot Country* (California, Oregon); *Hiking the Grand Canyon* (Arizona); *Hiking the Great Basin* (Rocky Mountain/Great Basin States, U.S.A.); *Hiking the North Cascades* (Washington); *Hiking the Old Dominion* (Virginia); *Hiking the Southwest* (U.S.A.); *Hiking the Teton Backcountry* (Wyoming); *Hiking the Yellowstone Backcountry* (Wyoming); *Starr's Guide to the John Muir Trail and the High Sierra Region* (California); *Timberline Country* (California); *To Walk with a Quiet Mind* (California).

Sierra Club National Parks Guides
Sierra Club Books

Each of these guidebooks is full of information on the specific park, its history, its facilities, its points of interest, its hiking paths, its natural history, and its geology. Beautiful photos, as well as information on trips and tours to take, and food and lodging is included.

Books currently available: *The Sierra Club Guide to the National Parks of the Desert Southwest* (U.S.A.); similar titles on: *The East and Middle West* (New England, Mid-Atlantic States, Midwest, South, U.S.A.); *The Pacific Northwest and Alaska* (U.S.A.); *The Pacific Southwest and Hawaii* (Southwest, Hawaii, U.S.A.); *The Rocky Mountains and Great Plains* (Midwest, Rocky Mountain/ Great Basin States, U.S.A.)

Sierra Club Natural Areas Guides
Sierra Club Books

The Natural Areas Guides include the national parks of the region, but go far beyond that to address the lesser-known public-domain lands such as Bureau of Land Management and U.S. forests, wildlife refuges, and other wilderness areas. A wealth of detail on each area's location, physical description, the wildlife of the area, the flora, recreational opportunities that await, and the resources and facilities available is included. These well-organized, thorough guides use the nationally accepted signs for camping, hiking, hunting, fishing, boating, walking, horseback riding, etc. to provide quick, visual clues as to the appropriateness of a given area to travelers' needs. These are wonderful guides for those who love the outdoors.

Books currently available: *The Sierra Club Guide to the Natural Areas of California*; similar titles on: *Colorado and Utah; Idaho, Montana and Wyoming; New Mexico, Arizona and Nevada; Oregon and Washington.*

Sierra Club Naturalist's Guides
Sierra Club Books

The Sierra Club series represents a fine choice for those travellers interested in the geology, natural history, and the flora and fauna of a particular region. The materials presented are well organized, well written, and fascinating. These are first-rate guides for the serious naturalist, as well as the merely curious.

Books currently available: *A Sierra Club Naturalist's Guide to the Deserts of the Southwest* (U.S.A.); similar titles on: *Middle Atlantic Coast* (Mid-Atlantic States, U.S.A.); *North Atlantic Coast* (Canada; New England, U.S.A.); *The North Woods of Michigan, Wisconsin, Minnesota and Southern Ontario* (Canada; Midwest, U.S.A.); *The Piedmont of Eastern North America* (Canada; Mid-Atlantic States, New England, South, U.S.A.); *Sierra Nevada* (California); *Southern New England* (U.S.A.)

Ski Tours of California
Wilderness Press

This series is reviewed under "California."

Books currently available: *Ski Tours in the Sierra Nevada, Vol. 1: Lake Tahoe;* similar titles on: *Carson Pass, Bear Valley and Pinecrest; Yosemite, Kings Canyon and Sequoia; East of the Sierra Crest.*

Sophisticated Traveler Guides
Random House, Viking Penguin

This wonderful series of travel guides was created by various staff writers for the *New York Times.* The level of writing is high and the style is that of the fine-tuned essay—a considerable amount of practical travel information and many specific tips are communicated through the narrative form. Among the historical notes and fascinating anecdotes are recommendations on the best sidewalk cafes, hotels, restaurants, and sights to see. The books are a delight to read, and are recommended to travelers looking for something more than the basics.

Books currently available: *The Sophisticated Traveler: Beloved Cities of Europe* (Europe as a Whole); similar titles on: *Enchanting Places and How to Find Them* (The World); *Great Tours and Detours* (The World); *Winter: Love It or Leave It* (The World).

Step-by-Step Guides
Faber and Faber, Inc.

The Step-by-Step Guides are a British series prepared by Christopher Turner, whose approach to each guide is "to put myself in the position of a complete stanger who, on arrival, wants to know *exactly* where to go and what route to take." And he has done a superb job. Offered are carefully constructed, thoroughly researched walking tours tied to clear detail maps, and filled with interesting notes on history and architecture. His work won him the 1985 Guide Book of the Year Award in Great Britain, which, given the vast number of guidebooks produced in Britain, says a great deal about the quality of his effort. (Note: *London Churches Step-by-Step* is reviewed separately.)

Books currently available: *Greenwich and East London Step-by-Step* (England); similar titles on: *Outer London* (England); *Windsor and Eton* (England).

Storie McOwen Insider's Guides
Storie/McOwen Publishing

Although these guides are a bit cluttered with advertisements, they do cover the bases comprehensively. Lodging, hotels, and sightseeing activities are all well addressed and every price range is included. When advertisements are accepted, questions arise as to the objectivity of the evaluations presented. Nevertheless, these guides serve a purpose by addressing areas not otherwise well covered.

Books currently available: *Insider's Guide to Charlotte, North Carolina*; similar titles on: *Southside Hampton Roads, Virginia; The Outer Banks of North Carolina; The Triangle of North Carolina; Williamsburg, Virginia.*

Sunset Travel Guides
Lane Publishing

These large-format guides from the publishers of *Sunset* magazine are best used as planning tools. The guides do contain some specific information on tours, lodging, activities, restaurants, etc., but these sorts of information are available in more detail elsewhere. The real strength of the books is the feel they give of an area, at least from the point of view of the mainstream traveler. They also contain nicely written overviews and oodles of color photographs. If your requirements are minimal, these guides may give you enough information.

Books currently available: *Sunset Travel Guide: Alaska; similar titles on: Arizona; Australia; California and the Gold Rush Country; Hawaii; Islands of the South Pacific* (Oceania as a Whole); *Maui* (Hawaii); *Mexico; New Zealand; Northern California; Oregon; Orient* (Asia as a Whole); *South Pacific* (Oceania as a Whole); *Southeast Asia; Southern California; Washington.* Also in the series: *Sunset: Discovery Trips in Europe.*

Tastes of Tahoe Guides
Tastes of Tahoe

This series is reviewed under "California."

Books currently available: *The Tastes of California Wine Country, Napa and Sonoma; The Tastes of California Wine Country, North Coast; The Tastes of Tahoe III.*

Texas Monthly Guides
Texas Monthly Press

This is a really first-rate series of guides to the Lone Star State. The only problem is that *Texas*, the biggest guidebook of the group, is thoroughly out-of-date at this time. Word is that the big, single-volume guide to the state may finally see a new edition in 1989. The other regional guides have been regularly updated. That aside, this series offers an excellent summary of what each city or area has to offer: what to do, where to go, tours, annual events, nightlife, shopping, the arts, and hotels and restaurants. The latter emphasize the moderate-and-up range, at least in the big cities, but there are some less expensive options as well. The write-ups are informative and each guide is enjoyable to read. (Note: *Hill Country: Discover the Secrets of the Texas Hill Country* is reviewed separately.)

Books currently available: *Austin: The Complete Guide to Texas' Capital City; Dallas: Your Compete Guide to a Vibrant Texas City; Houston: Your Complete Guide to Texas' Largest City; San Antonio: An Indispensible Guide to One of Texas' Favorite Cities; Texas Coast: Discover Delights Along the Gulf Coast of Texas; Texas: The Newest, the Biggest, the Most Complete Guide to All of Texas.*

Times Travel Library Guides
Hunter Publishing

These large-format guides with a heavy emphasis on color photography provide practical local tips, local trivia, do-it-yourself walks, excursions, and additional, useful details.

Books currently available: *The Times Travel Library: Bali* (Indonesia); similar titles on: *Jakarta* (Indonesia); *Kathmandu* (Nepal); *Seoul* (South Korea).

Touch of the City Guides
Talman Co.

Fine little guides for those with at least moderate-sized travel budgets. A number of sections are for those who plan a longer stay and include business, banking, schools, and health care. Fine sections on hotels and restaurants (again mostly moderate and up), shopping, nightlife, and sporting activities are included. The "Getting Started" chapter is particularly thorough and covers most every topic of potential concern.

Books currently available: *A Touch of Geneva Guide* (Switzerland); similar titles on: *Monaco and French Riviera* (France, Monaco); *Paris* (France).

Touchstone Hiking Guides
Touchstone Press

This quality series of hiking guides gives a fine overview of each hike, coupled with nice photographs and some detailed topographical maps. Information on each hike includes time needed, distance, elevation gains or losses, highest altitude point, best season to go, and other USGS maps recommended. The selected hikes are mostly one-day hikes of varying difficulty.

Books currently available: *Backcountry Roads and Trails: San Diego County* (California); *50 Hiking Trails: Lassen, Tahoe and Carson Pass* (California); *50 Hiking Trails: Portland and Northwest Oregon; 41 Hiking Trails: Northwest California; 60 Hiking Trails:*

Central Oregon Cascades; 62 Hiking Trails: Northern Oregon Cascades; 33 Hiking Trails: Southern Washington Cascades.

Travel Key Guides
Travel Keys Books

Peter Manston, the author of *Travel Key Europe*, has also penned three guides to the flea markets, antique fairs, and auctions of three European countries. His meticulously researched and clearly written books detail where to find the best markets, how to ship purchased goods home safely, how to deal with customs, how to bargain, plus other information useful to serious collectors and casual participants alike. The amount of information provided is remarkable and includes a number of detail maps and helpful contact numbers. Note: Do not confuse with Traveler's Key Guides below.

Books currently available: *Manston's Flea Markets, Antique Fairs and Auctions of Britain;* similar titles on: *France; Germany.*

Travel Survival Kits
Lonely Planet Publications

Lonely Planet, an Australian publisher, has in recent years burst on the travel scene, mainly on the strength of its Travel Survival Kit series. More recently, the books have tried to broaden their focus, leaving the true budget travel to their other series, On a Shoestring Guides, but they still have a flavor that seems most appropriate for the moderately young and adventurous, although any traveler can find much of value. They are almost always solidly done guides (Mexico is a current exception, though soon to be completely rewritten) and sometimes simply wonderful. The guides written by Tony Wheeler, the founder of the company, are some of the best. The other important issue is publication date. The company seems to be moving toward a stricter schedule of revisions every two years, but some titles may wait three years or more before updating. Even every two years can be a very long time in some of the volatile countries on Lonely Planet's list. So be careful in confirming the details until you are sure of the guidebook's track record, especially one with an older publication date. The guides themselves are comprehensive. History, natural history notes, sightseeing information, facts and figures on getting there and getting around (public transportation data is always included), hotel tips, and restaurants are all thoroughly covered. The sightseeing "what to see, what to do" sections are especially expansive. Price ranges are inexpensive and moderate. Plenty of detail maps and a great deal of practical information are included as well. Lonely Planet also welcomes your comments and criticisms, and publishes many letters in a quarterly book, *Lonely Planet Update* (priced at $3.95). This excellent series will be made even better as updates become more frequent. Several new titles are on the horizon for late 1988 or 1989. Especially welcome will be the new Eastern Europe guide. Also slated for publication are new titles on more of the South American countries and, probably, the country of Bhutan.

Books currently available: *Alaska; Australia; Baja California* (Mexico); *Bali and Lombok* (Indonesia); *Bangladesh; Burma; Canada; Chile and Easter Island; China; East Africa; Ecuador and Galapagos Islands; Egypt and Sudan; Fiji; Hong Kong, Macau and Canton; India; Indonesia; Japan; Kashmir, Ladakh and Zanskar* (India); *Kathmandu and Kingdom of Nepal; Korea* (South Korea); *Malaysia, Singapore and Brunei; Mexico; Micronesia* (Oceania); *New Zealand; Pakistan; Papua New Guinea; Peru; Philippines; Rarotonga and Cook Islands* (Oceania); *Sri Lanka; Syria and Jordan; Tahiti and French Polynesia* (Oceania); *Taiwan; Thailand; Tibet; Turkey; Yemen* (Northern and Southern Yemen).

Traveler's Key Guides
Alfred Knopf, Inc.

These sophisticated guides concentrate on the meaning of ancient art, architecture, sacred places, legends, etc. They are designed to help the traveler gain a greater appreciation of history, religion, and culture through the writings and tangible remains of more ancient civilizations. The results are fascinating and definitely recommended for the interested, motivated traveler. Note: Do not confuse with Travel Keys Guides above.

Books currently available: *The Traveler's Key to Ancient Egypt;* similar titles on: *Medieval France; Northern India; Sacred England.*

Traveller's Guides
Hunter Publishing

This series tries to touch all the bases of interest to the traveler and does so at the expense of providing any real depth on any one subject. The guides are best seen as an overview and orientation to each area with a bit of history, cultural notes, and sightseeing tips. There are short lists of hotels and restaurants but with little or no comment. These guides are certainly adequate, but not very exciting.

Books currently available: *Traveller's Guide to Central and Southern Africa;* similar titles on: *East Africa and Indian Ocean; Middle East* (Asia); *North Africa; West Africa.*

Visitor's Guides
Hunter Publishing

The strong suit of the Visitor's Guides is sightseeing. They contain a good deal of useful information on where to go, what to do, and what to see. Included are numerous suggested walks with adequate directions but few detail maps. There are, however, numerous photos and some general orientation maps. And, because the guides concentrate on a region (or a small country like Iceland), they cover a lot of ground in their 144 or so pages.

Books currently available: *The Visitor's Guide to the Black Forest* (West Germany); similar titles on: *Brittany* (France); *Cornwall* (England); *Cotswolds* (England); *Devon* (England); *Dordogne* (France); *East Anglia* (England); *Florence and Tuscany* (Italy); *French Coast* (France); *Guernsey, Alderney and Sark* (England); *Hampshire and Isle of Wight* (England); *Historic Places of Wales; Iceland; Kent* (England); *Lake District* (England); *Loire* (France); *Normandy* (France); *North Wales and Snowdonia; North Ireland; Peak District* (England); *Scottish Borders and Edinburgh* (Scotland); *Severn and Avon* (England); *Somerset and Dorset* (England); *South and West Wales; South of France; Sussex* (England); *Turkey; Tyrol* (Austria); *Welsh Borders* (Wales); *Yorkshire Dales* (England).

Walking Through Britain Guides
Hunter Publishing

The "walks" are really hikes in common parlance. Each is easily divisible into shorter hikes and walks. The primary thrust of the book is, however, on multi-day tramps through some of Britain's most scenic countryside. Included are hiking notes, maps, suggestions for places to stay, comments on history and archaeology, and useful drawings. This fine series provides some excellent hiking/walking ideas.

Books currently available: *Walking Through Northern England;* similar titles on: *Scotland; Lake District* (England); *Wales.*

Way-Ahead Guides
VLE Ltd.

In these guides, each city is arranged into several distinct walks. An overview map of the area is provided for purposes of orientation, then each walk is drawn out in a large scale and its points of interest are noted and briefly described in a logical, progressive fashion. These extremely light and very handy fold-out map/guides are a very simple, direct way to enjoy a walk through each city.

Map/Guides currently available: *Walks Through Barcelona* (Spain); similar titles on: *London* (England); *Madrid* (Spain); *Munich* (West Germany); *Paris* (France); *Rome* (Italy); *Seville* (Spain); *Stuttgart* (West Germany); *Vienna* (Austria); *Zurich* (Switzerland).

Webster's Wine Tours
Prentice Hall Press
   Comprehensive and thorough, each guide offers nicely written descriptions of a wide variety of vineyards organized along well-conceived touring routes. Tours are arranged by region and include good directions as well as maps which point out the most scenic byways between wineries. The representative wines of each vineyard are noted along with those of "particular reputation." Touring, tasting, and sales hours information is also included. There are also plenty of other practical facts, such as hotels, restaurants and tips on how to buy wine. The books are quite well done and the rapidly expanding series now covers all the major wine-producing regions of the world with the release of the Fall 1988 titles. In anticipation of their timely arrival, all of these are included in the text and listed below.
   Books currently available: *Webster's Wine Tours: Australia*; similar titles on: *California, Oregon and Washington*; *France*; *Germany* (West Germany); *Italy*; *Portugal*; *Spain.*

Western Tanager Hiking Guides
Western Tanager Press
   This series is reviewed under "California."
   Books currently available: *Hike Los Angeles* (2 volumes); *Hike the Santa Barbara Backcountry.*

Where to Go Guides
Hippocrene Books
   This popular British series focuses on helping travelers decide where to go. Each destination is previewed and discussed as to the ease of getting there, its scenery, the sights to see, special features, etc. An interesting chart system helps line up prospective destinations as to accessibility, scenery, eating out, sights, beaches, and other features. These guides are helpful as planning tools.
   Books currently available: *Where to Go in Greece*; *Where to Go in Greece: Athens and the North Aegean Islands*; *Where to Go in Greece: Corfu and the Ionian Islands*; *Where to Go in Greece: Rhodes and the Dodecanese Islands*; *Where to Go in Spain*; *Where to Go in Turkey.*

Wilderness Press Hiking Guides
Wilderness Press
   The many hiking guides from Wilderness Press are well done, thorough, and easy to use. Trail descriptions are particularly excellent and all the specifics as to distances, directions, elevation change, etc. are noted. The majority of the guides come with a full-sized,

separate topographical map of excellent quality. Several titles duplicate portions of topographical maps rather than providing a separate one. A few titles that concentrate on shorter hikes in more urban areas, have simplified trail maps for each hike and recommend U.S.G.S. maps. The "topos" produced by Wilderness Press are particularly excellent because the routes described in the guidebook are more clearly plotted than on the average U.S.G.S. map and are usually done in a bright color. This is a fine series.

Books currently available: *Afoot and Afield in San Diego County* (California); *Afoot and Afield in Orange County* (California); *Arizona Trails*; *Carson Iceberg Wilderness* (California); *Crater Lake National Park (Oregon)*; *Desolation Wilderness and South Lake Tahoe Basin* (California); *Hiking the Big Sur Country* (California); *Lassen Volcanic National Park* (California); *Marble Mountain Wilderness* (California); *San Bernardino Mountain Trails* (California); *Sawtooth National Recreation Area* (Idaho); *Self-Propelled in the Southern Sierra* (2 volumes; California); *Sierra North* (California); *Sierra South* (California); *South Bay Trails* (California); *The Tahoe Sierra* (California); *Trails of the Angeles* (California); *Trinity Alps* (California); *Yosemite National Park* (California).

Woodland Walks
Hunter Publishing

The six volumes of this comprehensive series detail over 400 walks in England, Scotland, and Wales. Included are color photographs, numerous maps, and considerable information on access, parking, the types of woodland, length and difficulty of each hike, woodland ecology, and more. All books are well organized and delightful to read.

Books currently available: *Woodland Walks in Central England*; similar titles on: *North of England*; *Scotland*; *South-East England*; *South-West England*; *Wales and The Marches*.

Zagat Survey
Zagat Survey

The Zagat Survey is conceived and executed in a manner different from most restaurant guides. Instead of giving just one person's opinion on the merits of particular restaurants, this survey employs thousands of people to provide factual information by which to judge each establishment. For example, the 1988 New York survey involved 3500 people dining out an average of 3.6 times a week. That's over 12,000 meals a week and 600,000 meals a year—a lot more than any one person could conceive of, let alone consume. Anyone can participate, and the guidebook has information on doing so. The sum total of all these meals leads to a rating system grading food, decor,

and service on a scale of 0 to 30. A separate cost column estimates
the tab for one dinner. A short commentary is also provided and
additional charts rate favorite restaurants, best buys, top food, top
decor, and top spots by cuisine. Here is the common man's opinion—
collectively. This is a very popular way to eat in the major cities the
Zagat Survey covers.

Books currently available: *Zagat Boston Restaurant Survey;* similar titles on: *Chicago* (Illinois); *Los Angeles* (California); *New Orleans* (Louisiana); *New York City* (New York); *San Francisco* (California); *Washington, D.C.* (District of Columbia).

General Travel Books

The following titles address important travel topics, but do not direct their primary focus toward particular destinations or geographic areas. Books of a similar nature that are specific to a particular area are listed under the specific geographic heading.

Affordable Travel: How to Travel and Vacation for Less—Anywhere in the World
by Marlin and Loris Bree, MarLor Press, 1983, 132 pages, paper, $5.95
   This book is chock-full of useful planning ideas and checklists for keeping costs down on transportation, lodging, food, entertainment, shopping, taking the kids, etc.

Bon Voyage! The Cruise Traveler's Handbook
by Gary Bannerman, Passport Books, 1984, 256 pages, paper, $9.95
   A detailed orientation to cruise ship travel that has enough information to satisfy both the first-time participant and the veteran. Entertaining to read, it contains all sorts of tips to help travelers make the most of cruise ship holidays.

Cheap/Smart Travel: Dependable Alternatives to Traveling Full Fare
by Theodore Fischer, M. Evans & Co., 1988 (2nd ed.), 193 pages, paper, $6.95
   This is a real "how-to" guide that includes information on "coping with travel agents" and "shopping at the air transportation flea market" as well as sections on ground transportation, lodging, food, and other "money matters." Well-organized, well-written and up-to-date, this new edition includes popular easy-to-read charts that show the pros and cons of each potential travel situation.

The Complete Guide for Motorcycle Travelers

by Erik Sandberg, Viking Productions, 1986, 222 pages, paper,
$6.95

This very entertaining, practical guide could be subtitled "every-thing you always wanted to know about touring, but were afraid to find out the hard way." Sandberg's book covers all the basics from starting out, camping, and mechanics, to food and portable bath-rooms. And while this is primarily a book on general motorcycle travel subjects, there is a large chapter on the specifics of traveling in Europe. A new, expanded edition is due out in 1989.

The Complete Trip Diary

MarLor Press, 1987, 80 pages, paper, $4.50

This is a good choice for an organized diary-type book—with sec-tions for expenses, schedules, and picture descriptions, and room to write observations.

Confessions of a Tour Leader

by Baxter and Corinne Geeting, Prima Publishing, 1987, 119 pages,
paper, $7.95

This book, winner of the National Book Writers Club Annual Book Competition, provides a real insight into the world of tours and tour guides. Travelers deciding between touring or going it alone will find this book helpful.

Discount Guide to Travelers Over 55

by Caroline and Walter Weintz, E. P. Dutton, 1988, 336 pages,
paper, $7.95

This comprehensive, recently updated listing, details senior citi-zen discounts on planes, rental cars, sightseeing, and hotels.

Do's and Taboos Around the World

by Roger Axtell, John Wiley & Sons, 1985, 183 pages, paper, $9.95

This fascinating guide, now published in three languages, details the vast differences in customs from country to country and the 1001 ways to unwittingly be rude, such as using a gesture that has a positive meaning back home but is highly insulting in another country, or toasting at the wrong point in the meal. Axtell has been through it all and helps to make these vagaries clear.

An Explorer's Handbook: An Unconventional Guide for Travelers to Remote Regions

by Christina Dodwell, Facts on File, 1986, 192 pages, paper, $8.95

For those who are headed *away* from civilization, this is a good general travel title covering such topics as how to deal with park animals, how to choose a campsite, how to prepare and cook game, campsite baking and housekeeping, health and first aid, and how not to breach local customs.

A Fieldbook of Nature Photography
by Patricia Maye, Sierra Club Books, 1974, 209 pages, paper, $8.95

This excellent popular photography guide is loaded with useful information on cameras, filters, and shutter speeds, and contains special sections on landscapes, close-ups, animals, and underwater photography. It comes in a small, easy-to-handle size and is a boon to travelers wanting to improve their vacation photography.

Fielding's Travel Photography Handbook
by Julian Calder and John Garrett, William Morrow & Co., 1985, 235 pages, paper, $14.95

This quality handbook provides information on choosing cameras, meters, film, filters, flash attachments, and coping with extremes of temperatures, as well as tips on the best ways to photograph cities, landscapes, portraits, children, animals, and closeups. The authors also include plenty of actual photographs to illustrate their points. A very helpful guide for travel photographers.

Fly There For Less: 70 Strategies to Save Money Flying Worldwide
by Bob Martin, Teak Wood Press, 1988, 136 pages, paper, $8.95

Included in this book are more strategies for saving money in the air than anyone ever thought possible. This is a great book for travelers looking for ways to avoid handing the airline industry more than they have to.

Frommer's Beat the High Cost of Travel
by Tom Brosnahan, Prentice Hall Press, 1988, 374 pages, paper, $6.95

This useful book explains a wide variety of ways to cut travel costs whether traveling on a shoestring or going first class. Brosnahan, author of five Frommer guides, shares his expertise on every travel issue: accommodations, transportation, dining, sightseeing, shopping, and more. He also provides information specific to seniors, students, singles, and families.

Frommer's Swap & Go
by Albert and Verna Beerbower, Prentice Hall Press, 1986, 246 pages, paper, $10.95

In this book the Beerbowers thoroughly address the subject of home exchanging, providing simple, step-by-step instructions on how to make a home exchange a part of any vacation.

Guide to the Best Buys in Package Tours
by Paige Palmer, Pilot Books, 1986, 48 pages, paper, $3.95
   In this book Palmer lists the best tours and gives useful descriptions of each. As such material can quickly become dated, updated editions should appear at regular intervals.

Gypsying After 40: A Guide to Adventure & Self-Discovery
by Robert Harris, John Muir Publications, 1987, 255 pages, paper, $12.95
   This enjoyable book will inspire the gypsy in any traveler but more than that, it provides utilitarian information. Adventure is possible after 40 and Harris shows you how.

Home Exchanging: A Complete Sourcebook for Travelers at Home or Abroad
by James Dearing, The Globe Pequot Press, 1986, 192 pages, paper, $9.95
   Dearing provides a very thorough analysis of absolutely everything there is to know about home swapping and how to get it done without suffering from a series of major headaches. Extensive appendices highlight this informed text.

How to Pack a Suitcase...and Other Travel Tips
by Cris Evatt, Fawcett, 1987, 47 pages, paper, $4.95
   The primary focus of this book is indeed how to pack your suitcase. The strategies for getting the most out of (and into) luggage are quite extensive. But it isn't just how much goes into a suitcase. The real questions are: "How easily accessible are those most used items?", and "How wrinkled are the clothes?" This handy little book is a real gem.

How to Take Great Trips With Your Kids
by Sanford and Joan Portnoy, The Harvard Common Press, 1983, 180 pages, paper, $8.95
   Planning, packing, and problem-solving are different when there are children along. As the Portnoys have learned first-hand, a successful vacation must allow for the limitations and needs of the children. This book insightfully describes the ABC's of family travel.

An Insider's Guide to the Travel Game
by John Seales, Rand Editions, 1983, 183 pages, paper, $7.95
   In this book Seales tells how to get the most for your travel dollar. Often complimented, it remains a thoughtful and well-written work full of sound advice on a wide array of travel topics.

The International Safe Travel Guide

by Robert Downes and William Bartman, Betterway Publications, 1987, 141 pages, paper, $6.95

Appropriately timed, given the general paranoia surrounding travel to some regions these days, this recent publication addresses the issue of how to play it safe regardless of the method of travel. It also helps to put the risk of a fatal terrorism attack in perspective by comparing the statistics on terrorism to other risks such as drowning, choking to death, and lightning strikes. Indeed, a traveler is nine times more likely to be killed by lightning than by a terrorist. That aside, these suggested strategies for keeping a low and safe profile while traveling are worth thinking about.

Kids and Cars: A Parent's Survival Guide for Family Travel

by Ellyce Field and Susan Shlom, Melius & Peterson Publishing, 1988, 200 pages, paper, $8.95

Family travel is not all fun and games. Things can sometimes be rough, especially in a crowded car. To the rescue comes *Kids and Cars*, a wise, insightful, and thoroughly practical book on dozens of important topics such as carsickness, rowdy kids, cranky kids, cranky adults, misbehavior, and restaurant survival. Besides hundreds of creative ideas and practical solutions, dozens of games for all ages and other educational activities are also included. This book is truly an oasis of help for those with family travel hassles.

Manston's Before You Leave on Your Vacation

by Robert Bynum and Paula Mazuski, Travel Keys Books, 1988, 96 pages, paper, $5.95

A new title, released after press time, on how to safeguard your home when you are away. Specific issues include: security suggestions; types and costs of alarm systems; house, pet, and yard sitters; lawn, garden, and pool care; mail and newspaper deliveries; and forms to organize emergency information for anyone looking after your home.

Money Saving Secrets of Smart Airline Travelers

by Richard Bodner, Betterway Publications, 1986, 129 pages, paper, $4.95

In this book, a veteran commercial pilot gives the rundown on the myriad ways travelers can save money by understanding airline fare codes including fares that are less than coach such as the Q fare (coach economy discounted), charter flights, coupon brokers, and how to help your travel agent. This is definitely a well-done, helpful compendium of ideas.

The Nature Observer's Handbook

by John Brainerd, The Globe Pequot Press, 1986, 272 pages, paper, $9.95

Brainerd's book is a mini-course in learning to observe and appreciate the world of nature in both urban and rural settings.

The New World of Travel

by Arthur Frommer, Prentice Hall Press, 1988, 384 pages, paper, $12.95

Anyone who has listened to Arthur Frommer speak is aware that this man *knows* what he is talking about. In this book he shares what he considers to be the most exciting, interesting, and money-saving travel ideas. These include such new, alternative modes of travel as politically oriented travel, personal growth centers, utopian communities, international institutes, study travel, work camps, feminist travel, and Elderhostel. Frommer covers 175 organizations that sponsor some type of innovative travel alternative. Also included are money-saving ideas for taking advantage of these new travel opportunities.

The New York Times Practical Traveler

by Paul Grimes, Times Books, 1985, 412 pages, paper, $10.95

Grimes, a former *New York Times* columnist, and currently news editor for Condé Nast's *Traveler*, offers an excellent collection of tips on everything related to travel: selecting hotels, customs, traveling with children, and discounts for seniors, to name a few.

Overcoming Jet Lag

by Dr. Charles Ehret and Lynne Scanlon, Berkley Books, 1983, 160 pages, paper, $4.95

Learn from a medical professional the strategy used by military and business executives of major corporations to overcome the plague of all long-distance travelers: jet lag.

Passport's Health Guide for International Travelers

by Thomas Sakmar, M.D., *et al.*, Passport Books, 1986, 143 pages, paper, $7.95

This top-quality health guide is divided into four major sections. The first section provides helpful reminders to be sure none of those necessary health items remain unpacked. The next section contains numerous tips and precautions, while the third section focuses on medical problems such as fever, blisters, animal bites, and diarrhea. And, not to forget that all travelers eventually go home, the fourth section contains useful information for the returning traveler.

The Pocket Doctor: A Carry-Along Guide for Healthy, Safe Traveling
by Stephen Bezruchka, M.D., The Mountaineers, 1988, 80 pages, paper, $2.50
This new title of interest was released after press time.

The Pocket Guide to Safe Travel
by Dr. Stephen Sloan, Contemporary Books, 1986, 96 pages, paper, $3.25
This tiny, pocket-sized book offers excellent advice on topics ranging from trip preparation and how to keep a low profile to coping when threats become reality.

The Portable Pet: How to Travel Anywhere With Your Dog or Cat
by Barbara Nicholas, The Harvard Common Press, 1983, 80 pages, paper, $5.95
This helpful reference for those traveling with their pets contains chapters on traveling by plane, car, train, bus, and ship. These cover a wide variety of topics in a question-and-answer format.

Survival Manual for the Independent Woman Traveler
by Roberta Mendel, Pin Prick Press, 1982, 118 pages, paper, $12.95
This homespun guide has some good helpful hints and strategies for women traveling alone, especially for the first time. The section on specific trips and resources, on the other hand, is very dated; a revised edition would certainly be welcome.

Things That Go Bump in the Flight: A Whiteknuckler's Guide to Air Travel
by Robert Welch, Betterway Publications, 1987, 156 pages, paper, $5.95
Robert Welch, a veteran pilot with 35 years experience in the airline industry, addresses all those "what if" questions that worry more than one traveler as the plane heads down the runway. He also discusses the weather, the airplane itself, and air traffic control in an effort to make air travel less frightening and more understandable. Welch also includes some thought-provoking proposals for making what is a safe system even safer.

Tips for the Savvy Traveler
by Deborah Burns and Sarah May Clarkson, Storey Communications, 1987, 216 pages, paper, $4.95
This widely praised book contains numerous of tips on every travel topic imaginable: shopping, photography, dining, lodging, traveling with children, to name a few. Most tips are arranged in short, stac-

cato paragraphs that seem to jump off the page—the type of layout that ensures that the little things don't get lost in the shuffle.

The Travel & Vacation Discount Guide
by Paige Palmer, Pilot Books, 1987, 64 pages, paper, $3.95
Lists, lists, and more lists, this book is full of listed information to help you save money when you travel.

Travel Easy: The Practical Guide for People Over 50
by Rosalind Massow, Scott, Foresman & Co., 1985, 263 pages, paper, $8.95
An American Association of Retired Persons book aimed at helping you get the most for your money. Information is included that will help you avoid misleading travel advertising claims, make the best use of travel agents, and find "don't miss" trips. This is essential background reading for those 50 years of age or older.

Travel for the Disabled: A Handbook of Travel Resources and 500 Worldwide Access Guides
by Helen Hecker, R.N., Twin Peaks Press, 1985, 185 pages, paper, $9.95
This is a first-rate book covering a wide variety of topics of interest and concern to the disabled traveler. This resource guide provides page after page of useful information on travel by car, bus, train, air, and ship; medical problems; respite service; camps; and access guides in cities throughout the world. Heckler has done a wonderful service for the disabled.

Travel for Two: The Art of Compromise
by Margot Biestman, Pergot Press, 1987, 192 pages, paper, $10.95
For all its fun, travel is stressful, particularly when you are on the go with no place to call home. Written with humor and warmth, this is one self-help book that provides practical techniques, insightful suggestions, and real-life examples to help you pull things together and cope with the realities you cannot change and restructure the ones you can. *Travel for Two* is a real contribution to the travel book field.

Travel Photography: Developing a Personal Style
by Lisl Dennis, Focal Press, 1983, 138 pages, paper, $19.50
This excellent, large-format guide, filled with color and black-and-white examples, will guide the serious amateur in the development of a personal photographic style. This is a great book for the amateur photographer.

Travel Safety
by Jack Adler and T. C. Tompkins, Hippocrene Books, 1988, 240 pages, paper, $14.95
This new title, released after press time, covers security safeguards at home and abroad.

Travel Well: A Comprehensive Guide to Your Health Abroad
by W. Scott Harkonen, M.D., Dodd, Mead & Co., 1984, 286 pages, paper, $11.95
This well-done guide covers pre-trip health preparations, immunizations, air sickness, coping with jct lag, finding health care abroad, tropical diseases and other maladies, water and food safety, disabled travelers, and other special problems. The large vaccination and health risk appendix is generally helpful, but will not always be up-to-date. To obtain current information, be sure to contact the local Health Department for the latest information from the Centers for Disease Control.

Travel Wise, Smart & Light: A Common Sense Guide to Vacation Planning
by Mary Nell York, Cobble & Mickle Books, 1986, 104 pages, paper, $6.95
This excellent, well-organized, down-to-earth guide gives information on how to avoid some major traveling mistakes. Topics include general planning, what to take, luggage do's and don'ts, money, documents, and useful lists.

Travel Writer's Handbook
by Louise Zobel, Writer's Digest Books, 1988 (2nd ed.), 274 pages, paper, $10.95
This well-done guide covers everything for the prospective travel writer, including how to pack like a writer, how to do research, and how to write the most popular kinds of travel articles. Zobel's tips will clarify the pitfalls and keep the aspiring writer focused on the goal—a published travel piece. Note: The new edition was released after press time; the listed price and number of pages are approximate.

Travel Writer's Markets
by Elaine O'Gara, Winterbourne Press, 1987, 181 pages, paper, $12.95
This well-done book contains the specifics on over 400 markets for travel articles. Each listing gives the name and address of the publication, the editor's name, pay rates, preferred article length, types of photos used, and other important information. A special

sections of "Washouts" lists publications that either do not accept freelance articles, do not pay well, or have foundered. This great source of detailed information provides mail label service and is updated every two years.

The Traveler's Challenge: The Sophisticated Globetrotter's Record Book

by George Blagowidow, Hippocrene Books, 1987, 240 pages, paper, $6.95

Listed in this unusual book are 1000 worthwhile travel objectives in absolutely every corner of the world. Also included is UNESCO's World Heritage List of natural features and works of man "that are of outstanding, universal value." This is an interesting way to summarize trips to date and plan future ones.

The Traveler's Medical Manual

by Angelo Scotti, Berkley Books, 1985, 244 pages, paper, $4.95

This book contains practical medical information on a wide array of possible diseases, immunizations (always check with the local Health Department for the latest requirements), and safe food. Scotti also provides a useful guide to the International Association for Medical Assistance to Travelers (IAMAT), an organization of English-speaking medical professionals throughout the world who meet the standards set by IAMAT and also agree to follow its fee structure.

Traveling Like Everybody Else: A Practical Guide for Disabled Travelers

by Jacqueline Freedman and Susan Gersten, Adama Books, 1987, 175 pages, paper, $11.95

This excellent reference for the disabled traveler contains a large appendix filled with helpful information plus some well-done chapters like "What, Me Travel?" and "What If Disaster Strikes?" Other chapters cover planning, staying healthy along the way, and what to do upon arrival.

Travels: The Traveller's Notebook

by Thomas Benedict, Teal Publishing, 1984, paper, $9.95

This is an elegant and simple travel diary for travel with a very sturdy cover and a ribbon marker. It is durable and has only a minimum of structured format.

The Tropical Traveller: An Essential Guide to Travel in Hot Climates
by John Hatt, Hippocrene Books, 1984, 254 pages, paper, $6.95

For those headed for high-temperature climes, this enjoyable classic how-to guide covers all the standard planning topics—equipment, money, flying, health, animal hazards, and photography. Heat can cause unique problems and this book tells how to avoid them.

Vagabond Globetrotting: State of the Art
by M. L. Endicott, Enchiridion International, 1984, 142 pages, paper, $8.95

"Traveling cheaply requires you to rely on others and to live as they do. It will spark ingenuity you never knew you had," states the author of this "new age" book. And, following the philosophy that a shoestring budget doesn't necessarily mean no travel, Endicott fills this book with practicalities that will make such a vagabond journey possible.

The Wandering Woman's Phrasebook
by Alison Owings, Shameless Hussy Press, 1987, 112 pages, paper, $6.95

Contained herein are those verbal retorts not found in other books to help the solo woman traveler make her feelings clearly known when the atmosphere is tense. Also included are phrases useful when meeting potential new friends and in other social situations. All phrases appear in French, Spanish, and Italian.

A World of Travel Tips
by Jean Nieman, Travel Interludes, 1982, 275 pages, paper, $8.95

Clear and commonsense advice on a wide range of travel topics, including tips on boat travel, air travel, train travel, health, hotels, tours, and car rentals, is contained in this book. These good ideas for a happy, trouble-free vacation will be of value to the veteran as well as the novice traveler.

Work Your Way Around the World
by Susan Griffith, Writer's Digest Books, 1987 (2nd ed.), 320 pages, paper, $10.95

In this book, veteran travelers who have worked their way around the world share their first-hand information. There are plenty of useful tips and, probably more importantly, cautions on the pitfalls. This valuable book allows potential workers to learn from the mistakes of others.

Writer's Market
  edited by Glenda Neff, Writer's Digest Books, 1987, 1047 pages, cloth, $21.95
  This is the famous, annual guide on publications of all types for writers. Considerable coverage is given to publications seeking travel articles, but this is not the focus of the book and there are fewer references on travel than a specialized title such as *Travel Writer's Marketplace* will have. The annual update is a real plus, however.

You Can Travel Free
  by Robert Kirk, Pelican Publishing, 1985, 191 pages, paper, $7.95
  Kirk, who has traveled free for over 15 years and covered more than 166,000 miles in the process, shares his experience in this book. Frequently gaining free lodging as well as free travel, Kirk's creative ideas run the gamut from earning a free trip as a trip organizer or participating in exchange programs to home exchanging or babysitting across Europe. The ideas are endless in this very creative effort.

The World

ABC Passenger Shipping Guide
ABC International, monthly editions, 300 pages, paper, $10.00
This comprehensive guide is updated monthly and widely used by travel agents. It contains up-to-date timetables of departures, plus all the necessary addresses and phone numbers for cruise ships and ferries around the world. This kind of information can be used to supplement a more standard cruise vacation guide.

Access to the World: A Travel Guide for the Handicapped
by Louise Weiss, Henry Holt & Co., 1986 (revised ed.), 220 pages, paper, $12.95
This is a respected resource for the disabled on air travel, buses, ships, planes, vehicles, lodging, tours, and more, with specific suggestions worldwide.

The Art of the Winemaker: A Guide to the World's Greatest Vineyards
edited by Serena Sutcliffe, Running Press, 1981, 256 pages, cloth, $25.00
This beautifully done, hardcover volume, filled with excellent color photographs as well as a well-written history, maps of every region, and detailed location maps for each of the 68 wineries selected, doubles as a coffee-table book. The countries of France, Germany, Italy, Australia, and the state of California are represented in this magnificent book, which is a guide and a great planning aid, but too cumbersome to carry along.

Baby Travel
Hippocrene Books, 1987, 357 pages, paper, $11.95
The topic of this British book is traveling with children. The book contains practical assessments of dozens of countries to aid in choos-

ing the best destination, details on the various modes of travel available (although most are British references), and a final section on "Baby Travel Know-How". This section is helpful but quite brief.

Backpacking and Camping in the Developing World

by Scott Graham, Wilderness Press, 1988, 160 pages, paper, $11.95

This new, practical guide, released after press time, is for those who would like to explore the developing countries of the world, but are unsure as to what is involved. Subjects covered include where to go, how to find inexpensive international flights, cooking and sleeping gear, health considerations, equipment checklists, and hundreds of suggestions based on the experience of the author and others.

Berlitz Complete Guide to Cruising

by Douglas Ward, Macmillan Publishing, 1986, 250 pages, paper, $12.95

Douglas Ward, the executive director of the International Cruise Passengers Association, provides a detailed analysis and rating of all the major ships afloat, as well as recommendations on where to cruise and how to choose between the many available options. A new edition has been announced.

Birding Around the World: A Guide to Observing Birds Everywhere You Travel

by Aileen Lotz, Dodd, Mead & Co., 1987, 266 pages, paper, $10.95

Aileen Lotz's book contains an extensive amount of helpful information for bird watchers. Her compendium of where-to guides to specific regions of the world is particularly useful.

Carol Haber's Discriminating Traveler: An Insider's Most Treasured Travel Tips

by Carol Haber, Charles Scribner's Sons, 1985, 406 pages, paper, $15.95

Focusing on the major cities of the world, Haber tells what to pack, the best guidebooks available, what tourist traps to bypass, and the best sightseeing. In addition, she suggests a small number of hotels and restaurants in various price ranges, shopping tips, and more. A down-to-earth, original guide.

Classic Walks of the World

edited by Walt Unsworth, Haynes Publications, 1985, 160 pages, cloth, $23.95

This is a book of major hikes in Kashmir, Japan, Peru, Africa, Greece, Nepal, New Zealand, Europe, and America. It is also part of the Classic Walks series, which is reviewed in more detail under "Series Reviews."

Culturgrams: The Nations Around Us
Garrett Park Press, 1987, unnumbered, paper, $14.00

Two volumes are available. Volume I covers North America, South America, and Europe. Volume II covers the Middle East, Asia, Africa and Oceania. Each is made up of four-page "culturgrams" from Brigham Young University, which summarize the customs and courtesies of each country and provide a brief synopsis on the people, the lifestyle, and the country as a whole. While pages are unnumbered, countries are arranged alphabetically so confusion only arises around countries with several common names. In all, this a good overview.

Dining Customs Around the World
by Alice Mothershead, Garrett Park Press, 1982, 131 pages, paper, $9.95

This simply prepared volume answers questions pertaining to the dining customs of 42 different countries.

Directory of Low-Cost Vacations With a Difference
Pilot Books, 1986, 70 pages, paper, $4.95

This book is essentially an extensive list of vacation possibilities, including everything from foreign families who will house travelers to budget travel clubs. Each reference includes a brief description of the services provided and the necessary addresses and phone numbers.

Eurail Guide: How to Travel Europe and All the World By Train
by Kathryn Turpin and Marvin Satzman, Eurail Guide Annual, 1987 (17th ed.), 816 pages, paper, $12.95

No single train guide covers more ground than this one. The authors of this book painstakingly assemble all the current schedules and other pertinent information on train travel in 141 countries each year. The book is comprehensive, but, as departure and arrival times change frequently, the authors admonish travelers to "always—without exception—before commencing each journey doublecheck the departure and arrival times given..." An annual guide can only offer what is current at the time of publication, but the approximations listed here are still very helpful.

Facts on File: Pocket Guide to the World

by Bernard Stonehouse, Facts on File, 1985, 496 pages, paper, $9.95

This is a traveler's reference book to anywhere containing notes on history, geography, weather, recent developments, general organization, and population statistics on each country. A gazetteer to geographic names and features is also included. For quick orientations to a multitude of localities, this is a useful reference.

Fielding's Worldwide Cruises

by Antoinette DeLand, William Morrow & Co., 1987 (3rd ed.), 469 pages, paper, $12.95

Well-regarded, this book rates over 100 ships (using the typical Fielding one-to-five-stars) including barges, river cruises, and other special trips. Ports of call covered include the Black Sea, Suez and the Red Sea, the Mississippi River, as well as more traditional world destinations.

Fodor's Views to Dine By Around the World

by Jerome Klein, Fodor's Travel Publications, 1986, 240 pages, paper, $9.95

Dining with a view is a novel idea in guidebooks. Available in different editions since 1961, this is one of Fodor's better titles. The author and his wife have personally experienced most of the restaurants and have written a good blurb on each, including all the practical information, though prices may be a little out-of-date. Prices range from quite moderate to very expensive.

Ford's Freighter Travel Guide

Ford's Travel Guides, 1987, 140 pages, paper, $7.95

A new edition of this guide is published every six months and is also available by subscription. Freighters are seldom thought of as modes of travel, but they offer accommodations for a maximum of 12 passengers, have no planned activities, no formal attire requirements, and provide an opportunity for complete relaxation. Cabins are often comparable to the best first-class cabins on a passenger liner and are available for as little as half the price. In addition, cabins are usually situated mid-ship—the quietest part of the ship. And because freighters carry such heavy cargo, they offer much smoother sailing than other ships. This book is full of great ideas for those considering setting sail.

Ford's International Cruise Guide

Ford's Travel Guides, 1987, 160 pages, paper, $8.95

This guide provides current information on over 100 ships. Black-and-white photos of each ship and a short description precede copi-

ous details on current trips available. Updated quarterly, this guide
can be obtained by subscription.

Frommer's Dollarwise Guide to Cruises
by Marilyn Springer and Don Schultz, Prentice Hall Press, 1987,
405 pages, paper, $12.95

This thorough, comprehensive review of more than 100 ships
includes advice on costs, how to get help from travel agents, how to
compare costs, when a bargain is worth its price, etc. Detailed reviews of ports of call in Alaska, Canada, the Caribbean, South America, Hawaii, Mexico, Panama, and the United States are provided.
This book is updated biennially.

Going Alone: The Woman's Guide to Travel Know-How
by Carole Chester, Hippocrene Books, 1987, 195 pages, paper, $8.95

Organized by continent and country, each section of this book will
provide the independent woman traveler with descriptions of "the
male attitude," where to stay, how to get around alone, eating and
drinking solo, "the safety factor," the "no-no's," and other essentials—all specifically from the lone female traveler's point of view.
Countries around the world are covered in 34 chapters. Well-organized and well-written, this book is recommended reading for the
woman who must or wishes to travel alone.

Guide Relais & Châteaux
Hunter Publishing, 1988, 200 pages, paper, $6.95

About half the selected castles, abbeys, and manor houses in this
guide now function as fine, charming inns in various spots throughout the world. The other half are in France. Additional review comments on this title are found in the section on France.

Guide to Health Spas Around the World
by Carol Wright, The Globe Pequot Press, 1988, 160 pages, paper,
$12.95

This new guide, expected out in the spring of 1988, covers specific
information on more than 150 spas and health resorts in 30 countries.

Guide to the Great Resorts of the World
by Steven Stern, Prentice Hall Press, 1985, 240 pages, paper, $14.95

Though not as up-to-date as possible, this guide is a very good idea
book for travelers hoping to vacation in one of the world's most
luxurious resorts. The chosen few are in every corner of the world
and each is a self-contained vacationland filled with restaurants,

sporting facilities, expansive holiday suites, etc. The appendixes contain all the facts and figures, circa 1985.

Half the Earth: Women's Experiences of Travel Worldwide
Routledge & Kegan Paul, 1986, 456 pages, paper, $10.95
More than 50 women share their stories about their travels in over 70 countries in this wonderful background book for the independent woman traveler.

Hideaways Guide
Hideaways International, 1988, 128 pages, paper, $9.95
Hideaways International, a membership travel club, makes available its semiannual guide on a single-copy basis. This guide is chockfull of fantastic rental possibilities throughout the world—each is described in detail and accompanied by a photo. Non-member rental of these wonderful spots is difficult. So if the spot is that appealing, it may be worthwhile to become a member. This is a cheap way to check out that possibility.

How to Get From the Airport to the City All Around the World
by Norman Crampton, M. Evans & Co., 1988 (7th ed.), 124 pages, paper, $4.95
Crampton's popular guide to airport transportation, now published for the first time by M. Evans & Co., provides indispensible, up-to-date information on cabs, limos, rentals and public transportation from airport to city. Updated annually since 1982, this book will now be revised biennially.

How to Go Around the World Overland
by Michael and Theresa Savage, Surface Travel Publications, 1988 (2nd ed.), 498 pages, paper, $14.95
In this guide the Savages show how to travel around the world using public transportation. The focus is on those who choose *not* to fly between destinations, preferring instead to stick to surface travel all the way around the globe. Even so, there is plenty of interest for travelers hopping around the world by air. The first edition contained useful tourist notes on 67 major cities and included lodging, food, sightseeing, and entertainment—all in the budget category. It was an ambitious effort for a self-published work, and the second edition can only be better.

The International Traveler's Security Handbook
by Anthony Herbert, Hippocrene Books, 1985, 330 pages, paper, $9.95
This useful book provides concise information about traveling safely and securely in 155 different countries.

The Jewish Travel Guide

edited by Sidney Lightman, Sepher-Herman Press, 1987, 308 pages, paper, $9.50

This annually published guide is full of information on kosher restaurants, hotels, synagogues, and places of historic interest throughout the world, including Eastern European countries and the Far East. The type is small, the format crowded, and the amount of information considerable.

The Jewish Traveler: Hadassah Magazine's Guide to the World's Jewish Communities and Sights

edited by Alan Tigay, Doubleday & Co., 1988, 360 pages, paper, $10.95

The focus of this nicely done, pleasantly written guidebook is on the major cities of the world. For each city, information on its history, its sights of Jewish interest, its places of worship, its kosher restaurants, and where to stay is included. The comments on restaurants and hotels are quite brief, however. Still, this is a good source of information for the Jewish traveler.

1988 Spas: The International Spa Guide

edited by Joseph Bain and Eli Dror, BDIT, Inc., 1987, 294 pages, paper, $12.95

It's all here: spas that feature medical treatments, beauty spas, mineral spas, hot springs, and those with fitness programs. And they are located in every corner of the world, including Eastern Europe. A good description of each spa location, the services available, the distance from the airport, the seasons they are open, and the length of specific treatments is included. More than 300 spas in 30 countries, including Eastern Europe, are described.

The Pan Am World Guide

McGraw-Hill, 1982 (26th ed.), 1163 pages, cloth, $11.95

This guide is a thick, but compact, hardback providing quick, encyclopedic looks at essentially every country in the world—its size, type of currency and expected exchange rate, transportation options, and what to see. This is a very useful book and one of the only general guides to the world currently in print. Although it has not been revised since 1982, this guide is worth perusing.

Passport's Guide to the Business Capitals of the World

edited by Graham Boynton, Passport Books, 1986, 320 pages, cloth, $29.95

This book covers 31 major cities, each with a several-page introduction followed by sections on where to stay, where to eat, nightlife, and how to get around. Selections, ranging upwards from moderately expensive, are given informative write-ups. This is a good single-volume guide to the meccas of world business.

Pat Dickerman's Adventure Travel Abroad

by Pat Dickerman, Henry Holt & Co., 1986, 222 pages, paper, $12.95

Contained herein are descriptions of over 340 trips, from rafting, cycling, and ballooning to horseback riding and trekking. All the pertinent facts of vacationing on every continent are included. Prices will, of course, be a bit higher now, but other than that almost all the information included is substantially correct. This is a great book for armchair adventurers as well as those who plan to "get up and go."

Pat Dickerman's Farm/Ranch and Country Vacations

by Pat Dickerman, Farm/Ranch Vacations, 1986, 215 pages, paper, $9.95

This book, which is revised every two to three years, contains specific information on numerous vacation possibilities out on the farm. Choices range from participating on operating farms to vacationing on sophisticated dude ranches. Emphasis here is on the United States, but there are possibilities all over the world.

Peterson's Learning Vacations: The All-Season Guide to Educational Travel

by Gerson Eisenberg, Peterson's Guides, 1986 (5th ed.), 249 pages, paper, $9.95

In this book, Eisenberg has assembled descriptions and contact information on seminars, workshops, arts, crafts, photography, and senior citizen's programs in many diverse locations. This is a great resource for planning a constructive vacation and perhaps earning a few college credits at the same time.

The Round-the-World Air Guide

by George McDonald and Katie Wood, E. P. Dutton, 1988, 976 pages, paper, $14.95

Released after press time, this large, comprehensive guide is for those who plan to buy a round-the-world airfare ticket and head on out to see it all. The many possible routing options and current air fare policies, as well as myriad other practicalities are discussed in a detailed, 200-page section. The remainder of the book covers the 50 main worldwide stop-off points, including information on such other topics as passports, visas, health, hotels, food, and sightseeing.

The Simon and Schuster Pocket Guide to Beer: The Connoisseur's Companion to the Fine Beers of the World
by Michael Jackson, Simon & Schuster, 1986, 155 pages, paper, $7.95
Serious beer drinkers should slip a copy of this book into their bags before leaving and attempt to collect as many different beers as possible on the journey. The print in this volume is small, but the information is well organized by country. A glossary of terms completes this look into the nuances of the world of beer.

Sobek's Adventure Vacations
edited by Christian Kallen, Running Press, 1986 (4th ed.), 140 pages, paper, $12.95
Sobek International, widely respected in the adventure travel field, sponsors raft trips, safaris, treks, mountaineering excursions, bicycling trips, educational trips, and natural history trips in the most exciting, exotic, mysterious places in the world. Excellent photos highlight hundreds of exciting vacation possibilities.

The Sophisticated Traveler: Enchanting Places and How to Find Them—From Pleasant Hill to Katmandu
edited by A. M. Rosenthal and Arthur Gelb, Random House, 1986, 419 pages, cloth, $15.95
The Sophisticated Traveler: Great Tours and Detours
edited by A. M. Rosenthal and Arthur Gelb, Random House, 1985, 544 pages, cloth, $15.95
The Sophisticated Traveler: Winter: Love It or Leave It
edited by A. M. Rosenthal and Arthur Gelb, Viking Penguin, 1984, 541 pages, paper, $8.95
These three titles in the Sophisticated Traveler Guides series are reviewed in more detail under "Series Reviews." Note that these finely crafted essays by *New York Times* staff are not all from the same publisher. Several of the titles in this Random House series (including *Beloved Cities of Europe*) are available in paperback from Penguin Books.

Spartacus Guide for Gay Men
by Bruno Gmünder, Inland Book Co., 1987 (16th ed.), 784 pages, paper, $24.95
This annually updated book is the number-one international guide for gay men. The brief notes on each country are in English only, but most of the book is a combination of four languages (German, French, Spanish, and English). Contained herein are listings of the best bars, clubs, saunas, beaches, hotels, restaurants, cafes, and bookshops worldwide. The coverage is massive.

Stern's Guide to the Cruise Vacation

by Steven Stern, Pelican Publishing, 1988, 222 pages, paper, $10.95

A busy lawyer part of the year, Stern spends from three to five months a year hopping from one ship to the next to keep this thoroughly comprehensive guide up-to-date. The guide includes details on planning, choosing a ship, what to bring, and what to expect, as well as descriptions of the major ports of call and suggestions for what to do while in port. Special sections on singles ("Love Boat" etiquette), and cruising with children round out this fine book. The appendix provides statistics on every cruise ship in service and at least one ship from each cruise ship line is rated for accommodations and service.

The Third World Guide

Grove Press, 1986, 642 pages, paper, $22.50

The *Third World Guide* is a look at the history, geography, economics, and politics of the diverse countries around the globe that function on the fringe of the international system. It has been assembled by a team of writers and editors from various countries, most of whom are also involved in the bi-monthly publication of the magazine, *Third World*.

Thomas Cook Overseas Timetable

Timetable Publishing, monthly editions, paper, $19.95

For up-to-date train schedules all over the world (except Europe, which is published separately as the *Thomas Cook European Timetable*), this is the best, most readily available source. This timetable, used in conjunction with any other train guide, will provide the most up-to-date information available. Forsyth Travel Library is the primary importer of these timetables in America (see Travel Bookstore appendix). Many travel bookstores carry these popular books, although not all will stock each of the monthly editions. Travel Books Unlimited is one store that does, as will other stores in the very largest cities.

The 300 Best Hotels in the World

by Rene Lecler, Prentice Hall Press, 1985, 220 pages, paper, $7.95

The premier (not to mention expensive) hotels selected for inclusion in this book represent 65 countries. Each is given an informative write-up, which includes all the necessary practical information— even the distance to the airport. (Note: some specifics may have changed since the publication date.)

The Times Books World Weather Guide
  by E. A. Pearch and Gordon Smith, Times Books, 1984, 480 pages,
  paper, $22.50
    This detailed, comprehensive work, consisting of more than 450
  charts and maps, covers weather facts city-by-city.

The Total Traveler by Ship
  by Ethel Blum, Hippocrene Books, 1988, 400 pages, paper, $13.95
    Ethel Blum is the president of the Society of American Travel
  Writers and is an acknowledged authority on ship travel. Her annual
  encyclopedia of travel covers most every type imaginable: luxury
  liner, freighter, cargoliner, riverboat, paddlewheeler, Nile cruising,
  Rhine cruising, and yacht charters. All are rated by a panel of 75
  experts. Copious details on ship etiquette, ports of call, customs,
  and lots more are also included. This is a comprehensive guide to
  the world of ship travel.

**The Traveler's Reading Guide: Ready-made Lists for the Armchair
  Traveler**
  edited by Maggy Simony, Facts on File, 1988, 831 pages, paper,
  $17.95
    Simony's laborious effort, an inspiration for our own work, which
  she previously published in three separate volumes, has been released in this single volume by Facts on File. Its strength is its
  background materials—novels, journals, historical works, and travel
  articles—on just about every destination imaginable. While there is
  some mention of selected guidebooks, the focus is on books for the
  armchair traveler contemplating a future trip. This is a complement
  to our own book that will work well; it will help prepare any traveler
  to get the most out of his or her vacation.

The Traveller's Handbook
  edited by Melissa Shales, The Globe Pequot Press, 1988 (5th ed.),
  820 pages, paper, $15.95
    This weighty book, popular with English travelers for years, is
  now available in America for the first time. Its first section is a series
  of helpful essays by various authorities on subjects ranging from
  booking air travel to coping with burglary abroad. A second section
  is packed with the names and addresses of helpful suppliers, organizations, embassies, etc., and details on health and visa requirements, driving conditions, climate, banking, shopping hours, and
  tipping.

Volunteer Vacations
by Bill McMillon, Chicago Review Press, 1987, 173 pages, paper, $11.95
  This book is for those who want to do something more than just soak up the good times on their next vacation. Described are plenty of worthwhile special projects that need volunteers. More than 500 opportunities in many parts of the world are included in this excellent resource.

Work, Study, Travel Abroad: The Whole World Handbook
by Council on International Educational Exchange, St. Martin's Press, 1988 (9th ed.), 416 pages, paper, $8.95
  Students and interested travelers of all ages will find more information in this one source on work/study/travel abroad than anywhere else. Crammed with information on grants, foreign exchanges, internships, traineeships, university programs, and cheap travel alternatives, this book covers the whole world, not just Europe, and includes expanded sections on New Zealand and Australia.

Work Your Way Around the World
by Susan Griffith, Writer's Digest Books, 1987, 383 pages, paper, $10.95
  This guide provides firsthand information from those who have worked their way to a travel adventure many times before. These veterans provide plenty of useful tips, cautions on pitfalls, and other useful facts to consider.

The World Class Executive
by Neil Chesanow, Bantam Books, 1985, 303 pages, paper, $9.95
  A vast amount of information is contained in this first-class, business-oriented book. It addresses the practical realities of major areas of the world—Europe, the Arabian Peninsula, the Orient, and Latin America—and makes clear the ground rules applicable to Americans visiting these foreign lands.

World Guide for the Jewish Traveler
by Warren Freedman, E. P. Dutton, 1984, 360 pages, paper, $8.95
  Covering over 100 countries, this book contains histories and lists of kosher restaurants and synagogues, as well as short sections on individual cities. The information is solid, but necessarily brief at times.

World Guide to Nude Beaches and Recreation
by Lee Baxandall, Crown Publishers, 1988, 240 pages, paper, $17.95
   This newly updated text containing plenty of photographs focuses on hundreds of clothing-optional spots—beaches and otherwise—in 60 countries on seven continents. This is the most comprehensive source of skinny-dipping information available.

Africa

AFRICA AS A WHOLE

See also "The World."

Africa On a Shoestring
by Geoff Crowther, Lonely Planet Publications, 1986 (4th ed.), 752 pages, paper, $14.95

This is one of the budget-oriented On a Shoestring Guide series, which is reviewed in more detail under "Series Reviews." The series is updated every two to three years.

African Safari: The Complete Travel Guide to Ten Top Game Viewing Countries
by Mark Nolting, Global Travel Publishers, 1987, 250 pages, paper, $15.95

This well-done, widely praised book can be used when planning a safari or on an organized safari trip. It includes lots of practical information, such as when to go, where to stay, regulations affecting travelers, and the animals to see.

Fielding's African Safaris
by Jane and Leah Taylor, William Morrow & Co., 1987, 608 pages, paper, $17.95

The Taylors have written an interesting book that details 65 African safaris in 16 different countries. All types of safaris are proposed, not just the typical ones that come to mind. For example, information on an artist's safari, a bicycling safari, and a bird watcher's safari is included. Background information on each country, as well as notes on planning, budgets, local customs, health tips, hotel prices, and travel documents also appear.

Fielding's Literary Africa
  by Jane and Leah Taylor, William Morrow & Co., 1988, 380 pages, paper, $12.95
  Here is an interesting and unusual book suggesting seven intriguing itineraries for viewing the African landscape based on seven famous books. This is a fascinating idea that will charm the literature buff.

A Hitchhiker's Guide to Africa and Arabia
  by David Childress, Chicago Review Press, 1984, 295 pages, paper, $8.95
  This is a thoroughly enjoyable narrative of a multi-year hitchhiking adventure. Childress' journal is one that also contains a lot of practical information on how to survive and cope with the "daily problems of money, sustenance, shelter, even sex." This is definitely a guide for the hearty traveler.

Staying Healthy in Asia, Africa and Latin America
  by Dirk Schroeder, Volunteers in Asia, 1988, 168 pages, paper, $7.95
  This wonderful guide offers tips on how to remain healthy in third world countries. Well-written chapters include pre-trip planning and preventing illness upon arrival. General health maintenance tips and guidelines for diagnosis and treatment of illness are offered as well as suggestion on how to deal with common health problems, infections, and diseases, including problems of heat, cold, and high altitude in areas where no doctor is available. Travelers heading for these continents—particularly the rural areas—should pick up a copy.

REGIONS OF AFRICA

CENTRAL AFRICA

See also "Africa as a Whole." Comprising Burundi, Central African Republic, Congo, Rwanda, and Zaire.

Backpacker's Africa: A Walker's Guide to East, Central, and Southern Africa
  Hunter Publishing, 1983 (2nd ed.), 204 pages, paper, $11.95
Backpacker's Africa-2: A Guide to West & Central Africa
  Hunter Publishing, 1988, 224 pages, paper, $11.95
  These are two titles in the Hunter Walking/Hiking Guide series, which is reviewed in more detail under "Series Reviews."

Traveller's Guide to Central and Southern Africa
Hunter Publishing, 1986, 248 pages, paper, $12.95
Part of the Traveller's Guide series which is reviewed in more
detail under "Series Reviews."

EASTERN AFRICA

See also "Africa as a Whole." Comprising Djibouti, Ethiopia, Somalia,
Sudan, Tanzania, and Uganda.

**Backpacker's Africa: A Walker's Guide to East, Central, and Southern
Africa**
Hunter Publishing, 1983 (2nd ed.), 204 pages, paper, $11.95
One of the Hunter Walking/Hiking Guide series, which is re-
viewed in more detail under "Series Reviews."

East Africa: A Travel Survival Kit
by Geoff Crowther, Lonely Planet Publications, 1987, 373 pages,
paper, $9.95
Considered the best guide to the region by many reviewers, this
book is definitely more oriented to the young and adventurous. It is
one of the Travel Survival Kit series, which is reviewed in more
detail under "Series Reviews." It is updated every two to three years.

Guide to East Africa: Kenya, Tanzania, The Seychelles
by Nina Casimati, Hippocrene Books, 1987 (3rd ed.), 191 pages,
paper, $11.95
This solid, thorough, all-purpose guidebook includes useful, practical information on day trips, shopping, and sightseeing. Hotels and
restaurants are briefly described and cover different price ranges
where available.

Traveller's Guide to East Africa and the Indian Ocean
Hunter Publishing, 1986, 234 pages, paper, $12.95
This is part of the Traveller's Guide series, which is reviewed in
more detail under "Series Reviews."

NORTHERN AFRICA

See also "Africa as a Whole." Comprising Algeria, Egypt, Libya, Mauritania, and the western Sahara.

ABC Air Europe, Middle East & North Africa
ABC International, monthly editions, 340 pages, paper, $10.00
This comprehensive monthly airline schedule is for those who
need to make numerous air connections in their travels and are
compelled by necessity to be their own travel agent.

Fodor's North Africa
Fodor's Travel Publications, 1987, 416 pages, paper, $16.95
This is one of the Fodor's Country/Regional Guide series, which is reviewed in more detail under "Series Reviews." It is updated annually.

Traveller's Guide to North Africa
Hunter Publishing, 1987, 192 pages, paper, $12.95
This book is part of the Traveller's Guide series, which is reviewed in more detail under "Series Reviews."

SOUTHERN AFRICA

See also "Africa as a Whole." Comprising Angola, Botswana, Lesotho, Malawi, Mozambique, Namibia, South Africa, Swaziland, Zambia, and Zimbabwe.

Backpacker's Africa: A Walker's Guide to East, Central, and Southern Africa
Hunter Publishing, 1983 (2nd ed.), 204 pages, paper, $11.95
This book is part of the Hunter Walking/Hiking Guide series, which is reviewed in more detail under "Series Reviews."

Traveller's Guide to Central and Southern Africa
Hunter Publishing, 1986, 248 pages, paper, $12.95
This book is part of the Traveller's Guide series, which is reviewed in more detail under "Series Reviews."

WESTERN AFRICA

See also "Africa as a Whole." Comprising Benin, Burkina Faso, Cameroon, Chad, Equatorial Guinea, Gabon, Gambia, Ghana, Guinea, Guinea-Bissau, Ivory Coast, Liberia, Mali, Niger, Nigeria, Sao Tome, Senegal, Sierra Leone, and Togo.

Backpacker's Africa-2: A Guide to West & Central Africa
Hunter Publishing, 1988, 224 pages, paper, $11.95
This is one of the Hunter Walking/Hiking Guide series, which is reviewed in more detail under "Series Reviews."

Traveller's Guide to West Africa
Hunter Publishing, 1986 (6th ed.), 274 pages, paper, $12.95
This book is part of the Traveller's Guide series, which is reviewed in more detail under "Series Reviews."

COUNTRIES OF AFRICA

Includes only those few African nations for which there are specific titles. For other African nations, see regional titles above.

The Azores: See "Islands of the Eastern and Northern Atlantic Ocean" under Europe.
Canary Islands: See "Islands of the Eastern and Northern Atlantic Ocean" under Europe.
Cape Verde: See "Islands of the Eastern and Northern Atlantic Ocean" under Europe.

EGYPT

See also "Northern Africa" and "Africa as a Whole."

Baedeker's Egypt
Prentice Hall Press, 1984, 384 pages, paper, $15.95
This is part of the Baedeker's Country/Regional Guide series, which is reviewed in more detail under "Series Reviews."

Berlitz: Egypt
Macmillan Publishing, 1980, 128 pages, paper, $6.95
This book is one of the small-format Berlitz Guide series, which is reviewed in more detail under "Series Reviews."

Blue Guide: Egypt
by Peter Stocks and Veronica Seton-Williams, W. W. Norton & Co., 1983, 768 pages, paper, $20.95
This book is part of the highly regarded Blue Guide series, which is reviewed in more detail under "Series Reviews."

Coptic Egypt: History and Guide
by Jill Kamil, Columbia University Press, 1987, 149 pages, paper, $16.00
This is an excellent guide to the history, evolution, and historic monuments of the Coptic Christian church, including a large chapter on the Coptic Museum, the most extensive collection of Coptic art in the world. Here are both broad overviews and detailed, comprehensive evaluations that should satisfy any traveler's interest.

Egypt and the Sudan: A Travel Survival Kit
by Scott Wayne, Lonely Planet Publications, 1987, 256 pages, paper, $8.95
This book is part of the Travel Survival Kit series, which is re-

viewed in more detail under "Series Reviews." It is updated every two to three years.

Fodor's Egypt
Fodor's Travel Publications, 1987, 272 pages, paper, $12.95
This book is part of Fodor's Country/Regional Guide series, which is reviewed in more detail under "Series Reviews." It is updated annually.

Frommer's Dollarwise Guide to Egypt
by Nancy McGrath, Prentice Hall Press, 1988, 264 pages, paper, $11.95
This book is one of Frommer's Dollarwise Guide series, which is reviewed in more detail under "Series Reviews." These guides emphasize selections in the moderate price range and are updated every two years.

Frommer's Touring Guide to Egypt
by Denise Basdevant, Prentice Hall Press, 1986, 166 pages, paper, $8.95
This book is part of Frommer's Touring Guide series, which is reviewed in more detail under "Series Reviews."

Guide to Cairo Including the Pyramids and Saqqara
by Michael Haag, Hippocrene Books, 1986, 144 pages, paper, $9.95
Michael Haag's first-rate travel guide provides excellent sightseeing information as well as lots of practical information, including informative comments on hotels and restaurants in all price ranges.

Guide to Egypt
by Michael Haag, Hippocrene Books, 1985 (2nd ed.), 345 pages, paper, $14.95
Considered by many the best and most comprehensive guide (albeit aging) on Egypt available, this book covers both the pleasures and practicalities of travel in Egypt.

Let's Go: Israel & Egypt (including Jordan)
by Harvard Student Agencies, St. Martin's Press, 1988, 464 pages, paper, $10.95
This book is part of the excellent, budget-oriented Let's Go Guide series, which is reviewed in more detail under "Series Reviews." Egypt is also included in *Let's Go: Europe*. This series is updated annually.

Nagel's Egypt
Passport Books, 1983, 815 pages, cloth, $49.95
This classic, cultural guide is part of the Nagel's Guide series, which is reviewed in more detail under "Series Reviews."

The Traveler's Key to Ancient Egypt: A Guide to the Sacred Places
by John Anthony West, Alfred Knopf, Inc., 1985, 480 pages, paper, $18.95
This title provides excellent detail while concentrating "on the inner meaning of the sacred art and architecture of ancient Egypt." It is part of the Traveler's Key Guide series, which is reviewed in more detail under "Series Reviews."

ISLANDS OF THE WESTERN INDIAN OCEAN

Comprising Madagascar, the Maldives, Mauritius, and the Seychelles. The Comoro Islands and Reunion are also included as part of the regional title listed below.

Berlitz: Sri Lanka and the Maldives
Macmillan Publishing, 1981, 128 pages, paper, $6.95
This book is part of the small-format Berlitz Guide series, which is reviewed in more detail under "Series Reviews."

Guide to Madagascar
Hunter Publishing, 1988, 224 pages, paper, $12.95
This may well be the only guide exclusively on Madagascar. It is a new title and was due to be published in mid-1988.

Hildebrand's Travel Guide: Mauritius
Hunter Publishing, 1985, 111 pages, paper, $8.95
Hildebrand's Travel Guide: Seychelles
Hunter Publishing, 1985, 126 pages, paper, $8.95
These are two titles in the Hildebrand's Guide series, which is reviewed in more detail under "Series Reviews."

Maldives
by Stuart Bevan, Publisher's Group West, 1985, 191 pages, paper, $8.95
This helpful, comprehensive guide provides an overview of the country, its history, politics, religion, holidays, festivals, music, and dance, as well as information on lodging, dining, and sightseeing. Published by Other People Publications in Australia, this book also includes a handy language section.

Traveller's Guide to East Africa and the Indian Ocean
Hunter Publishing, 1986, 234 pages, paper, $12.95
    This guide includes information on the Seychelles, the Comoro Islands, Madagascar, Mauritius, and Reunion. It is part of the Traveller's Guide series, which is reviewed in more detail under "Series Reviews."

KENYA

See also "Eastern Africa" and "Africa as a Whole."

Berlitz: Kenya
Macmillan Publishing, 1979, 128 pages, paper, $6.95
    This book is one of the small-format Berlitz Guide series, which is reviewed in more detail under "Series Reviews."

Fodor's Kenya
Fodor's Travel Guides, 1986, 240 pages, paper, $11.95
    This particular edition has been criticized for inaccuracy. It is part of Fodor's Country/Regional Guide series, which is reviewed in more detail under "Series Reviews."

Hildebrand's Travel Guide: Kenya
Hunter Publishing, 1986, 189 pages, paper, $10.95
    This book is one of the Hildebrand's Guide series, which is reviewed in more detail under "Series Reviews."

Insight Guide: Kenya
by Apa Productions, Prentice Hall Press, 1987, 315 pages, paper, $16.95
    This book is one of the widely praised Insight Guide series, which is reviewed in more detail under "Series Reviews."

Kenya: A Visitor's Guide
by Arnold Curtis, Hunter Publishing, 1985, 170 pages, paper, $12.95
    The strong point of this book is its author, a resident of Kenya since 1952, who shares his intimacy with the country in this quality guide. The book is filled with places to see and things to do and provides plenty of detail maps and color photos. Comments on hotels and restaurants, however, are quite general and Curtis refers travelers to other local books (not otherwise available in America) when choosing restaurants.

Mombasa and the Kenya Coast: A Visitor's Guide
by J. H. A. Jewel, Hunter Publishing, 1988, 200 pages, paper, $10.95

This guide covers the beautiful Indian Ocean area, well known for its reef-protected coastline and the exotic charm of the city of Mombasa, which has maintained a contact with both India and Arabia for centuries. Providing details on diving, fishing, sailing, shopping, and history, this new guide was due out in mid-1988; pages are approximate.

Rough Guide to Kenya
by Richard Trillo, Routledge & Kegan Paul, 1987, 300 pages, paper, $12.95

This book is part of the excellent Rough Guide series, which is reviewed in more detail under "Series Reviews." The series is updated every two to three years.

Visiting Kenya
by John Brigden, Hippocrene Books, 1987, 192 pages, paper, $8.95

This is a companion guide to Kenya, filled with history and an orientation to the Kenya of today. It includes general tips on what to take, what to wear, how to travel, and more.

Madagascar: See "Islands of the Western Indian Ocean" above.
Madeira: See "Islands of the Eastern and Northern Atlantic Ocean" under Europe.
Mauritius: See "Islands of the Western Indian Ocean" above.

MOROCCO
See also "Northern Africa" and "Africa as a Whole."

Berlitz: Morocco
Macmillan Publishing, 1979, 128 pages, paper, $6.95

This book is one of the small-format Berlitz Guide series, which is reviewed in more detail under "Series Reviews."

The Camper's Companion to Southern Europe
by Dennis and Tina Jaffe, Williamson Publishing, 1986, 287 pages, paper, $13.95

This guide includes camping opportunities in Morocco and is reviewed under "Europe as a Whole."

Frommer's Spain & Morocco on $40 a Day
by Darwin Porter, Prentice Hall Press, 1987, 552 pages, paper,
$10.95
This book is part of the budget-oriented Frommer's Dollar-a-Day
Guide series, which is reviewed in more detail under "Series Reviews." The series is updated every two years.

Let's Go: Spain, Portugal & Morocco
by Harvard Student Agencies, St. Martin's Press, 1988, 592 pages,
paper, $10.95
This book is one of the excellent, budget-oriented Let's Go Guide
series, which is reviewed in more detail under "Series Reviews."
Morocco is also included in *Let's Go: Europe*. The series is updated
annually.

Rough Guide to Morocco
by Mark Ellingham and Shaun McVeigh, Routledge & Kegan Paul,
1986, 232 pages, paper, $9.95
This book is part of the excellent Rough Guide series, which is
reviewed in more detail under "Series Reviews." The series is updated every two to three years.

Shopping in Exotic Morocco
by Ron Krannich, *et al.*, Impact Publications, 1988, 180 pages,
paper, $9.95
This book is part of the excellent Shopping in Exotic Places series,
which is reviewed in more detail under "Series Reviews." The series
is updated every two years. Released after press time, the number of
pages is approximate.

Seychelles: See "Islands of the Western Indian Ocean" above.

SOUTH AFRICA

See also "Southern Africa" and "Africa as a Whole."

Berlitz: South Africa
Macmillan Publishing, 1983, 128 pages, paper, $6.95
This book is one of the small-format Berlitz Guide series, which
is reviewed in more detail under "Series Reviews."

Hildebrand's Travel Guide: South Africa
Hunter Publishing, 1985, 153 pages, paper, $8.95
This book is part of the Hildebrand's Guide series, which is re-
viewed in more detail under "Series Reviews."

SUDAN

See also "Eastern Africa" and "Africa as a Whole."

Egypt and Sudan: A Travel Survival Kit

by Scott Wayne, Lonely Planet Publications, 1987, 256 pages, paper, $8.95

This book is part of the well-known Travel Survival Kit series, which is reviewed in more detail under "Series Reviews." The series is updated every two to three years.

TUNISIA

See also "Northern Africa" and "Africa as a Whole."

Berlitz: Tunisia

Macmillan Publishing, 1977, 128 pages, paper, $6.95

This book is one of the small-format Berlitz Guide series, which is reviewed in more detail under "Series Reviews."

Rough Guide to Tunisia

by Peter Morris, Routledge & Kegan Paul, 1986, 247 pages, paper, $7.95

This book is part of the excellent Rough Guide series, which is reviewed in more detail under "Series Reviews." The series is updated every two to three years.

Antarctica

Fodor's South America
Fodor's Travel Publications, 1987, 629 pages, paper, $14.95

There isn't a single guidebook *exclusively* on Antarctica. However, at the end of the chapter on Chile is a small section on travel to Antarctica. One of the options offered is through the Chilean military and includes accommodations in Antarctica's only hostelry: the 35-room Hotel Estrella Polar. *Fodor's South America* is updated annually.

Asia

ASIA AS A WHOLE

See also "The World."

ABC Air Asia, Australia & New Zealand

ABC International, monthly editions, 250 pages, paper, $7.00

This airline schedule is a must for travelers making many connections and compelled to play travel agent. Note that the Middle East is part of *ABC Air Europe, Middle East & Northern Africa*.

All-Asia Guide

Charles E. Tuttle Co., 1986 (14th ed.), 704 pages, paper, $12.95

The *All-Asia Guide*, produced by the *Far Eastern Economic Review*, has been a standard for many years. The guide covers 26 different countries and includes history, the practicalities and idiosyncrasies of each country, and sightseeing tips. Clear detail maps of major cities and a separate hotel guide supplement the work. Restaurant and hotel comments are brief, but still reasonably informative. This is the best single guide for travelers visiting a multitude of countries, but the use of additional guides for individual countries should be considered if they are available. Note: The Middle East and Eastern Russia are not included and the print is quite small.

Asia 101: History, Art and Culture for the Traveler

by John Gottberg, John Muir Publications, 1988, 352 pages, paper, $11.95

This new guide, released after press time, is produced in the same format as the classic *Europe 101*, which is reviewed under "Europe as a Whole."

Asia Through The Back Door
by Rick Steves and John Gottberg, John Muir Publications, 1986, 319 pages, paper, $11.95

Rick Steves has adapted his classic *Europe Through The Back Door* concept to the Asian continent. The result is an excellent strategy book especially useful for those wishing to travel cheaply. Included among the many practical subjects are separate sections on transportation, budget eating and sleeping, health, attitude adjustment, and 18 suggested "back doors"—ways to enter and experience the *real* Asia.

Best Places to Stay in Asia
by Jerome Klein, The Harvard Common Press, 1988, 600 pages, paper, $14.95

Released after press time, this addition to the Best Places to Stay Guide series (reviewed in more detail under "Series Reviews") is the only in-depth guidebook available on lodging in Asia. Written by the author of *Fodor's Views to Dine By Around the World*, it is organized country-by-country and includes the facts and figures on many types of lodging possibilities as well as interesting anecdotes, legends, and histories. No fees are accepted for inclusion.

Fielding's Far East
by Antoinette DeLand, William Morrow & Co., 1986, 592 pages, paper, $14.95

Typical of a number of other Fielding titles, this one is written in a somewhat uncomfortable omniscient style. Nonetheless, it contains plenty of information, especially on shopping, entertainment, and nightlife. The hotel write-ups are often too brochure-like and are rated with the well-known Fielding five-star system. This book is part of the Fielding's Travel Guide series, which is reviewed in more detail under "Series Reviews."

International Herald Tribune Guide to Business Travel in Asia
edited by Robert McCage, Passport Books, 1988, 208 pages, paper, $14.95

In this book, the *International Herald Tribune* expands on the theme of its popular European guide for the business traveler. Addressing the stated needs of the businessperson, the reporters and editors of this famous newspaper cover all the topics of importance for each of the 16 major business cities in considerable detail. This title was released after press time, but the European version is well known and well done. The cities and countries covered are: Bangkok, Beijing, Brunei, Canton, Hong Kong, Jakarta, Kuala Lampur, Macau,

Manila, Osaka, Seoul, Shanghai, Sherzhen, Singapore, Taipei, and Tokyo.

Staying Healthy in Asia, Africa and Latin America
by Dirk Schroeder, Volunteers in Asia, Inc., 1988, 168 pages, paper, $7.95

This great little book is reviewed under "Africa as a Whole."

Sunset Orient Travel Guide
Lane Publishing, 1986, 160 pages, paper, $9.95

This large-format guide is spotty in its coverage of the Orient and should only be used for vacation ideas. It is part of the Sunset Travel Guide series, which is reviewed in more detail under "Series Reviews."

Travel With Children: A Survival Kit for Travel in Asia
by Maureen Wheeler, Lonely Planet Publications, 1985, 96 pages, paper, $4.95

This guide is full of information for those contemplating traveling in Asia with children. Wheeler deals with myriad cultural issues and kid-related problems beginning with the most immediate ones of culture shock, health, food, and even diaper resources ("nappies" are not readily available everywhere; Wheeler lists the realities specific to each country). She then moves on to ways to keep the kids entertained. It may seem like an overwhelming idea to take a child to Asia, but it can be done and this little book will certainly help.

The Traveler's Guide to Asian Customs and Manners
by Elizabeth Devine and Nancy Braganti, St. Martin's Press, 1986, 315 pages, paper, $9.95

This useful book covers myriad topics from greetings, dress, meals, hotels, and business concerns to transportation needs, health issues, and helpful phrases for the traveler. Note that the authors have included Australia and New Zealand as well.

REGIONS OF ASIA

For clarity, only the commonly used regional designations are used: the Middle East and Southeast Asia. Other regional designations, such as Northeast Asia or West Asia, are much less clear as to what nations are included and the few titles in these categories are listed under each country covered.

THE MIDDLE EAST

See also "Asia as as Whole." Technically, the Middle East includes the nations of Southwestern Asia and North Africa from Libya on the west to Afghanistan on the east. The Asian nations are Afghanistan, Iran, Iraq, Israel, Jordan, Kuwait, Lebanon, Oman, Qatar, Saudi Arabia, Southern Yemen (People's Democratic Republic of Yemen), Syria, Turkey, United Arab Emirates, and Northern Yemen (Yemen Arab Republic). The African nations technically included are Egypt and Libya. However, we have elected to keep the African nations under the "Africa" section.

ABC Air Europe, Middle East & Northern Africa

ABC International, monthly editions, 340 pages, paper, $10.00

This is the airline schedule to have for travelers making many connections and compelled to play travel agent.

The Economist Business Traveller's Guides: Arabian Peninsula

Prentice Hall Press, 1987, 254 pages, paper, $17.95

This book is part of the excellent Economist Business Traveller's Guide series, which is reviewed in more detail under "Series Reviews."

A Hitchhiker's Guide to Africa and Arabia

by David Childress, Chicago Review Press, 1984, 295 pages, paper, $8.95

See "Africa as a Whole."

Nagel's Gulf Emirates

Passport Books, 1976, 191 pages, cloth, $39.95

This old but classic cultural guide is part of the Nagel Guides series, which is reviewed in more detail under "Series Reviews."

Traveller's Guide to the Middle East

Hunter Publishing, 1987, 190 pages, paper, $12.95

This book is part of the Traveller's Guide series, which is reviewed in more detail under "Series Reviews."

West Asia On A Shoestring

by Tony Wheeler, Lonely Planet Productions, 1986 (5th ed.), 368 pages, paper, $8.95

Including budget-oriented information on Afghanistan, Iran, Iraq, Israel, Jordan, Kuwait, Lebanon, Saudi Arabia, Syria, and Turkey, this book is part of the On A Shoestring Guides series, which is reviewed in more detail under "Series Reviews." The series is updated every two to three years.

SOUTHEAST ASIA

See also "Asia as as Whole." Comprising Brunei, Burma, Hong Kong, Indonesia, Kampuchea, Laos, Macau, Malaysia, the Philippines, Singapore, Thailand, and Vietnam. Note: At this writing, Kampuchea, Laos, and Vietnam are not encouraging tourism.

The Economist Business Traveller's Guide: Southeast Asia
Prentice Hall Press, 1988, 250 pages, paper, $17.95

This is a new, expected addition to the excellent Economist Business Traveller's Guide series, which is reviewed in more detail under "Series Reviews." As it was released after press time, the number of pages is approximate.

Fodor's Southeast Asia
Fodor's Travel Guides, 1987, 439 pages, paper, $15.95

This well-regarded volume in the Fodor series covers Hong Kong, the Philippines, Thailand, Singapore, Malaysia, Indonesia, Macau, Brunei, and Burma, as well as Taiwan. It is part of the Fodor's Country/Regional Guides series, which is reviewed in more detail under "Series Reviews." The series is updated annually.

Shopping In Exotic Places: Your Passport to Exciting Hong Kong, Korea, Thailand, Indonesia, and Singapore
by Ronald Krannich, *et al.*, Impact Publications, 1987, 469 pages, paper, $13.95

This is the first title in what now has become an excellent shopping series. The Shopping in Exotic Places series is reviewed in more detail under "Series Reviews." The series is updated every two years.

South-East Asia Handbook
by Stefan Loose and Renate Ramb, Riverdale Co., 1985 (2nd ed.), 558 pages, paper, $12.95

This well-done, comprehensive guide covers all price ranges and travel topics, but is especially useful for those traveling on a budget. Good detail maps are an added bonus. Countries covered are Brunei, Burma, Indonesia, Malaysia, Singapore, and Thailand. Note: Those traveling to Malaysia, Singapore, or Brunei will find more detail in Loose's *Malaysia, Singapore, Brunei Traveller's Handbook.*

South-East Asia On A Shoestring
by Tony Wheeler, Lonely Planet Publications, 1985 (5th ed.), 574 pages, paper, $9.95
 This is one of the books that made Lonely Planet famous, although at this point it is looking for its next update. Therefore, be sure to confirm all the details until the 6th edition arrives. The countries covered are Brunei, Burma, Hong Kong, Indonesia, Macau, Malaysia, Papua New Guinea, The Philippines, Singapore, Thailand, and, briefly, Vietnam, Laos, and Kampuchea. This is part of the budget-oriented On A Shoestring Guide series, which is reviewed in more detail under "Series Reviews." The series is generally updated every two to three years.

Sunset Southeast Asia Travel Guide
Lane Publishing, 1982, 160 pages, paper, $9.95
 This particular member of the Sunset Travel Guide series (reviewed in more detail under "Series Reviews") is pretty spotty in its coverage and is best used for ideas only.

COUNTRIES OF ASIA

Includes only those nations for which there are specific guidebooks, those nations that are included in other titles for regions not addressed under Regions of Asia, and those nations included in regional titles which, by our definition, are not considered technically a part of that region. For all other nations of Asia, see regional titles above.

BANGLADESH

See also "Asia as a Whole."

Bangladesh: A Travel Survival Kit
by Jose Santiago, Lonely Planet Publications, 1985, 136 pages, paper, $7.95
 This book is part of the popular Travel Survival Kit series, which is reviewed in more detail under "Series Reviews." Most titles in this series are updated every two to three years.

West Asia On A Shoestring
by Tony Wheeler, Lonely Planet Publications, 1986 (5th ed.), 368 pages, paper, $8.95
 Describing the overland route from Bangladesh to Turkey, this book is part of the budget-oriented On A Shoestring Guide series, which is reviewed in more detail under "Series Reviews." This series is updated every two to three years.

BAHRAIN

See also "The Middle East" and "Asia as a Whole."

Bahrain: A Meed Practical Guide

Routledge & Kegan Paul, 1983, 190 pages, paper, $19.95

This book is part of the Meed Guide series, which is reviewed in more detail under "Series Reviews."

BHUTAN

See also "Asia as a Whole."

West Asia On A Shoestring

by Tony Wheeler, Lonely Planet Publications, 1986 (5th ed.), 368 pages, paper, $8.95

Describing the overland route from Bangladesh to Turkey, this book is part of the budget-oriented On A Shoestring Guide series, which is reviewed in more detail under "Series Reviews." This series is updated every two to three years.

BRUNEI

See also "Southeast Asia" and "Asia as a Whole."

Malaysia, Singapore and Brunei: A Travel Survival Kit

by Geoff Crowther and Tony Wheeler, Lonely Planet Publications, 1988 (3rd ed.), 320 pages, paper, $9.95

This book is part of the popular Travel Survival Kit series, which is reviewed in more detail under "Series Reviews." This series is updated every two to three years.

Malaysia, Singapore, Brunei Traveller's Handbook

by Stefan Loose and Renate Ramb, Riverdale Co., 1986, 331 pages, paper, $9.95

See "Malaysia."

Time Travel in the Malay Crescent

by Wayne Stier, Meru Publishing, 1985, 312 pages, paper, $10.00

This excellent companion guide to a more standard guidebook is reviewed under "Malaysia."

BURMA

See also "Southeast Asia" and "Asia as a Whole."

Burma: A Travel Survival Kit
by Tony Wheeler, Lonely Planet Publications, 1988 (4th ed.), 192 pages, paper, $8.95

This is an excellent volume in the Travel Survival Kit series, which is reviewed in more detail under "Series Reviews." The series is updated every two to three years.

Burma: Asia's Secret Treasure Trove
by Caroline Courtauld, Passport Books, 1988, 208 pages, paper, $9.95

This book is part of the Passport Asian Guide series, which is reviewed in more detail under "Series Reviews."

Cadogan Guide: Thailand and Burma
by Frank Kusy and Frances Capel, The Globe Pequot Press, 1988, 350 pages, paper, $14.95

This is a new member of the highly regarded Cadogan Guides series, which is reviewed in more detail under "Series Reviews." The series is updated biennially. As it was released after press time, the number of pages is approximate.

Insight Guide: Burma
by Apa Productions, Prentice Hall Press, 1986, 332 pages, paper, $16.95

This book is one of the acclaimed Insight Guide series, which is reviewed in more detail under "Series Reviews."

Wide Eyes in Burma and Thailand: Finding Your Way
by Wayne Stier and Mars Cavers, Meru Publishing, 1983, 218 pages, paper, $7.50

Written in a personable and enjoyable style, this book covers the practicalities, a useful but not overwhelming amount of history, economics, and language, and contains informative discussions of things to see and do. Lodgings selected are in various price ranges, including budget. The types of good local food dishes are covered generally; there are a few specific restaurant selections. However, the publication date probably makes some of these specifics out-of-date.

CHINA

See also "Taiwan" and "Asia as a Whole."

All China
Passport Books, 1986, 143 pages, paper, $8.95

Beijing
> Passport Books, 1987, 144 pages, paper, $8.95
>
> These two titles are in the Passport China Guide series, which is reviewed in more detail under "Series Reviews."

Beijing Old and New
> by Zhou Shachen, China Books, 1984, 404 pages, paper, $7.95
>
> Written and published in Beijing, this is an historical guide to the city's interesting sites and the areas within one day's journey of the famous city. Included are color photos and good detail maps of some of the points of interest.

Berlitz: China
> Macmillan Publishing, 1986, 256 pages, paper, $8.95
>
> This is one of the larger volumes in the Berlitz Country Guide series, which is reviewed in more detail under "Series Reviews."

China: A Travel Survival Kit
> by Alan Samagalski and Robert Strauss, Lonely Planet Publications, 1988 (2nd ed.), 820 pages, paper, $17.95
>
> This book is one of the popular Travel Survival Kit series, which is reviewed in more detail under "Series Reviews." The series is updated every two to three years. This edition was released after press time; the number of pages is approximate.

The China Business Handbook
> by Arne de Keijzer, China Books, 1986, 217 pages, paper, $16.95
>
> One of the authors of the highly regarded *China Guidebook* has written this excellent, concise guide to doing business in China. It is considered a valuable resource to those expert in China trade.

China Companion: A Guide to 100 Cities, Resorts, and Places of Interest in the People's Republic
> by Evelyne Garside, Farrar, Straus, and Giroux, 1981, 276 pages, cloth, $14.95
>
> While this superbly done guidebook, winner of the prestigious Thomas Cook Guide Book Award in 1981, is clearly out-of-date on the specifics of hotels, restaurants, and shopping, its excellent sections on history, geography, art, and architecture make it a good choice as a companion guide.

China Guidebook
> by Fredric Kaplan, *et al.*, Eurasia Press, 1987 (8th ed.), 768 pages, paper, $15.95
>
> Long the best-selling guide to China, this book is considered one

of the best guides available by those knowledgeable in the travel industry and the best guide to take on a tour. It is authoritative, comprehensive, and well organized. No subject is neglected and special sections on cuisine, archaeology, shopping, and arts are included. This book is updated annually.

China in 22 Days
See *22 Days in China* below.

China, Solo: A Guide to Independent Travel in the People's Republic of China
by Barbara Letson, Jadetree Press, 1984, 213 pages, paper, $9.95
   This excellent book is a delight to read. Letson, who has been through it all, shares her mistakes and the wisdom she has gleaned from her solo travels. This really is a strategy book on "how to do it." Even sections on hotels and food deal primarily with the peculiarities facing travelers away from more familiar western hotels. Combined with another standard guide, *China, Solo* will more than pay for itself in helpful time-saving and headache-saving hints.

The Economist Business Traveller's Guide: China
Prentice Hall Press, 1988, 250 pages, paper, $17.95
   This book is a new addition to the respected Economist Business Traveller's Guide series, which is reviewed in more detail under "Series Reviews." As it was released after press time, the number of pages is approximate.

Fielding's People's Republic of China
by Ruth Malloy and Priscilla Hsu, William Morrow & Co., 1988, 400 pages, paper, $13.95
   This book is part of the Fielding's Travel Guide series, which is reviewed in more detail under "Series Reviews." The series is updated annually.

Fodor's Beijing, Guangzhou, and Shanghai
Fodor's Travel Publications, 1988, 224 pages, paper, $7.95
   This book is one of Fodor's City Guide series, which is reviewed in more detail under "Series Reviews." The series is updated annually.

Fodor's People's Republic of China
by John Summerfield, Fodor's Travel Publications, 1987, 595 pages, paper, $15.95
   This book is one of Fodor's Country/Regional Guide series, which

is reviewed in more detail under "Series Reviews." The series is updated annually.

Fujian
Passport Books, 1988, 144 pages, paper, $9.95
Guilin, Canton, Guangdong
Passport Books, 1988, 208 pages, paper, $9.95
Hangzhou & Zhejiang
Passport Books, 1987, 144 pages, paper, $8.95
    These are three titles in the Passport China Guide series, which is reviewed in more detail under "Series Reviews."

Hildebrand's Travel Guide: China
Hunter Publishing, 1985, 336 pages, paper, $11.95
    This book is part of the Hildebrand's Guide series, which is reviewed in more detail under "Series Reviews."

How to Tour China: The Newest Comprehensive Guidebook
China Books, 1986, 197 pages, paper, $9.95
    Written in China, this small guidebook covers all the standard tourist bases briefly but adequately. Plenty of color photos highlight the sights described. At press time, Kampmann & Company was listing a new edition at $12.95.

Insider's Guide to China
Hunter Publishing, 1987, 224 pages, paper, $12.95
    This book is part of the Hunter Insider's Guide series, which is reviewed in more detail under "Series Reviews."

Magnificent China: A Guide to Its Cultural Treasures
by Petra Haring-Kuan and Kuan Yu-Chien, China Books, 1987, 425 pages, cloth, $34.95
    The outstanding aspect of this well-done hardback book is its excellent descriptions of the important cultural sites throughout China. It provides an encyclopedic look at China's history, literature, religion, philosophy, art, and architecture. The detailed maps of towns and historic sites are superb and quality color photos supplement the text. As a sightseeing guide it is excellent. The book contains some practical information as well, but this is brief.

Nagel's China
Passport Books, 1984, 1504 pages, cloth, $49.95
    This classic, comprehensive cultural guide is part of the Nagel's Guide series, which is reviewed in more detail under "Series Reviews."

Nanjing & Jiangsu

Passport Books, 1988, 160 pages, paper, $8.95

This book is part of the Passport China Guide series, which is reviewed in more detail under "Series Reviews."

North-East Asia On A Shoestring

edited by Tony Wheeler, Lonely Planet Publications, 1985, 288 pages, paper, $7.95

Covering China, Hong Kong, Japan, Macau, South Korea, and Taiwan, with short notes on visiting North Korea, this book is part of the budget-oriented On A Shoestring Guide series, which is reviewed in more detail under "Series Reviews." The series is generally updated every two to three years. A new edition has been announced.

Rough Guide to China

by Catherine Sanders, Chris Stewart, and Rhonda Evans, Routledge & Kegan Paul, 1987, 595 pages, paper, $12.95

Already considered by many to be the best guide for independent travel in China, especially by the younger, more adventurous crowd, this book is part of the Rough Guides series, which is reviewed in more detail under "Series Reviews." The series is updated every two to three years.

Shanghai

Passport Books, 1987, 144 pages, paper, $8.95

This book is part of the Passport China Guide series, which is reviewed in more detail under "Series Reviews."

Shopping in China: Arts, Crafts & The Unusual

by Roberta Stalberg, China Books, 1986, 230 pages, paper, $9.95

This is a well-organized book that is fascinating to read; it covers 12 major cities and explains what to look for and where to look. It also offers detailed discussions on each "highly recommended" or "recommended" store. Widely praised, this book is ideal for the traveling shopper.

Southwest China Off the Beaten Track

by Mark Stevens and George Wehrfritz, Passport Books, 1988, 224 pages, paper, $12.95

Released after press time, this is the first title in a new series for "the adventuresome and independent traveler." It covers large cities, wilderness areas, small villages, and such practicalities as hitchhiking and the etiquette of crossing through closed areas. Numerous maps, including one large fold-out map of the four-province area, are provided.

Tibet
Passport Books, 1986, 208 pages, paper, $9.95
This book is part of the Passport China Guide series, which is reviewed in more detail under "Series Reviews."

Tibet: A Travel Survival Kit
by Michael Buckley and Robert Strauss, Lonely Planet Publications, 1986, 256 pages, paper, $7.95
This book is part of the popular Travel Survival Kit series, which is reviewed in more detail under "Series Reviews." The series is updated every two to three years.

22 Days in China: The Itinerary Planner
by Gaylon Duke and Zenia Victor, John Muir Publications, 1987, 141 pages, paper, $6.95
One of of a series of books modeled after the well-known *Europe In 22 Days* (now called *22 Days in Europe*). The Itinerary Planner series is reviewed in more detail under "Series Reviews." Note that the title change is recent; this book may also be entitled *China in 22 Days*.

Xi'an
Passport Books, 1988, 128 pages, paper, $7.95
The Yangzi River
Passport Books, 1985, 208 pages, paper, $9.95
Yunnan
Passport Books, 1987, 208 pages, paper, $9.95
These are three titles in the Passport China Guide series, which is reviewed in more detail under "Series Reviews."

HONG KONG

See also "Southeast Asia" and "Asia as a Whole."

The American Express Pocket Guide to Hong Kong, Singapore, and Bangkok
Prentice Hall Press, 1988, 200 pages, cloth, $9.95
This book is part of the respected American Express Pocket Guide series, which is reviewed in more detail under "Series Reviews." As it was released after press time, the number of pages is approximate.

Baedeker's Hong Kong
Prentice Hall Press, 1987, 168 pages, paper, $10.95
This book is part of Baedeker's City Guide series, which is reviewed in more detail under "Series Reviews."

Berlitz: Hong Kong
Macmillan Publishing, 1979, 128 pages, paper, $6.95
This book is part of the small-format Berlitz Guide series, which is reviewed in more detail under "Series Reviews."

Born to Shop: Hong Kong
by Suzy Gershman and Judith Thomas, Bantam Books, 1986, 240 pages, paper, $8.95
This book is one of the well-done Born to Shop Guide series, which is described in more detail under "Series Reviews."

The Complete Guide to Hong Kong Factory Bargains
by Dana Goetz, Delta Dragon Books, 1987, 234 pages, paper, $9.95
This is a tiny, handy shopping guide to Hong Kong, although it is not as extensive as other guides now available. What is covered has informative write-ups. Clear maps are also provided. Published in Hong Kong, this book has no American distributor at present. A reliable source is Wide World Books & Maps (see Travel Bookstore appendix); it may also be carried by other bookstores.

Fodor's Hong Kong and Macau
Fodor's Travel Publications, 1987, 271 pages, paper, $10.95
This book is part of Fodor's Country/Regional Guide series, which is reviewed in more detail under "Series Reviews." The series is updated annually.

Frommer's Dollarwise Guide to Japan & Hong Kong
by Beth Reiber, Prentice Hall Press, 1988, 384 pages, paper, $13.95
This book is part of Frommer's Dollarwise Guide series, which is reviewed in more detail under "Series Reviews." These series guides emphasize selections in the moderate price range and are updated every two years.

Hong Kong
Passport Books, 1986, 144 pages, paper, $8.95
This book is part of the Passport China Guide series, which is reviewed in more detail under "Series Reviews."

Hong Kong in Your Pocket
Barron's Educational Series, 1987, 176 pages, paper, $3.95
This small-format guide is part of the In Your Pocket Guide series, which is reviewed in more detail under "Series Reviews."

Hong Kong, Macau & Canton: A Travel Survival Kit

by Carol Clewlow and Alan Samagalski, Lonely Planet
Publications, 1986 (4th ed.), 256 pages, paper, $7.95

This book is one of the popular Travel Survival Kit series, which
is reviewed in more detail under "Series Reviews." The series is
updated every two to three years.

Insider's Guide to Hong Kong

Hunter Publishing, 1987, 176 pages, paper, $12.95

This book is part of Hunter's Insider's Guide series, which is
reviewed in more detail under "Series Reviews."

Insight Guide: Hong Kong (with Macau)

by Apa Productions, Prentice Hall Press, 1986, 338 pages, paper,
$16.95

This book is one of the widely praised Insight Guide series, which
is reviewed in more detail under "Series Reviews."

North-East Asia On A Shoestring

edited by Tony Wheeler, Lonely Planet Publications, 1985, 288
pages, paper, $7.95

Covering China, Hong Kong, Japan, Macau, South Korea, and Taiwan, with short notes on visiting North Korea, this book is part of
the budget-oriented On A Shoestring Guide series, which is reviewed
in more detail under "Series Reviews." Guides in this series are
generally updated every two to three years. A new edition for this
title has been announced.

Post Guide: Hong Kong

Hunter Publishing, 1987, 144 pages, paper, $8.95

This book is part of the Post Guide series, which is reviewed in
more detail under "Series Reviews."

Shopping in Exotic Hong Kong: Your Passport to Asia's Most Incredible Shopping Mall

by Ronald Krannich, *et al.*, Impact Publications, 1988, 180 pages,
paper, $9.95

Shopping In Exotic Places: Your Passport to Exciting Hong Kong, Korea, Thailand, Indonesia, and Singapore

by Ronald Krannich, *et al.*, Impact Publications, 1987, 469 pages,
paper, $13.95

Both of these titles are part of the excellent Shopping in Exotic
Places series, which is reviewed in more detail under "Series Reviews." The Hong Kong volume is an anticipated addition to the
series that will expand on the Hong Kong section of the second title.

The series is updated every two years. The Hong Kong volume was released after press time; the number of pages is approximate.

Shopwalks: Hong Kong
by Corby Kukmmer, Crown Publishing, 1987, fold-out map/guide, paper, $5.95
   This guide is part of the Shopwalks series, which is reviewed in more detail under "Series Reviews."

INDIA

See also "Asia as a Whole."

Berlitz: India
Macmillan Publishing, 1986, 256 pages, paper, $8.95
   This is a larger title in the Berlitz Country Guide series, which is reviewed in more detail under "Series Reviews."

The Best of India, From Budget to Luxury
by Paige Palmer, Pilot Books, 1987, 196 pages, paper, $7.95
   In a succinct, well-organized style, this book covers all the traveler's bases in less than 200 pages. A wide choice of lodging and restaurants in every price category, including choices appropriate for the backpacker, are included. From shopping to sightseeing, the book moves rapidly through the topics—with just enough detail to point travelers in the right direction. The author's considerable experience in almost every corner of India is evident.

Cadogan Guide: India
by Frank Kusy, The Globe Pequot Press, 1987, 406 pages, paper, $12.95
   This book is one of the highly regarded Cadogan Guide series, which is reviewed in more detail under "Series Reviews." The series is updated every two years.

Fodor's India, Nepal, and Sri Lanka
Fodor's Travel Publications, 1987, 520 pages, paper, $16.95
   This book is part of Fodor's Country/Regional Guide series, which is reviewed in more detail under "Series Reviews." The series is updated annually.

Frommer's India on $25 a Day
by Jan Aaron, Prentice Hall Press, 1988, 375 pages, paper, $10.95
   This book is part of the budget-oriented Frommer's Dollar-a-Day Guide series, which is reviewed in more detail under "Series Re-

views." The series is updated every two years. This edition was released after press time so the number of pages is approximate.

Guide to Rajasthan
by Kim Naylor, Hippocrene Books, 1988, 160 pages, paper, $11.95

Due out in mid-1988, this may be the only guide to the mystical, magical land of Rajasthan.

Hildebrand's Travel Guide: India and Nepal
Hunter Publishing, 1985, 224 pages, paper, $10.95

This book is part of the Hildebrand's Guide series, which is reviewed in more detail under "Series Reviews."

India: A Travel Survival Kit
by Geoff Crowther, *et al.*, Lonely Planet Publications, 1987 (3rd ed.), 801 pages, paper, $17.95

This is a huge, highly-regarded title in the popular Travel Survival Kit series, which is reviewed in more detail under "Series Reviews." The series is updated every two to three years.

India in 22 Days
See *22 Days in India* below.

India, Nepal & Sri Lanka: The Traveller's Guide
by Peter Meyer and Barbara Rausch, Riverdale Co., 1987, 656 pages, paper, $14.95

Brought to America for the first time in early 1988, this book is the fourth edition of a popular German travel guide. The focus of the book is on the young adventurer who wants to get by as cheaply as possible with a reasonable measure of cleanliness and safety. While the typesetting is rather utililitarian in an aesthestic sense, the information presented is solid, thorough, and first-class. Careful attention has been paid to all the important travel details and clear maps are provided.

Insight Guide: India
by Apa Productions, Prentice Hall Press, 1987, 359 pages, paper, $16.95

This book is part of the acclaimed Insight Guide series, which is reviewed in more detail under "Series Reviews."

Kashmir, Ladakh & Zanskar: A Travel Survival Kit
by Margaret and Rolf Schettler, Lonely Planet Publications, 1985 (2nd ed.), 204 pages, paper, $7.95

This book is part of the popular Travel Survival Kit series, which is reviewed in more detail under "Series Reviews." Generally, titles in this series are updated every two to three years. At press time, a new edition had not yet been announced.

Nagel's India & Nepal

Passport Books, 1983, 831 pages, cloth, $49.95

This classic, cultural guide is part of the Nagel's Guide series, which is reviewed in more detail under "Series Reviews."

The Traveler's Key to Northern India: A Guide to the Sacred Places of Northern India

by Alistair Shearer, Alfred Knopf, Inc., 1983, 546 pages, paper, $18.95

This book is an exploration of the legends, art, and architecture of Northern India. It is part of the finely crafted Traveler's Key Guide series, which is reviewed in more detail under "Series Reviews."

Trekking in the Indian Himalaya

by Gary Weare, Lonely Planet Publications, 1986, 160 pages, paper, $6.95

This is the first edition of a guide to this somewhat less popular trekking area of the Himalaya. Plans are already being made to add other trekking routes and regions, and to improve the current information in the next edition. This guide, however, appears well done, with clear, concise coverage of all the topics of importance to the trekker.

22 Days in India: The Itinerary Planner

by Anurag Mather, John Muir Publications, 1988, 136 pages, paper, $6.95

This book is a new title in the Itinerary Planner series, which is reviewed in more detail under "Series Reviews." It is modeled after the popular *Europe in 22 Days* (now called *22 Days in Europe*). Note that the title change is recent; this book may also be entitled *India in 22 Days*.

Visiting India

by Allan Stacey, Hippocrene Books, 1987, 192 pages, paper, $9.95

This is an illustrated guide focusing on the background information of use to the traveler: regional customs, the various religions of the country, the realities of transportation, flora and fauna, as well as suggestions for various side trips worth planning.

West Asia On A Shoestring

by Tony Wheeler, Lonely Planet Publications, 1986 (5th ed.), 368 pages, paper, $8.95

Describing the overland route from Bangladesh to Turkey, this book is part of the budget-oriented On A Shoestring Guide series, which is reviewed in more detail under "Series Reviews." The series is updated every two to three years.

INDONESIA

See also "Southeast Asia" and "Asia as a Whole."

Bali and Lombok: A Travel Survival Kit

by Mary Covernton and Tony Wheeler, Lonely Planet Publications, 1986, 208 pages, paper, $6.95

This book is one of the popular Travel Survival Kit series, which is reviewed in more detail under "Series Reviews." The series is updated every two to three years.

Hildebrand's Travel Guide: Indonesia

Hunter Publishing, 1985, 333 pages, paper, $10.95

This book is one of the Hildebrand's Guide series, which is reviewed in more detail under "Series Reviews."

Indonesia: A Travel Survival Kit

by Ginny Bruce, Mary Covernton, and Alan Samagalski, Lonely Planet Publications, 1986, 768 pages, paper, $14.95

This book is part of the well-known Travel Survival Kit series, which is reviewed in more detail under "Series Reviews." The series is updated every two to three years.

Indonesia Handbook

by Bill Dalton, Moon Publications, 1988 (4th ed.), 900 pages, paper, $17.95

One of the best travel guides ever written, this book is part of the first-rate Moon Handbooks series, which is reviewed in more detail under "Series Reviews." The series is updated every two years.

Insight Guide: Bali

by APA Productions, Prentice Hall Press, 1986, 275 pages, paper, $16.95

Insight Guide: Indonesia

by APA Productions, Prentice Hall Press, 1986, 418 pages, paper, $16.95

These two titles are in the acclaimed Insight Guide series, which is reviewed in more detail under "Series Reviews."

Post Guide: Indonesia
Hunter Publishing, 1987, 144 pages, paper, $8.95

This book is one of the Post Guide series, which is reviewed in more detail under "Series Revews."

Shopping in Exotic Indonesia
by Ron Krannich, *et al.*, Impact Publications, 1988, 180 pages, paper, $9.95

Shopping In Exotic Places: Your Passport to Exciting Hong Kong, Korea, Thailand, Indonesia, and Singapore
by Ronald Krannich, *et al.*, Impact Publications, 1987, 469 pages, paper, $13.95

Both of these titles are part of the excellent Shopping in Exotic Places series, which is reviewed in more detail under "Series Reviews." The Indonesia volume is an anticipated addition to the series that will expand on the Indonesia section of the second title. The series is updated every two years. The Indonesia volume was released after press time; the number of pages is approximate.

The Times Travel Library: Bali
Hunter Publishing, 1987, 104 pages, paper, $10.95

The Times Travel Library: Jakarta
Hunter Publishing, 1987, 104 pages, paper, $10.95

These two titles are in a new large-format series, The Times Travel Library Guides, which is reviewed in more detail under "Series Reviews."

IRAN
See also "The Middle East" and "Asia as a Whole."

Nagel's Iran
Passport Books, 1977, 391 pages, cloth, $39.95

This is an excellent cultural guide, but certainly about how things *used* to be. It is one of the well-known Nagel's Guide series, which is reviewed in more detail under "Series Reviews."

ISRAEL
See also "The Middle East" and "Asia as a Whole."

Baedeker's Israel
Prentice Hall Press, undated, 286 pages, paper, $14.95
This book is one of the Baedeker's Guide series, which is reviewed in more detail under "Series Reviews."

Baedeker's Jerusalem
Prentice Hall Press, 1987, 192 pages, paper, $10.95
This book is part of the Baedeker's City Guide series, which is reviewed in more detail under "Series Reviews."

Bazak Guide to Israel
Harper & Row, 1987, 468 pages, paper, $12.95
This has been the best-selling English-language guidebook on Israel for over 25 years. It offers suggested tours and good descriptions of important sites, but in a rather dry, impersonal style. Only general information on restaurants and hotels is provided. A standard, solid, but somehow unexciting guide. One strong point, however, is the inclusion of a large, separate, multi-colored map on which all sorts of historic sites and points of interest have been plotted.

Berlitz: Jerusalem & the Holy Land
Macmillan Publishing, 1979, 128 pages, paper, $6.95
This book is part of the small-format Berlitz Guide series, which is reviewed in more detail under "Series Reviews."

Carta's Official Guide to Israel: Complete Gazetteer to All Sites in the Holy Land
Hunter Publishing, 1983, 468 pages, paper, $15.95
This is truly the "official" guide, coming as it does from the Israel Ministry of Defence Publishing House. This useful gazetteer of the important sites in the Holy Land covers history and important archaeological sites; it is a good specialty guide for the interested traveler.

An Evangelical's Guide to the Holy Land
by Wayne Dehoney, Broadman Press, 1974, 162 pages, paper, $9.95
This is an older book but still useful for walking and driving tours of the places of importance to Christians. Each site is tied to biblical passages and supplemented with clearly drawn maps and numerous photos. Be sure to use this guide in conjunction with an up-to-date map.

Fodor's Israel
Fodor's Travel Publications, 1987, 320 pages, paper, $13.95

Fodor's Jordan and the Holy Land
Fodor's Travel Publications, 1986 (2nd ed.), 256 pages, paper,
$12.95
These are two titles in Fodor's Country/Regional Guide series,
which is reviewed in more detail under "Series Reviews." The Israel
guide is updated annually.

Frommer's Israel on $35 a Day
by Tom Brosnahan, Prentice Hall Press, 1988, 360 pages, paper,
$11.95
This book is part of the well-known Frommer's Dollar-a-Day
Guide series, which is reviewed in more detail under "Series Reviews." The series is updated every two years.

**The Heart of Jerusalem: A Handbook for Visitors, Newcomers, and
Foreign Residents**
by Arlynn Nellhaus, John Muir Publications, 1988, 320 pages,
paper, $12.95
Released after press time, this practical guide to "making the
Jerusalem experience more fulfilling and less exasperating" offers
tips on getting oriented, sightseeing, eating, sleeping, and more practical items like furnishing an apartment, shopping for shoes, or
getting a telephone installed.

Holy Places in Jerusalem
by Rabbi Menachem Hacohen, Franklin Watts, Inc., 1988, 208
pages, cloth, $18.95
A new guide, released after press time, from one of Israel's prom-
inent rabbis, covering all the holy places of Jerusalem—complete
with maps and histories of the important sites.

Insight Guide: Israel
by Apa Publications, Prentice Hall Press, 1986, 380 pages, paper,
$16.95
This book is part of the acclaimed Insight Guide series, which is
reviewed in more detail under "Series Reviews."

Israel: A Phaidon Art and Architecture Guide
Prentice Hall Press, 1987, 259 pages, cloth, $17.95
This book is one of the encyclopedic Phaidon Art and Architecture
Guide series, which is reviewed in more detail under "Series Re-
views."

The Israel Experience Book

by David Breakstone and Cindy Jochnowitz, Bloch Publishing, 1985, 248 pages, paper, $8.95

This unique book, designed to accompany a more standard guide-book, is filled with history, games, ideas, tips, and thoughts. Its focus is more for the student, especially the Jewish student, who will be exploring this historic land.

Israel On Your Own

by Harriet Greenberg, Passport Books, 1988, 509 pages, paper, $12.95

An essay on the essence and vitality of Israel by Kate Simon sets the tone for this exellent guide to independent travel throughout Israel. This comprehensive guide contains chapters on geography, history, the disabled traveler, traveling with children, and much more. The large, easy-to-read type is an added bonus. Hotel and, especially, restaurant selections are in all price ranges and are infor-mative. Many thoughtfully planned itineraries and walking tours describe what to see and do. One problem, however is that the text takes up so much space that there is no room for maps or photos. Regardless, this is a fine guidebook and well worth the added cost of a few maps (for Israel, additional maps are usually necessary anyhow).

Jerusalemwalks

by Nitza Rosovsky, Henry Holt & Co., 1982, 289 pages, paper, $10.95

This book is part of the well-done Citywalks series, which is reviewed in more detail under "Series Reviews."

Let's Go: Israel & Egypt (includes Jordan)

by Harvard Student Agencies, St. Martin's Press, 1988, 464 pages, paper, $10.95

This book is part of the excellent, budget-oriented Let's Go Guide series, which is reviewed in more detail under "Series Reviews." The series is updated annually. (Israel is also included in *Let's Go: Europe*.)

Michael's Guide: Jerusalem

by Michael Shichor, Hunter Publishing, 1987, 238 pages, paper, $8.95

This is a popular title in the Michael's Guide series, which is reviewed in more detail under "Series Reviews."

The New Holiday Guide to Israel
M. Evans & Co., 1988 (10th ed.), 160 pages, paper, $4.95
This book is one of the Holiday Guide series, which is reviewed in more detail under "Series Reviews."

A New Testament Guide to the Holy Land
John Kilgallen, S.J., Loyola University Press, 1987, 268 pages, cloth, $12.95
For the Christian traveler, this beautifully done hardback is light enough to carry along. This well-conceived, thoughtful work describes the geographic and archaeological importance of the many holy sites of Israel and ties them to the relevant Gospel passages. This is then followed by a commentary on the site's deeper religious significance.

Off the Beaten Track in Israel
by Ori Devir, Adama Books, 1986, 200 pages, cloth, $19.95
This book explores places in the cities and the countryside that are usually missed by the average tourist.

Rand McNally: Israel and the Holy Land
by Dymphna Byrne, Rand McNally & Co., 1985, 95 pages, paper, $5.95
This book is part of the small-format Rand McNally Pocket Guide series, which is reviewed in more detail under "Series Reviews."

Six New Testament Walks in Jerusalem
by I. Martin, Harper & Row, 1986, 240 pages, paper, $12.95
Written by a Jerusalem tour guide, this book offers interesting walks, highlighted by photos and line drawings, through the rich biblical history of Jerusalem. The text is easy to follow, but the detail maps provided may not prove enough for some.

JAPAN

See also "Asia as a Whole."

The American Express Pocket Guide: Tokyo
Prentice Hall Press, 1988, 200 pages, cloth, $9.95
This book is part of the American Express Pocket Guide series, which is reviewed in more detail under "Series Reviews." As it was released after press time, the number of pages is approximate.

Baedeker's Japan

Prentice Hall Press, undated, 352 pages, paper, $15.95
This book is one of the Baedeker's Guide series, which is reviewed in more detail under "Series Reviews."

Baedeker's Tokyo

Prentice Hall Press, 1987, 153 pages, paper, $10.95
This book is part of the Baedeker's City Guide series, which is reviewed in more detail under "Series Reviews."

Berlitz: Japan

Macmillan Publishing, 1986, 256 pages, paper, $8.95
This book is one of the small-format Berlitz Country Guide series, which is reviewed in more detail under "Series Reviews."

A Bird Watcher's Guide to Japan

by Mark Brazil, Kodansha International, 1988, 220 pages, paper, $13.95
This new title, released after press time, highlights the 60 best bird-watching areas of Japan.

Born to Shop: Tokyo

by Suzy Gershman and Judith Thomas, Bantam Books, 1987, 329 pages, paper, $9.95
This book is part of the well-done Born to Shop Guide series, which is reviewed in more detail under "Series Reviews".

Crown Insider's Guide: Japan

edited by Robert Fisher, Crown Publishers, 1987, 328 pages, paper, $10.95
This book is part of the Crown Insider's Guide series, which is reviewed in more detail under "Series Reviews."

Discovering Cultural Japan

by Boye De Mente, Passport Books, 1988, 152 pages, paper, $12.95
This book covers a wide variety of important topics such as crossing cultural barriers, the traditions of hospitality, the special joys of Japan, and the unique faces of the Japanese.

Eating Cheap in Japan: The Gaijin Gourmet's Guide to Ordering in Non-Tourist Restaurants

by Kimiko Nagasawa and Camy Condon, Charles E. Tuttle Co., 1972, 104 pages, paper, $9.95
This "old" book is definitely not out-of-date. Now in its 19th printing, this is not a book on specific restaurants but rather contains

the information necessary to dine in many wonderful (and relatively cheap) restaurants where English is neither on the menu nor spoken. Compact, with copious color photos of specific dishes, this little guide will greatly expand any traveler's culinary horizons.

The Economist Business Traveller's Guide: Japan

Prentice Hall Press, 1987, 256 pages, paper, $17.95

This book is part of the excellent Economist Business Traveller's Guide series, which is reviewed in more detail under "Series Reviews."

Fisher's World: Japan

by Robert Fisher, Fisher's World, Inc., 1988, 367 pages, paper, $14.95

This book is one of the Fisher's World Guide series, which is reviewed in more detail under "Series Reviews." The series is updated annually.

Fodor's Great Travel Values: Japan

Fodor's Travel Publications, 1988, 192 pages, paper, $6.95

This book is part of Fodor's Great Travel Values Guide series, which is reviewed in more detail under "Series Reviews." The series is updated annually.

Fodor's Japan

Fodor's Travel Publications, 1988, 544 pages, paper, $15.95

This book is part of Fodor 's Country/Regional Guide series, which is reviewed in more detail under "Series Reviews." The series is updated annually.

Fodor's Tokyo

Fodor's Travel Publications, 1988, 144 pages, paper, $6.95

This book is one of the Fodor City Guide series, which is reviewed in more detail under "Series Reviews." The series is updated annually.

Frommer's Dollarwise Guide to Japan and Hong Kong

by Beth Reiber, Prentice Hall Press, 1988, 384 pages, paper, $13.95

This book is part of Frommer's Dollarwise Guide series, which is reviewed in more detail under "Series Reviews." The series is updated every two years.

Good Tokyo Restaurants

by Rick Kennedy, Kodansha International, 1985, 268 pages, paper, $7.95

From among Tokyo's 77,000 restaurants Kennedy has chosen some of the best in varying price ranges and covering many different cuisines. The full range of Japanese foods is offered in 39 of these choices. Others offer Swiss, Swedish, French, and other types of food. Each restaurant chosen is given an informative, well-written, two-page review, including a hand-drawn map on which important buildings appear in three dimensions.

A Guide to Food Buying in Japan

by Carolyn Krouse, Charles E. Tuttle Co., 1986, 191 pages, paper, $9.50

This is an excellent guide to shopping for foodstuffs, not for what to eat in a restaurant. It is very helpful for those wishing to do their own cooking.

The Guide to Japanese Food and Restaurants

by Russel Marcus and Jack Plimpton, Charles E. Tuttle Co., 1984, 263 pages, paper, $12.95

In this well-organized guide containing excellent detail maps, the authors describe over 700 restaurants. Different types of cuisine are arranged by section and special tab markers are used for easy reference. Recommended restaurants are tied to specific maps. The Restaurant Finder inside the front cover is an added feature and the section on how to spot different types of restaurants is always handy in a crowded and unfamiliar place. Unfortunately, this guide will soon be out of date.

Hildebrand's Travel Guide: Japan

Hunter Publishing, 1985, 352 pages, paper, $10.95

This book is part of the Hildebrand's Guide series, which is reviewed in more detail under "Series Reviews."

How to Get Lost and Found in Japan

by John McDermott, Hunter Publishing, 1984, 271 pages, paper, $9.95

This book is part of the delightful Lost & Found Guides series, which is reviewed in more detail under "Series Reviews."

Insider's Guide to Japan

Hunter Publishing, 1987, 212 pages, paper, $12.95

This book is part of the Hunter's Insider's Guide series, which is reviewed in more detail under "Series Reviews."

Japan: A Travel Survival Kit
by Ian McQueen, Lonely Planct Publications, 1986 (2nd ed.), 520 pages, paper, $12.95
This book is one of the popular Travel Survival Kit series, which is reviewed in more detail under "Series Reviews." The series is updated every two to three years.

Japan At Night: A Complete Guide to Entertainment and Leisure in Japan
by Boye De Mente, Passport Books, 1987, 307 pages, paper, $7.95
This compact little book is crammed with plenty of information. It takes a little getting used to, but the write-ups are informative and the variety of topics is truly incredible for such a small book. Areas covered include recreational activities, spectator sports, personal services, spas, discos, and pleasure baths.

Japan for Westerners
Yes! Inc., 1986, 88 pages, paper, $5.95
This is a resource guide to books on Japan, including the topics of arts, music, literature, history, martial arts, cuisine, business, language, and travel. An update addendum is expected in 1988-89.

Japan Handbook
by J. D. Bisignani, Moon Publications, 1983, 505 pages, paper, $12.95
The new edition of this guide is due out in 1989. It is part of the superb Moon Handbook series, which is reviewed in more detail under "Series Reviews." Moon Publications has recently made a commitment to updating their various titles every two years.

Japan in 22 Days
See *22 Days in Japan* below.

Japan: Land of Many Faces
by Alan Booth, Passport Books, 1988, 288 pages, paper, $9.95
This book is part of the Passport Asian Guide series, which is reviewed in more detail under "Series Reviews."

Japan Solo: A Practical Guide for Independent Travelers
by Eiji Kanno and Constance O'Keefe, Warner Books, 1988, 400 pages, paper, $14.95
The authors of this book, both of whom have had considerable experience with the Japan National Tourist Organization, have created a book of great and lasting value for independent travelers. It is well organized and includes many walking tours, much sightseeing

information, and a large number of excellent detail maps. This edition covers the north and south islands and is printed in a small, more manageable size. Hotels are offered in all price ranges (comments are brief) and restaurant picks are selected to fit into various itineraries. This is one of the best guides to Japan.

Japan Today! A Westerner's Guide to the People, Language, and Culture of Japan

by Theodore Welch and Hiroki Kato, Passport Books, 1986, 115 pages, paper, $7.95

This title covers essential cultural information in an A-to-Z format. It is a handy reference work and includes an additional special language section.

Japan Unescorted: A Practical Guide to Discovering Japan On Your Own

by James Weatherly, Kodansha International, 1986, 200 pages, paper, $6.95

This delightful little guide is one of several well-done books on independent travel in Japan. It is full of helpful descriptions of hotels and restaurants in all price ranges, although the focus of the book is on "practicality and budget." The detail maps are helpful.

Kyoto: Seven Paths to the Heart of the City

by Diane Durston, Kodansha International, 1988, 64 pages, paper, $9.95

This large-format book, due for release after press time, focuses on seven districts "that best exemplify Japan's old imperial capital." Carefully drawn maps allow travelers to explore the narrow back streets of Kyoto even though most, in typical Japanese style, are nameless. Additional sections on cuisine, festivals, customs, and practical facts are also included. This author has also produced the excellent *Old Kyoto: A Guide to Traditional Shops, Restaurants, and Inns.*

National Parks of Japan

by Mary Sutherland and Dorothy Britton, Kodansha International, 1980, 148 pages, cloth, $19.95

This book, containing great descriptions of Japan's 27 national parks, is the kind of book that belongs on the coffee table. Combining clear maps and some fantastic photographs, this book will encourage even the most intinerary-oriented traveler to make changes to allow a visit to some of these magnificent spots.

North-East Asia On A Shoestring
edited by Tony Wheeler, Lonely Planet Publications, 1985, 288 pages, paper, $7.95

Covering China, Hong Kong, Japan, Macau, South Korea, and Taiwan, with short notes on visiting North Korea, this book is part of the budget-oriented On A Shoestring Guide series, which is reviewed in more detail under "Series Reviews." Titles in this series are generally updated every two to three years. A new edition has been announced.

Old Kyoto: A Guide to Traditional Shops, Restaurants, and Inns
by Diane Durston, Kodansha International, 1986, 240 pages, paper, $11.95

This is a thoroughly classy guide to the old section of this ancient city: its history; its shops of food goods, textiles, incense, tea, sweets, and dolls; its traditional inns and restaurants. This book will allow all travelers, even armchair travelers, to experience the real Kyoto.

Passport's Japan Almanac
by Boye De Mente, Passport Books, 1987, 319 pages, paper, $17.95

This large-format book takes Passport Books' other A-to-Z "compendium of all things Japanese" (*Japan Today!*) a step further. It is well written, pleasantly laid out, and covers almost 1000 subjects including art, education, social customs, and history. Too large to carry comfortably, this book will answer questions after the trip that the guidebooks didn't cover.

Post Guide: Japan
Hunter Publishing, 1987, 144 pages, paper, $8.95

This is one of the Post Guide series, which is reviewed in more detail under "Series Reviews."

Tokyo/Access
by Richard Saul Wurman, Prentice Hall Press, 1987, 225 pages, paper, $11.95

This is part of the Access Guide series, which is reviewed in more detail under "Series Reviews."

Tokyo City Guide
by Judith Conner and Mayumi Yoshida, Kodansha International, 1987 (revised ed.), 363 pages, paper, $15.95

This beautifully laid out and thoroughly comprehensive *Tokyo City Guide* contains information on accommodations, places to eat, the best shopping, entertainment, nightlife, the arts, sightseeing, and health-and-beauty resources. The multi-colored map section is particularly excellent in this wonderful resource.

Tokyo in Your Pocket

Barron's Educational Series, 1987, 160 pages, paper, $3.95

This is one of the small-format In-Your-Pocket Guide series, which is reviewed in more detail under "Series Reviews."

Top Shopping in Japan

Charles E. Tuttle Co., 1984, 303 pages, paper, $19.95

Produced in Japan for the tourist trade, this book is full of photos, good detail maps, and the occasional advertisement. It covers a little bit of everything, including eating spots, hotels, and sightseeing along the shopping trail. Its biggest plus, in spite of its age, is that it covers shopping areas not generally covered elsewhere. For Tokyo, it is a useful complement to the more detailed and up-to-date *Born to Shop* guide.

22 Days in Japan: The Itinerary Planner

by David Old, John Muir Publications, 1987, 133 pages, paper, $6.95

Rick Steves' famous *Europe in 22 Days* (now called *22 Days in Europe*) has spawned a whole Itinerary Planner series, which is reviewed in more detail under "Series Reviews." Note that the change in title is quite recent; this book may also be entitled *Japan in 22 Days*.

What's What in Japanese Restaurants

by Robb Satterwhite, Kodansha International, 1988, 144 pages, paper, $9.95

This new title, released after press time, delves into the specific cuisines of the Japanese, many of which are unfamiliar to westerners. The book contains a section on the Japanese menu designed to let travelers know what they are ordering and some very helpful chapters on beer, *sake*, and tourist traps.

JORDAN

See also "The Middle East" and "Asia as a Whole."

Fodor's Jordan and the Holy Land

Fodor's Travel Publications, 1986 (2nd ed.), 256 pages, paper, $12.95

This book is part of the Fodor's Guide series, which is reviewed in more detail under "Series Reviews."

Guide to Jordan
by Christine Osborne, Hippocrene Books, 1987, 225 pages, paper, $9.95

This interesting-sounding guide, released at press time, focuses on history, historic sites, Jordan's economy, its special foods, and "the pleasures of Aqaba."

Jordan: A Meed Practical Guide
Routledge & Kegan Paul, 1983, 282 pages, paper, $19.95

This book is part of the Meed Guide series, which is reviewed in more detail under "Series Reviews."

Let's Go: Israel & Egypt (including Jordan)
by Harvard Student Agencies, St. Martin's Press, 1988, 464 pages, paper, $10.95

This book is part of the excellent budget-oriented Let's Go Guide series, which is reviewed in more detail under "Series Reviews." The series is updated annually.

Syria & Jordan: A Travel Survival Kit
by Hugh Finlay, Lonely Planet Publications, 1987, 200 pages, paper, $8.95

This is one of the popular Travel Survival Kit series, which is reviewed in more detail under "Series Reviews." The series is updated every two to three years.

Korea: See "North Korea" and "South Korea."

MACAU

See also "Southeast Asia" and "Asia as a Whole."

Fodor's Hong Kong and Macau
Fodor's Travel Publications, 1987, 271 pages, paper, $10.95

This book is part of Fodor's Country/Regional Guide series, which is reviewed in more detail under "Series Reviews." The series is updated annually.

Hong Kong, Macau & Canton: A Travel Survival Kit
by Carol Clewlow and Alan Samagalski, Lonely Planet Publications, 1986 (4th ed.), 256 pages, paper, $7.95

This book is one of the popular Travel Survival Kit series, which is reviewed in more detail under "Series Reviews." The series is updated every two to three years.

Insight Guide: Hong Kong (with Macau)

by Apa Productions, Prentice Hall Press, 1986, 336 pages, paper, $16.95

This book is one of the acclaimed Insight Guide series, which is reviewed in more detail under "Series Reviews."

North-East Asia On A Shoestring

edited by Tony Wheeler, Lonely Planet Publications, 1985, 288 pages, paper, $7.95

Covering China, Hong Kong, Japan, Macau, South Korea, and Taiwan, with short notes on visiting North Korea, this book is part of the budget-oriented On A Shoestring Guide series, which is reviewed in more detail under "Series Reviews." The titles in this series are generally updated every two to three years. At press time, a new edition had not yet been announced.

MALAYSIA

See also "Southeast Asia" and "Asia as a Whole."

Insight Guide: Malaysia

by Apa Productions, Prentice Hall Press, 1986, 350 pages, paper, $16.95

This is one of the highly regarded Insight Guide series, which is reviewed in more detail under "Series Reviews."

Malaysia, Singapore and Brunei: A Travel Survival Kit

by Geoff Crowther and Tony Wheeler, Lonely Planet Publications, 1988 (3rd ed.), 320 pages, paper, $9.95

This is an excellent title in the popular Travel Survival Kit series, which is reviewed in more detail under "Series Reviews." The series is updated every two to three years. This edition was released after press time so the number of pages is approximate.

Malaysia, Singapore, Brunei Traveller's Handbook

by Stefan Loose and Renate Ramb, Riverdale Co., 1986, 331 pages, paper, $9.95

Translated from the German, this little book focuses on the budget-minded traveler, but covers price ranges from "luxurious to super cheap" in hotels, restaurants, and transportation. The layout is a little utilitarian, but the information on practicalities and pleasures is as enjoyable to read as it is helpful. Good detail maps are an added plus.

Post Guide: Malaysia

Hunter Publishing, 1987, 144 pages, paper, $8.95

This book is part of the Post Guide series, which is reviewed in more detail under "Series Reviews."

Shopping in Exotic Singapore and Malaysia

by Ronald Krannich, *et al.*, Impact Publications, 1988, 170 pages, paper, $9.95

This new book, released after press time, is part of the Shopping in Exotic Places series, which is reviewed in more detail under "Series Reviews." The series is updated every two years; the number of pages is approximate.

Time Travel In the Malay Crescent

by Wayne Stier, Meru Publishing, 1985, 312 pages, paper, $10.00

This enjoyable, informative book provides some real insight into the lands of Malaysia, Singapore, Borneo, and Brunei. It makes a terrific companion guide to supplement a more standard guide to this fascinating region of the world.

Maldives: See "Islands of the Western Indian Ocean" under "Africa."

NEPAL

See also "Asia as a Whole."

Berlitz: Nepal

Macmillan Publishing, 1988, 128 pages, paper, $6.95

This book is one of the small-format Berlitz Guide series, which is reviewed in more detail under "Series Reviews."

Fodor's India, Nepal and Sri Lanka

Fodor's Travel Publications, 1987, 520 pages, paper, $16.95

This book is part of the Fodor's Guide series, which is reviewed in more detail under "Series Reviews." The series is updated annually.

A Guide to Trekking in Nepal

by Stephen Bezruchka, The Mountaineers, 1985 (5th ed.), 352 pages, $10.95

This well-organized, well-written guide describes the best trekking routes in detail and provides additional notes on history and natural history. It is perfect for those trekking alone or with a group, offering excellent information on preparations, health care, and interacting with the Nepalese (including a good section on language and useful phrases for the trekker).

Hildebrand's Travel Guide: India and Nepal
Hunter Publishing, 1985, 224 pages, paper, $10.95
This book is part of the Hildebrand's Guide series, which is reviewed in more detail under "Series Reviews."

India, Nepal & Sri Lanka: A Traveller's Guide
by Peter Meyer and Barbara Rausch, Riverdale Co., 1987, 656 pages, paper, $14.95
This great budget guide for the young adventurer is reviewed under "India" above.

Insight Guide: Nepal
by Apa Productions, Prentice Hall Press, 1986, 351 pages, paper, $16.95
This book is part of the excellent Insight Guide series, which is reviewed in more detail under "Series Reviews."

Kathmandu & The Kingdom of Nepal: A Travel Survival Kit
by Prakash A Ray, Lonely Planet Publications, 1985 (5th ed.), 144 pages, paper, $7.95
This book is part of the popular Travel Survival Kit series, which is reviewed in more detail under "Series Reviews." The titles in this series are generally updated every two to three years. At press time, a new edition had not yet been announced.

Nagel's India and Nepal
Passport Books, 1983, 831 pages, cloth, $49.95
This old, classic, cultural guide is part of the Nagel's Guide series, which is reviewed in more detail under "Series Reviews."

The Times Travel Library: Kathmandu
Hunter Publishing, 1987, 104 pages, paper, $10.95
This book is part of the new large-format, photo-oriented Times Travel Library Guide series, which is reviewed in more detail under "Series Reviews."

The Trekker's Guide to the Himalaya and Karakoram
by Hugh Swift, Sierra Club Books, 1982, 352 pages, paper, $10.95
This quality guide is done in typical Sierra Club fashion, but is not as up-to-date on some issues as other guides to the area.

Trekking in the Nepal Himalaya
by Stan Armington, Lonely Planet Publications, 1985 (4th ed.), 200 pages, paper, $7.95

This solid guide emphasizes trek organization. It includes suggestions on routes, equipment needs, maps, and more.

West Asia On A Shoestring
by Tony Wheeler, Lonely Planet Publications, 1986 (5th ed.), 368 pages, paper, $8.95

Describing the overland route from Bangladesh to Turkey, this book is part of the budget-oriented On A Shoestring Guide series, which is reviewed in more detail under "Series Reviews." The series is updated every two to three years.

NORTH KOREA

North-East Asia On A Shoestring
edited by Tony Wheeler, Lonely Planet Publications, 1985, 288 pages, paper, $7.95.

Covering China, Hong Kong, Japan, Macau, South Korea, and Taiwan, with short notes on visiting North Korea, this book is part of the budget-oriented On A Shoestring Guide series, which is reviewed in more detail under "Series Reviews." Titles in this series are updated every two to three years. A new edition has been announced.

NORTHERN YEMEN (YEMEN ARAB REPUBLIC)
See also "The Middle East" and "Asia as a Whole."

Guide to North Yemen
by Christine Osborne, Hippocrene Books, 1987, 160 pages, paper, $11.95

In this book, the author traces various itineraries from Sana'a, the capital city, to the coast and into the mysterious inland mountains. Along the way she describes the historic sites, the flora and fauna of the area, and Yemeni cooking, and includes notes on history and the traditional Yemeni way of life.

Yemen: A Travel Survival Kit
by Pertti Hämäläinen, Lonely Planet Publications, 1988, 180 pages, paper, $8.95

Covering both Southern Yemen (the People's Democratic Republic of Yemen) and Northern Yemen (the Yemen Arab Republic), this book is part of the Travel Survival Kit series, which is reviewed in more detail under "Series Reviews." The series is updated every two to three years.

OMAN

See also "The Middle East" and "Asia as a Whole."

Oman: A Meed Practical Guide
Routledge & Kegan Paul, 1981, 198 pages, paper, $19.95
This book is part of the Meed Guide series, which is reviewed in more detail under "Series Reviews."

PAKISTAN

See also "Asia as a Whole."

Pakistan: A Travel Survival Kit
by Jose Santiago, Lonely Planet Publications, 1987 (3rd ed.), 240 pages, paper, $8.95
This book is part of the well-known Travel Survival Kit series, which is reviewed in more detail under "Series Reviews." The series is updated every two to three years.

West Asia On A Shoestring
by Tony Wheeler, Lonely Planet Publications, 1986 (5th ed.), 368 pages, paper, $8.95
Describing the overland route from Bangladesh to Turkey, this book is part of the budget-oriented On A Shoestring Guide series, which is reviewed in more detail under "Series Reviews." The series is updated every two to three years.

PAPUA NEW GUINEA

See also "Southeast Asia."

Bushwalking in Papua New Guinea
by Riall Nolan, Lonely Planet Publications, 1983, 136 pages, paper, $6.95
This well-done guide describes 11 walks and climbs through this fascinating, exotic land. All the practical information needed to enjoy a real outdoor adventure is included.

Papua New Guinea: A Travel Survival Kit
by Tony Wheeler, Lonely Planet Publications, 1985 (3rd ed.), 256 pages, paper, $8.95
This book is part of the popular Travel Survival Kit series, which is reviewed in more detail under "Series Reviews." Titles in this

series are generally updated every two to three years. At press time, a new edition had not yet been announced.

Shopping in the Exotic South Pacific: Your Passport to Exciting Australia, New Zealand, Papua New Guinea, Tonga, Fiji, Tahiti, and the Solomon Islands
by Ronald Krannich, *et al.*, Impact Publications, 1989, 450 pages, paper, $13.95
   Including Papua New Guinea, this book is a new, anticipated title in the excellent Shopping in Exotic Places series, which is reviewed in more detail under "Series Reviews." The price and number of pages are approximate.

People's Democratic Republic of Yemen: See "Southern Yemen."
People's Republic of China: See "China."

PHILIPPINES

See also "Southeast Asia" and "Asia as a Whole."

Hildebrand's Travel Guide: Philippines
Hunter Publishing, 1988, 240 pages, paper, $10.95
   This book is a new member of the Hildebrand's Guide series, which is reviewed in more detail under "Series Reviews."

Insight Guide: the Philippines
by Apa Productions, Prentice Hall Press, 1986, 335 pages, paper, $16.95
   This book is part of the acclaimed Insight Guide series ,which is reviewed in more detail under "Series Reviews."

Nagel's Philippines
Passport Books, 1982, 367 pages, cloth, $39.95
   This classic, cultural guide is part of the Nagel's Guide series, which is reviewed in more detail under "Series Reviews."

Philippines: A Travel Survival Kit
by Jens Peters, Lonely Planet Publications, 1987 (3rd ed.), 372 pages, paper, $8.95
   This book is part of the popular Travel Survival Kit series, which is reviewed in more detail under "Series Reviews." The series is updated every two to three years.

QATAR

See also "The Middle East" and "Asia as a Whole."

Qatar: A Meed Practical Guide
Routledge & Kegan Paul, 1983, 176 pages, paper, $19.95
This book is one of the Meed Guide series, which is reviewed in more detail under "Series Reviews."

SAUDI ARABIA

See also "The Middle East" and "Asia as a Whole."

Berlitz: Saudi Arabia
Macmillan Publishing, 1985, 128 pages, paper, $6.95
This book is part of the small-format Berlitz Guide series, which is reviewed in more detail under "Series Reviews."

Saudi Arabia: A Meed Practical Guide
Routledge & Kegan Paul, 1983, 350 pages, paper, $19.95
This book is one of the Meed Guide series, which is reviewed in more detail under "Series Reviews."

SINGAPORE

See also "Southeast Asia" and "Asia as a Whole."

The American Express Pocket Guide to Hong Kong, Singapore, and Bangkok
Prentice Hall Press, 1988, 200 pages, cloth, $9.95
This book is one of the respected American Express Pocket Guide series, which is reviewed in more detail under "Series Reviews." As it was released after press time, the number of pages is approximate.

Baedeker's Singapore
Prentice Hall Press, 1986, 112 pages, paper, $10.95
This book is part of Baedeker's City Guide series, which is reviewed in more detail under "Series Reviews."

Berlitz: Singapore
Macmillan Publishing, 1979, 128 pages, paper, $6.95
This book is part of the small-format Berlitz Guide series, which is reviewed in more detail under "Series Reviews."

Fodor's Singapore
Fodor's Travel Publications, 1987, 176 pages, paper, $7.95
This book is one of Fodor's City Guide series, which is reviewed in more detail under "Series Reviews." The series is updated annually.

Insight Guide: Singapore
by Apa Productions, Prentice Hall Press, 1986, 342 pages, paper,
$16.95
    This book is part of the acclaimed Insight Guide series, which is
reviewed in more detail under "Series Reviews."

Malaysia, Singapore and Brunei: A Travel Survival Kit
by Geoff Crowther and Tony Wheeler, Lonely Planet Publications,
1988 (3rd ed.), 320 pages, paper, $9.95
    This is an excellent title in the popular Travel Survival Kit series,
which is reviewed in more detail under "Series Reviews." The titles
in this series are updated every two to three years. This edition was
released after press time so the number of pages is approximate.

Malaysia, Singapore, Brunei Traveller's Handbook
by Stefan Loose and Renate Ramb, Riverdale Co., 1986, 331 pages,
paper, $9.95
    This budget-oriented book is reviewed under "Malaysia."

Post Guide: Singapore
Hunter Publishing, 1983, 144 pages, paper, $8.95
    This book is part of the Post Guide series, which is reviewed in
more detail under "Series Reviews."

**Shopping In Exotic Places: Your Passport to Exciting Hong Kong,
    Korea, Thailand, Indonesia, and Singapore**
by Ronald Krannich, *et al.*, Impact Publications, 1987, 469 pages,
paper, $13.95
Shopping in Exotic Singapore and Malaysia
by Ronald Krannich, *et al.*, Impact Publications, 1988, 170 pages,
paper, $9.95
    Both of these titles are part of the excellent Shopping in Exotic
Places series, which is reviewed in more detail under "Series Reviews." The Singapore and Malaysia volume is an addition to the
series and will expand on the Singapore section of the first title. The
Singapore and Malaysia volume was released after press time; the
number of pages is approximate. The series is updated every two
years.

SOUTH KOREA
See also "Asia as a Whole."

Fodor's Korea
Fodor's Travel Publications, 1988, 192 pages, paper, $10.95
This book is part of Fodor's Country/Regional Guide series, which is reviewed in more detail under "Series Reviews." The series is updated annually.

Hildebrand's Travel Guide: South Korea
Hunter Publishing, 1987, 255 pages, paper, $10.95
This book is part of the Hildebrand's Guide series, which is reviewed in more detail under "Series Reviews."

Insider's Guide to Korea
Hunter Publishing, 1987, 196 pages, paper, $12.95
This book is part of the Hunter Insider's Guide series, which is reviewed in more detail under "Series Reviews."

Insight Guide: Korea
by Apa Productions, Prentice Hall Press, 1986, 321 pages, paper, $16.95
This book is one of the acclaimed Insight Guide series, which is reviewed in more detail under "Series Reviews."

Korea: A Travel Survival Kit
by Geoff Crowther, Lonely Planet Publications, 1988, 200 pages, paper, $8.95
This new title, released after press time, is part of the popular Travel Survival Kit series, which is reviewed in more detail under "Series Reviews." The series is updated every two to three years; the number of pages listed above is approximate.

Korea Guide
by Edward Adams, Charles E. Tuttle Co., 1986, 360 pages, cloth, $19.50
This attractive, hardbound volume, replete with many beautiful photos, is an excellent planning tool. At the back of the book is a Tourist Directory that offers practical information and hotel selections (without detailed comment). However, the real strengths of this book are its coverage of history and cultural attributes, and the many suggested sightseeing tours described by a man who has lived and worked in Korea for several decades.

The Korea Guidebook
by Kyung Cho Chung, *et al.*, Eurasia Press, 1987, 528 pages, paper, $14.95
This comprehensive, well-written guide covers all the classic tour-

ist bases. Major sections on practicalities, doing business, history and culture, and various tours—each with recommended things to see, places to stay in different price ranges, and a few select restaurants—make this a great resource. Note: This edition was released in anticipation of the 1988 Olympics and officially recommended by the Olympic Committee.

Korea: The Land of Morning Calm
by Daniel Reid, Passport Books, 1988, 208 pages, paper, $9.95
This book is one of the Passport Asian Guide series, which is reviewed in more detail under "Series Reviews."

North-East Asia On A Shoestring
edited by Tony Wheeler, Lonely Planet Publications, 1985, 288 pages, paper, $7.95
Covering China, Hong Kong, Japan, Macau, South Korea, and Taiwan, with short notes on visiting North Korea, this book is part of the budget-oriented On A Shoestring Guide series, which is reviewed in more detail under "Series Reviews." Titles in this series are updated every two to three years. A new edition has been announced.

Seoul, 1988 Olympic Site
by Edward Adams, Charles E. Tuttle Co., 1984, 57 pages, paper, $4.00
Although the hotel recommendations certainly need updating, this little paperback remains a useful, compact guide to the capital city. Information includes a subway guide, what to see, what to eat (general strategies and suggested dishes), shopping, and entertainment. Detail maps are only adequate.

Shopping in Exotic Korea
by Ronald Krannich, *et al.*, Impact Publications, 1988, 180 pages, paper, $9.95
Shopping In Exotic Places: Your Passport to Exciting Hong Kong, Korea, Thailand, Indonesia, and Singapore
by Ronald Krannich, *et al.*, Impact Publications, 1987, 469 pages, paper, $13.95
Both of these titles are part of the excellent Shopping in Exotic Places series, which is reviewed in more detail under "Series Reviews." The Korea volume is an anticipated addition to the series and expands on the Korea section of the second title. The series is updated every two years. The Korea volume was released after press time so the number of pages is approximate.

South Korea Handbook
by Robert Nilsen, Moon Publications, 1988, 600 pages, paper, $14.95

This is a new edition, released after press time, to the superb Moon Handbook series, which is reviewed in more detail under "Series Reviews." The series is updated every two years.

The Times Travel Library: Seoul
Hunter Publishing, 1987, 104 pages, paper, $10.95

This book is part of the large-format, photo-oriented Times Travel Library series, which is reviewed in more detail under "Series Reviews."

SOUTHERN YEMEN
(PEOPLE'S DEMOCRATIC REPUBLIC OF YEMEN)
See also "The Middle East" and "Asia as a Whole."

Yemen: A Travel Survival Kit
by Pertti Hämäläinen, Lonely Planet Publications, 1988, 180 pages, paper, $8.95

Covering both Southern Yemen (the People's Democratic Republic of Yemen) and Northern Yemen (the Yemen Arab Republic), this book is part of the Travel Survival Kit series, which is reviewed in more detail under "Series Reviews." The series is updated every two to three years.

Soviet Union: All regions of the Soviet Union, whether technically in Europe or in Asia, are listed under Europe.

SRI LANKA
See also "Asia as a Whole."

Berlitz: Sri Lanka & the Maldives
Macmillan Publishing, 1981, 128 pages, paper, $6.95

This book is one of the small-format Berlitz Guide series, which is reviewed in more detail under "Series Reviews."

Fodor's India, Nepal, and Sri Lanka
Fodor's Travel Publications, 1987, 520 pages, paper, $16.95

This book is part of Fodor's Country/Regional Guide series, which is reviewed in more detail under "Series Reviews." This series is updated annually.

Hildebrand's Travel Guide: Sri Lanka

Hunter Publishing, 1985, 143 pages, paper, $8.95

This book is one of the Hildebrand's Guide series, which is reviewed in more detail under "Series Reviews."

India, Nepal & Sri Lanka: A Traveller's Guide

by Peter Meyer and Barbara Rausch, Riverdale Co., 1987, 656 pages, paper, $14.95

This excellent, budget guide for the young adventurer is reviewed under "India" above.

Insight Guide: Sri Lanka

by Apa Productions, Prentice Hall Press, 1985, 367 pages, paper, $16.95

This book is part of the widely praised Insight Guide series, which is reviewed in more detail under "Series Reviews."

Nagel's Ceylon

Passport Books, 1983, 271 pages, cloth, $39.95

This classic, cultural guide is part of the Nagel's Guide series, which is reviewed in more detail under "Series Reviews."

Post Guide: Sri Lanka

Hunter Publishing, 1983, 144 pages, paper, $8.95

This book is part of the Post Guide series, which is reviewed in more detail under "Series Reviews."

Sri Lanka: A Travel Survival Kit

by Tony Wheeler, Lonely Planet Publications, 1984 (4th ed.), 240 pages, paper, $8.95

This book is part of the popular Travel Survival Kit series, which is reviewed in more detail under "Series Reviews." Titles in this series are generally updated every two to three years. At press time, a new edition had not yet been announced.

West Asia On A Shoestring

by Tony Wheeler, Lonely Planet Publications, 1986 (5th ed.), 368 pages, paper, $8.95

Describing the overland route from Bangladesh to Turkey, this book is part of the budget-oriented On A Shoestring Guide series, which is reviewed in more detail under "Series Reviews." The series is updated every two to three years.

SYRIA

See also "The Middle East" and "Asia as a Whole."

Syria & Jordan: A Travel Survival Kit

by Hugh Finlay, Lonely Planet Publications, 1987, 200 pages, paper, $8.95

This book is part of the well-known Travel Survival Kit series, which is reviewed in more detail under "Series Reviews." The series is updated every two to three years.

TAIWAN

See also "Asia as a Whole."

Guide to Taipei and Taiwan

by Joseph Nerbonne, W. S. Heinman-Imported Books, 1988 (9th ed.), 330 pages, paper, $12.00

In this, perhaps the single best guide to Taiwan, Nerbonne, a long-time resident, provides a truly massive amount of sightseeing information, hotel and restaurant choices, and all sorts of practical facts and figures. This is a particularly helpful guide both for its excellent maps and for its inclusion of the Chinese and English language words for important streets, trains, etc. What this means is that travelers who are totally stuck can show the written word for the place or street they are seeking to the person they are asking directions of. The price and number of pages for the 1988 edition, not yet released at press time, are approximate.

Hildebrand's Travel Guide: Taiwan

Hunter Publishing, 1986, 190 pages, paper, $10.95

This book is part of the Hildebrand's Guide series, which is reviewed in more detail under "Series Reviews."

Insight Guide: Taiwan

by Apa Productions, Prentice Hall Press, 1986, 355 pages, paper, $16.95

This book is part of the acclaimed Insight Guide series, which is reviewed in more detail under "Series Reviews."

North-East Asia On A Shoestring

edited by Tony Wheeler, Lonely Planet Publications, 1985, 288 pages, paper, $7.95

Covering China, Hong Kong, Japan, Macau, South Korea, and Taiwan, with short notes on visiting North Korea, this book is part of the budget-oriented On A Shoestring Guides series, which is reviewed in more detail under "Series Reviews." Titles in this series are generally updated every two to three years. A new edition has been announced.

Taiwan: A Travel Survival Kit

by Robert Storey, Lonely Planet Publications, 1987, 250 pages, paper, $8.95

This book is one of the well-known Travel Survival Kit series, which is reviewed in more detail under "Series Reviews." The series is updated every two to three years.

THAILAND

See also "Southeast Asia" and "Asia as a Whole."

The American Express Pocket Guide to Hong Kong, Singapore, and Bangkok

Prentice Hall Press, 1988, 200 pages, cloth, $9.95

This book is one of the respected American Express Pocket Guide series, which is reviewed in more detail under "Series Reviews." As it was released after press time, the number of pages is approximate.

Baedeker's Bangkok

Prentice Hall Press, 1987, 144 pages, paper, $10.95

This book is part of Baedeker's City Guide series, which is reviewed in more detail under "Series Reviews."

Bangkok's Back Streets

by Bob Todd, Excogitations, 1986, 72 pages, paper, $9.95

This "guide to the pleasure of the world's most open city" is only for those seeking help surviving and enjoying Bangkok's red-light district.

Berlitz: Thailand

Macmillan Publishing, 1979, 128 pages, paper, $6.95

This book is one of the small-format Berlitz Guide series, which is reviewed in more detail under "Series Reviews."

Cadogan Guide: Thailand and Burma

by Frank Kusy and Frances Capel, The Globe Pequot Press, 1988, 350 pages, paper, $14.95

This is an expected new title in the highly regarded Cadogan Guide series, which is reviewed in more detail under "Series Reviews." The price and number of pages are approximate. The series is updated every two years; this title is due out in late 1988.

Frommer's Touring Guide to Thailand

Prentice Hall Press, 1988, 175 pages, paper, $9.95

This book is a new title in the latest Frommer series, Frommer's Touring Guides, which is reviewed in more detail under "Series Reviews."

Guide to Chiang Mai & Northern Thailand

by John Hoskin, Charles E. Tuttle Co., 1984, 180 pages, paper, $4.95

This book is considered by many to be the best guide to this region. It is written in an enjoyable style and is full of information on how to get there and what to see and do. The hotel listing is long and covers all price ranges, but additional comments are scant. The publication date means that some details need updating so be sure to confirm all time-sensitive information.

Hildebrand's Travel Guide: Thailand

by Dieter Rumpf, Hippocrene Books, 1985, 300 pages, paper, $10.95

This book is one of the Hildebrand's Guide series, which is reviewed in more detail under "Series Reviews."

Insight Guide: Thailand

by Apa Productions, Prentice Hall Press, 1987, 343 pages, paper, $16.95

This book is part of the excellent Insight Guide series, which is reviewed in more detail under "Series Reviews."

Nagel's Thailand

Passport Books, 1982, 383 pages, cloth, $39.95

This classic, cultural guide is part of the Nagel's Guide series, which is reviewed in more detail under "Series Reviews."

Post Guide: Thailand

Hunter Publishing, 1987, 144 pages, paper, $8.95

This book is part of the Post Guide series, which is reviewed in more detail under "Series Reviews."

Shopping In Exotic Places: Your Passport to Exciting Hong Kong, Korea, Thailand, Indonesia, and Singapore
by Ronald Krannich, *et al.*, Impact Publications, 1987, 469 pages, paper, $13.95

Shopping In Exotic Thailand
by Ronald Krannich, *et al.*, Impact Publications, 1988, 200 pages, paper, $10.95
Both of these titles are part of the excellent Shopping in Exotic Places series, which is reviewed in more detail under "Series Reviews." The Thailand volume is an anticipated addition to the series and expands on the Thailand section of the first title. The Thailand volume was released after press time, so the number of pages is approximate. The series is updated every two years.

Thailand: A Travel Survival Kit
by Joe Cummings, Lonely Planet Publications, 1987 (3rd ed.), 284 pages, paper, $8.95
This book is one of the popular Travel Survival Kit series, which is reviewed in more detail under "Series Reviews." The series is updated every two to three years.

Thailand: The Kingdom of Siam
by John Haskins, Passport Books, 1988, 224 pages, paper, $9.95
This book is part of the Passport Asian Guide series, which is reviewed in more detail under "Series Reviews."

The Traveler's Complete Guide to Pattaya and South-Eastern Thailand
by Steve Van Beek, Charles E. Tuttle Co., 1981, 150 pages, paper, $4.95
This guide is in need of an update, but is still useful for sightseeing and providing ideas for enjoying this popular place. Hotel selections are probably still useful—at least for the larger chains—although price ranges are undoubtedly higher now. The section on foods of the area will point out delicacies not to miss, but a few of the restaurants that are singled out may not exist anymore.

Wide Eyes in Burma and Thailand: Finding Your Way
by Wayne Stier and Mars Cavers, Meru Publishing, 1983, 218 pages, paper, $7.50
This book reviewed under "Burma."

Tibet: See "China."

TURKEY
See also "The Middle East" and "Asia as a Whole."

Baedeker's Istanbul
 Prentice Hall Press, 1987, 208 pages, paper, $10.95
 This book is part of Baedeker's City Guide series, which is reviewed in more detail under "Series Reviews."

Baedeker's Turkish Coast
 Prentice Hall Press, 1987, 301 pages, paper, $9.95
 This book is one of the Baedeker's Country/Regional Guide series, which is reviewed in more detail under "Series Reviews."

Berlitz: Istanbul & the Aegean Coast
 Macmillan Publishing, 1986, 128 pages, paper, $6.95
 This book is part of the small-format Berlitz Guide series, which is reviewed in more detail under "Series Reviews."

Berlitz: Turkey
 Macmillan Publishing, 1988, 256 pages, paper, $8.95
 This book is one of the small-format Berlitz Country Guide series, which is reviewed in more detail under "Series Reviews."

Blue Guide: Istanbul
 by John Freely, W. W. Norton & Co., 1987 (2nd ed.), 346 pages, paper, $18.95
 This book is one of the highly regarded Blue Guide series, which is reviewed in more detail under "Series Reviews."

Cadogan Guide: Turkey
 by Dana Facaros and Michael Pauls, The Globe Pequot Press, 1986, 394 pages, paper, $12.95
 This book is part of the highly regarded Cadogan Guides series, which is reviewed in more detail under "Series Reviews." The series is updated every two years.

The Camper's Companion to Southern Europe
 by Dennis and Tina Jaffe, Williamson Publishing, 1986, 287 pages, paper, $13.95
 This well-done camping guide to Europe includes camping opportunities in Turkey and is reviewed under "Europe as a Whole."

Essentially Turkey
by Carole and Chris Stewart, Hippocrene Books, 1987, 200 pages, paper, $8.95
This well-organized guide to history, historic sites, food, and wine includes plenty of useful travel tips specific to Turkey, as well as a practical vocabulary section.

Fodor's Turkey
Fodor's Travel Publications, 1987, 320 pages, paper, $16.95
This book is one of Fodor's Country/Regional Guide series, which is reviewed in more detail under "Series Reviews." The series is updated annually.

Frommer's Greece on $40 a Day (including Istanbul and Turkey's Aegean Coast)
by Kyle McCarthy and John Levy, Prentice Hall Press, 1987, 540 pages, paper, $11.95
Frommer's Turkey on $25 a Day
by Tom Brosnahan, Prentice Hall Press, 1988, 299 pages, paper, $10.95
Both of these titles are part of the budget-oriented Frommer's Dollar-a-Day Guide series, which is reviewed in more detail under "Series Reviews." The series is updated every two years.

Guide to Aegean and Mediterranean Turkey
by Diana Darke, Hippocrene Books, 1986, 296 pages, paper, $14.95
Guide to Eastern Turkey and the Black Sea Coast
by Diana Darke, Hippocrene Books, 1987, 320 pages, paper, $14.95
These two enjoyable, superbly detailed guides are first-rate for the subjects they cover. The second title covers the lands from Ankara eastward. Numerous itineraries are suggested and the necessary practical information and maps are provided. Thoughts on food and lodging choices, however, are general.

Let's Go: Greece (including Cyprus, the Turkish Coast, and Istanbul)
by Harvard Student Agencies, St. Martin's Press, 1988, 528 pages, paper, $10.95
This book is one of the excellent, budget-oriented Let's Go Guide series, which is reviewed in more detail under "Series Reviews." The series is updated annually. Note: Turkey is also included in *Let's Go: Europe.*

Nagel's Turkey

Passport Books, 1984, 799 pages, cloth, $49.95

This classic, cultural guide is part of the Nagel's Guide series, which is reviewed in more detail under "Series Reviews."

Strolling Through Istanbul: A Guide to the City

by Hilary Sumner-Boyd and John Freely, Methuen, Inc., 1987 (revised ed.), 537 pages, paper, $16.95

This classic guide was first printed in 1972 and has long been regarded as the best travel guide to Istanbul. The focus of the book is on the Byzantine and Ottoman antiquities of the city—art, architecture, and the history behind them—but, as the book states "the city is not treated as if it were merely an inhabited museum. Instead, the ancient monuments are described in the context of a living town...." This revised edition is superb.

Turkey: A Travel Survival Kit

by Tom Brosnahan, Lonely Planet Publications, 1988 (2nd ed.), 480 pages, paper, $12.95

This book is part of the popular Travel Survival Kit series, which is reviewed in more detail under "Series Reviews." The series is updated every two to three years.

The Visitor's Guide to Turkey

Hunter Publishing, 1987, 238 pages, paper, $9.95

This book is part of the Visitor's Guide series, which is reviewed in more detail under "Series Reviews."

West Asia On A Shoestring

by Tony Wheeler, Lonely Planet Publications, 1986 (5th ed.), 368 pages, paper, $8.95

Describing the overland route from Bangladesh to Turkey, this book is part of the budget-oriented On A Shoestring Guide series, which is reviewed in more detail under "Series Reviews." The series is updated every two to three years.

Where to Go in Turkey

Hippocrene Books, 1988, 140 pages, paper, $11.95

This is a new title in the Where to Go Guide series, which is reviewed in more detail under "Series Reviews." As it was released after press time, the number of pages is approximate.

UNITED ARAB EMIRATES

See also "The Middle East" and "Asia as a Whole."

UAE: A Meed Practical Guide
　Routledge & Kegan Paul, 1986, 360 pages, paper, $19.95
　　This book is one of the Meed Guide series, which is reviewed in more detail under "Series Reviews."

Yemen Arab Republic: See "Northern Yemen."

Australia

See also "The World." Australia includes the island of Tasmania.

ABC Air Asia, Australia & New Zealand
ABC International, monthly editions, 250 pages, paper, $7.00
This book contains airline schedules and is a lifesaver for travelers who must be their own travel agents.

The American Express Pocket Guide to Australia
by Tony Duboudin and Brian Courtis, Prentice Hall Press, 1988, 240 pages, cloth, $9.95
This book is an anticipated addition to the well-known American Express Pocket Guide series, which is reviewed in more detail under "Series Reviews." As it was released after press time, the number of pages is approximate.

Australia: A Travel Survival Kit
by Tony Wheeler, Lonely Planet Publications, 1986, paper, $14.95
This book is part of the Travel Survival Kit series, which is reviewed in more detail under "Series Reviews." The series is updated every two to three years.

Australian Art Guide
by Roslyn Keam, Robert Silver Associates, 1984, 132 pages, paper, $9.95
This book is part of the Robert Silver Art Guide series, which is reviewed in more detail under "Series Reviews."

Australia for Free
by Thomas King, Hippocrene Books, 1987, 196 pages, paper, $8.95
This handy reference, which is arranged regionally, provides lots of ideas about things to do—with or without the kids—that won't cost a cent.

Australia in 22 Days
See *22 Days in Australia* below.

Berlitz: Australia
Macmillan Publishing, 1986, 256 pages, paper, $8.95
This is a volume in the Berlitz Country Guide series, which is reviewed in more detail under "Series Reviews."

Blair's Guide to Victoria & Melbourne
written and published by Suzanne Blair, 1986 (3rd ed.), 288 pages, paper, $9.95
The Blair Guide bears an uncanny resemblance to a Michelin Green guide, with copious sightseeing information, historic notes, and a good range of ideas of what to do. However, where Michelin Green concentrates on sightseeing and culture only, the Blair Guide also covers restaurant selections and some general notes on the availability of various sorts of lodging. Well organized and easy-to-use, the book is published in Australia and, at present, has no American distributor, although it can be found in some travel bookstores.

Bushwalking in Australia
by John and Monica Chapman, Lonely Planet Publications, 1988, 180 pages, paper, $8.95
This new book, released after press time, covers the many different backpacking opportunities in Australia. Written by two experienced walkers, the book contains all the details of the very best walks in every state of Australia. The number of pages is approximate.

Cadogan Guide: Australia
by Nick Lush, The Globe Pequot Press, 1988, 512 pages, paper, $14.95
This book is part of the excellent Cadogan Guide series, which is reviewed in more detail under "Series Reviews." The series is updated every two years.

Explore Australia: Touring for Leisure and Pleasure
by Currey O'Neil, Salem House, 1987 (5th ed.), 400 pages, cloth, $29.95
This very popular, large-format, hardback guide is well suited for planning or auto travel. This comprehensive book covers 700 towns and provides a gazetteer of more than 9000 places of interest, including the Great Barrier Reef. More than 175 pages are devoted to maps. *Explore Australia* is also color-coded by state to make it easier to use.

Exploring the A.C.T. and Southeast N.S.W.

by J. K. Donald, ISBS, 1985, 192 pages, paper, $9.95

This well-done guide covers the sightseeing adventures of the region of New South Wales that is situated between Melbourne and Sydney and includes the Australian Capital Territory, the Snowy Mountains, and all sorts of towns packed with fascinating history.

Exploring the Hunter Region

by J. K. Donald and M. E. Hungerford, ISBS, 1984, 201 pages, paper, $8.95

From Sydney, this excellent guide heads north to Newcastle, the second area settled on mainland Australia, into the Hunter Region, a land filled with farms, vineyards, wineries, and mountains. Good directions for tours that can usually be done over several days from the Sydney starting point are provided.

Fisher's World: Australia, New Zealand, and the South Pacific

by John McLeod, Fisher's World, 1988, 336 pages, paper, $14.95

Including Fiji, the Samoas, and French Polynesia, this book is one of the Fisher's World Guide series, which is reviewed in more detail under "Series Reviews." The series is updated annually.

Fodor's Australia, New Zealand, and the South Pacific

Fodor's Travel Publications, 1987, 628 pages, paper, $15.95

This is a solidly done title in Fodor Country/Regional Guide series, which is reviewed in more detail under "Series Reviews." The series is updated annually.

Fodor's Sydney

Fodor's Travel Publications, 1987, 160 pages, paper, $7.95

This book is one of Fodor's City Guide series, which is reviewed in more detail under "Series Reviews." The series is updated annually.

Frommer's Australia on $30 a Day

by John Godwin, Prentice Hall Press, 1988, 280 pages, paper, $11.95

This book is one of the budget-oriented Frommer's Dollar-a-Day Guide series, which is reviewed in more detail under "Ser.ies Reviews." This edition was released after press time, so the number of pages is approximate. The series is updated every two years.

Frommer's Touring Guide to Australia
Prentice Hall Press, 1988, 175 pages, paper, $9.95
This is a new title in Frommer's latest series, the Frommer's Touring Guides, which is reviewed in more detail under "Series Reviews."

G'Day! Teach Yourself Australian in 20 Easy Lessons
by Colin Bowles, Salem House, 1987, 120 pages, paper, $5.95
This is a fun, funny, and very helpful book on slang and other idiosyncrasies of Australian English.

The Great Barrier Reef: A Guide to the Islands and Resorts
by Arne and Ruth Werchick, Wide World Publishing, 1986, 295 pages, paper, $9.95
This very helpful guide to the many islands of the Great Barrier Reef provides information on how to reach them, the facilities available, what to do, and tips on food and drink, as well as practical information on transportation, attire, weather, photography, safety, coral, and, of course, snorkeling and diving.

Hildebrand's Guide to Australia
Hunter Publishing, 1985, 336 pages, paper, $10.95
This book is part of the Hildebrand's Guide series, which is reviewed in more detail under "Series Reviews."

How to Get Lost & Found in Australia
by John McDermott, Orafa Publishing, 1984 (2nd ed.), 303 pages, paper, $9.95
This book is part of the delightfully different Lost & Found Guide series, which is reviewed in more detail under "Series Reviews."

The Hume: Australia's Highway of History
by Brian Carroll, ISBS, 1983, 176 pages, paper, $6.95
The Hume highway runs from Sydney to Melbourne and in the process cuts through a wide array of historic points for the sightseeing traveler. A freeway often runs adjacent to the old highway now, but most of the book is focused along the older and much more fascinating road. This is a well-organized, useful book for the visitor to the states of New South Wales and Victoria.

Insider's Guide to Australia
Hunter Publishing, 1987, 220 pages, paper, $12.95
This book is one of the Hunter Insider's Guide series, which is reviewed in more detail under "Series Reviews."

Insight Guide: Australia
by Apa Productions, Prentice Hall Press, 1987, 368 pages, paper, $16.95

This book is an excellent title in the much-praised Insight Guide series, which is reviewed in more detail under "Series Reviews."

Long Stays in Australia
by Maggie Driver, Hippocrene Books, 1987, 200 pages, paper, $19.95

This book is part of the Long Stays Guide series, which is reviewed in more detail under "Series Reviews."

The Maverick Guide to Australia
by Robert Bone, Pelican Publishing, 1988, 352 pages, paper, $11.95

This book is one of the acclaimed Maverick Guide series, which is reviewed in more detail under "Series Reviews." The guide is updated every two years.

The Outdoor Traveler's Guide to Australia
by Mark Kestigian, Stewart, Tabori & Chang, 1988, 400 pages, paper, $18.95

Released after press time, this new guide for "action-oriented travelers" to Australia includes information on the Australian park system, the Great Barrier Reef, numerous full-color maps, and 250 color photographs by noted wildlife photographers.

The Penguin Guide to Australia
edited by Alan Tucker, Viking Penguin, 1988, 224-448 pages, paper, $9.95-12.95

This book is one of the first eight anticipated titles in the Penguin Travel Guide series, which is reviewed in more detail under "Series Reviews." At press time, only price and page-count ranges for the entire series were available. The series will be updated annually.

Post Guide: Australia
Hunter Publishing, 1987, 144 pages, paper, $8.95

This book is part of the Post Guide series, which is reviewed in more detail under "Series Reviews."

Shopping in the Exotic South Pacific: Your Passport to Exciting Australia, New Zealand, Papua New Guinea, Tonga, Fiji, Tahiti, and the Solomon Islands
by Ronald Krannich, *et al.*, Impact Publications, 1989, 450 pages, paper, $13.95

This is an anticipated addition to the superb Shopping in Exotic

Places series, which is reviewed in more detail under "Series Reviews." The series is updated every two years.

Sunset: Australia Travel Guide
Lane Publishing, 1987, 128 pages, paper, $9.95

Primarily an orientation book, this is part of the Sunset Travel Guide series, which is reviewed in more detail under "Series Reviews."

Sydney by Ferry & Foot
by John Gunter, ISBS, 1985, 160 pages, paper, $7.95

This is a compact, helpful touring guide to this popular Australian city.

The Traveler's Guide to Asian Customs and Manners
by Elizabeth Devine and Nancy Braganti, St. Martin's Press, 1986, 315 pages, paper, $9.95

This useful book includes Australia and is reviewed under "Asia as a Whole."

22 Days in Australia: The Itinerary Planner
by John Gottberg, John Muir Publications, 1987, 136 pages, paper, $5.95

This book is part of the Itinerary Planner series, which is reviewed in more detail under "Series Reviews." This title is based on the successful *Europe in 22 Days* (now also called *22 Days in Europe*). Note that the change in title is recent and that this book may also be found under *Australia in 22 Days*.

Webster's Wine Tours: Australia
Prentice Hall Press, 1988/89, 200 pages, cloth (flexible), $15.95

This is an anticipated addition to the Webster's Wine Tours series, which is reviewed in more detail under "Series Reviews." As it was released after press time, the price and number of pages are approximate.

Central America

CENTRAL AMERICA AS A WHOLE

Note that Mexico is not part of Central America and is listed separately under "North America." Books on Central America do not include Nicaragua unless so noted.

Fodor's Central America
Fodor's Travel Publications, 1987, 340 pages, paper, $14.95
This is solidly done title in Fodor's Country/Regional Guide series, which is reviewed in more detail under "Series Reviews."

Latin America on Bicycle
by J. P. Panet, Passport Press, 1987, 156 pages, paper, $12.95
This fine "plain-wrapper" guide from Passport Press contains good sections on what to take, planning your trip, bicycle necessities over the less developed terrain of Latin America, and survival and health tips while on the road. These are followed by detailed accounts of different bicycle journeys that include plenty of facts that you can incorporate into your own itinerary and other travel tips. Countries covered are: Costa Rica, Dominican Republic, Guatemala, Venezuela, Chile, and Argentina. Very helpful.

Nagel's Central America
Passport Books, 1980, 319 pages, cloth, $39.95
This classic, cultural guide is part of the Nagel's Guide series, which is reviewed in more detail under "Series Reviews." Note: This title includes Nicaragua.

South America On a Shoestring (including Mexico & Central America)
by Geoff Crowther, Lonely Planet Publications, 1986 (3rd ed.), 734 pages, paper, $14.95
   This is book is one of the On a Shoestring Guide series, which is reviewed in more detail under "Series Reviews." This series is updated every two to three years.

The South American Handbook (including Caribbean, Mexico and Central America)
edited by John Brooks, Rand McNally & Co., 1988 (64th ed.), 1341 pages, cloth, $28.95
   This definitive single-volume guide to South America includes Central America as well. It is reviewed under "South America as a Whole," and includes Nicaragua. This book is updated annually.

Staying Healthy in Asia, Africa, and Latin America
by Dirk Schroeder, Volunteers in Asia, 1988, 168 pages, paper, $7.95
   This excellent third world health guide is reviewed under "Africa as a Whole."

COUNTRIES OF CENTRAL AMERICA

BELIZE

See also "Central America as a Whole."

Belize Guide
by Paul Glassman, Passport Press, 1987, 104 pages, paper, $11.95
   This book is one of the excellent Passport Press Guide series which is reviewed in more detail under "Series Reviews."

Birnbaum's Caribbean, Bermuda, and the Bahamas
edited by Stephen Birnbaum, Houghton Mifflin, 1987, 786 pages, paper, $12.95
   Including Belize, this book is part of the excellent Birnbaum's Guide series which is reviewed in more detail under "Series Reviews." The series is updated annually.

The Collier World Traveler Series: Mexico, Belize, Guatemala, and the French Antilles
by Philippe Gloaguen and Pierre Josse, Macmillan Publishing, 1985, 192 pages, paper, $6.95
   This book is part of the Collier World Traveler Guide series, which is reviewed in more detail under "Series Reviews."

Frommer's Mexico on $20 a Day
by Tom Brosnahan, Prentice Hall Press, 1986, 504 pages, paper, $10.95

Including sections on Belize and Guatemala, this book is part of Frommer's Dollar-a-Day Guide series, which is reviewed in more detail under "Series Reviews." The series is updated every two years; the 1988 edition was not available at press time.

Maya Sites of the Yucatan
by Jacques and Parney Van Kirk, Great Outdoors Publishing, 1987, 78 pages, paper, $14.95

Including sites in Belize, this book is reviewed under "Mexico" (see "North America").

COSTA RICA

See also "Central America as a Whole."

Costa Rica
by Paul Glassman, Passport Press, 1988 (2nd ed.), 196 pages, paper, $12.95

This book is one of the excellent Passport Press Guide series, which is reviewed in more detail under "Series Reviews."

The Costa Rica Traveler: Getting Around in Costa Rica
by Ellen Searby, Windham Bay Press, 1988, 256 pages, paper, $11.95

The Costa Rica Traveler is a fine travel guide covering all the major attractions of Costa Rica—its parks, volcanoes, flora, fauna, and cultural life—and includes good sections on history, geography, and social conditions, as well as the more classic tourist details such as planning, transportation, hotels, restaurants, shopping, and much more. The practical information sections are particularly excellent. Hotel and restaurant selections are informatively described and cover the various price ranges available. Some handy charts on hotels help with comparisons where the choices are many. The foldout map including downtown San Jose and Costa Rica is rather primitive; so obtaining a more detailed map is advised.

The New Key to Costa Rica
by Beatrice Blake, Publications in English, 1987 (7th ed.), 209 pages, paper, $8.95

While all the guides to Costa Rica are quite excellent, this particular guide, published in Costa Rica, provides the most detail on history, parks, flora, fauna, and local fruits and vegetables. It also has a very helpful do-it-yourself tour-planning chapter which charts the attractions available in the various regions. In addition, there are good regional maps and a foldout map of San Jose and Costa Rica at the back. Hotel and restaurant choices are in all price ranges, with brief but informative notes. A special walking tour of San Jose is also included. The book is updated annually, but has no American distributor at present. Various travel bookstores may carry this book. We located it at Easy Going (see Travel Bookstore appendix).

El Salvador: See "Central America as a Whole."

GUATEMALA

See also "Central America as a Whole."

The Collier World Traveler Series: Mexico, Belize, Guatemala & the French Antilles
by Philippe Gloaguen and Pierre Josse, Macmillan Publishing, 1985, 192 pages, paper, $6.95
   This book is part of the Collier World Traveler Guide series, which is reviewed in more detail under "Series Reviews."

Guatemala Guide
by Paul Glassman, Passport Press, 1988 (2nd ed.), 367 pages, paper, $16.95
   The new edition of the 1977 classic has finally arrived and is as wonderful as ever. This guide is part of the excellent Passport Press Guide series which is reviewed in more detail under "Series Reviews."

A Guide to Ancient Maya Ruins
by C. Brune Hunter, University of Oklahoma Press, 1986 (2nd ed.), 342 pages, paper, $12.95
   Including numerous areas in Guatemala, this book is reviewed under "Mexico" (see North America).

Frommer's Mexico on $20 a Day
by Tom Brosnahan, Prentice Hall Press, 1986, 504 pages, paper, $10.95
   Including a section on Belize and Guatemala, this book is part of Frommer's Dollar-a-Day Guide series, which is reviewed in more detail under "Series Reviews." The series is updated every two years; the 1988 edition was not available at press time.

Maya Sites of the Yucatan

by Jacques and Parney Van Kirk, Great Outdoors Publishing, 1987, 78 pages, paper, $14.95

Including sites in Guatemala, this book is reviewed under "Mexico" (see "North America").

The World of Tikal, Guatemala

by Jacques Van Kirk, Parney Van Kirk and Patricia Solis, Great Outdoors Publishing, 1985, 98 pages, paper, $14.95

This is a large-format guide to the most famous of the Mayan ruins in northern Guatemala. A useful, bilingual guide (English-Spanish), this book provides a large, fold-out map and good descriptions of various sites, the various plants and animals you may see along the way, as well as a brief section on practical tourist information.

HONDURAS

See also "Central America as a Whole."

A Guide to Ancient Maya Ruins

by C. Bruce Hunter, University of Oklahoma Press, 1986 (2nd ed.), 342 pages, paper, $12.95

Includes some areas of Honduras. Reviewed under "Mexico" (see North America).

Nicaragua: See "Central America as a Whole."

PANAMA

See also "Central America as a Whole."

Frommer's South America on $30 a Day

by Arnold and Harriet Greenberg, Prentice Hall Press, 1987, 432 pages, paper, $10.95

This book is one of the budget-oriented Frommer's Dollar-a-Day Guide series, which is reviewed in more detail under "Series Reviews." The series is updated every two years; this title includes Panama.

Europe

EUROPE AS A WHOLE

See also "The World." Most books on Europe limit their focus to Western Europe; consequently, those titles that also include Eastern European countries have been specially noted.

AA Bed and Breakfast in Europe
by the Automobile Association, Salem House, 1988, 192 pages, paper, $12.95

The British AA crams information on nearly 7000 places to stay in 19 countries into this handy, up-to-date reference. Budget-priced lodging is emphasized throughout this annually updated book.

AA Camping and Caravaning in Europe
by the Automobile Association, Salem House, 1988, 428 pages, paper, $18.95

This AA guide covers nearly 4000 selected sites in 19 European countries. All locations are clearly marked on extensive maps. Essential tourist information, including how to write ahead for bookings is included. This title is updated annually.

AA Europe Lodging Guide
by the Automobile Association, Random House, 1988, 431 pages, paper, $18.95

This book contains over 8000 rated lodgings in 21 European countries. This book, produced by the British AA and brought to the U.S. by the American Automobile Association, includes location maps and route planning information. It is updated annually.

AA Europe Travel Guide
by the Automobile Association, Random House, 1988, 568 pages, paper, $8.95

This good planning book is filled with information on 31 European countries. Produced by the British AA and brought to the U.S. by the American Automobile Association, this book contains notes on history, culture, customs and currency regulations, transportation, climate, special events, the "must see" spots, and more. Information on Eastern European countries is also included in this annually updated title.

AA Touring Guide for the Disabled
by the Automobile Association, Salem House, 1988, 140 pages, paper, $7.95

Contained herein are numerous planned tours of Europe and Great Britain, including suggested accommodations and details on access and facilities in AA-inspected lodging. This title is updated annually.

ABC Air Europe, Middle East & North Africa
ABC International, monthly editions, 340 pages, paper, $10.00

This book of airline schedules is perfect for travelers making many airline connections and compelled to be their own travel agent.

Alan Rogers' Selected Sites for Caravanning and Camping in Europe
by Alan Rogers, Luso-Brazilian Books, 1987, 224 pages, paper, $7.95

This is the 20th annual edition of this self-published work. The 1988 edition is to be the last; Rogers plans to sell the rights and retire after that time. Meanwhile, this book offers excellent, hand-picked selection of the best sites in Europe. Descriptions are substantial and informative and include all the practical details including travel directions. Note: This is a British book so all prices are in pounds.

Apple's Europe: An Uncommon Guidebook
by R. W. Apple, Jr., Atheneum, 1986, 264 pages, paper, $8.95

One of the best travel books available anywhere, this book is full of superbly crafted, enjoyable essays that provide specific travel tips and suggestions. This is not a book to skim, it is rather a book to really read. Because Apple has lived primarily in Britain while working as a correspondent for the *New York Times*, there is a strong emphasis on travels in Britain; however, many other European countries, including Eastern European destinations in Hungary, Romania, and the Soviet Union are described.

Atlas of European Architecture
by Brian Sacher, Van Nostrand, 1984, 369 pages, cloth, $14.45

Information on 3500 structures in Europe built since 4700 B.C. is arranged in catalog form in this delightful guide for the "architecture-phile." Notes on each structure includes the year in which it was built, the architect (if known), its architectural significance, and its address, with maps to individual countries that note the location of each entry.

The Audi Ski Guide
Ocean Publications Ltd., 1987, 362 pages, paper, $22.95

This is the European ski "Bible" published by the *Daily Mail* of London in conjunction with Ocean Publications. A large, substantial book, it covers more than 250 resorts in 15 European countries, including Romania, Yugoslavia, Norway, Sweden, Bulgaria, Andorra, Greece, Liechtenstein, Spain, and Scotland, as well as the better-known ski countries of Europe. Contained in this comprehensive guide is a large map of the ski areas of many resorts, good descriptions, and some après-ski and hotel recommendations. However, at present this annually updated book has no American distributor. Check the Travel Bookstore appendix for stores that might carry it; it has previously been available through Book Passage.

Backroads of Southern Europe
by David Yeadon, Harper & Row, 1981, 256 pages, paper, $8.95

This beautifully prepared guide to the nooks and crannies of Southern Europe captures and conveys a feeling for both the places and the people of the rural countryside.

Baedeker's Rail Europe
Prentice Hall Press, 1988, 296 pages, paper, $15.95

This guide, focusing on rail service in the 18 most popular countries of Europe, is something new from Baedeker. Details on types of rail service, special fares, passes, discounts, and train and station facilities, as well as sightseeing information, are included for each country. A fold-out map of Europe's entire rail system is also provided. As it was due out after press time, the number of pages in this book is approximate.

Berlitz Business Travel Guide to Europe
Macmillan Publishing, 1981, 365 pages, paper, $6.95

For a small-format book, this one delivers an amazing amount of practical information on topics of importance to the fast-moving businessperson. It covers 31 countries of Western and Eastern Europe, including Albania, East Germany, Romania, and the Soviet Union. Unfortunately, the book is quite old; watch for a new edition.

Berlitz European Menu for Travellers
Macmillan Publishing, 1982, 192 pages, paper, $6.95

This is the traveler's best choice for a single language reference, as it covers 14 Western and Eastern European languages. It is certainly adequate for travelers wishing to visit restaurants in these countries.

Berlitz Pocket Guide: Cities of Europe
Macmillan Publishing, 1986, 504 pages, paper, $8.95
Berlitz Pocket Guide: Europe
Macmillan Publishing, 1986, 480 pages, paper, $8.95

These guides provide a quick rundown, in a convenient small format, of the rules, regulations, visas, local customs, medicine, attractions, and embassies in Europe. The Cities of Europe volume concentrates on the major European cities; the Europe volume covers 31 countries of Western and Eastern Europe.

The Best European Travel Tips
by John Whitman, Meadowbrook, 1986 (4th ed.), 213 pages, paper, $6.95

Probably the most popular of its kind, this book crammed with useful tips on every conceivable travel topic, including travel documents, itineraries, transportation, packing, and health considerations. Seasoned travelers will find some new ideas here; the occasional or first-time traveler will find this book invaluable.

Bicycle Touring in Europe
by Karen and Gary Hawkins, Pantheon, 1980, 346 pages, paper, $7.95

Despite its need for a revision, this comprehensive volume has a lot to say on planning, buying, and equipping a touring bicycle, and where and how to tour in the countries of Western Europe.

Biking Through Europe: A Roadside Travel Guide with 17 Planned Cycle Tours
by Dennis and Tina Jaffe, Williamson Publishing, 1987, 317 pages, paper, $13.95

This excellent, well-organized, and well-researched book clearly presents each suggested tour, the recommended maps, road numbers, route descriptions, and distances in an easy-to-follow format. Also provided is a good planning section, country-specific cycling information, sights, lodging suggestions, and information on picnic spots.

The Jaffes have drawn on their 13 years of experience in Europe to create this quality book.

Birnbaum's Europe
edited by Stephen Birnbaum, Houghton Mifflin, 1987, 1232 pages, paper, $13.95
    This book is part of the excellent Birnbaum's Guide series, which is reviewed in more detail under "Series Reviews." It includes all Eastern European countries except Albania and is updated annually.

Birnbaum's Europe for Business Travelers
edited by Stephen Birnbaum, Houghton Mifflin, 1987, 560 pages, paper, $7.95
    This guide is for travelers whose business takes them to the major European cities. Updated annually, this guide provides an amazing amount of vital business information, listings of hotels and restaurants in moderate-to-expensive price ranges, exercise options including fitness centers and jogging, sightseeing, entertainment, and nightlife. A good detail map is included as well. In all, 34 cities are covered, including the larger Western European cities as well as Moscow, Leningrad, Prague, Budapest, Warsaw, and East and West Berlin.

The Camper's Companion to Northern Europe
by Dennis and Tina Jaffe, Williamson Publishing, 1986, 303 pages, paper, $13.95
The Camper's Companion to Southern Europe
by Dennis and Tina Jaffe, Williamson Publishing, 1986, 287 pages, paper, $13.95
    The authors of the excellent *Biking Through Europe* have written two equally high-quality guides for campers. Each has a good section on practical considerations for camping in Europe, followed by chapters on each country. Chapters include general information, helpful travel notes, and information on selected campsites. The northern guide covers Austria, Belgium, Denmark, Finland, Northern France, East and West Germany, Great Britain, Ireland, Luxembourg, the Netherlands, Norway, Sweden, and Switzerland. The southern guide covers Andorra, Bulgaria, Czechoslovakia, Southern France, Greece, Hungary, Italy, Morocco, Poland, Portugal, Romania, Spain, Tunisia, Turkey, and Yugoslavia.

The Catholic Shrines of Europe
by Gerald Sherry, Our Sunday Visitor Publishing, 1986, 119 pages, paper, $5.95
    The history and importance to Catholicism of Walsingham, Can-

terbury, Glastonbury, Santiago de Compostela, Zaragoza (Our Lady of the Pillar), Lourdes, Paris (Miraculous Medal Shrine), Fatima, Czestochowa, and Einsiedeln are all discussed in this helpful guide. Following the text is a meditation appropriate to the lessons pilgrims to these sites might learn.

Classic Walks in Europe
by Walt Unsworth, Haynes Publications, 1987, 144 pages, cloth, $23.95
This book is part of the Classic Walk Guide series, which is reviewed in more detail under "Series Reviews."

The Collier World Traveler Series: Northern and Central Europe
edited by Philippe Gloaguen and Pierre Josse, Macmillan Publishing, 1985, 192 pages, paper, $6.95
This book is part of the Collier World Traveler Guide series, which is reviewed in more detail under "Series Reviews." The countries covered are Holland, Denmark, Sweden, Norway, Finland and West Germany.

The Complete Guide for Motorcycle Travelers
by Erik Sandberg, Viking Productions, 1986, 222 pages, paper, $6.95
Described under "General Travel Books," this travel guide also includes a large section on motorcycling in Europe. A new edition, totalling over 300 pages, is expected out in 1989.

The Condo Lux Vacationer's Guide to Condominium Rentals in the Mountain Resorts
by Jill Little, Random House, 1986, 340 pages, paper, $9.95
This book is part of the Condo Lux Guide series, which is reviewed in more detail under "Series Reviews."

Country Inns and Back Roads: Continental Europe
by Norman Simpson, Harper & Row, 1987, 439 pages, paper, $10.95
This well-known, enjoyably written guide is part of a three-volume series, Country Inns and Back Roads, which is reviewed in more detail under "Series Reviews." It covers Austria, Denmark, France, Germany, Hungary, Italy, Norway, Portugal, Spain, Sweden, and Switzerland and is updated annually.

Cycling in Europe
by Nathaniel Crane, Haynes Publications, 1984, 324 pages, paper, $13.95
    This popular, well-researched guide covers all the bases on cycling in Europe. Topics include best routes, best mountain crossings, where to stay, and how to deal with myriad potential problems. This British book, widely praised by British reviewers when it first came out, is now beginning to age a bit on some of the time-dated material. Nonetheless, it is an excellent, useful book.

Eating Out: A Guide to European Dishes
by Sally Major, Grastorf & Lang, 1981, 87 pages, cloth, $7.95
    This sturdy, hardbound book is thin enough to slide into purse or pocket, yet covers nearly 3000 food-related terms and dishes in an A-to-Z format. Information focuses on the following countries: Austria, Belgium, France, Germany, Greece, Hungary, Italy, Luxembourg, Portugal, Spain, Switerland, and Turkey.

Egon Ronay's Guide to 500 Good Restaurants in the Major Cities of Europe
Salem House, 1987, 400 pages, paper, $18.95
    Using a concise description and rating system, Britain's Egon Ronay's team's work proves a worthwhile resource. Restaurants in all price categories are covered.

Eurail Guide: How to Travel Europe and All the World by Train
by Kathryn Turpin and Marvin Saltzman, Eurail Guide Annual, 1988 (18th ed.), 816 pages, paper, $12.95
    This first-class, annual guide actually covers a great deal more than the Eurail system and the railroads of eastern Europe. It is reviewed more fully under "The World."

Europe by Bike: 18 Tours Geared for Discovery
by Karen and Terry Whitehill, The Mountaineers, 1987, 248 pages, paper, $10.95
    This quality guide provides good planning notes, plenty of information on each country, good descriptions, distances, maps, and what not to miss along the way. The text is enjoyably written and considerably detailed.

Europe by Eurail: How to Tour Europe by Train
by George and LaVerne Ferguson, The Globe Pequot Press, 1988 (13th ed.), 640 pages, paper, $11.95
    This excellent, well-written, annual volume combines the economy of the Eurailpass with the Ferguson's time-tested "Base City-

Day Excursion" method of touring Europe. Combined with the recommended Thomas Cook European Timetable (reviewed separately),
Europe by Eurail details how to get the most out of a Eurailpass
adventure. This title is updated every two years.

Europe by Rail

by Eberhard Fohrer, Riverdale Co., 1985 (3rd ed.), 634 pages, paper,
$12.95

Translated from the German, this fine guidebook is for those
exploring Europe on a limited budget. It includes the best towns to
stop in, tips for an inexpensive night's rest (including youth hostels,
student hotels, cheap pensions, and camping areas), cheap restaurants and cafes, fun nightlife spots, the neatest rail lines to try, and
reams of facts on discounts, health, bike rentals, buses, hiking, and
important addresses. Composed and researched with typical German
thoroughness, this is an excellent helping hand for those on a
shoestring budget. Eastern European countries included are Hungary
and Romania.

Europe by Train: The Insider's Guide to Budget Train Travel

by Katie Wood and George McDonald, E. P. Dutton, 1987, 448
pages, paper, $11.95

A truly budget guide to British and continental European train
travel, this book includes information on how to cut train travel
costs as well as where to stay and eat inexpensively along the way.
It also contributes useful sightseeing and train station information.

Europe for Free

by Brian Butler, Mustang Publishing, 1987, 389 pages, paper, $9.95

Here is a great idea book with literally thousands of things to do
all over Europe that won't cost "one single pfennig, franc or lira."
Travelers on a shoestring budget will find ideas on exhibits, brewery
tours, rose gardens, museums, botanical gardens, and many other
activities particularly helpful.

Europe for One: A Complete Guide for Solo Travelers

by Neil Chesanow, E. P. Dutton, 1982, 362 pages, paper, $8.25

Chesanow extends a helping hand to the person traveling alone
by discussing many of the unique problems of the solo traveler, such
as how to meet others and how to make dining alone a pleasure.
This book is thoughtfully done and useful to travelers venturing
forth without a traveling partner.

Europe Free! The Car, Van & RV Travel Guide
by David Shore and Patty Campbell, Shore-Campbell
Publications,1987, 96 pages, paper, $5.95
   This annually updated, self-published guide is a helpful tool for
those who buy, lease, or rent a vehicle in order to travel in Europe—
particularly a van or RV. The authors draw on their experience to
give good suggestions on what to take along, selecting "sleepsites,"
food shopping and cooking in Europe, and RV security.

Europe in 22 Days
See *22 Days in Europe* below.

Europe Off the Wall
by Kristan Lawson and Anneli Rufus, John Wiley & Sons, 1988,
314 pages, paper, $10.95
   This unusual new guide, released after press time, describes "many
of the most unique, bizarre, and entertaining attractions in Europe."

Europe 101: History and Art for the Traveler
by Rick Steves and Gene Openshaw, John Muir Publications, 1987
(revised ed.), 368 pages, paper, $11.95
   Thorough yet concise, *Europe 101* is a frequently humorous book
covering an incredible amount of history and art (a.k.a. culture) in
an enjoyable and marvelously digestable form. This is a real classic;
don't miss it.

Europe Through the Back Door
by Rick Steves, John Muir Publications, 1988 (8th ed.), 384 pages,
paper, $12.95
   This popular, annually updated guidebook is fast becoming a classic for the adventurous, independent, budget-oriented traveler. Dealing with myriad day-to-day travel strategies necessary for staying
within a budget, this book provides helpful chapters on planning,
transportation, budgeting (including eating and sleeping cheaply),
money, dealing with language barriers, health, and the single woman
traveler. Also included is plenty of information on where to go and
what to see. Some information on Bulgaria and Moscow is included.

Europe: Where the Fun Is
by Bruce Jacobsen and Rollin Riggs, Mustang Publishing, 1987, 172
pages, paper, $8.95
   This book is strictly a supplement to standard travel guides—it is
a guide to where the action is in all the major cities of Europe. It
leads travelers to "the wildest bars, the hottest beaches, the most

fun restaurants, cheapest flea markets, and the most romantic cafes" all over Europe.

European Country Cuisine: Romantic Inns and Recipes
Travel Press, 1987, 263 pages, paper, $10.95

For those who like to choose their inns by their recipes, the creators of the wonderful Karen Brown's Country Inns series have pooled their information from their various other titles, added the best of the recipes these inns have provided, and arranged them into a format that allows a one-page write-up on each inn with a line drawing and recipe. The inns selected number more than 100 and are found in 18 European countries.

European Country Inns: Best on a Budget
Travel Press, 1988, 370 pages, paper, $12.95

New for 1988 from Travel Press is a collection of the most budget-oriented inns of the many other titles of the Karen Brown's Country Inns series, which is reviewed in more detail under "Series Reviews." Inns selected cover 18 European countries.

Europe's Wonderful Little Hotels and Inns
by Hilary Rubinstein, St. Martin's Press, 1988, 900 pages, paper, $17.95

A most enjoyable, annually updated guide of over 1200 small hotels and inns in 21 European countries (including Great Britain). Each selection is carefully reviewed each year; inns must measure up to remain a part of this popular guide. The guide depends as well on feedback from travelers who stay in each inn. The result is an excellent, up-to-date list of charming, comfortable places full of the authentic atmosphere of Europe. No fees are charged, nor "freebies" accepted for inclusion.

Fielding's Discover Europe Off the Beaten Path
by Margaret Zellers, William Morrow & Co., 1987, 511 pages, paper, $12.95

Zellers, one of the truly excellent travel writers today, explores the quaint places generally missed by tourists in major cities, villages and rural areas of 23 European countries. This annually updated guide is an excellent resource for probing the nooks and crannies of Europe.

Fielding's Economy Europe
by Joseph and Judith Raff, William Morrow & Co., 1987, 592 pages, paper, $9.95

In this budget guide to 18 European countries, the Raffs first discuss all the essentials from planning and transportation to tipping and student travel, then cover each country in separate sections. Within each of these sections are tips specific to that country, where to go, and fairly brief but informative notes on lodging, restaurants, sightseeing, and shopping. However, it is important to note that each section concentrates on only one or two major cities with much briefer notes on other towns. This is a solid effort filled with lots of useful information that is updated annually.

Fielding's Europe
by Joseph Raff, William Morrow & Co., 1987, 846 pages, paper, $12.95

This book is part of the Fielding's Travel Guide series, which is reviewed in more detail under "Series Reviews." The series is updated annually.

Fielding's Europe with Children
by Leila Hadley, William Morrow & Co., 1984, 384 pages, paper, $12.95

In this excellent guide for parents visiting Europe with the kids, Hadley gives lots of ideas on how to find places for family fun, things the children can do on their own, and all sorts of other practicalities.

Fielding's Motoring and Camping Europe
by Patricia and Robert Foulke, William Morrow & Co., 1986, 240 pages, paper, $8.95

The authors of this useful guide for motorists and campers have designed eight different routes, each requiring from nine to 22 days to travel. Each route interlinks with others to give maximum flexibility in trip organization. Camping opportunities, suggested activities, and other useful tips are discussed.

Fielding's Select Shopping Guide to Europe
by Joseph and Judith Raff, William Morrow & Co., 1988, 329 pages, paper, $8.95

Presented in this annually updated guide are more than 1400 of the best shops and markets in 17 European countries. Information on shopping by mail is also included.

Fisher's World: Europe
by Edmund Antrobus, *et al.*, Fisher's World, Inc., 1988, 798 pages, paper, $17.95

This book is part of the Fisher's World Guide series, which is reviewed in more detail under "Series Reviews." The series is updated annually.

Fly/Ride Europe

Consumer Reports Books, 1987, 295 pages, paper, $13.00

The British Consumers Union has made a reputation for giving honest, clear assessments of value in products of every kind. In this book, distributed by its American counterpart, the BCU analyzes "how to get the best transportation values to and around Europe." Note that they include travel within Europe, not just getting there. This book is revised annually so the facts will always be as up-to-date as possible.

Fodor's Budget Europe

Fodor's Travel Publications, 1988, 592 pages, paper, $12.95

This book is part of Fodor's Great Travel Values series, which is reviewed in more detail under "Series Reviews." The only volume in the series to retain the older "budget" title, this book includes all the Eastern European countries, except Albania and the Soviet Union. Fodor publishes a separate volume on the Soviet Union and covers Albania in *Fodor's Europe*. The series is updated annually.

Fodor's Europe

Fodor's Travel Publications, 1988, 816 pages, paper, $14.95

This book is part of Fodor's Country/Regional Guide series, which is reviewed in more detail under "Series Reviews." This annually updated title covers all Eastern European countries except the Soviet Union, for which there is a separate volume.

Fodor's Selected Hotels of Europe

Fodor's Travel Publications, 1987, 372 pages, paper, $14.95

In this book Fodor's covers 500 hotels and lodgings of every sort (inns, converted castles and abbeys, stately homes) in 17 Western European countries and does so in depth. The write-ups are both informative and interesting; the hotels selected cover all price ranges, and include all the necessary practical data.

Frommer's Dollarwise Guide to Skiing in Europe: The Top Resorts in Austria, France, Italy, and Switzerland

by Catherine and Peter Foreht, Prentice Hall Press, 1986, 276 pages, paper, $12.95

This solid guide to skiing options among all the recognized resorts of Europe's Alps addresses every category important to the skier: where to stay, where to eat, the skiing options, après ski activities, and important services. As the guide is updated every two years, the 1988 edition was unavailable before press time.

Frommer's Europe on $30 a Day

by Arthur Frommer, Prentice Hall Press, 1988 (31st ed.), 782 pages, paper, $13.95

This book, while part of the Dollar-a-Day series, is structured differently and deserves a separate description and review. It is definitely a budget guide; the goal is to keep costs to $30 per person per day. Given the wild fluctuations of the dollar, that may or may not be possible. The book focuses only on major European cities, 21 in all, rather than on individual countries. A good planning/general tips section is followed by chapters on each of these cities that include general information, hotels, restaurants, sightseeing, nightlife, etc. By limiting the scope of the book in this way, the authors can devote more space to the cities covered. Discussions of hotels and restaurants are extensive and very informative. Additional comments submitted by travelers are sprinkled throughout and a separate section, "A Tale of Many Cities," is made up solely of quotes from readers with suggestions and recommendations on many other cities as well as those covered. The book is updated annually.

Getting High in Europe

by Bernard Winn, Incline Press, 1985, 150 pages, paper, $6.95

This fun little book describes 328 "high places" in 218 Western European cities which provide the best views of the landscape or city below.

The Good Skiing Guide

Consumer Reports Books, 1987, 608 pages, paper, $12.00

This guide provides well-written critical assessments of over 200 resorts throughout Europe. Bulgaria and Romania are included. Update annually.

Great European Itineraries

by Michael Spring, Doubleday & Co., 1987, 420 pages, paper, $9.95

This book is designed to show travelers "how to make do with a little money and spoil yourself with a lot." Day-to-day planned trips include information on hotels and restaurant selections in every price range. Additional notes on art, architecture, sightseeing, trips to do with the kids, and general travel information in each country are provided.

A Guide to Central Europe
by Richard Bassett, Viking Penguin, 1987, 244 pages, cloth, $19.95

This superb book is the only one to treat Central Europe as a distinct entity. Special emphasis is given to Vienna, Budapest, Eastern Hungary, Transylvania, Western Hungary, Prague, Bohemia, Moravia, Slovakia, Carlsbad, and Trieste. The book is written in narrative form and contains dozens of practical pearls, including hotels, food, special nooks and crannies, and neglected places where time has moved more slowly. A good index completes this helpful and beautifully written book.

A Guide to Christian Europe
by C. J. McNaspy, S.J., Loyola University Press, 1984, 280 pages, cloth, $9.95

This thoughtfully prepared book deals strictly with the cities, shrines, cathedrals, and art most important to the Christian traveler. Each country is given a succinct, yet carefully written overview. Included are the following Eastern European destinations: Moscow, Czestochowa, Budapest, Bucharest, and Prague.

Guide to Jewish Europe: Western Europe Edition
by Asher Israelowitz, Talman Co., 1987, 230 pages, paper, $9.95

An up-to-date guide to monuments, synagogues, youth hostels and other lodging, kosher restaurants, bakeries, and other Jewish establishments in Western Europe.

Guide to the Recommended Castle & Palace Hotels of Europe
by Pamela Barrus, The Globe Pequot Press, 1988, 300 pages, paper, $12.95

This well-written guide makes delightful reading for the armchair traveler as well as the traveler on the go. Barrus, a veteran traveler, has visited more than 100 countries in her journeys. This kind of experience lends credence to her selection of the 120 grand lodging opportunities included here. Descriptions are detailed and contain all the practical data; some inexpensive.selections are included as well. This is a new title for Globe Pequot and it will probably adhere to their general revision policy of every 18-24 months plus minor updates with each printing.

Hiking and Walking Guide to Europe
by Arthur Howcroft and Richard Sale, Passport Books, 1984, 137 pages, paper, $7.95

This is a good planning guide for travelers interested in Europe's long-distance footpaths and other hiking trails. Rather than the details of each hike, it offers an overview of each country, the best areas to consider for walks, climate considerations, the maps available, and the addresses needed to obtain maps, hiking details, and other tourist information. Information is included for the British Isles; somewhat limited information is included for Eastern Europe.

The Hitchhiker's Guide to Europe
by Ken Walsh, Grove Press, 1986, 412 pages, paper, $7.95

This guide is frequently updated and has been widely used since the early 1970s. Whether hitchhiking or just struggling with a hitchhiker-sized budget, travelers will find this guide a gold mine. The first 82 pages offer a wide array of advice on how to hitch, what to take, and how to survive. This is followed by an enjoyably written text on each European country that includes where to eat and sleep and what to see and do on a shoestring. Final chapters cover working in Europe, photography, and a useful language compendium.

How to Camp Europe By Train
by Lenore Baken, Ariel Publications, 1988 (5th ed.), 378 pages, paper, $12.95

Grab a small tent and a backpack, hop a train, and let this guide do the rest. This is an ultra-budget traveler's rail and camping guide all in one. It's chock full of facts about all sorts of things: walking tours, hikes, sightseeing, food options (including the nearest market), even the local laundromat's location. And it includes plenty of suggestions from reader's letters. The hand-drawn maps are very well done. Baken's quality guide will prove a great aid for travelers looking to take a trip on a shoestring without all the headaches. Hungary is the one Eastern European destination included.

How to Europe: The Complete Travelers Handbook
by John Bermont, Murphy and Broad, 1988 (2nd ed.), 502 pages, paper, $9.95

This useful compendium of travel tips is arranged by subject rather than country and addresses "those practical questions that many guides overlook—riding the trains, plugging in an electric shaver, making a phone call..."

Ian Keown's European Hideaways
by Ian Keown, Crown Publishers, 1980, 416 pages, paper, $7.95

This guide was not going to be included, because of age, when its Caribbean counterpart appeared on the scene in a new, 1988 edition. This welcome event raises hopes that Keown's European guidebook will also be revised. At present, it is too old to be of much help, although it once was a very popular guide to more than 150 romantic hideaways rated for their food, facilities, and romantic ambiance. If a new guide is released, its price will be approximately $12.95.

Insight Guide: Continental Europe
by Apa Productions, Prentice Hall Press, 1985, 388 pages, paper, $15.95

This book is part of the excellent Insight Guide series, which is reviewed in more detail under "Series Reviews."

The Insult Dictionary: How to Give 'Em Hell in Five Different Languages
Passport Books, 1988 (2nd ed.), 128 pages, paper, $4.95

This is the book for travelers who have been in situations in which they wished they could chew someone out but didn't know the right words. The five languages are: French, German, Italian, Spanish, and English.

International Herald Tribune Guide to Business Travel and Entertainment in Europe
by Peter Graham, Henry Holt & Co., 1984, 224 pages, paper, $9.95

Inspired by the many questions asked by business travelers, the foremost international English-language newspaper has written excellent overviews of major European cities—the pleasures and problems of each business center, essential facts on airport transportation, buses, subways, money, and much more. In addition, selected lists of accommodations, restaurants, entertainment, and shopping, as well as good ideas for spending the weekends off the beaten path, are included. Useful annotated maps are provided, but note the publication date.

Keep One Suitcase Empty: The Bargain Shopper's Guide to the Finest Factory Outlets in Europe
by Judith McQuown, Arbor House, 1987, 323 pages, paper, $8.95

This companion to McQuown's similarly titled volume is reviewed under "Great Britain."

Let's Go: Europe
by Harvard Student Agencies, St. Martin's Press, 1988, 896 pages, paper, $11.95

This book is part of the excellent, budget-oriented Let's Go Guide series, which is reviewed in more detail under "Series Reviews." The Europe volume covers 31 countries in all, including Egypt, Israel, Jordan, Morocco, Tunisia, Turkey, and the Soviet Union. The Eastern European countries, except Albania, are covered as well. The series is updated annually.

The Liberated Traveller's Guide to Europe
by Alan and Phyllis Kingery, Chicago Review, 1985, 319 pages, paper, $9.95
The lengthy sub-title says a lot about the emphasis of this excellent guidebook: "How to See Europe Intelligently, Independently, Inexpensively—the Way Europeans Do." The last revision was written at the time of the strong U.S. dollar; unfortunately, times have changed. Nonetheless, the author's in-depth look at strategies on every important travel issue will help travelers structure the best possible vacation within their allotted budgets. Intelligently written for the intelligent traveler, this is an excellent planning tool.

The Lover's Dictionary: How to Be Amorous in Five Delectable Languages
Passport Books, 1988, 128 pages, paper, $4.95
This book details how to address mysterious strangers on enchanted evenings in French, Spanish, Italian, German, and English.

Manston's Travel Key Europe
by Peter Manston, Travel Keys Books, 1987, 428 pages, paper, $9.95
A favorite "guide to the practical" for European travel, this near classic details it all: how to use any type of phone in any country (including Eastern Europe), what all those confusing noises on the phone mean, what supplies are needed for doing laundry, opening and closing times to expect at banks, shops, and government offices in each country, security, public transportation, using a car, location of the local library, flea market and street market times, and almost everything else under the sun. This is a great book to have along, and all of the countries of Eastern Europe are included.

Mennonite Tourguide to Western Europe
by Jan Gleysteen, Herald Press, 1984, 340 pages, paper, $17.95
A very well written guide, emphasizing those parts of Europe of particular relevance to Mennonite history, but also filled with good planning notes, walking tours, well-drawn maps of principal cities, and a considerable amount of general commentary and interesting historical notes. All information pertaining to the Anabaptist-Mennonite movement is clearly marked. Countries covered are Austria, Belgium, France, Germany, Holland, Italy, Liechtenstein, Luxembourg, and Switzerland.

Mermaids of Chenonceaux and 828 Other Stories: An Anecdotal Guide to Europe

by Phyllis Méras, Congdon & Weed, 1984, 322 pages, paper, $12.95

Instead of typical travel information, this guide contains interesting, sometimes amusing anecdotes—literary, historical, musical, artistic and legendary—that will evoke a new feeling for hundreds of cities and villages throughout Europe.

Michelin Red Guide: Main Cities—Europe

Michelin Guides and Maps, 1988, 448 pages, cloth (flexible), $16.95

A hotel and restaurant guide, this is the only guide in the Michelin Red Guide series that is written in English. This annually updated series is reviewed in more detail under "Series Reviews."

Mona Winks: A Guide to Enjoying Europe's Top Museums

by Rick Steves and Gene Openshaw, John Muir Publications, 1988, 300 pages, paper, $11.95

It seems only fitting that John Muir Publications, publisher of the classic VW repair manual "for the compleat idiot," should release a museum guide of the same ilk. This is the guide for those who "haven't studied art history and don't speak French," the poor wandering visitor who spends so long in the Louvre trying to find Mona that he or she can hardly make it back to the hotel. This book contains Steves' and Openshaw's cure for ignorance: 90-minute, intelligently planned tours of the most interesting of Europe's museums, castles, and palaces. Included are instructions on how to get there, hours, costs, and floor plans.

Motorcycle Touring in Europe

by Roger Hicks, William Collins Sons, 1985, 318 pages, paper, $10.95

This motorcyclist's guide to travel through Europe covers topics ranging from suggested routes, information on the mechanical requirements of motorcycle travel, places to stay and eat along the way, and some basic vocabulary for each country visited. Collins is an English publisher and, at present, there is no American distributor for this book, although it is commonly found in travel bookstores, including Travel Market (see Travel Bookstores appendix).

Music Lover's Europe: Guidebook and Companion

by Kenneth Bernstein, Charles Scribner's Sons, 1983, 202 pages, cloth, $12.95

This book covers the major festivals, concert halls, and museums of 24 European countries and includes sightseeing information on numerous composers. It explores both the famous and the offbeat and is a useful companion for the music lover, in spite of the clear need for an update. Included are Eastern European festivals in Bulgaria, Czechoslovakia, Hungary, Poland, and the Soviet Union.

Nino LoBello's Guide to Offbeat Europe
by Nino LoBello, Chicago Review Press, 1985, 203 pages, paper, $8.95

Here is an exciting and fascinating array of the fun, the unusual, and the unique—talking windmills, a clean tour of the Brighton sewers, a smuggler's museum, a street car that serves wine. This is a great book for every traveler to take along. Included Eastern European countries are Czechoslovakia, East Germany, Hungary, Poland, and the Soviet Union.

The Ocean Ferryliners of Europe—Southern Seas
by Michael and Laura Murphy, Hippocrene Books, 1986, 260 pages, paper, $12.95

The Ocean Ferryliners of Europe—Northern Seas
by Michael and Laura Murphy, Hippocrene Books, 1986, 260 pages, paper, $12.95

These two books are chock-full of information about the hundreds of ferry liners available to the traveler. Plenty of addresses and telephone and telex numbers for the individual ferry lines or their agents are included, so travelers can get the most up-to-date details ahead of time.

132 Unusual Museums in Europe That Most People Don't Know About
Traveler's Library, 1987, 27 pages, paper, $5.00

The knowledgable people who publish the exclusive travel newsletter, *Passport*, have gathered together an interesting little booklet of fascinating places to include on a European journey. A descriptive paragraph is devoted to each of these strange, exotic, or simply obscure museums.

The Palace Under the Alps
by William Bryson, St. Martin's Press, 1985, 256 pages, cloth, $16.95

This is an entertaining guide to over 200 spots throughout Europe that tourists usually miss. This book covers the gamut from interesting and intriguing sightseeing options, including off-beat villages and unusual museums, to resorts with special places for children.

Passport to Europe's Small Hotels and Inns

by Beverly Beyer, John Wiley & Sons, 1988 (27th ed.), 253 pages, paper, $6.95

An excellent selection of cozy, small hotels, castles, country inns, and other charming lodging is contained in this guide, which been updated and expanded since 1960. This small-format book covers 850 selected places in 23 countries and avoids all those symbols and tiny print. Eastern European countries included are Czechoslovakia, Hungary, and the Soviet Union. The book is updated annually.

Patty's On-the-Road Gourmet

by Patty Campbell, Shore-Campbell Publications, 1986, 64 pages, paper, $5.95

This is a companion volume to *Europe Free! The Car, Van & RV Travel Guide*. Providing invaluable practical recipes for van and RV preparation, this little booklet lists food shopping and cooking tips specific to England, France, Germany, Greece, Holland, Italy, Scandinavia, Spain, and Yugoslavia.

The Penguin Guide to Medieval Europe

by Richard Barber, Viking Penguin, 1984, 379 pages, paper, $11.95

A very comprehensive work, this book explores the medieval world by surveying its surviving images—both monuments well-known to the tourist and those rarely visited. Organized thematically rather than geographically, this book makes an excellent companion to a primary travel guide and provides insight into the medieval culture that produced so many of these sights.

Pilgrimages: A Guide to the Holy Places of Europe for Today's Traveler

by Paul Higgins, Prentice Hall Press, 1984, 146 pages, paper, $7.95

This compact guide to selected places of religious interest throughout Europe contains history and the necessary touring information—including how to reach each location and some comments, perhaps dated, on where to stay upon arrival.

RAC Continental Hotel Guide

Sheridan House, 1988, 300 pages, paper, $13.95

This is the Royal Automobile Club's official hotel guide to the European continent (a separate guide is published for Great Britain and Ireland). Like the guides of automobile clubs everywhere, this is a compilation of more than 2000 places meeting the club's standards. Each is given short, descriptive comments about amenities and the general orientation of the hotel or inn. Particularly helpful is information on whether or not English is spoken and prices, phone numbers, and other specifics. Areas are keyed to maps at the back of the book. Nothing exotic or fancy here, but it covers a lot of ground. Included are the countries of Western Europe, Yugoslavia, and Turkey.

Romantik Hotels and Restaurants: Charming Historic Hotels in Europe and the United States
edited by the Romantik Hotel and Restaurant Association, The Harvard Common Press, 1988, 290 pages, paper, $6.95
    In order for a hotel to be affiliated with the Romantik Hotel and Restaurant Association it must meet high and uniform standards— it must be located in an historic building, be under the personal management of the owner, and have first-class food, friendly service, and a pleasant and comfortable atmosphere. Over 150 hotels in Europe and the U.S. meet these criteria and are described in this book. Also included are itineraries for each country, detailed maps to each hotel, and color photos on every page.

The Senior Citizen's Guide to Budget Travel in Europe
by Paige Palmer, Pilot Books, 1985, 48 pages, paper, $3.95
    Useful for seniors planning a trip, this booklet contains lots of good tips and planning advice, as well as a list of 250 budget-priced hotels and inns in the major European tourist areas.

Ski Europe: A Comprehensive Guide to Skiing Europe's Best Resorts
by Charles Leocha and William Walker, World Leisure Corp., 1987, 384 pages, paper, $11.95
    In order to help traveling skiers get the best value for their dollar, this book provides all manner of information on mountain ratings, lift ticket and ski school prices, child care, and brief notes on hotels and restaurants. Included are many of the resorts of Austria, France, Italy, Germany, Spain, Switzerland, and Yugoslavia. The Eastern European country of Bulgaria is included as well.

The Sophisticated Traveler: Beloved Cities of Europe
Viking Penguin, 1985, 469 pages, paper, $8.95
    This book is part of the wonderful travel essay series, Sophisticated Traveler Guides, from the correspondents of the *New York Times*. This series is reviewed in more detail under "Series Reviews."

Sunset: Discovery Trips in Europe
Lane Publishing, 1980, 144 pages, paper, $7.95
    Despite the age of this text, it is still a helpful planning and idea book that suggests 60 self-guided tours emphasizing smaller, less

crowded tourist areas. The crowds may be larger now, but there is plenty of food for thought.

Thomas Cook European Timetable

Timetable Publishing, 1988 (monthly editions), paper, $16.95

Because a new timetable is published every month, this is the finest single-volume source of up-to-the-minute railroad timetables throughout all of Europe and Great Britain. It is an essential companion to any rail guidebook and even includes a summer supplement in anticipation of warm weather changes. Published in England, it is imported by Forsyth Travel Library (see the Travel Bookstore appendix). Many travel bookstores stock the timetable as well, although not necessarily every monthly edition. Stores in the largest cities, including Travel Books Unlimited, are most likely to carry every edition. In addition, Timetable Publishing puts out a timetable for the rest of the world called the *Thomas Cook Overseas Timetable* (see "The World"). However, if traveling exclusively in Great Britain, try the monthly *ABC Rail Guide* described under "Great Britain" instead.

Touring Guide to Europe

edited by Richard Quilter, Henry Holt & Co., 1985, 463 pages, paper, $10.95

This thorough guidebook, published in conjunction with the Youth Hostels Association, has a decidedly budget orientation. The focus is on history, culture, and customs in the form of numerous tours, walking and otherwise, through the most interesting sections of 21 countries. This is not a guide to lodging and restaurants. There are some general thoughts on types of foods to try in each country and other practical points, but the emphasis is on planned, interesting itineraries and on that point they excel. Lodging is assumed to be the local youth hostel or other cheap accommodations that are listed in other publications.

Tramping Through Europe: A Walking Guide

by J. Sydney Jones, Prentice Hall Press, 1984, 231 pages, paper, $7.95

This practical, comprehensive guide for the walker in Europe features both long and short jaunts through the countryside, the necessary practical information, and suggested maps. This guide is well researched and clearly presented, and thoroughly covers all the bases.

Traveler's Guide to European Customs and Manners
by Nancy Braganti and Elizabeth Devine, Meadowbrook, 1984, 273
pages, paper, $6.95
This guide to how it's done in different European countries (including most of Eastern Europe) will teach the interested traveler
each country's "rules" on manners, conversation, tipping, bargain-
ing, dress, doing business, and more. It is a handy summary designed
to help travelers avoid headaches and prevent faux pas.

Traveler's Guide to Jewish Landmarks in Europe
by Bernard Postal and Samuel Abramson, Fleet Press, 1971, 335
pages, paper, $11.95
Covering a large number of Jewish landmarks throughout Eastern
and Western Europe, this guide, arranged by city, provides information about a diverse array of shrines, synagogues, parks, memorials,
birthplaces, and cemeteries. The book is old, but still a useful resource.

Traveler's Guide to the Great Art Treasures of Europe
by David Morton, G. K. Hall & Co., 1987, 562 pages, paper, $12.95
Focusing on the best of Europe's sculpture, painting, and architecture, this well-written book is designed to help travelers remember
what they learned in school as they stand before a great work of art.
Detailed explanations of the history behind and the significance of
each work of art make this an incredibly comprehensive and thoroughly fascinating single-volume work. The book contains no photographs, however, as it is a companion guide to works that must
be experienced first-hand. This book is also available in a hardbound
version for $45.00.

Turn Right at the Fountain
by George Oakes and Alexandra Chapman, Henry Holt & Co.,
1981 (4th ed.), 352 pages, paper, $9.95
This travel book classic and the most famous guidebook on walking tours anywhere was most recently updated by Alexandra Chapman after Oakes's death. Providing travelers the chance to discover
the feel of different major European cities through thoughtfully arranged walks, each with explicit directions keyed to simple maps,
this guide also contains concise descriptions of the sights and interesting historical notes.

22 Days in Europe: The Itinerary Planner
by Rick Steves, John Muir Publications, 1987 (revised ed.), 144
pages, paper, $5.95
This three-week itinerary for a European holiday is part of a new

series of Itinerary Planners, which is reviewed in more detail under "Series Reviews." Note that the title is a new one and copies with the old title of *Europe in 22 Days* will be on the bookstore shelf for some time to come.

Walking Europe From Top to Bottom: A Sierra Club Travel Guide to the Grande Randonnée Cinq

by Susan Margolis and Ginger Harmon, Sierra Club Books, 1986, 276 pages, paper, $10.95

This book plots a 107-day journey through the Netherlands, Belgium, Luxembourg, Switzerland, and France. It is primarily for those who plan to tackle the entire trip in one fell swoop, but the casual walker or seasoned traveler in search of a shorter hike will also find it informative. Each day is thoroughly described and the appropriate topographical maps needed clearly pointed out.

Where to Watch Birds in Britain and Europe

by John Gooders, Passport Books, 1988, 288 pages, paper, $17.95

This new, 1988 book is for the avid bird enthusiast headed for Europe. It provides the details, including maps, on over 200 sites for both novices and experienced birdwatchers.

The Wine Roads of Europe

by Marc and Kim Millon, Simon & Schuster, 1984, 288 pages, paper, $9.95

This well-done, detailed, regionally organized guide to a wide variety of wine country holidays provides all the necessary facts on travel, lodging, tours, itineraries, and phone numbers. Covered are the wine regions of France, Germany, Italy, Austria, Spain and Portugal. However, due to publication date, be sure to confirm any details before venturing forth.

Wings of History: The Air Museums of Europe

by Louis and Judy Divone, Oakton Hills Publications, 1988, 325 pages, paper, $21.95

This new, unique guide, released after press time, tells the story of aviation in Europe through the aircraft that still exist in the museums and collections of Western and Eastern Europe. From the famous to the obscure, *Wings of History* describes thirty-five of the most interesting of these museums and collections and provides an appendix listing the names and addresses of over 125 additional museums, with an inventory of their collections. More than 125 photographs complement this informative text. A handy table of key aviation terms and aircraft names is done in twelve languages. This book is a real must for the interested traveler.

REGIONS OF EUROPE

Two regions of Europe are useful to separate out: Eastern Europe and Scandinavia. As noted under "Europe as a Whole" above, the "region" of Western Europe is what most travelers mean when they speak of "Europe" and titles limiting themselves to Western Europe constitute most of the books included in that section.

EASTERN EUROPE

See also "Europe as a Whole." The countries of Eastern Europe are Albania, Bulgaria, Czechoslovakia, East Germany, Hungary, Poland, Romania, and the Soviet Union. Only those few titles exclusively on Eastern Europe are listed below. Titles on Europe that include one or more Eastern European countries are noted as such and are listed in "Europe as a Whole" above. Since there are so few titles on Eastern Europe, be advised that a major, much anticipated title on Eastern Europe from Lonely Planet's Travel Survival Kit series is due for release in late 1988 or early 1989.

Fodor's Eastern Europe
Fodor's Travel Publications, 1988, 512 pages, paper, $16.95
Covering Bulgaria, Czechoslovakia, Hungary, Poland, and Romania, this is one of the titles in Fodor's Country/Regional Guide series ,which is reviewed in more detail under "Series Reviews." Fodor publishes a separate volume on the Soviet Union, and Albania is covered in *Fodor's Europe*. East Germany is included in both *Fodor's Europe* and *Fodor's Budget Europe*. The series is updated annually.

Frommer's Eastern Europe on $25 a Day
by Morris Hadley and Adam Tanner, Prentice Hall Press, 1987, 547 pages, paper, $10.95
Covering Bulgaria, Czechoslovakia, East Germany, Hungary, Poland, Romania, and Yugoslavia, this book is part of Frommer's Dollar-a-Day Guide series, which is reviewed in more detail under "Series Reviews." The series is updated every two years.

SCANDINAVIA

See also "Europe as a Whole." Scandinavia includes, in its broadest definition, Denmark, the Faroe Islands, Finland, Iceland, Norway, and Sweden. Most books on Scandinavia exclude Iceland and the Faroe Islands, and a few exclude Finland. For clarity, unless otherwise noted the titles below will be assumed to include Denmark, Finland, Norway, and Sweden. Any exceptions to this rule will so noted.

Baedeker's Scandinavia
>   Prentice Hall Press, undated, 344 pages, paper, $14.95
>   This is one of the Baedeker's Country/Regional Guide series, which is reviewed in more detail under "Series Reviews."

Fodor's Scandinavia
>   Fodor's Travel Publications, 1987, 480 pages, paper, $14.95
>   Including Iceland, this book is part of Fodor's Country/Regional Guide series, which is reviewed in more detail under "Series Reviews." The series is updated annually.

Fodor's Stockholm, Copenhagen, Oslo, Helsinki, Reykjavik
>   Fodor's Travel Publications, 1987, 160 pages, paper, $6.95
>   Including Reykjavik, Iceland, this book is one of Fodor's City Guide series, which is reviewed in more detail under "Series Reviews." The series is updated annually.

Frommer's Scandinavia on $50 a Day
>   by Darwin Porter, Prentice Hall Press, 1987, 574 pages, paper, $10.95
>   Including Iceland, this book is part of Frommer's Dollar-a-Day Guide series, which is reviewed in more detail under "Series Reviews." The series is updated every two years.

The New Holiday Guide to Scandinavia
>   M. Evans & Co., 1988 (10th ed.), 160 pages, paper, $4.95
>   Excluding Finland, this book is part of the Holiday Guide series, which is reviewed in more detail under "Series Reviews."

Rand McNally: Scandinavia
>   by Sylvie Nickels, Rand McNally & Co., 1983, 128 pages, paper, $5.95
>   This is one of the small-format Rand McNally Pocket Guide series, which is reviewed in more detail under "Series Reviews."

Scandinavia in 22 Days
>   See *22 Days in Scandinavia* below.

Scandinavian Country Inns and Manors
>   by Clara and Karen Brown, Travel Press, 1988, 270 pages, paper, $12.95
>   This is one of the widely praised Karen Brown's Country Inns series, which is reviewed in more detail under "Series Reviews."

The Scandinavian Guide
edited by Peter Cowie, New York Zoetrope, 1988, 296 pages, paper, $13.95

This quality guide with a definite business orientation covers all the essential tourist bases with good information on sightseeing, hotels, restaurants, the arts, politics, and more. Price ranges tend toward the expensive and a separate business section includes recommended locations for business meetings. This excellent guide for those with company business to attend to includes Iceland and is the only travel book reviewed here that provides travel information on the Faroe Islands, the famed ornithological paradise midway between Norway and Iceland. The book is updated annually.

22 Days in Scandinavia: The Itinerary Planner
by Rick Steves, John Muir Publications, 1988, 136 pages, paper, $5.95

This is one of the growing Itinerary Planner series, which is reviewed in more detail under "Series Reviews." The series is based on the successful *Europe in 22 Days* (now called *22 Days in Europe*). Note that the title has recently changed and this book may also be found under *Scandinavia in 22 Days* or *Norway, Sweden, Denmark in 22 Days*. This work excludes Finland.

COUNTRIES OF EUROPE

ALBANIA

See also "Eastern Europe" and "Europe as a Whole." Albania is included in *Fodor's Europe*.

Albania: A Travel Guide
by Philip Ward, Hippocrene Books, 1988, 166 pages, paper, $16.50

Travelers willing to work out the logistics of visiting Albania will find this guide well written, informative, and enjoyable to read—particularly for historic notes, sightseeing ideas, and excellent practical tips for negotiating this most rigid Marxist country. Recently picked up by Hippocrene, this is a new edition of Ward's original 1983 book, released after press time.

ANDORRA

See also "Europe as a Whole." Andorra is included in *Birnbaum's Europe* and *Fodor's Europe*.

Walks and Climbs in the Pyrenees
by Kev Reynolds, Hunter Publishing, 1988 (3rd ed.), 206 pages, paper, $12.95
This is one of the Hunter Mountain Walks series, which is reviewed in more detail under "Series Reviews."

AUSTRIA

See also "Europe as a Whole." Austria is included in the following major, all-purpose guides to Europe: *Birnbaum's Europe; Fielding's Europe; Fielding's Economy Europe; Fisher's World: Europe; Fodor's Europe; Fodor's Budget Europe; Frommer's Europe on $30 a Day; Let's Go: Europe.*

Adventuring in the Alps: The Sierra Club Travel Guide to the Alpine Regions of France, Switzerland, Germany, Austria, Liechtenstein, Italy, and Yugoslavia
by William and Marylou Reifsnyder, Sierra Club Books, 1986, 278 pages, paper, $10.95
This is one of the excellent Sierra Club Adventure Travel Guide series, which is reviewed in more detail under "Series Reviews."

Austria: A Phaidon Art and Architecture Guide
Prentice Hall Press, 1985, 560 pages, cloth, $17.95
This is one of the encyclopedic Phaidon Art and Architecture Guide series, which is reviewed in more detail under "Series Reviews."

Austrian Country Inns and Castles
by Clare Brown, Travel Press, 1988 (revised ed.), 200 pages, paper, $12.95
This is one of the wonderful Karen Brown's Country Inns series which is reviewed in more detail under "Series Reviews."

Baedeker's Austria
Prentice Hall Press, 1985, 304 pages, paper, $14.95
This book is part of Baedeker's Country/Regional Guide series, which reviewed is reviewed in more detail under "Series Reviews."

Baedeker's Vienna
Prentice Hall Press, 1987, 192 pages, paper, $10.95
This book is part of Baedeker's City Guide series, which is reviewed in more detail under "Series Reviews."

Berlitz: Tyrol
Macmillan Publishing, 1982, 128 pages, paper, $6.95
Berlitz: Vienna
Macmillan Publishing, 1984, 128 pages, paper, $6.95
These books are part of the small-format Berlitz Guide series, which is reviewed in more detail under "Series Reviews."

Blue Guide: Austria
edited by Ian Robertson, W. W. Norton & Co., 1987 (2nd ed.), 408 pages, paper, $18.95
Part of the highly regarded Blue Guide series, which is reviewed in more detail under "Series Reviews."

The Children's Treasure Hunt Travel Guide to Austria, Germany, Switzerland
Hippocrene Books, 1979, 200 pages, paper, $6.95
This handy, little book, to help keep kids six years and up entertained along the way, is part of the Children's Treasure Hunt Guide series, which is reviewed in more detail under "Series Reviews."

Exploring Rural Austria
Passport Books, 1988/89, 200 pages, paper, $12.95
This is an anticipated new title in the Exploring Rural Europe Guide series, which is reviewed in more detail under "Series Reviews." The price and number of pages are approximate.

Fodor's Austria
Fodor's Travel Publications, 1987, 368 pages, paper, $12.95
This is one of the Fodor's Country/Regional Guide series, which is reviewed in more detail under "Series Reviews." The series is updated annually.

Fodor's Vienna
Fodor's Travel Publications, 1987, 128 pages, paper, $6.95
This is part of Fodor's City Guide series, which is reviewed in more detail under "Series Reviews." The series is updated annually.

Frommer's Dollarwise Guide to Austria and Hungary
by Darwin Porter, Prentice Hall Press, 1987, 600 pages, paper, $11.95
This is one of Frommer's Dollarwise Guide series, which is reviewed in more detail under "Series Reviews." This series emphasizes selections in the moderate price range and is updated every two years.

Germany, Austria, Switzerland in 22 Days
See *22 Days in Germany, Austria, Switzerland.*

Michelin Green Guide: Austria
Michelin Guides and Maps, 1986 (7th ed.), 176 pages, paper, $10.95
    This is part of the leading sightseeing guide series, the Michelin Green Guides, reviewed in more detail under "Series Reviews."

Mountain Walking in Austria
by Cecil Davies, Hunter Publishing, 1988, 176 pages, paper, $12.95
    This is one of Hunter Mountain Walks series, which is reviewed in more detail under "Series Reviews."

100 Hikes in the Alps
by Ira Spring and Harvey Edwards, The Mountaineers, 1985, 224 pages, paper, $9.95
    This book is part of the excellent Mountaineers Hiking Guide series, which is reviewed in more detail under "Series Reviews."

Rand McNally: Austria and Switzerland
by Shirley and John Harrison, Rand McNally & Co., 1983, 128 pages, paper, $4.95
    This is part of the small-format Rand McNally Pocket Guide series, which is reviewed in more detail under "Series Reviews."

22 Days in Germany, Austria, Switzerland: The Itinerary Planner
by Rick Steves, John Muir Publications, 1987, 133 pages, paper, $5.95
    This is one of the Itinerary Planner series ,which is reviewed in more detail under "Series Reviews." The title for this book has recently changed and may also be found under the title *Germany, Austria, Switzerland in 22 Days.*

Viennawalks
by J. Sydney Jones, Henry Holt & Co., 1985, 289 pages, paper, $10.95
    This is one of the Citywalks series, which is reviewed in more detail under "Series Reviews."

The Visitor's Guide to Austria
Hunter Publishing, 1988, 240 pages, paper, $10.95
    This is one of the New Visitor's Guide series, which is reviewed in more detail under "Series Reviews."

The Visitor's Guide to The Tyrol
by Alan Proctor, Hunter Publishing, 1984, 138 pages, paper, $9.95
   This book is part of the Visitor's Guide series, which is reviewed in more detail under "Series Reviews."

Walking Austria's Alps: Hut to Hut
by Jonathan Hurdle, The Mountaineers, 1988, 240 pages, paper, $10.95
   This new title was released after press time. However, The Mountaineers are known for their quality books and this new title will probably be no exception.

Walking in Austria
by Brian Spencer, Hunter Publishing, 1988, 192 pages, paper, $10.95
Walking in the Alps
by Brian Spencer, Hunter Publishing, 1986, 192 pages, paper, $9.95
   These two titles are in the Hunter Walks series, which is reviewed in more detail under "Series Reviews."

Walks Through Vienna
by Bert Lief, VLE Limited, undated, fold-out map/guide, paper, $2.00
   This is one of the Way-Ahead Walks series, which is reviewed in more detail under "Series Reviews."

Whole Europe Escape Manual: Germany, Austria, Switzerland
by James Kitfield and William Walker, World Leisure Corp., 1985, 160 pages, paper, $6.95
   This book is part of the unique Escape Manual series, which is reviewed in more detail under "Series Reviews."

Azores: See "Islands of the Eastern and Northern Atlantic Ocean" below.

BELGIUM

See also "Europe as a Whole." Belgium is included in the following major, all-purpose guides to Europe: *Birnbaum's Europe; Fielding's Europe; Fielding's Economy Europe; Fisher's World: Europe; Fodor's Europe; Fodor's Budget Europe; Frommer's Europe on $30 a Day; Let's Go: Europe.*

Baedeker's Brussels
Prentice Hall Press, 1987, 148 pages, paper, $10.95
This is one of Baedeker's City Guide series, which is reviewed in more detail under "Series Reviews."

Baedeker's Netherlands, Belgium and Luxembourg
Prentice Hall Press, undated, 325 pages, paper, $14.95
This book is part of Baedeker's Country/Regional Guide series, which is reviewed in more detail under "Series Reviews."

Berlitz Travel Guides: Brussels
Macmillan Publishing, 1988, 128 pages, paper, $6.95
This book is part of the small-format Berlitz Guide series, which is reviewed in more detail under "Series Reviews."

Blue Guide: Belgium & Luxembourg
edited by John Tomes, W. W. Norton & Co., 1983 (6th ed.), 312 pages, paper, $15.95
This is one of the highly respected Blue Guide series, which is reviewed in more detail under "Series Reviews."

The Children's Treasure Hunt Guide to Belgium and France
Hippocrene Books, 1979, 228 pages, paper, $6.95
This book is part of the Children's Treasure Hunt Guide series, which is reviewed in more detail under "Series Reviews."

Day Trips in Holland, Belgium and Luxembourg: 40 One-Day Adventures by Rail, Bus or Car
by Earl Steinbicker, Hastings House, 1988, 250 pages, paper, $10.95
This is a new title, released after press time, in the excellent Earl Steinbicker's Day Trips series, which is reviewed in more detail under "Series Reviews." The number of pages is approximate.

Fodor's Belgium and Luxembourg
Fodor's Travel Publications, 1987, 288 pages, paper, $12.95
This book is part of Fodor's Country/Regional Guide series, which is reviewed in more detail under "Series Reviews." The series is updated annually.

Frommer's Dollarwise Guide to Belgium, Holland, and Luxembourg
by Susan Poole, Prentice Hall Press, 1987, 319 pages, paper, $11.95
This book is part of Frommer's Dollarwise Guide series, which is reviewed in more detail under "Series Reviews." The series is updated every two years.

Long Stays in Belgium and Luxembourg
by Carole Hazelwood, Hippocrene Books, 1987, 200 pages, cloth, $19.95
This is one of the Long Stays Guide series, which is reviewed in more detail under "Series Reviews."

Michael's Guide: Brussels and Antwerp
by Michael Shichor, Hunter Publishing, 1988, 224 pages, paper, $7.95
This is one of the Michael's Guide series, which is reviewed in more detail under "Series Reviews." Released after press time, the number of pages is approximate.

Michelin Red Guide: Benelux
Michelin Guides & Maps, 1987, 407 pages, cloth, $16.95
Containing detailed hotel and restaurant information, this book is part of the Michelin Red Guide series, which is reviewed in more detail under "Series Reviews." The series is updated annually.

Rand McNally: Holland, Belgium and Luxembourg
by Carole Chester, Rand McNally & Co., 1986, 128 pages, paper, $5.95
This is one of the small-format Rand McNally Pocket Guide series, which is reviewed in more detail under "Series Reviews."

Whole Europe Escape Manual: France, Holland, Belgium with Luxembourg
by Kerry Green and Peter Bythiner, World Leisure Corp, 1985, 160 pages, paper, $6.95
This book is part of the unique Escape Manual series, which is reviewed in more detail under "Series Reviews."

BULGARIA

See also "Eastern Europe" and "Europe as a Whole. " Bulgaria is included in *Fodor's Europe* and *Fodor's Budget Europe*.

Bulgaria: A Guide
by Dimiter Mihailov and Pancho Smolenov, Hippocrene Books, undated, 246 pages, paper, $6.95
This useful little guidebook, written and published in Bulgaria fairly recently, is now distributed in America. It contains informative sections on history, economics, arts, nature, music, architecture, useful words and phrases, and a wide variety of sightseeing itineraries. Good color photos supplement the fairly dry writing style. No

hotel or restaurant recommendations are made, but information on reservation services is provided.

Nagel's Encyclopedia Guide: Bulgaria
Passport Books, 1981, 527 pages, cloth, $39.95
This classic, cultural guide is part of the Nagel's Guide series, which is reviewed in more detail under "Series Reviews."

Sophia: A Guide
by Dimiter Mihailov and Pancho Smolenov, Hippocrene Books, 1988, 233 pages, paper, $7.95
The authors of *Bulgaria: A Guide* have produced a new book on the Bulgarian capital, which was released after press time.

CYPRUS

See also "Europe as a Whole." Cyprus is included in the following major, all-purpose guides to Europe: *Birnbaum's Europe; Fielding's Europe; Fielding's Economy Europe; Fisher's World: Europe; Fodor's Europe; Fodor's Budget Europe; Let's Go: Europe.*

Baedeker's Mediterranean Islands
Prentice Hall Press, 1985, 223 pages, paper, $14.95
This volume, covering Cyprus, Malta, and the islands of Spain, France, Italy, and Greece, is part of the Baedeker's Country/Regional Guide series, which is reviewed in more detail under "Series Reviews."

Berlitz: Cyprus
Macmillan Publishing, 1985, 128 pages, paper, $6.95
This book is part of the small-format Berlitz Guide series, which is reviewed in more detail under "Series Reviews."

Blue Guide: Cyprus
edited by Ian Robertson, W. W. Norton & Co., 1984, 196 pages, paper, $17.95
This is one of the highly regarded Blue Guide series, which is reviewed in more detail under "Series Reviews."

Landscapes of Cyprus
by Geoff Daniel, Hunter Publishing, 1986, 128 pages, paper, $9.95
This book is part of the Countryside Guide series, which is reviewed in more detail under "Series Reviews."

Let's Go: Greece (including Cyprus, the Turkish Coast, and Istanbul)
by Harvard Student Agencies, St. Martin's Press, 1988, 528 pages, paper, $10.95
This book is part of the excellent, budget-oriented Let's Go Guide series, which is reviewed in more detail under "Series Reviews." The series is updated annually.

Canary Islands: See "Islands of the Eastern and Northern Atlantic Ocean" below.

CZECHOSLOVAKIA

See also "Eastern Europe" and "Europe as a Whole." Czechoslovakia is included in the following major, all-purpose guides to Europe: *Birnbaum's Europe; Fodor's Europe; Fodor's Budget Europe; Let's Go: Europe.*

Baedeker's Prague
Prentice Hall Press, 1987, 156 pages, paper, $10.95
This is one of the Baedeker's City Guide series, which is reviewed in more detail under "Series Reviews."

Berlitz: Prague
Macmillan Publishing, 1988, 128 pages, paper, $6.95
This is one of the small-format Berlitz Guide series, which is reviewed in more detail under "Series Reviews."

Guide to Czechoslovakia
by Simon Hayman, Hippocrene Books, 1987, 192 pages, paper, $11.95
Hayman, a frequent visitor to Czechoslovakia, has written a useful, all-purpose guide for travelers containing information on where to stay, sightseeing, transportation, and details on activities like canoeing, hiking, climbing, and caving. Included are trail maps and other pertinent details for hikers.

Nagel's Encyclopedia Guide: Czechoslovakia
Passport Books, 1975, 480 pages, cloth, $39.95
This classic, cultural guide is part of the Nagel's Guide series, which is reviewed in more detail under "Series Reviews."

DENMARK

See also "Scandinavia" and "Europe as a Whole." Denmark is included in the following major, all-purpose guides to Europe: *Birnbaum's Europe; Fielding's Europe; Fielding's Economy Europe; Fisher's World:*

Europe; Fodor's Europe; Fodor's Budget Europe; Frommer's Europe on $30 a Day; Let's Go: Europe.

Baedeker's Copenhagen
Prentice Hall Press, 1987, 120 pages, paper, $10.95
This is one of Baedeker's City Guide series, which is reviewed in more detail under "Series Reviews."

Baedeker's Denmark
Prentice Hall Press, 1987, 191 pages, paper, $14.95
This is one of the Baedeker's Country/Regional Guide series, which is reviewed in more detail under "Series Reviews."

Berlitz: Copenhagen
Macmillan Publishing, 1982, 128 pages, paper, $6.95
This book is part of the small-format Berlitz Guide series, which is reviewed in more detail under "Series Reviews."

Drive Around Denmark
by Robert Spark, Trafton Publishing, 1986 (2nd ed.), 144 pages, cloth, $10.95
This solid, practical guide, filled with suggested driving itineraries and sightseeing in and around Denmark, contains a general orientation to food and lodging. Published in England, the book currently has no American distributor. It has been carried by Traveller's Bookstore and Wide World Books and Maps. See Travel Bookstore appendix for other stores that might carry it.

Lett's Guide: Denmark
by Harold Dennis-Jones, Prima Publishing, 1981, 96 pages, paper, $5.95
This book is part of the Letts Guide series, which is reviewed in more detail under "Series Reviews."

Nagel's Encyclopedia Guide: Denmark and Greenland
Passport Books, 1980, 594 pages, cloth, $39.95
This classic, cultural guide is one of the Nagel's Guide series, which is reviewed in more detail under "Series Reviews."

EAST GERMANY (GERMAN DEMOCRATIC REPUBLIC)

See also "Eastern Europe" and "Europe as a Whole." East Germany is included in the following major, all-purpose guides to Europe: *Birnbaum's Europe; Fodor's Europe; Fodor's Budget Europe; Frommer's Europe on $30 a Day; Let's Go: Europe.*

Baedeker's Berlin
Prentice Hall Press, 1987, 168 pages, paper, $10.95
Including East Berlin, this book is part of the Baedeker's City Guide series, which is reviewed in more detail under "Series Reviews."

Fodor's Germany
Fodor's Travel Guides, 1987, 512 pages, paper, $14.95
Including East Germany, this is one of Fodor's Country/Regional Guide series, which is reviewed in more detail under "Series Reviews." The series is updated annually.

Frommer's Dollarwise Guide to Germany
by Darwin Porter, Prentice Hall Press, 1988, 655 pages, paper, $12.95
Including East Germany, this book is part of the Frommer's Dollarwise Guide series, which is reviewed in more detail under "Series Reviews." The series is updated every two years.

Germany At Its Best
by Robert Kane, Passport Books, 1988, 352 pages, paper, $12.95
Including East Germany, this is one of the At Its Best Guide series, which is reviewed in more detail under "Series Reviews."

Marling Menu-Master for Germany
by William and Clare Marling, Altarinda Books, 1970, 88 pages, plasticized cover, $5.95
This is one of the superb Marling Menu-Masters series, which is reviewed in more detail under "Series Reviews."

Signposts: Germany
by Edith and Margaret Wightman, Cambridge University Press, 1982, 99 pages, paper, $5.95
This useful, informative guide covers over 100 road signs and notices travelers will encounter while traveling in Germany.

England: See the section on England under "Great Britain."
Federal Republic of Germany: See "West Germany."

FINLAND

See also "Scandinavia" and "Europe as a Whole." Finland is included in the following major, all-purpose guides to Europe: *Birnbaum's Europe; Fielding's Europe; Fielding's Economy Europe; Fisher's World: Europe; Fodor's Europe; Fodor's Budget Europe; Let's Go: Europe.*

Berlitz Travel Guide: Helsinki & South Finland
Macmillan Publishing, 1980, 128 pages, paper, $6.95
    This book is part of the small-format Berlitz Guide series, which is reviewed in more detail under "Series Reviews."

Helsinki, Turku, Tampere and Lapland: A Guide
by Dimiter Mihailov and Pancho Smolenov, Hippocrene Books, 1988, 228 pages, paper, $14.95
    In this book the authors of the solidly done *Bulgaria: A Guide* have turned their attention to the far north. This title was released after press time.

Nagel's Encyclopedia Guide: Finland
Passport Books, 1980, 367 pages, cloth, $34.95
    This classic, cultural guide is one of the Nagel's Guide series, which is reviewed in more detail under "Series Reviews."

FRANCE

See also "Europe as a Whole." France is included in the following major, all-purpose guides to Europe: *Birnbaum's Europe; Fielding's Europe; Fielding's Economy Europe; Fisher's World: Europe; Fodor's Europe; Fodor's Budget Europe; Frommer's Europe on $30 a Day; Let's Go: Europe.*

AA Traveler's Guide to France
by the Automobile Association, Salem House, 1988, 140 pages, paper, $11.95
    This directory covers over 2000 hotels and 500 recommended garages in 1000 French towns and villages, all rated in typical AA fashion. Location maps and town plans are also included in this annually updated guide.

Adventuring in the Alps: The Sierra Club Travel Guide to the Alpine Regions of France, Switzerland, Germany, Austria, Liechtenstein, Italy, and Yugoslavia
by William and Marylou Reifsnyder, Sierra Club Books, 1986, 278 pages, paper, $10.95
    This is one of the excellent Sierra Club Adventure Travel Guide series, which is reviewed in more detail under "Series Reviews."

Alexis Lichine's Guide to the Wines and Vineyards of France
by Alexis Lichine, Alfred Knopf, Inc. 1984 (revised ed.), 453 pages, paper, $9.95
    This widely praised book contains information on wine tours,

itineraries, hotel recommendations, and the pick of the restaurants, although the time-dated material should be verified. In any case, this book will certainly enhance any traveler's enjoyment of the French wine country.

The American Express Pocket Guide to Paris
by Christopher McIntosh, Prentice Hall Press, 1983, 224 pages, cloth, $8.95
The American Express Pocket Guide to the South of France
by John Ardagh, Prentice Hall Press, 1987, 256 pages, cloth, $8.95
   Both of these titles are part of the highly regarded American Express Pocket Guide series, which is reviewed in more detail under "Series Reviews."

Americans in Paris
by Brian Morton, The Olivia & Hill Press, 1984, 425 pages, paper, $14.95
   This fascinating street-by-street guide describes how Paris has influenced and has likewise been influenced by more than 300 Americans who have lived and worked there since 1776.

Baedeker's France
Prentice Hall Press, undated, 320 pages, paper, $14.95
Baedeker's Loire
Prentice Hall Press, 1985, 159 pages, paper, $9.95
Baedeker's Mediterranean Islands
Prentice Hall Press, 1985, 223 pages, paper, $14.95
   These three titles are part of the Baedeker's Country/Regional Guide series, which is reviewed in more detail under "Series Reviews." The volume on the Mediterranean islands covers Cyprus, Malta, and the islands of France, Spain, Italy, and Greece.

Baedeker's Paris
Prentice Hall Press, 1987, 190 pages, paper, $10.95
   This book is part of Baedeker's City Guide series, which is reviewed in more detail under "Series Reviews."

Baedeker's Provence and Cote d'Azur
Prentice Hall Press, 1985, 231 pages, paper, $9.95
   This book is part of Baedeker's Country/Regional Guide series, which is reviewed in more detail under "Series Reviews."

Berlitz: Brittany
Macmillan Publishing, 1985, 128 pages, paper, $6.95
This is one of the small-format Berlitz Guide series, which is reviewed in more detail under "Series Reviews."

Berlitz: France
Macmillan Publishing, 1987, 256 pages, paper, $8.95
This is one of the small-format Berlitz Country Guide series, which is reviewed in more detail under "Series Reviews."

Berlitz: French Riviera
Macmillan Publishing, 1982, 128 pages, paper, $6.95
Berlitz: Loire Valley
Macmillan Publishing, 1982, 128 pages, paper, $6.95
Berlitz: Normandy
Macmillan Publishing, 1987, 128 pages, paper, $6.95
Berlitz: Paris
Macmillan Publishing, 1987, 128 pages, paper, $6.95
All of these titles are part of the small-format Berlitz Guide series, which is reviewed in more detail under "Series Reviews." The Paris guide contains an additional 16-page supplement on hotels and restaurants. The Paris and French Riviera guides are also available in the new "Berlitz Deluxe Guide" series. See additional notes on this series under "Series Reviews."

The Best of France
by Henri Gault and Christian Millau, Crown Publishers, 1986 (revised ed.), 605 pages, paper, $14.95
The Best of Paris
by Henri Gault and Christian Millau, Crown Publishers, 1986 (revised ed.), 517 pages, paper, $14.95
Both of these food, entertainment, and hotel guides are part of the Gault/Millau 'Best Of' Guide series, which is reviewed in more detail under "Series Reviews."

Birnbaum's France
edited by Stephen Birnbaum, Houghton Mifflin, 1987, 786 pages, paper, $12.95
This is one of the excellent Birnbaum's Guide series, which is reviewed in more detail under "Series Reviews." The series is updated annually.

Blue Guide: Corsica
by Roland Grant, W. W. Norton & Co., 1987, 168 pages, paper, $18.95

Blue Guide: France
 edited by Ian Robertson, W. W. Norton & Co., 1984, 923 pages,
 paper, $19.95
Blue Guide: Paris and Environs
 edited by Ian Robertson, W. W. Norton & Co., 1985 (6th ed.), 354
 pages, paper, $16.95
  All three of these titles are part of the highly regarded Blue Guide
 series, which is reviewed in more detail under "Series Reviews."

Born to Shop: France
 by Suzy Gershman and Judith Thomas, Bantam Books, 1987 (2nd
 ed.), 348 pages, paper, $8.95
  This book about shopping in Paris and the south of France is part
 of the Born to Shop Guide series, which is reviewed in more detail
 under "Series Reviews."

Cadogan Guide: The South of France
 by Barbara Mandell, The Globe Pequot Press, 1986, 232 pages,
 paper, $12.95
  This is one of the well-done Cadogan Guide series, which is reviewed in more detail under "Series Reviews." The series is updated
 every two years.

Cheap Eats in Paris
 by Sandra Gustafson and William Poole, Cobble & Mickle Books,
 1988, 101 pages, paper, $8.95
  This great little book offers information on 100 of the most inexpensive yet thoroughly enjoyable restaurants, brasseries, and bistros in Paris. The evaluations are informative and a pleasure to read.
 A quick reference chart shows which restaurants are near which
 major tourist attractions, as well as which ones are open on Sunday
 and during the month of August, when most Parisians have headed
 for the beach.

Cheap Sleeps in Paris
 by Sandra Gustafson and William Poole, Cobble & Mickle Books,
 1988, 85 pages, paper, $8.95
  This quality guide from the authors of *Cheap Eats in Paris*, describes an excellent selection of 75 relatively inexpensive (not to
 mention "clean, comfortable and, often, charming") hotels in the
 various *arrondissements*, or districts, of Paris. A quick reference
 chart locates each hotel and gives its proximity to important tourist
 attractions.

The Children's Treasure Hunt Guide to Belgium and France
Hippocrene Books, 1979, 228 pages, paper, $6.95
This is one of the Children's Teasure Hunt Guide series, which is reviewed in more detail under "Series Reviews."

Classic Walks in France
by Rob Hunter and David Wickers, Haynes Publications, 1985, 136 pages, paper, $12.95
This book is part of the Classic Walks Guide series, which is reviewed in more detail under "Series Reviews." Hunter recommends his earlier work, *Walking in France* (see below), to provide the added detail needed to thoroughly pre-plan a successful "classic walk" in France. Keep in mind that these "walks" are more aptly termed hikes in America.

Collier World Traveler Series: In and Around Paris
edited by Philippe Gloaguen and Pierre Josse, Macmillan Publishing, 1986, 224 pages, paper, $6.95
This book is part of the Collier World Traveler Guide series, which is reviewed in more detail under "Series Reviews."

The Companion Guide to Paris
by Anthony Glyn, Prentice Hall Press, 1985, 362 pages, paper, $10.95
The Companion Guide to the South of France
by Archibald Lyall, Prentice Hall Press, 1983, 272 pages, paper, $9.95
These two titles are part of the superb Companion Guide series, which is reviewed in more detail under "Series Reviews."

Country Hotels and Inns of France
Faber & Faber, 1987, 272 pages, paper, $10.95
Known as *Logis et Auberges de France* on the continent, this annual volume is published by the National Federation of Hotels and Auberges of France. A helpful directory, it lists 4500 small and medium-sized family-operated hotels located primarily in small towns and villages with a population of less than 5000. Each hotel or inn meets the Federation's standards for comfort, cleanliness, friendliness, service, and cooking. Though it is printed entirely in French, a simple code will allow you to understand the very brief descriptions.

Crown Insider's Guide: France
by Helmut Koenig, Crown Publishers, 1987, 336 pages, paper, $10.95
One of the Crown Insider's Guide series, which is reviewed in more detail under "Series Reviews."

Cruising French Canals and Rivers
by Hugh McKnight, Seven Seas Press, 1984, 288 pages, cloth, $29.95
This magnificent book, winner of the 1984 Thomas Cook Guide Book Award, provides an exceedingly in-depth, comprehensive look at the nearly 8000 km of navigable waterways in France. Photos and maps are included, as are all the practical details, such as boats for hire, the best moorings, and recommended restaurants and shops along each river or canal. This is a great book for boat travelers in France.

Day Trips in France: 40 One-Day Adventures by Rail, Bus or Car
by Earl Steinbicker, Hastings House, 1988 (revised ed.), 256 pages, paper, $10.95
This book is part of the Earl Steinbicker's Day Trips series, which is reviewed in more detail under "Series Reviews." The number of pages for the 1988 edition is approximate.

DuMont Guide to the French Riviera
by Rolf Legler, Stewart, Tabori & Chang, 1986, 344 pages, paper, $14.95
DuMont Guide to Paris and the Ile de France
by Klaus Bussman, Stewart, Tabori & Chang, 1984, 520 pages, paper, $14.95
DuMont Guide to the Loire Valley
by Wilfried Hansmann, Stewart, Tabori & Chang, 1986, 300 pages, paper, $14.95
These three titles are part of the DuMont Guide series, which is reviewed in more detail under "Series Reviews."

The Economist Business Traveller's Guide: France
Prentice Hall Press, 1988, 250 pages, cloth, $17.95
This is a new title in the excellent Economist Business Traveller's Guide series, which is reviewed in more detail under "Series Reviews." This volume was released after press time so the number of pages is approximate.

Eperon's French Wine Tour: A Traveler's Guide to Tasting and Buying Wine in France
by Arthur Eperon, Hunter Publishing, 1987, 256 pages, paper, $12.95

A companion to Eperon's popular *The French Selection* (below), this guide looks at each of the 16 wine-growing regions of France. A map, an introduction to the area, food and lodging tips, and a recommended touring route are provided for each area. Various wines of each region are described and evaluated in this excellent guide to the French wine country.

Exploring Rural France
by Andrew Sanger, Passport Books, 1988, 208 pages, paper, $12.95

This is one of the new Exploring Rural Europe Guide series, which is reviewed in more detail under "Series Reviews."

Fisher's World: France
edited by Robert Fisher, Fisher's World, Inc., 1988, 335 pages, paper, $14.95

Fisher's World: Paris
edited by Robert Fisher, Fisher's World, Inc., 1988, 123 pages, paper, $10.95

These two titles are part of the Fisher's World Guide series, which is reviewed in more detail under "Series Reviews." The series is updated annually.

Fodor's France
Fodor's Travel Publications, 1987, 544 pages, paper, $13.95

This is one of the Fodor's Country/Regional Guide series, which is reviewed in more detail under "Series Reviews." The series is updated annually.

Fodor's Fun in Paris
Fodor's Travel Publications, 1987, 128 pages, paper, $6.95

Fodor's Fun on the Riviera
Fodor's Travel Publications, 1987, 128 pages, paper, $6.95

These two titles are part of the Fodor's Fun Guide series, which is reviewed in more detail under "Series Reviews." The series is updated annually.

Fodor's Great Travel Values: France
Fodor's Travel Publications, 1987, 176 pages, paper, $5.95

Part of the budget-oriented Fodor's Great Travel Values Guide series which is reviewed in more detail under "Series Reviews." Updated annually.

Fodor's Loire Valley
Fodor's Travel Publications, 1987, 163 pages, paper, $8.95
This different little guide among the many Fodor titles deserves a separate writeup. Enjoyably written, it provides a brief introduction, including general architectural notes and a review of the history of the region. The majority of the book is a gazetteer with a map of each town, notes on the chateaux of the area and other sights of interest, and a useful short list of hotels and restaurants.

Fodor's Paris
Fodor's Travel Publications, 1987, 256 pages, paper, $8.95
This book is part of Fodor's City Guide series, which is reviewed in more detail under "Series Reviews." The series is updated annually.

The Food Lover's Guide to France
by Patricia Wells, Workman Publishing, 1987, 559 pages, paper, $14.95
This newer companion volume to Wells's critically acclaimed guide to Paris described below is structured in similar fashion. Containing well-written descriptions and critiques, practical information, information on when to visit the different regions of France, schedules of markets and festival days, travel directions, a French/English food glossary, beautiful photos, and 65 great recipes, this book covers the gamut. Every type of food establishment is represented including bistros, boulangeries, creperies, charcuteries, even gastronomic museums.

The Food Lover's Guide to Paris
by Patricia Wells, Workman Publishing, 1984, 320 pages, paper, $8.95
This classic but aging guide thoroughly covers Wells's picks among Parisian restaurants, cafés, tea salons, wine bars, markets, pastry shops, cheese shops, shops offering prepared foods to go, and chocolate shops. Also provided are 50 great recipes from some of her selected establishments. This is an exceptional book.

France: A Phaidon Art and Architecture Guide
Prentice Hall Press, 1985, 864 pages, paper, $16.95
This book is part of the encyclopedic Phaidon Art and Architecture Guide series, which is reviewed in more detail under "Series Reviews."

France At a Glance
by Inge and James Moore, Hippocrene Books, 1984, 192 pages, paper, $7.95
This is a useful book presenting facts on a host of practical travel topics that will make travel to France as close to carefree as possible.

France At Its Best
by Robert Kane, Passport Books, 1986, 432 pages, paper, $9.95
This is one of the widely praised At Its Best Guide series, which is reviewed in more detail under "Series Reviews."

France on Backroads: The Motorist's Guide to the French Countryside
Hunter Publishing, 1986, 256 pages, paper, $12.95
Despite its dry style of writing, this is a well-done book with lots of great touring ideas. It describes over 50 one- and two-day driving tours in 30 different locations, with good maps and notes on history, restaurants, recreation, sightseeing, picnic spots, walks, and even places to swim.

France on Your Own: Making the Most of Local Food and Drink
by Arthur and Barbara Eperon, Hippocrene Books, 1987, 158 pages, paper, $9.95
This helpful volume is designed for those planning an extended stay in France. It is part of the On Your Own Guide series, which is reviewed in more detail under "Series Reviews."

French Country Inns and Château Hotels
by Karen Brown, Travel Press, 1988 (5th ed.), 288 pages, paper, $12.95
This is one of the excellent Karen Brown's Country Inns series, which is reviewed in more detail under "Series Reviews."

French Country Welcome: Bed and Breakfast Guide
Faber and Faber, 1987, 384 pages, paper, $11.95
More than 6000 B&Bs are briefly described and rated, using a 1-to-3 system, in this informative book. To fit so many selections in, however, the editors used very small type and a variety of symbols. Each location is coded to the appropriate Michelin map. This is a French book that has been fully translated.

French Entrée 3: Normandy
by Patricia Fenn, ISBS, Inc., 1985, 221 pages, paper, $7.95
French Entrée 4: Calais and the North
by Patricia Fenn, ISBS, Inc., 1985, 173 pages, paper, $7.95

French Entrée 5: Brittany
by Patricia Fenn, ISBS, Inc., 1985, 192 pages, paper, $7.95
French Entrée 6: Boulogne, Pays D'Opal and Picardy
by Patricia Fenn, ISBS, Inc., 1987, 208 pages, paper, $7.95
These are the four currently available titles in this very popular British series. Each book concentrates on a small geographic area and provides oodles of information. After an introduction, each town is briefly overviewed, and recommended hotels and restaurants discussed, in excellent, although opinionated, detail. Numerous letters from other travelers are also quoted to provide more than one person's comments on many of the establishments. Towns are listed alphabetically and coded to a clear map of the area.

French Farm and Village Holiday Guide
by J. H. McCartney, Hunter Publishing, 1988, 384 pages, paper, $12.95
This annual catalog provides information on French farms in country villages available for rent for short or long vacation stays. Among its other details, this handy guide provides a small photograph, and the necessary prices and details—including whether English is spoken by others working on the farm.

French Leave Favorites
by Richard Binns, Boerum Hill Books, 1986, 208 pages, cloth, $14.95
Fans of Richard Binns are always disappointed to learn that his *French Leave 3* and *France a la Carte* are no longer available, although sometimes copies can be found on bookstore shelves. However, Binns fans will be happy to learn that *French Leave Favorites* is available and distributed in America. In this book, Binns presents critical assessments of his favorite lodging and dining spots, some located in those nooks and crannies that most tourists miss. In addition, other thoughtful suggestions from this respected, veteran traveler and practical tips are included. Note: Binns's *Best of Britain* is also still available, but somewhat older.

The French Selection: Arthur Eperon's Guide to the Best of French Hotels
by Arthur Eperon, Hunter Publishing, 1984, 158 pages, paper, $12.95
This is Arthur Eperon's very popular guide to his choice of the 50 best hotels in France. Each has a fine, informative, enjoyable evaluation, including food and drink, and is accompanied by color photos and recommended driving tours of the neighboring countryside. The practical details are here, too, and, while prices may have gone up

somewhat, be confident that, for the most part, hotels of this caliber have retained their quality over the years.

The French Way: An Insider's Guide to the Hotels and Restaurants of France

by Roland Escaig and Maurice Beaudoin, Warner Books, 1988, 672 pages, paper, $14.95

Released after press time, this is one of a number of new titles in Warner Books' Traveler's Bookshelf. The *French Way* is a very popular, annual French guide now translated into English for the first time.

Frommer's Dollarwise Guide to France

by Darwin Porter, Prentice Hall Press, 1987, 656 pages, paper, $11.95

This book is part of Frommer's Dollarwise Guide series, which is reviewed in more detail under "Series Reviews." The series emphasizes selections in the moderate price range and is updated every two years.

Frommer's Guide to Paris

by Darwin Porter, Prentice Hall Press, 1987, 218 pages, paper, $5.95

This is one of the Frommer's City Guide series, which is reviewed in more detail under "Series Reviews." The series is updated every two years.

Frommer's Touring Guide to Paris

Prentice Hall Press, 1986, 158 pages, paper, $8.95

This book is part of Frommer's Touring Guide series, which is reviewed in more detail under "Series Reviews."

Good Value France

Prentice Hall Press, 1988, 304 pages, paper, $10.95

This is the new name for the long-popular *Relais Routiers* guide, an annual French guide first begun in the 1930s as a guide for truckers in search of inexpensive but good-quality food. Each establishment chosen for the guide has a "Les Routiers" sign posted outside. To be in Relais Routiers, each dining spot must commit itself to offering a full meal at a reasonable price. *Good Value France*, the guide to wayside inns for travelers, is updated annually.

The Good Value Guide to Paris
by Francoise and Bernard Delthil, Hunter Publishing, 1985, 237
pages, paper, $10.95
This English edition, a translation of the famous *Paris Pas Cher*,
describes all sorts of opportunities for discounts on just about anything, and lists 230 restaurants and 60 hotels that are considered
"best value" for the money—in both the inexpensive and moderate
price range.

Grape Expeditions in France
by Sally Taylor, Sally Taylor & Friends, 1986 (2nd ed.), 120 pages,
paper, $9.00
This very useful little book offers 12 different bicycling tours
(automobile drivers will also find this guide useful), each with its
own map, description, and details that include type of terrain, distance covered, types of grapes grown in each region, suggestions for
food, lodging or camping, and the nearest bicycle rental or repair
shop.

A Guide to the Dordogne
by James Bentley, Viking Penguin, 1985, 184 pages, cloth, $18.95
This finely written companion guide will bring the Dordogne, that
beautiful region of the Massif Central, to life. But more than just
exploring the area's history and beauty, this guide will also present
its food and wine, its markets, and hidden treasures. Tips are imbed-
ded in the engrossing text. And, while there are no sections on dining
recommendations or other practical topics, the index outlines the
specifics. This title is now also available in paperback for $7.95.

Guide Relais & Châteaux
Hunter Publishing, 1988, 200 pages, paper, $6.95
The *Relais et Châteaux* are small castles, abbeys, and manor
houses that have been converted into charming, history-filled inns,
each with its own fine restaurant. Each establishment (372 in this
edition) must maintain the highest standards to be included in this
annual publication. Judged on comfort, cuisine, and courtesy, those
selected are succinctly described and each is shown with a color
photograph. About half the inns are in France; the rest are sprinkled
throughout the world.

The Hachette Guide to France: The Only Guide You'll Ever Need
Random House, 1988, 896 pages, paper, $16.95
The Hachette Guide to Paris: The Only Guide You'll Ever Need
Random House, 1988, 104 pages, paper, $5.95
These two titles are part of the popular French Hachette Guide

series, which is reviewed in more detail under "Series Reviews." The series is updated annually.

Hildebrand's Travel Guide: France

Hunter Publishing, 1988, 384 pages, paper, $10.95

This book is part of the Hildebrand's Guide series, which is reviewed in more detail under "Series Reviews."

Historic Houses, Castles and Gardens in France: The Official Guide to Sites Open to the Public

edited by Bertrand Du Vignaud, Hunter Publishing, 1986, 376 pages, paper, $15.95

The Ministry of Culture in Paris surveyed the owners of the many historic monuments throughout France and compiled the answers. The result is this handy reference guide that includes numerous photos (some in color), descriptions, a bit of history, and the hours each site is open to the public.

Holiday Which? Guide: France

Consumer Reports Books, 1988, 480 pages, paper, $12.00

Released after press time, this is a source of consumer-oriented information on history, sightseeing, and food.

Insight Guide: France

by Apa Productions, Prentice Hall Press, 1986, 324 pages, paper, $16.95

This is one of the highly regarded Insight Guide series, which is reviewed in more detail under "Series Reviews."

Just Off the Autoroute

by Monique Riccardi-Cubitt, Hippocrene Books, 1983, 256 pages, paper, $8.95

This handy guide to traveling the high-speed toll roads of France covers what to see and where to stay and eat—all just a short distance off the highway. Unfortunately, this book is in need of an update, so be sure to double-check information.

The Knopf Traveler's Guide to Art: France

by Mitchell Jacobs and Paul Stirton, Alfred Knopf, Inc., 1984, 304 pages, cloth, $14.95

This book is part of the superb Knopf Guides to Art series, which is reviewed in more detail under "Series Reviews."

La Creme de la Creme
by Barry Bone and Joanne Donsky, Harper & Row, 1986, 208 pages, cloth, $10.95

In this book nineteen of the finest French restaurants are carefully described and evaluated in detail based on first-hand experiences. Only one is outside the French borders: the spectacular Fredy Girardet's at the Hotel de Ville in a small suburb of Lausanne, Switzerland. Some wonderful ideas are included here and a full 42 pages cover the do's and don't's of dining at the classy, four-star level. This is a book for travelers not worried about the cost of their dining experience.

Les Routiers Guide to France
See *Good Value France* above.

Let's Go: France
by Harvard Student Agencies, St. Martin's Press, 1988, 624 pages, paper, $10.95

This is one of the excellent, budget-oriented Let's Go Guide series, which is reviewed in more detail under "Series Reviews." The series is updated annually.

Lett's Guide: France
by Harold Dennis-Jones, Prima Publishing, 1981, 96 pages, paper, $5.95

This book is part of the Letts Guide series, which is reviewed in more detail under "Series Reviews."

The Loire Valley: A Phaidon Art and Architecture Guide
Prentice Hall Press, 1986, 260 pages, cloth, $14.95

This is one of the encyclopedic Phaidon Art and Architecture Guide series, which is reviewed in more detail under "Series Reviews."

Long Walks in France
by Adam Nicolson, Crown Publishers, 1983, 288 pages, cloth, $17.95

Nine charming and exciting hikes covering more than 1000 miles through rural France are detailed in this book. Many photographs and plenty of practical information on clothing and food accompany the enjoyable and insightful descriptions of places and people.

Manston's Flea Markets, Antique Fairs and Auctions of France
by Peter Manston, Travel Keys Books, 1987, 195 pages, paper,
$9.95
    This book is part of the Travel Keys Guide series, which is re-
viewed in more detail under "Series Reviews."

The Marling Menu-Master for France
by William and Clare Marling, Altarinda Books, 1971, 112 pages,
plasticized cover, $5.95
    This is one of the superb Marling Menu Masters series, which is
reviewed in more detail under "Series Reviews."

Mediterranean Island Hopping—The Italian Islands, Corsica, Malta:
A Handbook for the Independent Traveler
by Dana Facaros and Michael Pauls, Hippocrene Books, 1982, 491
pages, paper, $12.95
    One of the few guidebooks to the French island of Corsica, this
book is part of the Island Hopping Guide series, which is reviewed
in more detail under "Series Reviews."

Michael's Guide: Paris
by Michael Shichor, Hunter Publishing, 1987, 160 pages, paper,
$6.95
    This is one of the Michael's Guide series, which is reviewed in
more detail under "Series Reviews."

Michelin Green Guide: Brittany
Michelin Guides & Maps, 1987, 226 pages, paper, $9.95
Michelin Green Guide: Burgundy
Michelin Guides & Maps, 1988, 182 pages, paper, $10.95
Michelin Green Guide: Châteaux of the Loire
Michelin Guides & Maps, 1985 (2nd ed.), 176 pages, paper, $9.95
Michelin Green Guide: Dordogne
Michelin Guides & Maps, 1984 (4th ed.), 192 pages, paper, $9.95
Michelin Green Guide: French Riviera
Michelin Guides & Maps, 1985 (9th ed.), 172 pages, paper, $9.95
Michelin Green Guide: Normandy
Michelin Guides & Maps, 1985 (6th ed.), 177 pages, paper, $9.95
Michelin Green Guide: Paris
Michelin Guides & Maps, 1986 (6th ed.), 206 pages, paper, $10.95
Michelin Green Guide: Provence
Michelin Guides & Maps, 1985 (3rd ed.), 139 pages, paper, $9.95
    All of the above are titles in the premier sightseeing series, the
Michelin Green Guides, which is reviewed in more detail under
"Series Reviews." Note that only those titles available in English

are included. A substantial number of additional titles are available in America for those who read French.

Michelin Red Guide: France
Michelin Guides & Maps, 1988, 1278 pages, cloth, $17.95
Michelin Red Guide: Paris
Michelin Guides & Maps, 1988, 70 pages, paper, $3.95
   Both of these hotel and restaurant guides are part of the annual Michelin Red Guide series, which is reviewed in more detail under "Series Reviews."

Museums of Paris
by Eloise Danto, Eldan Press, 1987, 112 pages, paper, $9.95
   This book is part of the Eldan Museum Guide series, which is reviewed in more detail under "Series Reviews."

Nagel's Encyclopedia Guide: France
Passport Books, 1983, 1248 pages, cloth, $49.95
   This classic, cultural guide is part of the Nagel's Guide series, which is reviewed in more detail under "Series Reviews."

The New Holiday Guide to France
M. Evans & Co., 1988 (10th ed.), 160 pages, paper, $4.95
The New Holiday Guide to Paris
M. Evans & Co., 1988 (10th ed.), 160 pages, paper, $4.95
   These titles are part of the Holiday Guide series, which is reviewed in more detail under "Series Reviews."

Nicholson: Guide to Brittany
Salem House, 1985, 160 pages, paper, $5.95
Nicholson: Guide to Loire Region
Salem House, 1985, 144 pages, paper, $5.95
Nicholson: Guide to Normandy
Salem House, 1985, 144 pages, paper, $5.95
   These three titles are part of the Nicholson Guide series, which is reviewed in more detail under "Series Reviews."

100 Hikes In the Alps
by Ira Spring and Harvey Edwards, The Mountaineers, 1985, 224 pages, paper, $8.95
   This is one of the excellent Mountaineers Hiking Guide series, which is reviewed in more detail under "Series Reviews."

Paris: A Literary Companion
by Ian Littlewood, Franklin Watts, Inc., 1987, 246 pages, paper, $16.95
Littlewood, a lecturer at the University of Sussex in England, weaves excerpts from the writings of many famous writers whose experience in Paris formed the basis for their work, with his own most enjoyable commentary. Focusing on each district of the city, he brings the past to life through its literature and the history of the times that produced each piece. Thoroughly fascinating and completely engrossing,, this book is a real must for the traveler seeking something more than practicalities and typical sightseeing notes.

Paris/Access
by Richard Saul Wurman, Prentice Hall Press, 1987, 181 pages, paper, $14.95
This book is part of the popular Access Guide series, which is reviewed in more detail under "Series Reviews." This guide is one of three in the series produced in a handy spiral binding.

Paris and the Ile de France: A Phaidon Art and Architecture Guide
Prentice Hall Press, 1987, 259 pages, cloth, $17.95
This book is part of the encyclopedic Phaidon Art and Architecture Guide series, which is reviewed in more detail under "Series Reviews."

Paris Art Guide
Robert Silver Associates, 1988, 128 pages, paper, $10.95
This is one of the Robert Silver Art Guide series, which is reviewed in more detail under "Series Reviews."

Paris at Its Best
by Robert Kane, Passport Books, 1987, 232 pages, paper, $9.95
This book is part of the widely praised At Its Best Guide series, which is reviewed in more detail under "Series Reviews."

Paris in Your Pocket
Barron's Educational Series, 1987, 208 pages, paper, $3.95
This is one of the small-format In-Your-Pocket Guide series, which is reviewed in more detail under "Series Reviews."

Paris par Arrondissement
Editions L'Indispensable, 1987, 158+ pages, paper, $14.95
This classic, little book, contains mostly maps and is small enough to fit into a back pocket. Each street is listed alphabetically and tied to its *arrondissement* or district. Behind the numbered pages are an

equal number of pages with maps, each tabbed for easy reference to its particular district. The system works well, and that's important, since the districts and streets of Paris can be confusing. Also included are many pages of addresses of all sorts of important traveler's services, museums, theatres, etc.—each tied in, again, to the particular district in which it is located. Published in Paris, this book currently has no American distributor, but some travel bookstores do stock it, including Travel Books Unlimited and Book Passage (see Travel Bookstore appendix).

Paris Rendez-Vous

by Alexandre Lazareff, Prentice Hall Press, 1988, 256 pages, paper, $10.95

Released after press time, this interesting-sounding book focuses on the best places to meet for different types of occasions: brunch with friends, tea at four, afternoon cocktails, romantic dinners, or all-night dancing. Lazareff is a Parisian food critic and writes a column for the French newspaper *Le Figaro*.

Pariswalks

by Alison and Sonia Landes, Henry Holt & Co., 1982, 256 pages, paper, $9.95

This is one of the Citywalks series, which is reviewed in more detail under "Series Reviews."

Pauper's Paris: How to Spend More Time in Paris Without Spending More Francs

by Miles Turner, St. Martin's Press, 1986, 241 pages, paper, $8.95

Recently brought to America, *Pauper's Paris* was first published in Britain. Focusing on the adventurous soul traveling with very few funds, this book does a fine job covering the cheapest sources of food, sleep, shopping, sightseeing, and entertainment. Every selection is given an excellent evaluation and plenty of helpful hints are included. Previous editions have come most every year, so information will hopefully be kept fresh and current.

The Penguin Guide to France

edited by John Ardagh, Viking Penguin, 1985, 336 pages, cloth, $22.50

This thorough, enjoyable cultural and tourist guide covers many travel topics, including foods, wines, festivals, architecture, and arts and crafts.

The Penguin Guide to France
edited by Alan Tucker, Viking Penguin, 1988, 228-448 pages, paper, $9.95-12.95

This is another *Penguin Guide to France*. The new Penguin Travel Guide series (which is reviewed in more detail under "Series Reviews") had not been released at press time and the titles for the series were supposed to be as listed. Obviously, given the previous title of the same name, there may have to be some fine tuning changes. Nonetheless, watch for these new, much anticipated guides. At press time only a range of prices and page counts for the entire series were available.

Permanent Parisians: An Illustrated Guide to the Cemeteries of Paris
by Judi Culbertson and Tom Randall, Chelsea Green Publishing, 1986, 230 pages, paper, $15.95

This beautifully designed, delightfully written guide provides information on the final resting places of both the famous and the obscure. Nineteen walking tours, combined with the help of well-drawn maps and selected photos, will lead interested travelers to the graves of Balzac, Modigliani, Isadora Duncan, Jim Morrison, Chopin, Oscar Wilde, and many, many more. At every stop along the way the authors' historic notes will bring those long dead alive.

The Pleasures of Paris: A Gastronomic Companion
by Michael Bond, Crown Publishers, 1988, 208 pages, paper, $9.95

In this book, released after press time, Bond shares his favorite Parisian restaurants, selected during his ten years in the city. The full range of price categories is represented.

Provence and the Cote d'Azur: A Phaidon Art and Architecture Guide
Prentice Hall Press, 1986, 259 pages, cloth, $14.95

This book is part of the encyclopedic Phaidon Art and Architecture Guide series, which is reviewed in more detail under "Series Reviews."

Rand McNally: Paris
by Anne Corbierre, Rand McNally & Co., 1983, 128 pages, paper, $5.95

This is one of the small-format Rand McNally Pocket Guide series, which is reviewed in more detail under "Series Reviews."

Rough Guide to Brittany & Normandy
by Greg Ward, Routledge & Kegan Paul, 1987, 250 pages, paper, $11.95

Rough Guide to France
by Kate Baillie, Tim Salmon, and Andrew Sanger, Routledge &
Kegan Paul, 1986, 475 pages, paper, $10.95
Rough Guide to Paris
by Kate Baillie and Tim Salmon, Routledge & Kegan Paul, 1987,
254 pages, paper, $10.95
These three titles are part of the excellent Rough Guide series,
which is reviewed in more detail under "Series Reviews." The series
is updated every two to three years. The Brittany and Normandy
volume had not been released at press time, so the number of pages
is approximate.

The Serious Shopper's Guide to Paris
Prentice Hall Press, 1987, 384 pages, paper, $14.95
This book is part of the Serious Shopper's Guide series, which is
reviewed in more detail under "Series Reviews."

Shopwalks: Paris
by Jane Magidson and Nancy Marshak, Crown Publishing, 1985,
fold-out map/guide, paper, $4.95
This book is part of the Shopwalks series, which is reviewed in
more detail under "Series Reviews."

Signposts: French
by Edith Baer and Margaret Wightman, Cambridge University
Press, 1982, 100 pages, paper, $5.95
This book contains over 400 photographs of signs and various
notices that appear along the highways and byways of France.

Small Museums of the French Riviera
by Eloise Danto, Eldan Press, 1985, 104 pages, paper, $9.95
This is one of the Eldan Museum Guide series, which is reviewed
in more detail under "Series Reviews."

Three Rivers of France (Dordogne, Lot, Tarn)
by Freda White, Faber & Faber, 1984 (reprint of 1952 ed.), 232
pages, paper, $9.95
This true travel classic was rereleased in 1984 in its first-edition
form. Entertaining and well written, it remains an excellent introduction and tour guide to an area of France filled with beautiful,
meandering rivers and quaint villages. This area of the Massif Central is still relatively undiscovered by American travelers.

A Touch of Monaco and the French Riviera Guide
edited by David Ward-Perkins, Talman Co., 1986, 242 pages, paper, $7.95

A Touch of Paris Guide
edited by Pierre Salinger, *et al.*, Talman Co., 1986, 242 pages, paper, $7.95

Both of these titles are part of the Touch of the City Guide series, which is reviewed in more detail under "Series Reviews."

Tour of Mount Blanc: A Walking Guide
by Andrew Harper, Hunter Publishing, 1988, 100 pages, paper, $9.95

This book is part of the Hunter Mountain Walks series, which is reviewed in more detail under "Series Reviews."

The Traveler's Key to Medieval France: A Guide to the Sacred Architecture of Medieval France
by John James, Alfred Knopf, Inc., 1986, 316 pages, cloth, $18.95

This is one of the excellent Traveler's Key Guide series, which is reviewed in more detail under "Series Reviews."

Travels in Provence
by Marion Deschamps, David & Charles, 1988, 176 pages, paper, $13.95

Travels in the Dordogne
by Fiona Fennell, David & Charles, 1988, 158 pages, paper, $13.95

The two authors are specialists in food, Deschamps a well-known food writer, and Fennell a British restaurateur. Each presents you with a thoroughly planned itinerary for a several week vacation in these two delightful regions. There are personal picks of restaurants, hotels, and places to visit. These were released after our deadline, but certainly sound wonderful.

The Visitor's Guide to Brittany
by Neil Lands, Hunter Publishing, 1984, 142 pages, paper, $8.95

This is one of the Visitor's Guide series, which is reviewed in more detail under "Series Reviews."

The Visitor's Guide to Corsica
Hunter Publishing, 1987, 230 pages, paper, $9.95

This book is part of the New Visitor's Guide series, which is reviewed in more detail under "Series Reviews."

The Visitor's Guide to the Dordogne
by Neil Lands, Hunter Publishing, 1986, 160 pages, paper, $8.95

The Visitor's Guide to the French Coast
  by Martin Collins, Hunter Publishing, 1985, 160 pages, paper,
  $8.95
The Visitor's Guide to the Loire
  by Norman Brangham, Hunter Publishing, 1985, 160 pages, paper,
  $8.95
The Visitor's Guide to Normandy
  by Martin Collins, Hunter Publishing, 1986, 151 pages, paper,
  $8.95
The Visitor's Guide to the South of France
  by Norman Brangham, Hunter Publishing, 1984, 159 pages, paper,
  $8.95
    Five titles in the Visitor's Guide series which is reviewed in more
  detail under "Series Reviews."

Walking in France
  by Rob Hunter, Haynes Publications, 1982, 218 pages, paper, $9.95
    Hunter has written an excellent introduction to hiking in France.
  There is plenty of information to help you with your plans. Each
  region is well described. Descriptions include topography, climate,
  national parks, nearby footpaths, where to find information on accommodations and camping in each area, transportation options,
  available maps and guides, the wildlife of the area, and useful information centers where you can seek additional details specific to your
  needs.

Walking in Northern France
  by Martin Collins, Hunter Publishing, 1987, 192 pages, paper,
  $8.95
Walking in the Alps
  by Brian Spencer, Hunter Publishing, 1986, 192 pages, paper, $9.95
    Two titles in the Hunter Walks series, which is reviewed in more
  detail under "Series Reviews."

Walks and Climbs in the Pyrenees
  by Kev Reynolds, Hunter Publishing, 1988 (3rd ed.), 206 pages,
  paper, $12.95
    Part of the Hunter Mountain Walks series, which is reviewed in
  more detail under "Series Reviews."

Walks Through Paris
  by Bert Lief, VLE Limited, undated, fold-out map/guide, paper,
  $2.00
    One of the Way-Ahead Guide series, which is reviewed in more
  detail under "Series Reviews."

Webster's Wine Tours: France
   Prentice Hall Press, 1987, 208 pages, cloth (flexible), $15.95
   Part of a the rapidly growing Webster's Wine Tours series, which
is reviewed in more detail under "Series Reviews."

**Whole Europe Escape Manual: France, Holland, Belgium with
Luxembourg**
   by Kerry Green and Peter Bythiner, World Leisure Corp., 1985, 160
pages, paper, $6.95
   Part of the unique Escape Manual series, which is reviewed in
more detail under "Series Reviews."

The Wine Lover's Guide to France
   by Michael Busselle, Little, Brown & Co., 1986, 255 pages, cloth,
$24.95
   A beautiful, hardbound book, filled with classic color photographs,
which clearly describes 26 tours through all of France's wine-growing
regions. For each region there are helpful wine buying notes, plus a
very useful calendar of annual events for each region. A finely done
guide for the true wine lover.

German Democratic Republic: See "East Germany."
Germany: See "East Germany" and "West Germany."
Gibraltar: See "Europe as a Whole." Gibraltar is included in *Birnbaum's
Europe* and *Fodor's Europe*.

GREAT BRITAIN

See also "Europe as a Whole. " Great Britain is the most commonly
used reference by travelers to this region. It comprises England, Scotland, and Wales. Technically, Great Britain is part of the United Kingdom of Great Britain and Ireland, a political entity that also includes
Northern Ireland. However, for the purposes of this book, Great Britain
is used as the primary designation and Northern Ireland is listed separately. The first books listed below cover two or all of the countries
of Great Britain. Immediately following are separate sections on England, Scotland, and Wales which list books focusing exclusively on
each of these countries. Great Britain is included in the following major,
all-purpose guides to Europe: *Birnbaum's Europe; Fielding's Europe;
Fielding's Economy Europe; Fisher's World: Europe; Fodor's Europe;
Fodor's Budget Europe; Let's Go: Europe.*

AA Bed and Breakfast in Britain
   by the Automobile Association, Salem House, 1988, 471 pages,
paper, $14.95
   The Automobile Association has put together a comprehensive

directory of more than 3000 bed and breakfast establishments that they feel offer good value in each price range. They have even included information on guesthouses, farmhouses, and inns. Good maps and plenty of details are also provided.. Comments on each selection are brief and details are summarized with the use of symbols because of the amount of information crammed into this annually updated volume.

AA Best Value Britain

by the Automobile Association, Salem House, 1988, 252 pages, paper, $12.95

The AA asked its inspectors where they would stay and eat if they were spending their own money. The result is this valuable collection of "Best Value" selections in all price ranges. Packed with solid, informative information on each establishment, this book also contains special sections on "good value" lunches in London and Birmingham's Chinese restaurants.

AA Book of British Villages

by the Automobile Association, W. W. Norton & Co., 1983, 447 pages, cloth, $27.95

This big, beautiful hardback covers 700 of Britain's most interesting and attractive villages in considerable detail. Typical AA maps are included.

AA Book of Country Walks

by the Automobile Association, W. W. Norton & Co., 1986, unnumbered, paper, $29.95

This large notebook-style book has its many walks on pages that can be removed for easier use.

AA Britain for Free

by the Automobile Association, Salem House, 1986, 190 pages, paper, $9.95

This great resource book of more than 1000 places throughout Britain that cost nothing to visit includes everything from stately homes, art galleries, museums, and cathedrals to cider mills, craft workshops, and lavender distilleries. Brief comments are made on each and every entry is coded to the numerous maps at the back that will at least generally indicate their location. Some of the larger cities are given additional detail maps, which are very well done.

AA Camping and Caravaning in Britain
by the Automobile Association, Salem House, 1988, 304 pages, paper, $14.95

This no-words-wasted directory from the British Automobile Association covers 1000 of Britain's best sites in all the regions of Great Britain. Each entry includes a basic description of each facility, what amenities are available (described through space-saving symbols), and what restrictions are in force. Each is also easily located using the excellent location atlas included in the book. This title is updated annually.

AA Discovering Britain: Where to See the Best of Our Countryside
by the Automobile Association, W. W. Norton & Co., 1986, 415 pages, cloth, $27.95

This is yet another great hardback from the Automobile Association on dozens of the best touring locations, complete with numerous photographs and maps.

AA Family Days Out in Britain
by the Automobile Association, Salem House, 1988, 224 pages, paper, $15.95

This useful guide is full of ideas on the whole issue of where to go and what to do when traveling with children in Britain.

AA Guide to Golf in Britain
by the Automobile Association, Salem House, 1988, 264 pages, paper, $21.95

This comprehensive directory offers information on a massive number of courses through Britain (1600 in all), including locations, prices, and nearby accommodations. An interesting introduction by one of the best golfers in the world, Seve Ballesteros, kicks off this interesting book.

AA Guide to National Trust Properties in Britain
by the Automobile Association, Salem House, 1983, 192 pages, paper, $17.95

The National Trust owns castles, large expanses of countryside and coastline, and beautiful gardens of every description, all of which are open to the public. This large-format book serves well as a planning guide to help travelers select the places they would most like to see.

AA Holiday Homes, Cottages, and Apartments in Britain
by the Automobile Association, Salem House, 1988, 288 pages, paper, $14.95
 The Automobile Association has assembled thousands of suggestions for vacation rentals in rural settings as well as in the middle of London. All the needed practical information is detailed in typical AA fashion in this annually updated book.

AA Hotels and Restaurants in Britain
by the Automobile Association, Salem House, 1988, 824 pages, paper, $22.95
 This AA-style directory, which is very popular in Britain, is crammed with essential information on over 5000 places to stay and eat in every price range. All are graded using the AA's respected star-rating system. This is an incredibly comprehensive, annually updated guide.

AA Illustrated Guide to Britain: A Journey of Discovery through England, Wales, and Scotland
by the Automobile Association, 1979, 400 pages, cloth, $27.95
AA Illustrated Guide to Britain's Coast
by the Automobile Association, 1983, 303 pages, cloth, $27.95
AA Illustrated Guide to Country Towns and Villages of Britain
by the Automobile Association, 1986, 448 pages, cloth, $29.95
 These three fantastic hardbacks are filled with photographs, informative commentary, and plenty of maps.

AA Seaside Accommodations in Britain
by the Automobile Association, Salem House, 1986, 251 pages, paper, $12.95
 This directory is packed, using numerous symbols and small print, with more than 2000 entries, all graded in standard AA fashion.

AA Secret Britain
by the Automobile Association, Salem House, 1986, 320 pages, paper, $24.95
 This is a beautifully done, thoroughly engaging guide to the "unexpected, unexplored, mysterious, exotic and eccentric things and places of Britain." As is usual with an AA guidebook, good maps and color photos supplement the textual materials. Arranged regionally, this book a good planning tool for visiting lesser-known places where the bizarre legends and unusual traditions have taken place. Visits to more familiar spots are suggested, too, but only in the context of some unusual story or undiscovered nook or cranny. This book is great fun to read and definitely a wonderful planning aid.

AA Stately Homes, Museums, Castles, and Gardens in Britain
by the Automobile Association, Salem House, 1986, 310 pages, paper, $14.95
Good information on the multitude of sightseeing and touring options through the museums, castles, gardens, and stately homes of Britain is included in this guide.

AA The Second Touring Guide to Britain
by the Automobile Association, Salem House, 1984, 192 pages, paper, $18.95
This large-format companion volume to the *Touring Guide to Britain* below details an additional 80 driving tours, primarily short one-day loops.

AA Touring Book of Britain
by the Automobile Association, Salem House, 1984, 320 pages, paper, $27.95
This useful, large-format travel guide/directory details over 2000 places to visit, day trips, and "special features on areas of outstanding interest." Good road maps, plenty of color photos, and an enjoyably informative text complete this book.

AA Touring Guide to Britain
by the Automobile Association, Salem House, 1982, 256 pages, paper, $19.95
This large-format guide offers 112 suggested tours through the best of Britain. Most are structured as one-day driving loops. Good maps, photos and practical information supplement this useful text.

AA Traveller's Guide for the Disabled
by the Automobile Association, Salem House, 1988, 140 pages, paper, $7.95
Included in this helpful guide are planned tours of hundreds of British and European tourist attractions along with suggested accommodations and the various details needed on access and facilities in AA-inspected lodgings. This guide is updated annually.

AA Treasures of Britain
by the Automobile Association, W. W. Norton & Co., 1986 (4th ed.), 680 pages, cloth, $27.95
This large, beautifully done hardback is filled with color photographs of the riches of Britain and Ireland. Each treasure is tied to maps and an informative text.

AA 250 Tours of Britain
by the Automobile Association, 1986, 415 pages, cloth, $29.95
This excellent collection of automobile tours in a large-format, hardback book includes copious maps, photographs, and a good narrative.

AA Where to Go In Britain
by the Automobile Association, Salem House, 1980, 224 pages, paper, $19.95
This worthwhile idea and planning book is an A-to-Z listing of hundreds of the most famous places to visit in Britain, complete with an informative text, color photos, and good road maps.

AA Where to Go In the British Countryside
by the Automobile Association, Salem House, 1985, 320 pages, paper, $21.95
This is another large-format idea book detailing 500 places to visit in rural Britain, including nature reserves and national parks. This book is a good planning tool, has lots of beautiful photos, and is fun to read besides.

ABC Rail Guide
ABC International, monthly editions, 650 pages, paper, $12.00
The most comprehensive and complete railroad information for Great Britain is contained in this famous monthly timetable, first published in 1853. The primary focus of the guide is on London and service throughout Southern England, but all areas are covered. Also included are London trains for European destinations via hovercraft or car ferries. These schedules are available directly from the publishers or from British Travel Bookshop (see Travel Bookstore appendix).

The Ackerman Guide to the Best Restaurants and Hotels in the British Isles
by Roy Ackerman, Viking Penguin, 1987, 448 pages, paper, $12.95
Ackerman offers excellent, opinionated evaluations of restaurants as only a chef and restaurateur can. The restaurants reviewed fall into every price range. The guide is very well done with nice graphics and drawings, some of which are in color. The organization of the book is by region, with an additional "Best of" section.

The American Express Pocket Guide to England and Wales
by John Tomes and Michael Jackson, Prentice Hall Press, 1984, 272 pages, cloth, $8.95
This is one of the the well-done American Express Pocket Guide series, which is reviewed in more detail under "Series Reviews."

The American Guide to Britain
by the Automobile Association, 1987, 298 pages, cloth, $24.95

Part history and part travel guide, this book focuses on Britain from the perspective of the American traveler. A detailed gazetteer with over 1500 places felt to be of greatest interest to an American, 75 color maps, and town plans to facilitate the book's use make this a helpful reference.

An American's Guide to Britain
by Robin Winks, Charles Scribner's Sons, 1984 (revised ed.), 412 pages, paper, $11.95

In this truly superb book, Robin Winks, a Yale historian and former cultural attaché to the U.S. Embassy in London, shares his intimate knowledge of Britain's most fascinating places—often the very ones tourists miss. Winks presents his pick of cathedrals, castles, parks, art galleries, museums and shops. His descriptions are excellent—clear, crisp, and informative. Winks's "How to Survive" chapter covers all sorts of practicalities—food, drink, travel, phones, money, etc. Suggested tour itineraries of various lengths, which can be done by car or public transportation, are offered. Some specific, time-dated facts may, however, no longer be true.

Ashley Courtenay's Hotel Guide: Let's Halt Awhile in Great Britain
by Ashley Courtenay, The Talman Co., 1987 (54th ed.), 704 pages, paper, $12.95

This annual volume has been published for more than half a century. Carefully and personally researched by 28 inspectors who spend their lives keeping this volume up-to-date by visiting every establishment, this independent guide gives thorough coverage of 1500 hotels. The writeups are sharp, opinionated, and very helpful. Selections cover a wide range of prices and all the needed practical details are given. In addition, readers of this excellent reference are invited to join the "Circle" and offer their own feedback.

Baedeker's Great Britain
Prentice Hall Press, undated, 432 pages, paper, $14.95

This book is part of Baedeker's Country/Regional Guide series, which is reviewed in more detail under "Series Reviews."

The Bed and Breakfast Guide to Great Britain
Consumers Reports Books, 1988, 384 pages, paper, $12.00

This new book, expected during 1988 but released after press time, covers B&Bs in all price ranges throughout Britain. Other titles by Consumers Reports and its sister organization in Great Britain, the

Association for Consumer Research, have been of high quality, so there is no reason to expect less from this one.

The Best Bed & Breakfast In The World: England, Scotland, & Wales

by Sigourney Welles and Jill Darbey, The Globe Pequot Press, 1988, 340 pages, paper, $12.95

This informative title groups over 900 bed and breakfast selections by county—with a separate section for London. A brief description of each county and its most interesting sights, and a short, but very helpful, gazetteer precede the listing of local B&Bs. The B&B descriptions are well done. Additional information noted in checklist style includes price range (in pounds), whether children and/or pets are welcome, and whether evening meals are offered. An orientation map of each county is also provided. A booking service is available and instructions are given for making reservations from overseas. All establishments are members of the World Wide Bed and Breakfast Association. The orientation to each area is a welcome touch and make just reading this guide a lot of fun.

Best of Britain

by Richard Binns, Atheneum, 1984, 144 pages, cloth, $8.95

Binns provides useful hotel and restaurant information and other practical facts in this sturdy, pocket-sized hardback volume. This quality book will also guide travelers on all sorts of exciting journeys into the rural nooks and crannies of Britain. Be sure to check all time-dated material.

The Best Pubs of Great Britain

edited by Neil Hanson, The Globe Pequot Press, 1986 (14th ed.), 320 pages, paper, $9.95

Hansen takes us Yankees by the hand and offers an enjoyable orientation to the realities of British beer—its history, its breweries (both large and small), its modern-day chemical additives (only in some and definitely to be avoided), and the *real* ales. More than 500 pubs are listed, with use of symbols and short notes. This is the only pub guide in the U.K. that is done exclusively with independent volunteers and without advertising support; each volunteer lives in the area he or she describes. This is an excellent resource book.

Birdwatcher's Britain

edited by John Parslow, Hunter Publishing, 1983, 256 pages, paper, $12.95

This good, comprehensive guide to the best birdwatching walks contains good maps, a general orientation, the best seasons to visit each location, and what to look for while there.

Birnbaum's Great Britain and Ireland

edited by Stephen Birnbaum, Houghton Mifflin, 1987, 848 pages, paper, $12.95

Beginning in 1989, this volume will split into two separate titles— Great Britain and Ireland. It is part of the excellent Birnbaum's Guide series, which is reviewed in more detail under "Series Reviews." The series is updated annually.

Blue Guide: Cathedrals and Abbeys of England and Wales

by Kenneth Spence, W. W. Norton & Co., 1984, 320 pages, paper, $16.95

Spence has assembled copious information on the history and description of numerous cathedrals and abbeys throughout England and Wales in this most helpful book.. Numerous floor plans are provided. This is a special edition in the Blue Guide series, which is reviewed in more detail under "Series Reviews."

Blue Guide: Literary Britain and Ireland

by Ian Ousby, W. W. Norton & Co., 1985, 424 pages, paper, $14.95

Ousby's work discusses 180 famous British writers and the places they knew and wrote about. It is arranged by author and suggests numerous tours of the places described. Many of the tours are designed for walkers. This book is a special title in the Blue Guide series, which is reviewed in more detail under "Series Reviews."

A Book of British Music Festivals

by Richard Adams, Riverdale Co., 1986, 224 pages, cloth, $23.95

Adams has created a superb survey of the nearly 200 classical music festivals held each year in England, Scotland, and Wales. Included are strictly music festivals and other types of festivals in which music plays a major role, such as festivals for youth, organ festivals, festivals in churches and cathedrals, early music festivals, and contemporary music festivals. A detailed appendix offers addresses and phone numbers for each festival so specifics on any given year's event can be obtained.

Britain At Its Best

by Robert Kane, Passport Books, 1986, 424 pages, paper, $9.95

This book is part of the quality At Its Best Guide series, which is reviewed in more detail under "Series Reviews."

Britain Before the Conquest: Celtic Britain

by Lloyd and Jennifer Laing, Hunter Publishing, 1987, 256 pages, paper, $9.95

Britain Before the Conquest: The Origins of Britain

by Lloyd Laing, Hunter Publishing, 1987, 256 pages, paper, $9.95

These are two titles in the Britain Before the Conquest Guide series, which is reviewed in more detail under "Series Reviews."

Britain by Britrail

by George and LaVerne Ferguson, The Globe Pequot Press, 1988 (9th ed.), 320 pages, paper, $10.95

This excellent, annual resource guide offers considerable help in planning tours of Britain by train. The Fergusons offer a truly comprehensive guide filled with knowledgeable recommendations, suggested excursions from London, Edinburgh, and Glasgow, and special itineraries including ferry crossings to Ireland and the continent, as well as schedules, fares and prices. This is a great resource.

Britain by Train

by Patrick Goldring, Salem House, 1987 (revised ed.), 208 pages, paper, $8.95

This is another solid book for those using the Britrail Pass. It includes lots of tips on how to use the trains in Britain and the most interesting itineraries.

Britain Off the Motorway

by Christopher Pick, Salem House, 1988, 352 pages, paper, $9.95

Discover the many attractions located no more than six miles from the major motorways using this book. Organized by highway and junction (exit) number, this guide is particularly useful for those with little time or a fear of driving down the smaller highways on the "wrong" side of the street.

British Railway Journeys

by Caroline Dakers, Salem House, 1986, 400 pages, paper, $12.95

In this great book for train travelers, Dakers describes the things that can be seen from the windows of the trains that run along all the most popular routes from London.

The British Selection: Arthur Eperon's Guide to the Best of British Hotels

by Arthur Eperon, Hunter Publishing, 1985, 164 pages, paper, $12.95

Please refer to the review of the identically formatted companion volume, *The French Selection*, that is reviewed under "France."

The Cambridge Guide to the Museums of Britain and Ireland
by Kenneth Hudson and Ann Nicholls, Cambridge University
Press, 1987, 435 pages, cloth, $24.95
This comprehensive and totally fascinating guide lists over 2000
museums and art galleries of every imaginable sort: puppets, cars,
anthropology, zoology, dental, cycling, maritime, children's, and art.
Each collection is briefly and intelligently described, practical information is provided, including the hours open to the public as well
as what amenities are available—museum shop, refreshments,
wheelchair facilities, picnic area, guided tours, free admission, etc.
Of particular help is the extensive, well-constructed subject index.
This is a incredible planning resource.

Charming Small Hotel Guide: Britain & Ireland
edited by Chris Gill, Hunter Publishing, 1988, 192 pages, paper,
$9.95
This is one of two volumes currently published (the other is on
Italy) in what will become a series on those small hotels that are so
memorable, because of their atmosphere, their caring service, and
good food at a fair price—in short, charming. Featuring 300 hotels,
many with a color photograph, this book provides an informative
review and all the needed practical details. These are not just the
hotels found in the most popular tourist places, but the ones in the
tiny hamlets, the nooks and the crannies that remain to this day
relatively undiscovered also.

The Children's Treasure Hunt Travel Guide to Britain
Hippocrene Books, 1979, 200 pages, paper, $6.95
Containing travel entertainment ideas for ages six and up, this
book is part of the Children's Treasure Hunt Guide series, which is
reviewed in more detail under "Series Reviews."

Classic Walks in Great Britain
by Bill Birkett, Haynes Publications, 1987, 183 pages, cloth, $23.95
Including walks and hikes (11 long-distance hikes and 22 day hikes
or walks), this book is part of the Classic Walks Guide series, which
is reviewed in more detail under "Series Revews."

Collier World Traveler Series: Great Britain and Ireland
edited by Philippe Gloaguen and Pierre Josse, Macmillan
Publishing, 1986, 192 pages, paper, $6.95
This is one of the Collier World Traveler Guide series, which is
reviewed in more detail under "Series Reviews."

Collins Book of British Gardens
by George Plumptre, Salem House, 1985, 463 pages, paper, $13.95
This beautifully done book contains excellent descriptions and all the practical information, including phone numbers so be sure to confirm the hours each is open.

Collins Guide to Cathedrals, Abbeys and Priories of England and Wales
by Henry Thorold, Salem House, 1987, 332 pages, cloth, $24.95
This comprehensive guide covers 48 cathedrals and a multitude of abbeys and priories, all of which are still in use today. Included are historical notes, detailed descriptions, special features unique to each building, and over 300 black-and-white photographs.

Country Inns and Back Roads: Britain and Ireland
by Norman Simpson, Harper & Row, 1988 (5th ed.), 320 pages, paper, $11.95
This book is part of the popular Country Inns and Back Roads series, which is reviewed in more detail under "Series Reviews." It is updated annually.

Country Inns, Lodges & Historic Hotels: Great Britain
by Eileen and Eugene O'Reilly, Burt Franklin–Publisher, 1988 (8th ed.), pages, paper, $8.95
This excellent resource is one of the Compleat Traveler's Companion series, which is reviewed in more detail under "Series Reviews." This annually updated title accepts no fees for inclusion.

Crown Insider's Guide to Britain
by Pat and Lester Brooks, Crown Publishers, 1987, 338 pages, paper, $10.95
This is one of the Crown Insider's Guide series, which is reviewed in more detail under "Series Reviews."

CTC Route Guide to Cycling in Britain and Ireland
by Christa Gausden and Nicholas Crane, Haynes Publishing, 1982 (revised ed.), 432 pages, cloth, $15.95
This is the official guide of the Cyclists' Touring Club of Britain. The authors have selected the best possible network of 365 interlinking routes to take the cyclist through the most beautiful parts of the British countryside. Using this network, tours of one day or several weeks can be plotted. Clear detail maps with references to more detailed road maps, distances, plenty of notes about points of interest along each route, and other practical data are all included.

Cyclist's Britain: A Complete Guide to On and Off-Highway Cycle Routes
Hunter Publishing, 1985, 302 pages, paper, $12.95
This solid cycling guidebook contains numerous suggested routes, good maps, and a few suggested lodging and eating options along the way.

Day Trips in Britain: 60 One-Day Adventures by Rail, Bus or Car from London and Edinburgh
by Earl Steinbicker, Hastings House, 1988, 300 pages, paper, $10.95
This is a new title, released after press time, in the Earl Steinbicker's Day Trips series, which is reviewed in more detail under "Series Reviews." The number of pages and price are approximate.

Derek Johansen's Recommended Hotels in Britain
by Derek Johansen, Salem House, 1988, 380 pages, paper, 24.95
This glossy, rather pretentious large-format guide is a good resource for descriptions of over 300 of the finest—not to mention most expensive—country hotels in Britain. Full color photographs of both interior and exterior views of each of these luxurious establishments make this a beautiful book. Specific reviews of particular establishments, however, must be found elsewhere.

The Economist Business Traveller's Guide: Britain
Prentice Hall Press, 1987, 256 pages, cloth, $17.95
This is one of the excellent Economist Business Traveller's Guide series, which is reviewed in more detail under "Series Reviews."

Egon Ronay's Guide to Healthy Eating Out
Salem House, 1988, 350 pages, paper, $14.95
This new guide in the Egon Ronay fold is for the health-conscious traveler. Information on over 500 restaurants, cafes, wine bars and pubs throughout Britain offering "whole food," including vegetarian cuisine, is provided. A helpful paragraph on each establishment details prices, locations, sample dishes, and types of food. Each establishment is also coded as to its status: restaurant, pub, or "quick bite" spot. The book is arranged alphabetically in five sections: London, England, Scotland, Wales, and the Channel Islands; prices are in pounds.

Egon Ronay's Hotels and Restaurants (Great Britain & Ireland)
Salem House, 1988, 864 pages, paper, $19.95
This is one of Britain's most famous food and lodging guides. Annually updated, it covers over 2500 places to stay or eat. Hotels are graded on a scale of 100; restaurants are rated with a star system.

Most hotels are illustrated and good location maps are provided. Prices are in pounds.

Egon Ronay's Just A Bite
Salem House, 1988, 384 pages, paper, $18.95

An annual volume, *Just a Bite* provides information on over 900 places in which travelers can eat well and cheaply. Everything from bistros, pubs, and tea rooms to wine bars and health food restaurants is included with the more standard cafes and restaurants. Typical menus are described and location maps are provided. This book is useful for travelers trying to stick to a careful budget. Prices are in pounds.

Egon Ronay's Pubs & Bar Food
Salem House, 1988, 320 pages, paper, $18.95

Pubs are more than just a place to drink and the Egon Ronay team, now in its 31st year, has identified 1000 of the best, chosen specifically for their good food, comfortable overnight accommodations, and pleasant atmosphere. Information included covers prices, types of food, rooms available, types of beer available, and details on each pub and its history.

English, Welsh, and Scottish Country Inns
by Karen and June Brown, Travel Press, 1988, 290 pages, paper, $12.95

This book is part of the popular Karen Brown's Country Inns series, which is reviewed in more detail under "Series Reviews."

Exploring Britain: 1001 Places to Visit
Sheridan House, 1986, 216 pages, paper, $19.95

This very large-format book (10" x 14") bridges the gap between maps and guidebooks. Plenty of quality road maps and equally as many ideas of things to do are contained within this volume. Each map is linked to a gazetteer. Interesting sights are marked on the map, then described in the adjacent gazetteer. This is definitely a great book to have on the back seat of the car.

The Farm Holiday Bureau Bed & Breakfast & Self Catering Holidays in Britain
Salem House, 1988, 260 pages, paper, $7.95

Contained herein are hundreds of suggestions for comfortable lodging in traditional British farmhouses with real home cooking at budget prices, and lodgings that can be rented for the whole family where travelers can cater their own meals. Details include rates, locations, and the general ambiance of each farm.

The Farm Holiday Guide to Holidays in England, Wales, Ireland, Channel Islands

Hunter Publishing, 1988, 568 pages, paper, $14.95

This popular, annually updated guide lists hundreds of B&Bs, farm and country houses that take in guests, village inns, camping, and activities in all the rural tourist areas.

Fisher's World: Britain

edited by Robert Fisher, Fisher's World, Inc., 1988, 335 pages, paper, $14.95

This book is part of the Fisher's World Guide series, which is reviewed in more detail under "Series Reviews." The series is updated annually.

Fodor's Great Britain

Fodor's Travel Publications, 1987, 512 pages, paper, $13.95

This book is part of Fodor's Country/Regional Guide series, which is reviewed in more detail under "Series Reviews." The series is updated annually.

Fodor's Great Travel Values: Britain

Fodor's Travel Publications, 1987, 224 pages, paper, $5.95

This is one of the budget-oriented Fodor's Great Travel Values Guide series, which is reviewed in more detail under "Series Reviews." The series is updated annually.

Fodor's Royalty Watching: Where to Find Britain's Royal Family

by Andrew Morton, Fodor's Travel Publications, 1987, 182 pages, paper, $9.95

This delightful new title from Fodor, introduced to considerable fanfare, is clearly a break from the standard formula of most other Fodor titles. The outlook is fresh and the execution commendable. In addition to month-by-month charts of what the royal family does, and tips on where they like to eat, shop, and play, this book provides information about the various royal palaces, the private royal homes, the royal yacht, and more.

Frommer's Dollarwise Guide to England and Scotland

by Darwin Porter, Prentice Hall Press, 1988, 718 pages, paper, $11.95

This is one of Frommer's Dollarwise Guide series, which is reviewed in more detail under "Series Reviews." This series emphasizes selections in the moderate price range and is updated every two years.

Frommer's Scotland and Wales on $40 a Day
by Arthur Frommer, Prentice Hall Press, 1988, 562 pages, paper, $11.95

This book is part of the budget-oriented Frommer's Dollar-A-Day Guide series, which is reviewed in more detail under "Series Reviews." The series is updated every two years.

Good Food Guide
edited by Drew Smith, Consumers Reports Books, 1988, 672 pages, paper, $15.00

This annual book, consistently well received by British reviewers, covers a large number of eating establishments rated by a highly refined point system. This is a top-quality restaurant guide prepared through Consumers Reports' sister organization in Britain.

The Good Pub Guide
edited by Alisdair Aird, Consumer Reports Books, 1987, 928 pages, paper, $17.00

Here are informative evaluations of over 1200 pubs, with readers' recommendations on over 3000 more. This guide includes the Channel Islands, and it is updated annually.

Good Value Britain
Prentice Hall Press, 1988, 432 pages, paper, $10.95

This is the new name for *Les Routiers Guide to Britain*, the famous budget guide from France. For more on this great guide, read the review of its companion volume, *Good Value France*.

Great Britain and Ireland: A Phaidon Art and Architecture Guide
Prentice Hall Press, 1985, 644 pages, cloth, $16.95

This is one of the encyclopedic Phaidon Art and Architecture Guide series, which is reviewed in more detail under "Series Reviews."

Great Britain in 22 Days
See *22 Days in Great Britain* below.

A Guide to Ancient Sites in Great Britain
by Janet and Colin Bord, Hunter Publishing, 1987, 192 pages, paper, $12.95
A Guide to Anglo-Saxon Sites
by Nigel and Mary Kerr, Hunter Publishing, 1987, 210 pages, paper, $12.95

These are two practical field guides to the monuments of history, with detailed directions to each site, its historical background, the pertinent archaeological facts, interesting folklore, etc. Each book is copiously illustrated with numerous maps and drawings.

Guide to Antique Shops of Britain

edited by R. Ferguson, Apollo Books, 1988, 900 pages, paper, $25.00

This up-to-date, comprehensive guide to antique shops, galleries, and "trade only" locations includes all the particulars.

A Guide to Norman Sites in Britain

by Nigel and Mary Kerr, Hunter Publishing, 1987, 192 pages, paper, $12.95

This is the third volume in in the Guide to British Sites series. See *A Guide to Ancient Sites in Great Britain* above.

Guide to Scotland and the Lake District

Consumers Reports Books, 1987, 171 pages, paper, $13.00

This is an exceptional guide to hotels, pubs, and restaurants in Scotland and the Lake District of Northern England. The write-ups are very well done and most informative. They describe what the keen eye of the Consumer's Association of Great Britain sees as "best values" in all price ranges. All the essential, practical details, as well as some finely done detail maps, are included in this annually updated volume.

The Hachette Guide to Great Britain: The Only Guide You'll Ever Need

Random House, 1988, 672 pages, paper, $16.95

This book is part of the popular French series, the Hachette Guides, which is reviewed in more detail under "Series Reviews." The series is updated annually.

Historic Country House Hotels: Great Britain

by Sigourney Welles and Jill Darbey, The Globe Pequot Press, 1988, 179 pages, paper, $11.95

An excellent review of many of the charming house hotels throughout Britain, which date from the 11th to the 19th century. Some are small and charming, others exceedingly grand. All are historically and architecturally interesting. All the essentials are included and a full-page photo of each establishment will help you choose. The selections are arranged by county. Each county is described as well, and a useful gazetteer is included. Updated annually.

Historic Houses, Castles & Gardens Open to the Public
Hunter Publishing, 1988, 246 pages, paper, $12.95
This comprehensive directory to over 1300 properties that are open to the public is organized by region and includes everything from cottages to castles. Up-to-date opening times, admission charges, special attractions, and maps are provided.

Historic Walks in London, Bath, Oxford, and Edinburgh
by Betty Reveley and Allan Wendt, Salem House, 1985, 216 pages, paper, $8.95
This book describes many interesting walks through history and is well worth the price of an added detail map or two, which they seem to have forgotten to include.

Holiday Which? Good Walks Guide
Consumers Reports Books, 1988, 608 pages, paper, $12.00
Released after press time, this new guide from the respected people at Consumers Reports and their British sister organization covers more than 200 inland and coastal walking paths throughout Britain.

Hotels & Restaurants of Britain
Prentice Hall Press, 1988 (60th ed.), 507 pages, paper, $12.95
This is one of those official guides—from the British Hotels, Restaurants, & Caterers Association. It covers more than 1700 establishments, each with a color photo, and manages to do so with the help of various space-saving symbols. The write-ups are short and rather bland.

Insight Guide: Great Britain
by Apa Productions, Prentice Hall Press, 1985, 364 pages, paper, $15.95
This is one of the acclaimed Insight Guide series, which is reviewed in more detail under "Series Reviews."

The Intelligent Traveller's Guide to Historic Britain
by Philip Crowl, Congdon & Weed, 1983, 832 pages, paper, $19.95
In this classic travel guide, Crowl discusses in great depth the historical context of more than 1000 places in Britain, each cross-referenced to a gazetteer that locates it and evaluates its attractiveness for the traveler. Travelers interested in the history behind the places will find no finer work than this.

Keep One Suitcase Empty: The Bargain Shopper's Guide to the Best Factory Outlets in England, Ireland, Scotland, and Wales
by Judith McQuown, Arbor House, 1987, 248 pages, paper, $7.95

Everything from cashmere sweaters and tweed jackets to hand-blown glass and silverware can be bought for less with the aid of this excellent book. McQuown has done an excellent job in assembling a vast array of outlets for the bargain shopper. Each is carefully described; just browsing through this book is an educational experience. The basics are there too: the best products to look for in each country, size conversion charts, addresses, hours open, credit cards accepted, and other currency and charge card realities. Note: There is a companion volume on Europe of similar title.

The Knopf Traveler's Guide to Art: Great Britain and Ireland
by Michael Jacobs and Paul Stirton, Alfred Knopf, Inc., 1984, 304 pages, cloth, $14.95

This is one title in the excellent Knopf Guides to Art series, which is reviewed in more detail under "Series Reviews."

Les Routiers Guide to Britain
See *Good Value Britain* above.

Let's Go: Britain and Ireland
by Harvard Student Agencies, St. Martin's Press, 1988, 576 pages, paper, $10.95

This book is part of the excellent, budget-oriented Let's Go Guide series, which is reviewed in more detail under "Series Reviews." The series is updated annually.

Literary Britain
by Frank Morley, Harper & Row, 1980, 509 pages, paper, $9.95

This wonderful guide provides voluminous information on British writers and landmarks. The book is arranged by the six arterial roadways that traverse Great Britain in radial fashion from London. For the well-read traveler touring by car this is a "must have" resource. The book is, however, a little hard to use because of its prose style, and it lacks maps, bold print, or any eye-catching aids to help orient the reader. Fortunately, the two indices of places and names are very helpful in solving this user-friendly issue.

Manston's Flea Markets, Antique Fairs and Auctions of Britain
by Peter Manston, Travel Keys Books, 1987, 277 pages, paper, $9.95

This book is part of the excellent Travel Keys Guide series, which is reviewed in more detail under "Series Reviews."

Manston's Travel Key Britain
by Peter Manston, Travel Keys Books, 1988, 288 pages, paper, $9.95
Released after press time, this is a companion volume to *Manston's Travel Key Europe* (see "Europe as a Whole").

Michelin Red Guide: Great Britain and Ireland
Michelin Guides and Maps, 1988, 652 pages, cloth, $16.95
This annual hotel and restaurant guide is part of Michelin Red Guide series, which is reviewed in more detail under "Series Reviews."

The Most Romantic Hotels and Inns in Britain
by Richard Nissen, St. Martin's Press, 1985, 192 pages, paper, $9.95
This great little book contains informative descriptions of 74 of the most charming hotels and inns in Britain. Sketches of the establishments accompany all the practical facts travelers will need.

Museums & Galleries in Great Britain and Ireland
Hunter Publishing, 1988, 184 pages, paper, $10.95
Organized by region, this annual directory offers information on every sort of museum imaginable—over 1200 of them. Brief descriptions of each museum and the pertinent facts on hours, admission, etc. accompany a special exhibition calendar for the coming year. This is a very handy reference.

Nagel's Encyclopedia Guide: Great Britain
Passport Books, 1985, 1195 pages, cloth, $49.95
This classic, cultural guide is part of the Nagel's Guide series, which is reviewed in more detail under "Series Reviews."

The National Trust Atlas
The National Trust and The National Trust for Scotland, Sheridan House, 1987 (3rd ed.), 224 pages, cloth, $29.95
This is a beautiful, large-format book detailing the many properties of the National Trust and the National Trust for Scotland. Arranged regionally, including a chapter on Northern Ireland, it provides well-written descriptions, numerous color photos, and excellent maps. Each property is coded to the appropriate road map. In addition, a county-by-county index of the various properties is provided. The National Trust owns some of the most historic and beautiful property in all of Britain.

National Trust Book of Long Walks in England, Scotland, and Wales
by Adam Nicolson, Crown Publishers, 1981, 291 pages, cloth,
$16.95
This beautifully done, illustrated guide to the best long walks (i.e.,
hikes) throughout Great Britain includes helpful maps and an excellent narrative.

The New Holiday Guide to Britain
M. Evans & Co., 1988 (10th ed.), 160 pages, paper, $4.95
This book is part of the Holiday Guide series, which is reviewed
in more detail under "Series Reviews."

Oxford Literary Guide to the British Isles
by Dorothy Eagle and Hilary Carnell, Oxford University Press,
1977, 468 pages, paper, $9.95
In this fascinating book the authors carefully describe myriad
places throughout the British Isles, all in terms of their relationship
to literature. The location of each important place is provided to
assist travelers in their own explorations.

The Penguin Guide to England and Wales
edited by Alan Tucker, Viking Penguin, 1988, 224-448 pages, paper,
$9.95-12.95
This is one of the new, anticipated titles in the Penguin Travel
Guide series, which is reviewed in more detail under "Series Reviews." The series is updated annually; only a range of prices and
page counts for the entire series were available at press time.

The Penguin Guide to Prehistoric England and Wales
by James Dyer, Viking Penguin, 1981, 373 pages, paper, $7.95
Dyer gives the inquisitive traveler detailed descriptions of the
places and structures important to the prehistory era of England and
Wales. Photographs and information on recent excavations and discoveries are included.

The Penguin Guide to the Landscape of England and Wales
by Paul Coones and John Patten, Viking Penguin, 1986, 348 pages,
paper, $8.95
This detailed and comprehensive survey of the cultural landscape
of England and Wales analyzes the interrelationship of geologic,
demographic, industrial, and social influences on the world as it it
now seen. Highly motivated travelers interested in understanding
the evolution of the visual scenes around them will find this book
an informative and scholarly guide.

Play the Best Courses: Great Golf in the British Isles

by Peter Allen, David & Charles, 1988, 210 pages, cloth, $39.95

From the scores of golf courses in Britain, Allen has selected the best 115. Some are private but others are there to play. Allen's entertaining hole-by-hole descriptions give an accurate picture of what each course is like, to enable traveling golfers to find the course that best suits their abilities.

Premier Hotels of Great Britain

by William McMinnies, Pelican Publishing, 1987 (49th ed.), 406 pages, paper, $12.95

The focus of this thoroughly researched, annually updated guide is on top-quality, premier hotels. Many selections in the major cities are included, along with stately country mansions, country inns, and seaside resorts. Brief histories of each selected establishment, good directions, numerous color photos, interesting features unique to each spot, nearby attractions, and practical details complete this well-done guide.

RAC Hotel Guide

by the Royal Automobile Club, Sheridan House, 1988, 704 pages, paper, $18.95

A different British automobile club publishes this annual tome, crammed with quick descriptions of nearly 6000 recommended hotels. Each description is followed by various symbols that summarize the amenities available and all the practical details. Photos of many hotels and numerous detail maps are included, as well as a large road map section to which each hotel is coded. The directory includes both the Republic of Ireland and Northern Ireland.

Rand McNally: Britain

by Nicole Swengley, Rand McNally & Co., 1984, 128 pages, paper, $5.95

This is one title in the small-format Rand McNally Pocket Guide series, which is reviewed in more detail under "Series Reviews."

Recommended Country Hotels of Britain
Hunter Publishing, 1988, 150 pages, paper, $6.95
Recommended Wayside Inns of Britain
Hunter Publishing, 1988, 150 pages, paper, $6.95

These are two annual reviews of distinguished historic hotels located in the British countryside and small, charming, often historic inns, respectively. Both were released after press time.

The Shell Book of British Walks

edited by John Whatmore, David & Charles, 1988, 368 pages, cloth, $34.95

Over 100 walking routes are carefully described and arranged on a thematic basis: walks along railway tracks, walks along canals, etc. An unusual chapter provides walks based on myths and legends. Included are numerous photos, drawings, and maps. Walking enthusiasts will find this a quality volume filled with many good ideas.

The Shell Book of Inland Waterways

by Hugh McKnight, David & Charles, 1988, 493 pages, cloth, $29.95

The waterways of Britain crisscross the landscape everywhere. This new edition of a long-popular book provides the information needed by travelers interested in boating the canals, walking the towpath, looking for an interesting day hike, or just learning about the waterway system. Included are a series of color photos and drawings as well as maps of the entire sytem.

Through Britain on Country Roads

by Peter Brereton, Crown Publishers, 1982, 320 pages, cloth, $12.95

This beautifully illustrated book, presenting 18 different driving tours through the nooks and crannies of rural Britain, includes good route descriptions and mileages, which should still be substantially accurate.

A Tour of British Bird Preserves

by Valerie Russell, Longwood Publishing, 1986, 191 pages, cloth, $25.95

This excellent guide provides an interesting and enthusiastic description of over 50 British bird preserves. An evaluation of each reserve, its location and access, the species to be seen and their habitats, and other important facts about each location are included. Bird watchers will find this very enjoyable reading.

Travel Guide to British/American English

by Norman Moss, Passport Books, 1986, 192 pages, paper, $3.95

Even though it is the same language, the number of differences in the English versus the American vocabulary can create a real language barrier for travelers. This handy little guide is a recommended addition to the travel library of those wanting to understand (and be understood by) the British.

22 Days in Great Britain: The Itinerary Planner

by Rick Steves, John Muir Publications, 1987, 125 pages, paper, $5.95

This is one of a series of guidebooks modeled after Rick Steves's well-known *Europe in 22 Days* (now called *22 Days in Europe*). The Itinerary Planner series is reviewed in more detail under "Series Reviews." Note that the title has recently been changed and this book may also be found under *Great Britain in 22 Days.*

Unforgettable British Weekends

by Angela Lansbury, Hippocrene Books, 1988, 148 pages, paper, $11.95

Released after press time, this interesting title from the well-known Angela Lansbury is designed for the visitor who has only a few days in Britain and wants to do something out of the ordinary. Lansbury gives her personal recommendations, including the hotel and restaurant best suited for any occasion.

Walker's Britain

Hunter Publishing, 1982, 336 pages, paper, $12.95

This is a well-written description of walks all over England, Wales, and Scotland, primarily in the countryside. Good directions are provided.

Walking Ancient Trackways

by Michael Dunn, Hunter Publishing, 1986, 232 pages, cloth, $17.95

Here are 34 walks that explore the old, even prehistoric, byways that remain to this day in rural Britain. Included are some famous walks: the Pilgrim's Way, the Fosse Way, the Old Craven Way, and Watling Street, to name a few. Each is carefully described, including history and other points of interest along the path. Numerous maps are included. This is a great book for history buffs on foot.

Whole Europe Escape Manual: UK/Ireland

by Kerry Green and Charles Leocha, World Leisure Corp., 1984, 160 pages, paper, $6.95

This book is part of the unique Escape Manual series, which is reviewed in more detail under "Series Reviews."

Woodland Walks in Britain

by Gerald Walkinson, Henry Holt & Co., 1985, 320 pages, cloth, $19.95

Using color British Ordnance Survey maps, Walkinson details over

400 great walks through the woodlands of Britain in this quality book.

England

See also "Great Britain" and "Europe as a Whole." Books listed below are exclusively on England. England is also included in the following major, all-purpose guides to Europe: *Birnbaum's Europe; Fielding's Europe; Fielding's Economy Europe; Fisher's World: Europe; Fodor's Europe; Fodor's Budget Europe; Frommer's Europe on $30 a Day; Let's Go: Europe.*

AA Day Trips: North West England

by the Automobile Association, Salem House, 1988, 120 pages, paper, $14.95

AA Day Trips: West Midlands

by the Automobile Association, Salem House, 1988, 120 pages, paper, $14.95

In these books are dozens of leisure journeys by car or even on foot, in and around each region. Good notes and clear maps point travelers in the right direction.

AA Holiday Guide: The West Country

by the Automobile Association, Salem House, 1988, 192 pages, paper, $11.95

Britain's Automobile Association has produced this factual guide to a popular vacation area. It contains information on lodging of every sort (hotels, B&Bs, even camping), restaurants, and plenty of sightseeing notes, including maps and town plans.

AA London: Where to Go, What to Do

by the Automobile Association, Salem House, 1988, 128 pages, paper, $12.95

This is a comprehensive London guide, including Automobile Association–inspected hotels and restaurants, detailed sections on sightseeing, shopping, and general orientation, and plenty of full-color maps.

AA/Ordnance Survey Leisure Guide: Channel Islands

by the Automobile Association, Salem House, 1987, 120 pages, paper, $19.95

AA/Ordnance Survey Leisure Guide: Cornwall
by the Automobile Association, Salem House, 1987, 120 pages, paper, $19.95

AA/Ordnance Survey Leisure Guide: Devon and Exmoor
by the Automobile Association, Salem House, 1988, 120 pages, paper, $19.95

AA/Ordnance Survey Leisure Guide: Isle of Wight
by the Automobile Association, Salem House, 1988, 112 pages, paper, $19.95

AA/Ordnance Survey Leisure Guide: Lake District
by the Automobile Association, Salem House, 1984, 120 pages, paper, $18.95

AA/Ordnance Survey Leisure Guide: London
by the Automobile Association, Salem House, 1987, 120 pages, paper, $19.95

AA/Ordnance Survey Leisure Guide: New Forest
by the Automobile Association, Salem House, 1983, 96 pages, paper, $18.95

AA/Ordnance Survey Leisure Guide: North Yorkshire Moors
by the Automobile Association, Salem House, 1985, 120 pages, paper, $18.95

AA/Ordnance Survey Leisure Guide: Northumbria
by the Automobile Association, Salem House, 1987, 120 pages, paper, $19.95

AA/Ordnance Survey Leisure Guide: Peak District
by the Automobile Association, Salem House, 1987, 120 pages, paper, $19.95

AA/Ordnance Survey Leisure Guide: South Downs
by the Automobile Association, Salem House, 1988, 112 pages, paper, $19.95

AA/Ordnance Survey Leisure Guide: The Cotswolds
by the Automobile Association, Salem House, 1986, 120 pages, paper, $18.95

AA/Ordnance Survey Leisure Guide: Wessex
by the Automobile Association, Salem House, 1988, 120 pages, paper, $19.95

AA/Ordnance Survey Leisure Guide: Wye Valley and Forest of Dean
by the Automobile Association, Salem House, 1988, 112 pages, paper, $19.95

AA/Ordnance Survey Leisure Guide: Yorkshire Dales
by the Automobile Association, Salem House, 1985, 120 pages, paper, $18.95

All of the above titles are part of the AA/Ordnance Survey Leisure Guide series, which is reviewed in more detail under "Series Reviews."

AA Pocket Guide to London
by the Automobile Association, Salem House, 1988, 176 pages, paper, $7.95

Hard facts on a world-class city: how to get around, London airports, shopping, sports, royal pageantry, how to drive, how to park, and a car tour of the city are contained in this petite book. An A-to-Z section on major sites, hotel information, good maps, and a street index are included.

AA Touring England: Central England/East Anglia
by the Automobile Association, Salem House, 1987, 176 pages, paper, $19.95
AA Touring England: North Country
by the Automobile Association, Salem House, 1987, 152 pages, paper, $19.95
AA Touring England: South and South East England
by the Automobile Association, Salem House, 1987, 176 pages, paper, $19.95
AA Touring England: The West Country
by the Automobile Association, Salem House, 1987, 152 pages, paper, $19.95

These four titles are part of the AA Regional Touring Guide series, which is reviewed in more detail under "Series Reviews."

AA Town and City Guide: Cambridge
by the Automobile Association, Salem House, 1988, 120 pages, paper, $18.95
AA Town and City Guide: York
by the Automobile Association, Salem House, 1988, 120 pages, paper, $18.95

These two titles are part of the AA Town and City Guide series, which is reviewed in more detail under "Series Reviews."

Alec Clifton-Taylor's Buildings of Delight
edited by Denis Moriarty, David & Charles, 1988, 260 pages, cloth, $34.95

This is a great planning tool for those interested in the magnificent architecture of England. Too big to carry, it is best used for reading up on Clifton-Taylor's 100 favorite buildings, which include castles, abbeys, mills, farmhouses, churches, bridges, and railway stations. Plenty of photographs are provided.

The American Express Pocket Guide to London
by Michael Jackson, Prentice Hall Press, 1986, 224 pages, cloth, $8.95

This is one of the American Express Pocket Guide series, which is reviewed in more detail under "Series Reviews."

Antiques: A Buyer's Guide to London
Paige Publications, 1987, 159 pages, paper, $6.95

This is a comprehensive listing, updated annually, of antique dealers of every description. Listings are arranged by London postal districts—a separate listing arranges dealers by their specialties. Information on all the major London fairs, along with suggestions in every price range of where to stay and eat is also provided in this excellent resource.

Baedeker's London
Prentice Hall Press, 1987, 186 pages, paper, $10.95

This is one of Baedeker's City Guide series, which is reviewed in more detail under "Series Reviews."

Berlitz: Channel Islands
Macmillan Publishing, 1986, 128 pages, paper, $6.95
Berlitz: London
Macmillan Publishing, 1979, 128 pages, paper, $6.95
Berlitz: Oxford and Stratford
Macmillan Publishing, 1981, 128 pages, paper, $6.95

These three titles are part of the small-format Berlitz Guide series, which is reviewed in more detail under "Series Reviews."

The Best of London
by Henri Gault and Christian Millau, Crown Publishing, 1985, 352 pages, paper, $13.95

This food, entertainment and hotel guide is part of the Gault/Millau 'Best Of' Guide series, which is reviewed in more detail under "Series Reviews."

Blue Guide: Channel Islands
edited by Peter Eadie, W. W. Norton & Co., 1987, 130 pages, paper, $16.95
Blue Guide: England
edited by Stuart Rossiter, W. W. Norton & Co., 1980 (9th ed.), 720 pages, paper, $14.95
Blue Guide: London
edited by Stuart Rossiter, W. W. Norton & Co., 1986 (12th ed.), 416 pages, paper, $15.95

Blue Guide: Museums and Galleries of London
by Malcolm Rogers, W. W. Norton & Co., 1986 (2nd ed.), 375
pages, paper, $16.95
Blue Guide: Oxford and Cambridge
edited by Mercia Mason, W. W. Norton & Co., 1987 (3rd ed.), 219
pages, paper, $14.95
Blue Guide: Victorian Architecture in England
by Julia Orbach, W. W. Norton & Co., 1988, 300 pages, paper,
$19.95

All of the above titles are part of the highly regarded Blue Guide
series, which is reviewed in more detail under "Series Reviews."
Note that the Channel Islands, off the southeastern coast of England,
include Guernsey and Jersey. The title on England is overdue for an
update; one should be out soon. The Museums and Galleries title is
a specialized volume that includes the history, descriptions, and floor
plans of many of the museums and galleries of London. The Victorian
Architecture title was released after press time; the price and number
of pages are approximate.

The Blue Plaque Guide to London
by Caroline Dakers, W. W. Norton & Co., 1982, 318 pages, cloth,
$17.95

This is a fascinating guide to the official historic buildings and
monuments of London. Each site is marked by a conspicuous blue
plaque that will easily catch the traveler's eye on sightseeing jaunts
throughout the city.

Born to Shop: London
by Suzy Gershman and Judith Thomas, Bantam Books, 1987 (2nd
ed.), 295 pages, paper, $8.95

This book is part of the Born to Shop Guide series, which is
reviewed in more detail under "Series Reviews."

Britain Before the Conquest: Anglo-Saxon England
by Lloyd and Jennifer Laing, Hunter Publishing, 1987, 256 pages,
paper, $9.95

This historical archaeological tour is part of the Britain Before the
Conquest Guide series, which is reviewed in more detail under
"Series Reviews."

Channel Island Hopping: A Handbook for the Independent Traveler
by Mary Gladwin, Hippocrene Books, 1984, 240 pages, paper,
$12.95

This book is part of the Island Hopping Guide series, which is
reviewed in more detail under "Series Reviews."

The Children's Guide to London
by Christopher Pick, Salem House, 1985, 224 pages, paper, $11.95
This comprehensive guide to all those things kids and would-be kids like to do in London includes lots of walks the whole family will enjoy, as well as a directory of activities. Be sure to check any time-dated material.

The Companion Guide to London
by David Piper, Prentice Hall Press, 1983, 520 pages, paper, $12.95
The Companion Guide to Shakespeare Country
by Jonathan Keates, Prentice Hall Press, 1983, 320 pages, paper, $7.95
These two titles are part of the superb Companion Guide series, which is reviewed in more detail under "Series Reviews."

County Companion: Cornwall
Salem House, 1984, 224 pages, paper, $9.95
County Companion: Cumbria
Salem House, 1985, 224 pages, paper, $9.95
County Companion: Devon
Salem House, 1984, 224 pages, paper, $9.95
County Companion: Dorset
Salem House, 1986, 224 pages, paper, $9.95
County Companion: Kent
Salem House, 1983, 224 pages, paper, $9.95
County Companion: Somerset & Avon
Salem House, 1985, 224 pages, paper, $9.95
County Companion: Surrey
Salem House, 1984, 224 pages, paper, $9.95
County Companion: Sussex
Salem House, 1984, 224 pages, paper, $9.95
County Companion: Yorkshire & Humberside
Salem House, 1986, 224 pages, paper, $9.95
These are all the titles in this small-format series from the Cadogan Publications group in England. Each book provides an A-to-Z listing of the towns and villages in the areas, including a bit of history and orientation, followed by a directory section with maps (each town being coded to a particular map), a list of activities and important points of interest that are then further described in the third section, and another A-to-Z listing of leisure activities from fishing and golf courses to historic museums and castles. For some volumes in the series, time-dated material in this section bears scrutiny. This series is a good resource of information, but as far as sightseeing goes, the only geographic orientations are the small town maps.

Day Trips from London: 50 One-Day Adventures by Rail, Bus or Car
by Earl Steinbicker, Hastings House, 1986, 256 pages, paper, $9.95
This is one of the Earl Steinbicker's Day Trips series, which is reviewed in more detail under "Series Reviews."

Days Out, In and Around London
by Pauline Gorman, Little, Brown & Co., 1986, 283 pages, paper, $5.95
This is an A-to-Z format of information on oodles of places to visit in and around London with information on how to get there (including rail and underground options), what it will cost, and the facilities available, including those for the disabled. Writeups are short but informative.

England by Bus and Coach
by Elizabeth Gundrey, Salem House, 1988, 416 pages, paper, $12.95
In this book, Elizabeth Gundrey shows travelers on tiny budgets how to meet the people of England without going broke in the process. Lots of practical information, including timetables and frequency of services, and plenty of sightseeing tips are included in this useful book.

Exploring England by Canal
by David Owen, David & Charles, 1986, 208 pages, cloth, $25.95
This fine resource for those interested in exploring the canals of England includes notes on the history of each canal, as well as practical details on renting boats, dealing with locks and tunnels, and more. Suggested routes to travel and information on the sights to see along the way are provided.

Exploring Rural England
Passport Books, 1988/89, 200 pages, paper, $12.95
This is an anticipated, new title in the Exploring Rural Europe Guide series, which is reviewed in more detail under "Series Reviews." The price and number of pages are approximate.

Fisher's World: London
by Edmund Antrobus, Fisher's World, Inc., 1988, 109 pages, paper, $10.95
This book is part of the Fisher's World Guide series, which is reviewed in more detail under "Series Reviews." The series is updated annually.

Fodor's Fun In London

Fodor's Travel Publications, 1987, 128 pages, paper, $6.95

This book is part of Fodor's Fun Guide series, which is reviewed in more detail under "Series Reviews." The series is updated annually.

Fodor's Great Travel Values: London

Fodor's Travel Publications, 1987, 176 pages, paper, $5.95

This is one of the budget-oriented Fodor's Great Travel Values Guide series, which is reviewed in more detail under "Series Reviews." The series is updated annually.

Fodor's London

Fodor's Travel Publications, 1987, 256 pages, paper, $8.95

This book is part of Fodor's City Guide series, which is reviewed in more detail under "Series Reviews." The series is updated annually.

Frommer's England on $40 a Day

by Darwin Porter, Prentice Hall Press, 1987, 550 pages, paper, $11.95

This is one of the budget-oriented Frommer's Dollar-a-Day Guide series, which is reviewed in more detail under "Series Reviews." The series is updated every two years.

Frommer's Guide to London

by Darwin Porter, Prentice Hall Press, 1988, 218 pages, paper, $5.95

This book is part of the Frommer's City Guide series, which is reviewed in more detail under "Series Reviews." The series is updated every two years.

Frommer's Touring Guide to London

Prentice Hall Press, 1986, 158 pages, paper, $8.95

This book is part of the Frommer's Touring Guide series, which is reviewed in more detail under "Series Reviews."

Greenwich and East London Step-by-Step

by Christopher Turner, Faber and Faber, 1987, 82 pages, paper, $4.95

This is one of the Step-by-Step Guide series, which is reviewed in more detail under "Series Reviews."

Guide to Greater London: Hotels, Pubs, and Restaurants

Consumers Reports Books, 1987, 234 pages, paper, $13.00

This is an exceptional guide to hotels, pubs, and restaurants from the Consumers Association of Great Britain. The writeups are well written, informative and describe "best values" in all price ranges. Necessary practical information is included, as well as good detail maps. The guide also covers Brighton, Cambridge, Canterbury, Oxford, Windsor, and Eton.

The Hachette Guide to London: The Only Guide You'll Ever Need

Random House, 1988, 104 pages, paper, $5.95

This is one of the Hachette Guide series, which is reviewed in more detail under "Series Reviews." The series is updated annually.

Here's England: A Highly Informal Guide

by Ruth McKenney and Richard Bransten, Harper & Row, 1971 (3rd ed.), 336 pages, cloth, $18.95

Few travel books have endured as well as *Here's England*. Its third edition is ancient history now, yet its delightful blend of history, architecture, and practical points are more often up-to-date than not. It is a great "companion guide" to a more conventional guidebook.

Hertfordshire: A Shell Guide

by R. M. Healey, Faber and Faber, 1982, 192 pages, paper, $11.95

This good sightseeing guide to this small and picturesque English county contains numerous black-and-white photos and an informative text.

The Historic Country Hotels of England: A Selective Guide

by Wendy Arnold, Henry Holt & Co., 1986, 96 pages, paper, $11.95

The Historic Hotels of London: A Selective Guide

by Wendy Arnold, Henry Holt & Co., 1987, 96 pages, paper, $11.95

These are two visually magnificent books on some of the most classic lodging in England. The strongest assets of these books are the copious color photographs portraying the interiors and exteriors of these wonderful structures and, sometimes, the surrounding countryside of the more rurally placed hotels. The write-ups are informative and all the practical details are included. None of these accommodations comes too cheaply, however, with prices for two (even before the more recent devaluation of the dollar) running from $75 to nearly $300 per night (including continental breakfast). Full English breakfast and other meals will add still further to the bill.

How to Get Lost and Found in London
by John and Bobbye McDermott, Orafa Publishing, 1988, 307
pages, paper, $9.95
This book is part of the delightfully different Lost and Found Guide
series, which is reviewed in more detail under "Series Reviews."

In Our Grandmothers' Footsteps: A Walking Tour of London
by Jennifer Clarke, Atheneum, 1984, 168 pages, paper, $7.95
This unique gazetteer of the London area emphasizes the remarkable accomplishments of over 200 Englishwomen. The majority of
the book is given over to the details of each woman's life. At the
back are area-by-area guides arranged into "as walkable a route as
possible." However, this information must be plotted on a map
obtained separately. This lack of maps is unusual for a book billed
as a walking tour. Nonetheless, this is a fine resource of information.

Kid's London
by Elizabeth Holt and Molly Perham, St. Martin's Press, 1985 (2nd
ed.), 221 pages, paper, $5.95
The authors have gathered together literally hundreds of things
for kids (and the kid in everyone) to do while in London. Specific
information on how to get to each selected activity, what events are
free, the days and hours open, and where the hungry horde can grab
a snack or have a picnic along the way is included.

London/Access
by Richard Saul Wurman, Prentice Hall Press, 1987, 182 pages,
paper, $14.95
This book is part of the well-done Access Guide series, which is
reviewed in more detail under "Series Reviews." This is one of three
new guides produced with a handy spiral binding.

London Art and Artist's Guide
by Heather Waddell, Robert Silver Associates, 1983 (3rd ed.), 141
pages, paper, $6.95
This book is part of the Robert Silver Art Guide series, which is
reviewed in more detail under "Series Reviews."

London At Its Best
by Robert Kane, Passport Books, 1987, 209 pages, paper, $9.95
This book is part of the widely praised At Its Best Guide series,
which is reviewed in more detail under "Series Reviews."

London Churches Step-by-Step

by Christopher Turner, Faber and Faber, 1987, 240 pages, cloth, $14.95

A member of the Step-by-Step Guide series, this title is a little different, focusing specifically on churches. It is a very well done, small-print guide to 132 selected churches throughout London, including directions on how to reach each by public transportation, the hours each is open, and what to do to see those churches otherwise unavailable for public viewing. A short history and a description of the main attractions of each church are followed by a more detailed tour of the exterior and interior. This series is reviewed in more detail under "Series Reviews."

London for the Independent Traveler

by Ruth Humleker, MarLor Press, 1987, 208 pages, paper, $12.95

This is a well-organized, well-thought-out book that will allow travelers to see the parts of London of most interest to them in a short space of time. The book is arranged into different theme chapters such as Art Lover's London, Royal London, Shopper's London, and Children's London. Each of these chapters describes a three-day tour of London emphasizing the particular topic of interest with occasional notes on what to do with an extra day. Good detail maps and other practical information supplement this quality book.

London in Your Pocket

Barron's Educational Series, 1987, 152 pages, paper, $3.95

This is one of the In Your Pocket Guide series, which is reviewed in more detail under "Series Reviews." The series is updated every two years.

London Man

by Francis Chichester, Warner Books, 1988, 220 pages, cloth, $11.95

This guide for the upper crust is part of the new Francis Chichester Guide series, which was released after press time. For more details see the "Series Reviews."

London Walkabouts with Kate Lucas

by Kate Lucas, Hippocrene Books, 1983, 124 pages, paper, $6.95

In this book, Kate Lucas offers lots of ideas for walking tours—including places to eat along the way—while visiting the top ten tourist attractions of London.

London Woman
  by Francis Chichester, Warner Books, 1988, 204 pages, cloth,
  $11.95
  This guide for the upper crust is part of the new Francis Chichester
  Guide series, which was released after press time. For more details
  see the "Series Reviews."

Londonwalks
  by Anton Powell, Henry Holt & Co., 1982, 224 pages, paper, $9.95
  This is one of the Citywalks series, which is reviewed in more
  detail under "Series Reviews."

The Luxury Shopping Guide to London
  by Nicholas Courtney, Vendome Press, 1987, 186 pages, paper,
  $17.95
  Here is a guide to the famous shops of London "known for their
  excellence of design, workmanship, and service." The jewelry stores
  of Bond Street, the department stores of Piccadilly, and the gourmet
  food shops of Soho and Covent Garden are all here.

Michelin Green Guide: London
  Michelin Guides & Maps, 1985 (4th ed.), 192 pages, paper, $10.95
Michelin Green Guide: West Country England
  Michelin Guides & Maps, 1985, 232 pages, paper, $10.95
  Both of these titles are part of the premier sightseeing guide series,
  Michelin Green Guides, which is reviewed in more detail under
  "Series Reviews."

Michelin Red Guide: Greater London
  Michelin Guides & Maps, 1987, 78 pages, paper, $3.95
  This annual hotel and restaurant guide is part of the Michelin Red
  Guide series, which is reviewed in more detail under "Series Re-
  views."

Mystery Reader's Walking Guide: England
  by Alzina Dale and Barbara Hendershott, Passport Books, 1988,
  320 pages, cloth, $19.95
Mystery Reader's Walking Guide: London
  by Alzina Dale and Barbara Hendershott, Passport Books, 1987,
  294 pages, cloth, $16.95
  Each of these fascinating titles provides 11 unusual walks focused
  around the paths of "the most widely read mystery writers, their
  sleuths and characters." Copious information is included with each
  walk, as well as notes on good places to eat nearby. Hand-drawn
  maps guide the way.

The New Bell's Cathedral Guide: Canterbury Cathedral
Salem House, 1987, 192 pages, paper, $14.95
The New Bell's Cathedral Guide: Coventry Cathedral
Salem House, 1988, 192 pages, paper, $14.95
The New Bell's Cathedral Guide: St. Paul's Cathedral
Salem House, 1988, 192 pages, paper, $14.95
The New Bell's Cathedral Guide: Salisbury Cathedral
Salem House, 1988, 192 pages, paper, $14.95
The New Bell's Cathedral Guide: Wells Cathedral
Salem House, 1988, 192 pages, paper, $14.95
The New Bell's Cathedral Guide: Westminster Abbey
Salem House, 1987, 192 pages, paper, $14.95
These six titles represent the full series to date. Each book focuses on a specific famous cathedral and, with photo and text, describes the architecture and fascinating history of each. A useful resource for the cathedral buff.

The New Holiday Guide to London
M. Evans & Co., 1988 (10th ed.), 160 pages, paper, $4.95
This is one of the Holiday Guide series, which is reviewed in more detail under "Series Reviews."

The New Penguin Guide to London
by F. R. Banks, Penguin Books, 1986 (revised ed.), 608 pages, paper, $6.95
This excellent book, now revised, was the winner of the London Tourist Board Guide Book of the Year Award in 1984. It is an all-purpose guide with useful and perceptive information on hotels, restaurants, museums, parks, transportation, and many other topics.

Nicholson: Access in London
by Gordon Couch and William Forrester, Salem House, 1984, 176 pages, paper, $6.95
Written by Londoners for disabled visitors or those who have problems getting around, this useful book provides a wealth of information on emergencies, wheelchair repairs, getting around, accommodations, entertainment, sightseeing, pubs, restaurants, and more.

Nicholson: Guide to English Churches
Salem House, 1986, 240 pages, paper, $14.95
This is a comprehensive survey of the magnificent churches and cathedrals of England.

Nicholson: Holiday Guide to Devon
Salem House, 1986, 208 pages, paper, $11.95
Nicholson: Holiday Guide to the Lake District and Cumbria
Salem House, 1986, 152 pages, paper, $11.95
   These two titles are part of the Nicholson Guide series, which is reviewed in more detail under "Series Reviews."

Nicholson: London by Bus and Tube
Salem House, 1988, 144 pages, paper, $9.95
   Included in this book is up-to-date information on London's famous transportation system with an A-to-Z guide of all the sights and how to get there by bus or tube. Information on London tours by bus and subway, and all the practical data needed to use the system to its utmost is provided as well. Color maps of the bus and underground systems are included.

Nicholson: London Guide
Salem House, 1986, 224 pages, paper, $6.95
   Far and away London's best-selling guide, this concise, everything-you-need-to-know guide to London is part of the Nicholson Guide series, which is reviewed in more detail under "Series Reviews."

Nicholson: London Pub Guide
Salem House, 1985, 176 pages, paper, $6.95
   This book covers 600 of London's best drinking/eating establishments. The entries are arranged by area for ease of use, with each pub briefly described.

Nicholson: London Shopping Guide & Streetfinder
Salem House, 1988, 96 pages, paper, $6.95
   Newly revised, this book is designed to help travelers locate, using Nicholson's famous maps and street index, the most famous stores, the best stores for a particular item, the stores that provide the best value for the money, and the stores that are the most fun to shop in.

Nicholson: Royal London Guide & Streetfinder
Salem House, 1988, 96 pages, paper, $6.95
   This good, up-to-date guide for royalty watchers includes all the goings on, even where today's and yesterday's royalty do their shopping. Color maps and the street index system for which the Nicholson Guides are justifiably famous are included.

Nicholson: The Good Tour Guide
Salem House, 1988, 176 pages, paper, $8.95
This book summarizes the myriad guided tours available in London.

Nicholson: Tourist London
Salem House, 1987, 98 pages, paper, $3.95
This small, pocket guide is another of the many Nicholson guides to London. Packed with practical facts and notes on sightseeing, shopping, museums, markets, pubs, parks, restaurants, and tours, this book contains a little bit of everything. More than half the book features a large-scale street atlas, maps of the underground transportation system and the theater district, and a full street index.

Nicholson: Visitor's Guide
Salem House, 1986, 128 pages, paper, $5.95
An abridged version of the *Nicholson: London Guide*, sufficient for a short visit, this book is part of the Nicholson Guide series, which is reviewed in more detail under "Series Reviews."

Outer London Step-by-Step
by Christopher Turner, Faber and Faber, 1986, 264 pages, paper, $7.95
This is one of the Step-by-Step Guide series, which is reviewed in more detail under "Series Reviews."

Passport's Guide to Ethnic London
by Ian McAuley, Passport Books, 1987, 224 pages, paper, $11.95
In this well-done guidebook to a different sort of London, McAuley explores the London world of its eight major ethnic groups, with separate chapters on Chinese, Asian, Polish, Italian, Jewish, Irish, Cypriot, and Afro-Caribbean neighborhoods. Each chapter covers history, shopping, restaurants, places of worship, museums, art galleries, and other topics of interest including famous members of each group. Good detail maps of important locations are included, although a pocket street atlas is recommended.

Peter Brereton's Touring Guide to English Villages
by Peter Brereton, Prentice Hall Press, 1984, 224 pages, paper, $9.95
Here are 52 scenic tours of over 300 villages, with plenty of practical notes. Be aware, though, that the food and lodging information is probably too old to be of much value.

A Photographer's Guide to London

by Kevin MacDonnell, Gower Publishing, 1986, 127 pages, paper, $13.50

With notes on cameras and the best places to capture the worthwhile photograph, MacDonnell will lead you on delightfully enjoyable tours of the city and its many nooks and crannies. The text is lively and supplemented with excellent photos. Even if you leave your camera back at the hotel, this is a most delightful tour guide.

Rand McNally: London

by George Kay, Rand McNally & Co., 1984, 128 pages, paper, $5.95

One of the small-format Rand McNally Pocket Guide series which is reviewed in more detail under "Series Reviews."

The Rose Gardens of England

by Michael Gibson, The Globe Pequot Press, 1988, 160 pages, cloth, $19.95

England is, of course, known worldwide for its penchant for roses and for its talent in raising them. This new guide takes you on an illustrated tour of 70 of the most renowned rose gardens in England. But this is not just a coffee-table book. It is arranged by county to facilitate its use as a guide, and each garden is described in terms of its practical points: driving directions, visiting hours, etc. And there is plenty of historical information included, too—on the landscapes, the estates, and the neighborhood surrounding them.

Serious Shopper's Guide to London

by Ruth Reiber, Prentice Hall Press, 1987, 384 pages, paper, $14.95

Part of the Serious Shopper's Guide series, which is reviewed in more detail under "Series Reviews."

Shopwalks: London

by Francis Ehrlich, Crown Publishers, 1985, fold-out map/guide, paper, $4.95

One of the Shopwalks series, which is reviewed in more detail under "Series Reviews."

Short Walks in English Towns

by Bryn Frank, Crown Publishers, 1987, 192 pages, cloth, $19.95

This is primarily a photographic walking tour of ten of England's most picturesque towns: Bath, Canterbury, Cambridge, Cheltenham, Durham, Norwich, Oxford, Salisbury, Winchester, and York. Maps of each town are included, making this book usable as a companion guide.

Staying Off the Beaten Track

by Elizabeth Gundrey, Salem House, 1988 (6th ed.), 479 pages, paper, $12.95

This is an excellent resource of over 300 friendly, moderately priced inns, small hotels, farms, and country houses specializing in good home cooking and located in the "tranquil depths of England's rural places." Each charming spot is well covered with great write-ups and all the facts you will need. Many include pen-and-ink drawings. Elizabeth Gundrey's name has become almost a verb in England—people speak of "going Gundreying". The bottom line is that Gundrey has an uncanny eye for quality at a fair price.

Traveler's Key to Sacred England: A Guide to the Legends, Lore, and Landscape of England's Sacred Places

by John Mitchell, Alfred Knopf, Inc., 1988, 416 pages, cloth, $18.95

The fourth title in the superb Traveler's Key Guide series, which is reviewed in more detail under "Series Reviews."

Turn Left at the Pub: Walking Tours of the English Countryside

by George Oakes, Congdon & Weed, 1985, 192 pages, paper, $8.95

This is a truly excellent travel guide, a companion volume to the classic *Turn Right at the Fountain* (see "Europe"), which together stand as a lasting tribute to this famous writer. The walking tours offered will guide you on an exploration of some of the most beautiful places in England. The walks are well described and keyed to simple maps, and are supplemented with informative historical notes.

The Virgin Guide to London

Random House, 1986, 288 pages, paper, $7.95

Taking a very critical and selective approach, the authors of the *Virgin Guide* break the London area down into different neighborhoods and within each select and describe the best of the main attractions. They specifically avoid an excess of history, churches, statues, and the like, in favor of a much smaller, select grouping to assist you in cutting through the vast number of tourist attractions available in this world-class city. Basic survival tips are included, as well as restaurant selections in all price ranges. This is a useful and enjoyably written guide.

A Visitor's Guide to Cornwall and the Isles of Scilly

by Rita Pope, Hunter Publishing, 1988, 220 pages, paper, $9.95

A Visitor's Guide to Devon
by Brian LeMessurier, Hunter Publishing, 1983, 156 pages, paper, $8.95
A Visitor's Guide to East Anglia
by Clive Tully, 1984, Hunter Publishing, 156 pages, paper, $8.95
A Visitor's Guide to Guernsey, Alderney & Sark
by Victor Coysh, Hunter Publishing, 1983, 143 pages, paper, $8.95
A Visitor's Guide to Hampshire & the Isle of Wight
by John Barton, Hunter Publishing, 1985, 160 pages, paper, $8.95
A Visitor's Guide to Kent
by Kev Reynolds, Hunter Publishing, 1985, 160 pages, paper, $8.95
A Visitor's Guide to Severn & Avon
by Lawrence Garner, Hunter Publishing, 1986, 160 pages, paper, $8.95
A Visitor's Guide to Somerset & Dorset
by Alan Proctor, Hunter Publishing, 1983, 133 pages, paper, $8.95
A Visitor's Guide to Sussex
by Jim Cleland, Hunter Publishing, 1985, 160 pages, paper, $8.95
A Visitor's Guide to the Cotswolds
by Richard Sale, Hunter Publishing, 1987, 143 pages, paper, $8.95
A Visitor's Guide to the Lake District
by Brian Spencer, Hunter Publishing, 1988, 139 pages, paper, $9.95
A Visitor's Guide to the Peak District
by Lindsay Porter, Hunter Publishing, 1984, 154 pages, paper, $8.95
A Visitor's Guide to Yorkshire Dales
by Brian Spencer, Hunter Publishing, 1984, 160 pages, paper, $8.95
All of the above are titles in the Visitor's Guide series, which is reviewed in more detail under "Series Reviews."

Walking Through Northern England
by Charlie Emett and Mike Hutton, Hunter Publishing, 1987, 208 pages, paper, $10.95
Walking Through the Lake District
by Michael Dunn, Hunter Publishing, 1987, 224 pages, paper, $10.95
These are two titles in the Walking Through Britain Guide series which is reviewed in more detail under "Series Reviews."

Walks Through London
by Bert Lief, VLE Limited, undated, fold-out map/guide, paper, $2.00
One of the Way-Ahead Guide series which is reviewed in more detail under "Series Reviews."

Windsor and Eton Step by Step
by Christopher Turner, Faber and Faber, 1986, 72 pages, paper, $4.95
Part of the Step-by-Step Guide series which is reviewed in more detail under "Series Reviews."

Woodland Walks in Central England
by Gerald Wilkinson, Hunter Publishing, 1987, 128 pages, paper, $9.95
Woodland Walks in South-East England
by Gerald Wilkinson, Hunter Publishing, 1987, 128 pages, paper, $9.95
Woodland Walks in South-West England
by Gerald Wilkinson, Hunter Publishing, 1987, 128 pages, paper, $9.95
Woodland Walks in the North of England
by Gerald Wilkinson, Hunter Publishing, 1987, 128 pages, paper, $9.95
These are four titles in the Woodland Walks series, which is reviewed in more detail under "Series Reviews."

Scotland

See also "Great Britain" and "Europe as a Whole." Those books listed below are exclusively on Scotland. Scotland is also included in the following major, all-purpose guides to Europe: *Birnbaum's Europe; Fielding's Europe; Fielding's Economy Europe; Fisher's World: Europe; Fodor's Europe; Fodor's Budget Europe; Let's Go: Europe.*

AA Holiday Guide: Scotland
by the Automobile Association, Salem House, 1988, 192 pages, paper, $11.95
This is a companion guide to *AA Holiday Guide: The West Country,* which is reviewed under "England."

AA/Ordnance Survey Leisure Guide: Scottish Highlands
by the Automobile Association, Salem House, 1988, 120 pages, paper, $18.95
This book is part of the AA/Ordnance Survey Leisure Guide series, which is reviewed in more detail under "Series Reviews."

AA Scotland: Where to Go, What to Do
by the Automobile Association, Salem House, 1982, 240 pages, paper, $9.95
This is an overview of things Scottish, with numerous color road

maps, and reams of tiny-print detail on where to go and what to do. Some details may be out of date.

AA Touring Scotland
by the Automobile Association, Salem House, 1987, 152 pages, paper, $19.95
This is one of the AA Regional Touring Guide series, which is reviewed in more detail under "Series Reviews."

AA Town and City Guide: Edinburgh
by the Automobile Association, Salem House, 1988, 120 pages, paper, $18.95
AA Town and City Guide: Glasgow
by the Automobile Association, Salem House, 1988, 120 pages, paper, $18.95
These two titles are part of the AA Town and City Guide series, which is reviewed in more detail under "Series Reviews."

Berlitz: Scotland
Macmillan Publishing, 1982, 128 pages, paper, $6.95
This book is part of the small-format Berlitz Guide series, which is reviewed in more detail under "Series Reviews."

Blue Guide: Scotland
edited by John Tomes, W. W. Norton & Co., 1986 (9th ed.), 550 pages, paper, $19.95
This is one of the highly regarded Blue Guide series, which is reviewed in more detail under "Series Reviews."

Cadogan Guide: Scotland
by Richenda Miers, The Globe Pequot Press, 1987, 474 pages, paper, $12.95
This book is part of the widely praised Cadogan Guide series, which is reviewed in more detail under "Series Reviews." The series is updated every two years.

Chambers Guide to the Castles of Scotland
by Susan Ross, Cambridge University Press, 1988, 144 pages, paper, $12.95
This new title, released after press time, is aimed at the "sophisticated traveler." Illustrated with numerous photographs, this guide focuses on the history, architecture, and touring information of 250 Scottish castles, fortified houses, and ruins.

Exploring Rural Scotland

Passport Books, 1988, 200 pages, paper, $12.95

This is an anticipated, new title in the Exploring Rural Europe Guide series, which is reviewed in more detail under "Series Reviews." Price and number of pages are approximate.

The Farm Holiday Guide to Holidays in Scotland

Hunter Publishing, 1988, 96 pages, paper, $5.95

This is a companion volume to the similarly titled work reviewed under "Great Britain."

Fodor's Scotland

Fodor's Travel Publications, 1987, 288 pages, paper, $12.95

This book is part of Fodor's Country/Regional Guide series, which is reviewed in more detail under "Series Reviews." The series is updated annually.

Frommer's Scotland and Wales on $40 a Day

by Darwin Porter, Prentice Hall Press, 1988, 562 pages, paper, $11.95

This is one of the Frommer's Dollar-a-Day Guide series, which is reviewed in more detail under "Series Reviews." The series is updated every two years.

Good Golf Guide to Scotland

by David Hamilton, Pelican Publishing, 1982, 168 pages, cloth, $11.95

This is a fine little hardback, still basically up-to-date in its information, on all the best courses, their location, history, a general description, and notes on whether visitors are welcome and what to do to gain access. In addition, tips on appropriate dress, the weather (an important subject in Scotland), the rules of play, and the history of golf in its birthplace are included.

The Intelligent Traveller's Guide to Historic Scotland

by Philip Crowl, Congdon & Weed, 1986, 625 pages, cloth, $35.00

This superb book is the sequel and companion to Crowl's classic work, *The Intelligent Traveller's Guide to Historic Britain*. The first 371 pages comprise a detailed and engrossing narrative history. Then, what has been detailed in chronological order in part 1 is arranged in geographical order in part 2, the gazetteer. Each section is cross-referenced to the other, making this otherwise weighty hardback a useful travel guide for the motivated person. For travelers who love to learn about the history of the things they will see in Scotland, this guide is as good as they get.

Michael's Guide: Scotland
by Michael Shichor, Hunter Publishing, 1988, 224 pages, paper, $7.95

This book is part of the Michael's Guide series, which is reviewed in more detail under "Series Reviews."

Michelin Green Guide: Scotland
Michelin Guides and Maps, 1985, 230 pages, paper, $10.95

This is one of the premier sightseeing guide series, the Michelin Green Guides, which is reviewed in more detail under "Series Reviews."

Scotland: Camping and Caravan Parks
Salem House, 1988, 96 pages, paper, $8.95

This is a new directory from Britain aimed at those who would like to camp out during their stay in Scotland.

Scotland for the Motorist
Salem House, 1988, 184 pages, paper, $5.95

This is a handy reference to numerous driving tours of the best of Scotland's scenery and history.

Scotland: Home of Golf
Salem House, 1988, 180 pages, paper, $5.95

This updated directory contains plenty of information to help golfers plan the perfect golfing vacation.

Scotland: 1001 Things to See
by Scottish Tourist Board, Salem House, 1985, 206 pages, paper, $7.95

This is a useful, quick-reference directory to many of the sightseeing opportunities in Scotland.

Scotland: Walks and Trails
Salem House, 1985, 72 pages, paper, $4.50

Plenty of suggestions for day hikes and walks of every sort are contained herein.

Scotland: Where to Stay, Bed and Breakfast
Scottish Tourist Board, Salem House, 1988, 232 pages, paper, $8.95

Over 2000 bed and breakfast selections are detailed here, with a clear emphasis on places that offer a warm welcome at a budget price.

Scotland: Where to Stay, Hotels and Guesthouses
Scottish Tourist Board, Salem House, 1988, 308 pages, paper, $11.95

This is a collection of over 2000 places to stay that meet the standards of the Scottish Tourist Board. Choices are for all budgets, and many of them are illustrated.

Scottish Island Hopping: A Handbook for the Independent Traveler
by Jemina Tindall, Hippocrene Books, 1982 (2nd ed.), 320 pages, paper, $12.95

This book is part of the Island Hopping Guide series, which is reviewed in more detail under "Series Reviews."

Scottish Museums & Galleries Guide
by the Scottish Museums Council, Salem House, 1987, 112 pages, paper, $8.95

This detailed listing of nearly 400 museums and galleries throughout the country provides the practical information needed on everything from folk museums to neo-classical galleries.

Shell Guide to Northern Scotland and the Islands
by Francis Thompson, Stephen Greene Press, 1987, 224 pages, paper, $14.95

This is a comprehensive volume on the history and points of interest in Northern Scotland. Many color photos accompany the informative text.

The South Clyde Estuary: An Illustrated Architectural Guide to Inverclyde and Renfrew
Longwood Publishing, 1987, 152 pages, paper, $7.25

This detailed architectural guide explores the districts of Inverclyde and Renfrew to the west and southwest of Glasgow, both of which contain a fascinating blend of old and new structures. Each interesting building is introduced with a photograph, its location noted, and all pertinent facts and history discussed—sometimes in considerable detail.

The Visitor's Guide to the Scottish Borders & Edinburgh
by Roger Smith, Hunter Publishing, 1983, 131 pages, paper, $8.95

This is one of the titles in the Visitor's Guide series, which is reviewed in more detail under "Series Reviews."

Walking Through Scotland
  by David and Kathleen MacInnes, Hunter Publishing, 1987, 192
  pages, paper, $10.95
    This is one of the Walking Through Britain Guide series, which
  is reviewed in more detail under "Series Reviews."

Woodland Walks in Scotland
  by Gerald Wilkinson, Hunter Publishing, 1986, 96 pages, paper,
  $9.95
    This book is part of the Woodland Walks series, which is reviewed
  in more detail under "Series Reviews."

Wales

See also "Great Britain" and "Europe as a Whole." Those books listed
below are exclusively on Wales. Wales is also included in the following
major, all-purpose guides to Europe: *Birnbaum's Europe; Fielding's Europe; Fielding's Economy Europe; Fisher's World: Europe; Fodor's Europe; Fodor's Budget Europe; Frommer's Europe on $30 a Day; Let's Go: Europe.*

AA Castles in Wales
  by the Automobile Association, Salem House, 1982, 192 pages,
  paper, $19.95
    This survey of over 80 castles in Wales via 15 suggested tours is
  replete with maps and details of the castle grounds, interior decor,
  and architecture.

AA Touring Wales: The Complete Touring Guide
  by the Automobile Association, Salem House, 1987, 152 pages,
  paper, $19.95
    This book is part of the AA Regional Touring Guide series, which
  is reviewed in more detail under "Series Reviews."

Blue Guide: Wales and the Marches
  edited by John Tomes, W. W. Norton & Co., 1979, (6th ed.), 402
  pages, paper, $16.95
    This is one of the highly regarded Blue Guide series, which is
  reviewed in more detail under "Series Reviews."

Frommer's Scotland and Wales on $40 a Day
  by Darwin Porter, Prentice Hall Press, 1988, 562 pages, paper,
  $11.95
    This is one of the Frommer's Dollar-A-Day Guide series, which is
  reviewed in more detail under "Series Reviews." The series is updated every two years.

Going Places: Motor Touring Guide to Wales
Salem House, 1986, 72 pages, paper, $4.95
This helpful guide to sightseeing by car includes suggested tours, maps, and information on places of interest.

Tourist Guide: Mid-Wales
Salem House, 1987, 72 pages, paper, $3.95
Tourist Guide: North Wales
Salem House, 1987, 72 pages, paper, $3.95
Tourist Guide: South Wales
Salem House, 1987, 72 pages, paper, $3.95
These compact regional guidebooks provide information on where to go and what to see, with general tips on food and lodging.

The Visitor's Guide to Historic Places in Wales
by W. T. Barber, Hunter Publishing, 1984, 160 pages, paper, $8.95
The Visitor's Guide to North Wales and Snowdonia
by Colin Macdonald, Hunter Publishing, 1983, 144 pages, paper, $8.95
The Visitor's Guide to South and West Wales
by Peter Gibson, Hunter Publishing, 1985, 142 pages, paper, $8.95
The Visitor's Guide to Welsh Borders
by Lawrence Garner, Hunter Publishing, 1984, 154 pages, paper, $8.95
All of these are titles in the Visitor's Guide series, which is reviewed in more detail under "Series Reviews."

Wales: Bed and Breakfast
by the Wales Tourist Board, Salem House, 1988, 112 pages, paper, $6.95
The emphasis here is on value—enjoyable bed and breakfasts at a reasonable price. All the practical details are included.

Wales: Walking
Salem House, 1985, 108 pages, paper, $4.95
Wales is a real rambler's paradise and this compact guide is a helpful resource to fascinating walks of varied length.

Wales: Where to Stay
by the Wales Tourist Board, Salem House, 1988, 320 pages, paper, $10.95
This is a useful guide to all manner of accommodations: expensive hotels, moderately priced bed and breakfasts, caravan parks, and camp sites. Classified by the Wales Tourist Board, many establish-

ments are illustrated in color. Practical details include 1988 prices. This book is updated annually.

Walking Through Wales

by David and Kathleen MacInnes, Hunter Publishing, 1987, 172 pages, paper, $10.95

This is one of the Walking Through Britain Guide series, which is reviewed in more detail under "Series Reviews."

Woodland Walks in Wales and the Marches

by Gerald Wilkinson, Hunter Publishing, 1987, 128 pages, paper, $9.95

This book is part of the Woodland Walks series, which is reviewed in more detail under "Series Reviews."

GREECE

See also "Europe as a Whole." Greece is included in the following major, all-purpose guides to Europe: *Birnbaum's Europe; Fielding's Europe; Fielding's Economy Europe; Fisher's World: Europe; Fodor's Europe; Fodor's Budget Europe; Frommer's Europe on $30 a Day; Let's Go: Europe.*

The American Express Pocket Guide to Greece

by Peter Sheldon, Prentice Hall Press, 1987, 240 pages, cloth, $8.95

This is one of the well-known American Express Pocket Guide series, which is reviewed in more detail under "Series Reviews."

Athens and Attica: A Phaidon Art and Architecture Guide

Prentice Hall Press, 1986, 259 pages, cloth, $14.95

This book is part of the encyclopedic Phaidon Art and Architecture Guide series, which is reviewed in more detail under "Series Reviews."

Baedeker's Athens

Prentice Hall Press, 1987, 160 pages, paper, $10.95

This book is part of Baedeker's City Guide series, which is reviewed in more detail under "Series Reviews."

Baedeker's Greece

Prentice Hall Press, undated, 296 pages, paper, $14.95

Baedeker's Greek Islands

Prentice Hall Press, 1987, 288 pages, paper, $10.95

Baedeker's Mediterranean Islands

Prentice Hall Press, 1985, 223 pages, paper, $14.95

These three titles are part of the Baedeker's Country/Regional Guide series, which is reviewed in more detail under "Series Reviews." The volume on the Mediterranean islands covers Cyprus and Malta, as well as the islands of Greece, Italy, Spain, and France.

Berlitz: Athens
Macmillan Publishing, 1982, 128 pages, paper, $6.95
Berlitz: Corfu
Macmillan Publishing, 1979, 128 pages, paper, $6.95
Berlitz: Crete
Macmillan Publishing, 1977, 128 pages, paper, $6.95
Berlitz: Greek Islands of the Aegean
Macmillan Publishing, 1979, 128 pages, paper, $6.95
Berlitz: Peloponnese
Macmillan Publishing, 1985, 128 pages, paper, $6.95
Berlitz: Rhodes
Macmillan Publishing, 1976, 128 pages, paper, $6.95
Berlitz: Salonica and Northern Greece
Macmillan Publishing, 1980, 128 pages, paper, $6.95
All of these titles are part of the small-format Berlitz Guide series, which is reviewed in more detail under "Series Reviews."

Blue Guide: Athens and Environs
edited by Stuart Rossiter, W. W. Norton & Co., 1981 (2nd ed.), 192 pages, paper, $14.95
Blue Guide: Crete
by Pat Cameron, W. W. Norton & Co., 1988 (5th ed.), 128 pages, paper, $14.95
Blue Guide: Greece
by Robin Barber, W. W. Norton & Co., 1987 (5th ed.), 792 pages, paper, $19.95
These three titles are part of the highly regarded Blue Guide series, which is reviewed in more detail under "Series Reviews."

Cadogan Guide: Greek Islands
by Dana Facaros, The Globe Pequot Press, 1986, 396 pages, paper, $12.95
Dana Facaros, a first-class travel book writer, contributes this volume to the quality Cadogan Guide series, which is reviewed in more detail under "Series Reviews." The series is updated every two years.

Collier World Traveler Series: Greece and Yugoslavia
Macmillan Publishing, 1985, 192 pages, paper, $6.95
    This book is part of the Collier World Traveler Guide series, which
is reviewed in more detail under "Series Reviews."

DuMont Guide to the Greek Islands
by Evi Melas, Stewart, Tabori & Chang, 1985, 440 pages, paper,
$14.95
    This book is part of the DuMont Guide series, which is reviewed
in more detail under "Series Reviews."

Eperon's Guide to the Greek Islands
by Arthur Eperon, Hunter Publishing, 1988, 224 pages, paper,
$14.95
    The well-known, veteran travel writer Arthur Eperon now offers
a new guide to 55 of the Greek islands, concentrating on areas less
frequented by travelers. Included are hotel, restaurant, and sightseeing information, and numerous color photos. Although it was released after press time, expect the high quality of Eperon's other
guides.

Exploring Rural Greece
Passport Books, 1988/89, 200 pages, paper, $12.95
    This is an anticipated, new title in the Exploring Rural Europe
series, which is reviewed in more detail under "Series Reviews."
The price and number of pages are approximate.

Fisher's World: Greece
by Alex and Jane Eliot, Fisher's World, Inc., 1988, 261 pages, paper,
$14.95
    This is one of the Fisher's World Guide series, which is reviewed
in more detail under "Series Reviews." The series is updated annually.

Fodor's Greece
Fodor's Travel Publications, 1987, 384 pages, paper, $13.95
    This is one of the Fodor's Country/Regional Guide series, which
is reviewed in more detail under "Series Reviews." The series is
updated annually.

**Frommer's Greece on $40 a Day (Including Istanbul and Turkey's
Aegean Coast)**
by Kyle McCarthy and John Levy, Prentice Hall Press, 1987, 540
pages, paper, $11.95
    This book is part of the budget-oriented Frommer's Dollar-A-Day

Guide series, which is reviewed in more detail under "Series Reviews." The series is updated every two years.

Frommer's Guide to Athens
by Darwin Porter, Prentice Hall Press, 1987, 218 pages, paper, $5.95

This book is part of the Frommer City Guide series, which is reviewed in more detail under "Series Reviews." The series is updated every two years.

Greece: A Phaidon Art and Architecture Guide
Prentice Hall Press, 1985, 600 pages, cloth, $16.95

This book is part of the encyclopedic Phaidon Art and Architecture Guide series, which is reviewed in more detail under "Series Reviews."

Greece—Mainland and Islands—On Your Own: Making the Most of Local Food and Drink
by Florica Kyriacopoulos and Tim Salmon, Hippocrene Books, 1986, 155 pages, paper, $9.95

For those staying in Greece for a while, this is a useful survival kit. It is part of the On Your Own Guide series, which is reviewed in more detail under "Series Reviews."

Greece On Foot: Mountain Treks, Islands Trails
by Marc Dubin, The Mountaineers, 1986, 240 pages, paper, $10.95

Dubin, a contributor to the top-rate Rough Guide series, has put together an excellent assortment of hikes, 50 in all, ranging from two-hour day trips to journeys of several weeks. An informative section on traveling in Greece and on issues of importance to the hiker, such as maps, available backpacking foods, health hazards, and finding trails when there are none, is provided. Hiking directions are clear and concise as well as very detailed.

Greek Island Hopping: A Handbook for the Independent Traveler
by Dana Facaros, Hippocrene Books, 1982 (2nd ed.), 352 pages, paper, $12.95

This book is part of the Island Hopping Guide series, which is reviewed in more detail under "Series Reviews."

Guide to Greece
by Michael Haag and Neville Lewis, Hippocrene Books, 1985 (2nd ed.), 319 pages, paper, $12.95

This well-produced, quality cultural tour guide is filled with history and practical information clearly and concisely organized by region.

Landscapes of Corfu
by Noel Rochford, Hunter Publishing, 1987, 128 pages, paper, $9.95
Landscapes of Eastern Crete
by Jonnie Godfrey and Elizabeth Karslake, Hunter Publishing, 1986, 128 pages, paper, $9.95
Landscapes of Rhodes
by Noel Rochford, Hunter Publishing, 1983, 128 pages, paper, $9.95
Landscapes of Western Crete
by Jonnie Godfrey and Elizabeth Karslake, Hunter Publishing, 1987, 128 pages, paper, $9.95
All four of these titles are part of the Countryside Guide series, which is reviewed in more detail under "Series Reviews."

Let's Go: Greece (including Cyprus, the Turkish Coast and Istanbul)
by Harvard Student Agencies, St. Martin's Press, 1988, 528 pages, paper, $10.95
This is one of the excellent, budget-oriented Let's Go Guide series, which is reviewed in more detail under "Series Reviews." The series is updated annually.

Lett's Guide: Greece, the Mainland
Prima Publishing, 1980, 96 pages, paper, $5.95
Lett's Guide: Greek Islands
Prima Publishing, 1981, 96 pages, paper, $5.95
These two titles are part of the Letts Guide series, which is reviewed in more detail under "Series Reviews."

Michelin Green Guide: Greece
Michelin Guides and Maps, 1987, 235 pages, paper, $10.95
This is one title in the premier sightseeing guide series, the Michelin Green Guides, which is reviewed in more detail under "Series Reviews."

The Mountains of Greece: A Walker's Guide
by Tim Salmon, Hunter Publishing, 1988, 176 pages, paper, $12.95
This book is part of the Hunter Mountain Walks series, which is reviewed in more detail under "Series Reviews."

The New Holiday Guide to Greece and Aegean Islands
M. Evans & Co., 1988 (10th ed.), 160 pages, paper, $4.95
This is one of the Holiday Guide series, which is reviewed in more detail under "Series Reviews."

Nicholson: Guide to the Greek Islands
Salem House, 1986, 208 pages, paper, $9.95
Covering more than 50 islands, this book is part of the Nicholson Guide series, which is reviewed in more detail under "Series Reviews."

Pilgrimages to Rome and Beyond
by Paul Higgins, Prentice Hall Press, 1985, 130 pages, paper, $8.95
This excellent guide for the interested traveler describes the holy places of Italy, the Vatican, Greece, Spain, Portugal, and Yugoslavia. Higgins's enjoyable and highly informative commentary evokes vivid images of these important religious sites.

Rand McNally: Greece and the Aegean Islands
by John and Shirley Harrison, Rand McNally & Co., 1981, 128 pages, paper, $5.95
This book is part of the small-format Rand McNally Pocket Guide series, which is reviewed in more detail under "Series Reviews."

Rough Guide to Greece
by Mark Ellingham, *et al.*, Routledge & Kegan Paul, 1987, 375 pages, paper, $10.95
This book is part of the top-notch Rough Guide series, which is reviewed in more detail under "Series Reviews."

Where to Go In Greece
by Trevor Webster, Hippocrene Books, 1986, 128 pages, paper, $8.95
Where to Go In Greece: Athens Mainland and the North Aegean Islands
by Trevor Webster, Hippocrene Books, 1987, 75 pages, paper, $9.95
Where to Go In Greece: Corfu and the Ionian Islands
by Trevor Webster, Hippocrene Books, 1987, 67 pages, paper, $9.95
Where to Go In Greece: Rhodes and the Dodecanese Islands
by Trevor Webster, Hippocrene Books, 1987, 83 pages, paper, $9.95
All of these titles are part of the Where to Go Guide series, which is reviewed in more detail under "Series Reviews."

Whole Europe Escape Manual: Italy, Greece
by Kerry Green and Charles Leocha, World Leisure Corp., 1986,
160 pages, paper, $6.95
This book is part of the unique Escape Manual series, which is
reviewed in more detail under "Series Reviews."

Holland: See the "Netherlands."

HUNGARY

See also "Eastern Europe" and "Europe as a Whole." Hungary is in-
cluded in the following major, all-purpose guides to Europe: *Birnbaum's
Europe; Fielding's Europe; Fodor's Europe; Fodor's Budget Europe; Let's
Go: Europe.*

Baedeker's Budapest
Prentice Hall Press, 1987, 176 pages, paper, $10.95
This is one of the Baedeker's Country/Regional Guide series,
which is reviewed in more detail under "Series Reviews."

Berlitz: Budapest
Macmillan Publishing, 1982, 128 pages, paper, $4.95
This book is part of the small-format Berlitz Guide series, which
is reviewed in more detail under "Series Reviews."

Berlitz: Hungary
Macmillan Publishing, 1983, 192 pages, paper, $8.95
This book is part of the small-format Berlitz Country Guide series,
which is reviewed in more detail under "Series Reviews."

Budapest: A Complete Guide
Hippocrene Books, 1982, 200 pages, paper, $12.95
Although getting older, this book is still a useful guide to Budapest.
Its strong suit is sightseeing, which makes it a little less old than it
appears. A useful section of practical facts for the traveler is also
included.

Fodor's Hungary
Fodor's Travel Publications, 1986, 208 pages, paper, $9.95
This book is part of the Fodor's Country/Regional Guide series,
which is reviewed in more detail under "Series Reviews." The series
is updated annually.

Frommer's Dollarwise Guide to Austria and Hungary
by Darwin Porter, Prentice Hall Press, 1987, 600 pages, paper, $11.95

This is one of Frommer's Dollarwise Guide series, which is reviewed in more detail under "Series Reviews." The series is updated every two years.

Hungary: A Complete Guide
Hippocrene Books, 1985, 320 pages, paper, $14.95

This guide has plenty of good, practical information and sightseeing ideas. General strategies on food and lodging are also included in this decent, if unexciting, guidebook.

Iceland: See "Islands of the Eastern and Northern Atlantic Ocean" below.

IRELAND

See also "Europe as a Whole." Ireland is included in the following major, all-purpose guides to Europe: *Birnbaum's Europe; Fielding's Europe; Fielding's Economy Europe; Fisher's World: Europe; Fodor's Europe; Fodor's Budget Europe; Let's Go: Europe.*

AA/Ordnance Survey Leisure Guide: Ireland
Salem House, 1988, 176 pages, paper, $19.95

This is one of the AA/Ordnance Survey Leisure Guide series, which is reviewed in more detail under "Series Reviews."

AA Town and City Guide: Dublin
Salem House, 1988, 120 pages, paper, $18.95

This book is part of the AA Town and Country Guide series, which is reviewed in more detail under "Series Reviews."

AA Treasures of Britain
by the Automobile Association, W. W. Norton & Co., 1986 (4th ed.), 680 pages, cloth, $27.95

This large, hardbound book includes descriptions, color photographs, and maps of the many riches of Ireland, as well as those of Britain.

Baedeker's Ireland
Prentice Hall Press, 1987, 236 pages, paper, $14.95

This is one of the Baedeker's Country/Regional Guide series, which is reviewed in more detail under "Series Reviews."

Berlitz: Ireland
Macmillan Publishing, 1981, 128 pages, paper, $6.95
This is one of the small-format Berlitz Guide series, which is reviewed in more detail under "Series Reviews."

Birnbaum's Great Britain and Ireland
edited by Stephen Birnbaum, Houghton Mifflin, 1987, 848 pages, paper, $12.95
Beginning with the 1989 edition, this title will be split into two guidebooks—one on Ireland and the other on Great Britain. Depending on size, the title on Ireland may actually cost less. Both titles are part of the excellent Birnbaum's Guide series, which is reviewed in more detail under "Series Reviews." The series is updated annually.

Blue Guide: Ireland
edited by Ian Robertson, W. W. Norton & Co., 1987 (5th ed.), 401 pages, paper, $17.95
This is one title in the excellent Blue Guide series, which is reviewed in more detail under "Series Reviews."

Blue Guide: Literary Britain and Ireland
by Ian Ousby, W. W. Norton & Co., 1985, 424 pages, paper, $14.95
See "Great Britain."

Cadogan Guide: Ireland
by Catherine Day, The Globe Pequot Press, 1986, 320 pages, paper, $12.95
This book is part of the widely praised Cadogan Guide series, which is reviewed in more detail under "Series Reviews." The series is updated every two years.

The Cambridge Guide to the Museums of Britain and Ireland
by Kenneth Hudson and Ann Nicholls, Cambridge University Press, 1987, 435 pages, cloth, $24.95
This excellent, comprehensive guide is reviewed under "Great Britain."

Charming Small Hotel Guide: Britain and Ireland
edited by Chris Gill, Hunter Publishing, 1988, 224 pages, paper, $9.95
This is one of two titles in what will become a full series on small hotels known for their emphasis on atmosphere, service, good food, and good value. The other volume currently available covers Italy.

Collier World Traveler Series: Great Britain and Ireland
edited by Philippe Gloaguen and Pierre Josse, Macmillan
Publishing, 1986, 192 pages, paper, $6.95
This book is part of the Collier World Traveler Guide series, which
is reviewed in more detail under "Series Reviews."

Companion Guide to Ireland
by Brendan Lehane, Prentice Hall Press, 1985, 516 pages, paper,
$10.95
This is one of the superb Companion Guide series, which is reviewed in more detail under "Series Reviews."

Country Inns and Back Roads: Britain and Ireland
by Norman Simpson, Harper & Row, 1988 (5th ed.) 317 pages,
paper, $10.95
This quality guide is part of the Country Inns and Back Roads
series, which is reviewed in more detail under "Series Reviews." It
is updated annually.

Country Inns, Castles & Historic Hotels: Ireland
by Eileen and Eugene O'Reilly, Burt Franklin–Publisher, 1988 (7th
ed.), 246 pages, paper, $8.95
This fine resource is part of the Compleat Traveler's Companions
series, which is reviewed in more detail under "Series Reviews."
The series is updated annually. No fees were accepted for inclusion.

CTC Route Guide to Cycling in Britain and Ireland
by Christa Gansden and Nicolas Cramer, Haynes Publishing, 1982
(revised ed.), 432 pages, cloth, $15.95
This top-notch cycling guide is reviewed under "Great Britain."

DuMont Guide to Ireland
by Wolfgang Ziegler, Stewart, Tabori & Chang, 1984, 302 pages,
paper, $12.95
A guide to art, architecture, and history, this book is part of the
DuMont Guide series, which is reviewed in more detail under "Series Reviews."

Egon Ronay's Hotels and Restaurants (Great Britain and Ireland)
Salem House, 1988, 864 pages, paper, $19.95
One of the most famous hotel and restaurant guides in the United
Kingdom, this book is reviewed under "Great Britain."

Exploring Rural Ireland
Passport Books, 1988/89, 200 pages, paper, $12.95
   This is one of the new, anticipated additions to the Exploring Rural Europe series, which is reviewed in more detail under "Series Reviews." The price and number of pages are approximate.

The Farm Holiday Guide to Holidays in England, Wales, Ireland, Channel Islands
Hunter Publishing, 1988, 568 pages, paper, $14.95
   This annual guide is described under "Great Britain."

Fisher's Ireland
by Patricia and John Preston, Fisher's World, Inc., 1988, 432 pages, paper, $14.95
   This book is part of the Fisher's World Guide series, which is reviewed in more detail under "Series Reviews." The series is updated annually.

Fodor's Ireland
Fodor's Travel Publications, 1987, 320 pages, paper, $13.95
   This book is part of the Fodor's Country/Regional Guide series, which is reviewed in more detail under "Series Reviews." The series is updated annually.

Frommer's Guide to Dublin and Ireland
by Susan Poole, Prentice Hall Press, 1987, 230 pages, paper, $5.95
   This is one of the Frommer's City Guide series, which is reviewed in more detail under "Series Reviews." The series is updated every two years.

Frommer's Ireland on $30 a Day
by Susan Poole, Prentice Hall Press, 1986, 360 pages, paper, $10.95
   This book is part of the budget-oriented Frommer's Dollar-A-Day Guide series, which is reviewed in more detail under "Series Reviews." The series is updated every two years.

Great Britain and Ireland: A Phaidon Art and Architecture Guide
Prentice Hall Press, 1985, 644 pages, cloth, $16.95
   This is one of the encyclopedic Phaidon Art and Architecture Guide series, which is reviewed in more detail under "Series Reviews."

The Holiday Guide to Ireland
M. Evans & Co., 1988 (10th ed.), 160 pages, paper, $4.95
This book is part of the Holiday Guide series, which is reviewed in more detail under "Series Reviews."

Ireland's Pubs
by Sybil Taylor, Viking Penguin, 1983, 256 pages, paper, $7.95
This is a charmingly presented guide, arranged by county, that presents "the life and lore of Ireland through its finest pubs." Taylor's book is a delight to read even for those who never anticipate having a drink in an Irish pub, but travelers planning a visit will find plenty of practical information here. Most of the practical information in this guide should still be substantially correct, as the finest pubs in a land that values them so highly are not likely to change their ways rapidly. So, despite the need of an update, this is a fine book.

Irish Country Inns and Cottages
by June Brown, Travel Press, 1988, 256 pages, paper, $12.95
This book is part of the delightful Karen Brown's Country Inns series, which is reviewed in more detail under "Series Reviews."

Irish Museums Guide
edited by Sean Popplewell, Irish Books & Media, 1983, 207 pages, paper, $7.95
This is a fine resource, although some hours and prices may have changed, to dozens of museums of every description. Each is given a good overview and other practical details, such as handicapped access, are noted. Separate chapters on historic houses, gardens, and libraries make this a helpful planning resource.

Irish Touring Guide: What to Do, Where to Go, What to See
The Globe Pequot Press, 1988, 128 pages, paper, $14.95
This large-format guide, filled with color photographs and numerous road and detailed town maps, is useful in planning an Irish holiday. Included are sections on driving tours, dining, shopping, transportation, lodging, sights not to miss, history, and culture.

Joyce's Dublin: A Walking Guide to Ulysses
by Jack McCarthy, Irish Books & Media, 1986, 80 pages, paper, $6.95
This delightful book traces the routes the main characters of Joyce's *Ulysses* took through Dublin, in an attempt to clarify what may not have been at all clear in the classic book itself—what characters went which way. This premise makes for a fascinating

journey and this well-done guide, with its clear maps and carefully laid-out text, makes traveling these paths today possible.

The Knopf Traveler's Guide to Art: Great Britain and Ireland

by Michael Jacobs and Paul Stirton, Alfred Knopf, Inc., 1984, 304 pages, cloth, $14.95

This superb guide is part of the Knopf Guides to Art series, which is reviewed in more detail under "Series Reviews."

Let's Go: Great Britain and Ireland

by Harvard Student Agencies, St. Martin's Press, 1988, 576 pages, paper, $10.95

This book is part of the highly regarded, budget-oriented Let's Go Guide series, which is reviewed in more detail under "Series Reviews." The series is updated annually.

Michelin Red Guide: Great Britain and Ireland

Michelin Guides and Maps, 1988, 652 pages, cloth, $16.95

This annual hotel and restaurant guide is part of the Michelin Red Guide series, which is reviewed in more detail under "Series Reviews."

Museums & Galleries in Great Britain and Ireland

Hunter Publishing, 1988, 184 pages, paper, $10.95

This annual large-format directory is reviewed under "Great Britain."

Nagel's Encyclopedia Guide: Ireland

Passport Books, 1980, 352 pages, cloth, $39.95

This classic, cultural guide is one of the Nagel's Guide series, which is reviewed in more detail under "Series Reviews."

Nicholson: Guide to Ireland

Salem House, 1983, 160 pages, paper, $11.95

This book is part of the Nicholson Guide series, which is reviewed in more detail under "Series Reviews."

Oxford Literary Guide to the British Isles

by Dorothy Eagle and Hilary Carnell, Oxford University Press, 1977, 468 pages, paper, $9.95

This book is reviewed in more detail under "Great Britain."

The Penguin Guide to Ireland
edited by Alan Tucker, Viking Penguin, 1988, 224-448 pages, paper, $9.95-12.95

This is one of the first titles in the new Penguin Travel Guide series, which is reviewed in more detail under "Series Reviews." Only the price and page count range for the entire series were available at press time.

RAC Hotel Guide
by the Royal Automobile Club, Sheridan House, 1988, 704 pages, paper, $18.95

This book is updated annually, and is reviewed in more detail under "Great Britain."

Rand McNally: Ireland
by John and Shirley Harrison, Rand McNally & Co., 1986, 126 pages, paper, $5.95

This is one of the small-format Rand McNally Pocket Guide series, which is reviewed in more detail under "Series Reviews."

See Ireland by Train
by Fergus Mulligan, Irish Books & Media, 1986, 96 pages, paper, $5.95

This compact guide describes the main train routes of Ireland, along with what to look for as the train moves through the Irish countryside. Included also are ideas for what to see and do in and around the various train stops.

A Visitor's Guide to the Dingle Peninsula
by Steve MacDonagh and Pat Langan, Longwood Publishing, 1985, 104 pages, paper, $4.95

This large-format book provides a history and an orientation to the many archaeological sites and the rich heritage of the fascinating Dingle Peninsula at the extreme southwest of Ireland. A practical information section is included.

What to Do In and Around Dublin
by Hugh Oran, Irish Books & Media, 1984, 72 pages, paper, $5.95

This pocket-sized little book helps travelers decide what to do when visiting the Dublin area and the immediately surrounding counties. Some small, but useful, orientation maps are included.

Whole Europe Escape Manual: UK/Ireland
by Kerry Green and Charles Leocha, World Leisure Corp., 1984,
160 pages, paper, $6.95
This book is part of the unique Escape Manual series, which is
reviewed in more detail under "Series Reviews."

ISLANDS OF THE EASTERN AND
NORTHERN ATLANTIC OCEAN

Comprising the Azores, Canary Islands, and Madeira, plus Greenland
and Iceland. Note: England's Channel Islands are included under "England," the Faroe Islands under "Scandinavia," and the Shetland Islands
under "Scotland."

Azores, Canary Islands, and Madeira

Berlitz: Canary Islands
Macmillan Publishing, 1977, 128 pages, paper, $6.95
Berlitz: Madeira
Macmillan Publishing, 1982, 128 pages, paper, $6.95
These two titles are part of the small-format Berlitz Guide series,
which is reviewed in more detail under "Series Reviews."

**Canary Island Hopping (The Azores, Madeira): A Handbook for the
Independent Traveler**
by Judith Hayter, Hippocrene Books, 1984, 319 pages, paper, $12.95
This book is part of the Island Hopping Guide series, which is
reviewed in more detail under "Series Reviews."

Frommer's Dollarwise Guide to Portugal, Madeira and the Azores
by Darwin Porter, Prentice Hall Press, 1988, 312 pages, paper,
$12.95
This book is part of Frommer's Dollarwise Guide series, which is
reviewed in more detail under "Series Reviews." This series emphasizes selections in the moderate price range and is updated every
two years.

Frommer's Spain and Morocco plus the Canary Islands on $40 a Day
by Darwin Porter, Prentice Hall Press, 1987, 552 pages, paper,
$10.95
This is one of Frommer's Dollar-a-Day Guide series, which is
reviewed in more detail under "Series Reviews." The series is updated every two years.

Landscapes of Madeira
by John and Pat Underwood, Hunter Publishing, 1983, 120 pages, paper, $9.95

Landscapes of Gran Canaria (Canary Islands)
by Noel Rochford, Hunter Publishing, 1986, 128 pages, paper, $9.95

Landscapes of Tenerife (Canary Islands)
by Noel Rochford, Hunter Publishing, 1984, 176 pages, paper, $9.95

These three titles are part of the Countryside Guide series, which is reviewed in more detail under "Series Reviews."

Cape Verde

Traveller's Guide to Western Africa
Hunter Publishing, 1986 (6th ed.), 274 pages, paper, $12.95

Including Cape Verde, this book is part of the Traveller's Guide series, which is reviewed in more detail under "Series Reviews."

Greenland

Nagel's Encyclopedia Guide: Denmark and Greenland
Passport Books, 1980, 594 pages, cloth, $39.95

This classic, cultural guide is part of the Nagel's Guide series, which is reviewed in more detail under "Series Reviews."

Iceland

See also "Europe as a Whole." Iceland is included in the following major, all-purpose guides to Europe: *Birnbaum's Europe; Fodor's Europe; Fodor's Budget Europe; Let's Go: Europe.*

Hiking and Walking Guide to Europe
by Arthur Howcroft and Richard Sale, Passport Books, 1984, 137 pages, paper, $7.95

Including Iceland, this book is reviewed under "Europe as a Whole."

Iceland: The Visitor's Guide
by David Williams, Stacey International, 1985, 264 pages, cloth, $19.95

This is an excellent guide, well written, with beautiful photographs and plenty of information on sights, driving itineraries, history, and culture. Hotel recommendations are lists only, but in all other respects this is a fine guidebook. Published in England, this book currently has no American distributor. However, it can be found in many travel bookstores, including Travel Books Unlimited and Wide World Books and Maps (see Travel Bookstore appendix).

Nagel's Encyclopedia Guide: Iceland
Passport Books, 1984, 190 pages, cloth, $29.95
   This classic, cultural guide is part of the Nagel's Guide series, which is reviewed in more detail under "Series Reviews."

The Visitor's Guide to Iceland
by Don Philpott, Hunter Publishing, 1985, 160 pages, paper, $10.95
   This book is part of the Visitor's Guide series, which is reviewed in more detail under "Series Reviews."

ITALY

See also "Europe as a Whole." Italy is included in the following major, all-purpose guides to Europe: *Birnbaum's Europe; Fielding's Europe; Fielding's Economy Europe; Fisher's World: Europe; Fodor's Europe; Fodor's Budget Europe; Frommer's Europe on $30 a Day; Let's Go: Europe.*

The Adventure Guide to Italy
Hunter Publishing, 1988, 224 pages, paper, $12.95
   This book is part of the Hunter Adventure Guide series, which is reviewed in more detail under "Series Reviews."

The Adventure Guide to the Alps: The Sierra Club Travel Guide to the Alpine Regions of France, Switzerland, Germany, Austria, Liechtenstein, Italy, and Yugoslavia
by William and Marylou Reifsnyder, Sierra Club Books, 1986, 278 pages, paper, $10.95
   This is one of the Sierra Club Adventure Travel Guide series, which is reviewed in more detail under "Series Reviews."

The American Express Pocket Guide to Florence and Tuscany
by Sheila Hale, Prentice Hall Press, 1987, 224 pages, cloth, $9.95
The American Express Pocket Guide to Rome
by Anthony Pereira, Prentice Hall Press, 1986, 224 pages, cloth, $8.95
The American Express Pocket Guide to Venice
by Sheila Hale, Prentice Hall Press, 1988, 208 pages, cloth, $9.95
   These three titles are part of the well-done American Express Pocket Guide series, which is reviewed in more detail under "Series Reviews."

Backpacking and Walking in Italy
by Stefano Ardito, Hunter Publishing, 1987, 224 pages, paper, $11.95
   This is one of the Hunter Walking/Hiking Guide series, which is reviewed in more detail under "Series Reviews."

Baedeker's Florence
Prentice Hall Press, 1987, 168 pages, paper, $10.95
This is one of the Baedeker's City Guide series, which is reviewed in more detail under "Series Reviews."

Baedeker's Italy
Prentice Hall Press, undated, 368 pages, paper, $14.95
Baedeker's Mediterranean Islands
Prentice Hall Press, 1985, 223 pages, paper, $14.95
These two titles are part of the Baedeker's Country/Regional Guide series, which is reviewed in more detail under "Series Reviews." The Mediterranean Islands guide covers Cyprus, Malta, and the islands of Italy, France, Spain, and Greece.

Baedeker's Rome
Prentice Hall Press, 1987, 190 pages, paper, $10.95
This book is part of Baedeker's City Guide series, which is reviewed in more detail under "Series Reviews."

Baedeker's Tuscany
Prentice Hall Press, 1985, 247 pages, paper, $9.95
This book is part of Baedeker's Country/Regional Guide series, which is reviewed in more detail under "Series Reviews."

Baedeker's Venice
Prentice Hall Press, 1987, 125 pages, paper, $11.95
This is one title in the Baedeker's City Guide series, which is reviewed in more detail under "Series Reviews."

Berlitz: Florence
Macmillan Publishing, 1988, 128 pages, paper, $6.95
Berlitz: Italian Adriatic
Macmillan Publishing, 1982, 128 pages, paper, $6.95
Berlitz: Italian Riviera
Macmillan Publishing, 1982, 128 pages, paper, $6.95
These three titles are part of the small-format Berlitz Guide series, which is reviewed in more detail under "Series Reviews."

Berlitz: Italy
Macmillan Publishing, 1988, 256 pages, paper, $8.95
This is one of the small-format Berlitz Country Guide series, which is reviewed in more detail under "Series Reviews."

Berlitz: Rome
Macmillan Publishing, 1988, 128 pages, paper, $6.95

Berlitz: Sicily
Macmillan Publishing, 1982, 128 pages, paper, $6.95
Berlitz: Venice
Macmillan Publishing, 1977, 128 pages, paper, $6.95
These three titles are part of the small-format Berlitz Guide series, which is reviewed in more detail under "Series Reviews." The books on Rome and Venice can also be found as part of the new Berlitz Deluxe Guide series. For additional notes, see "Series Reviews."

Best of Italy
by Henri Gault and Christian Millau, Crown Publishers, 1984, 408 pages, paper, $13.95
This food, entertainment, and hotel guide is one of the Gault/Millau 'Best Of ' Guide series, which is reviewed in more detail under "Series Reviews." This fine guide is just too old at present, but watch for a new edition.

Birnbaum's Italy
edited by Stephen Birnbaum, Houghton Mifflin, 1987, 686 pages, paper, $12.95
This is one of the excellent Birnbaum's Guide series, which is reviewed in more detail under "Series Reviews." The series is updated annually.

Blue Guide: Florence
edited by Alta Macadam, W. W. Norton & Co., 1988 (4th ed.), 240 pages, paper, $15.95
Blue Guide: Rome and Environs
edited by Alta Macadam, W. W. Norton & Co., 1985 (3rd ed.), 384 pages, paper, $16.95
Blue Guide: Northern Italy: From the Alps to Rome
edited by Alta Macadam, W. W. Norton & Co., 1985, 679 pages, paper, $19.95
Blue Guide: Sicily
edited by Alta Macadam, W. W. Norton & Co., 1982 (2nd ed.), 191 pages, paper, $16.95
Blue Guide: Southern Italy: From Rome to Calabria
edited by Paul Blanchard, W. W. Norton & Co., 1986 (6th ed.), 376 pages, paper, $16.95
Blue Guide: Venice
edited by Alta Macadam, W. W. Norton & Co., 1986 (3rd ed.), 271 pages, paper, $15.95
All of these titles are part of the highly regarded Blue Guide series, which is reviewed in more detail under "Series Reviews."

Born to Shop: Italy
by Suzy Gershman and Judith Thomas, Bantam Books, 1987 (2nd ed.), 297 pages, paper, $8.95
This guide to shopping in Rome, Florence, Venice, and Milan is part of the Born to Shop Guide series, which is reviewed in more detail under "Series Reviews."

Cadogan Guide: Italian Islands
by Dana Facaros and Michael Pauls, The Globe Pequot Press, 1986, 366 pages, paper, $12.95
Cadogan Guide: Italy
by Dana Facaros and Michael Pauls, The Globe Pequot Press, 1988, 512 pages, paper, $14.95
Two fine travel writers have contributed these titles to the well-done Cadogan Guide series, which is reviewed in more detail under "Series Reviews." The series is updated every two years.

Charming Small Hotel Guide: Italy, Sicily & Sardinia
edited by Chris Gill, Hunter Publishing, 1988, 192 pages, paper, $9.95
This new guide in a upcoming series focuses on small hotels emphasizing atmosphere, service, good food, and good value. The other currently available volume is on Great Britain and Ireland. This volume, covering 240 hotels, was released after press time.

The Children's Treasure Hunt Travel Guide to Italy
by Frances Goldstein, Hippocrene Books, 1980, 222 pages, paper, $6.95
Providing on-the-road entertainment for kids six and up, this book is part of the Children's Treasure Hunt Guide series, which is reviewed in more detail under "Series Reviews."

Collier World Traveler Series: Italy
edited by Philippe Gloaguen and Pierre Josse, Macmillan Publishing, 1986, 192 pages, paper, $6.95
This is one of the Collier World Traveler Guide series, which is reviewed in more detail under "Series Reviews."

The Companion Guide to Rome
by Georgina Masson, Prentice Hall Press, 1983 (6th ed.), 541 pages, paper, $12.95
The Companion Guide to Venice
by Hugh Honour, Prentice Hall Press, 1983, 288 pages, paper, $9.95
Hugh Honour's guide is acknowledged to be one of the classic

travel guides. Both titles are part of the superb Companion Guide series, which is reviewed in more detail under "Series Reviews."

Crown Insider's Guide to Italy

by Barbara Hults, Hunter Publishing, 1988, 336 pages, paper, $10.95

This is one of the Crown Insider's Guide series, which is reviewed in more detail under "Series Reviews."

Day Trips in Italy: 50 One-Day Adventures by Rail, Bus or Car

by Earl Steinbicker, Hastings House, 1987, 304 pages, paper, $10.95

This book is part of the Earl Steinbicker's Day Trips series, which is reviewed in more detail under "Series Reviews."

Exploring Rural Italy

by Michael Leach, Passport Books, 1988, 208 pages, paper, $12.95

This is one of a new series, Exploring Rural Europe Guides, which is reviewed in more detail under "Series Reviews."

Fisher's World: Italy

by Wilma Pezzini, Fisher's World, Inc., 1988, 342 pages, paper, $14.95

This book is part of the Fisher's World Guide series, which is reviewed in more detail under "Series Reviews." The series is updated annually.

Florence and Tuscany: A Phaidon Art and Architecture Guide

Prentice Hall Press, 1986, 259 pages, cloth, $14.95

This is one of the encyclopedic Phaidon Art and Architecture Guide series, which is reviewed in more detail under "Series Reviews."

Florencewalks

by Anne Holler, Henry Holt & Co., 1982, 192 pages, paper, $9.95

This is one of the Citywalks series, which is reviewed in more detail under "Series Reviews."

Fodor's Florence and Venice

Fodor's Travel Publications, 1987, 304 pages, paper, $9.95

This is one title in Fodor's City Guide series ,which is reviewed in more detail under "Series Reviews." The series is updated annually.

Fodor's Great Travel Values: Italy
Fodor's Travel Publications, 1987, 160 pages, paper, $5.95

This book is part of the budget-oriented Fodor's Great Travel Values Guide series, which is reviewed in more detail under "Series Reviews." The series is updated annually.

Fodor's Italy
Fodor's Travel Publications, 1987, 432 pages, paper, $13.95

This is one title in Fodor's Country/Regional Guide series, which is reviewed in more detail under "Series Reviews." The series is updated annually.

Fodor's Rome
Fodor's Travel Publications, 1987, 256 pages, paper, $8.95

This book is part of Fodor's City Guide series, which is reviewed in more detail under "Series Reviews." The series is updated annually.

Frommer's Dollarwise Guide to Italy
by Darwin Porter, Prentice Hall Press, 1988, 373 pages, paper, $11.95

This is one of the Frommer's Dollarwise Guide series, which is reviewed in more detail under "Series Reviews." The series emphasizes selections in the moderate price range and is updated every two years.

Frommer's Guide to Rome
by Darwin Porter, Prentice Hall Press, 1987, 234 pages, paper, $5.95

This is one of the Frommer's City Guide series, which is reviewed in more detail under "Series Reviews." The series is updated every two years.

Frommer's Touring Guide to Florence
Prentice Hall Press, 1986, 158 pages, paper, $8.95
Frommer's Touring Guide to Venice
Prentice Hall Press, 1986, 158 pages, paper, $8.95

These books are part of Frommer's Touring Guide series, which is reviewed in more detail under "Series Reviews."

A Guide to Tuscany
by James Bentley, Viking Penguin, 1987, 255 pages, cloth, $19.95

This exceptionally wonderful book is written in the same vein as Bentley's popular volume, *A Guide to the Dordogne*. For more comments, see the review of this other work under "France."

The Hachette Guide to Italy: The Only Guide You'll Ever Need
Random House, 1988, 896 pages, paper, $16.95
 This is one of the Hachette Guide series, which is reviewed in more detail under "Series Reviews." The series is updated annually.

Holiday Which? Guide: Italy
Consumers Reports Books, 1988, 560 pages, paper, $12.00
 Released after press time, this is a guide to consumer-oriented information on history, sightseeing, and food from the reliable people at Consumers Reports.

Insight Guide: Italy
by Apa Productions, Prentice Hall Press, 1985, 337 pages, paper, $16.95
 This book is part of the acclaimed Insight Guide series, which is reviewed in more detail under "Series Reviews."

Italian Country Inns and Villas
by Karen Brown and Clare Brown, Travel Press, 1988, 224 pages, paper, $12.95
 This is one of the delightful Karen Brown's Country Inns series, which is reviewed in more detail under "Series Reviews."

Italy
by Edmund Swinglehurst, David & Charles, 1988, 175 pages, cloth, $29.95
 This new guide, due out after press time, addresses a wide variety of travel subjects ranging from history, architecture, and art to Italy's people, traditions, and cuisine. Arranged by region, the book focuses not only on the familiar tourist landmarks, but also on more obscure locations usually missed by travelers. Detailed sections on major cities as well as the countryside, including walks, driving tours, and good restaurants, complete this volume.

Italy: A Phaidon Art and Architecture Guide
Prentice Hall Press, 1985, 832 pages, cloth, $16.95
 This is one of the encyclopedic Phaidon Art and Architecture Guide series, which is reviewed in more detail under "Series Reviews."

Italy At Its Best
Robert Kane, Passport Books, 1985, 417 pages, paper, $9.95
 This book is part of the popular At Its Best Guide series, which is reviewed in more detail under "Series Reviews."

Italy On Your Own: Making the Most of Local Food and Drink
by Susan Grossman, Hippocrene Books, 1987, 184 pages, paper, $9.95

This book, for those planning longer stays in Italy, is part of the On Your Own Guide series, which is reviewed in more detail under "Series Reviews."

The Knopf Traveler's Guide to Art: Italy
by Helen Langdon, Alfred Knopf, Inc., 1984, 304 pages, cloth, $14.95

This is one of the titles in the excellent Knopf Guides to Art series, which is reviewed in more detail under "Series Reviews."

Let's Go: Italy
by Harvard Student Agencies, St. Martin's Press, 1988, 592 pages, paper, $10.95

This book is part of the top-quality, budget-oriented Let's Go Guide series, which is reviewed in more detail under "Series Reviews." The series is updated annually.

Marling Menu-Master for Italy
by William and Clare Marling, Altarinda Books, 1971, 108 pages, plasticized cover, $5.95

This is one of the excellent, small-format Marling Menu-Masters series, which is reviewed in more detail under "Series Reviews."

Mediterranean Island Hopping—Italian Islands, Corsica, Malta: A Handbook for the Independent Traveler
by Dana Facaros and Michael Pauls, Hippocrene Books, 1982 (revised ed.), 491 pages, paper, $12.95

This is one of the Island Hopping Guide series, which is reviewed in more detail under "Series Reviews." The Italian island portion of this aging title is now part of the Cadogan Guide series in a new, updated version.

Michelin Green Guide: Italy
Michelin Guides and Maps, 1983 (10th ed.), 290 pages, paper, $10.95
Michelin Green Guide: Rome
Michelin Guides and Maps, 1985, 216 pages, paper, $10.95

These are part of the premier sightseeing guide series, the Michelin Green Guides, which is reviewed in more detail under "Series Reviews."

Michelin Red Guide: Italia
Michelin Guides and Maps, 1988, 694 pages, cloth, $17.95

This annual hotel and restaurant guide is one of the Michelin Red Guide series, which is reviewed in more detail under "Series Reviews."

Milan Alive
by Arnold and Harriet Greenberg, Alive Publications, 1988, 300 pages, paper, $10.95

This is one of the titles in the revival of the Alive Guide series, which is reviewed in more detail under "Series Reviews." As it was released after press time, the number of pages is approximate.

Museums of Florence
by Eloise Danto, Eldan Press, 1987 (10th ed.), 80 pages, paper, $9.95

This small-format book is part of the Eldan Museum Guide series, which is reviewed in more detail under "Series Reviews."

The New Holiday Guide to Italy
M. Evans & Co., 1988, 160 pages, paper, $4.95

The New Holiday Guide to Rome
M. Evans & Co., 1988 (10th ed.), 160 pages, paper, $4.95

Both of these volumes are part of the Holiday Guide series, which is reviewed in more detail under "Series Reviews."

Nino LoBello's Guide to the Vatican
by Nino LoBello, Chicago Review Press, 1987, 240 pages, paper, $9.95

LoBello's book is a great help for those visiting the Vatican. Describing the treasures of the Vatican and including their historic significance, this book is an excellent companion guide for those looking for more than the standard tour. LoBello also offers all sorts of fascinating anecdotes and information on how to gain entrance into areas of the Vatican not normally open to the public.

100 Hikes In The Alps
by Ira Spring and Harvey Edwards, the Mountaineers, 1985, 224 pages, paper, $8.95

This book is part of the Mountaineers Hiking Guide series, which is reviewed in more detail under "Series Reviews."

The Penguin Guide to Italy
Viking Penguin, 1988, 224-448 pages, paper, $9.95-12.95
    This is one title in the much-anticipated Penguin Travel Guide series, which is reviewed in more detail under "Series Reviews." Only price and page-count ranges for the entire series were available at press time.

Pilgrimages to Rome and Beyond
by Paul Higgins, Prentice Hall Press, 1985, 130 pages, paper, $8.95
    This guide to Christian holy places, including sites in Rome and the Vatican, is reviewed under "Greece."

Places In Between
by Kate Simon, Harper & Row, 1984, 384 pages, paper, $9.95
    This delightful book, written in Simon's always enjoyable style, emphasizes many of the towns that lie quietly and relatively forgotten between the major tourist destinations in Italy and the "places in between." Each fascinating destination is discussed at great length, complete with points of interest, suggested walks, and sights to see. Some notes on hotels and restaurants may be helpful, but be aware of the publication date.

Rome/Access
by Richard Saul Wurman, Prentice Hall Press, 1987, 181 pages, paper, $14.95
    This book is part of the widely praised Access Guide series, which is reviewed in more detail under "Series Reviews."

Rand McNally: Italy
by Dorothy Daly, Rand McNally & Co., 1985, 128 pages, paper, $5.95
Rand McNally: Rome
by David and Marie-Claire Willey, Rand McNally & Co., 1985, 128 pages, paper, $5.95
Rand McNally: Venice
by Edmund and Jan Swinglehurst, Rand McNally & Co., 1987, 128 pages, paper, $5.95
    These three titles are part of the small-format Rand McNally Pocket Guide series, which is reviewed in more detail under "Series Reviews."

Rome and Latium: A Phaidon Art and Architecture Guide
Prentice Hall Press, 1987, 323 pages, cloth, $17.95
    This is one of the encyclopedic Phaidon Art and Architecture Guide series, which is reviewed in more detail under "Series Reviews."

Romewalks
by Anya Shetterly, Henry Holt & Co., 1984, 242 pages, paper, $9.95
This book is part of the excellent Citywalks series, which is reviewed in more detail under "Series Reviews."

Serious Shopper's Guide to Italy
by Robert Jine, Prentice Hall Press, 1988, 450 pages, paper, $14.95
This book is one of the Serious Shopper's Guide series, which is reviewed in more detail under "Series Reviews."

Shopwalks: Milan
by Frances Ehrlich, Crown Publishers, 1987, fold-out map/guide, paper, $5.95
This guide is part of the Shopwalks series, which is reviewed in more detail under "Series Reviews."

Venice for Pleasure
by J.G. Links, Farrar, Straus, Giroux, 1984 (4th ed.), 272 pages, paper, $9.95
The unique reality of Venice is that most of the streets of this city are built on water; there is little bothersome car traffic. Links's classic work takes advantage of the relative lack of cars by offering all sorts of intriguing and slow-paced walks through this historic city—including frequent opportunities to relax in picturesque cafes. Illustrations show the Venice of old, providing a fine historic perspective. A separate chapter, "Venice for Children's Pleasure," is an additional delight.

The Visitor's Guide to Corsica
Hunter Publishing, 1987, 232 pages, paper, $9.95
This book is part of the New Visitor's Guide series, which is reviewed in more detail under "Series Reviews."

The Visitor's Guide to Florence and Tuscany
by Phil Whitney, Hunter Publishing, 1986, 160 pages, paper, $8.95
This is one of the Visitor's Guide series, which is reviewed in more detail under "Series Reviews."

The Visitor's Guide to the Italian Lakes
Hunter Publishing, 1988, 240 pages, paper, $10.95
This book is part of the New Visitor's Guide series, which is reviewed in more detail under "Series Reviews."

Walking in the Alps
by Brian Spencer, Hunter Publishing, 1986, 192 pages, paper, $9.95
This book is part of the Hunter Walks series, which is reviewed in more detail under "Series Reviews."

Walking Through Rome
by Bert Lief, VLE Limited, fold-out map/guide, paper, $2.00
This is one of the Way-Ahead Guide series, which is reviewed in more detail under "Series Reviews."

Webster's Wine Tours: Italy
Prentice Hall Press, 1988/89, 200 pages, cloth (flexible), $15.95
This is an anticipated, new volume in the expanding Webster's Wine Tours series, which is reviewed in more detail under "Series Reviews." The price and number of pages are approximate.

Whole Europe Escape Manual: Italy/Greece
by Kerry Green and Charles Leocha, World Leisure Corp., 1986, 160 pages, paper, $6.95
This is one of the delightfully different Escape Manual series, which is reviewed in more detail under "Series Reviews."

LIECHTENSTEIN

See also "Europe as a Whole." Liechtenstein is included in the following major, all-purpose guides to Europe: *Birnbaum's Europe; Fielding's Europe; Fodor's Europe; Let's Go: Europe.*

Adventuring in the Alps: A Sierra Club Travel Guide to the Alpine Regions of France, Switzerland, Germany, Austria, Liechtenstein, Italy, and Yugoslavia
by William and Marylou Reifsnyder, Sierra Club Books, 1986, 278 pages, paper, $10.95
This book is part of the Sierra Club Adventure Travel Guide series, which is reviewed in more detail under "Series Reviews."

Frommer's Dollarwise Guide to Switzerland and Liechtenstein
by Darwin Porter, Prentice Hall Press, 1987, 503 pages, paper, $12.95
This is one of the Frommer's Dollarwise Guide series, which is reviewed in more detail under "Series Reviews." This series emphasizes selections in the moderate price range and is updated biennially.

100 Hikes in the Alps

by Ira Spring and Harvey Edwards, The Mountaineers, 1985, 224 pages, paper, $8.95

This is one of the Mountaineers Hiking Guide series, which is reviewed in more detail under "Series Reviews."

LUXEMBOURG

See also "Europe as a Whole." Luxembourg is included in the following major, all-purpose guides to Europe: *Birnbaum's Europe; Fielding's Europe; Fielding's Economy Europe; Fisher's World: Europe; Fodor's Europe; Fodor's Budget Europe; Let's Go: Europe.*

Baedeker's Netherlands, Belgium & Luxembourg

Prentice Hall Press, undated, 325 pages, paper, $14.95

This is one of the Baedeker's Country/Regional Guide series, which is reviewed in more detail under "Series Reviews."

Blue Guide: Belgium & Luxembourg

edited by John Tomes, W. W. Norton & Co., 1983 (6th ed.), 312 pages, paper, $15.95

This book is part of the highly regarded Blue Guide series, which is reviewed in more detail under "Series Reviews." This edition is apparently no longer available, but a new edition may be available soon.

Day Trips in Holland, Belgium and Luxembourg: 40 One-Day Adventures by Rail, Bus or Car

by Earl Steinbicker, Hastings House, 1988, 300 pages, paper, $10.95

This is a new title in the Earl Steinbicker Day Trips series, which is reviewed in more detail under "Series Reviews." As it was released after press time, the price and number of pages are approximate.

Fodor's Belgium & Luxembourg

Fodor' Travel Publications, 1987, 288 pages, paper, $13.95

This is one of Fodor's Country/Regional Guide series, which is reviewed in more detail under "Series Reviews." The series is updated annually.

Frommer's Dollarwise Guide to Belgium, Holland, and Luxembourg

by Susan Poole, Prentice Hall Press, 1987, 319 pages, paper, $11.95

This is one of the Frommer's Dollarwise Guide series, which is reviewed in more detail under "Series Reviews." The series is updated every two years.

Long Stays in Belgium and Luxembourg
by Carole Hazlewood, Hippocrene Books, 1987, 200 pages, cloth, $19.95
This book is part of the Long Stays Guide series, which is reviewed in more detail under "Series Reviews."

Michelin Red Guide: Benelux
Michelin Guides and Maps, 1988, 407 pages, cloth, $16.95
This annual hotel and restaurant guide is part of the Michelin Red Guide series, which is reviewed in more detail under "Series Reviews."

Rand McNally: Holland, Belgium, & Luxembourg
by Carole Chester, Rand McNally & Co., 1986, 128 pages, paper, $5.95
This is one of the small-format Rand McNally Pocket Guide series, which is reviewed in more detail under "Series Reviews."

Whole Europe Escape Manual: France/Holland/Belgium/with Luxembourg
by Kerry Green and Peter Bythiner, World Leisure Corp., 1985, 160 pages, paper, $6.95
This book is part of the unique Escape Manual series, which is reviewed in more detail under "Series Reviews."

Madeira: See "Islands of the Eastern and Northern Atlantic Ocean."

MALTA

See also "Europe as a Whole." Malta is included in the following major, all-purpose guides to Europe: *Birnbaum's Europe; Fodor's Europe; Fodor's Budget Europe.*

Baedeker's Mediterranean Islands
Prentice Hall Press, 1985, 223 pages, paper, $14.95
This title, covering Malta, Cyprus, and the islands of Italy, Greece, France and Spain, is part of Baedeker's Country/Regional Guide series, which is reviewed in more detail under "Series Reviews."

Berlitz: Malta
Macmillan Publishing, 1980, 128 pages, paper, $6.95
This book is part of the small-format Berlitz Guide series, which is reviewed in more detail under "Series Reviews."

Blue Guide: Malta
> edited by Peter Endie, W. W. Norton & Co., 1979, (2nd ed.), 130 pages, paper, $10.95
>
> This book is one of the highly regarded Blue Guide series, which is reviewed in more detail under "Series Reviews."

Mediterranean Island Hopping—Italian Islands, Corsica, Malta: A Handbook for the Independent Traveler
> by Dana Facaros and Michael Pauls, Hippocrene Books, 1982, 491 pages, paper, $12.95
>
> This book is part of the Island Hopping Guide series, which is reviewed in more detail under "Series Reviews."

Nagel's Encyclopedia Guide: Malta
> Passport Books, 1978, 223 pages, cloth, $29.95
>
> This classic, cultural guide is part of the Nagel's Guide series, which is reviewed in more detail under "Series Reviews."

MONACO

See also "Europe as a Whole." Monaco is included in the following major, all-purpose guides to Europe: *Birnbaum's Europe; Fielding's Europe; Fodor's Europe.*

A Touch of Monaco and the French Riviera Guide
> edited by David Ward-Perkins, Talman Co., 1986, 242 pages, paper, $7.95
>
> This is one of the Touch of the City Guide series, which is reviewed in more detail under "Series Reviews."

NETHERLANDS (HOLLAND)

See also "Europe as a Whole." The Netherlands is included in the following major, all-purpose guides to Europe: *Birnbaum's Europe; Fielding's Europe; Fielding's Economy Europe; Fisher's World: Europe; Fodor's Europe; Fodor's Budget Europe; Frommer's Europe on $30 a Day; Let's Go: Europe.*

The American Express Pocket Guide to Amsterdam
> Prentice Hall Press, 1988, 240 pages, cloth, $9.95
>
> This book is part of the American Express Pocket Guide series, which is reviewed in more detail under "Series Reviews." Released after press time, the number of pages is approximate.

Amsterdam Art Guide
by Christian Reinewald, Robert Silver Associates, 1986, 194 pages, paper, $10.95

This is one of the Robert Silver Art Guide series, which is reviewed in more detail under "Series Reviews."

Baedeker's Amsterdam
Prentice Hall Press, 1987, 139 pages, paper, $10.95

This book is part of Baedeker's City Guide series, which is reviewed in more detail under "Series Reviews."

Baedeker's Netherlands, Belgium, and Luxembourg
Prentice Hall Press, undated, 325 pages, paper, $14.95

This book is part of Baedeker's Country/Regional Guide series, which is reviewed in more detail under "Series Reviews."

Berlitz: Amsterdam
Macmillan Publishing, 1987, 128 pages, paper, $6.95

This is one of the small-format Berlitz Guide series, which is reviewed in more detail under "Series Reviews." This edition includes an extra 16-page supplement on hotels and restaurants. *Berlitz: Amsterdam* is also available in the new Berlitz Deluxe Guide series. For additional information, see the "Series Reviews."

Blue Guide: Holland
edited by John Tomes, W. W. Norton & Co., 1987 (4th ed.), 440 pages, paper, $19.95

This title is part of the highly regarded Blue Guide series, which is reviewed in more detail under "Series Reviews."

Day Trips in Holland, Belgium and Luxembourg: 40 One-Day Adventures by Rail, Bus or Car
by Earl Steinbicker, Hastings House, 1988, 300 pages, paper, $10.95

This is a new title in the Earl Steinbicker Day Trips series, which is reviewed in more detail under "Series Reviews." As it was released after press time, the price and number of pages are approximate.

Fodor's Amsterdam
Fodor's Travel Publications, 1987, 128 pages, paper, $6.95

This is one of the Fodor's City Guide series, which is reviewed in more detail under "Series Reviews." The series is updated annually.

Fodor's Holland
Fodor's Travel Publications, 1987, 320 pages, paper, $13.95
This book is part of Fodor's Country/Regional Guide series, which is reviewed in more detail under "Series Reviews." The series is updated annually.

Frommer's Dollarwise Guide to Belgium, Holland, and Luxembourg
by Susan Poole, Prentice Hall Press, 1987, 319 pages, paper, $11.95
This is one of the Frommer's Dollarwise Guide series, which is reviewed in more detail under "Series Reviews." The series is updated every two years.

Frommer's Guide to Amsterdam and Holland
by Darwin Porter, Prentice Hall Press, 1987, 216 pages, paper, $5.95
This book is part of Frommer's City Guide series, which is reviewed in more detail under "Series Reviews." The series is updated every two years.

A Guide to Jewish Amsterdam
by Jan Stoutenbeek and Paul Vigeveno, Sepher-Hermon Press, 1985, 156 pages, paper, $13.95
This good-quality book details walks through historic Jewish Amsterdam. Well-selected photographs supplement an informative text.

Holland: A Phaidon Art and Architecture Guide
Prentice Hall Press, 1987, 290 pages, cloth, $17.95
This book is part of the encyclopedic Phaidon Art and Architecture Guide series, which is reviewed in more detail under "Series Reviews."

Holland At Its Best
by Robert Kane, Passport Books, 1988, 252 pages, paper, $9.95
This is a new addition to the widely praised At Its Best Guide series, which is reviewed under "Series Reviews."

Lett's Guide: Holland
by Harold Dennis-Jones, Prima Publishing, 1981, 96 pages, paper, $5.95
This book is part of the Letts Guide series, which is reviewed in more detail under "Series Reviews."

Michael's Guide: Amsterdam

by Michael Shichor, Hunter Publishing, 1988, 200 pages, paper, $7.95

This is a new title in the Michael's Guide series, which is reviewed in more detail under "Series Reviews." As it was released after press time, the number of pages is approximate.

Michelin Red Guide: Benelux

Michelin Guides and Maps, 1988, 407 pages, cloth, $14.95

This annual hotel and restaurant guide is part of the Michelin Red Guide series, which is reviewed in more detail under "Series Reviews."

Rand McNally: Amsterdam

by Carole Chester, Rand McNally & Co., 1986, 95 pages, paper, $5.95

Rand McNally: Holland, Belgium and Luxembourg

by Carole Chester, Rand McNally & Co., 1986, 128 pages, paper, $5.95

These two titles are part of the small-format Rand McNally Pocket Guide series, which is reviewed in more detail under "Series Reviews."

Rough Guide to Amsterdam

by Martin Dunford and Jack Holland, Routledge & Kegan Paul, 1987, 176 pages, paper, $9.95

Including sections on North and South Holland, Rotterdam, and The Hague, this book is part of the excellent Rough Guide series, which is reviewed in more detail under "Series Reviews." The series is updated every two to three years.

The Visitor's Guide to Holland

Hunter Publishing, 1987, 288 pages, paper, $9.95

This book is part of the New Visitor's Guide series, which is reviewed in more detail under "Series Reviews."

Whole Europe Escape Manual: France/Holland/Belgium/with Luxembourg

by Kerry Green and Peter Bythiner, World Leisure Corp., 1985, 160 pages, paper, $6.95

This is one of the unique Escape Manual series, which is reviewed in more detail under "Series Reviews."

NORTHERN IRELAND

See also "Ireland" and "Europe as a Whole." Except for regional titles, almost all books on Ireland contain a section on Northern Ireland. Northern Ireland is included in the following major, all-purpose guides to Europe: *Birnbaum's Europe; Fodor's Europe; Let's Go: Europe.*

An American's Guide to Britain
by Robin Winks, Charles Scribner's Sons, 1984 (revised ed.), 432 pages, paper, $9.95
This classic travel guide, reviewed under "Great Britain," includes Northern Ireland.

Baedeker's Great Britain
Prentice Hall Press, undated, 432 pages, paper, $14.95
This is one of Baedeker's Country/Regional Guide series, which is reviewed in more detail under "Series Reviews." Northern Ireland is included.

The National Trust Atlas
The National Trust and The National Trust for Scotland, Sheridan House, 1987 (3rd ed.), 224 pages, cloth, $29.95
Detailing the properties of the National Trust, including those in Northern Ireland, this title is reviewed under "Great Britain."

Northern Ireland: All the Places to Stay
by the Automobile Association, Salem House, 1988, 124 pages, paper, $4.95
In this book, the British Automobile Association does its typically solid, if sometimes utilitarian, job of detailing lodging options in all price categories.

RAC Hotel Guide
by the Royal Automobile Club, Sheridan House, 1988, 704 pages, paper, $18.95
Including Northern Ireland, this book is reviewed under "Great Britain."

The Visitor's Guide to Northern Ireland
Hunter Publishing, 1987, 240 pages, paper, $10.95
This is one of the Visitor's Guide series, which is reviewed in more detail under "Series Reviews."

Whole Europe Escape Manual: UK/Ireland

by Kerry Green and Charles Leocha, World Leisure Corp., 1984, 160 pages, paper, $6.95

This book is part of the unique Escape Manual series, which is reviewed in more detail under "Series Reviews."

NORWAY

See also "Scandinavia" and "Europe as a Whole." Norway is included in the following major, all-purpose guides to Europe: *Birnbaum's Europe; Fielding's Europe; Fielding's Economy Europe; Fisher's World: Europe; Fodor's Europe; Fodor's Budget Europe; Frommer's Europe on $30 a Day; Let's Go: Europe.*

Berlitz: Oslo and Bergen

Macmillan Publishing, 1981, 128 pages, paper, $6.95

This is one of the small-format Berlitz Guide series, which is reviewed in more detail under "Series Reviews."

Motoring in Norway

by E. Welle-Strande, Arthur Vanous Co., 1986, 156 pages, cloth, $14.50

This handy guide covers a large number of possible touring routes for those traveling by car. Color road maps and brief write-ups of things to do along the way are included. Although each route is not developed in any great depth, this will prove a useful planning resource.

The Visitor's Guide to Norway

Hunter Publishing, 1987, 240 pages, paper, $9.95

This is one of the New Visitor's Guide series, which is reviewed in more detail under "Series Reviews."

POLAND

See also "Eastern Europe" and "Europe as a Whole." Poland is included in the following major, all-purpose guides to Europe: *Birnbaum's Europe; Fodor's Europe; Fodor's Budget Europe; Let's Go: Europe.*

Nagel's Encyclopeda Guide: Poland

Passport Books, 1978, 399 pages, cloth, $39.95

This classic, cultural guide is part of the Nagel's Guide series, which is reviewed in more detail under "Series Reviews."

Poland
by Marc Heine, Hippocrene Books, 1987, 182 pages, paper, $8.95

This book is a guided tour of both cities and the countryside, primarily in southeast Poland (the Warsaw-Lublin-Cracow triangle), the area most likely to be visited by tourists. Heine's accounts are filled with history and his special interest in architecture is evident. Practical information is limited (he recommends using the Polish Travel Office), but a good chapter on getting the most out of Polish food and drink is included.

PORTUGAL

See also "Europe as a Whole." Portugal is included in the following major, all-purpose guides to Europe: *Birnbaum's Europe; Fielding's Europe; Fielding's Economy Europe; Fisher's World: Europe; Fodor's Europe; Fodor's Budget Europe; Frommer's Europe on $30 a Day; Let's Go: Europe.* Note: Portugal's two nearby Atlantic Ocean islands, the Azores and Madeira, are covered under "Islands of the Eastern and Northern Atlantic Ocean."

Baedeker's Portugal
Prentice Hall Press, undated, 261 pages, paper, $14.95

This book is part of Baedeker's Country/Regional Guide series, which is reviewed in more detail under "Series Reviews."

Berlitz: Algarve
Macmillan Publishing, 1980, 128 pages, paper, $6.95
Berlitz: Lisbon
Macmillan Publishing, 1982, 128 pages, paper, $6.95

Both of these titles are part of the small-format Berlitz Guide series, which is reviewed in more detail under "Series Reviews."

Birnbaum's Portugal
edited by Stephen Birnbaum, Houghton Mifflin, 1989, 500 pages, paper, $12.95

This is an anticipated, new title in the Birnbaum's Guide series, which is reviewed in more detail under "Series Reviews." The series is updated annually; the price and number of pages are approximate.

Blue Guide: Portugal
edited by Ian Robertson, W. W. Norton & Co., 1988 (3rd ed.), 320 pages, paper, $17.95

This book is part of the highly regarded Blue Guide series, which is reviewed in more detail under "Series Reviews."

Exploring Rural Portugal

Passport Books, 1988/89, 200 pages, paper, $12.95

This is an anticipated, new title in the Exploring Rural Europe series, which is reviewed in more detail under "Series Reviews." The price and number of pages are approximate.

Fisher's World: Spain and Portugal

Patricia and Lester Brooks, Fisher's World, Inc., 1988, 435 pages, paper, $14.95

This book is part of the Fisher's World Guide series, which is reviewed in more detail under "Series Reviews." The series is updated annually.

Fodor's Lisbon

Fodor's Travel Publications, 1987, 128 pages, paper, $6.95

This is one of Fodor's City Guide series, which is reviewed in more detail under "Series Reviews." The series is updated annually.

Fodor's Portugal

Fodor's Travel Publications, 1987, 336 pages, paper, $13.95

This book is part of Fodor's Country/Regional Guide series, which is reviewed in more detail under "Series Reviews." The series is updated annually.

Frommer's Dollarwise Guide to Portugal, Madeira, and the Azores

by Darwin Porter, Prentice Hall Press, 1987, 312 pages, paper, $12.95

This book is part of Frommer's Dollarwise Guide series, which is reviewed in more detail under "Series Reviews." This series emphasizes selections in the moderate price range and is updated every two years.

Frommer's Lisbon, Madrid & Costa del Sol

by Darwin Porter, Prentice Hall Press, 1987, 234 pages, paper, $5.95

This is one of the Frommer's City Guide series, which is reviewed in more detail under "Series Reviews." The series is updated every two years.

Let's Go: Spain, Portugal and Morocco

by Harvard Student Agencies, St. Martin's Press, 1988, 592 pages, paper, $10.95

Including a particularly superb section on Portugal, this book is part of the excellent, budget-oriented Let's Go Guide series, which is reviewed in more detail under "Series Reviews." The series is updated annually.

Lett's Guide: Portugal
by Harold Dennis-Jones, Prima Publishing, 1981, 96 pages, paper, $5.95
This book is part of the Letts Guide series, which is reviewed in more detail under "Series Reviews."

Long Stays in Portugal
by Roger Hicks and Francis Schultz, Hippocrene Books, 1988, 200 pages, cloth, $19.95
This is one of the Long Stays Guide series, which is reviewed in more detail under "Series Reviews."

Michelin Green Guide: Portugal
Michelin Guides and Maps, 1985 (4th ed.), 161 pages, paper, $10.95
This is one of the premier sightseeing guide series, the Michelin Green Guides, which is reviewed in more detail under "Series Reviews."

Michelin Red Guide: España-Portugal
Michelin Guides and Maps, 1988, 510 pages, cloth, $16.95
This annual hotel and restaurant guide is part of the Michelin Red Guide series, which is reviewed in more detail under "Series Reviews."

Pilgrimages to Rome and Beyond
by Paul Higgins, Prentice Hall Press, 1985, 130 pages, paper, $8.95
This guide to Christian holy places, including sites in Portugal, is reviewed under "Greece."

Portugal
by Thornton Cox, Hippocrene Books, 1987, 176 pages, paper, $8.95
In this solid, useful, thoroughly prepared guide, the veteran travel writer Thornton Cox covers Portuguese history and culture in some depth before carefully assessing each region of the country in terms of travelers' needs, including detailed notes on hotels, other forms of lodging, and restaurants.

Portugal On Your Own: Making the Most of Local Food and Drink
by Carol Wright, Hippocrene Books, 1986, 150 pages, paper, $9.95
This useful book is part of the On Your Own Guide series, which is reviewed in more detail under "Series Reviews."

Portuguese Country Inns and Pousadas

by Cynthia and Ralph Kite, Travel Press, 1988, 330 pages, paper, $12.95

This book is part of the delightful Karen Brown's Country Inns series, which is reviewed in more detail under "Series Reviews."

Pousadas of Portugal: Unique Lodging in State-owned Castles, Palaces, Mansions, and Hotels

by Sam and Jane Ballard, The Harvard Common Press, 1986, 173 pages, paper, $8.95

Portugal has created enchanting and affordable accommodations out of spectacular old palaces, castles, and other more modern structures. Dining is available at each location and is generally superb. A good introduction to making reservations, planning, and other practical facts is included along with 13 thoughtfully arranged itineraries in both Portugal and Spain for those touring by car from seven up to as many as 52 days (see *Paradores of Spain* for lodging in that country). Additional touring notes are sprinkled throughout the enjoyable text.

Rand McNally: Portugal

by R.A.N. Dixon, Rand McNally & Co., 1984, 128 pages, paper, $5.95

This is one of the small-format Rand McNally Pocket Guide series, which is reviewed in more detail under "Series Reviews."

Rough Guide to Portugal

by Mark Ellingham, et al., Routledge & Kegan Paul, 1986, 224 pages, paper, $10.95

This book is part of the excellent Rough Guide series, which is reviewed in more detail under "Series Reviews." The series is updated every two to three years.

Spain and Portugal in 22 Days

See *22 Days in Spain* below.

Travellers' Portugal

by Anthony Hogg, Luso-Brazilian Books, 1986, 278 pages, paper, $15.95

The excellent 50-page introduction on history, customs, and language in this book is followed by six well-described itineraries, each beginning at Santander, where the Brittany Ferries arrive from Plymouth, England, and ending at the coastal town of Oporto. Suggested flying/driving tours from the towns of Oporto; Lisbon; and Seville, Spain through Portugal's southern province, the Algarve, follow. This widely praised travel guide is a wonderful blend of amusing personal tales and hard practical tourist information.

22 Days in Spain and Portugal: The Itinerary Planner

by Rick Steves, John Muir Publications, 1987, 125 pages, paper, $5.95

This is one of the growing Itinerary Planner series, modeled after the successful *Europe in 22 Days* (now called *22 Days in Europe*). The series is reviewed in more detail under "Series Reviews." Note that the title has recently changed and this book may also be found under *Spain and Portugal in 22 Days*.

Webster's Wine Tours: Portugal

Prentice Hall Press, 1988, 200 pages, cloth (flexible), $15.95

This is a new, anticipated title in the expanding Webster's Wine Tours series, which is reviewed in more detail under "Series Reviews." The price and number of pages are approximate.

Whole Europe Escape Manual: Spain/Portugal

by Peter Bythiner and Charles Leocha, World Leisure Corp., 1986, 160 pages, paper, $6.95

This is one of the uniquely different Escape Manual series which is reviewed in more detail under "Series Reviews."

ROMANIA

See also "Eastern Europe" and "Europe as a Whole." Romania is included in the following major, all-purpose guides to Europe: *Birnbaum's Europe; Fodor's Europe; Fodor's Budget Europe; Let's Go: Europe.*

Nagel's Encyclopedia Guide: Rumania

Passport Books, 1980, 399 pages, cloth, $29.95

This classic, cultural guide is one of the Nagel's Guide series, which is reviewed in more detail under "Series Reviews."

San Marino: See "Europe as a Whole." San Marino is included in *Birnbaum's Europe.*

Scotland: See Scotland section under "Great Britain."

SOVIET UNION

See also "Eastern Europe" and "Europe as a Whole." The Soviet Union is included in *Birnbaum's Europe* and *Let's Go: Europe.* Note: For convenience, all books on the Soviet Union, to both European and Asian destinations, are listed below.

Alma-Ata: A Guide
by I. Malyar, Imported Publications, 1983, 62 pages, cloth, $6.95
   This is one of the Guides from Russia series, which is reviewed in more detail under "Series Reviews."

An American's Guide to the Soviet Union
by Lydle Brinkle, Hippocrene Books, 1988, 224 pages, paper, $14.95
   This is a new title, released after press time, from American geography professor Lydle Brinkle.

American's Tourist Manual for the U.S.S.R.
compiled by John Felber, International Intertrade, 1986 (15th ed.), 224 pages, paper, $8.95
   This is one of the original guides to the Soviet Union, first published in 1954. The book is unusual in that four separate, rather uniquely drawn maps bulge from within (they cover Moscow, the Kremlin, Leningrad, and Kiev) and there is no table of contents—it just seems to start in with visas, currency, orientation, tours, transportation, etc. But a further look will show that on the back page is the index/table of contents. This comprehensive manual for the American tourist contains a real wealth of information and practical tips, gained from years of experience. Orientation to food, hotels, and shopping is general, not specific to individual places. Sightseeing details, including various walking tours, are extensive. The hand-drawn maps take a little getting used to, but are quite helpful and detailed in the final analysis.

Ashkhabad: A Guide
by I. Pasevyev, Imported Publications, 1982, 103 pages, cloth, $6.95
   This is one of the Guides from Russia series, which is reviewed in more detail under "Series Reviews."

Baedeker's Moscow
Prentice Hall Press, 1987, 137 pages, paper, $10.95
   This book is part of Baedeker's City Guide series, which is reviewed in more detail under "Series Reviews."

Berlitz: Moscow and Leningrad
Macmillan Publishing, 1985, 128 pages, paper, $6.95
   This book is part of the small-format Berlitz Guide series, which is reviewed in more detail under "Series Reviews."

The Black Sea Coast of the Caucasus: A Guide
by G. Khutsishvili, Imported Publications, 1980, 207 pages, cloth,
$7.95
  This book is part of the Guides from Russia series, which is
reviewed in more detail under "Series Reviews."

Blue Guide: Moscow and Leningrad
by Evan and Margaret Mawdsley, W. W. Norton & Co., 1984, 392
pages, paper, $17.95
  This is one of the highly praised Blue Guide series, which is
reviewed in more detail under "Series Reviews."

Burkhara: A Guide
by V. Tiurikov, Imported Publications, 1982, 79 pages, cloth, $4.95
  This book is part of the Guides from Russia series, which is
reviewed in more detail under "Series Reviews."

Coping With Russia: A Beginner's Guide to the U.S.S.R.
by Robert Daglish, Basil Blackwell, Inc., 1987, 176 pages, paper,
$7.95
  This new, comprehensive guide covers traveling in the Soviet
Union with an emphasis on the first-time visitor.

Discovering Moscow: Architecture, History, Art
by Helen Semler, Hippocrene Books, 1987, 212 pages, paper, $14.95
  This well-written guide describes 11 different excursions to explore the art and architecture of the city and the history behind
them. Also included are short lists of recommended hotels, restaurants, theaters, and shops.

Dushanbe: A Guide
by M. Davidzon and V. Yurlov, Imported Publications, 1983, 88
pages, cloth, $6.95
  This book is part of the Guides from Russia series, which is
reviewed in more detail under "Series Reviews."

Fodor's Soviet Union
Fodor's Travel Publications, 1987, 448 pages, paper, $16.95
  This is one of Fodor's Country/Regional Guide series, which is
reviewed in more detail under "Series Reviews." The series is updated annually.

From Moscow to Vladivostok
by Alexander Niven, IIAS, 1985, 17 pages, paper, $8.00

This helpful, large-format booklet provides an historical, geographical, and economic overview of numerous points along the Trans-Siberian Railroad.

Frunze: A Guide
by B. Prokhorov, Imported Publications, 1984, 123 pages, cloth, $6.95

Greater Yalta: A Guide
by O. Volobuyev, Imported Publications, 1978, 200 pages, cloth, $8.45

These two titles are part of the Guides from Russia series, which is reviewed in more detail under "Series Reviews."

Hermitage: An Illustrated Guide
Imported Publications, 1983, 215 pages, cloth, $9.95

This is an interesting guide to one of the most fantastic art collections in the world and the largest collection in the Soviet Union—2,700,000 pieces of art are contained in the five-building complex. The guide boasts numerous photos of the museum itself as well as of some of the art works displayed. The Hermitage contains one of the finest collections of Impressionist art in the world (much to France's dismay).

Information Moscow: Western Edition
edited by Anya Kucharev, U.S. Information Moscow, 1987 (7th ed.), 491 pages, paper, $20.00

This up-to-date, annual guide is strongly oriented toward East-West trade. Its appearance on the travel bookshelf would be most uncommon, but it is well worth seeking out, since it contains more current information of interest to the prospective traveler to Moscow than any other guide. The first 160 pages are packed with useful facts on making travel arrangements, currency, customs, getting to the hotel, plus detailed listings of hotels, restaurants, cafes, places to shop, transportation services, and cultural and recreational activities. The remainder of the book, more than 300 additional pages, covers every aspect of doing business in Moscow. Included are lengthy lists of every conceivable address and phone number.

Irkutsk: A Guide
by M. Sergeyev, Imported Publications, 1986, 69 pages, cloth, $7.95

Kiev: A Guide
by H. Levitsky, Imported Publications, 1980, 190 pages, cloth, $8.45

Kishinev: A Guide
　by M. Hazin, Imported Publications, 1985, 110 pages, cloth, $6.95
　　These three titles are part of the Guides from Russia series, which
　is reviewed in more detail under "Series Reviews."

Leningrad: Art and Architecture
　by V. Schwarz, Imported Publications, 1981, 311 pages, cloth,
　$8.95
　　Translated from the Russian, this book provides a good overview
　of the monuments and buildings, both historic and modern, of Len-
　ingrad. The book is generally arranged in chronological order, so the
　tourist is forced to first determine what the monument is, then use
　the index to find its description. It is somewhat difficult to use but
　does have merit.

Louis Motorist's Guide to the Soviet Union
　Pergamon Press, 1987 (2nd ed.), 625 pages, paper, $40.00
　　This is an expensive, comprehensive guide to the Soviet Union,
　written for those who plan to see this massive nation by automobile.
　Automobile travel is not without its restrictions, but it can be done.

Minsk: A Guide
　by Anatoli Andrukhovich, Imported Publications, 1980, 80 pages,
　cloth, $6.45
Moldavia: A Guide
　by M. Shukhat, Imported Publications, 1986, 150 pages, cloth,
　$7.95
Moscow-Leningrad-Kiev: A Guide
　by L. Dubinskaya, Imported Publications, 1981, 215 pages, cloth,
　$7.45
　　These three titles are part of the Guides from Russia series, which
　is reviewed in more detail under "Series Reviews."

Motorists' Guide to the Soviet Union
　by Leonid Zadvorny, Imported Publications, 1980, 391 pages, cloth,
　$12.95
　　Contrary to the general view, there are indeed ways to see the
　Soviet Union by car. Unfortunately, this manual, produced in the
　U.S.S.R., has continued to age without a sign of a new edition. In
　fact, it is difficult to find a copy or even order one at the present
　time. Nonetheless, this is a good book that could help to foster
　greater understanding between the Soviet Union and other nations.
　Ask the people at the nearest travel bookstore to find out the current
　status of this valuable book.

Museums in and Around Moscow

by I. Baikova, Imported Publications, 1983, 197 pages, cloth, $8.95

This is a small, useful guidebook to 67 different museums in the general vicinity of Moscow. A fair number of color photos are included as well as practical information such as locations, metro stops, and telephone numbers. Admission hours should be double-checked because of the publication date.

Nagel's Encyclopedia Guide: U.S.S.R.

Passport Books, 1985, 1103 pages, cloth, $49.95

This classic, cultural guide is one of the Nagel's Guide series, which is reviewed in more detail under "Series Reviews."

Next Time You Go to Russia

by Charles Ward, Charles Scribner's Sons, 1980, 142 pages, paper, $9.95

The focus is on sightseeing in this nicely prepared but aging title. Although some specifics on museums and such have no doubt changed, it is still a very handy, well-prepared, touring guide. Plenty of useful maps, including museum floor plans are included.

Odessa: A Guide

by G. Kononova, Imported Publications, 1985, 191 pages, cloth, $7.95

Petrozavodsk and Kizhi: A Guide

by A. Frolov, Imported Publications, 1983, 167 pages, cloth, $6.95

Pskov: A Guide

by Yelena Morozkina, Imported Publications, 1984, 192 pages, cloth, $7.95

Riga: A Guide

by M. Debrer, Imported Publications, 1982, 156 pages, cloth, $6.95

These four titles are part of the Guides from Russia series, which is reviewed in more detail under "Series Reviews."

The Russian Museum: A Guide

by A. Gubarev, Imported Publications, 1981, 175 pages, cloth, $5.95

The Russian Museum in Leningrad is one of the world's largest with over 320,000 paintings, sculptures, and other works of art. This little book gives an overview of the museum and its major works of art plus the layout of its many rooms.

Smolensk: A Guide
by Mikhail Dunaev, Imported Publications, 1982, 102 pages, cloth, $5.95
This book is part of the Guides from Russia series, which is reviewed in more detail under "Series Reviews."

The Soviet Union: A Guide and Reference Book
by Lidiya Dubinskaya, Imported Publications, 1985, 350 pages, cloth, $12.95
Another of the many titles translated from the Russian, this may prove the most useful, since it is generally more up-to-date than those on individual cities and contains an overview—from the perspective of the Soviet Union, of course—of history, geography and daily life, followed by separate chapters on sightseeing in the 15 Soviet Republics (only one of which is technically "Russia"). Each gives a respectable overview of things to see, transportation notes, and useful addresses to hotels, theaters, shops, and the like. A short but useful section on practical information for the traveler completes this guide.

Suzdal: A Guide
by A. Milovsky, Imported Publications, 1981, 139 pages, cloth, $7.45
Tallinn: A Guide
by H. Gustavson and R. Pullat, Imported Publications, 1980, 68 pages, cloth, $6.95
Tashkent: A Guide
by V. Tyurikov, Imported Publications, 1985, 94 pages, cloth, $7.95
These three titles are part of the Guides from Russia series, which is reviewed in more detail under "Series Reviews."

Trans-Siberian Rail Guide
by Robert Strauss, Hunter Publishing, 1987, 207 pages, paper, $11.95
This great guide for the trans-Siberian journey, combines practical facts with culture and history. Strauss delves into the history of Siberia and the building of the railroad before launching into specific planning and preparation requirements. He discusses nine European and Oriental gateways to the trans-Siberian rail system and provides 25 easy-to-follow strip maps that cover the full length of the 9000-km journey. Amidst the practical details are fascinating and enjoyable tales from other travelers on this historic railroad—from the turn of the century up to the present time.

Ulyanovsk: A Guide
by Jean Mindubayev, Imported Publications, 1980, 75 pages, cloth, $4.95
   This is one of the Guides from Russia series, which is reviewed in more detail under "Series Reviews."

U.S.S.R.: From an Original Idea by Karl Marx
by Marc Polonsky and Russell Taylor, Faber and Faber, 1986, 172 pages, paper, $ 8.95
   In this very funny book, the authors, who previously guided tours of the U.S.S.R., show the human (i.e., the "sweaty, pig-headed, exasperating, and endearingly incompetent") face of Socialism. At the same time, Polonsky and Taylor point out a wide range of basic survival skills helpful when it comes to food, drink, shopping, entertainment, transportation, and meeting the masses.

Vladimir: A Guide
by Sergei Gordeyev, Imported Publications, 1983, 143 pages, cloth, $7.95

Volgograd: A Guide
by N. T. Morozova and N. D. Monakhova, Imported Publications, 1979, 162 pages, cloth, $8.95
   These two titles are part of the Guides from Russia series, which is reviewed in more detail under "Series Reviews."

SPAIN

See also "Europe as a Whole." Spain is included in the following major, all-purpose guides to Europe: *Birnbaum's Europe; Fielding's Europe; Fielding's Economy Europe; Fisher's World: Europe; Fodor's Europe; Fodor's Budget Europe; Frommer's Europe on $30 a Day; Let's Go: Europe.* Note: Spain's nearby Canary Islands are covered under "Islands of the Eastern and Northern Atlantic Ocean."

The American Express Pocket Guide to Spain
by Herbert Livesey, Prentice Hall Press, 1984, 240 pages, cloth, $8.95
   This book is part of the quality American Express Pocket Guide series, which is reviewed in more detail under "Series Reviews."

Baedeker's Madrid
Prentice Hall Press, 1987, 137 pages, paper, $10.95
   This is one of the Baedeker's City Guide series, which is reviewed in more detail under "Series Reviews."

Baedeker's Mediterranean Islands
Prentice Hall Press, 1985, 223 pages, paper, $14.95
Baedeker's Spain
Prentice Hall Press, undated, 304 pages, paper, $14.95
   Both of these titles are part of Baedeker's Country/Regional Guide
series, which is reviewed in more detail under "Series Reviews."
The Mediterranean Islands volume covers Cyprus, Malta, and the
islands of Greece, France, Spain, and Italy.

Berlitz: Barcelona and Costa Dorada
Macmillan Publishing, 1988, 128 pages, paper, $6.95
Berlitz: Costa Blanca
Macmillan Publishing, 1980, 128 pages, paper, $6.95
Berlitz: Costa Brava
Macmillan Publishing, 1988, 128 pages, paper, $6.95
Berlitz: Costa del Sol and Andalusia
Macmillan Publishing, 1982, 128 pages, paper, $6.95
Berlitz: Ibiza and Formentera
Macmillan Publishing, 1982, 128 pages, paper, $6.95
Berlitz: Madrid
Macmillan Publishing, 1977, 128 pages, paper, $6.95
Berlitz: Majorca and Minorca
Macmillan Publishing, 1982, 128 pages, paper, $6.95
   All of these titles are part of the small-format Berlitz Guide series,
which is reviewed in more detail under "Series Reviews." The Bar-
celona title is also available in the new Berlitz Deluxe Guide series.
For more information, see "Series Reviews."

Birnbaum's Spain
edited by Stephen Birnbaum, Houghton Mifflin, 1989, 600 pages,
paper, $12.95
   This new title is part of the excellent Birnbaum's Guide series,
which is reviewed in more detail under "Series Reviews." Because
this title will appear for the first time beginning with the 1989
editions, the number of pages and price are approximate.

Blue Guides: Spain, The Mainland
edited by Ian Robertson, W. W. Norton & Co., 1980 (4th ed.), 576
pages, paper, $17.95
   This is one title in the highly regarded Blue Guide series, which
is reviewed in more detail under "Series Reviews."

Cadogan Guide: Spain
by Dana Facaros and Michael Pauls, The Globe Pequot Press, 1987, 484 pages, paper, $12.95
   Two fine travel writers have teamed up for this volume in the Cadogan Guide series, which is reviewed in more detail under "Series Reviews." The series is updated every two years.

The Companion Guide to Madrid and Central Spain
by Alastair Boyd, Prentice Hall Press, 1986 (revised ed.), 474 pages, paper, $12.95
   This is one of the superb Companion Guide series, which is reviewed in more detail under "Series Reviews."

Everything Under the Sun: Barcelona
edited by Erica Witschey, Passport Books, 1987, 176 pages, paper, $6.95
Everything Under the Sun: Cordoba
edited by Erica Witschey, Passport Books, 1988, 176 pages, paper, $6.95
Everything Under the Sun: Granada
edited by Erica Witschey, Passport Books, 1988, 176 pages, paper, $6.95
Everything Under the Sun: Madrid
edited by Erica Witschey, Passport Books, 1988, 192 pages, paper, $6.95
Everything Under the Sun: Marbella
edited by Erica Witschey, Passport Books, 1987, 160 pages, paper, $6.95
Everything Under the Sun: Palma de Majorca
edited by Erica Witschey, Passport Books, 1988, 176 pages, paper, $6.95
Everything Under the Sun: Salamanca
edited by Erica Witschey, Passport Books, 1988, 176 pages, paper, $6.95
Everything Under the Sun: Seville
edited by Erica Witschey, Passport Books, 1987, 176 pages, paper, $6.95
Everything Under the Sun: Toledo
edited by Erica Witschey, Passport Books, 1987, 176 pages, paper, $6.95
   These are all of the available titles in a new, comprehensive travel series on Spain, published in collaboration with the National Tourist Board of Spain. Each book is an excellent, compact, all-purpose guide on basic facts, sightseeing, walking tours, culture and history. Each book also contains rated excursions to areas nearby, rated lodging

and dining in various price ranges (each selection is well described using symbols and short paragraphs), and unusual "aerial view" maps. By employing small type, the editor has managed to pack an incredible amount of information into these remarkable little books.

Exploring Rural Spain

by Jan McGirk, Passport Books, 1988, 178 pages, paper, $12.95

This is one of three 1988 titles in a new series, Exploring Rural Europe, which is reviewed in more detail under "Series Reviews."

Fisher's World: Spain and Portugal

by Patricia and Lester Brooks, Fisher's World, Inc., 1988, 435 pages, paper, $14.95

This book is part of the Fisher's World Guide series, which is reviewed in more detail under "Series Reviews." The series is updated annually.

Fodor's Great Travel Values: Spain

Fodor's Travel Publications, 1988, 176 pages, paper, $5.95

This book is part of the budget-oriented Fodor's Great Travel Values Guide series, which is reviewed in more detail under "Series Reviews." The series is updated annually.

Fodor's Madrid

Fodor's Travel Publications, 1988, 128 pages, paper, $6.95

This book is part of Fodor's City Guide series, which is reviewed in more detail under "Series Reviews." The series is updated annually.

Fodor's Spain

Fodor's Travel Publications, 1988, 512 pages, paper, $13.95

This book is part of Fodor's Country/Regional Guide series, which is reviewed in more detail under "Series Reviews." The series is updated annually.

Frommer's Guide to Lisbon, Madrid and Costa del Sol

by Darwin Porter, Prentice Hall Press, 1987, 234 pages, paper, $5.95

This is one of the Frommer's City Guide series, which is reviewed in more detail under "Series Reviews." The series is updated every two years.

Frommer's Spain and Morocco (plus the Canary Islands) on $40 a Day

by Darwin Porter, Prentice Hall Press, 1987, 552 pages, paper, $10.95

This book is part of the budget-oriented Frommer's Dollar-a-Day

Guide series, which is reviewed in more detail under "Series Reviews." The series is updated every two years.

Insight Guide: Spain
by Apa Productions, Prentice Hall Press, 1987, 339 pages, paper, $16.95
   This book is part of the widely praised Insight Guide series, which is reviewed in more detail under "Series Reviews."

Landscapes of Mallorca
by Valerie Crespi-Green, Hunter Publishing, 1984, 168 pages, paper, $9.95
   This book is part of the Countryside Guide series, which is reviewed in more detail under "Series Reviews."

Let's Go: Spain, Portugal and Morocco
by Harvard Student Agencies, St. Martin's Press, 1988, 592 pages, paper, $10.95
   This is one of the superb, budget-oriented Let's Go Guide series, which is reviewed in more detail under "Series Reviews." The series is updated annually.

Lett's Guide: Costa Brava and Costa Dorada
by Harold Dennis-Jones, Prima Publishing, 1981, 96 pages, paper, $5.95
Lett's Guide: Costa del Sol
by Harold Dennis-Jones, Prima Publishing, 1981, 96 pages, paper, $5.95
Lett's Guide: Spanish Islands
by Harold Dennis-Jones, Prima Publishing, 1981, 96 pages, paper, $5.95
   These three titles are part of the Letts Guide series, which is reviewed in more detail under "Series Reviews."

Marling Menu-Master for Spain
by William and Clare Marling, Altarinda Books, 1973, 112 pages, plasticized cover, $5.95
   This book is part of the excellent, small-format Marling Menu-Master series, which is reviewed in more detail under "Series Reviews."

Mediterranean Island Hopping—The Spanish Islands: A Handbook for the Independent Traveler
by Dana Facaros and Michael Pauls, Hippocrene Books, 1982 (2nd ed.), 304 pages, paper, $12.95
   This is one of the Island Hopping Guide series, which is reviewed in more detail under "Series Reviews."

Michael's Guide: Madrid
by Michael Shichor, Hunter Publishing, 1988, 192 pages, paper, $7.95
   This book is part of the Michael's Guide series, which is reviewed in more detail under "Series Reviews."

Michelin Green Guide: Spain
Michelin Guides and Maps, 1987 (5th ed.), 290 pages, paper, $10.95
   This book is part of the premier sightseeing guide series, the Michelin Green Guides, which is reviewed in more detail under "Series Reviews."

Michelin Red Guide: España-Portugal
Michelin Guides and Maps, 1988, 510 pages, cloth, $16.95
   This annual hotel and restaurant guide is part of the Michelin Red Guide series, which is reviewed in more detail under "Series Reviews."

The New Holiday Guide to Spain
B. Evans & Co., 1988 (10th ed.), 160 pages, paper, $4.95
   This is one of the Holiday Guide series, which is reviewed in more detail under "Series Reviews."

Paradores of Spain: Unique Lodgings in State-owned Castles, Convents, Mansions and Hotels
by Sam and Jane Ballard, The Harvard Common Press, 1986, 240 pages, paper, $8.95
   This is an excellent guide to the state-owned and operated inns of Spain. Spain has built beautiful modern inns in spectacular places, and renovated old palaces, mansions, convents, and castles to provide historic, unusual lodging at reasonable prices. The Ballards also provide many intriguing travel itineraries through Spain and Portugal—13 by car and five by train—that will make the best use of the parador system for trips of six to 52 days (see *Pousadas of Portugal* for lodging in Portugal). Plenty of thoughtful and informative touring notes, as well as all the needed practical information, is included in this first-rate book.

Pilgimages to Rome and Beyond

by Paul Higgins, Prentice Hall Press, 1985, 130 pages, paper, $8.95

This guide to Christian holy places, including sites in Spain, is reviewed under "Greece."

Rand McNally: Spain

by R. A. Dixon, Rand McNally & Co., 1980, 128 pages, paper, $5.95

This book is part of the small-format Rand McNally Pocket Guide series, which is reviewed in more detail under "Series Reviews."

Rough Guide to Spain

by Mark Ellingham and John Fisher, Routledge & Kegan Paul, 1986, 250 pages, paper, $7.95

This is one of the top-notch Rough Guide series, which is reviewed in more detail under "Series Reviews." The series is updated every two to three years.

Spain: A Phaidon Art and Architecture Guide

Prentice Hall Press, 1985, 600 pages, cloth, $16.95

This book is part of the encyclopedic Phaidon Art and Architecture Guide series, which is reviewed in more detail under "Series Reviews."

Spain and Portugal in 22 Days

See *22 Days in Spain and Portugal* below.

Spain At Its Best

by Robert Kane, Passport Books, 1988, 352 pages, paper, $12.95

This book is part of the widely praised At Its Best Guide series, which is reviewed in more detail under "Series Reviews."

Spanish Country Inns and Paradors

by Cynthia and Ralph Kite, Travel Press, 1988, 270 pages, paper, $12.95

This book is part of the excellent Karen Brown's Country Inns series, which is reviewed in more detail under "Series Reviews."

22 Days in Spain and Portugal: The Itinerary Planner

by Rick Steves, John Muir Publications, 1987, 125 pages, paper, $5.95

This is one of the Itinerary Planner series modeled after Rick Steves' successful *Europe In 22 Days* (now called *22 Days in Europe*). The series is reviewed in more detail under "Series Reviews." Note that the title was recently changed and this book may be found under *Spain and Portugal in 22 Days.*

Walks and Climbs in the Pyrenees
by Kev Reynolds, Hunter Publishing, 1988 (3rd ed.), 206 pages, paper, $12.95
This is one of the Hunter Mountain Walks series, which is reviewed in more detail under "Series Reviews."

Walks Through Barcelona
by Bert Lief, VLE Limited, undated, fold-out map/guide, paper, $2.00
Walks Through Madrid
by Bert Lief, VLE Limited, undated, fold-out map/guide, paper, $2.00
Walks Through Seville
by Bert Lief, VLE Limited, undated, fold-out map/guide, paper, $2.00
All of these titles are part of the Way-Ahead Guide series, which is reviewed in more detail under "Series Reviews."

Webster's Wine Tours: Spain
Prentice Hall Press, 1988/89, 200 pages, cloth (flexible), $15.95
This is a new, anticipated title in the growing Webster's Wine Tours series, which is reviewed in more detail under "Series Reviews." The price and number of pages are approximate.

Where to Go in Spain
by Harold Dennis-Jones, Hippocrene Books, 1988, 140 pages, paper, $11.95
This is a new addition to the Where to Go Guide series, which is reviewed in more detail under "Series Reviews."

Whole Europe Escape Manual: Spain/Portugal
by Peter Bythiner and Charles Leocha, World Leisure Corp., 1986, 160 pages, paper, $6.95
This is one of the unique Escape Manual series, which is reviewed in more detail under "Series Reviews."

SWEDEN

See also "Scandinavia" and "Europe as a Whole." Sweden is included in the following major, all-purpose guides to Europe: *Birnbaum's Europe; Fielding's Europe; Fielding's Economy Europe; Fisher's World:*

Europe; Fodor's Europe; Fodor's Budget Europe; Frommer's Europe on $30 a Day; Let's Go: Europe.

Berlitz: Stockholm
Macmillan Publishing, 1982, 128 pages, paper, $6.95
This is one of the small-format Berlitz Guide series, which is reviewed in more detail under "Series Reviews."

Drive Around Sweden
by Robert Spark, Trafton Publishing, 1986, 144 pages, cloth, $10.95
This solid, practical guide contains selected itineraries, sights to see along the way, and a general orientation to food and lodging. Published in England, this book currently has no American distributor. It can be found in a some travel bookstores, including the Traveller's Bookstore and Wide World Books and Maps (see Travel Bookstores appendix).

Fodor's Sweden
Fodor's Travel Publications, 1988, 128 pages, paper, $6.95
This is one of the Fodor's Country/Regional Guide series, which is reviewed in more detail under "Series Reviews." The series is updated annually.

Nagel's Encyclopedia Guide: Sweden
Passport Books, 1974, 448 pages, cloth, $39.95
This classic, cultural guide is part of the Nagel's Guide series, which is reviewed in more detail under "Series Reviews."

The Visitor's Guide to Sweden
Hunter Publishing, 1987, 210 pages, paper, $9.95
This book is part of the New Visitor's Guide series, which is reviewed in more detail under "Series Reviews."

SWITZERLAND

See also "Europe as a Whole." Switzerland is included in the following major, all-purpose guides to Europe: *Birnbaum's Europe; Fielding's Europe; Fielding's Economy Europe; Fisher's World: Europe; Fodor's Europe; Fodor's Budget Europe; Frommer's Europe on $30 a Day; Let's Go: Europe.*

Adventuring in the Alps: The Sierra Club Travel Guide to the Alpine Regions of France, Switzerland, Germany, Austria, Liechtenstein, Italy, and Yugoslavia
by William and Marylou Reifsnyder, Sierra Club Books, 1986, 278 pages, paper, $10.95

This is one of the excellent Sierra Club Adventure Travel Guide series, which is reviewed in more detail under "Series Reviews."

Baedeker's Switzerland
Prentice Hall Press, undated, 323 pages, paper, $14. 95

This is one of Baedeker's Country/Regional Guide series, which is reviewed in more detail under "Series Reviews."

Berlitz: Switzerland
Macmillan Publishing, 1985, 192 pages, paper, $8.95

This is one of the Berlitz Country Guide series, which is reviewed in more detail under "Series Reviews."

Bernina Express: Across the Alps in a Sight-Seeing Train
by Henning Wall, Seven Hills Books, 1988, 56 pages, paper, $12.50

This large-format guidebook covers one of the most scenic train routes in the world—from Chur, Switzerland, over the Alps via the Bernina Pass to Tirano, Italy. Notes on the history of the famous route, the incredible effort that built it, the train equipment used, and the points of interest and beauty along the way are all contained in this interesting book. A great companion guide for the trip itself, this book is full of photographs, drawings, technical facts, and information on scheduling and services.

Blue Guide: Switzerland
edited by Ian Robertson, W. W. Norton & Co., 1987 (4th ed.), 345 pages, paper, $18.95

This is one of the highly regarded Blue Guide series, which is reviewed in more detail under "Series Reviews."

The Children's Treasure Hunt Guide to Austria, Germany, Switzerland
Hippocrene Books, 1979, 200 pages, paper, $6.95

This book is part of the Children's Treasure Hunt Guide series, which is reviewed in more detail under "Series Reviews."

The Famous Glacier Express of Switzerland
by Hans Schweers, Seven Hills Books, 1985, 64 pages, paper, $12.50

The famous Glacier Express is the narrow-gauge, 290-km railroad from St. Moritz to Zermatt. Passing over 291 bridges and through 91 tunnels as it traverses some of the most spectacular scenery in the world, this run is a traveler's delight. This enjoyable and informative book describes the railroad's development, the cars used both past and present, and important scenic points along the way.

Fodor's Switzerland
Fodor's Travel Publications, 1988, 368 pages, paper, $13.95
This book is part of Fodor's Country/Regional Guide series, which is reviewed in more detail under "Series Reviews." The series is updated annually.

Footloose in the Swiss Alps: A Hiker's Guide to the Mountain Inns and Trails of Switzerland
by William Reifsnyder, Sierra Club Books, 1974, 444 pages, paper, $10.95
This is one of the Sierra Club Hiking Totebook series, which is reviewed in more detail under "Series Reviews."

Frommer's Dollarwise Guide to Switzerland and Liechtenstein
by Darwin Porter, Prentice Hall Press, 1988, 503 pages, paper, $12.95
This is one title in the Frommer's Dollarwise Guide series, which is reviewed in more detail under "Series Reviews." This series emphasizes selections in the moderate price range and is updated every two years.

Germany, Austria, and Switzerland in 22 Days
See *22 Days in Germany, Austria, and Switzerland* below.

Lett's Guide: Switzerland
by Harold Dennis-Jones, Prima Publishing, 1981, 96 pages, paper, $5.95
This is one of the Letts Guide series, which is reviewed in more detail under "Series Reviews."

Michelin Green Guide: Switzerland
Michelin Guides and Maps, 1985 (8th ed.), 217 pages, paper, $10.95
This is one of the premier sightseeing guide series, the Michelin Green Guides, which is reviewed in more detail under "Series Reviews."

100 Hikes In The Alps
by Ira Spring and Harvey Edwards, The Mountaineers, 1985, 224 pages, paper, $8.95

Ths book is part of the Mountaineers Hiking Guide series, which is reviewed in more detail under "Series Reviews."

Rand McNally: Austria and Switzerland
by John and Shirley Harrison, Rand McNally & Co., 1983, 128 pages, paper, $5.95

This book is part of the small-format Rand McNally Pocket Guide series, which is reviewed in more detail under "Series Reviews."

Swiss Country Inns and Chalets
by Karen and Clare Brown, Travel Press, 1988, 260 pages, paper, $12.95

This book is part of the excellent Karen Brown's Country Inns series, which is reviewed in more detail under "Series Reviews."

Switzerland: A Phaidon Art and Architecture Guide
Prentice Hall Press, 1985, 436 pages, cloth, $17.95

This is one of the encyclopedic Phaidon Art and Architecture Guide series, which is reviewed in more detail under "Series Reviews."

Switzerland At Its Best
by Robert Kane, Passport Books, 1987, 266 pages, paper, $9.95

This book is part of the well-done At Its Best Guide series, which is reviewed in more detail under "Series Reviews."

A Touch of Geneva Guide
edited by Mary Krienke, Talman Co., 1986, 245 pages, paper, $7.95

This is one of the Touch of the City Guide series, which is reviewed in more detail under "Series Reviews."

22 Days in Germany, Austria, and Switzerland: The Itinerary Planner
by Rick Steves, John Muir Publications, 1987, 136 pages, paper, $5.95

This book is part of the Itinerary Planner series, which is reviewed in more detail under "Series Reviews." The guide is formatted after the successful *Europe in 22 Days* (now called *22 Days in Europe*). Please note that the title has recently been changed; this book can sometimes still be found under the title *Germany, Austria, and Switzerland in 22 Days*.

Walking in Switzerland
by Brian Spencer, Hunter Publishing, 1986, 205 pages, paper, $9.95
Walking in the Alps
by Brian Spencer, Hunter Publishing, 1986, 192 pages, paper, $9.95
These two titles are part of the Hunter Walks series, which is reviewed in more detail under "Series Reviews."

Walking Switzerland—the Swiss Way—from Vacation Apartments, Hotels, Mountain Inns and Huts
by Marcia and Philip Lieberman, The Mountaineers, 1987, 272 pages, paper, $10.95
Swiss hikers prefer to organize their walks around lodging rather than taking the chance of having to camp. This well-done book describes walking the Swiss way—renting a vacation apartment and venturing out from there, organizing walks between different lodging stops each night, or using trams, trains, and buses to bridge the gap between interesting walking areas. Beginning with an informative section on tips and basics, the book then continues with a section of planned walks from specific cities where vacation apartments are available, followed by planned tours between picturesque inns. Each segment is well described, including distance, difficulty rating, other maps needed, and expected hiking time. Options for the use of trams and other transportation are pointed out where available. The next night's lodging options are clearly described and the phone numbers listed.

Walks and Climbs in the Engadine
Hunter Publishing, 1988, 192 pages, paper, $12.95
This is one of the Hunter Mountain Walks series, which is reviewed in more detail under "Series Reviews."

Walks Through Zurich
by Bert Lief, VLE Limited, undated, fold-out map/guide, paper, $2.00
This guide is part of the Way-Ahead Guide series, which is reviewed in more detail under "Series Reviews."

Whole Europe Escape Manual: Germany/Austria/Switzerland
by James Kitfield and William Walker, World Leisure Corp., 1985, 160 pages, paper, $6.95
This is one of the delightfully different Escape Manual series, which is reviewed in more detail under "Series Reviews."

United Kingdom: See "Great Britain" and "Northern Ireland."
Wales: See the Wales section under "Great Britain."

WEST GERMANY (FEDERAL REPUBLIC OF GERMANY)

See also "Europe as a Whole." West Germany is included in the following major, all-purpose guides to Europe: *Birnbaum's Europe; Fielding's Europe; Fielding's Economy Europe; Fisher's World: Europe; Fodor's Europe; Fodor's Budget Europe; Frommer's Europe on $30 a Day; Let's Go: Europe.*

Baedeker's Berlin
   Prentice Hall Press, 1987, 168 pages, paper, $10.95
Baedeker's Cologne
   Prentice Hall Press, 1987, 144 pages, paper, $10.95
Baedeker's Frankfurt
   Prentice Hall Press, 1987, 176 pages, paper, $10.95
   These three titles are part of Baedeker's City Guide series, which is reviewed in more detail under "Series Reviews."

Baedeker's Germany
   Prentice Hall Press, undated, 320 pages, paper, $14.95
   This is one of the Baedeker's Country/Regional Guide series, which is reviewed in more detail under "Series Reviews."

Baedeker's Hamburg
   Prentice Hall Press, 1987, 192 pages, paper, $10.95
Baedeker's Munich
   Prentice Hall Press, 1987, 240 pages, paper, $10.95
   Both of these titles are part of Baedeker's City Guide series, which is reviewed in more detail under "Series Reviews."

Baedeker's Rhine
   Prentice Hall Press, 1985, 288 pages, paper, $9.95
   This book is part of the Baedeker's Country/Regional Guide series, which is reviewed in more detail under "Series Reviews."

Baedeker's Stuttgart
   Prentice Hall Press, 1987, 175 pages, paper, $10.95
   This is one of the Baedeker's City Guide series, which is reviewed in more detail under "Series Reviews."

Berlin Art Guide
   by Irene Blumenfeld, Robert Silver Associates, 1986, 146 pages, paper, $10.95
   This book is part of the Robert Silver Art Guide series, which is reviewed in more detail under "Series Reviews."

Berlitz: Berlin
Macmillan Publishing, 1983, 128 pages, paper, $6.95
Berlitz: Munich
Macmillan Publishing, 1982, 128 pages, paper, $6.95
Berlitz: Rhine Valley from Cologne to Mainz
Macmillan Publishing, 1982, 128 pages, paper, $6.95
    These three titles are part of the small-format Berlitz Guide series, which is reviewed in more detail under "Series Reviews."

The Children's Treasure Hunt Travel Guide to Austria, Germany, Switzerland
Hippocrene Books, 1979, 222 pages, paper, $6.95
    This book is part of the Children's Treasure Hunt Guide series, which is reviewed in more detail under "Series Reviews."

Day Trips in Germany: 50 One Day Adventures by Rail or Car
by Earl Steinbicker, Hastings House, 1987 (2nd ed.), 288 pages, paper, $9.95
    This book is part of the Earl Steinbicker Day Trips series, which is reviewed in more detail under "Series Reviews."

The Economist Business Traveller's Guide: West Germany
Prentice Hall Press, 1988, 250 pages, cloth, $17.95
    This is one of the highly regarded Economist Business Traveller's Guide series, which is reviewed in more detail under "Series Reviews." As it was released after press time, the number of pages is approximate.

Exploring Rural Germany
Passport Books, 1988/89, 200 pages, paper, $12.95
    This is a new, anticipated title in the Exploring Rural Europe series, which is reviewed in more detail under "Series Reviews." The price and number of pages are approximate.

Fisher's World: Germany
by Helmut Koenig, Fisher's World, Inc., 1987, 336 pages, paper, $14.95
    This book is part of the Fisher's World Guide series, which is reviewed in more detail under "Series Reviews." The series is updated annually.

Fodor's Germany

Fodor's Travel Publications, 1987, 512 pages, paper, $13.95

This book is part of Fodor's Country/Regional Guide series, which is reviewed in more detail under "Series Reviews." The series is updated annually.

Fodor's Great Travel Values: Germany

Fodor's Travel Publications, 1987, 192 pages, paper, $5.95

This is one of the budget-oriented Fodor's Great Travel Values Guide series, which is reviewed in more detail under "Series Reviews." The series is updated annually.

Fodor's Munich

Fodor's Travel Publications, 1987, 128 pages, paper, $6.95

This is one of Fodor's City Guide series, which is reviewed in more detail under "Series Reviews." The series is updated annually.

Frommer's Dollarwise Guide to Germany

by Darwin Porter, Prentice Hall Press, 1988, 655 pages, paper, $12.95

This book is part of Frommer's Dollarwise Guide series, which is reviewed in more detail under "Series Reviews." This series emphasizes selections in the moderate price range and is updated every two years.

German Country Inns and Castles

by Karen and June Brown, Travel Press, 1988, 250 pages, paper, $12.95

This is one of excellent Karen Brown's Country Inns series, which is reviewed in more detail under "Series Reviews."

Germany: A Phaidon Art and Architecture Guide

Prentice Hall Press, 1985, 832 pages, cloth, $16.95

This is one of the encyclopedic Phaidon Art and Architecture Guide series, which is reviewed in more detail under "Series Reviews."

Germany At Its Best

by Robert Kane, Passport Books, 1988, 352 pages, paper, $12.95

This is one of the highly regarded At Its Best Guide series, which is reviewed in more detail under "Series Reviews."

Germany, Austria, and Switzerland in 22 Days

See *22 Days in Germany, Austria, and Switzerland* below.

Insight Guide: Germany
by Apa Productions, Prentice Hall Press, 1988, 359 pages, paper, $16.95
This is a new title in the acclaimed Insight Guide series, which is reviewed in more detail under "Series Reviews."

Manston's Flea Markets, Antique Fairs and Auctions of Germany
by Peter Manston, Travel Keys Books, 1987, 297 pages, paper, $9.95
This is one of the excellent titles in the Travel Key Guide series, which is reviewed in more detail under "Series Reviews."

The Marling Menu-Master for Germany
by William and Clare Marling, Altarinda Books, 1970, 88 pages, plasticized cover, $5.95
This is one of the superb Marling Menu-Masters series, which is reviewed in more detail under "Series Reviews."

Michelin Green Guide: Germany
Michelin Guides and Maps, 1987 (7th ed.), 282 pages, paper, $10.95
This is one of the premier sightseeing guide series, the Michelin Green Guides, which is reviewed in more detail under "Series Reviews."

Michelin Red Guide: Deutschland
Michelin Guides and Maps, 1987, 878 pages, cloth, $17.95
This annual hotel and restaurant guide is part of the Michelin Red Guide series, which is reviewed in more detail under "Series Reviews."

Nagel's Encyclopedia Guide: German Federal Republic
Passport Books, 1981, 943 pages, cloth, $39.95
This classic, cultural guide is part of the Nagel's Guide series, which is reviewed in more detail under "Series Reviews."

The New Holiday Guide to West Germany
F. Evans & Co., 1988 (10th ed.), 160 pages, paper, $4.95
This book is part of the Holiday Guide series, which is reviewed in more detail under "Series Reviews."

100 Hikes In the Alps
by Ira Spring and Harvey Edwards, The Mountaineers, 1985, 224 pages, paper, $8.95
This book is part of the well-done Mountaineers Hiking Guide series, which is reviewed in more detail under "Series Reviews."

Rand McNally: Germany
by Carole Chester, Rand McNally & Co., 1985, 128 pages, paper, $5.95
This book is part of the Rand McNally Pocket Guide series, which is reviewed in more detail under "Series Reviews."

Signposts: German
by Edith Baer and Margaret Wightman, Cambridge University Press, 1982, 99 pages, paper, $5.95
This is a useful and informative guide to over 100 road signs and notices along the roads of Germany.

22 Days in Germany, Austria, and Switzerland: The Itinerary Planner
by Rick Steves, John Muir Publications, 1987, 136 pages, paper, $5.95
This book is part of the Itinerary Planner series, which is reviewed in more detail under "Series Reviews." Note that the title has recently been changed and this book may be found under the title *Germany, Austria, and Switzerland in 22 Days.*

The Visitor's Guide to Bavaria
Hunter Publishing, 1987, 240 pages, paper, $9.95
This is one of the New Visitor's Guide series, which is reviewed in more detail under "Series Reviews."

The Visitor's Guide to the Black Forest
by George Wood, Hunter Publishing, 1984, 140 pages, paper, $9.95
This book is part of the Visitor's Guide series, which is reviewed in more detail under "Series Reviews."

The Visitor's Guide to the Rhine, Mosel & Eifel
Hunter Publishing, 1988, 240 pages, paper, $9.95
This book is one of the New Visitor's Guide series, which is reviewed in more detail under "Series Reviews."

Walks Through Munich
by Bert Lief, VLE Limited, undated, fold-out map/guide, paper, $2.00
Walks Through Stuttgart
by Bert Lief, VLE Limited, undated, fold-out map/guide, paper, $2.00
These two titles are part of the Way-Ahead Guide series, which is reviewed in more detail under "Series Reviews."

Webster's Wine Tours: Germany
Prentice Hall Press, 1988/89, 200 pages, cloth (flexible), $15.95
   This is a new, anticipated title in the growing Webster's Wine Tours series, which is reviewed in more detail under "Series Reviews." The price and number of pages are approximate.

Whole Europe Escape Manual: Germany/Austria/Switzerland
by James Kitfield and William Walker, World Leisure Corp., 1985, 160 pages, paper, $6.95
   This is one of the unique Escape Manual series, which is reviewed in more detail under "Series Reviews."

YUGOSLAVIA

See also "Europe as a Whole." Yugoslavia is included in the following major, all-purpose guides to Europe: *Birnbaum's Europe, Fisher's World: Europe; Fodor's Europe; Fodor's Budget Europe; Let's Go: Europe.*

Adventuring in the Alps: The Sierra Club Travel Guide to the Alpine Regions of France, Switzerland, Germany, Austria, Liechtenstein, Italy, and Yugoslavia
by William and Marylou Reifsnyder, Sierra Club Books, 1986, 278 pages, paper, $10.95
   This is one of the excellent Sierra Club Adventure Travel Guide series, which is reviewed in more detail under "Series Reviews."

Baedeker's Yugoslavia
Prentice Hall Press, undated, 280 pages, paper, $14.95
   This book is part of the Baedeker's Country/Regional Guide series, which is reviewed in more detail under "Series Reviews."

Berlitz: Dubrovnik and Southern Dalmatia
Macmillan Publishing, 1982, 128 pages, paper, $6.95
Berlitz: Istria and Croatian Coast
Macmillan Publishing, 1977, 128 pages, paper, $6.95
Berlitz: Split and Dalmatia
Macmillan Publishing, 1977, 128 pages, paper, $6.95
   These three titles are part of the small-format Berlitz Guide series, which is reviewed in more detail under "Series Reviews."

Berlitz: Yugoslavia
Macmillan Publishing, 1988, 256 pages, paper, $8.95
   This is a new title in the Berlitz Country Guide series, which is reviewed in more detail under "Series Reviews."

Collier World Traveler Series: Greece and Yugoslavia
Macmillan Publishing, 1985, 192 pages, paper, $6.95
This book is part of the Collier World Traveler Guide series, which is reviewed in more detail under "Series Reviews."

The Companion Guide to Jugoslavia
by J. A. Cuddon, Prentice Hall Press, 1984, 480 pages, paper, $12.95
This is one of the superb Companion Guide series, which is reviewed in more detail under "Series Reviews."

Fodor's Yugoslavia
Fodor's Travel Publications, 1988, 320 pages, paper, $14.95
This is a respected title in Fodor's Country/Regional Guide series, which is reviewed in more detail under "Series Reviews." The series is updated annually.

Frommer's Eastern Europe on $25 a Day
by Morris Hadley and Adam Tanner, Prentice Hall Press, 1987, 547 pages, paper, $10.95
Including Yugoslavia, this book is part of Frommer's Dollar-a-Day Guide series, which is reviewed in more detail under "Series Reviews." The series is updated every two years.

100 Hikes in the Alps
by Ira Spring and Harvey Edwards, The Mountaineers, 1985, 224 pages, paper, $8.95
This is one of the fine Mountaineers Hiking Guide series, which is reviewed in more detail under "Series Reviews." Hikes in Yugoslavia are included.

Pilgrimages to Rome and Beyond
by Paul Higgins, Prentice Hall Press, 1985, 130 pages, paper, $8.95
This guide to the Christian holy places, including sites in Yugoslavia, is reviewed under "Greece."

Rough Guide to Yugoslavia
by Martin Dunford and Jack Holland, Routledge & Kegan Paul, 1986, 224 pages, paper, $9.95
This is one of the excellent Rough Guide series, which is reviewed in more detail under "Series Reviews." The series is updated every two to three years.

Treasures of Yugoslavia, An Encyclopedic Touring Guide
Hippocrene Books, 1986, 664 pages, cloth, $29.95
    This beautiful, large-format book organized by republic or province, covers myriad significant cultural and historical landmarks, works of art, and other treasures. It is big, bulky, and heavy—not a book to carry around. However, for those traveling by car, this book is an excellent source of information. For armchair travelers, it is a great adornment for the coffee table.

The Visitor's Guide to Yugoslavia, Adriatic Coast
Hunter Publishing, 1987, 220 pages, paper, $10.95
    This is one of the New Visitor's Guide series, which is reviewed in more detail under "Series Reviews."

North America

NORTH AMERICA AS A WHOLE

See also "The World." North America comprises Canada, Mexico, and the United States. Because Central America, technically part of North America, is generally viewed as its own specific area, it is listed under its own heading.

Affordable Bed and Breakfasts for $40 or Less for Two People
by Loris Bree, MarLor Press, 1987, 165 pages, paper, $9.95
Surprisingly, there are quite a lot of budget B&Bs throughout the U.S. and Canada. This book gives short descriptions and practical information on each and includes B&B registration service networks also.

America On Display: A Guide to Unusual Museums and Collections in the United States and Canada
by Joyce Jurnovoy and David Jenness, Facts on File, 1987, 280 pages, cloth, $24.95
This is an unusual book on an unusual subject. The list of extraordinary museums and collections is seemingly endless and this book offers some fascinating descriptions. All the practical information is included, such as location, hours open to the public, admission costs, and wheelchair accessibility.

America's Grand Resort Hotels: 80 Classic Resorts in the U.S. and Canada
by Rod Fensom, The Globe Pequot Press, 1985, 226 pages, paper, $10.95
This book describes first-class lodging in 30 states and five Canadian provinces. All the practical details are included in this excellent planning book.

Bed & Breakfast American Style
by Norman Simpson, Harper & Row, 1988, 446 pages, paper, $10.95

This annually updated book on bed and breakfasts, first published in 1981, was an early entry in the B&B guide field and was partly responsible for feeding the continent's rising passion for B&Bs. The reviews are personal, opinionated, and quite extensive. Each is based almost always upon on-site visits, rather than on information submitted by the B&B itself. Travel bookstore personnel indicate, however, that the inns included must belong to the author's organization. Be that as it may, all the practical data, including good directions, are provided. Coverage includes the U.S., Canada, Mexico, and the Caribbean.

Bed & Breakfast Coast to Coast
by Bernice Chesler, The Stephen Greene Press, 1986, 416 pages, paper, $12.95

This book contains evaluations of more than 200 B&B reservation services representing more than 15,000 establishments throughout the United States and Canada. Reservation services are a helping hand to many travelers, acting as a sort of a travel agent for the bed and breakfast trade. This is a superb resource for travelers interested in these services.

The Bed & Breakfast Directory
by Barbara Nortarius, John Wiley & Sons, 1988, 416 pages, paper, $12.95

In this guide, released after press time, the founder of Bed and Breakfast USA provides the details on over 1000 B&Bs in the U.S. and Canada.

The Bed & Breakfast Guide
by Phyllis Featherston and Barbara Ostler, Talman Co., 1987 (3rd ed.), 457 pages, paper, $11.95

This is a comprehensive directory, with some photos and illustrations, of all the members of the National Bed & Breakfast Association, whose membership now totals more than 1100 B&Bs. Included are brief narrative descriptions containing the essentials.

Bed & Breakfast: North America
by Norma Buzan, Betsy Ross Publications, 1987 (4th ed.), 549 pages, paper, $14.95

Here are short, informative reviews and the practical information on hundreds of interesting B&Bs and B&B reservation service organizations in the U.S., Canada, Mexico, the Virgin Islands, and Jamaica. The reader feedback chapter in this frequently updated guide is also very helpful.

Bed & Breakfast U.S.A.
by Betty Rundback and Nancy Kramer, E. P. Dutton, 1988, 650 pages, paper, $10.95
This popular book covers a large number of B&Bs throughout the U.S., with some coverage of Canada, Puerto Rico, and the Virgin Islands. Although this has been the bestselling B&B guidebook, the reviews are not very informative. It should be noted that those listed pay a fee to be part of an association. This book is updated annually.

The Benenson Restaurant Guide
by Edward Benenson, Sterling Publishing, 1987, 224 pages, paper, $7.95
This useful, amazingly compact guide for the traveler on the move contains capsule reviews of more than 1200 restaurants in almost all the major U.S. and Canadian cities. The emphasis is on fine gourmet cuisine, but a good range of prices is represented. The author's favorites are specifically noted. Each entry is understandably small, but each is informative and includes a specific rating for food, wine, service, and ambiance.

Best Low Cost Things to See and Do
MarLor Press, 1988, 224 pages, paper, $9.95
Released after press time, this is a guide to inexpensive (less than $5) or free attractions in the U.S. and Canada.

The Best Places to Eat in America: 50 Food Writers Pick the Don't Miss Restaurants in 50 Cities in the U.S. and Canada
by Janice Okun and Eleanor Ostman, Harper & Row, 1987, 416 pages, paper, $9.95
This book is the result of a poll of newpaper food editors, writers, and reviewers who were asked where to find the best breakfasts, business lunches, fish, steak, and ethnic food, as well as the places to take the kids and to eat late at night, and the most romantic spots in their own territories. Included are excellent descriptions and evaluations of the everything from the most informal and inexpensive hamburger joint to the full-blown, expensive coat-and-tie affair.

The Best Ski Touring in America
by Steve Barnett, Sierra Club Books, 1987, 288 pages, paper, $10.95
In this book, Barnett has selected 31 of the best skiing sites throughout the continent, based on his assessment of terrain, conditions, difficulty, and geographic diversity. Areas covered are the

U.S. (including Alaska), Canada, and Mexico. Tours range in difficulty from day trips to intense adventures far into the backcountry. Plenty of the practical data is provided, including access, climate, the best time to go, lodging, and supplies.

Bob Damron's Address Book
Bob Damron Enterprises, 1988, 413 pages, paper, $12.00
This is an annual, small-format directory for gay men, which lists services and entertainment in the United States, Canada, Mexico, Puerto Rico, and the Virgin Islands.

Celebrations: America's Best Festivals, Jamborees, Carnivals & Parades
by Judith Young, Capra Press, 1986, 183 pages, paper, $10.95
All the facts about good times and holidays celebrated throughout the U.S. and Canada are contained in this wonderful vacation planning guide.

Cheap/Smart Weekends: Dependable Alternatives to Vacationing Full Fare
by Theodore Fischer, M. Evans & Co., 1988, 192 pages, paper, $6.95
The focus of this title is on the U.S., Canada, Mexico, and the Caribbean, and the myriad strategies, specific resources, and destinations that will make for a memorable weekend without draining the coffers dry. Included are the best travel deals—travel by air, train, bus, or car rental, as well as bargain packages through B&Bs and various hotels—and specific ideas for weekends accentuating a particular activity, such as bicycling, boating, canoeing, dude ranches, tennis, golf, hunting, fishing, even nudist resorts. This is a vast, thoroughly researched array of planning tools.

The Complete Guide to Bed & Breakfasts, Inns & Guesthouses in the United States and Canada
by Pamela Lanier, John Muir Publications, 1988, 624 pages, paper, $12.95
This is one of the big ones when it comes to directories of B&Bs. No critical comments are included, rather this book is a straightforward listing of over 4800 available inns and B&Bs in the U.S. and Canada. This is an excellent reference directory, but a fee is charged for inclusion. Descriptions are necessarily very brief but include the practical details. Helpful separate lists group these inns into other categories, such as spas, gourmet, antiques, outstanding, romantic, special, skiing, etc. This title is updated annually.

Country Inns and Back Roads: North America
by Norman Simpson, Harper & Row, 1988 (23rd ed.), 432 pages, paper, $10.95
This is one of three volumes in the famous Country Inns and Back Roads series, which is reviewed in more detail under "Series Reviews." The series is updated annually.

Directory of Free Vacation & Travel Information
edited by Raymond Carlson, Pilot Books, 1985, 48 pages, paper, $3.95
This is a handy collection of addresses for visitor's bureaus, chambers of commerce, travel commissions, National Park and Recreation information offices, and foreign tourist offices located in the U.S. All 50 states, Canada, and Puerto Rico are covered.

Ferryliner Vacations in North America: Ocean Travel and Inland Cruising
by Michael and Laura Murphy, E. P. Dutton, 1988, 277 pages, paper, $10.95
The authors of the *Ocean Ferryliners of Europe* tackle the North American continent in this well-done look at vacation options on the ferryliners of North America. Included are prices, facilities, booking information, land and sea itineraries, and on-shore sightseeing and accommodation tips.

Fitness on the Road: Where to Stay to Stay Fit
by John Winsor, Shelter Publications, 1986, 218 pages, paper, $7.95
This book is most helpful for those hoping to maintain their fitness routine while traveling in the large cities of North America. A suggested jogging route, the places to stay that make fitness equipment available, available public swimming pools, and a special section on 50 fitness vacation resorts in 23 states, Canada, and Mexico are listed for each of 33 cities.

Fodor's Bed & Breakfast Guide
Fodor's Travel Publications, 1987, 597 pages, paper, $9.95
Nice descriptions to 750 B&Bs in the U.S., Canada, and Mexico are contained in this helpful, solidly researched guide. Pertinent information includes rates, whether children and/or pets are welcome, whether smoking is permitted, and types of breakfast served.

Fodor's Ski Resorts of North America
Fodor's Travel Publications, 1986, 391 pages, paper, $14.95

Fodor's offers a comprehensive listing of a wide variety of ski resorts all over the U.S. and Canada. Information, in typical succinct Fodor fashion, covers all the essentials of the ski resorts themselves, lodging, food, entertainment, and transportation.

Frommer's Bed & Breakfast North America
by Hal Gieseking, Prentice Hall Press, 1987, 361 pages, paper, $8.95

This is another quality B&B guide, with some unique features such as a section on locating B&Bs in other countries, including Czechoslovakia and Yugoslavia, and a large section describing what it terms the 100 best B&B homes in North America, as nominated by the various B&B reservation services. More traditionally, this guide also includes a section on reservation services (more than 150 of the ones judged most reliable), and a section on more than 200 B&B inns across North America. The descriptions are fairly short, but informative, and all practical information is clearly listed. This book is updated every two years.

Frommer's Guide to Honeymoon Destinations
by Risa Weinreh, Prentice Hall Press, 1987, 628 pages, paper, $12.95

Weinreh, the travel editor of *Modern Bride*, shares her intimate knowledge of the most romantic spots throughout the U.S., Canada, Mexico, the Caribbean, Bermuda, and the Bahamas—those perfect destinations for any honeymoon. All the practical details from transportation to accommodations are included, and selections fit any budget. There is even a chapter on offbeat ideas like ballooning or chartering a yacht. This practical book with an eye on romance is a great idea.

Gardens of North America and Hawaii: A Traveler's Guide
by Irene and Walter Jacob, Timber Press, 1985, 268 pages, cloth, $24.95

This is a well-done, comprehensive guide to over 1400 public gardens in the United States and Canada, over 900 of which charge no admission. Included are location, principal plant collections, special notes of interest, facilities and handicap access, visiting hours, and more. A 4-star rating system makes this a helpful title for the plant lover.

Gayellow Pages, National Edition
Renaissance House, 1988, 256 pages, paper, $8.95
   This is an annual guide to services and entertainment for the gay man in the United States and Canada. Renaissance House also publishes regional editions.

The Ghostly Register: Haunted Dwellings, Active Spirits—A Journey to America's Strangest Landmarks
by Arthur Myers, Contemporary Books, 1986, 378 pages, paper, $9.95
   For those interested in the strange, the bizarre, and the unexplained, Myers has assembled a wonderful collection of incredible tales. The *Ghostly Registry* can also be used as a guidebook. Locations and directions are provided, as well as the best time to witness the strange goings-on. This is a unique book among travel guides.

Guide to Budget Motels
by Loris Bree, MarLor Press, 1988, 261 pages, paper, $8.95
   This is a no-nonsense listing of more than 3600 inexpensive rooms for the night in the U.S. and Canada. Included in each compact write-up are services offered, the exit to take off the freeway, and location. Oriented to the automobile traveler, this handy guide is updated each tourist season.

How to Get Lost & Found in California and Other Lovely Places
by John McDermott, Orafa Publishing, 1982, 295 pages, paper, $9.95
   The title is a little deceiving, since destinations all over North America are included. However, a strong emphasis is placed on California. This book is part of the Lost and Found Guide series, which is reviewed in more detail under "Series Reviews." Note that this title is not distributed by Hunter Publishing, as are the others in the series. It should be obtained directly from Orafa Publishing.

National Directory of Budget Motels
edited by Raymond Carlson, Pilot Books, 1987, 80 pages, paper, $3.95
   This is an annually revised listing of over 2200 low-cost, chain motel accommodations in the U.S. and Canada. Included are location, freeway exit information, and phone numbers.

Natural Attractions: A Select Guide to Experiencing North America's Unique Wildlife and Wonders
by John Thaxton, Warner Books, 1987, 299 pages, paper, $8.95
   This wonderfully unique book concentrates on the animals seen in North America. Each chapter covers a particular animal—hawks,

bears, waterfowl, wolves, bats, whooping cranes, etc. Within each chapter is information on how to best view the particular animal and where to go to do it, and specific recommendations on where to stay while experiencing these wonders of the continent.

North American Indian Travel Guide
edited by Ralph and Lisa Woo Shanks, Costano Books, 1987, 278 pages, paper, $14.95

This book contains informative chapters on the unique aspects of life in Indian Country and major trends and issues among the Indians. These are followed by a state-by-state, province-by-province guide to the parks, museums, cemeteries, villages, pueblos, research centers, and other locations that are open to the public. Each is accompanied by addresses and phone numbers. This is truly a vast store of information, including short pieces on each Indian tribe. This great resource covers all of the U.S. and Canada.

Pat Dickerman's Adventure Travel North America
by Pat Dickerman, Henry Holt & Co., 1986 (15th ed.), 256 pages, paper, $12.95

This classic resource guide to specific adventure plans is a compendium of information on each company offering adventure travel of one sort or another: rafting, kayaking, hiking, climbing, jeeping, horseback packing, canoeing, ballooning, dogsledding, or whatever. Informative descriptions, not just information off the back of a brochure, and all the practical facts are provided. This wonderful planning tool is updated every two to three years.

Places for Men
Ferrari Publications, 1987, 336 pages, paper, $8.00

This is an annual gay men's guide to North America, including Mexico and the Caribbean, that lists bars, restaurants, religious organizations, erotica, and much more. This useful directory is published in a compact pocket-sized format.

Places of Interest: Atlas of Gay Travel
Ferrari Publications, 1987 (8th ed.), 200 pages, paper, $10.00

This is a single-volume guide for both gay men and women to hotels, bars, restaurants, bookstores, and religious organizations in a wide variety of cities in the U.S., Canada, Mexico, and the Caribbean. It is an excellent source of information.

Places of Interest to Women: Guide to Women's Travel
Ferrari Publications, 1987, 204 pages, paper, $7.00
This is an annual gay women's guide to North America, including Mexico and the Caribbean. Organized like *Places for Men* but in a slightly larger format, it provides important city-by-city information on all services of interest to the gay woman traveler.

Quilt Collections: A Directory for the United States and Canada
by Lisa Oshins, Acropolis Books, 1987, 255 pages, paper, $18.95
This is a delightful directory of over 700 quilt collections totalling more than 25,000 quilts. Housed in museums, historical societies, galleries, museum parks, or other spots, this helpful book tells how to see them all, whether by appointment or during regular visiting hours. Oshins includes notes on the types of quilts in each collection. Exploring folk history can be fun and informative.

Rail Ventures: The Comprehensive Planning Guide to Rail Travel in the United States, Canada, and Mexico
Wayfinder Press, 1988 (3rd ed.), 352 pages, paper, $12.95
This comprehensive book gives detailed information on the need for reservations, services available, accommodations, distances traveled and the time needed to do so, as well as great running logs of each trip that describe things to be seen from the train and the approximate arrival and departure from intermediate cities along the route. Suggestions for time spent in various cities—where the train station is (a map is included), where to catch a cab, sights to see, places to stay—are included. This most detailed book is helpful for the train traveler.

Rand McNally RV Park & Campground Directory
Rand McNally & Co., 1987, 863+ pages, paper, $12.95
This is a heavy, large-format directory to thousands of campgrounds in America, Mexico, and Canada. Rather than rating each facility as others do, Rand McNally groups campgrounds, both public and private, into color-coded regional charts which compare fees, facilities, recreational possibilities, etc. Each is coded to a colored Rand McNally road map. An extensive RV service section is also included in this annually updated guide.

The Senior Citizen's Guide to Budget Travel in the United States and Canada
by Paige Palmer, Pilot Books, 1987, 62 pages, paper, $3.95
This helpful planning booklet for seniors provides information on doing travel homework, how to get there, where to stay, package

tours, where to eat, and sightseeing. Plenty of good strategies to take the best advantage of what resources are available are outlined.

Train Trips: Exploring America by Rail (includes Canada)
by William Scheller, The Globe Pequot Press, 1984, 286 pages, paper, $9.95
This delightful book gives a history of American passenger trains and plenty of tips on where to stay, what to do, and public transportation options in the cities visited.

The Traveler's Almanac, North America: Planning Your Vacation Around the Weather
by Harold Bernard, Jr., Riverdale Co., 1987, 216 pages, paper, $11.95
This book assembles copious facts into easy-to-use charts and combines them with good descriptions of salient points to remember about the weather's track record. The odds of a better vacation increase with the use of this great resource book.

What to Do With the Kids This Year: 100 Family Vacation Places With Time Off for You!
by Jane Wilford, The Globe Pequot Press, 1986, 267 pages, paper, $8.95
Contained herein are excellent descriptions of all sorts of great destinations with recreational activities for both the kids and the grownups. Family-oriented places that have not only good food and attractive surroundings, but also such pluses as babysitting services, are also included.

Where to Eat in America
by William Rice and Barbara Goldman, Charles Scribner's Sons, 1987 (3rd ed.), 379 pages, paper, $12.95
Rice, a columnist for *The Chicago Tribune* and previously editor-in-chief of *Food and Wine* magazine, has joined forces with food consultant Barbara Goldman to produce this compendium of restaurant selections covering all 50 states and five major Canadian cities. The selections are necessarily few for most cities and the review comments, while apt, are quite brief. Nonetheless, as a national directory, this is a fine book, especially since it covers many smaller cities in addition to major metropolitan destinations.

The White Book of Ski Areas
by Robert Enzel, Inter-Ski Services, 1987 (12th ed.), 390 pages, paper, $13.95
This comprehensive, annual guide is low on interesting prose and

absolutely loaded with facts. For more than 900 ski resorts, up-to-date details on the area's statistics, instruction, rentals, transportation options, plus general notes on the availability of lodging, restaurants, and après-ski spots are provided. For some areas the ski slope map is reproduced. Details include prices and phone numbers. No single guidebook covers more.

Woodall's Campground Directory
Woodall Publishing, 1987, 828 pages, paper, $12.95
    This heavy, large-format, annually-updated book is filled with a huge number of camping choices, including public and private campgrounds, RV service locations, and selected attractions in the U.S., Canada, and Mexico. All private campgrounds are inspected each year by one of Woodall's 30 husband/wife teams who rate each facility on a 1-to-5 scale. Information on facilities, recreational activities, driving directions, etc. are provided.

COUNTRIES OF NORTH AMERICA

CANADA

See also "North America as a Whole."

Adventuring in the Rockies: The Sierra Club Travel Guide to the Rocky Mountain Region of the United States and Canada
by Jeremy Schmidt, Sierra Club Books, 1986, 320 pages, paper, $10.95
    This book is part of the Sierra Club Adventure Travel Guide series, which is reviewed in more detail under "Series Reviews."

Alaska-Yukon Handbook, including the Canadian Rockies
by David Stanley, Moon Publications, 1988, 450 pages, paper, $10.95
    This is another excellent volume in the Moon Handbook series, which is reviewed in more detail under "Series Reviews."

The American Garden Guidebook
by Everitt Miller and Jay Cohen, M. Evans & Co., 1987, 293 pages, paper, $8.95
    Including the four eastern Canadian provinces, this book is reviewed under "New England" (U.S.A.).

Bed and Breakfast Home Directory: California, Oregon, Washington
by Diane Knight, Knighttime Publications, 1986 (4th ed.), 230 pages, paper, $8.95
   Including southwestern British Columbia, this book is reviewed under the "The Southwest" (U.S.A.).

Bed & Breakfast in Michigan and Surrounding Areas
by Norma Buzan and Bert Howell, Betsy Ross Publications, 1985, 120 pages, paper, $8.25
   Including selections in Ontario, Canada, this book is reviewed under "The Midwest" (U.S.A.).

The Bed and Breakfast Traveler: Touring the West Coast
by Lewis Green, The Globe Pequot Press, 1987, 288 pages, paper, $10.95
   Including Vancouver and Victoria, this book is reviewed under "The Pacific Northwest" (U.S.A.).

Berlitz: Canada
Macmillan Publishing, 1988, 256 pages, paper, $8.95
   This book is part of the small-format Berlitz Country Guide series, which is reviewed in more detail under "Series Reviews."

Berlitz: Montreal
Macmillan Publishing, 1978, 128 pages, paper, $6.95
Berlitz: Toronto
Macmillan Publishing, 1986, 128 pages, paper, $6.95
   These two titles are part of the small-format Berlitz Guide series, which is reviewed in more detail under "Series Reviews."

The Best Places to Eat in America: 50 Food Writers Pick the Don't Miss Restaurants in 50 Cities in the U.S. and Canada
by Janice Okun and Eleanor Ostman, Harper & Row, 1987, 416 pages, paper $9.95
   See "North America as a Whole."

Best Places to Stay in the Pacific Northwest
by Marilyn McFarlane, The Harvard Common Press, 1988, 400 pages, paper, $14.95
   Including British Columbia, this is one of the excellent Best Places to Stay Guide series, which is reviewed in more detail under "Series Reviews." No fees were accepted for inclusion.

Bicycling the Pacific Coast
by Tom Kirkendall and Vicky Spring, The Mountaineers, 1984, 224 pages, paper, $9.95

Including British Columbia, this book is reviewed under "The Pacific Northwest" (U.S.A.).

Biking the Great Lakes Islands
by Kathleen and Lawrence Abrams, Entwood Publishing, 1985, 164 pages, paper, $8.95

Including several Canadian islands, this book is reviewed under "Michigan."

Birnbaum's Canada
edited by Stephen Birnbaum, Houghton Mifflin, 1988, 626 pages, paper, $12.95

This is one of the excellent Birnbaum Guide series, which is reviewed in more detail under "Series Reviews." The series is updated annually.

Canada
by Nina Nelson, Hippocrene Books, 1987, 139 pages, paper, $8.95

This is a pleasantly readable introduction to the diverse Canadian scene, including descriptions of museums, churches, parks and other sightseeing/touring ideas in each location. Some hotel and restaurant selections are also provided, but this is not the primary focus of the book.

Canada: A Travel Survival Kit
by Mark Lightbody, Lonely Planet Publications, 1986 (2nd ed.), 384 pages, paper, $9.95

This book is part of the well-known Travel Survival Kit series, which is reviewed in more detail under "Series Reviews." The series is updated every two to three years.

Canada's National Parks: A Visitor's Guide
by Marylee Stephenson, Prentice Hall Press, 1984, 308 pages, paper, $11.95

This is a comprehensive guide to the Canadian parks with natural history notes, information on hiking trails, facilities, programs, and campsites. Some materials may be dated and trail maps are quite basic.

The Canadian Bed and Breakfast Book

by Patricia Wilson, William Street Press, 1987, 220 pages, paper, $7.95

This title contains solid evaluations of Canadian B&Bs in most provinces (except the far north) and in all price ranges.

The Canadian Bed and Breakfast Guide

by Gerda Pantel, Chelsea Green Publishing, 1987 (3rd ed.), 305 pages, paper, $10.95

This is a comprehensive directory of B&B possibilities throughout Canada. All the needed information is here, but there are no reviews. This is a thorough compilation of information from returned questionnaires.

The Coastal Kayaker: Kayak Camping on the Alaska and B.C. Coast

by Randel Washburne, The Globe Pequot Press, 1983, 224 pages, paper, $10.95

This is a comprehensive handbook on kayaking along the northern Pacific coast that includes seven sample tours.

The Complete Guide to Bed & Breakfasts, Inns & Guesthouses in the United States and Canada

by Pamela Lanier, John Muir Publications, 1988, 624 pages, paper, $12.95

See "North America as a Whole."

The Complete Guide to Bicycling in Canada

by Elliot Katz, Sierra Club Books, 1987, 231 pages, paper, $10.95

Good descriptions of numerous routes, plus the maps and other helpful guidebooks on specific areas of Canada to obtain are listed in this title.

The Complete Guide to Cross-Country Skiing in Canada

by John Peaker, Doubleday & Co., 1986, 246 pages, paper, $10.95

Plenty of information is provided here, but only about 100 pages of the book is actually on the best places to ski throughout the country. The first 140 pages are on things like equipment and technique.

Country Inns, Lodges & Historic Hotels: Canada

by Anthony Hitchcock and Jean Lindgren, Burt Franklin–Publisher, 1988 (8th ed.), 246 pages, paper, $8.95

This is one of the Compleat Traveler Companions series, which is reviewed in more detail under "Series Reviews." The series is updated annually. No fees were accepted for inclusion.

Country Walks Near Montreal
by William Scheller, Appalachian Mountain Club, 1982, 152 pages, paper, $7.95
This book is part of the AMC Hiking Guide series, which is reviewed in more detail under "Series Reviews."

Cross-Country Ski Inns of the Eastern U.S. and Canada
by Marge Lamy, The Stephen Greene Press, 1986, 128 pages, paper, $12.95
See "New England" (U.S.A.).

An Explorer's Guide: British Columbia
by Harry McKeever, Chronicle Books, 1982 (revised ed.), 192 pages, paper, $8.95
This detailed, well-written guide to tourist and sightseeing attractions throughout British Columbia. also addresses the needs of the fisherman, boatman, and backpacker. Sprinkled throughout are lots of historic details. The book is well done, but some information may be quite dated.

Exploring Manning Park
The Mountaineers, 1979, 128 pages, paper, $6.95
This is a guide to the trails, accesses, and facilities of this popular British Columbia park.

Fisher's World: Canada
by Robert Turnbull, Fisher's World, Inc., 1988, 313 pages, paper, $14.95
Fisher's World: Pacific Northwest
by Barry and Hilda Anderson, Fisher's World, Inc., 1988, 320 pages, paper, $14.95
Both of these volumes are part of the Fisher's World Guide series, which is reviewed in more detail under "Series Reviews." The Pacific Northwest title includes Western Canada. The series is updated annually.

Fodor's Canada
Fodor's Travel Publications, 1987, 547 pages, paper, $13.95
This book is part of Fodor's Country/Regional Guide series, which is reviewed in more detail under "Series Reviews." The series is updated annually.

Fodor's Canada's Maritime Provinces plus Newfoundland and Labrador
Fodor's Travel Publications, 1987, 154 pages, paper, $6.95
Basically a section from the larger *Fodor's Canada* volume, this book is part of the Fodor's Country/Regional Guides series, which is reviewed in more detail under "Series Reviews." The series is updated annually.

Fodor's Fun in Montreal
Fodor's Travel Publications, 1987, 128 pages, paper, $5.95
This is one of Fodor's Fun Guide series, which is reviewed in more detail under "Series Reviews." The series is updated annually.

Fodor's Great Travel Values: Canada
Fodor's Travel Publications, 1987, 224 pages, paper, $6.95
This book is part of the budget-oriented Fodor's Great Travel Values Guide series, which is reviewed in more detail under "Series Reviews." The series is updated annually.

Fodor's Pacific North Coast
Fodor's Travel Publications, 1987, 352 pages, paper, $9.95
Fodor's Province of Quebec
Fodor's Travel Publications, 1986, 214 pages, paper, $8.95
Fodor's Rockies
Fodor's Travel Publications, 1987, 256 pages, paper, $8.95
All of these titles are part of Fodor's Country/Regional Guide series, which is reviewed in more detail under "Series Reviews." The Pacific North Coast title includes British Columbia. The Rockies title includes the mountainous regions of Alberta and British Columbia. The series is updated annually.

Fodor's Toronto
Fodor's Travel Publications, 1987, 176 pages, paper, $7.95
This is part of Fodor's City Guide series which is reviewed in more detail under "Series Reviews." It is updated annually.

Frommer's Dollarwise Guide to Canada
by John Goodwin, Prentice Hall Press, 1988, 672 pages, paper, $12.95
Part of Frommer's Dollarwise Guide series, which is reviewed in more detail under "Series Reviews." This series emphasizes selections in the moderate price range. Updated every two years.

Frommer's Dollarwise Guide to Skiing: USA East
by I. William Berry, Prentice Hall Press, 1988, 266 pages, paper, $11.95

Frommer's Dollarwise Guide to Skiing: USA West
by Lois Friedland, Prentice Hall Press, 1988, 320 pages, paper, $11.95

Both titles include ski areas located in Eastern and Western Canada repectively. Reviewed under "New England" (East) and "Rocky Mountain/Great Basin States" (West).

Frommer's Dollarwise Guide to the Northwest
by Marylyn Springer and Don Schultz, Prentice Hall Press, 1987, 408 pages, paper, $11.95

Including Vancouver and Victoria, this guide is part of Frommer's Dollarwise Guide series which is reviewed in more detail under "Series Reviews." This series emphasizes selections in the moderate price range. Updated every two years.

Frommer's Guide to Montreal & Quebec City
by Tom Brosnahan, Prentice Hall Press, 1987, 200 pages, paper, $5.95

Part of Frommer's City Guide series which is reviewed in more detail under "Series Reviews." Updated every two years.

Glacier-Waterton Explorer's Guide
by Carl Schreier, Homestead Publishing, 1983, 48 pages, paper, $4.95

This is part of the Park Explorer's Guide series, which is reviewed in more detail under "Series Reviews."

Going Places: Family Getaways in the Pacific Northwest
by John Biegelow and Breck Longstreth, Seattle's Child Publications, 1985, 139 pages, paper, $7.95

Includes British Columbia. Reviewed under "The Pacific Northwest" (U.S.A.).

The Great Lakes Guidebook: Lake Huron and Eastern Lake Michigan
by George Cantor, The University of Michigan Press, 1985, 196 pages, paper, $7.95

The Great Lakes Guidebook: Lakes Ontario and Erie
by George Cantor, The University of Michigan Press, 1985, 238 pages, paper, $7.95

The Great Lakes Guidebook: Lake Superior and Western Lake Michigan

by George Cantor, The University of Michigan Press, 1980, 226 pages, paper, $6.95

All three titles cover numerous Canadian locations. Reviewed under "The Midwest" (U.S.A.).

The Great Towns of the West

by David Vokac, West Press, 1985, 464 pages, paper, $14.95

Including towns in Alberta and British Columbia as well as 10 western states, this book is part of the Great Towns Guide series, which is reviewed in more detail under "Series Reviews."

Guide to Eastern Canada

by Frederick Pratson, The Globe Pequot Press, 1986 (2nd ed.), 484 pages, paper, $10.95

The widely praised *Guide to Eastern Canada*, now in its second edition, has been joined by a welcome companion volume, *Guide to Western Canada* (below). Both of these guides are excellent, very enjoyable books in their own right, "rich in detail and extremely accurate" as knowledgeable reviewers have said. Each is full of a diverse selection of well-chosen restaurants, lodging, scenic and recreational attractions as well as helpful hints, transportation options, historical sketches, shopping ideas, and more.

A Guide to the Queen Charlotte Islands

by Neil Carey, Alaska Northwest Publishing, 1986 (8th ed.), 90 pages, paper, $6.95

A popular, frequently updated book on these remote islands off the British Columbia coast, which witnessed the zenith of the Haida Indian culture. Abandoned Haida villages and totem poles are sprinkled throughout the islands and this guide offers all sorts of information on exploring every corner—whether by auto, boat, or plane. There are detailed maps, including a large separate one, as well as the practical information on weather, what to wear, where to go, and how to get there. This guide is very well done.

The Guide to Vancouver's Chinese Restaurants

by Ginger Chang, Hancock House Publishers, 1985, 136 pages, paper, $7.95

Chang has chosen to provide a descriptive guide to the highly diverse selection of Chinese food available in Vancouver, rather than one with rated reviews. But you will find her writeups very helpful nonetheless in choosing the Chinese restaurant that fits your needs. All price ranges are covered; all the details you need are included, though some may be drifting out-of-date. Well done and deserving of a revised edition.

Guide to Western Canada
by Frederick Pratson, The Globe Pequot Press, 1987, 372 pages, paper, $10.95
   This is a companion volume to the highly regarded *Guide to Eastern Canada* reviewed above.

Hot Springs and Hot Pools of the Northwest
by Jayson Loam and Marjorie Gersh, Wilderness Press, 1986, (2nd ed.), 196 pages, paper, $12.95
   Including southwestern Canada, this book is reviewed under "The Pacific Northwest" (U.S.A.).

Insight Guide: Canada
by Apa Productions, Prentice Hall Press, 1986, 364 pages, paper, $16.95
   This book is part of the acclaimed Insight Guide series, which is reviewed in more detail under "Series Reviews."

Island Treasures: An Insider's Guide to Victoria, Vancouver Island and the Gulf Islands
by Carolyn Thomas and Jill Stewart, Harbour Publishing, 1986, 188 pages, paper, $9.95
   Written in a chatty style by two women—one a restaurant columnist, the other in radio and a travel writer. While one constructs her comments around what her "doting mother" used to say, the other plays off her seemingly dense mother-in-law's comments. The result is a fun read. Though the guide is a bit hard to use at times it is certainly well worth the effort. This comprehensive source includes hotel and restaurant selections in a variety of price ranges with an emphasis on those moderately priced.

James Barber's Personal Guide to the Best Eating in Vancouver
by James Barber, Solstice Press, 1985, 152 pages, paper, $7.95
   James Barber is a delight to read. His introduction alone is worth the price of the book. There are no "ratings on a scale of one to ten, and no cute little groupings of knives and forks," rather a guide to the best of Vancouver's nearly 2,000 restaurants. They are all "the best" for one reason or another. Grouped by type of food or type of restaurant (café, deli, family, cappuccino bar), this wonderful book covers a wide range of tantalizing choices in every price range.

Let's Go: Pacific Northwest, Western Canada & Alaska
by Harvard Student Agencies, St. Martin's Press, 1988, 464 pages, paper, $10.95
This book is part of the excellent, budget-oriented Let's Go Guide series, which is reviewed in more detail under "Series Reviews." It is updated annually.

Michelin Green Guide: Canada
Michelin Guides & Maps, 1985 (2nd ed.), 242 pages, paper, $10.95
This is one of the renowned Michelin Green Guide sightseeing series, which is reviewed in more detail under "Series Reviews."

The Milepost
Alaska Northwest Publishing, 1988 (38th ed.), 530 pages, paper, $14.95
The "bible of north country travel" is reviewed under "Alaska," and includes all the provinces of western Canada. Updated annually.

Nagel's Canada
Passport Books, 1981, 735 pages, cloth, $39.95
This classic, cultural guide, part of the Nagel's Guide series, is reviewed in more detail under "Series Reviews."

National Parks of the Rocky Mountains
by Kent and Donna Dannen, Rocky Mountain Nature Association, 1986, 120 pages, cloth, $14.95
Including Waterton National Park, this book is reviewed under "The Rocky Mountain/Great Basin States" (U.S.A.).

94 Hikes in the Canadian Rockies
by Vicky Spring and Dee Urbick, The Mountaineers, 1983, 224 pages, paper, $9.95
This is one of the Mountaineers Hiking Guide series, which is reviewed in more detail under "Series Reviews."

Northwest Best Places
by David Brewster and Kathryn Robinson, Sasquatch Books, 1987, 544 pages, paper, $14.95
This superb resource for hotels, restaurants, and much more in British Columbia and the Pacific Northwest, is reviewed under "The Pacific Northwest" (U.S.A.). It is updated every two years.

Northwest Mileposts
Alaska Northwest Publishing, 1987, 496 pages, paper, $14.95
Including western Canada, this is an annually updated companion guide to the famous *Milepost*, the "bible of north country travel," and is reviewed under "The Pacific Northwest" (U.S.A.).

Northwest Trails: A Hiker's Guide to National Parks and Wilderness Areas
by Ira Spring and Harvey Manning, The Mountaineers, 1982, 192 pages, paper, $9.95
100 Hikes in the Inland Northwest
by Rich Landers and Ida Dolphin, The Mountaineers, 1987, 224 pages, paper, $9.95
103 Hikes in Southwestern B.C.
by Mary and David Macaree, The Mountaineers, 1987 (3rd ed.), 224 pages, paper, $9.95
109 Walks in B.C.'s Lower Mainland
by David and Mary Macaree, The Mountaineers, 1983, 192 pages, paper, $9.95
All of these are part of the Mountaineers Hiking Guide series, which is reviewed in more detail under "Series Reviews."

The Penguin Guide to Canada
edited by Alan Tucker, Viking Penguin, 1988, 224-448 pages, paper, $9.95-12.95
One of the new, anticipated titles in the Penguin Travel Guide series, which is reviewed in more detail under "Series Reviews." This series is updated annually. Only price and page-count ranges for the entire series were available at press time.

Quilt Collections: A Directory for the United States and Canada
by Lisa Oshins, Acropolis Books, 1987, 255 pages, paper, $18.95
This book is reviewed under "North America as a Whole."

Rafting in British Columbia
by D. Van Dine, Hancock House, 1984, 72 pages, paper, $6.95
This is a guide to numerous potential river trips in British Columbia for raft, canoe, or kayak.

Rail Ventures: The Comprehensive Planning Guide to Rail Travel in the United States, Canada and Mexico
Wayfinder Press, 1988 (3rd ed.), 352 pages, paper, $12.95
This guide is reviewed under "North America as a Whole."

Rand McNally Pocket Guides: Eastern Canada
by Carole Chester, Rand McNally & Co., 1987, 128 pages, paper, $5.95

This book is part of the small-format Rand McNally Pocket Guide series, which is reviewed in more detail under "Series Reviews."

The Senior Citizen's Guide to Budget Travel in the United States and Canada
by Paige Palmer, Pilot Books, 1987, 62 pages, paper, $3.95

This guide is reviewed under "North America as a Whole."

Shopwalks: Montreal
by Francis Ehrlich, Crown Publishers, 1988, fold-out map/guide, paper, $5.95

This is one of the Shopwalks series, which is reviewed in more detail under "Series Reviews."

The Sierra Club Naturalist's Guide to the North Atlantic Coast: Cape Cod to Newfoundland
by Michael and Deborah Berrill, 1981, 512 pages, paper, $12.95

The Sierra Club Naturalist's Guide to the North Woods of Michigan, Wisconsin, Minnesota, and Southern Ontario
by Glenda Daniel and Jerry Sullivan, Sierra Club Books, 1981, 384 pages, paper, $10.95

Both of these titles are part of the Sierra Club Naturalist's Guide series, which is reviewed in more detail under "Series Reviews."

Special Places for the Discerning Traveler in Oregon, Washington, Idaho, Montana, British Columbia, California Wine Country
by Fred and Mardi Nystrom, Graphic Arts Center Publishing, 1986, 216 pages, paper, $13.95

This title is reviewed under "Pacific Northwest" (U.S.A.).

The Toronto Underground Restaurant Book: Your Guide to the Best and Cheapest Neighborhood Restaurants in Toronto
by Cynthia Wine, Doubleday & Co., 1986, 188 pages, paper, $9.95

Despite a difficult-to-use format, this book lists 180 excellent restaurants in all price ranges, with an emphasis on the bargain range.

Train Trips: Exploring America by Rail (includes Canada)
by William Scheller, The Globe Pequot Press, 1984, 286 pages, paper, $9.95

This book is reviewed under "North America as a Whole."

The Vancouver Guide
by Terri Wershler, Douglas McIntyre, Ltd., 1985, 239 pages, paper, $8.95

This is a very complete, nicely written, well laid out guidebook containing plenty of information on a wide array of hotels, restaurants, and essential services.

The Vancouver Guide Book
by Ginny and Beth Evans, Chronicle Books, 1986 (revised ed.), 310 pages, paper, $5.95

This is a solid guide to the Vancouver area. All the tourist categories are covered here: transportation, touring the city, cultural opportunities, shopping, sports, and entertainment. The list of accommodations is quite diverse and in all price ranges. Notes on each lodging choice are fairly brief. The "Eating Out" section is particularly well done, covering all price ranges and needs (family, take-out, etc.). There is also a good section of tours out from the city.

Vancouver Island Traveler: Great Adventures on Canada's West Rim
by Sandy Bryson, Windham Bay Press, 1988, 208 pages, paper, $10.95

This is a wonderful, adventure-oriented travel guide to the pleasures of Vancouver Island. Bryson's enjoyable text captures the essence of this fascinating place through the words and thoughts of those who live and work there—the artists, the fishermen, the backcountry guides. There are separate chapters on history, art, and exciting people, places, and events, as well as bicycling, caving, diving, fishing, golfing, hiking, sailing, and wildlife and habitat. And the practical details are here, including specific ideas for each adventure possibility, as well as hotels, restaurants, reading suggestions, and maps. Great reading, thoroughly researched, *Vancouver Island Traveler* is one first-rate guidebook as well as a great reading adventure.

Vancouver Rainy Day Guide
by Paula Brook, Chronicle Books, 1984, 128 pages, paper, $6.95

This is one of the Rainy Day Guide series, which is reviewed in more detail under "Series Reviews."

The Vancouver Super Shopper
by Anne Garber, JASI, 1986 (3rd ed.), 206 pages, paper, $8.95

This is a popular, frequently revised shopping guide to "the best bargains and the best places to find them," as the *Vancouver Sun* put it. Provided are good, informative write-ups on a wide range of shops. Some selections are directed toward local residents, but there are plenty for the tourist as well.

Water Escapes: Great Waterside Vacation Spots in the Northeast
by Betsy Wittemann and Nancy Webster, Wood Pond Press, 1987, 418 pages, paper, $12.95

Including some Canadian destinations, this book is reviewed under the "New England" (U.S.A.).

Western Trips and Trails
by E. M. Sterling, Pruett Publishing, 1987 (2nd ed.), 325 pages, paper, $10.00

Including some Canadian trips and trails, this book is reviewed under "The Rocky Mountain/Great Basin States" (U.S.A.).

Woodall's Tenting Directory
Woodall Publishing, 1987, 168 pages, paper, $7.95

This annual, large-format guide to campsites appropriate for tent camping includes some Canadian destinations and is done in the same fashion as their full directory, which is reviewed under "North America as a Whole."

Woodall's Western Campground Directory
Woodall Publishing, 1987, 642+ pages, paper, $8.95

This large-format guide to camping in the west, including western Canada, is a section of their full directory, which is reviewed under "North America as a Whole." This guide is oriented to RV and car camping and is updated annually.

Greenland: See "Islands of the Eastern and Northern Atlantic Ocean" under "Europe".

MEXICO
See also "North America as a Whole."

Adventuring Along the Gulf of Mexico: The Sierra Club Guide to the Gulf Coast of the United States and Mexico from the Florida Keys to Yucatan
by Donald Schueler, Sierra Club Books, 1986, 320 pages, paper, $10.95

This book is part of the excellent Sierra Club Adventure Travel Guide series, which is reviewed in more detail under "Series Reviews."

The American Express Pocket Guide to Mexico

by James Tickell, Prentice Hall Press, 1988, 220 pages, cloth, $9.95

This is one of the respected American Express Pocket Guide series, which is reviewed in more detail under "Series Reviews." This edition was released after press time, so the number of pages is approximate.

Backcountry Mexico: A Traveler's Guide and Phrase Book

by Bob Burleson and David Riskind, University of Texas Press, 1986, 311 pages, cloth, $12.95

In this book, the authors help travelers "hire a guide and a burro, navigate rural roads and trails, and communicate with the friendly and, sometimes, unfriendly folks you are likely to meet in a rural setting." The well-written text covers myriad topics, such as eating and staying well, camping, canoeing, rural Mexican village life, and car repair in the middle of nowhere. Interspersed throughout is a real crash course in Spanish. This should be required reading for those heading for the Mexican hinterland.

Baedeker's Mexico

Prentice Hall Press, undated, 328 pages, paper, $14.95

This book is part of the Baedeker's Country/Regional Guide series, which is reviewed in more detail under "Series Reviews."

The Baja Adventure Book

by Walt Peterson, Wilderness Press, 1987, 246 pages, paper, $16.95

The author of this book has gathered together a remarkable amount of information on all those fun things to do in Baja California and where to do them, whether it be diving, fishing, boating, bicycling, hiking, kayaking, hunting, surfing, shell and mineral collecting, or cave exploring. Good maps and interesting photos supplement this top-notch guide.

The Baja Book III

by Tom Miller and Carol Hoffman, Baja Trail Publications, 1987 (14th ed.), 180 pages, paper, $11.95

A top-quality, often-praised, all-purpose guide, this is probably the best-known of the Baja books. It covers the practical essentials well and uses NASA space photos overlaid with maps of various sections of the peninsula to orient the traveler. All sorts of useful information is tied to kilometer markers along the way.

Baja California: A Travel Survival Kit
by Scott Wayne, Lonely Planet Publications, 1988, 192 pages, paper, $8.95

This is one of the popular Travel Survival Kit series, which is reviewed in more detail under "Series Reviews." The series is updated every two to three years.

Baja California Diver's Guide
by Michael and Lauren Farley, Marcor Publishing, 1984, 220 pages, paper, $12.95

This is a carefully prepared, comprehensive guide to the many excellent diving areas of Baja.

Berlitz: Mexico City
Macmillan Publishing, 1978, 128 pages, paper, $6.95

This is one of the small-format Berlitz Guide series, which is reviewed in more detail under "Series Reviews."

The Best Mexican Travel Tips
by John Whitman, Harper & Row, 1986, 387 pages, paper, $7.95

In this book, the author of the well-known *Best European Travel Tips* turns his experience and attention south of the border. The result is a vast collection of information that will help even veteran travelers save "money, time, and trouble." This very helpful work includes local customs, laws, and weather information.

Best Places to Stay in Mexico
by Bill and Cheryl Jamison, The Harvard Common Press, 1989, 400 pages, paper, $14.95

This is an anticipated addition to the excellent Best Places to Stay Guide series, which is reviewed in more detail under "Series Reviews." No fees are accepted for inclusion; the price and number of pages were approximate at press time.

Best Ski Touring in America
by Steve Barnett, Sierra Club Books, 1987, 288 pages, paper, $10.95

Including locations in Mexico, this book is reviewed under "North America as a Whole."

Birnbaum's Caribbean, Bermuda & the Bahamas
edited by Stephen Birnbaum, Houghton Mifflin, 1987, 786 pages, paper, $12.95

Birnbaum's Mexico
edited by Stephen Birnbaum, Houghton Mifflin, 1987, 558 pages, paper, $12.95

Both of these titles are part of the excellent Birnbaum's Guide series, which is reviewed in more detail under "Series Reviews." The Caribbean volume includes Mexico's Caribbean coast. These titles are updated annually.

Border Towns of the Southwest: Shopping, Dining, Fun & Adventure From Tijuana to Juarez
by Rick Cahill, Pruett Publishing, 1987, 200 pages, paper, $9.95
In this excellent idea for a guidebook, author Cahill provides the reader with a good overview of each town and, usually, a map. Recommended restaurants are nicely discussed and the few recommended hotels are listed without further comment (sometimes, in the smaller towns, there aren't any to recommend at all). Particularly in the more populous areas, there follows a very informative section on shopping.

Collier World Traveler Series: Mexico, Belize, Guatemala & the French Antilles
edited by Philippe Gloaguen and Pierre Josse, Macmillan Publishing, 1985, 192 pages, paper, $6.95
This book is part of the Collier World Traveler Guide series, which is reviewed in more detail under "Series Reviews."

Crown Insider's Guide to Mexico
by Michelle Richmond and Florence Lemkowitz, Crown Publishing, 1987, 336 pages, paper, $10.95
This is one of the Crown Insider's Guide series, which is reviewed in more detail under "Series Reviews."

Diver's Guide to Underwater Mexico
by Michael and Lauren Farley, Marcor Publishing, 1986, 270 pages, paper, $14.95
This is a comprehensive, well-researched diver's almanac to the excellent diving areas of Cozumel, Cancun, Isla Mujeres, the Sea of Cortez, Veracruz, Mexico's west coast, and Baja.

Diving and Snorkeling Guide to Cozumel
by George Lewbel, PBC International, 1984, 96 pages, paper, $9.95
This book is part of the Pisces Diving/Snorkeling Guide series, which is reviewed in more detail under "Series Reviews."

Eating Your Way Through Baja
by Tom Miller, Baja Trail Publications, 1986, 94 pages, paper, $4.95
After a quick primer on Spanish and an equally brief guide to picking up food in a grocery store or at a restaurant, the major part

of the book is spent detailing specific feeding spots—from taquerias and taco stands to cafeterias, steakhouses, and restaurants. Each is given an informative description and a rating.

Fielding's Mexico
by Lynne and Lawrence Foster, William Morrow & Co., 1988, 729 pages, paper, $12.95
This book is part of the Fielding's Travel Guide series, which is reviewed in more detail under "Series Reviews." The series is updated annually.

Fisher's World: Mexico
by Florence Lomkowitz, Fisher's World, Inc., 1988, 421 pages, paper, $14.95
This is one of the Fisher's World Guide series, which is reviewed in more detail under "Series Reviews." The series is updated annually.

Fodor's Cancun, Cozumel, Merida, and the Yucatan
Fodor's Travel Publications, 1987, 160 pages, paper, $8.95
This book is part of Fodor's City Guide series, which is reviewed in more detail under "Series Reviews." The series is updated annually.

Fodor's Fun in Acapulco
Fodor's Travel Publications, 1987, 128 pages, paper, $6.95
This is one of the Fodor's Fun Guide series, which is reviewed in more detail under "Series Reviews." The series is updated annually.

Fodor's Great Travel Values Mexico
Fodor's Travel Publications, 1987, 224 pages, paper, $6.95
This book is part of the budget-oriented Fodor's Great Travel Values Guide series, which is reviewed in more detail under "Series Reviews." The series is updated annually.

Fodor's Mexico's Baja & Puerto Vallarta, Mazatlan, Manzanillo, Copper Canyon
Fodor's Travel Publications, 1987, 160 pages, paper, $7.95
Fodor's Mexico
Fodor's Travel Publications, 1987, 532 pages, paper, $13.95
These two titles are part of Fodor's Country/Regional Guide series, which is reviewed in more detail under "Series Reviews." The series is updated annually.

Fodor's Mexico City and Acapulco

Fodor Travel Publications, 1987, 128 pages, paper, $6.95

This is one of Fodor's City Guide series, which is reviewed in more detail under "Series Reviews." The series is updated annually.

Frommer's Guide to Cancun, Cozumel, and the Yucatan

by Tom Brosnahan, Prentice Hall Press, 1987, 224 pages, paper, $5.95

Frommer's Guide to Mexico City and Acapulco

by Tom Brosnahan, Prentice Hall Press, 1987, 218 pages, paper, $5.95

These two titles are part of the Frommer's City Guide series, which is reviewed in more detail under "Series Reviews." The series is updated every two years.

Frommer's Mexico on $20 a Day

by Tom Brosnahan, Prentice Hall Press, 1986, 504 pages, paper, $10.95

This book is part of the Frommer's Dollar-a-Day Guide series, which is reviewed in more detail under "Series Reviews." Including sections on Belize and Guatemala, this title is updated every two years.

The Gringo's Guide to Acapulco

by Charles "Carlos" Winkler, Dialogue Publications, 1985, 110 pages, paper, $5.75

Winkler, a Chicago lawyer, has created a compact guide replete with detailed lists of recommended places to eat, sleep, visit, and play in various price ranges. It contains lots of good ideas and some excellent planning hints.

A Guide to Ancient Maya Ruins

by C. Bruce Hunter, University of Oklahoma Press, 1986 (2nd ed.), 342 pages, paper, $12.95

Hunter has provided a rich, scholarly work for the serious traveler interested in delving deep into the fascinating history and culture of these ancient Mexico, Guatemala, and Honduras.

Guide to the Yucatan Peninsula

by Chicki Mallan, Moon Publications, 1986, 300 pages, paper, $10.95

This may be the best guide to the Yucatan at present, particularly for the younger and slightly more adventurous crowd traveling without a car. It is a wonderfully constructed, all-purpose guide on every travel topic imaginable. Although the title is different, its similar format and content make it part of the excellent Moon Handbook series, which is reviewed in more detail under "Series Reviews."

Hidden Mexico: Adventurer's Guide to the Beaches and Coasts
by Rebecca Bruns, Ulysses Press, 1987, 433 pages, paper, $12.95
    This is a fine, well-reviewed addition to the growing Hidden Places Guide series, inspired by and modeled after the famous *Hidden Hawaii*. The series is reviewed in more detail under "Series Reviews" and is updated every two years.

Hildebrand's Travel Guide: Mexico
Hunter Publishing, 1986, 367 pages, paper, $10.95
    This book is part of the Hildebrand's Guide series, which is reviewed in more detail under "Series Reviews."

Insight Guide: Mexico
by Apa Productions, Prentice Hall Press, 1983, 423 pages, paper, $15.95
    This book is part of the acclaimed Insight Guide series, which is reviewed in more detail under "Series Reviews."

Let's Go: California & Hawaii
by Harvard Student Agencies, St. Martin's Press, 1988, 528 pages, paper, $10.95
Let's Go: Mexico
by Harvard Student Agencies, St. Martin's Press, 1988, 560 pages, paper, $10.95
    Both of these titles are part of the excellent, budget-oriented Let's Go Guide series, which is reviewed in more detail under "Series Reviews." The Mexico volume is particularly well known for its comprehensiveness, including a great deal of cultural information and detailed notes on ruins and museums. The California and Hawaii title includes Baja California. The series is updated annually.

The Magnificent Peninsula: The Only Absolutely Essential Guide to Mexico's Baja California
written and published by H. J. Williams, 1986, 248 pages, paper, $14.95
    In this self-published, excellent, all-purpose guide to Baja, Williams provides clear and useful information on numerous important topics, as well as a good overview of the entire area. Covered are transportation options, boating, fishing, hotels, border information, geology, vegetation, wildlife, and a large section on touring through Baja—from the border to Cabo San Lucas. Interesting side trips are

pointed out along the way, as well as special information concerning local history, geology, etc.

Maya Sites of the Yucatan
by Jacques and Parney Van Kirk, Great Outdoors Publishing, 1987, 78 pages, paper, $14.95

This large-format book contains short but informative descriptions of 31 Maya sites, principally in the Yucatan, but also in Guatemala and Belize. These are tied to a large fold-out map that shows general locations only. Numerous photos are provided and, interestingly, the text is in French and English. Mileage between sites is given and the string of 31 sites is given in logical travel order. More detailed travel information is not included.

Mexico: A Travel Survival Kit
by Doug Richmond, Lonely Planet Publications, 1985 (2nd ed.), 256 pages, paper, $7.95

This is one of the well-known Travel Survival Kit series, which is reviewed in more detail under "Series Reviews." Unfortunately, it is one title in the series that seems to get more than a few complaints. A new author is at work on a much larger, new edition which is expected out in late 1988 or 1989. The series is updated every two to three years.

Mexico in 22 Days
See *22 Days in Mexico* below.

Mexico: Places and Pleasures
by Kate Simon, Harper & Row, 1979 (3rd ed.), 408 pages, paper, $7.95

This wonderful book was still available at last report. The respected author, Kate Simon, possesses a clear depth of understanding of Mexico. She conveys her insights into the unique characteristics of this land, its geography, its archaeology, and its people. The practical tips may be totally out-of-date, but this beautifully written guide still has much to offer.

Motoring Mexico: The Best of Mexico's Auto Tours
by Joanne Harrier Barker and Jack Stone, Doubleday & Co., 1987, 442 pages, paper, $12.95

Helping travelers plan the best auto trips, these authors include information on the distances involved and time needed, and rate the highways for safety. They also provide a general orientation to each possible trip. Towns are rated and the places to stay and things to do well-detailed.

Nagel's Mexico
Passport Books, 1978, 576 pages, cloth, $39.95
This classic, cultural guide is part of the Nagel's Guide series, which is reviewed in more detail under "Series Reviews."

The New Holiday Guide to Mexico
M. Evans & Co., 1988 (10th ed.), 160 pages, paper, $4.95
This book is part of the Holiday Guide series, which is reviewed in more detail under "Series Reviews."

Pacific Boating Almanac: Southern California, Arizona, & Mexico
Western Marine Enterprises, 1987, 432 pages, paper, $10.95
This annual guide to the "how and where" of boating is part of the Boating Almanac series, which is reviewed in more detail under "Series Reviews."

The Pacific Coast of Mexico From Mazatlan to Ixtapa-Zihuatanejo: A Traveller's Guide
by Memo Barroso, Crown Publishers, 1986, 211 pages, paper, $8.95
Solid and well organized, covering all the topics of interest, this book is nonetheless a little dry. Hotel and restaurant selections are in all price ranges, but descriptions and evaluations are very short.

The People's Guide to Mexico
by Carl Franz, John Muir Publications, 1986 (6th ed.), 555 pages, paper, $13.95
This is one of those rare books that combine consistently enjoyable prose with hard, practical facts. It is a pleasure to read sections such as "Car Repairs," "Health," and the "Tourist and the Law." Franz covers it all—transportation, camping, restaurants, hotels, and more—with an emphasis on traveling inexpensively. Rather than choosing specific lodging or restaurants, he gives a first-class primer on *how* to choose.

Rail Ventures: The Comprehensive Planning Guide to Rail Travel in the United States, Canada and Mexico
Wayfinder Press, 1988 (3rd ed.), 352 pages, paper, $12.95
See "North America as a Whole."

Rand McNally: Mexico
by Mona King, Rand McNally & Co., 1986, 128 pages, paper, $5.95
This book is part of the Rand McNally Pocket Guide series, which is reviewed in more detail under "Series Reviews."

Romantic Inns of Mexico: A Selective Guide
by Toby Smith, Chronicle Books, 1986, 142 pages, paper, $7.95
Enjoyable, informative narratives on more than 40 of the best and most charming inns of Mexico are contained in this book. Two or three pages is spent describing each inn and a photo and all the practicalities accompany the text. Price ranges run the gamut, but are approximate, given the volatile Mexican economy.

The Rough Guide to Mexico
by John Fisher, Routledge & Kegan Paul, 1986, 232 pages, paper, $9.95
This is one of the consistently excellent Rough Guide series, which is reviewed in more detail under "Series Reviews." The series is updated every two to three years.

Schell's Guide to Yucatan and Neighboring States
by Rolfe and Lois Schell, Island Press, 1986, 288 pages, paper, $4.95
This little book would definitely not win a beauty contest, but there really is some quality inside. The crazy fluctuations of the peso will make prices difficult to interpret, but the information remains quite useful. There is a good overview on each area, including accommodations and restaurants in a variety of price ranges, transportation options, and sightseeing ideas, some of them less known to the tourist population.

South America On a Shoestring (including Mexico & Central America)
by Geoff Crowther, Lonely Planet Publications, 1986, 734 pages, paper, $14.95
See "South America as a Whole." This book is part of the budget-oriented On a Shoestring Guide series, which is reviewed in more detail under "Series Reviews." The series is updated every two to three years.

The South American Handbook (including Caribbean, Mexico and Central America)
edited by John Brooks, Rand McNally & Co., 1988 (64th ed.), 1341 pages, cloth, $28.95
This definitive, single-volume guide to South America, including Mexico, is reviewed under "South America as a Whole."

Staying Healthy in Asia, Africa, and Latin America
by Dirk Schroeder, Volunteers in Asia, 1988, 168 pages, paper, $7.95
This exellent health guide is reviewed under "Africa as a Whole."

Sunset: Mexico Travel Guide

Lane Publishing, 1983, 160 pages, paper, $9.95

Basically a planning and orientation book, this title is part of the Sunset Travel Guide series, which is reviewed in more detail under "Series Reviews."

Traveling Texas Borders: A Guide to the Best of Both Sides

by Ann Ruff, Gulf Publishing, 1983, 119 pages, paper, $9.95

Including Mexican border towns, this book is reviewed under "Texas."

22 Days in Mexico: The Itinerary Planner

by Steve Rogers and Tina Rosa, John Muir Publications, 1987, 136 pages, paper, $6.95

This is one of the Itinerary Planner series, which is reviewed in more detail under "Series Reviews." The title of this book is new, so it may also be found under *Mexico in 22 Days*.

Woodall's Tenting Directory

Woodall Publishing, 1987, 168 pages, paper, $7.95

This large-format guide to campsites appropriate for tent camping throughout the West includes locations in Mexico and is done in the same fashion as *Woodall's Campground Directory*, which is reviewed under "North America as a Whole." This book is updated annually.

Woodall's Western Campground Directory

Woodall Publishing, 1987, 642 pages, paper, $8.95

This large-format guide to camping in the West includes Mexico and is a section of *Woodall's Campground Directory*, which is reviewed under "North America as a Whole." Oriented to RV and car camping, this title is updated annually.

The Yucatan: A Guide to the Land of Maya Mysteries

by Antoinette May, Wide World Publishing, 1987, 251 pages, paper, $9.95

This is a respected guide to the Yucatan, emphasizing culture, orientation, and an better understanding of the area and its people. Such practicalities as hotels, restaurants, and shopping are not neglected, but these are clearly not the focus of the book. This is a lovely guide, especially for those who want something more than just nuts-and-bolts travel facts.

Yucatan, Mexico's Hidden Beaches and Ruins: A Traveller's Guide
by Memo Barroso, Crown Publishers, 1983, 189 pages, paper, $8.95
   The hotel and restaurant information in this book is long overdue
for an update, but the sightseeing information is still solid and well
organized.

Zihuatanejo & Ixtapa
by Grover Tate and B. Gaspard-Michel, Maverick Publications,
1986, 118 pages, paper, $5.95
   This well-written resource guide contains a bit of history and
thoughts on shopping, transportation, and regional foods, as well as
descriptive lists of bars, restaurants, and lodging—without any attempt to rate each place discussed. The text is bilingual; from page
89 on it is all in Spanish, repeating the first section in a more
condensed fashion.

UNITED STATES

United States as a Whole

See also "North America as a Whole."

All-Suite Hotel Guide: The Definitive Directory
by Pamela Lanier, John Muir Publications, 1987, 308 pages, paper,
$11.95
   This is a handy resource of hotels offering only suites (i.e., at least
two rooms with a closeable door in-between), sometimes at very
reasonable prices. Costs range from as low as $30 a night to terribly
expensive. But suites in all-suite hotels are almost always less expensive than the equivalent in a regular hotel—hence their charm.
Lanier describes over 600 suites, including all the essentials. No
critiques or ratings are evident and travel bookstores say that Lanier
charges a fee for inclusion.

**America On Display: A Guide to Unusual Museums and Collections
in the United States and Canada**
by Joyce Jurnovoy and David Jenness, Facts on File, 1987, 280
pages, cloth, $24.95
   See "North America as a Whole."

The American Garden Guidebook
by Everitt Miller and Jay Cohen, M. Evans & Co., 1987, 293 pages,
paper, $8.95
   This guide covers the eastern regions of the U.S. and Canada and
is reviewed under "New England."

America's Grand Resort Hotels: 80 Classic Resorts in the U.S. and Canada
by Rod Fensom, The Globe Pequot Press, 1985, 226 pages, paper, $10.95
Reviewed under "North America as a Whole."

America's Greatest Walks: A Traveler's Guide to 100 Scenic Adventures
by Gary Yanker and Carol Tarlow, Addison-Wesley Publishing, 1986, 257 pages, paper, $10.95
A wonderful collection of all sorts of walks for every need: challenging walks, casual walks, short walks, beach walks, mountain walks, city walks. Each walk selected is well described and accompanied by a good map. Also noted are length, difficulty, best times to go, and other special notes.

America's Historic Battlefields
by Irvin Haas, Hippocrene Books, 1987, 158 pages, paper, $14.95
This large-format book provides copious details on the many battlefields throughout America, including maps and photos.

America's Wonderful Little Hotels and Inns: Eastern Edition
edited by Sandra Soule, St. Martin's Press, 1988, 512 pages, paper, $13.95
America's Wonderful Little Hotels and Inns: Western Edition
edited by Sandra Soule, St. Martin's Press, 1988, 464 pages, paper, $13.95
These two fine guidebooks are reviewed under the U.S. Regionals: the Eastern Edition under "New England"; the Western Edition under "Rocky Mountain/Great Basin States."

Bed & Breakfast American Style
by Norman Simpson, Harper & Row, 1988, 446 pages, paper, $10.95
This book covers more than America and is reviewed under "North America as a Whole."

Bed & Breakfast Cookbook
by Pamela Lanier, Running Press, 1985, 142 pages, paper, $9.95
Lanier has collected some great recipes from nearly 200 B&Bs into this book. In the margin beside each recipe are the name, address, phone number, cost range (expensive, moderate, inexpensive), credit cards accepted, and a short description of the B&B from which the recipe came. If kept up-to-date, this may prove a fun way to choose your lodging.

Bed & Breakfast U.S.A.
by Betty Rundback and Nancy Kramer, E. P. Dutton, 1988, 650 pages, paper, $10.95
This book covers the U.S. and Canada and is reviewed under "North America as a Whole."

Berlitz: USA
Macmillan Publishing, 1986, 256 pages, paper, $8.95
This is one of the Berlitz Country Guide series, which is reviewed in more detail under "Series Reviews."

Best of the Best in the U.S.
National Bestseller Corp., 1988, 223 pages, paper, $14.95
Here are lots of specific vacation ideas arranged into chapters covering regal resorts, historic landmarks, theme and amusement parks, health spas, fishing and hunting spots, ethnic and historic villages, and high adventure. Within each chapter, selections are arranged regionally, and each is given an informative write-up, including the practical details and, often, a color photograph.

The Best Places to Eat in America: 50 Food Writers Pick the Don't Miss Restaurants in 50 Cities in the U.S. and Canada
by Janice Okun and Eleanor Ostman, Harper & Row, 1987, 416 pages, paper, $9.95
See "North America as a Whole."

Best Places to Stay in America's Cities: Unique Hotels, City Inns, and Bed and Breakfasts
edited by Kenneth Hale-Wehmann, The Harvard Common Press, 1986, 404 pages, paper, $9.95
This excellent guide covers 250 "best places" in varying price ranges in 42 of America's major cities. Among hotels, the focus is on the non-chain variety. This title is one of the Best Places to Stay Guide series, which is reviewed in more detail under "Series Reviews." No fees were collected for inclusion.

The Best Ski Touring in America
by Steve Barnett, Sierra Club Books, 1987, 288 pages, paper, $10.95
Covering Canada and Mexico, this book is reviewed under "North America as a Whole."

Bicycling Across America
by Robert Winning, Wilderness Press, 1988, 160 pages, paper, $11.95
Released after press time, this book contains route slips (46 in all)

for a trip from Santa Monica, California to Washington, D.C. A narrative section on points of interest, a schematic road map, and an elevation profile are included along with plenty of practical information on trips of any length.

Birnbaum's United States
edited by Stephen Birnbaum, Houghton Mifflin, 1024 pages, paper, $12.95

This book is part of the excellent Birnbaum's Guide series, which is reviewed in more detail under "Series Reviews." The series is updated annually.

Birnbaum's USA for Business Travelers
edited by Stephen Birnbaum, Houghton Mifflin, 1987, 614 pages, paper, $8.95

This typically classy Birnbaum book covers hotels, restaurants, business services, fitness centers, jogging routes, sightseeing, and special events in all the major business centers—information for the businessperson on the go. The structure and format of this book are similar to other Birnbaum titles and reading the review of Birnbaum's Guides in the "Series Reviews" section is suggested. This annually updated book is full of first-class selections in the moderate to expensive price range.

The Bus Traveler's Guide to the U.S.A.
On Our Way, Inc., 1986, 305 pages, paper, $12.95

Concise bus information, plus inexpensive places to stay and things to see and do along the route are contained in this real resource for the traveler by bus. Updates will need to be frequent to maintain the usefullness of this book.

Celebrations: America's Best Festivals, Jamborees, Carnivals & Parades
by Judith Young, Capra Press, 1986, 183 pages, paper, $10.95

Covering Canada, this book is reviewed under "North America as a Whole."

The Complete Guide to American Bed and Breakfast
by Rik and Nancy Barnes, Pelican Publishing, 1987 (2nd ed.), 600 pages, paper, $11.95

This edition covers about 1700 inns across America. All the practical data and some special features are noted, but information is scant on each, due to space limitations. This is a solid effort for a directory but perhaps covering fewer inns and more description from personal experience would make it a better book.

The Complete Guide to Cabins & Lodges in America's State and National Parks
by George Zimmerman, Little, Brown & Co., 1985, 475 pages, paper, $12.95
    This is a comprehensive, thoroughly researched listing and evaluation of overnight accommodations in nearly 300 state parks and 36 national parks. Zimmerman divides the book by region and provides some history of the park, its setting and facilities, activities available, some natural history notes, and infomation on lodging by the day or week.

The Economist Business Traveller's Guide: United States
Prentice Hall Press, 1987, 250 pages, paper, $17.95
    This book is part of the highly regarded Economist Business Traveller's Guide series, which is reviewed in more detail under "Series Reviews."

Elegant Small Hotels: A Connoisseur's Guide
by Pamela Lanier, John Muir Publications, 1987, 196 pages, paper, $13.95
    In this book, small means fewer than 200 rooms, and that usually means expensive. This is certainly the case here. However, as a resource on elegant, somewhat smaller hotels, this is a good one. Good descriptions, photographs, and all the practical data are included. The main drawback is a lack of critical reviews—each of these write-ups could easily be made up of part of the hotel's brochure.

Experiencing America's Past: A Travel Guide to Museum Villages
by Gerald and Patricia Gutek, John Wiley & Sons, 1986, 263 pages, paper, $12.95
    America's fascination with its past has stimulated the growth of special museum villages where the traveler can go to experience what life might have been like in an earlier era. Participants not only dress the part, but actually work and create, using the authentic methods of the time period. Gutek's guide provides the background information and complete details needed to plan a visit to over 40 of these special, historic places.

Exploring Our National Parks and Monuments
by Devereux Butcher, The Harvard Common Press, 1985 (8th ed.), 389 pages, paper, $14.95
    This classic volume, in print since 1947, describes 47 national parks, 26 national nature monuments, and 18 national archaeological monuments, including Alaska's newer parks. Each is well described

and accompanied by carefully selected photographs. This is a good single-source overview of the national parks and monuments system.

Ferries of America: A Guide to Adventurous Travel
by Sarah Wright, Peachtree Publishers, 1987, 347 pages, paper, $12.95

This is not so much a travel guide as a directory for the ferry enthusiast—an incredible assemblage of information on 270 possible ferry trips in 39 states. All the practical details are here, on the most famous to the most humble and obscure, and delightful anecdotes make browsing through this unique travel book a total delight.

Festivals U.S.A.
by Kathleen Hill, John Wiley & Sons, 1988, 242 pages, paper, $12.95

This great little book evolved out of the author's previous self-published book on festivals. The original title covered only the western states. The new title covers the entire country and lists over 1000 of the best festivals from the author's file of more than 9000. Every imaginable gathering worth its salt is described, including the pertinent details. Music festivals are a major category, but festivals of absolutely every sort are included. This is a fantastic planning directory.

The Field Guide to U.S. National Forests: Enchanted Lands for Hikers and Campers
by Robert Mohlenbrock, Congdon & Weed, 1984, 324 pages, paper, $11.95

This helpful, single-source resource to America's 153 National Forests provides a quick rundown on each, arranged regionally, including the types of terrain, wildlife, and activities, and where to write to get maps and brochures from the forest supervisor. Specific topographical maps are not detailed.

Fielding's Family Vacations USA
by Diane Torrens, William Morrow & Co., 1985, 544 pages, paper, $12.95

This book contains oodles of ideas for the best family vacations and the specific planning tools to make them a reality.

Fielding's Havens and Hideaways USA
by Thomas Tracy and James Ward, William Morrow & Co., 1983, 384 pages, paper, $7.95

This is a useful idea book but too dated to be much more. Included are interesting lodging options in those out-of-the-way, off-the-beaten-path kinds of places.

Fisher's World: USA

edited by Robert Fisher, Fisher's World, Inc., 1988, 800 pages, paper, $17.95

This is one of the Fisher's World Guide series, which is reviewed in more detail under "Series Reviews." This particular volume does not include a travel planner section as described in the series review. The series is updated annually.

Fodor's Great Travel Values: American Cities

Fodor's Travel Publications, 1987, 565 pages, paper, $13.95

This book is part of Fodor's Great Travel Values Guide series, which is reviewed in more detail under "Series Reviews." The series is updated annually.

Fodor's Selected Resorts and Hotels of the U.S.

Fodor's Travel Publications, 1987, 320 pages, paper, $10.95

Fodor seems to be branching out these days, and the quality of their special titles has been quite good. This is another solid effort with selections ranging from luxury suites to romantic country inns to beach resorts that welcome children. Also included are tennis and golf resorts, spas, guest ranches, and other family-oriented hotels.

Fodor's USA

Fodor's Travel Publications, 1987, 848 pages, paper, $15.95

This book is part of Fodor's USA Guide series, which is reviewed in more detail under "Series Reviews." The series is updated annually.

Frommer's Where to Stay USA

by the Council on International Educational Exchange, Prentice Hall Press, 1988, 480 pages, paper, $10.95

For those on a strict budget, here is an up-to-date guide to over 1700 places to stay priced from $3 to $30 a night. Included are dorms, YMCAs, hostels, B&Bs, motels, hotels, and campsites. Information on access for the disabled and special discounts for students and seniors is also included. The authors, the CIEE for short, have been instrumental in assisting students with their travel needs for over four decades. This is another one of those great resource guides that show up every now and then.

A Guide to America's Indians: Ceremonials, Reservations, and Museums

by Arnold Marquis, The University of Oklahoma Press, 1974, 267 pages, paper, $14.95

A finely written section on America's Indians and their history, arts, and politics, is followed by informational chapters on Indian ceremonials, buying arts and crafts, and camping with the Indians in this well-written cultural guide. The tribes of each of the five major regions of the country are discussed in some detail, and lists of major events are included. In spite of the age of this book, a considerable amount of its factual data should still be helpful.

Guide to Free Attractions

by Don Wright, Williamson Publishing, 1987, 635 pages, paper, $14.95

Arranged on a state-by-state basis, this thoroughly researched book lists more than 6000 free things to do while traveling. Even those not on a tight budget will find lots of great ideas for fun and entertainment.

Guide to Free USA Campgrounds

by Don Wright, Williamson Publishing, 1988, 640 pages, paper, $14.95

Designed as a supplement to the major campground directories, this helpful guide lists some 5000 no-charge campgrounds offering approximately 100,000 camping spaces. Many of the campgrounds offer hot showers and other "luxury" features at no charge. And free campgrounds have another plus: because they are not in the business of making money, they are often located in some of the prettiest, out-of-the-way places. This fine resource deserves a place in the glove compartment.

Great American Bridges and Dams

by Donald Jackson, Preservation Press, 1988, 360 pages, paper, $16.95

Released after press time, this is a unique travel guide, arranged regionally, to more than 300 of the best examples of bridges and dams across America. More than 550 illustrations are included.

Great American Movie Theatres

by David Naylor, Preservation Press, 1987, 276 pages, paper, $16.95

Copiously illustrated, this is the first in what will become a series on unique types of American architecture and design (see *Great American Bridges and Dams* above.) This guide focuses on those wonderful movie theaters that still abound. It is arranged regionally and is specifically intended for the traveler. Future titles of this type will look at lighthouses, interior spaces, roadside architecture, and gardens.

Great Vacations With Your Kids
by Dorothy Jordon and Marjorie Cohen, E. P. Dutton, 1988, 314 pages, paper, $9.95

Jordan and Cohen share their insights on traveling with children in this new title, released after press time.

The Healthiest Dining in America: A Guide to Wholesome Meals When Traveling
by Dee Ashley, Melius & Peterson Publishing, 1986, 231 pages, paper, $11.95

This is a guide to more than 200 restaurants, cafeterias, and even university food services, located coast-to-coast, that can adapt to a wide variety of diets—sodium-free, low fat, high fiber, gluten-free, etc.—and help travelers follow the doctor's orders while on the road. Some vegetarian choices are included. A few selections are available in almost every state.

Hosteling USA: The Official American Youth Hostels Handbook
The Globe Pequot Press, 1985 (3rd ed.), 208 pages, paper, $7.95

This book is a detailed listing of more than 270 lodges run by American Youth Hostels. Included are maps, directions, and descriptions of each facility.

Insight Guide: Crossing America
by Apa Productions, Prentice Hall Press, 1986, 338 pages, paper, $15.95

This book is part of the acclaimed Insight Guide series, which is reviewed in more detail under "Series Reviews."

Let's Go: USA
by Harvard Student Agencies, St. Martin's Press, 1988, 976 pages, paper, $11.95

This wonderful piece of work, chock full of value, is part of the excellent, budget-oriented Let's Go Guide series, which is reviewed in more detail under "Series Reviews." The series is updated annually.

Mariani's Coast-to-Coast Dining Guide
edited by John Mariani, Times Books, 1986, 866 pages, paper, $12.95

Restaurant critics from each locale offer their choices of the best restaurants in 50 major U.S. cities in this great resource guide for people who visit many of the major U.S. cities in their travels. These are not just the expensive spots that can eat up a month's savings in several hours. Rather, a wide range of appealing choices, including inexpensive hometown food that accentuates the best dishes of each region, is listed. The evaluations are crisp and informative, and will hopefully be kept up-to-date.

Mobil Travel Guide: Major Cities
Prentice Hall Press, 1988, 441 pages, paper, $8.95
This is one of the Mobil Travel Guide series, which is reviewed in more detail under "Series Reviews." The series is updated annually.

National Directory of Free Tourist Attractions
edited by Raymond Carlson and Maria Maiorino, Pilot Books, 1987, 78 pages, paper, $3.95
This directory lists more than 1100 no-charge things to do throughout America. Included are addresses, phone numbers, and hours open to the public.

The National Seashores: The Complete Guide to America's Scenic Coastal Parks
by Ruthe and Walt Wolverton, Woodbine House, 1988, 200 pages, paper, $9.95
The nation's ten national seashores are featured in this new title, released after press time. For each park, historical background information and overviews of the special attractions at each location are listed.

Official Guide to American Historic Bed & Breakfast Inns and Guesthouses
Association of American Historic Inns, 1987, 288 pages, paper, $14.95
This is a directory of historic lodging spots, with more than 2000 member inns briefly described, including line drawings of many. An additional appendix lists other non-member inns located in historic buildings. These are not reviews but helpful summaries of the most historic locations to stay.

Quilt Collections: A Directory for the United States and Canada
by Lisa Oshins, Acropolis Books, 1987, 255 pages, paper, $18.95
See "North America as a Whole."

Rail Ventures: The Comprehensive Planning Guide to Rail Travel in the United States, Canada and Mexico
Wayfinder Press, 1988 (3rd ed.), 352 pages, paper, $12.95
See "North America as a Whole."

Rand McNally National Park Guide
by Michael Frome, Rand McNally & Co., 1987 (21st ed.), 246 pages, paper, $11.95
This is an annual volume on the entire National Park system. A good overview is provided, sometimes with the appropriate Rand McNally road map, followed by a practical guide, generally of several pages, on things like trails, visitor's centers, camping, accommodations, and things to see and do nearby. Separate chapters on historical areas, archaeological sites, natural and recreational areas, and a guide to lodging in and near the National Parks are included in this good overview of the complete system.

Rand McNally Vacation Places Rated: Finding the Best Vacation Places in America
by Sylvia McNair, Rand McNally & Co., 1986, 218 pages, paper, $12.95
Rating 107 potential vacation spots, this book uses a scoring system that gives points for the categories of Blessings of Nature, Fun in the Great Outdoors, Basic Necessities, Discovering Our Heritage, Feeding the Mind and Spirit, and Entertainment for All. Some favor wild, outdoor settings, while others favor cities, but the results basically say there are no real losers in the entire list.

Reader's Digest: Off the Beaten Path—A Guide to More Than 1000 Scenic & Interesting Places Still Uncrowded and Inviting
The Reader's Digest Association, 1987, 384 pages, cloth, $23.95
The editors of this *Reader's Digest* project have compiled an excellent selection of things to do that are either literally off the beaten path or are unusual or less frequented places in towns or well-known parks throughout the country. The layout is arranged regionally.

Roadfood and Goodfood
by Jane and Michael Stern, Alfred Knopf, Inc., 1986, 561 pages, paper, $10.95
In this highly praised book, the Sterns offer excellent descriptions/ evaluations of restaurants of every sort, each selected to reflect the best quality and value as well as the best of regional cuisine specialties. Most selections are in a very reasonable price range.

Romantik Hotels and Restaurants: Charming Historic Hotels in Europe and the United States

by the Romantik Hotel and Restaurant Association, The Harvard Common Press, 1988, 290 pages, paper, $6.95
See "Europe as a Whole."

The Senior Citizen's Guide to Budget Travel in the United States and Canada

by Paige Palmer, Pilot Books, 1987, 62 pages, paper, $3.95
See "North America as a Whole."

State and National Parks: Lodges and Cabins

by John Thaxton, Burt Franklin–Publisher, 1987, 623 pages, paper, $9.95

This is a very comprehensive, annually produced guide to accommodations in our state and national parks. Each park is briefly described as to its size, general features, facilities, and types of activities, and is followed by a summary of the types of lodging to choose from and instructions on how to make reservations.

Steam Passenger Service Directory

Empire State Railway Museum, 1987, 213 pages, paper, $6.50

This is an illustrated directory listing tourist railroad, trolley, and museum operations with regularly scheduled or intermittent service throughout the United States.

Traveling Jewish in America: The Complete Guide for Business & Pleasure

edited by Ellen Chernofsky, Wandering You Press, 1987 (2nd ed.), 472 pages, paper, $9.95

This thorough, no-nonsense, up-to-date guide to cities and towns throughout America includes synagogues, temples, accommodations, and food sources (either local stores with the best selection of kosher products or places to eat out where available). No city is too small to be included in this most comprehensive work. For practical detail to the essentials of U.S. travel in a single volume, this is the best and most up-to-date resource.

USA by Bus and Train

by Gary Hawkins, Pantheon Books, 1985, 396 pages, paper, $9.95

This is a well-written, thorough description of 27 different tours of America by bus and/or train. Included are descriptions of things to see and do in the towns along the way, and other practical advice. Hawkins writes in an entertaining style; his "face to face" sections on various destinations are most enjoyable. A directory section of resources, services, and useful addresses is quite extensive.

Vagabonding in the U.S.A.: A Guide to Independent Travel
written and published by Ed Buryn, 1983, 423 pages, paper, $10.95

Vagabonding, according to author Ed Buryn, is first an attitude, then a technique. With this philosophy, Buryn provides a lot of practical, down-to-earth information for would-be, latter-day hippies. Some real nuts-and-bolts stuff is here, if a little crazily (not to mention hilariously) presented at times. This is a unique and positively wonderful guidebook—and fun to read, too.

Where to Eat in America
by William Rice and Barbara Goldman, Charles Scribner's Sons, 1987, 379 pages, paper, $12.95

Covering Canada as well as the United States, this book is reviewed under "North America as a Whole."

The Woman's Travel Guide
by Jane Lasky and Brenda Fine, G. K. Hall & Co., 1986, 534 pages, paper, $12.95

Tips on local customs, restaurants, clubs, transportation, shopping, and hotels in 25 major American cities are contained in this resource.

Regions of the United States
Regions are arranged geographically from east to west. Please note the composition of each region.

NEW ENGLAND
See also "United States as a Whole." The New England States are Connecticut, Maine, Massachusetts, New Hampshire, Rhode Island, and Vermont.

The American Garden Guidebook
by Everitt Miller and Jay Cohen, M. Evans & Co., 1987, 293 pages, paper, $8.95

This comprehensive guide to 339 gardens in 28 eastern states and four eastern Canadian provinces is crammed with data on each garden, its location, its special attributes, hours, fees, tours, and wheelchair access. This guide is a great help for narrowing down the choices, with "don't miss" and "excellent" categories.

American Jewish Landmarks: A Travel Guide and History, Volume 1: The East
by Bernard Postal and Lionel Koppman, Fleet Press, 1977, 400 pages, paper, $18.95
    This book is part of the four-volume American Jewish Landmarks series, which is reviewed in more detail under "Series Reviews."

America's Wonderful Little Hotels and Inns: Eastern Edition
edited by Sandra Soule, St. Martin's Press, 1988, 512 pages, paper, $13.95
    The highly regarded Eastern Edition covers states east of the Mississippi, states along the Mississippi's western bank, Puerto Rico, and eastern Canadian provinces. The book depends heavily on reader feedback. No inn is listed that has not had a favorable review from its guests. Sometimes reader's letters are not very specific in their assessment, but the comments offered are honest and often very revealing. The book is updated annually.

Appalachian Whitewater, Volume III: The Northern Mountains
by John Connelly and John Porterfield, Menasha Ridge Press, 1987, 140 pages, paper, $13.95
    This large-format guide to the premier canoeing and kayaking streams of Connecticut, Massachusetts, Vermont, New Hampshire, Maine, and Eastern New York State is part of the Appalachian Whitewater Guide series, which is reviewed in more detail under "Series Reviews."

The Art Museums of New England
by S. Lane Faison, Jr., David Godine—Publisher, 1982, 463 pages, cloth, $35.00
The Art Museums of New England: Connecticut & Rhode Island
by S. Lane Faison, Jr., David Godine—Publisher, 1982, 111 pages, paper, $8.95
The Art Museums of New England: New Hampshire, Vermont & Maine
by S. Lane Faison, Jr., David Godine–Publisher, 1982, 101 pages, paper, $8.95
The Art Museums of New England: Massachusetts
by S. Lane Faison, Jr., David R. Godine–Publisher, 1982, 251 pages, paper, $9.95
    This is one of three paperbacks that have been drawn from the superb, hardbound *Art Museums of New England*, which is reviewed under "New England."
    These books come in either one hardback volume or three paperback volumes (the fourth is listed under Massachusetts). In whatever

format, this beautifully done, superbly crafted, comprehensive work—a publishing work of art—is an authoritative guide to the more than 100 museums housing the art treasures of the New England area. The detail and the amount of research in these books in astonishing. Although some changes have no doubt occurred since its last revision, this book is clearly *the* resource to buy.

Away for the Weekend, New England: Great Getaways for Every Season of the Year Throughout the Six New England States

by Eleanor Bermon, Crown Publishers, 1985, 288 pages, paper, $9.95

Away for the Weekend, New York: Great Getaways Less Than 200 Miles from New York City for Every Season of the Year

by Eleanor Bermon, Crown Publishers, 1988 (2nd revised ed.), 256 pages, paper, $11.95

These books are part of the Away for the Weekend Guide series, which is reviewed in more detail under "Series Reviews." The New York title includes various New England destinations in Connecticut, Rhode Island, and Massachusetts.

Bed & Breakfast Guide: East Coast

by Roberta Garner, *et al.*, Prentice Hall Press, 1986, 160 pages, paper, $12.95

This book covers 119 inns in the New England and Mid-Atlantic states. Each is given a good description with practical details, directions, and interior and exterior color photographs.

Bed and Breakfast in New England

by Bernice Chesler, The Globe Pequot Press, 1987, 494 pages, paper, $11.95

The companion volume to *Bed & Breakfast in the Mid-Atlantic States*, this popular book has been called the best of all the B&B guides. Although places selected are charged a fee for inclusion, Chesler's honest and thorough appraisals have won her a wide following. Included here are 210 that meet her specifications (10 or fewer rooms, a common room, no public restaurant or bar on the premises, owner occupants, breakfast included with the rate). An index of 300 reservation services in the U.S. and Canada (no fee charged for inclusion) is also included in this fun-to-read and informative guide that is updated every two years.

Bed and Breakfast Inns of New England
by Deborah Patton, Yankee Books, 1987, 192 pages, paper, $9.95
    This informative book describes slightly under 100 B&Bs and gives each an excellent two-page write-up. Small, homey places as well as larger, historic inns in all price ranges are included.

The Best of Daytripping & Dining in Southern New England and Nearby New York
by Betsy Witteman and Nancy Webster, Wood Pond Press, 1985, 186 pages, paper, $7.95
    These two experienced authors have a real knack for assembling great itineraries for outings of every sort. This book offers 25 day trips in Massachusetts, Rhode Island, Connecticut, and adjacent areas of New York. They are thoughtfully arranged and include places to see, locations to eat, and clear, hand-drawn detail maps.

Best Places to Stay in New England
by Christina Tree and Bruce Shaw, The Harvard Common Press, 1988 (revised ed.), 456 pages, paper, $14.95
    This book is part of the excellent Best Places to Stay Guide series, which is reviewed in more detail under "Series Reviews." Each selection has been carefully evaluated and no fee has been accepted for inclusion.

Budget Dining & Lodging in New England
by Fran and Frank Sullivan, The Globe Pequot Press, 1988, 288 pages, paper, $9.95
    This book is a must for travelers seeing the New England countryside on a tight budget. It covers hundreds of delightful places to stay and eat, proving that reasonably priced selections are everywhere in New England.

Canoe Camping Vermont & New Hampshire Rivers
by Roioli Schweiker, Backcountry Publications, 1985 (2nd ed.), 128 pages, paper, $6.95
Canoeing Massachusetts, Rhode Island and Connecticut
by Ken Weber, Backcountry Publications, 1986, 160 pages, paper, $7.95
    Both of these guides are part of the Backcountry Canoeing Guide series, which is reviewed in more detail under "Series Reviews."

Classic Diners of the Northeast
by Donald Kaplan and Alan Bellink, Faber and Faber, 1980, 160 pages, paper, $9.95
    This wonderful little guide was unfortunately not updated when

it was reprinted in 1986. As the new introduction says, "Many places described within these pages may be renovated beyond recognition as a classic diner." And, of course, prices have changed as well. Nonetheless, this remains a worthwhile little guide, emphasizing as it does the history and atmosphere of each old-fashioned diner described. The photos included reveal the classic architecture; the narrative provides some down-home talk with the equally classic folks inside. This books covers New England, New Jersey and New York.

Coastal Daytrips in New England
by Harriet Webster, Yankee Books, 1986 (2nd ed.), 192 pages, paper, $9.95
Yankee Books has another "Daytrips" book, but this one sticks firmly to the New England coastline. *Coastal Daytrips* includes many interesting, well-researched suggestions for fun along the New England coast.

The Condo Lux Vacationer's Guide to Condominium Rentals in the Mountain Resorts
by Jill Little, Random House, 1986, 340 pages, paper, $9.95
Including Vermont and New Hampshire, this book is part of the Condo Lux Guide series, which is reviewed in more detail under "Series Reviews."

Country Inns of America: Lower New England (Connecticut, Massachusetts, and Rhode Island)
Henry Holt & Co., 1985 (revised ed.), 112 pages, paper, $10.95
Country Inns of America: Upper New England (Maine, New Hampshire, and Vermont)
Henry Holt & Co., 1985 (revised ed.), 112 pages, paper, $10.95
The strength of these books lies in the number of color photographs, revealing each inn both inside and out, that they contain. Both titles are part of the large-format Country Inns of America Guide series, which is reviewed in more detail under "Series Reviews."

Country Inns, Lodges & Historic Hotels: New England States
by Anthony Hitchcock and Jean Lindgren, Burt Franklin–Publisher, 1987 (10th ed.), 284 pages, paper, $8.95
This book is part of the Compleat Traveler's Companions series, which is reviewed in more detail under "Series Reviews." No fees are accepted for inclusion in this annually updated guide.

A Critical Guide to Cross-Country Ski Areas: The Best of New England's Touring Centers

by Raymond Elman, Viking Penguin, 1987, 159 pages, paper, $9.95

This critical, well-organized overview of many of the best ski touring centers in New England has plenty of practical information on getting there, food, lodging, and prices.

Cross-Country Ski Inns of the Eastern U.S. and Canada

by Marge Lamy, The Stephen Greene Press, 1986, 128 pages, paper, $12.95

This beautiful, large-format book is filled with color photos and has an informative text to help skiers choose among some wonderful possibilities.

A Cyclist's Guide: New England Over the Handlebars

by Michael Farny, Little, Brown & Co., 1975, 174 pages, paper, $9.95

Old, but still available, this guide provides some good ideas for cycling trips—38 in all—from a few hours to four days in length. A mileage log and personal observations are included.

Day Trips and Budget Vacations in New England

by Patricia & Robert Foulke, The Globe Pequot Press, 1988 (2nd ed.), 264 pages, paper, $8.95

This book describes fourteen thorough, flexible, dependable itineraries for vacation fun. Everything is included—from things the kids might enjoy to ways to stay within a tight budget. Destinations are both well-known and off the beaten path.

Earth Treasures, Volume 1: The Northeastern Quadrant

by Allen Eckert, Harper & Row, 1987, 336 pages, cloth (flexible), $14.95

This guide to collecting minerals, rocks, and fossils is part of the comprehensive Earth Treasures series, which is reviewed in more detail under "Series Reviews."

Factory Store Guide to All New England

by A. Miser and A. Pennypincher, The Globe Pequot Press, 1984 (6th ed.), 249 pages, paper, $5.95

Long a popular guide to inexpensive shopping, this edition, though getting old, covers 600 factory stores, outlets, and complexes in rapid-fire fashion. Each has been visited and assessed on an anonymous basis. Included are essential details like hours and directions, along with features of note for each store.

Favorite Daytrips in New England
by Michael Schuman, Yankee Books, 1987 (4th ed.), 192 pages, paper, $9.95
A New England favorite now in its fourth edition, this well-written little guide presents 40 interesting trips calculated to take a day or less. Thorough and well-researched, these outings are for the whole family or for only two.

Favorite Weekends in New England
by Harriet Webster, Yankee Books, 1986, 192 pages, paper, $8.95
This book presents a diverse, well-organized collection of suggested trips for the weekend, such as ski tours, museums, and summer theatres. Information on how to get there and appropriate phone numbers is also included.

Fisher's World: New England
by Sylvia McNair, Fisher's World, Inc., 1988, 309 pages, paper, $14.95
This book is part of the Fisher's World Guide series, which is reviewed in more detail under "Series Reviews." The series is updated annually.

Fodor's I-95
Fodor's Travel Publications, 1986, 215 pages, paper, $6.95
Covering I-95 from Maine to Miami, this book is part of Fodor's Interstate Guide series, which is reviewed in more detail under "Series Reviews."

Fodor's New England
Fodor's Travel Publications, 1987, 496 pages, paper, $11.95
This book is part of Fodor's Country/Regional Guide series, which is reviewed in more detail under "Series Reviews." The series is updated annually.

Frommer's Dollarwise Guide to New England
by Tom Brosnahan, Prentice Hall Press, 1988, 408 pages, paper, $12.95
This book is part of Frommer's Dollarwise Guide series, which is reviewed in more detail under "Series Reviews." This series emphasizes selections in the moderate price range and is updated every two years.

Frommer's Dollarwise Guide to Skiing USA East
by I. William Berry, Prentice Hall Press, 1988, 266 pages, paper, $11.95

This book covers ski resorts throughout the eastern U.S. and eastern Canada, including those of Massachusetts, Maine, New Hampshire, and Vermont. Arranged in identical fashion to the western edition of the same name, which is reviewed under "The Rocky Mountain/Great Basin States," this guide is updated every two years.

Getaways for Gourmets in the Northeast
by Nancy Webster and Richard Woodworth, Wood Pond Press, 1988 (2nd ed.), 474 pages, paper, $12.95

While covering places to stay, this book is primarily a gourmet's guide to good food in those out-of-the-way places. The descriptions and evaluations are extensive and, besides lodging choices, other gourmet treats for each of the 18 getaway spots selected are listed. This is an excellent book.

Great Family Trips in New England and Its Neighbors
by Harriet Webster, Yankee Books, 1988, 192 pages, paper, $9.95

Released after press time, this new guidebook covers more than 100 attractions of interest to children.

The Great Weekend Escape Book from Virginia to Vermont
by Michael Spring, E. P. Dutton, 1987 (3rd ed.), 417 pages, paper, $10.95

Written in a friendly style, this excellent book covers the gamut: major attractions, the arts, antiques and crafts, tours, walks, biking, fishing, riding, skiing, golf, things for kids, after-hours options, and, of course, food and lodging.

Guide to Cross-Country Skiing in New England
by Lyn and Tony Chamberlain, The Globe Pequot Press, 1986, 216 pages, paper, $8.95

New England may be small but it is a skier's paradise, for this region alone has 161 ski touring centers. The authors of this excellent resource guide have carefully and thoroughly organized all the essential information, including a well-written narrative, to help ski enthusiasts choose among so many options.

A Guide to New England's Landscape
by Neil Jorgensen, The Globe Pequot Press, 1977, 256 pages, paper, $7.95

This easy-to-understand guide to New England's geography, geology, and botany is written in a pleasing and entertaining style.

Guide to the National Park Areas: Eastern States
by David and Kay Scott, The Globe Pequot Press, 1987 (2nd ed.), 272 pages, paper, $10.95
See "The South."

Guide to the Recommmended Country Inns of New England
by Elizabeth Squier, The Globe Pequot Press, 1987 (10th ed.), 453 pages, paper, $10.95
This is a widely acclaimed title in the respected Recommended Country Inns series, which is reviewed in more detail under "Series Reviews." The author has visited and evaluated every inn and has accepted no payment for inclusion. This book is updated every two years.

Guide to the Restaurants of New England
by New England Monthly, Little, Brown & Co., 1987, 181 pages, paper, $8.95
This book is a compilation of more than 300 restaurant reviews from the *New England Monthly* magazine. Each is well written, with good descriptions of food and atmosphere along with the occasional complaint. Practical facts are included: hours, credit cards accepted, and location. Price run the gamut.

A Guide to Writers' Homes in New England
by Miriam Levine, Applewood Books, 1984, 186 pages, paper, $10.95
Nineteen homes of famous writers are chronicled in this interesting work. A pretty line drawing of the home and a photo of the writer precedes some history on the house, its relationship to the writer's life, a bibliographic essay, and other notes. The goal is to "give the traveler and reader a complete picture of what life must have been like in these houses..." The writing style is a bit short and matter-of-fact, but this is nonetheless a fine book. Information on visiting (address, phone, hours, admission fees) is included. Check first, though, for some of these details may have changed.

The Handbook for Beach Strollers from Maine to Cape Hatteras
by Donald Zinn, The Globe Pequot Press, 1985 (2nd ed.), 246 pages, paper, $9.95
Providing a wonderful compendium of botanical and zoological information to enhance any sojourn to the eastern seaboard by the budding naturalist, this book is for the thalassopsammonphile (a.k.a. beach lover). The book is somewhat "textbook" in its syntax, yet the author's love of the subject shines through, keeping it readable

even for the non-scientist. It is arranged by types of ocean life and even includes the author's sea-source recipes.

Hiking from Inn to Inn: Wilderness Walking Tours with Comfortable Overnight Lodging from Maine to Virginia
by David and Kathleen MacInnes, The Globe Pequot Press, 1982, 191 pages, paper, $7.95

This book is well conceived and well executed, although clearly in need of revision. Thirteen routes are described step-by-step, with a bit of history and lore thrown in. Mileage and elevations are included for each route.

Indian Mounds of the Atlantic Coast: A Guide to Sites from Maine to Florida
by Jerry McDonald and Susan Woodward, McDonald and Woodward Publishing, 1987, 162 pages, paper, $12.95

See "The Mid-Atlantic States."

INNSpiration Northeast: A Guide to Small Country Inns
edited by Robert Bendix, Inns-piration Guide Publishing, 1986, 301 pages, paper, $12.95

Each inn selected for inclusion here meets Robert Bendix's exacting criteria (15 rooms or less, one or more common rooms, quality breakfasts and dinners, quiet and attractive setting, and absence of commercialism). Each of the 88 chosen are given a photo, a thumbnail sketch of all essentials, the author's own astute comments, and comments from two house guests. No fees or gratuities are accepted for inclusion. The result is an excellent, thoroughly researched guide to the very best small country inns of the Northeast. Note: Rhode Island is not included in this edition, but, a second edition is due out May, 1989.

Inn Spots & Special Places in New England
by Nancy Webster and Richard Woodworth, Wood Pond Press, 1986, 334 pages, paper, $11.95

Thirty recommended places to visit, 200 places to stay, 300 places to eat, and 400 sights to see and things to do are outlined in this book. The descriptions and evaluations are thorough, very personal, and most helpful.

Inside Outlets: The Best Bargain Shopping in New England
by Naomi Rosenberg and Marianne Sekulow, The Harvard Common Press, 1985, 204 pages, paper, $8.95

This comprehensive guide to factory outlets throughout New England provides a vast array of choices in every price range for most every type of good imaginable, all at prices that are up to 75% less than retail. The authors have also assembled shopping itineraries for particularly scenic areas of New England. They give plenty of tips on what to look for, what to avoid, and where the very best "Blue Ribbon" stores are—though time may have had its effect on some.

Insight Guide: New England
by Apa Productions, Prentice Hall Press, 1986, 344 pages, paper, $15.95
This is one of the acclaimed Insight Guide series, which is reviewed in more detail under "Series Reviews."

The Interstate Gourmet: New England
by Neal Weiner and David Schwartz, Summit Books, 1986, 300 pages, paper, $6.95
Unfortunately, at press time this title was out of print. It has been included because it is part of the excellent Interstate Gourmet Guide series, which is reviewed in more detail under "Series Reviews." Perhaps there will be a new edition soon.

Island Hopping in New England
by Mary Maynard, Yankee Books, 1986, 176 pages, paper, $8.95
Here is a well-organized guide to the dozens of offshore hideaways on the many islands along the New England coast, with good descriptions and revealing photos. How to access each island, where to stay, and what to do upon arrival are all addressed.

Land's Edge: A Natural History of Barrier Beaches from Maine to North Carolina
by Michael Hoel, The Globe Pequot Press, 1986, 140 pages, paper, $6.95
This interesting field book details how the early inhabitants used the barrier beaches, how the beaches were formed, how dunes and pocket marshes develop, and introduces travelers to the plants and animals that live in these areas, the effects of storms on the area, and loads of other intriguing facts.

Marilyn Wood's Wonderful Weekends
by Marilyn Wood, Prentice Hall Press, 1987, 680 pages, paper, $11.95
This is definitely one of the great getaway guides for those living in the New York area. It describes 25 general destination areas in detail, offering travelers an incredible variety of choices for events, lodging, dining, walking tours, sightseeing, and other activities. Included are knowledgeable, extensive reviews of more than 450 inns

and 700 restaurants. The maps are clear and well done. This is a wonderful resource to destinations within 200 miles of the Big Apple.

Michelin Green Guide: New England
Michelin Guides and Maps, 1986 (3rd ed.), 214 pages, paper, $10.95
This is one of the excellent titles in the Michelin Green Guide sightseeing series, which is reviewed in more detail under "Series Reviews."

Mobil Travel Guide: Lodging for Less, Northeast and Midwest
Prentice Hall Press, 1988, 250 pages, paper, $5.95
This series is something new from Mobil in 1988: an annual guide to inexpensive lodging, fully inspected and star-rated in the typical Mobil fashion. This new, three-volume series, Mobil Lodging for Less Guides, is reviewed in more detail under "Series Reviews."

Mobil Travel Guide: Northeastern States
Prentice Hall Press, 1988, 370 pages, paper, $8.95
This book is part of the well-known, large-format Mobil Travel Guide series, which is reviewed in more detail under "Series Reviews." The series is updated annually.

New England Bed & Breakfast Book
by Corinne Ross, The Globe Pequot Press, 1986, 192 pages, paper, $8.95
This is one of the Bed & Breakfast Book series, which is reviewed in more detail under "Series Reviews."

New England Gardens Open to the Public
by Rolce Payne, David Godine–Publisher, 1979, 230 pages, cloth, $20.00
Excellent descriptions and illustrations of 150 gardens available to the public are included in this first-rate though somewhat dated resource. Information on the seasons each is open, hours, and admission charges, if any, is provided. Considering the publication date, call ahead and determine current hours and admission charges. Phone numbers are listed for those places charging an admission fee, and many locations are without any charges at all.

New England in 22 Days
See *22 Days in New England* below.

New England's Special Places: A Daytripper's Guide
by Michael Schuman, The Countryman Press, 1986, 192 pages, paper, $10.95
This wonderful guidebook contains short, beautifully crafted essays on 44 New England destinations that offer a real insight into the New England character, can be reached from almost anywhere in New England in a day's time, and are all of such quality that the author feels he could recommend them to a friend. What he has chosen covers a wide range: colonial New England locations, presidents' homes, special historic sites like the New England Maple Museum or the Saugus Iron Works National Historic Site, castles, mansions, even special sports and games museums. This great selection will delight the whole family.

One-Day Adventures by Car: A Guide to Day Trips from New York City
by Lida Newberry and Joy Johannessen, Hastings House, 1986 (5th ed.), 348 pages, paper, $10.95
Including trips into Connecticut and Massachusetts, this book is reviewed under "New York."

Oscar Israelowitz's Guide to Jewish U.S.A., Volume I: The Northeast
by Oscar Israelowitz, Talman Co., 1987, 334 pages, paper, $9.95
This is an excellent resource for both the Jewish history of this region and current lists of kosher restaurants, hotels, butchers, bakeries, synagogues, milvehs, chabad houses, museums, landmarks, etc. An added intriguing feature is a chapter on "The Old Neighborhoods" for those who would like to find the still extant old synagogues from the original communities now used for other purposes.

Secluded Islands of the Atlantic Coast
by David Yeadon, Crown Publishers, 1984, 224 pages, paper, $8.95
In this book, David Yeadon directs his considerable talent toward an array of little-known and relatively unspoiled islands along the Atlantic seaboard. His illustrations and charming, informative writing illuminate some interesting vacation ideas.

The Sierra Club Guide to the National Parks of the East and Middle West
Sierra Club Books, 1984, 300 pages, cloth, $14.95
This book is part of the Sierra Club National Parks Guide series, which is reviewed in more detail under "Series Reviews."

The Sierra Club Naturalist's Guide to the Middle Atlantic Coast: Cape Hatteras to Cape Cod
by Bill Perry, Sierra Club Books, 1985, 448 pages, paper, $12.95
The Sierra Club Naturalist's Guide to the North Atlantic Coast: Cape Cod to Newfoundland
by Michael and Deborah Berrill, Sierra Club Books, 1981, 512 pages, paper, $12.95
The Sierra Club Naturalist's Guide to Southern New England
by Neil Jorgensen, Sierra Club Books, 1978, 448 pages, paper, $12.95
The Sierra Club Naturalist's Guide to the Piedmont of Eastern North America
by Michael Godfrey, Sierra Club Books, 1980, 432 pages, paper, $9.95

These four titles are part of this excellent natural history series, Sierra Club Naturalist's Guides, which is reviewed in more detail under "Series Reviews."

Special Museums of the Northeast: A Guide to Uncommon Collections from Maine to Washington, D.C.
by Nancy Frazier, The Globe Pequot Press, 1985, 304 pages, paper, $9.95

This is a good overview of 144 smaller but nonetheless fascinating museums covering a vast array of subjects, such as locks, soups, computers, antique toys, baseball, photography, dogs, and almost everything else imaginable.

Trips for Those Over 50
by Harriet Webster, Yankee Books, 1988, 176 pages, paper, $9.95

The title doesn't tell you, but this book, released after press time, lists more than two dozen New England destinations "for every season and lifestyle."

22 Days in New England: The Itinerary Planner
by Arnold Schuchter, John Muir Publications, 1988, 136 pages, paper, $6.95

This one of the Itinerary Planner series, which is reviewed in more detail under "Series Reviews." As the title of this book is new, it may also be found under *New England in 22 Days*.

Water Escapes: Great Waterside Vacation Spots in the Northeast
by Betsy Wittemann and Nancy Webster, Wood Pond Press, 1987, 418 pages, paper, $12.95

Two seasoned travel writers present 36 waterside holiday ideas, including all the information needed to arrange an itinerary—where to stay, where to eat, what to do, camping, boating, shopping, hikes, nature walks, and more. Every selection is given an extensive and very informative write-up.

Watertrips: A Guide to East Coast Cruise Ships, Ferryboats, and Island Excursions
by Theodore Scull, International Marine Publishing, 1987, 264 pages, paper, $12.95
Covering the coast from Maine to Virginia, this guide is reviewed under "The Mid-Atlantic States."

Weekending in New England: A Selective Guide to the Most Appealing Destinations for All Seasons
by Betsy Wittemann and Nancy Webster, Wood Pond Press, 1988, (3rd ed.), 242 pages, paper, $10.95
This is a new edition of the first book from the well-known authors of the excellent *Water Escapes* previously reviewed. *Weekending in New England*, a popular book in its own right with 55,000 copies sold in previous editions, is a fine assemblage of ideas for wonderful weekends in New England. The 1988 edition was released after press time so the price and number of pages are approximate.

THE MID-ATLANTIC STATES

See also "United States as a Whole." The Mid-Atlantic States are Delaware, Maryland, New Jersey, New York, Pennsylvania, Virginia, West Virginia, plus the District of Columbia.

Adventure Vacations in Five Mid-Atlantic States
by Carolyn Mulford and Betty Ford, EPM Publications, 1987, 198 pages, paper, $9.95
It's not exactly about adventures in the sense of being off-beat or unusual, but for travelers interested in recreational activity (hiking, cycling, riding, sailing, etc.) in Maryland, North Carolina, Pennsylvania, Virginia, or West Virginia. This book provides the whats, whens, and wheres. Price references are too broad and approximate to be very useful, but the remainder of the information is helpful.

The American Garden Guidebook
by Everitt Miller and Jay Cohen, M. Evans & Co., 1987, 293 pages, paper, $8.95
Including all the Mid-Atlantic states, this book is reviewed under "New England."

American Jewish Landmarks: A Travel Guide and History, Volume 1: The East
by Bernard Postal and Lionel Koppman, Fleet Press, 1977, 400 pages, paper, $18.95
 This is one of the four-volume American Jewish Landmarks series, which is reviewed in more detail under "Series Reviews."

America's Wonderful Little Hotels and Inns: Eastern Edition
edited by Sandra Soule, St. Martin's Press, 1988, 512 pages, paper, $13.95
 See "New England."

Appalachian Whitewater, Volume II: The Central Mountains
by Ed Grove, *et al.*, Menasha Ridge Press, 1987, 206 pages, paper, $13.95
 This large-format guide to the premier canoeing and kayaking streams of Pennsylvania, West Virginia, Maryland, Delaware, and Virginia is part of the Appalachian Whitewater Guide series, which is reviewed in more detail under "Series Reviews."

Away for the Weekend, New York: Great Getaways Less Than 200 Miles from New York City for Every Season of the Year
by Eleanor Bermon, Crown Publishers, 1988 (2nd ed.), 256 pages, paper, $11.95
Away for the Weekend, Washington, D.C.: 52 Great Getaways Within 200 Miles of Washington D.C.
by Eleanor Bermon, Crown Publishers, 1987, 288 pages, paper, $11.95
 This is one of the Away for the Weekend Guide series, which is reviewed in more detail under "Series Reviews." The New York volume covers destinations in New York, Connecticut, Massachusetts, Pennsylvania, Delaware, New Jersey, and Rhode Island. The Washington, D.C., volume covers destinations in Delaware, Maryland, New Jersey, Pennsylvania, West Virginia, and Virginia.

Bed & Breakfast Guide: East Coast
by Roberta Garner, *et al.*, Prentice Hall Press, 1986, 160 pages, paper, $12.95
 This book covers 119 inns in the New England and Mid-Atlantic states. Each is given a good description with practical details and directions, including interior and exterior color photographs.

Bed & Breakfast in the Mid-Atlantic States
by Bernice Chesler, The Globe Pequot Press, 1987, 343 pages, paper, $10.95

In this book, Bernice Chesler, a respected authority on the subject of B&Bs, reviews 330 of the best in D.C., Delaware, Maryland, New Jersey, New York, Pennsylvania, Virginia, and West Virginia. Criteria for selection include: 10 or fewer rooms, a common room, no public restaurant or bar on the premises, owner occupants, breakfast included with the rate. Each is given an informative one-page write-up. Chesler states clearly that each must pay a "processing fee" for inclusion. While this policy not ideal, the author has made her reputation on honesty and her written words speak for themselves. There is also an index of 300 reservation services in the U.S. and Canada (no fee charged). This book, the companion volume of *Bed and Breakfast in New England*, is updated every two years.

Canoeing the Delaware: A Guide to the River and Shore
by Gary Letcher, Rutgers University Press, 1985, 170 pages, paper, $9.95

This is a comprehensive guide to the pleasures of navigating the Delaware.

Circuit Hikes in Virginia, West Virginia, Maryland, and Pennsylvania
Potomac Appalachian Trail Club, 1986 (4th ed.), 88 pages, paper, $5.00

This book is part of the Circuit Hikes Guide series, which is reviewed in more detail under "Series Reviews."

Classic Diners of the Northeast
by Donald Kaplan and Alan Bellink, Faber and Faber, 1980, 160 pages, paper, $9.95

Including New Jersey and New York, this book is reviewed under "New England."

Country Inns of America: New York & Mid-Atlantic
Henry Holt & Co., 1986, 96 pages, paper, $11.95
Country Inns of America: Southeast
Henry Holt & Co., 1982, 96 pages, paper, $10.25

These two titles are part of the Country Inns of America series, which is reviewed in more detail under "Series Reviews." The Southeast title includes Virginia and West Virginia. Each title is filled with beautiful color photos and even the older title can still be helpful as a supplement to a more up-to-date guide.

Country Inns, Lodges & Historic Hotels: Mid-Atlantic States
by Anthony Hitchcock and Jean Lindgren, Burt Franklin–Publisher, 1988 (10th ed.), 244 pages, paper, $8.95
This is one of the Compleat Traveler's Companions series, which is reviewed in more detail under "Series Reviews." No fees are accepted for inclusion in this annually updated guide.

Country Walks Near Washington
by Alan Fisher, Rambler Books, 1984, 210 pages, paper, $7.95
This book is part of the excellent Rambler Walks series, which is reviewed in more detail under "Series Reviews."

A Cruising Guide to the Chesapeake
by William Stone and Fessenden Blanchard, Dodd, Mead & Co., 1983 (revised ed.), 320 pages, cloth, $19.95
This is the authoritative guide to the waterways of the Chesapeake as well as the passages from Long Island Sound to the New Jersey coast and the Inland Waterway. In print for more than 30 years, this guide has earned the label "classic." The detail is immense and well written. Even the veteran will find new facts and ways to enjoy this popular water playground in this informative book.

Daytrips, Getaway Weekends, and Budget Vacations in the Mid-Atlantic States
by Patricia and Robert Foulke, The Globe Pequot Press, 1986, 453 pages, paper, $10.95
Eight flexible, thoughtfully planned itineraries in the Mid-Atlantic states (excluding the Virginias) are the focus of this nicely illustrated guide. The emphasis is on automobile travel and the narrative is chock-full of history, architecture and art. Points of interest are noted clearly in the wide margins alongside the text and phone numbers are listed where useful. Several helpful appendices cover available campgrounds and bed and breakfasts.

Earth Treasures, Volume 1: Northeastern Quadrant
by Allan Eckert, Harper & Row, 1987, 336 pages, cloth (flexible), $14.95
Earth Treasures, Volume 2: Southeastern Quadrant
by Allan Eckert, Harper & Row, 1987, 336 pages, cloth (flexible), $14.95
These two titles are part of the Earth Treasures series, a guide to collecting minerals, rocks, and fossils. The Mid-Atlantic states are divided into these two volumes.

Elegant Lodging: A Guide to Country Mansions & Manor Houses in Virginia, Maryland & Pennsylvania
by Caroline Lancaster and Candyce Stapen, Washington Book Trading Co., 1985, 157 pages, paper, $5.95

The private homes of yesteryear, even homes built as long ago as the 17th century, are still private homes today. However, many of the occupants take in a few guests at a time to enjoy the elegant, usually expansive private surroundings, and often their own private entrance. Prices can be expensive, but some are quite moderate and breakfast is usually included (sometimes continental, sometimes full). And, there is history for the asking. These great ideas are well described and personally evaluated by this writing team.

Fodor's Chesapeake
Fodor's Travel Publications, 1986, 176 pages, paper, $7.95

This book is part of Fodor's Country/Regional Guide series, which is reviewed in more detail under "Series Reviews." The series is updated annually.

Fodor's I-80
Fodor's Travel Publications, 1986, 240 pages, paper, $6.95
Fodor's I-95
Fodor's Travel Publications, 1986, 215 pages, paper, $6.95

These two titles are part of Fodor's Interstate Guide series, which is reviewed in more detail under "Series Reviews." One title covers I-95 from Maine to Miami, the other I-80 from New York City to San Francisco.

Frommer's Dollarwise Guide to Skiing USA East
by I. William Berry, Prentice Hall Press, 1988, 266 pages, paper, $11.95

This guide includes the ski resorts of New York and other Mid-Atlantic states and is arranged in identical fashion to the western edition of a similar name, which is reviewed under "The Rocky Mountain/Great Basin States." The book is updated every two years.

Frommer's Dollarwise Guide to the Mid-Atlantic
by Patricia and John Preston, Prentice Hall Press, 1987, 396 pages, paper, $12.95

This book is part of Frommer's Dollarwise Guide series, which is reviewed in more detail under "Series Reviews." The book is updated every two years.

Getaways for Gourmets in the Northeast
by Nancy Webster and Richard Woodworth, Wood Pond Press, 1988 (2nd ed.), 474 pages, paper, $12.95
Including destinations in New York, New Jersey, Delaware, and Pennsylvania, this book is reviewed under "New England."

The Great Weekend Escape Book from Virginia to Vermont
by Michael Spring, E. P. Dutton, 1987 (3rd ed.), 417 pages, paper, $10.95
See "New England."

The Greater Washington Area Bicycle Atlas
edited by Ken Moskowitz, Potomac Area Council AYH, Inc., 1987 (3rd ed.), 254 pages, paper, $9.95
Here are 62 possible tours of the District of Columbia, Virginia, and Maryland area. Offered are tours with an emphasis on leisure enjoyment, safe, low-traffic roads, scenic beauty, and other attractive points of interest. Only the most knowledgeable local cyclist could begin to arrange such well-designed adventures. Plenty of practical up-to-date data, such as an overview, distances, difficulty rating, and food and lodging along the way, is also provided.

Guide to the National Park Areas: Eastern States
by David and Kay Scott, The Globe Pequot Press, 1987, 272 pages, paper, $10.95
See "The South."

Guide to the Recommended Country Inns of the Mid-Atlantic States
by Brenda Chapin, The Globe Pequot Press, 1987 (2nd ed.), 311 pages, paper, $9.95
This is one of the excellent Recommended Country Inns series, which is reviewed in more detail under "Series Reviews." The author has visited and reviewed each inn and has accepted no fee for inclusion. The book is updated every two years.

The Handbook for Beach Strollers from Maine to Cape Hatteras
by Donald Zinn, The Globe Pequot Press, 1985 (2nd ed.), 246 pages, paper, $9.95
See "New England."

Hikes in the Washington Area: Part C: District of Columbia and Prince George's, Charles, and Calvert Counties in Maryland
Potomac Appalachian Trail Club, 1986, 110 pages, paper, $5.00
This is one of the first-rate, small-format Potomac Hiking Guide series, which is reviewed in more detail under "Series Reviews."

Hiking From Inn to Inn: Wilderness Walking Tours with Comfortable Overnight Lodging from Maine to Virginia
by David and Kathleen MacInnes, The Globe Pequot Press, 1982, 191 pages, paper, $7.95
  See "New England."

Indian Mounds of the Atlantic Coast: A Guide to Sites from Maine to Florida
by Jerry McDonald and Susan Woodward, McDonald and Woodward Publishing, 1987, 162 pages, paper, $12.95
  This is a unique guide to the extant, publicly accessible prehistoric mounds and mound-like features of the Atlantic coast region. The archaeological features of 42 mounds from Maine to Florida, along with directions on how to find them and visitor information, are carefully described. For the interested traveler, this introductory material on mounds, from geographic, archaeological and cultural perspectives, will prove invaluable.

Inns of the Southern Mountains: 100 Scenic and Historic Hostelries from Virginia to Georgia
by Patricia Hudson, EPM Publications, 1985, 160 pages, paper, $8.95
  Including Virginia and West Virginia, this book is reviewed under "South."

INNSpiration Northeast: A Guide to Small Country Inns
edited by Robert Bendix, The Globe Pequot Press, 1986, 301 pages, paper, $12.95
  This excellent guide to the Mid-Atlantic states of Maryland, New York, Pennsylvania, and Virginia is reviewed under "New England."

The Interstate Gourmet: Mid-Atlantic
by Neal Weiner and David Schwartz, Summit Books, 1986, 217 pages, paper, $6.95
The Interstate Gourmet: Southeast
by Neal Weiner and David Schwartz, Summit Books, 1985, 329 pages, paper, $6.95
  These two titles are part of the excellent Interstate Gourmet series, which is reviewed in more detail under "Series Reviews." The Mid-Atlantic volume covers the region except for West Virginia and the District of Columbia. The Southeast volume includes West Virginia and additional parts of Virginia.

Land's Edge: A Natural History of Barrier Beaches from Maine to North Carolina
by Michael Hoel, The Globe Pequot Press, 1986, 140 pages, paper, $6.95
See "New England."

Marilyn Wood's Wonderful Weekends
by Marilyn Wood, Prentice Hall Press, 1987, 680 pages, paper, $11.95
Including destinations in Delaware, New Jersey, New York, and Pennsylvania, this book is reviewed under "New England."

The Mid-Atlantic Bed and Breakfast Book
by Corinne Ross, The Globe Pequot Press, 1986, 224 pages, paper, $8.95
This book is part of the Bed and Breakfast Book series, which is reviewed in more detail under "Series Reviews."

Mobil Travel Guide: Lodging for Less, Northeast and Midwest
Prentice Hall Press, 1988, 250 pages, paper, $5.95
Mobil Travel Guide: Lodging for Less, The South
Prentice Hall Press, 1988, 250 pages, paper, $5.95
These two titles are part of the new Mobil Lodging for Less series, which is reviewed in more detail under "Series Reviews." The series is updated annually.

Mobil Travel Guide: Middle Atlantic States
Prentice Hall Press, 1988, 319 pages, paper, $8.95
This book is part of the Mobil Travel Guide series, which is reviewed in more detail under "Series Reviews." The series is updated annually.

More Country Walks Near Washington
by Alan Fisher, Rambler Books, 1985, 219 pages, paper, $7.95
This is one of the excellent Rambler Walks series, which is reviewed in more detail under "Series Reviews."

New York Walk Book
by the N.Y.-N.J. Trail Conference, Doubleday & Co., 1984 (5th ed.), 393 pages, paper, $15.00
Including hikes in New York and New Jersey, this book is reviewed under "New York."

One-Day Adventures by Car: A Guide to Day Trips from New York City
by Lida Newberry and Joy Johannessen, Hastings House, 1986 (5th ed.), 348 pages, paper, $10.95
Including trips in New Jersey, Pennsylvania, and New York, this book is reviewed under "New York."

Secluded Islands of the Atlantic Coast
by David Yeadon, Crown Publishers, 1984, 224 pages, paper, $8.95
See "New England."

The Sierra Club Guide to the National Parks of the East and Middle West
Sierra Club Books, 1986, 395 pages, cloth, $14.95
This book is part of the Sierra Club National Park Guide series, which is reviewed in more detail under "Series Reviews."

The Sierra Club Naturalist's Guide to the Middle Atlantic Coast: Cape Hatteras to Cape Cod
by Bill Perry, Sierra Club Books, 1985, 448 pages, paper, $9.95
The Sierra Club Naturalist's Guide to the Piedmont of Eastern North America
by Michael Godfrey, Sierra Club Books, 1980, 432 pages, paper, $9.95
These two titles are part of the excellent natural history series, Sierra Club Naturalist's Guides, which is reviewed in more detail under "Series Reviews."

Special Museums of the Northeast: A Guide to Uncommon Collections from Maine to Washington, D.C.
by Nancy Frazier, The Globe Pequot Press, 1985, 304 pages, paper, $9.95
See "New England."

A Traveler's Guide to the Smoky Mountains Region
by Jeff Bradley, The Harvard Common Press, 1985, 272 pages, paper, $10.95
Including portions of Virginia, this excellent guide is reviewed under "The South."

Trips to Beauty & Bounty: 150 Natural Attractions In and Around Washington, D.C.
by Jane Smith, EPM Publications, 1983, 262 pages, paper, $8.95
This book is part of the One-Day Trip Books series, which is reviewed in more detail under "Series Reviews."

Walks and Rambles on the Delmarva Peninsula: A Guide for Hikers and Naturalists
by Jay Abercrombie, Backcountry Publications, 1985, 195 pages, paper, $8.95
The Delmarva Peninsula is the landmass made up of portions of Delaware, Maryland, and Virginia. It is a land ripe for walkers and hikers and this guide is a well-conceived effort to make some of the best hikes available to visitors. Long and short hikes are included. Each is well described, with its access and length noted. A trail map is included and other, more detailed maps available are described.

The Washington One-Day Trip Book: 101 Offbeat Excursions In and Around the Nation's Capital
by Jane Smith, EPM Publications, 1984 (3rd ed.), 228 pages, paper, $7.95
This book is part of the One-Day Trip Books series, which is reviewed in more detail under "Series Reviews."

Watertrips: A Guide to East Coast Cruise Ships, Ferryboats, and Island Excursions
by Theodore Scull, International Marine Publishing, 1987, 264 pages, paper, $12.95
This unique and wonderful guide gives all the data necessary to arrange a trip by water anywhere from Maine to Virginia. Scull provides a well-written overview for each of these inspired vacation ideas as well as practicalities such as where to park the car and costs.

Weekender's Guide to the Four Seasons
by Robert Shosteck, Pelican Publishing, 1988 (8th ed.), 512 pages, paper, $11.95
All sorts of ideas for what to do on the weekend in the states of Delaware, Pensylvania, Maryland, New Jersey, North Carolina, Virginia, and West Virginia are contained in this book. All trips are within a 200-mile radius of Richmond, Baltimore, or Washington, D.C. A good appendix with a month-by-month calendar of events is provided.

THE SOUTH —————————————————————————

See also "United States as a Whole." The Southern States are Alabama, Arkansas, Florida, Georgia, Kentucky, Louisiana, Mississippi, North Carolina, South Carolina, Tennessee.

Adventuring Along the Gulf of Mexico: The Sierra Club Guide to the Gulf Coast of the United States and Mexico from the Florida Keys to Yucatan
by Donald Schueler, Sierra Club Books, 1986, 320 pages, paper, $10.95
This book is part of the excellent Sierra Club Adventure Travel Guide series, which is reviewed in more detail under "Series Reviews."

The American Garden Guidebook
by Everitt Miller and Jay Cohen, M. Evans & Co., 1987, 293 pages, paper, $8.95
Including all the Southern states, this book is reviewed under "New England."

American Jewish Landmarks: A Travel Guide and History, Volume 2: The South and Southwest
by Bernard Postal and Lionel Koppman, Fleet Press, 1977, 400 pages, paper, $18.95
This is one of the four-volume American Jewish Landmarks series, which is reviewed in more detail under "Series Reviews."

America's Wonderful Little Hotels and Inns: Eastern Edition
edited by Sandra Soule, St. Martin's Press, 1988, 512 pages, paper, $13.95
Including all the Southern states, this book is reviewed under "New England."

Appalachian Whitewater, Volume I: The Southern Mountains
by Bob Sehlinger, *et al.*, Menasha Ridge Press, 1986, 159 pages, paper, $13.95
This large-format guide to the premier canoeing and kayaking streams of Kentucky, Tennessee, Alabama, Georgia, North Carolina, and South Carolina is part of the Appalachian Whitewater Guide series, which is reviewed in more detail under "Series Reviews."

Back Roads of the Carolinas
by Earl Thollander, Crown Publishing, 1985, 192 pages, paper, $12.95
This is one of the Earl Thollander's Back Roads series, which is reviewed in more detail under "Series Reviews."

Beachcomber's Guide to Gulf Coast Marine Life
by Nick Fotheringham, Gulf Publishing, 1980, 124 pages, paper,
$9.95
 This popular naturalist's guide will enhance any visit to the fascinating gulf coast.

Bed and Breakfast in the Deep South
by Sarah-Margaret Brown and Ruth Bruns, Variety House, 1985, 86
pages, paper, $6.70
 This is a homemade, but very detailed, look at B&Bs and inns in
Alabama, Louisiana, Mississippi, Florida, Tennessee, and Texas. Information on reservation services with a supplement to update important information is included.

Blue Ridge Mountain Pleasures: An A-Z Guide to North Georgia,
Western North Carolina, and the Upcountry of South Carolina
by Donald Wenberg, The Globe Pequot Press, 1988 (2nd ed.), 288
pages, paper, $9.95
 This compendium of ideas has a table of contents that reads like
many other guidebook's indices. An A-Z format delivers list upon
list of interesting activities and events. Lest a letter be left out, "X"
is for "X-tra, X-tra" which covers miscellaneous events, and "Y" is
for "You Wouldn't Believe," a category of trivia items.

The Condo Lux Vacationer's Guide to Condominium Rentals in the
Southeast
by Jill Little, Random House, 1986, 300 pages, paper, $9.95
 This is one of the Condo Lux Guide series, which is reviewed in
more detail under "Series Reviews."

Country Inns, Lodges, & Historic Hotels: The South
by Anthony Hitchcock and Jean Lindgren, Burt Franklin–Publisher,
1988 (10th ed.), 283 pages, paper, $8.95
 This book is part of the Compleat Traveler's Companions series,
which is reviewed in more detail under "Series Reviews." No fees
are accepted for inclusion in this annually updated guide.

Country Inns of America: The Mississippi
Henry Holt & Co., 1983, 96 pages, paper, $10.25
Country Inns of America: Southeast
Henry Holt & Co., 1982, 96 pages, paper, $10.25
 These two older titles are filled with beautiful photos that could
prove a useful supplement to a more current guide. Both are part of
the Country Inns of America series, which is reviewed in more detail
under "Series Reviews." The Mississippi title includes Louisiana,

Mississippi, Alabama, Arkansas, and Tennessee. The Southeast title includes the remainder of the Southern states.

Earth Treasures, Volume 2: Southeastern Quadrant
by Allan Eckert, Harper & Row, 1987, 336 pages, cloth (flexible), $14.95

This guide to collecting minerals, rocks, and fossils is part of the Earth Treasures series, which is reviewed in more detail under "Series Reviews."

Fisher's World: Southeast
by Sylvia McNair, Fisher's World, Inc., 1988, 290 pages, paper, $14.95

This book is part of the Fisher's World Guide series, which is reviewed in more detail under "Series Reviews." The series is updated annually.

Fodor's Carolinas and the Georgia Coast
Fodor's Travel Publications, 1987, 256 pages, paper, $8.95

This book is part of Fodor's USA Guide series, which is reviewed in more detail under "Series Reviews." Updated annually.

Fodor's I-10
Fodor's Travel Publications, 1986, 208 pages, paper, $6.95
Fodor's I-55
Fodor's Travel Publications, 1986, 160 pages, paper, $6.95
Fodor's I-75
Fodor's Travel Publications, 1986, 224 pages, paper, $6.95
Fodor's I-95
Fodor's Travel Publications, 1986, 215 pages, paper, $6.95

These four titles are part of Fodor's Interstate Guide series, which is reviewed in more detail under "Series Reviews." They cover the following: I-10 from Florida to Los Angeles; I-55 from Chicago to New Orleans; I-75 from Michigan to Miami; and I-95 from Maine to Miami.

Fodor's South
Fodor's Travel Publications, 1987, 448 pages, paper, $12.95

This book is part of Fodor's Country/Regional Guide series, which is reviewed in more detail under "Series Reviews." This annually updated guide includes Virginia, but does not cover Arkansas or Kentucky.

Frommer's Dollarwise Guide to Skiing USA East
by I. William Berry, Prentice Hall Press, 1988, 266 pages, paper, $11.95
Including ski resorts in the Southern states, this book is arranged in identical fashion to the western edition of similar name, which is reviewed under "The Rocky Mountain/Great Basin States." This title is updated every two years.

Frommer's Dollarwise Guide to the Southeast and New Orleans
by Susan Poole, Prentice Hall Press, 1987, 396 pages, paper, $11.95
This is one of the Frommer's Dollarwise Guide series, which is reviewed in more detail under "Series Reviews." This series emphasizes selections in the moderate price range and is updated every two years.

The Greatest Ozark Guidebook
by Harry and Phyl Dark, Greatest Graphics, 1980 (2nd ed.), 240 pages, paper, $7.95
See "Missouri."

Guide to the National Park Areas: Eastern States
by David and Kay Scott, The Globe Pequot Press, 1987 (2nd ed.), 272 pages, paper, $10.95
This guide, one of a two-part series, covers all states east of the Mississippi. It provides a fairly brief, but quite informative rundown on the 200 areas operated by the National Park Service. Each write-up gives a location map (including the whereabouts of the visitor's center), what facilities are available, camping options, whether fishing is allowed, where the best trails (if any) are, and where to obtain additional information.

Guide to the Recommended Country Inns of the South
by Sara Pitzer, The Globe Pequot Press, 1987, 313 pages, paper, $9.95
This book is part of the highly regarded Recommended Country Inns series, which is reviewed in more detail under "Series Reviews." The author has visited and reviewed each inn and has accepted no fee for inclusion. This title is updated every two years.

Hiker's Guide to the Smokies
by Dick Murlless and Constance Stallings, Sierra Club Books, 1973, 375 pages, paper, $10.95
This small-format book that includes a large, fold-out topographical map of the region is part of the Sierra Club Hiking Totebooks series, which is reviewed in more detail under "Series Reviews."

Indian Mounds of the Middle Ohio Valley: A Guide to Adena and Ohio Hopewell Sites
by Susan Woodward and Jerry McDonald, McDonald and Woodward Publishing, 1986, 130 pages, paper, $9.95
Including sites in Kentucky, this book is reviewed under "The Midwest."

Inns of the Southern Mountains: 100 Scenic and Historic Hostelries from Virginia to Georgia
by Patricia Hudson, EPM Publications, 1985, 160 pages, paper, $8.95
Written by a magazine journalist who discovered the charm and economy of staying in inns during her frequent travels, *Inns of the Southern Mountains* offers descriptions that include not only all the necessities, but a bit of the history and lore surrounding each inn. It will surely help to meet the author's goal of luring people off the interstates and into mountain communities where their experiences will enable them to see beyond the hillbilly stereotype. This is a wonderful book covering the states of Georgia, Kentucky, North Carolina, Tennessee, Virginia, and West Virginia.

The Interstate Gourmet: Southeast
by Neal Weiner and David Schwartz, Summit Books, 1985, 329 pages, paper, $6.95
This is one of the excellent Interstate Gourmet series, which is reviewed in more detail under "Series Reviews." This volume covers Florida, Georgia, Kentucky, North Carolina, South Carolina, Tennessee, Virginia, and West Virginia.

Joy in the Mountains
by Lou Winokur, Alice Winokur and Patricia Hope, Joy Publishing, 1985, 191 pages, paper, $7.95
Joy in the Mountains #2
by Lou and Alice Winokur, Joy Publishing, 1981, 192 pages, paper, $7.95
The first volume addresses the mountainous corner surrounding the Blue Ridge Parkway, which is made up of portions of North Carolina, Tennessee, and Virginia. The second volume focuses on Gatlinburg and the Great Smoky Mountains region of Tennessee, Kentucky, and North Carolina. Each is a directory addressing a wide array of activities and where and when to pursue each. Lists include plenty of annual events organized month-by-month. Activities run the gamut: arts, crafts, horse shows, swimming, skating, train rides, auctions, etc. Be sure to confirm dates and prices.

Land's Edge: A Natural History of Barrier Beaches from Maine to North Carolina
by Michael Hoel, The Globe Pequot Press, 1986, 140 pages, paper, $6.95
See "New England."

Mobil Travel Guide: Lodging for Less, South
Prentice Hall Press, 1988, 250 pages, paper, $5.95
This is one of the Mobil Lodging for Less series, which is reviewed in more detail under "Series Reviews." The series is updated annually.

Mobil Travel Guide: Middle Atlantic States
Prentice Hall Press, 1988, 319 pages, paper, $8.95
Mobil Travel Guide: Southeastern States
Prentice Hall Press, 1988, 301 pages, paper, $8.95
These are part of the Mobil Travel Guide series, which is reviewed in more detail under "Series Reviews." The series is updated annually.

Mountain Getaways in Georgia, North Carolina, and Tennessee
by Rusty Hoffland, On the Road Publishing, 1988, 160 pages, paper, $5.95
Dividing the Great Smokies and Blue Ridge Mountains into eight distinct regions, this book provides helpful and informative descriptions of various tours, inns, restaurants, things to do, and sights to see along each route. Useful maps are interspersed throughout. An annual calendar of events helps with planning. This great little book is up-to-date and eminently useful.

A Naturalist's Blue Ridge Parkway
by David Catlin, The University of Tennessee Press, 1984, 208 pages, paper, $7.95
See "North Carolina."

Old South: A Traveler's Guide to Virginia, North Carolina and South Carolina
by Dana Facaros and Michael Pauls, Hippocrene Books, 1987 (revised ed.), 124 pages, paper, $5.95
This budget-oriented book is for the independent traveler. Information on the history, cuisine, specialties, and festivities of the Old South, as well as where to find the best accommodations, are provided by these two respected travel writers.

The Pelican Guide to the Ozarks
 by Bet Hampel, Pelican Publishing, 1982, 160 pages, paper, $4.95
 See "Missouri."

Secluded Islands of the Atlantic Coast
 by David Yeadon, Crown Publishers, 1984, 224 pages, paper, $8.95
 See "New England."

The Sierra Club Guide to the National Parks of the East and Middle West
 Sierra Club Books, 1986, 395 pages, cloth, $14.95
 This book is part of the Sierra Club National Parks Guide series, which is reviewed in more detail under "Series Reviews."

The Sierra Club Naturalist's Guide to the Piedmont of Eastern North America
 by Michael Godfrey, Sierra Club Books, 1980, 432 pages, paper, $9.95
 This is one of the excellent natural history series, Sierra Club Naturalist's Guides, which is reviewed in more detail under "Series Reviews."

The Southern Bed and Breakfast Book
 by Corinne Ross, The Globe Pequot Press, 1986, 192 pages, paper, $8.95
 This is one of the Bed and Breakfast Book series, which is reviewed in more detail under "Series Reviews."

Travel Guide to the Natchez Trace Parkway Between Natchez, Mississippi and Nashville, Tennessee
 Natchez Trace Parkway Association, 1984, 100 pages, paper, $7.95
 See "Mississippi."

A Traveler's Guide to the Smoky Mountains Region
 by Jeff Bradley, The Harvard Common Press, 1985, 272 pages, paper, $10.95
 What makes this book stand out from all the rest is the author's ability to capture the unique flavor of each region through the stories and rich history with which he embellishes the basic facts. Reviewer James Dickey, a native of the area and the author of *Deliverance*, finds it "...a new exploration of a fascinating region. It's destined to become indispensable....a thoroughly delightful guide." Portions of Tennessee, North Carolina, Georgia, and Virginia are included.

Traveling Texas Borders: A Guide to the Best of Both Sides
by Ann Ruff, Gulf Publishing, 1983, 119 pages, paper, $9.95
See "Texas."

Walks in the Great Smokies
by Rodney and Priscilla Albright, The Globe Pequot Press, 1979,
189 pages, paper, $7.95
This book is part of the small-format Globe Pequot Hiking Guide
series, which is reviewed in more detail under "Series Reviews."

Whitewater Home Companion: Southeastern Rivers (Volume I)
by William Nealy, Menasha Ridge Press, 1981, 156 pages, paper,
$8.95
Whitewater Home Companion: Southeastern Rivers (Volume II)
by William Nealy, Menasha Ridge Press, 1981, 165 pages, paper,
$8.95
These two great river guides are widely respected for their accuracy, but are reminiscent of the cartoon books of the flower-child
era. The guides focus specifically on kayaking and are laced with
Nealy's sense of humor. These guides are fun to read and first-class
reference books for the whitewater paddler.

Woodall's Tenting Directory, Western Edition
Woodall Publishing, 1987, 168 pages, paper, $7.95
Including Louisiana and Arkansas, this annually updated, large-
format book on campsites appropriate for tent camping is similar in
format to their full directory, which is reviewed under "North America as a Whole."

THE MIDWEST ───────────────────────────────

See also the "United States as a Whole." The Midwest States are
Illinois, Indiana, Iowa, Kansas, Michigan, Minnesota, Missouri, Nebraska, North Dakota, Ohio, South Dakota, Wisconsin.

The American Garden Guidebook
by Everitt Miller and Jay Cohen, M. Evans & Co., 1987, 293 pages,
paper, $8.95
Including the Midwest states east of the Mississippi River, this
book is reviewed under "New England."

**American Jewish Landmarks: A Travel Guide and History, Volume 3:
The Middlewest**
by Bernard Postal and Lionel Koppman, Fleet Press, 1984, 352
pages, paper, $12.95

American Jewish Landmarks: A Travel Guide and History, Volume 4: The West
by Bernard Postal and Lionel Koppman, Fleet Press, 1986, 320 pages, paper, $12.95
   Both of these titles are part of the four-volume American Jewish Landmarks series, which is reviewed in more detail under "Series Reviews."

America's Wonderful Little Hotels and Inns: Eastern Edition
edited by Sandra Soule, St. Martin's Press, 1988, 512 pages, paper, $13.95
America's Wonderful Little Hotels and Inns: Western Edition
edited by Sandra Soule, St. Martin's Press, 1988, 464 pages, paper, $13.95
   The geographic dividing line between the Eastern and Western editions of this title is the Mississippi River (with states along the river's western border being included in the Eastern Edition). Both are written in an identical fashion and are reviewed under either "New England" or "The Rocky Mountain/Great Basin States." Both are updated annually.

Bed and Breakfast in Michigan and Surrounding Areas
by Norma Buzan and Bert Howell, Betsy Ross Publications, 1985, 120 pages, paper, $8.25
   This is a homey, nicely prepared evaluation of numerous inns, private homes, and B&Bs in the Great Lakes region. Photos, drawings, and practical information are included.

Canals of Mid-America
by Leslie Swanson, Swanson Publishing, 1984, 53 pages, paper, $3.00
   This is one of Swanson's several great little booklets on a fascinating and historic aspect of Midwestern life and landscape. Written with obvious care, the text is supplemented with good photos. For those wishing to visit these remaining canals, the author suggests a number of organizations to contact.

Country Inns of America: The Mississippi
Henry Holt & Co., 1983, 93 pages, paper, $10.95
Country Inns of America: The Great Lakes
Henry Holt & Co., 1981, 96 pages, paper, $8.95
   These two older volumes, still useful as supplements to more up-to-date guides, are part of the Country Inns of America series, which is reviewed in more detail under "Series Reviews."

Country Inns, Lodges & Historic Hotels: The Midwest and Rocky Mountain States
by Anthony Hitchcock and Jean Lindgren, Burt Franklin–Publisher, 1988 (10th ed.), 241 pages, paper, $8.95
This book is part of the Compleat Traveler's Companions series, which is reviewed in more detail under "Series Reviews." No fees are accepted for inclusion in this annually updated title.

Covered Bridges in Illinois, Iowa, and Wisconsin
by Leslie Swanson, Swanson Publishing, 1970, 48 pages, paper, $3.00
This is a great little booklet on the many covered bridges remaining in these midwestern states.

Earth Treasures, Volume 1: The Northeastern Quadrant
by Allan Eckert, Harper & Row, 1987, 336 pages, cloth (flexible), $14.95
Earth Treasures, Volume 3: The Northwestern Quadrant
by Allan Eckert, Harper & Row, 1987, 632 pages, cloth (flexible), $16.95
Each of these guides for collecting minerals, rocks, and fossils covers some of the Midwestern states, with the Mississippi River being the dividing line. They are part of the Earth Treasures series, which is reviewed in more detail under "Series Reviews."

Fielding's Lewis and Clark Trail
by Gerald Olmsted, William Morrow & Co., 1986, 305 pages, paper, $12.95
Following the famous trail from Missouri to the Pacific Northwest, this book is one of the Fielding's Trail Guide series, which is reviewed in more detail under "Series Reviews."

Fodor's I-55
Fodor's Travel Publications, 1986, 160 pages, paper, $6.95
Fodor's I-75
Fodor's Travel Publications, 1986, 224 pages, paper, $6.95
Fodor's I-80
Fodor's Travel Publications, 1986, 240 pages, paper, $6.95
These three titles cover interstate highways passing through the Midwest—I-55 running from Chicago to New Orleans, I-75 running from Miami to Michigan, and I-80 running from New York City to San Francisco. These are part of Fodor's Interstate Guide series, which is reviewed in more detail under "Series Reviews."

Golfer's Travel Guide: Great Lakes Edition
edited by Roy Rasmussen, RSG Publishing, 1987, 208 pages, paper, $12.95
 This is a handy resource guide to golfing options through the Great Lakes region.

The Great Lakes Guidebook: Lake Huron and Eastern Lake Michigan
by George Cantor, The University of Michigan Press, 1985 (2nd ed.), 196 pages, paper, $7.95
The Great Lakes Guidebook: Lake Ontario and Erie
by George Cantor, The University of Michigan Press, 1985 (2nd ed.), 238 pages, paper, $7.95
The Great Lakes Guidebook: Lake Superior and Western Lake Michigan
by George Cantor, The University of Michigan Press, 1980, 226 pages, paper, $6.95
 These three books, two of which have been revised, collectively make up a fantastic assemblage of the best attractions in the Great Lakes region, including this region's fascinating history. All sorts of driving tours and walking tours, plus numerous and exceptionally well-prepared detail maps are included.

Guide to Art Museums: Midwest Edition
by Michael Beatty and James Nulty, And Books, 1984, 268 pages, paper, $9.95
 This handy, though aging, guide to art museums in Kentucky, Ohio, Illinois, Indiana, Iowa, Michigan, Minnesota, Missouri, and Wisconsin contains brief descriptions of more than 150 museums of all types. Hours and admission charges are provided.

Guide to the National Park Areas: Eastern States
by David and Kay Scott, The Globe Pequot Press, 1987, 272 pages, paper, $9.95
Guide to the National Park Areas: Western States
by David and Kay Scott, The Globe Pequot Press, 1987, 272 pages, paper, $9.95
 These two guides cover all the areas run by the National Park Service. The guide to the eastern states covers all states east of the Mississippi and is reviewed under "The South." The guide to the western states covers states west of the Mississippi and is reviewed under "The Southwest."

Guide to the Recommended Country Inns of the Midwest

by Bob Puhala, The Globe Pequot Press, 1987, 312 pages, paper,
$9.95

This is one of the excellent Recommended Country Inns series,
which is reviewed in more detail under "Series Reviews." The author
has visited and evaluated each inn himself; no payment of any kind
has been accepted for the inclusion of any inn in this book. States
covered are: Illinois, Indiana, Iowa, Michigan, Minnesota, Missouri,
Ohio, and Wisconsin. This book is updated every two years.

Indian Mounds of the Middle Ohio Valley: A Guide to Adena and Ohio Hopewell Sites

by Susan Woodward and Jerry McDonald, McDonald and
Woodward Publishing, 1986, 130 pages, paper, $9.95

This is a well-done guide to the "most conspicuous elements of
prehistoric American Indian culture." The numerous sites are carefully described, a clear map provided, directions to each site are
given, and the hours of public access noted.

The Interstate Gourmet: Midwest

by Neal Weiner and David Schwartz, Summit Books, 1986, 287
pages, paper, $6.95

This book is part of the excellent Interstate Gourmet series, which
is reviewed in more detail under "Series Reviews." The Midwest
volume covers Illinois, Indiana, Iowa, Michigan, Minnesota, Missouri, Ohio, Wisconsin, and portions of Kentucky.

Landmarks of the West: A Guide to Historic Sites

by Kent Ruth, The University of Nebraska Press, 1986, 309 pages,
paper, $17.50

Including all Midwestern states west of the Mississippi River, this
book is reviewed under "Rocky Mountain/Great Basin States."

Mobil Travel Guide: Lodging for Less, Northeast and Midwest

Prentice Hall Press, 1988, 250 pages, paper, $5.95

This book is part of the Mobil Lodging for Less series, which is
reviewed in more detail under "Series Reviews." The series is updated annually.

Mobil Travel Guide: Great Lakes Area

Prentice Hall Press, 1988, 339 pages, paper, $8.95

Mobil Travel Guide: Northwest and Great Plains States

Prentice Hall Press, 1988, 333 pages, paper, $8.95

Mobil Travel Guide: Southwest and South Central

Prentice Hall Press, 1988, 322 pages, paper, $8.95

These three titles are part of the Mobil Travel Guide series, which is reviewed in more detail under "Series Reviews." The Great Lakes edition covers Illinois, Indiana, Michigan, Ohio, and Wisconsin. The Northwest and Great Plains States edition includes Iowa, Minnesota, Nebraska, North Dakota, and South Dakota. The Southwest and South Central edition includes Kansas and Missouri. The series is updated annually.

Old Mills in the Mid-West
by Leslie Swanson, Swanson Publishing, 1985, 48 pages, paper, $3.00

This booklet is a unique guide to some truly classic structures of old. It is full of the history of these still surviving mills, their towns, and their owners. The author relates the workings of the mills and their architecture as well as recent preservation efforts. Good photos and some semblance of directions complete the book.

The Sierra Club Guide to the National Parks of the East and Middle West
Sierra Club Books, 1986, 395 pages, cloth, $14.95
The Sierra Club Guide to the National Parks of the Rocky Mountains and the Great Plains
Sierra Club Books, 1984, 272 pages, cloth, $14.95

These two titles are part of the Sierra Club National Park Guide series, which is reviewed in more detail under "Series Reviews."

The Sierra Club Naturalist's Guide to the North Woods of Michigan, Wisconsin, Minnesota, and Southern Ontario
by Glenda Daniel and Jerry Sullivan, Sierra Club Books, 1981, 384 pages, paper, $10.95

This book is part of the Sierra Club Naturalist's Guide series, which is reviewed in more detail under "Series Reviews."

Ski Minnesota: A Cross-Country Skier's Guide to Minnesota, Northern Wisconsin, and Michigan's Upper Peninsula
by Elizabeth and Gary Noren, Nodin Press, 1985, 424 pages, paper, $11.95

See "Minnesota."

Woodall's Tenting Directory: Western Edition
Woodall Publishing, 1987, 168 pages, paper, $7.95

This large-format book on public and private campgrounds appropriate for tent camping covers all states west of the Mississippi, Western Canada, and Mexico. Done in a fashion similar to their full directory, which is reviewed under "North America as a Whole," this book is updated annually.

Woodall's Western Campground Directory
Woodall Publishing, 1987, 642 pages, paper, $8.95

This large-format book covers all states west of the Mississippi except Arkansas, Iowa, Louisiana, Minnesota, and Missouri. This less expensive section of their full guide is reviewed under "North America as a Whole" and is updated annually.

THE ROCKY MOUNTAIN/GREAT BASIN STATES ──────────

See also "United States as a Whole." The Rocky Mountain/Great Basin States are Colorado, Idaho, Montana, Nevada, Utah, Wyoming.

Adventuring in the Rockies
by Jerry Schmidt, Sierra Club Books, 1986, 320 pages, paper, $10.95

This is one of the Sierra Club Adventure Travel Guide series, which is reviewed in more detail under "Series Reviews."

American Jewish Landmarks: A Travel Guide and History, Volume 4: The West
by Bernard Postal and Lionel Koppman, Fleet Press, 1986, 320 pages, paper, $12.95

This book is part of the four-volume American Jewish Landmarks series, which is reviewed in more detail under "Series Reviews."

American Southwest in 22 Days
See *22 Days in the American Southwest* below.

America's Wonderful Little Hotels and Inns: Western Edition
edited by Sandra Soule, St. Martin's Press, 1988, 464 pages, paper, $13.95

This newer western edition has joined the highly regarded eastern edition to cover the states west of the Mississippi (excluding those along the river's western border) and the western Canadian provinces. As it depends heavily on reader feedback, readers of this book are encouraged to share their experiences with others. No inn is listed that has not had a favorable review from its guests. Sometimes readers' letters are not very specific in their assessment, but the comments offered are honest and often very revealing. This book is updated annually.

Ancient Cities of the Southwest: A Practical Guide to the Major Prehistoric Ruins of Arizona, New Mexico, Utah, and Colorado
by Buddy Mays, Chronicle Books, 1982, 132 pages, paper, $7.95
  See "The Southwest."

Best Places to Stay in the Pacific Northwest
by Marilyn McFarlane, The Harvard Common Press, 1988, 400 pages, paper, $14.95
  Including Idaho and Montana, this book is part of the excellent Best Places to Stay Guide series, which is reviewed in more detail under "Series Reviews." Each selection has been carefully reviewed; no fee has been charged for inclusion.

Bicycle Touring in the Western United States
by Karen and Gary Hawkins, Random House, 1982, 390 pages, paper, $9.95
  This title contains more than 100 pages on equipment, preparation, planning, the hazards of the road, and camping out. Beginning with the ABCs of touring, this book plots some great tours through all of the western states: the Southwest, Great Basin, Rocky Mountains, and Pacific Northwest. Each tour is fully described, down to the nearest grocery store.

Budget Skiers Guidebook, Western U.S.
by Michael Studebaker, Glastonbury Press, 1985, 148 pages, paper, $6.95
  This well-done budget ski guide is a great planning aid. All the major ski resorts of the western U.S. are addressed, with a rundown of inexpensive food and lodging for each. States covered are: Arizona, California, Colorado, Idaho, Montana, Nevada, New Mexico, Oregon, Utah, Washington, and Wyoming.

Budget Vacationers Guidebook, Western U.S.
by Michael Studebaker, Glastonbury Press, 1986, 318 pages, paper, $8.95
  What this guide lacks in literary style it makes up for in its usefulness to the budget traveler. The author's vast experience shows through in the myriad ideas presented. Each town covered includes free or inexpensive things to do, campgrounds (many free), lodging, and restaurants—all presented in no-nonsense, rapid-fire fashion. This compact catalog of money-saving tips covers the same states as the *Budget Skiers Guidebook* above.

The Condo Lux Vacationer's Guide to Condominium Rentals in the Mountain Resorts
by Jill Little, Random House, 1986, 338 pages, paper, $9.95
   Including resort locations in Colorado, Nevada, Idaho, Wyoming, and Utah, this is one of the Condo Lux Guide series, which is reviewed in more detail under "Series Reviews."

Country Inns, Lodges & Historic Hotels: The Midwest and Rocky Mountain States
by Anthony Hitchcock and Jean Lindgren, Burt Franklin–Publisher, 1988 (10th ed.), 241 pages, paper, $8.95
   This book is part of the Compleat Traveler's Companions series, which is reviewed in more detail under "Series Reviews." No fees are accepted for inclusion in this annually updated guide.

Country Inns of America: Rocky Mountains
Henry Holt & Co., 1983, 96 pages, paper, $10.95
   This book is part of the Country Inns of America series, which is reviewed in more detail under "Series Reviews."

Earth Treasures, Volume 3: The Northwestern Quadrant
by Allan Eckert, Harper & Row, 1987, 632 pages, cloth (flexible), $16.95
Earth Treasures, Volume 4: The Southwestern Quadrant
by Allan Eckert, Harper & Row, 1987, 740 pages, cloth (flexible), $16.95
   These two guides to collecting minerals, rocks, and fossils are part of the Earth Treasures series, which is reviewed in more detail under "Series Reviews." Among the Rocky Mountain/Great Basin states, the Northwestern edition contains Idaho, Montana, and Wyoming; the Southwestern edition contains Colorado, Nevada, and Utah.

A Field Guide to Yellowstone's Geysers, Hot Springs and Fumaroles
by Carl Schreier, Homestead Publishing, 1987, 96 pages, paper, $9.95
   See "Wyoming."

Fielding's Lewis and Clark Trail
by Gerald Olmsted, William Morrow & Co., 1986, 305 pages, paper, $12.95
   Following the famous trail from Missouri to the Pacific Northwest, this is one of the Fielding's Trail Guide series, which is reviewed in more detail under "Series Reviews."

Fisher's World: West
by Frank and Elfriede Riley, Fisher's World, Inc., 1988, 290 pages, paper, $14.95
Including Nevada, Utah, Arizona, and California, this book is part of the Fisher's World Guide series, which is reviewed in more detail under "Series Reviews." The series is updated annually.

Fodor's Far West
Fodor's Travel Publications, 1987, 544 pages, paper, $12.95
This book is part of Fodor's Country/Regional Guide series, which is reviewed in more detail under "Series Reviews." Including Idaho, Montana, Nevada, Utah, and Wyoming, this book is updated annually.

Fodor's I-80
Fodor's Travel Publications, 1986, 240 pages, paper, $6.95
Describing services along the interstate highway from New York City to San Francisco, this book is part of Fodor's Interstate Guide series, which is reviewed in more detail under "Series Reviews."

Fodor's Rockies
Fodor's Travel Publications, 1987, 256 pages, paper, $8.95
This book is part of Fodor's Country/Regional Guides series, which is reviewed in more detail under "Series Reviews." The series is updated annually.

Frommer's Dollarwise Guide to Skiing USA West
by Lois Friedland, Prentice Hall Press, 1988, 320 pages, paper, $11.95
This is a well-done guide that rates and describes ski resorts throughout the regions of the Pacific Northwest, the Southwest, the Rocky Mountain/Great Basin states, and western Canada. Lodging and restaurants in all price ranges are recommended and each entry is thoroughly reviewed. This guide is updated every two years.

Ghost Towns of the Northwest
by Norman Weis, Caxton Printers, 1981, 319 pages, cloth, $11.95
Covering numerous sites in Idaho, Montana, and Wyoming, this book is reviewed under "The Pacific Northwest."

The Great American Runner's Guide: Western States Edition
by Edward Moore, Beaufort Books, 1985, 141 pages, paper, $6.95
Travelers who are used to taking their morning run will find this possible while visiting the major cities of the west with the help of this well-done guide. The excellently drawn maps of suggested run-

ning paths include the locations of all the major hotels nearby. A helpful narrative on each run, as well as addresses and phone numbers of nearby racquetball facilities and athletic goods stores, are also included. The guide covers major towns in the entire Rocky Mountain/Great Basin region, as well as Alaska (Anchorage only), Arizona, California, Hawaii (Honolulu only), and New Mexico (Albuquerque only).

Great Hot Springs of the West
by Bill Kaysing, Capra Press, 1984, 208 pages, paper, $9.95

This is a comprehensive guide to hot springs in Arizona, California, Colorado, Idaho, Montana, Nevada, New Mexico, Oregon, Utah, Washington, and Wyoming. Provided are locations, descriptions, whether bathing suits are needed, prices and phone numbers (when there are any), and an appendix filled with good detail maps. Over 200 hot springs are described; nearly 1700 can be located on the detail maps.

The Great Towns of the West
by David Vokac, West Press, 1985, 464 pages, paper, $14.95

Including the entire Rocky Mountain/Great Basin region, this book is part of the Great Towns Guide series, which is reviewed in more detail under "Series Reviews."

Guide to the National Park Areas: Western States
by David and Kay Scott, The Globe Pequot Press, 1987 (2nd ed.), 341 pages, paper, $10.95

Covering all areas run by the National Park Services west of the Mississippi River, this book is reviewed under "Southwest."

Guide to the Recommended Country Inns of the Rocky Mountain Region
by Doris Kennedy, The Globe Pequot Press, 1987, 300 pages, paper, $9.95

This book is part of the excellent Recommended Country Inns series, which is reviewed in more detail under "Series Reviews." The author has visited and reviewed each inn selected and has accepted no payment for inclusion of any inn. The book is updated every two years.

Hiking the Great Basin: The High Desert Country of California, Oregon, Nevada, and Utah
by John Hart, Sierra Club Books, 1981, 369 pages, paper, $9.95

Hiking the Yellowstone Backcountry
by Orville Bach, Jr., Sierra Club Books, 1973, 240 pages, paper, $8.95
Both of these titles are part of the Sierra Club Hiking Totebook series, which is reviewed in more detail under "Series Reviews."

Hot Springs and Hot Pools of the Northwest
by Jayson Loam and Marjorie Gersh, Wilderness Press, 1986 (2nd ed.), 196 pages, paper, $12.95
This edition, covering all states of the Rocky Mountain/Great Basin region except Nevada, is reviewed under "The Pacific Northwest."

Insight Guide: The Rockies
by Apa Productions, Prentice Hall Press, 1985, 384 pages, paper, $15.95
This book is part of the excellent Insight Guide series, which is reviewed in more detail under "Series Reviews."

Journey to the High Southwest: A Traveler's Guide
by Robert Casey, The Globe Pequot Press, 1988 (3rd ed.), 450 pages, paper, $16.95
This superb guide to the Four Corners region of Arizona, New Mexico, Colorado, and Utah, and the Santa Fe, New Mexico area is reviewed under "The Southwest."

Landmarks of the West: A Guide to Historic Sites
by Kent Ruth, The University of Nebraska Press, 1986, 309 pages, paper, $17.50
This popular guide has been recently updated. Beautifully designed, well-written, and with a fascinating collection of new and old photographs and drawings, this is a thoroughly classy, completely intriguing guide to dozens of historic sites throughout the entire West—all the states west of the Mississippi River except Louisana. For history buffs, this is definitely recommended reading.

Mobil Travel Guide: Lodging for Less, West
Prentice Hall Press, 1988, 250 pages, paper, $5.95
This book is part of the Mobil Lodging for Less series, which is reviewed in more detail under "Series Reviews." The series is updated annually.

Mobil Travel Guide: California and the West
Prentice Hall Press, 1988, 274 pages, paper, $8.95

Mobil Travel Guide: Southwest and South Central
Prentice Hall Press, 1988, 322 pages, paper, $8.95
Mobil Travel Guide: Northwest and Great Plains States
Prentice Hall Press, 1988, 333 pages, paper, $8.95
These titles are part of the Mobil Travel Guide series, which is reviewed in more detail under "Series Reviews." The Rocky Mountain/Great Basin states are included as follows: the California and the West edition includes Nevada and Utah; the Southwest and South Central edition includes Colorado; the Northwest and Great Plains states edition includes Idaho, Montana, and Wyoming. The series is updated annually.

Myrna Oakley's Bed and Breakfast Northwest
by Myrna Oakley, Solstice Press, 1987, 113 pages, paper, $7.95
Containing selections from Idaho, Montana, and northern Nevada, this book is reviewed under "The Pacific Northwest."

National Parks of the Rocky Mountains
by Kent and Donna Dannen, Rocky Mountain Nature Association, 1986, 120 pages, cloth, $14.95
This beautiful, hardbound book contains a large number of prize-winning photos. Its information section gives an overview of several pages on each of the five parks, including its history, a description, how to get there, accommodations (general orientation and contact information), activities, special events, and a park map.

Northwest Mileposts
Alaska Northwest Publishing, 1987, 496 pages, paper, $14.95
This annually updated, large-format book, which includes Idaho and Montana, is reviewed under "The Pacific Northwest."

Northwest Trails: A Hiker's Guide to National Parks and Wilderness Areas
by Ira Spring and Harvey Manning, The Mountaineers, 1982, 192 pages, paper, $9.95
100 Hikes in the Inland Northwest
by Rich Landers and Ida Rowe Dolphin, The Mountaineers, 1987, 224 pages, paper, $9.95
The Northwest Trails volume includes trails in Idaho, Montana, and Wyoming. The Inland Northwest volume includes hikes in Idaho and Montana as well as Washington and British Columbia. Both are part of the Mountaineers Hiking Guide series, which is reviewed in more detail under "Series Reviews."

Recreation On the Colorado River
Sail Sales Publishing, 1985, 112 pages, paper, $9.95
 This large-format, spiral-bound guide provides a general overview of recreational opportunities along the Colorado River from California to Colorado. Parks and other access points are briefly described, and a large detail map is included. Useful campground information and boat launch ramp locations are provided.

River Runners' Guide to Utah and Adjacent Areas
by Gary Nichols, University of Utah Press, 1986, 168 pages, paper, $14.95
 Including several rivers in areas immediately adjacent to Utah in Idaho, Wyoming, Colorado, and Arizona, this book is reviewed under "Utah."

Roadside Geology of Yellowstone Country
by William Fritz, Mountain Press, 1985, 160 pages, paper, $8.95
 This book is part of the excellent Roadside Geology Guide series, which is reviewed in more detail under "Series Reviews."

The Sierra Club Guide to the National Parks of the Rocky Mountains
Sierra Club Books, 1984, 261 pages, cloth, $12.95
 This book is part of the Sierra Club National Parks Guide series, which is reviewed in more detail under "Series Reviews."

The Sierra Club Guide to the Natural Areas of Colorado and Utah
by John and Jane Perry, Sierra Club Books, 1985, 416 pages, paper, $9.95
The Sierra Club Guide to the Natural Areas of Idaho, Montana, and Wyoming
by John and Jane Perry, Sierra Club Books, 1988, 416 pages, paper, $10.95
 These two titles are part of the Sierra Club Natural Areas Guide series, which is reviewed in more detail under "Series Reviews."

The Sierra Club Naturalist's Guide to the Deserts of the Southwest
by Peggy and Lane Larson, Sierra Club Books, 1977, 288 pages, paper, $9.95
 This book is part of the Sierra Club Naturalist's Guide series, which is reviewed in more detail under "Series Reviews."

Special Places for the Discerning Traveler in Oregon, Washington, Idaho, Montana, British Columbia, California Wine Country
by Fred and Mardi Nystrom, Graphic Arts Center Publishing, 1986, 216 pages, paper, $13.95
See "The Pacific Northwest."

22 Days in the American Southwest: The Itinerary Planner
by Richard Harris, John Muir Publications, 1988, 136 pages, paper, $6.95
Including Colorado, Utah, and Nevada as well as New Mexico and Arizona, this book is part of the Itinerary Planner series, which is reviewed in more detail under "Series Reviews." Note that the title has recently been changed, and that this book may be found under *American Southwest in 22 Days.*

Visiting Our Western National Parks
by George Perkins, Perkins Publishing, 1987, 166 pages, paper, $12.95
This is a good overview of the parks west of the continental divide, including the Great Basin National Park in Nevada—our newest park. Each park and its history are briefly covered, as well as the campgrounds and adjacent facilities available. A general map, a brief note on hiking opportunities, and a listing of all the important, practical data are included. This handy, up-to-date resource guide is also filled with beautiful photographs, mostly in color. States covered are Idaho, Arizona, California, Colorado, Idaho, Montana, Nevada, Oregon, Utah, Washington, and Wyoming.

Western Trips & Trails
by E. M. Sterling, Pruett Publishing, 1987 (2nd ed.), 325 pages, paper, $10.00
The author's personal survey of each carefully chosen destination in 11 western states and Canada lends real credibility and a personal touch to this excellent outdoor guide. The style is relaxed and warm, with considerable attention paid both to details and the need to stop and smell the flowers along the way. The occasional hiker, the automobile traveler looking for a pretty place to walk, and even experienced backpacker will find this book a wealth of good ideas. States covered are: Arizona, California, Colorado, Idaho, New Mexico, Montana, Nevada, Oregon, Utah, Washington, Wyoming, along with several areas of the Canadian Rockies.

Woodall's California/Nevada/Mexico Campground Directory
Woodall Publishing, 1987, 240 pages, paper, $3.95

This large-format book is made up of different sections (not numbered consecutively) form their full directory, which is reviewed under "North America as a Whole." Oriented to RV and car camping, this title is updated annually.

Woodall's Tenting Directory: Western Region
Woodall Publishing, 1987, 168 pages, paper, $7.95

This large-format book on private and public campsites appropriate for tent camping covers all states west of the Mississippi plus western Canada and Mexico. Done in much the same way as their full guide, which is reviewed under "North America as a Whole," this book is updated annually.

Woodall's Western Campground Directory
Woodall Publishing, 1987, 642 pages, paper, $8.95

This large-format book covers all states west of the Mississippi except Arkansas, Iowa, Louisiana, Minnesota, and Missouri. This less expensive section of their full directory, which is reviewed under "North America as a Whole," is oriented to RV and car camping and updated annually.

Yellowstone Explorer's Guide
by Carl Schreier, Homestead Publishing, 1983, 52 pages, paper, $4.95

This is one of the Park Explorer's Guide series, which is reviewed in more detail under "Series Reviews."

THE SOUTHWEST

See also "United States as a Whole." The Southwest States are: Arizona, California, New Mexico, Oklahoma, Texas.

American Jewish Landmarks: A Travel Guide and History, Volume 4: The West
by Bernard Postal and Lionel Koppman, Fleet Press, 1986, 320 pages, paper, $12.95

This book is part of the four-volume American Jewish Landmarks series, which is reviewed in more detail under "Series Reviews."

American Southwest in 22 Days
See *22 Days in American Southwest* below.

America's Wonderful Little Hotels and Inns: Western Edition
edited by Sandra Soule, St. Martin's Press, 1988, 464 pages, paper, $13.95
See "Rocky Mountain/Great Basin States."

Ancient Cities of the Southwest: A Practical Guide to the Major Prehistoric Ruins of Arizona, New Mexico, Utah, and Colorado
by Buddy Mays, Chronicle Books, 1982, 132 pages, paper, $7.95
In this beautifully done book, Mays offers thoughtful descriptions of each ruin in the local and national monuments, tribal parks, primitive areas, and national parks of four western states. Included are notes on location, access, and, where applicable, a rather dated summary of the hours, facilities, and interpretive services available. This is an excellent overview.

Best Places to Stay in the Southwest
by Gail Rickey, The Harvard Common Press, 1988, 400 pages, paper, $14.95
Covering the states of Arizona, New Mexico, Oklahoma, and Texas, this book is part of the excellent "Best Places to Stay Guide" series, which is reviewed in more detail under "Series Reviews." Each selection is carefully inspected; no fee is accepted for inclusion.

Bicycle Touring in the Western United States
by Karen and Gary Hawkins, Random House, 1982, 390 pages, paper, $9.95
Including Arizona and New Mexico, this book is reviewed under "The Rocky Mountain/Great Basin States."

Budget Skiers Guidebook, Western U.S.
by Michael Studebaker, Glastonbury Press, 1985, 148 pages, paper, $6.95
See "The Rocky Mountain/Great Basin States."

Budget Vacationers Guidebook, Western U.S.
by Michael Studebaker, Glastonbury Press, 1986, 318 pages, paper, $8.95
See "The Rocky Mountain/Great Basin States."

The Condo Lux Vacationer's Guide to Condominium Rentals in the Mountain Resorts
by Jill Little, Random House, 1986, 338 pages, paper, $9.95
The Condo Lux Vacationer's Guide to Condominium Rentals in the Southwest and Hawaii
by Jill Little, Random House, 1986, 330 pages, paper, $9.95

The Mountain Resorts title includes New Mexico. Both are part of the Condo Lux Guide series, which is reviewed in more detail under "Series Reviews."

Country Inns, Lodges & Historic Hotels: The Midwest and Rocky Mountain States

by Anthony Hitchcock and Jean Lindgren, Burt Franklin–Publisher, 1988 (10th ed.), 241 pages, paper, $8.95

Including Arizona and New Mexico, this book is part of the Compleat Traveler's Companions series, which is reviewed in more detail under "Series Reviews." The West Coast volume is listed under California and the Pacific Northwest. No fees are accepted for inclusion in this annually updated guide.

Country Inns of America: Southwest

Henry Holt & Co., 1982, 96 pages, paper, $10.25

This book is part of the Country Inns of America series, which is reviewed in more detail under "Series Reviews."

Earth Treasures, Volume 4: The Southwestern Quadrant

by Allan Eckert, Harper & Row, 1987, 740 pages, cloth (flexible), $16.95

This guide to collecting minerals, rocks, and fossils is part of the Earth Treasures series, which is reviewed in more detail under "Series Reviews."

Fielding's Spanish Trails in the Southwest

by Lynn and Lawrence Foster, William Morrow & Co., 1986, 302 pages, paper, $12.95

This is one of Fielding's Trail Guide series, which is reviewed in more detail under "Series Reviews."

Fisher's World: Southwest

by Connie Sherley, Fisher's World, Inc., 1988, 386 pages, paper, $14.95

Fisher's World: West

by Frank and Elfriede Riley, Fisher's World, Inc., 1988, 290 pages, paper, $14.95

The Southwest volume includes New Mexico, Oklahoma, and Texas. The West volume includes Arizona and California. Both are part of the Fisher's World Guide series, which is reviewed in more detail under "Series Reviews." The series is updated annually.

Fodor's I-10

Fodor's Travel Publications, 1986, 208 pages, paper, $6.95

Fodor's I-80
Fodor's Travel Publications, 1986, 240 pages, paper, $6.95
These guides, describing services and supplies along I-10 from Los Angeles to Florida and I-80 from San Francisco to New York City, are part of Fodor's Interstate Guide series, which is reviewed in more detail under "Series Reviews."

Fodor's Far West
Fodor's Travel Publications, 1987, 536 pages, paper, $12.95
This single guide on Arizona, California, Idaho, Montana, Nevada, Oregon, Utah, Washington, and Wyoming is part of Fodor's Country/Regional Guide series, which is reviewed in more detail under "Series Reviews." The series is updated annually.

Frommer's Dollarwise Guide to Skiing USA West
by Lois Friedland, Prentice Hall Press, 1988, 320 pages, paper, $11.95
Including the skiing areas of the Southwest, this book is reviewed under "Rocky Mountain/Great Basin States" and updated every two years.

Frommer's Dollarwise Guide to the Southwest
by Roy Bongertz, Prentice Hall Press, 1986, 528 pages, paper, $11.95
This book is part of Frommer's Dollarwise Guide series, which is reviewed in more detail under "Series Reviews." This series emphasizes selections in the moderate price range and is updated every two years.

The Great American Runner's Guide: Western States Edition
by Edward Moore, Beaufort Books, 1985, 141 pages, paper, $6.95
Including Arizona, California, and New Mexico, this book is reviewed under "Rocky Mountain/Great Basin States."

Great Hot Springs of the West
by Bill Kaysing, Capra Press, 1984, 208 pages, paper, $9.95
Including Arizona, California, and New Mexico, this book is reviewed under "Rocky Mountain/Great Basin States."

The Great Towns of the West
by David Vokac, West Press, 1985, 464 pages, paper, $14.95
Including Arizona, California, and New Mexico, this book is part of the Great Towns Guide series, which is reviewed in more detail under "Series Reviews."

Guide to the National Park Areas: Western States
by David and Kay Scott, The Globe Pequot Press, 1987, 341 pages, paper, $10.95

This well-organized guide gives a good rundown on basically every area run by the National Park Service that is west of the Mississippi. More than just parks, these areas include monuments, seashores, historic sites, recreation areas, and military parks—a total of 170 in all. All are of national importance, but not necessarily uniformly popular and crowded. Included is a good description, the location, where to find the visitor's center, hiking trails of interest, facilities available, camping options, and whether (and where) fishing is permitted. This is an excellent, thoughtfully prepared resource to the national park system. A companion guide to the eastern states is reviewed under "The South."

Guide to the Recommended Country Inns of Arizona, New Mexico, and Texas
by Eleanor Morris, The Globe Pequot Press, 1987, 290 pages, paper, $9.95

This is one of the excellent Recommended Country Inns series, which is reviewed in more detail under "Series Reviews." The author has visited and reviewed each inn personally; no payments have been accepted for inclusion. This book is updated every two years.

Hiking the Southwest: Arizona, New Mexico and West Texas
by Dave Ganci, Sierra Club Books, 1983, 384 pages, paper, $9.95

This is a small-format title in the Sierra Club Hiking Totebook series, which is reviewed in more detail under "Series Reviews."

Hot Springs and Hot Pools of the Southwest
by Jayson Loam and Gary Sohler, Wilderness Press, 1985 (2nd ed.), 192 pages, paper, $12.95

This is a good resource to available hot tubs/spas in motels and inns, with good descriptions of improved and unimproved hot pools throughout Arizona, California, Nevada, and New Mexico. Good location maps and interesting photos supplement this quality guide.

Indian Villages of the Southwest: A Practical Guide to the Pueblo Indian Villages of New Mexico and Arizona
by Buddy Mays, Chronicle Books, 1985, 105 pages, paper, $8.95

This is a thoughtfully prepared guide to 18 picturesque small Indian pueblos, all but one of which is located in New Mexico. A bit of history and thought-provoking discussion is combined with practical information on access, when non-Indians can visit, any admission charges or permission needed to enter, what types of photography are permissible, any available interpretive services, special ceremonies, and arts and crafts produced by the pueblo.

Insight Guide: American Southwest
by Apa Productions, Prentice Hall Press, 1985, 384 pages, paper, $15.95

This book is part of the excellent Insight Guide series, which is reviewed in more detail under "Series Reviews."

The Interstate Gourmet: Texas and the Southwest
by Barbara Rodriguez and Tom Miller, Summit Books, 1986, 232 pages, paper, $6.95

This is one of the excellent Interstate Gourmet series, which is reviewed in more detail under "Series Reviews."

Journey to the High Southwest: A Traveler's Guide
by Robert Casey, The Globe Pequot Press, 1988 (3rd ed.), 450 pages, paper, $16.95

This classic guide to the Four Corners region and the Santa Fe area has got even better in this third, expanded edition. This edition includes tour information to the Flagstaff, Arizona and Albuquerque, New Mexico areas, the new Anasazi Heritage Center near Dolores, Colorado, and a revised and greatly expanded shopping and buying guide for southwestern Indian arts and crafts. This is an exciting tour of the natural wonders, archaeological ruins, Indian reservations, parks, and historic sites of this magnificent region.

Landmarks of the West: A Guide to Historic Sites
by Kent Ruth, The University of Nebraska Press, 1986, 309 pages, paper, $17.50

This superb book, including all the states of the Southwest, is reviewed under "The Rocky Mountain/Great Basin States."

Mobil Travel Guide: Lodging for Less, West
Prentice Hall Press, 1988, 250 pages, paper, $5.95

This is one of the Mobil Lodging for Less series, which is reviewed in more detail under "Series Reviews." The series is updated annually.

Mobil Travel Guide: California and the West
Prentice Hall Press, 1988, 274 pages, paper, $8.95
Mobil Travel Guide: Southwest and South Central
Prentice Hall Press, 1988, 322 pages, paper, $8.95

These two large-format guides are part of the well-known Mobil Travel Guide series, which is reviewed in more detail under "Series

Reviews." The California and the West volume includes Arizona and California. The Southwest and South Central volume includes Oklahoma, Texas, and New Mexico. The series is updated annually.

Myrna Oakley's Bed and Breakfast Northwest
by Myrna Oakley, Solstice Press, 1987, 113 pages, paper, $7.95
   Containing some selections in northern California, this book is reviewed under "Pacific Northwest."

Pacific Boating Almanac: Northern California & Nevada
Western Marine Enterprises, 1987, 432 pages, paper, $10.95
Pacific Boating Almanac: Southern California, Arizona, & Mexico
Western Marine Enterprises, 1987, 432 pages, paper, $10.95
   These two annually published guides on the how and where of boating are part of the Boating Almanac series, which is reviewed in more detail under "Series Reviews."

Senior Guide: Day-Hiking in the Southwestern National Parks and Monuments
by James Campbell, WestPark Books, 1986, 220 pages, paper, $11.95
   If you are a novice or fairly inexperienced hiker, senior citizen or not, Campbell has a lot of words of experience to share with you. Nearly half of this book is spent on an excellent discussion of planning, equipment and clothing needs, hiking hardware that is worth the weight, and safe hiking strategies for hikers of all ages and abilities. Campbell, an ecologist and former park ranger, shares his selection of the best day-hike trails throughout the national parks and monuments of the southwest. He grades each hike, gives the elevations, distances, best seasons to go, plants and animals to look for, and other special considerations, such as the presence or absence of water.

The Sierra Club Guide to the National Parks of the Desert Southwest
Sierra Club Books, 1984, 352 pages, cloth, $14.95
The Sierra Club Guide to the National Parks of the Pacific Southwest and Hawaii
Sierra Club Books, 1984, 261 pages, cloth, $14.95
   These two titles are part of the Sierra Club National Parks Guide series, which is reviewed in more detail under "Series Reviews."

The Sierra Club Guide to the Natural Areas of New Mexico, Arizona, and Nevada
by John and Jane Perry, Sierra Club Books, 1985, 412 pages, paper, $10.95
This is one of the Sierra Club Natural Areas Guide series which is reviewed in more detail under "Series Reviews."

The Sierra Club Naturalist's Guide to the Deserts of the Southwest
by Peggy and Lane Larson, Sierra Club Books, 1977, 288 pages, paper, $9.95
The Sierra Club Naturalist's Guide to the Sierra Nevada
by Stephen Whitney, Sierra Club Books, 1979, 544 pages, paper, $10.95
These two titles are part of the Sierra Club Naturalist's Guide series, which is reviewed in more detail under "Series Reviews."

Sunset Highway Services Exit-by-Exit: Southwest Edition
Lane Publishing, 1987, 288 pages, paper, $12.95
This large-format guide to the limited access highways of Arizona, New Mexico, and Texas contains detailed exit diagrams pinpointing food, lodging, and other services.

Traveling Texas Borders: A Guide to the Best of Both Sides
by Ann Ruff, Gulf Publishing, 1983, 119 pages, paper, $9.95
This book describes interesting things to do along the Texas-Oklahoma and Texas-New Mexico borders.

22 Days in the American Southwest: The Itinerary Planner
by Richard Harris, John Muir Publications, 1988, 136 pages, paper, $6.95
Including Colorado, Utah, and Nevada as well as New Mexico and Arizona, this book is part of the Itinerary Planner series, which is reviewed in more detail under "Series Reviews." Note that the title has recently been changed, and that this book may be found under *American Southwest in 22 Days.*

Visiting Our Western National Parks
George Perkins, Perkins Publishing, 1987, 166 pages, paper, $12.95
Including the parks of California and Arizona, this book is reviewed under "Rocky Mountain/Great Basin States."

Western Trips & Trails
by E. M. Sterling, Pruett Publishing, 1987 (2nd ed.), 325 pages, paper, $10.00
This excellent guide to hikes and camping in 11 western states

and Canada is reviewed under "Rocky Mountain/Great Basin States."

Woodall's California/Nevada/Mexico Campground Directory
Woodall Publishing, 1987, 240 pages, paper, $3.95

This large-format guide, made up of sections (not numbered consecutively) from their full directory, is reviewed under "North America as a Whole." Oriented to RV and car camping, this book is updated annually.

Woodall's Tenting Directory: Western Edition
Woodall Publishing, 1987, 168 pages, paper, $7.95

This large-format guide to public and private campgrounds appropriate for tent camping, is done in a similar fashion to their full directory, which is reviewed under "North America as a Whole." All states west of the Mississippi, western Canada, and Mexico are covered in this annually updated guide.

Woodall's Western Campground Directory
Woodall Publishing, 1987, 642 pages, paper, $8.95

This is a large-format, less expensive section of their full directory, which is reviewed under "North America as a Whole." This one covers 19 western states, western Canada, and Mexico, and is oriented to RV and car camping. This title is updated annually.

THE PACIFIC NORTHWEST

See also "United States as a Whole." The Pacific Northwest States are Oregon, Washington.

The Adventure Guide to the American Northwest
Hunter Publishing, 1988, 224 pages, paper, $12.95

This book is part of the Hunter Adventure Guide series, which is reviewed in more detail under "Series Reviews."

Bed and Breakfast Guide: West Coast
by Courtia Worth and Terry Berger, Prentice Hall Press, 1986, 160 pages, paper, $12.95

The authors provide plenty of color photographs of each selection with both interior and exterior views, in addition to good descriptions and the necessary practical details and directions for 115 inns in Oregon, Washington, and California. The photographs are particularly helpful in giving visual clues to the best spot to choose.

Bed and Breakfast Homes Directory: California, Oregon, Washington
by Diane Knight, Knighttime Publications, 1988 (5th ed.), 280
pages, paper, $9.95
Knight's popular guide provides a different focus from other B&B
guides—it covers actual homes travelers can stay in rather than B&B
inns. The British began bed and breakfasts by inviting travelers into
their homes. The homes selected in this directory, located all along
the Pacific coast as well as in southwestern British Columbia, have
chosen to carry on this British-style tradition. Knight provides a good
description of each—she has visited every home included in this
guide—and all the facts needed to choose between them. Every price
range is represented, but moderately priced locations are emphasized.
For those who want the old-fashioned B&B experience, this is a great
guide. The 1988 edition has added a quick rundown of recommended
dining spots in each area. This title is updated every two years.

The Best Places to Kiss in the Northwest: A Romantic Travel Guide
by Paula Begoun, Beginning Press, 1986, 113 pages, paper, $7.95
This guide to those romantic spots is part of the Romantic Travel
Guide series, which is reviewed in more detail under "Series Reviews."

Best Places to Stay in the Pacific Northwest
by Marilyn McFarlane, The Harvard Common Press, 1988, 400
pages, paper, $14.95
Covering Washington (including the San Juan islands), Oregon,
Idaho, Montana, and British Columbia, this book is part of the excellent Best Places to Stay Guide series, which is reviewed in more
detail under "Series Reviews." Each selection has been carefully
reviewed; no fee has been charged for inclusion.

Bicycle Touring in the Western United States
by Karen and Gary Hawkins, Random House, 1982, 390 pages,
paper, $9.95
See "The Rocky Mountain/Great Basin States."

Bicyling the Pacific Coast
by Tom Kirkendall and Vicky Spring, The Mountaineers, 1984, 224
pages, paper, $9.95
The guide is organized north-to-south, beginning in British Columbia and ending at the Mexican border, all the while hugging the
coastline of B.C., Washington, Oregon, and California. This nearly
2000-mile journey is broken into segments approximately 50 miles
long—a decent day's ride for the touring cyclist. Along the way are
plenty of side trips. Each segment is carefully discussed and followed

by a detailed trip log. Scenic areas, campground possibilities, and potential hazards are all noted in this well-organized and thorough, yet compact, guide.

Budget Skiers Guidebook, Western U.S.
by Michael Studebaker, Glastonbury Press, 1985, 148 pages, paper, $6.95
Including Oregon and Washington, this book is reviewed under "The Rocky Mountain/Great Basin States."

Budget Vacationers Guidebook, Western U.S.
by Michael Studebaker, Glastonbury Press, 1986, 318 pages, paper, $8.95
Including Oregon and Washington, this book is reviewed under "The Rocky Mountain/Great Basin States."

Country Inns, Lodges & Historic Hotels: California, Oregon & Washington
by Anthony Hitchcock and Jean Lindgren, Burt Franklin–Publisher, 1988 (10th ed.), 281 pages, paper, $8.95
This book is part of the Compleat Traveler's Companions series, which is reviewed in more detail under "Series Reviews." No fees are accepted for inclusion in this annually updated guide.

Country Inns of America: Pacific Northwest
Henry Holt & Co., 1981, 96 pages, paper, $9.95
Older but still helpful as a supplement to a more up-to-date guide, this book is part of the Country Inns of America series, which is reviewed in more detail under "Series Reviews." Many beautiful color photographs are included.

Earth Treasures, Volume 3: The Northwestern Quadrant
by Allen Eckert, Harper & Row, 1987, 632 pages, cloth (flexible), $16.95
This guide to collecting minerals, rocks, and fossils is part of the Earth Treasures series, which is reviewed in more detail under "Series Reviews."

Fielding's Lewis and Clark Trail
by Gerald Olmsted, William Morrow & Co., 1986, 305 pages, paper, $12.95
Following the famous trail from Missouri to the Pacific Northwest, this is one of the Fielding's Trail Guide series, which is reviewed in more detail under "Series Reviews."

Fisher's World: Pacific Northwest
by Barry and Hilda Anderson, Fisher's World, Inc., 1988, 320 pages, paper, $14.95
Covering Oregon, Washington, western Canada, and Alaska, this book is part of the Fisher's World Guide series, which is reviewed in more detail under "Series Reviews." The series is updated annually.

Fodor's Far West
Fodor's Travel Publications, 1987, 536 pages, paper, $12.95
Fodor's Pacific North Coast
Fodor's Travel Publications, 1987, 352 pages, paper, $9.95
These two titles are part of Fodor's Country/Regional Guide series, which is reviewed in more detail under "Series Reviews." The Far West title covers Arizona, California, Idaho, Montana, Nevada, Oregon, Utah, Washington, and Wyoming. The Pacific North Coast includes the Pacific Northwest and British Columbia. The series is updated annually.

Foraging Along the Pacific Coast
by Peter Howorth, Capra Press, 1986, 213 pages, paper, $9.95
See "California."

Frommer's Dollarwise Guide to Skiing USA West
by Lois Friedland, Prentice Hall Press, 1988, 320 pages, paper, $11.95
See "Rocky Mountain/Great Basin States." This title is updated every two years.

Frommer's Dollarwise Guide to the Northwest
by Marylyn Springer and Don Schultz, Prentice Hall Press, 1987, 408 pages, paper, $11.95
This book is part of Frommer's Dollarwise Guide series, which is reviewed in more detail under "Series Reviews." The series emphasizes moderately priced selections and is updated every two years.

Ghost Towns of the Northwest
by Norman Weis, Caxton Printers, 1981, 319 pages, cloth, $11.95
This interesting guide to all sorts of existing ghost towns in Idaho, Montana, Oregon, Washington, and Wyoming provides general location maps, although the going is often tough along old, rutted paths. The author shares the history and anecdotes behind each of these old, abandoned towns. This three-year research project is a wealth of information and includes many fascinating photographs. It is an excellent guide for the ghost-town nut.

Going Places: Family Getaways in the Pacific Northwest
by John Biegelow and Breck Longstreth, Seattle's Child
Publications, 1985, 139 pages, paper, $7.95
Good descriptions of lots of family-oriented places to stay and play
in Oregon, Washington, Idaho, and British Columbia are contained
in this well-thought-out guide from the publishers of *Seattle's Child*,
a monthly guide for parents. Included are lists of things to do at each
resort/hotel selected and in the surrounding area, the amenities
available, comments from families who have used the facilities, and
other practical facts useful for planning a vacation of family fun.

The Great American Runner's Guide: Western States Edition
by Edward Moore, Beaufort Books, 1985, 141 pages, paper, $6.95
Including Oregon and Washington, this book is reviewed under
"The Rocky Mountain/Great Basin States."

Great Hot Springs of the West
by Bill Kaysing, Capra Press, 1984, 208 pages, paper, $9.95
Including Oregon and Washington, this book is reviewed under
"The Rocky Mountain/Great Basin States."

The Great Towns of the Pacific Northwest
by David Vokac, West Press, 1987, 304 pages, paper, $8.95
The Great Towns of the West
by David Vokac, West Press, 1985, 464 pages, paper, $14.95
These two titles are part of the Great Towns Guide series, which
is reviewed in more detail under "Series Reviews." The West volume
includes Oregon and Washington.

Guide to the National Park Areas: Western States
by David and Kay Scott, The Globe Pequot Press, 1987 (2nd ed.),
341 pages, paper, $10.95
Including Oregon and Washington, this book is reviewed under
"Southwest."

Guide to the Recommended Country Inns of the West Coast
by Julianne Belote, The Globe Pequot Press, 1986, 394 pages,
paper, $10.95
Including Oregon and Washington, this is one of the excellent
Recommended Country Inns series, which is reviewed in more detail
under "Series Reviews." The author has visited and evaluated each
inn personally; no payment has been accepted for inclusion. This
book is updated every two years.

Hot Springs and Hot Pools of the Northwest

by Jayson Loam and Marjorie Gersh, Wilderness Press, 1986 (2nd ed.), 196 pages, paper, $12.95

This guide lists the available hot tubs/spas in motels and inns and describes the improved and unimproved natural hot pools throughout Colorado, Idaho, Montana, Oregon, Utah, Washington, Wyoming, and southwestern Canada. Good location maps and interesting photos supplement this helpful resource guide.

Insight Guide: The Pacific Northwest

by Apa Productions, Graphic Arts Center Publishing, 1986, 330 pages, paper, $15.95

Thid book is part of the excellent Insight Guide series, which is reviewed in more detail under "Series Reviews." This title is distributed by Graphic Arts Center Publishing; the remainder of the series is distributed by Prentice Hall Press.

The Interstate Gourmet: California and the Pacific Northwest

by Neal Weiner and David Schwartz, Summit Books, 1986, 222 pages, paper, $6.95

This is one of the highly regarded Interstate Gourmet series, which is reviewed in more detail under "Series Reviews."

Let's Go: Pacific Northwest, Western Canada, and Alaska

by Harvard Student Agencies, St. Martin's Press, 1988, 464 pages, paper, $10.95

This book is part of the excellent, budget-oriented Let's Go Guide series, which is reviewed in more detail under "Series Reviews." The series is updated annually.

Mobil Travel Guide: Lodging for Less, West

Prentice Hall Press, 1988, 250 pages, paper, $5.95

Including Oregon and Washington, this is one of the Mobil Lodging for Less series, which is reviewed in more detail under "Series Reviews." The series is updated annually.

Mobil Travel Guide: Northwest and Great Plains States

Prentice Hall Press, 1987, 333 pages, paper, $8.95

This annually updated, large-format guide is part of the well-known Mobil Travel Guide series, which is reviewed in more detail under "Series Reviews."

Myrna Oakley's Bed & Breakfast Northwest
by Myrna Oakley, Solstice Press, 1987, 197 pages, paper, $9.95
After clearly listing all of the essentials, the author artfully recreates the atmosphere of each of the many inns selected. Suggestions of things to do and a smattering of the history of each region is included. This excellent guide covers not only Oregon and Washington but Idaho and British Columbia as well—with a sampling of inns from southeast Alaska, Montana, northern California, and northern Nevada.

Northwest Best Places
by David Brewster and Kathryn Robinson, Sasquatch Books, 1987, 544 pages, paper, $14.95
Thorough, comprehensive, and accurate, *Northwest Best Places* is the most respected guidebook to the Pacific Northwest. The primary focus is on the hotels and restaurants of Oregon, Washington, and British Columbia. The authors are able to provide a detailed evaluation of over 1500 listings, each rated on a scale of 0 to 4 stars. Very few receive a full four stars yet every entry has merit and is worthy of consideration. The descriptions are truly excellent and the selections run from inexpensive to expensive, with the emphasis on moderate and up. All the practical details are also included. In addition, numerous touring suggestions are provided and, while this aspect of the book takes a back seat to the hotel and restaurant reviews, the touring information is not to be missed—there are some real pearls. This guide is updated every two years.

Northwest Golfer: A Guide to the Public Golf Courses of Washington & Oregon
by Kiki Canniff, KI-2 Enterprises, 1987, 188 pages, paper, $9.95
This guide contains a brief run-down on the 250 golf courses allowing public play in Oregon and Washington. Included are descriptions, difficulty of the course, hours, fees, and general scenic features of each course.

Northwest Mileposts
Alaska Northwest Publishing, 1987, 496 pages, paper, $14.95
This large-format, annually updated guide is structured along the lines of its more famous companion guide, *The Milepost*, long the standard guide to Alaska. This is an extremely comprehensive work in spite of the sometimes irritating congestion of ads. It is organized by highway routes throughout the region—which includes Idaho, Oregon, Montana, and Washington, as well as Southwestern Canada. The mile-by-mile log provides an abundance of information on sights, fishing, camping, and exit services available, and brief, inter-

esting historical notes. This is a wealth of good, up-to-date information.

Northwest Trails: A Hiker's Guide to National Parks and Wilderness Areas
by Ira Spring and Harvey Manning, The Mountaineers, 1982, 192 pages, paper, $9.95

This is one of the excellent Mountaineers Hiking Guide series, which is reviewed in more detail under "Series Reviews."

Northwest Wine Country
by Ronald and Glenda Holden, Holden Pacific, 1986, 282 pages, paper, $12.95

In this guide, the Holdens, well known in northwest wine country circles, profile and rate each and every winery in Idaho, Oregon, and Washington. The ratings are two-fold, judging both value as a tourist attraction and quality of wine. Their informative evaluations include a bit of history on each winery, a discussion of what it's like to visit, wine tasting recommendations, special events each winery holds, hours open, and clear directions on how to get there.

100 Hikes in the Inland Northwest
by Rich Landers and Ida Rowe Dolphin, The Mountaineers, 1987, 224 pages, paper, $9.95

Including hikes in Idaho, Montana, Washington, and British Columbia, this book is part of the Mountaineers Hiking Guide series, which is reviewed in more detail under "Series Reviews."

Pacific Boating Almanac: Pacific Northwest & Alaska
Western Marine Enterprises, 1987 (23rd ed.), 432 pages, paper, $10.95

This annual guide on the how-to and where-to of boating is part of the Boating Almanac series, which is reviewed in more detail under "Series Reviews."

Pacific Northwest in 22 Days
See *22 Days in the Pacific Northwest* below.

Parks of the Pacific Coast
by Doug and Bobbe Tatreau, The Globe Pequot Press, 1985, 160 pages, paper, $10.95

This large-format guide to 34 national and historic parks in California, Oregon, and Washington contains numerous photos, helpful maps along with a general overview of each park, its access, services, etc. A quick-glance chart at the back compares each park by specific types of services and recreation available. All park addresses and phone numbers are included.

The Sierra Club Guide to the National Parks of the Pacific Northwest and Alaska
Sierra Club Books, 1985, 400 pages, cloth, $14.95
This is one of the Sierra Club National Parks Guide series, which is reviewed in more detail under "Series Reviews."

The Sierra Club Guide to the Natural Areas of Oregon and Washington
by John and Jane Perry, Sierra Club Books, 1983, 360 pages, paper, $9.95
This book is part of the Sierra Club Natural Areas Guide series, which is reviewed in more detail under "Series Reviews."

Special Places for the Discerning Traveler in Oregon, Washington, Idaho, Montana, British Columbia, California Wine Country
by Fred and Mardi Nystrom, Graphic Arts Center Publishing, 1986, 216 pages, paper, $13.95
In this guide, the authors have assembled their picks of the very best places to play, stay, or eat a memorable meal. Those selected are an exclusive group—there are only 48—and each is well described and evaluated, with pertinent details made clear and often beautiful photos included. This select list ranges in price from moderate to quite expensive.

22 Days in the Pacific Northwest: The Itinerary Planner
by Richard Harris, John Muir Publications, 1988, 136 pages, paper, $6.95
This is one of the Itinerary Planner series, which is reviewed in more detail under "Series Reviews." Note that this is a recent title change, and that this book may be found under *Pacific Northwest in 22 Days.*

Visiting Our Western National Parks
by George Perkins, Perkins Publishing, 1987, 166 pages, paper, $12.95
Including Oregon and Washington, this book is reviewed under "Rocky Mountain/Great Basin States."

Webster's Wine Tours: California, Oregon and Washington
by Bob Thompson, Prentice Hall Press, 1987, 200 pages, cloth
(flexible), $15.95
    This book is part of the Webster's Wine Tours series, which is
reviewed in more detail under "Series Reviews."

Western Trips & Trails
by E. M. Sterling, Pruett Publishing, 1987 (2nd ed.), 325 pages,
paper, $10.00
    Including Oregon and Washington, this book is reviewed under
"Rocky Mountain/Great Basin States."

Woodall's Tenting Directory
Woodall Publishing, 1987, 168 pages, paper, $7.95
    This large-format guide to campsites appropriate for tent camping
in all states west of the Mississippi is done in the same fashion as
their full directory, which is reviewed under "North America as a
Whole." This title is updated annually.

Woodall's Western Campground Directory
Woodall Publishing, 1987, 642 pages, paper, $8.95
    This is a large-format guide to camping in 19 western states,
western Canada, and Mexico. It is a section of their full directory,
which is reviewed under "North America as a Whole." Oriented to
RV and car camping, this title is updated annually.

States and Federal District of the United States

ALABAMA ───
See also "The South" and "United States as a Whole."

Eating Out in Alabama...Still!: A Guide to the Best Restaurants
by "Hungry" Herman Moore, Title Books, 1988, 201 pages, paper,
$6.95
    This is a great gastronomic guidebook, frequently updated, that
will provide travelers to Alabama with excellent, informative eval-
uations/descriptions of everything from fancy coat-and-tie restaurants to down-home cookin' at the corner café. Included are all the
practical facts and figures—even appropriate dress, parking, and reservation requirements.

ALASKA ──
See also "United States as a Whole."

Adventuring in Alaska: The Sierra Club Travel Guide to the Great Land
by Peggy Wayburn, Sierra Club Books, 1988 (revised ed.), 352 pages, paper, $10.95

This book is part of the excellent Sierra Club Adventure Travel Guide series, which is reviewed in more detail under "Series Reviews."

The Alaska Adventure Book
Graphic Arts Center Publishing, 1987, 116 pages, paper, $12.95

This is a good collection of specific vacation ideas, with helpful descriptions and practical information on parks, refuges, lodges, cruises, museums, ski touring, climbing, biking, birding, sailing, rafting, fishing, and horseback riding. Plenty of color photographs are included.

Alaska in 22 Days
See *22 Days in Alaska* below.

Alaska's Parklands: The Complete Guide
by Nancy and Lange Simmerman, The Mountaineers, 1983, 336 pages, paper, $15.95

Here in one book is a brief overview of over 110 state and national parks and wild areas—their location, the topographical maps needed, the best times to visit, elevations, camping, facilities, outdoor activities available, etc.

Alaska's Southeast: Touring the Inside Passage
by Sarah Eppenbach, The Globe Pequot Press, 1988 (3rd ed.), 304 pages, paper, $11.95

This is a beautifully written, well-researched, well-organized guide to the land of the Inside Passage. Travelers venturing to Alaska via state ferry, cruise ship, or private means will find information on what to bring, when to go, geography, weather, history, native cultures, sightseeing, shopping, and more. Hotels and restaurants are briefly covered.

The Alaska Wilderness Milepost
Alaska Northwest Publishing, 1988, 494 pages, paper, $14.95

This was the first issue of what should be a frequently updated "supplement" to the famous *The Milepost*. It is a comprehensive work for both business and recreational travelers on 250 remote towns and villages. Locations, how to get there, private plane landing requirements, and what visitor's facilities are available are all outlined in this great book.

Alaska-Yukon Handbook (including the Canadian Rockies)

by David Stanley and Deke Castleman, Moon Publications, 1988, 450 pages, paper, $10.95

Part of the superb Moon Handbook series, which is reviewed in more detail under "Series Reviews," this new edition is greatly expanded and includes the western national parks of Canada.

Berlitz Cruise Guide: Alaska

Macmillan Publishing, 1986, 160 pages, paper, $6.95

This small-format book of cruising options along the Inside Passage includes where to go, how to enjoy a cruise, the ports of call, and a general overview. Not as up-to-date as other cruise guides, this is still a worthwhile, inexpensive overview.

Camping Alaska and Canada's Yukon: The Motorist's Handbook to North Country Campgrounds and Roadways

by Mike and Marilyn Miller, The Globe Pequot Press, 1987, 187 pages, paper, $10.95

Filled with suggestions, this is one of those books that will really help travelers organize their plans for camping in the northern climes. Included are notes on planning, what to wear, campground descriptions and fees, places to fish, and the nearest churches along the way. Information is arranged geographically.

The Coastal Kayaker: Kayak Camping on the Alaska and B.C. Coast

by Randel Washburne, The Globe Pequot Press, 1983, 224 pages, paper, $10.95

This comprehensive handbook covers kayaking along the northern Pacific coast. Seven sample tours are included.

55 Ways to the Wilderness of Southcentral Alaska

by Nancy Simmerman, The Mountaineers, 1985 (3rd ed.), 176 pages, paper, $9.95

This book is part of the well-done Mountaineers Hiking Guide series, which is reviewed in more detail under "Series Reviews."

Fisher's World: Pacific Northwest

by Barry and Hilda Anderson, Fisher's World, Inc., 1988, 320 pages, paper, $14.95

Including Alaska and western Canada, this book is part of the Fisher's World Guide series, which is reviewed in more detail under "Series Reviews." The series is updated annually.

Fodor's Alaska
Fodor's Travel Publications, 1988, 218 pages, paper, $8.95
This book is part of Fodor's Country/Regional Guide series, which is reviewed in more detail under "Series Reviews." The series is updated annually.

Frommer's Dollarwise Guide to Alaska
by John Anderson, Prentice Hall Press, 1987, 336 pages, paper, $12.95
This is one of Frommer's Dollarwise Guide series, which is reviewed in more detail under "Series Reviews." This series emphasizes selections in the moderate price range and is updated every two years.

Glacier Bay National Park: A Backcountry Guide to the Glaciers and Beyond
by Jim DuFresne, The Mountaineers, 1987, 152 pages, paper, $8.95
This book is part of the Mountaineers National Park Guide series, which is reviewed in more detail under "Series Reviews."

Great American Runner's Guide: Western Edition
by Edward Moore, Beaufort Books, 1985, 141 pages, paper, $6.95
Including Alaska, this book is reviewed under "The Rocky Mountain/Great Basin States."

How to Cruise to Alaska Without Rocking the Boat Too Much
by Walt Woodward, Nor'Westing, Inc., 1985, 186 pages, paper, $11.95
This book will help travelers enjoy cruising their own boat to Alaska. Included is information on the needed charts, the best overnight resting spots, clothes and food to take, interesting side trips, and other facts important in boat travel.

The Inside Passage Traveler
by Ellen Searby, Windham Bay Press, 1988 (11th ed.), 192 pages, paper, $7.95
This is a solid guide to the Alaska Marine Highway System and the towns of the Inside Passage. For each town the author has included an extensive list of things to see and do, recommended hotels, transportation options, campgrounds, boat rentals/charters, facilities available (such as laundromats, propane, dump stations, hospitals, etc.), and special events. A small section on the southwestern Alaska ferry system is also part of this annually updated guide.

Insight Guide: Alaska
by Apa Productions, Prentice Hall Press, 1987, 331 pages, paper, $15.95
This book is part of the excellent Insight Guide series, which is reviewed in more detail under "Series Reviews."

Juneau Trails: Recreational Opportunity Guide
Alaska Natural History Association, 1985, 61 pages, paper, $2.00
This helpful little booklet, done in cooperation with the U.S. Forest Service, gives a wide array of hiking ideas in and around the Juneau area. The trails noted vary in length from 0.5 to 12 miles.

Let's Go: Pacific Northwest, Western Canada & Alaska
by Harvard Student Agencies, St. Martin's Press, 1988, 464 pages, paper, $10.95
This is one of the excellent, budget-oriented Let's Go Guide series, which is reviewed in more detail under "Series Reviews." The series is updated annually.

The Milepost
Alaska Northwest Publishing, 1988 (40th ed.), 530 pages, paper, $14.95
Since 1949, this "bible of north country travel" has helped those headed to Alaska and the provinces of western Canada. Compared to many guidebooks, it seems cluttered with advertisements, but the contents are valuable. Here is a mile-by-mile guide to all the highways of the north, including what to see, what to do, where to camp or find a hotel, where to eat, etc. Updated annually through field editor research and plenty of reader feedback, this is deservedly one of the leading Alaska guides—along with the newer *Wilderness Milepost.*

Myrna Oakley's Bed & Breakfast Northwest
by Myrna Oakley, Solstice Press, 1987, 197 pages, paper, $9.95
Including some selections in southeastern Alaska, this book is reviewed under "The Pacific Northwest."

Pacific Boating Almanac: Pacific Northwest & Alaska
Western Marine Enterprises, 1987 (23rd ed.), 432 pages, paper, $10.95
This annual guide on the how-to and where-to of boating is part of the Boating Almanac series, which is reviewed in more detail under "Series Reviews."

Ride Guide to the Historic Alaska Railroad

by Laura Zahn and Anita Williams, Turnagain Products, 1987, 64 pages, paper, $3.95

The Alaska railroad is a wonderful ride. Beginning in Seward, it hits the big city of Anchorage, heads north through the beautiful Alaska backcountry into Denali National Park (lucky travelers will see Mt. McKinley as they approach the park) and on to Fairbanks. This handy booklet provides an informative mile-by-mile account of interesting facts and anecdotes to make the trip more fun.

Roadside Geology of Alaska

by Cathy Conner and Daniel O'Hare, Mountain Press, 1988, 256 pages, paper, $11.95

This book is part of the excellent Roadside Geology Guide series, which is reviewed in more detail under "Series Reviews."

The Sierra Club Guide to the National Parks of the Pacific Northwest and Alaska

Sierra Club Books, 1985, 400 pages, cloth, $14.95

This book is part of the Sierra Club National Parks Guide series, which is reviewed in more detail under "Series Reviews."

The Student's Guide to the Best Summer Jobs in Alaska

by Josh Groves, Mustang Publishing, 1986, 159 pages, paper, $7.95

Summer in Alaska is a popular idea among students, and this guide provides plenty of concrete ideas and general job-hunting strategies.

Sunset: Alaska Travel Guide

Lane Publishing, 1988 (4th ed.), 120 pages, paper, $9.95

This older, large-format book, useful primarily for planning ideas, is part of the Sunset Travel Guide series, which is reviewed in more detail under "Series Reviews."

A Tourist Guide to Mount McKinley

by Bradford Washburn, Alaska Northwest Publishing, 1980 (revised ed.), 80 pages, paper, $5.95

This is an excellent, large-format booklet on the great mountain of North America, "Denali." Here is a mile-by-mile account for travelers of the Park Highway which details, among other things, the many spectacular views of Mt. McKinley. Washburn's love and enthusiasm for the subject is obvious and makes for a first-rate book.

22 Days in Alaska: The Itinerary Planner
by Pamela Lanier, John Muir Publications, 1988, 136 pages, paper, $6.95

This is a recent title in the expanding Itinerary Planner series, which is reviewed in more detail under "Series Reviews." Note that the title has recently changed, and that this book may be found under *Alaska in 22 Days.*

ARIZONA

See also "The Southwest" and "United States as a Whole."

Arizona Hideaways
by Thelma Heatwole, Golden West Publishers, 1986, 126 pages, paper, $4.50

This is a good list of tiny towns in which to spend a tranquil day or two hiding away.

Arizona Off the Beaten Path!
by Thelma Heatwole, Golden West Publishers, 1982, 142 pages, paper, $4.50

In this book, a veteran reporter for the *Arizona Republic* details her favorite out-of-the-way corners of Arizona. The descriptions of her adventures are interesting, and simple maps will help pinpoint the location, but additional maps may be necessary.

Arizona Outdoor Adventure
by Ernest Snyder, Golden West Publishers, 1985, 126 pages, paper, $5.00

Arizona ranges from a few hundred feet above sea level to more than 12,600 feet. And with mountains, deserts, canyons, and rivers, choices for outdoor fun are many. Snyder helps travelers understand what they are seeing by providing interesting information on plants, animals, geology, rocks, natural environments, and land forms.

Arizona Trails: 100 Hikes in Canyon and Sierra
by David Mazel, Wilderness Press, 1985 (2nd ed.), 312 pages, paper, $12.95

This book is part of the excellent Wilderness Press Hiking Guide series, which is reviewed in more detail under "Series Reviews."

Arizona Traveler's Handbook
by Bill Weir, Moon Publications, 1986, 450 pages, paper, $10.95

This book is part of the superb Moon Handbook series, which is reviewed in more detail under "Series Reviews." The series is updated every two years.

Best Choices in Arizona

by Lance Machamer, Gable & Gray, 1987, 322 pages, paper, $12.95

This book is part of the Gable & Gray Best Choices Guide series, which is reviewed in more detail under "Series Reviews."

Explore Arizona!

by Rick Harris, Golden West Publishers, 1986, 126 pages, paper, $5.00

This is a good collection of ideas for the explorer—ghost towns, old forts, cliff dwellings, caves, hot springs, ruins, pottery, and lots more. Each adventure idea is accompanied by a useful location map and special notes (which are often reminders to look, enjoy, and leave the artifacts for the next person to see).

Fodor's Arizona

Fodor's Travel Publications, 1987, 224 pages, paper, $7.95

This book is part of Fodor's Country/Regional Guide series, which is reviewed in more detail under "Series Reviews." The series is updated annually.

Grand Canyon River Guide

by Buzz Belknap, Westwater Books, 1969, 52 pages, paper (waterproof), $10.95

This classic guide for Grand Canyon river rats describes every rapid and other points of interest and provides historical notes throughout. A non-waterproof version is available for $6.95.

A Guide to the Architecture of Metro Phoenix

by Central Arizona Chapter A.I.A., Gibbs M. Smith, Inc., 1985, 200 pages, paper, $12.95

This is one of the Gibbs M. Smith Architecture Guide series, which is reviewed in more detail under "Series Reviews."

Guide to the Recommended Country Inns of Arizona, New Mexico, and Texas

by Eleanor Morris, The Globe Pequot Press, 1987, 290 pages, paper, $9.95

This is one of the excellent Recommended Country Inns series, which is reviewed in more detail under "Series Reviews." The author has visited and reviewed each inn personally; no payments have been accepted for inclusion.

The Hiker's Guide to Arizona
by Stewart Aitchison and Bruce Grubbs, Falcon Press, 1987, 157 pages, paper, $9.95

This book is part of the Falcon Press Hiking Guide series, which is reviewed in more detail under "Series Reviews."

Hiking the Grand Canyon
by John Annerino, Sierra Club Books, 1986, 320 pages, paper, $10.95

This is one of the small-format Sierra Club Hiking Totebook series, which is reviewed in more detail under "Series Reviews."

100 Best Restaurants in Arizona
by John and Joan Bogert, A.D.M. Inc., 1987 (11th ed.), 208 pages, paper, $3.95

Actually, 172 places are described in this popular guide. The emphasis is on inexpensive yet gourmet dining and the prices range from cheap to moderate. This guide is written by authors who dined anonymously several times at each establishment so chances are they experienced the same kind of evening any traveler will. This first-class book contains all the practical data, including access for disabled. The guide is updated annually.

On Foot in the Grand Canyon: Hiking the Trails of the South Rim
by Sharon Spangler, Pruett Publishing, 1986, 194 pages, paper, $11.95

In this interpretive guide, a hiker shares her adventures. But there are enough practical facts here to help hikers plan their own hikes as well—including appendices that mention water availability , topographical maps, basic geology, and some day-hike suggestions.

Outdoors in Arizona: A Guide to Camping
by Bob Hirsch, Arizona Highways, 1986, 128 pages, paper, $12.95

This book combines plenty of camping ideas, with enough beautiful color photos, location maps, and charts of practical facts of importance to make a very useful compendium.

Outdoors in Arizona: A Guide to Hiking and Backpacking
by John Annerino, Arizona Highways, 1987, 136 pages, paper, $12.95

This book, from the author of the Sierra Club's *Hiking the Grand Canyon*, contains 48 suggested hikes, many with topographical map reproductions. Photos are also included.

Pacific Boating Almanac: Southern California, Arizona, & Mexico
Western Marine Enterprises, 1987, 432 pages, paper, $10.95
This annually published guide on the how and where of boating is part of the Boating Almanac series, which is reviewed in more detail under "Series Reviews."

River Runners' Guide to Utah and Adjacent Areas
by Gary Nichols, University of Utah Press, 1986, 168 pages, paper, $14.95
Including Arizona, this book is reviewed under "Utah."

River Runner's Guide to the History of the Grand Canyon
by Kim Crumbo, Johnson Books, 1981, 96 pages, paper, $5.95
This fine take-along guide tells about the fascinating geology and the storied past of the Grand Canyon.

Roadside Geology of Arizona
by Halka Chronic, Mountain Press, 1983, 314 pages, paper, $9.95
This book is part of the excellent Roadside Geology Guide series, which is reviewed in more detail under "Series Reviews."

Shifra Stein's Day Trips From Phoenix, Tucson, and Flagstaff: Getaways Less Than 2 Hours Away
by Pam Hait, The Globe Pequot Press, 1986, 190 pages, paper, $8.95
This book is part of the Shifra Stein's Day Trips series, which is reviewed in more detail under "Series Reviews."

The Sierra Club Guide to the Natural Areas of New Mexico, Arizona, and Nevada
by John and Jane Perry, Sierra Club Books, 1985, 412 pages, paper, $10.95
This is one of the Sierra Club Natural Areas Guide series, which is reviewed in more detail under "Series Reviews."

Ski Touring Arizona: Plateaus of Snow
by Dugald Bremner, Northland Press, 1987, 136 pages, paper, $11.95
This excellently prepared guidebook offers over 40 ski tours for beginners and experts. Each is rated, with distances noted. A good map, directions to the starting point, suggestions of other maps needed, and a well-written discussion of each trip are provided. Planning notes on equipment needs, winter hazard warnings, even suggestions for that most pleasurable of skiing ideas—moonlight touring—are included.

The State Parks of Arizona

by John Young, University of New Mexico Press, 1986, 204 pages, paper, $11.95

This is a well-written orientation to the numerous state parks of Arizona. Helpful photographs accompany an enjoyable text on the history of each park and sights of local interest. Specific information on campsites, motels, etc. is not included.

Sunset: Arizona Travel Guide

Lane Publishing, 1985, 128 pages, paper, $8.95

Best used as a idea and planning tool, this book is part of the Sunset Travel Guide series, which is reviewed in more detail under "Series Reviews."

This Is Tucson: Guidebook to the Old Pueblo

by Peggy Lockard, Pepper Publishing, 1988 (3rd ed.), 294 pages, paper, $9.95

Well-written, and full of useful information and exceptionally good maps, this award-winning book covers history, cultural activities, walking and driving tours of the historic districts, sightseeing, hiking, picnicking, seasonal events, tours of the surrounding areas, shopping, 65 restaurants, and more. Every city should have such a superb guide available.

Travel Arizona: Full Color Tours of the Grand Canyon State

by Joseph Stocker, Arizona Highways, 1987 (5th ed.), 128 pages, paper, $8.95

This book offers 16 interesting tours of one to three days' duration for the automobile traveler. The text is informative and the beautiful color photos in this large-format book are typical of those that made *Arizona Highways* magazine famous. A small section of suggested day hikes is included.

ARKANSAS

See also "The South" and "United States as a Whole."

The Arkansas Handbook

by Diann Smith, Emerald City Press, 1984, 480 pages, paper, $11.95

This wonderful but aging book tells everything about Arkansas—right down to the Razorbacks' scores for every season since 1894.

The Greatest Ozarks Guidebook
by Harry and Phyl Dark, Greatest Graphics, 1979, 240 pages, paper, $7.95
Including the Ozarks of Arkansas, this book is reviewed under "Missouri."

Landmarks of the West: A Guide to Historic Sites
by Kent Ruth, The University of Nebraska Press, 1986, 309 pages, paper, $17.50
This superb book, which includes Arkansas's Fort Smith, is reviewed under "The Rocky Mountain/Great Basin States."

The Pelican Guide to the Ozarks
by Bet Hampel, Pelican Publishing, 1982, 160 pages, paper, $4.95
Including the Ozarks of Arkansas, this book is reviewed under "Missouri."

CALIFORNIA
See also "The Southwest" and "United States as a Whole."

Adventures on & off Interstate 80
by Eleanor Huggins and John Olmstead, Tioga Publishing, 1985, 254 pages, paper, $12.95
Journey from San Francisco, across the Sierra, and into the Nevada desert on a trip through natural and human history that will turn these mindless miles into pleasure and adventure. This book contains so many suggestions for side trips, vista stops, and other explorations that travelers would probably never get to the end of them all. Each side trip is carefully explained (with clear directions) and each point of history or comment on native flora or fauna is well presented and fascinating to read. This thoroughly delightful book is a great companion guide to this stretch of highway.

Adventuring in the California Desert: The Sierra Club Travel Guide to the Great Basin, Mojave, and Colorado Desert Regions of California
by Lynne Foster, Sierra Club Books, 1987, 438 pages, paper, $12.95
Adventuring in the San Francisco Bay Area: The Sierra Club Guide to San Francisco, Marin, Sonoma, Napa, Solano, Contra Costa, Alameda, Santa Clara, San Mateo Counties, and the Bay Islands
by Peggy Wayburn, Sierra Club Books, 1987, 422 pages, paper, $10.95
These two great titles are part of the Sierra Club Adventure Travel Guide series, which is reviewed in more detail under "Series Reviews."

Afoot and Afield in Orange County
by Jerry Schad, Wilderness Press, 1988, 224 pages, paper, $14.95
Afoot and Afield in San Diego County
by Jerry Schad, Wilderness Press, 1986, 290 pages, paper, $12.95
    These two excellent hiking guides are part of the Wilderness Press Hiking Guide series, which is reviewed in more detail under "Series Reviews." The Orange County guide describes 60 hiking opportunities and was released after press time; the price and number of pages are approximate. The San Diego County guide includes 176 hikes. Both volumes contain a number of short and easy walks for ramblers of all ages.

All Around the Bay: A Shoreline Guide to San Francisco Bay
by Ruth Jackson, Chronicle Books, 1987, 119 pages, paper, $7.95
    Around the perimeter of the great San Francisco Bay resides every pleasure. From pristine marshes and quiet places of solitude to bustling wharfs and trips to Alcatraz, there is a lot to do, and this quality guide has great ideas. Suggestions on places to eat are included.

The American Express Pocket Guide to California
by Bob Thompson, Prentice Hall Press, 1987 (2nd ed.), 256 pages, cloth, $9.95
    This book is part of the first-rate American Express Pocket Guide series, which is reviewed in more detail under "Series Reviews."

The Anza-Borrego Desert Region: A Guide to the State Park and the Adjacent Areas
by Lowell and Diana Lindsay, Wilderness Press, 1985 (2nd ed.), 179 pages, paper, $9.95
    The large fold-out map shows all the jeep trails, paved roads,and hiking routes throughout this large desert playground. After introductory chapters on climate, geologic history, desert life, and the do's and don'ts of desert exploration, comes a very detailed account of all the roads—paved, dirt, and four-wheel-drive-only—as well as hiking trails within the four major regions of Anza-Borrego. Like all Wilderness Press books, this is a very useful, first-class effort.

Architecture in Los Angeles: A Compleat Guide
by Harold Kirker, Gibbs M. Smith, Inc., 1985, 528 pages, paper, $14.95
    This is one of the Gibbs M. Smith Architecture Guide series, which is reviewed in more detail under "Series Reviews."

Away for the Weekend: Los Angeles—Great Getaways Less Than 250 Miles from Los Angeles
by Michele and Tom Grimm, Crown Publishers, 1986, 288 pages, paper, $10.95
   This book is part of the Away for the Weekend Guide series, which is reviewed in more detail under "Series Reviews."

Backcountry Roads & Trails: San Diego County
by Jerry Schad, The Touchstone Press, 1986 (revised ed.), 96 pages, paper, $6.95
   This well-done guide is part of the Touchstone Hiking Guide series, which is reviewed in more detail under "Series Reviews."

Backroad Wineries of California: A Discovery Tour of California's Country Wineries
by Bill Gleeson, Chronicle Books, 1985, 168 pages, paper, $7.95
   This is a wonderful collection of wineries situated in all the northern and central California wine-growing regions that are less discovered than the rest. Many are the kind of places travelers should call the day before in order to arrange to do some tasting. Otherwise, the staff may be in the fields. A few of these wineries may be a little more frequented now, but the information contained herein is still quite pertinent.

Back Roads of California: A Sunset Pictorial
by Earl Thollander, Lane Publishing, 1988 (3rd ed.), 208 pages, paper, $12.95
   This is one of the Earl Thollander's Back Roads series, which is reviewed in more detail under "Series Reviews." Note that this is the only title from Lane Publishing (Sunset Books). The remainder of this series is from Crown Publishing.

Baedeker's San Francisco
Prentice Hall Press, 1987, 172 pages, paper, $10.95
   This book is part of the well-known Baedeker's City Guide series, which is reviewed in more detail under "Series Reviews."

The Beach Towns: A Walker's Guide to L.A.'s Beach Communities
by Robert Pierson, Chronicle Books, 1985, 144 pages, paper, $7.95
   Here are some well-described walks in towns all along the L.A. coast: Santa Monica, Venice, Manhattan Beach, Palos Verdes Estates, and San Pedro. Not only are the sights well described; Pierson has lots of good words for places travelers may want to check out more closely—bakeries, bars, restaurants, and tobacco shops, to name a

few. Each walk has good directions, where to park, how to get there on the bus, distance traveled, duration, and other notes.

Bed and Breakfast: California—A Selective Guide
by Linda Bristow, Chronicle Books, 1985 (revised ed.), 230 pages, paper, $8.95
This book is great for those traveling to California and planning to stay in a B&B. Provided are well-written, enjoyable evaluations of each of the 101 establishments, including all the practical data for places in every price range.

Bed and Breakfast Guide: West Coast
by Courtia Worth and Terry Berger, Prentice Hall Press, 1986, 160 pages, paper, $12.95
Beautiful color photographs of both interior and exterior views of each B&B supplement an informative text. Practical details and directions are included in this handsome volume. The guide covers 155 inns in California, Oregon, and Washington, and the photos in this guide make it much easier to choose between them.

Bed and Breakfast Homes Directory: California, Oregon, Washington
by Diane Knight, Knighttime Publications, 1988 (5th ed.), 280 pages, paper, $9.95
See "The Pacific Northwest."

Bed and Breakfast in California
by Kathy Strong, The Globe Pequot Press, 1988 (3rd ed.), 224 pages, paper, $9.95
Although the title has changed from the last edition (it used to be *The California Bed & Breakfast Book*), this book is part of the Bed and Breakfast Book series, which is reviewed in more detail under "Series Reviews."

The Bed and Breakfast Traveler: Touring the West Coast
by Lewis Green, The Globe Pequot Press, 1987, 288 pages, paper, $10.95
Including the area from San Francisco to Victoria, Canada, this book is reviewed under "The Pacific Northwest."

Berlitz: California
Macmillan Publishing, 1982, 128 pages, paper, $6.95
This book is part of the small-format Berlitz Guide series, which is reviewed in more detail under "Series Reviews."

Best Choices in Northern California
by Linda McCurry, Gable & Gray, 1987, 602 pages, paper, $12.95
Best Choices in Northern California, Bay Area Edition
by Tom Baker, Gable & Gray, 1987, 815 pages, paper, $12.95
Best Choices in Orange County
by Patty Mitchell, Gable & Gray, 1987, 370 pages, paper, $12.95
Best Choices in San Diego
by Sharon Holloway, Gable & Gray, 1988, 276 pages, paper, $12.95
These four titles are part of the Gable & Gray Best Choices Guide
series, which is reviewed in more detail under "Series Reviews."

The Best of Los Angeles
by Henri Gault and Christian Millau, 1987, 352 pages, paper,
$14.95
This book is part of the Gault-Millau 'Best of' Guide series, which
is reviewed in more detail under "Series Reviews." Unfortunately,
if the Washington, D.C. edition is any indication, other reviewers
are now doing the bulk of the work in America for this famous
French team, whose sharp, opinionated reviews earned them their
now-considerable reputation.

The Best of San Diego
by Judy Kennedy and Judi Strada, Metropolitan Press, 1985 (2nd
ed.), 230 pages, paper, $6.95
This book of the "best of" all sorts of things includes good ideas
on camping, bed and breakfast, ice cream, hikes, wine shops, hotels,
etc.

The Best of San Francisco
by Don and Betty Martin, Chronicle Books, 1986, 192 pages, paper,
$7.95
Not to be confused with the Gault/Millau title of the same name
(see below), this is a local San Francisco effort. Assembled are the
Martin's ten top choices in a wide range of categories, such as attractions, photo spots, restaurants (in many specific classes), wines,
pubs, nightlife, festivals, museums, hotels, architecture, as well as
a section on the ten most overlooked pleasures the city has to offer.
Each choice includes a good review and all the practical details.

The Best of San Francisco
by Henri Gault and Christian Millau, Prentice Hall Press, 1987,
352 pages, paper, $14.95
See note under *The Best of Los Angeles* above. This book is part
of the Gault-Millau 'Best of' Guide series, which is reviewed in
more detail under "Series Reviews."

The Best of the Gold Country
by Don and Betty Martin, Pine Cone Press, 1987, 208 pages, paper, $9.95

This is a first-class guide to the gold country of the Sierra foothills of northern California. Thorough, opinionated, and accurate evaluations are done anonymously and with no fees paid by the restaurants. Lodging, campgrounds, and the attractions of this enjoyable tourist playground are also described. Well-written, with a bit of whimsy and a smattering of history, this is a most helpful companion to the land that Sutter's Mill and Mark Twain made famous. In addition, 50 cents from the price of every book is donated to non-profit organizations "working to preserve the area's historic treasures."

The Best Places to Kiss in Los Angeles: A Romantic Travel Guide
by Paula Begoun, Beginning Press, 1988, 78 pages, paper, $7.95
The Best Places to Kiss in San Francisco and the Bay Area: A Romantic Travel Guide
by Paula Begoun, Beginning Press, 1986, 78 pages, paper, $7.95

These two titles are part of the Romantic Travel Guide series, which is reviewed in more detail under "Series Reviews."

Bicycling Country Roads from San Jose to Santa Barbara
by Joanne Rife, Western Tanager Press, 1982, 124 pages, paper, $6.95

This good collection of 50 different rides off the beaten path along the quiet roads of central coastal California contains helpful maps, descriptions, distances, and ratings.

Bicycling the Pacific Coast
by Tom Kirkendall and Vicky Spring, The Mountaineers, 1984, 224 pages, paper, $9.95

This excellent cycling guide, which details a trip from British Columbia to San Diego, is reviewed under "The Pacific Northwest."

A Bicyclist's Guide to Bay Area History
by Carol O'Hare, Fair Oaks Publishing, 1989 (revised ed.), 160 pages, paper, $8.95

This great guidebook to San Francisco has a different twist—cycling tours of historic sites in the Bay area. Each of the 15 tours described includes a good map, the distance traveled, difficulty rating, highlights of the tour, and plenty of historic notes and good directions. Rides for every level of cycling skill are included. And travelers can drive or even walk all or part of each itinerary. The new edition of this guide is due out in July, 1989; the price and number of pages are approximate.

Birnbaum's Disneyland
edited by Stephen Birnbaum, Houghton Mifflin, 1988, 160 pages, paper, $6.95
This book is similar in content and format to *Birnbaum's Walt Disney World,* which is reviewed under "Florida." The title is updated annually.

California Coastal Access Guide
by the California Coastal Commission, University of California Press, 1983, 288 pages, paper, $10.95
Unfortunately, this guide has not been updated in some time. Nonetheless, it is a good resource for determining where California's many public beach areas are and how to reach them.

California Downhill: A Skier's Handbook
by Stephen Metzger, Moon Publications, 1986, 144 pages, paper, $7.95
Metzger divides the state downhill skiing opportunities into four districts—Northern, Central, Southern, and Lake Tahoe—and gives the low-down on each district and the ski resorts in it. Included are discussions of the facilities, lodging, food, package deals, how to get there, shuttle services, even cross-country skiing nearby. Moon Publications recently made a commitment to update their travel books every two years, so a new edition of this title may be out sometime soon.

California in 22 Days
See *22 Days in California* below.

California State Parks
by Kim Heacox, Falcon Press, 1987, 128 pages, paper, $14.95
This is primarily an idea book with plenty of beautiful color photographs to supplement informative descriptions of some of the best park areas. The variety of environments within the state park system is enormous. A section at the back briefly describes the details of each state park, including facilities and features, in a chart format.

California State Parks Guide
Olympus Press, 1987, 232 pages, paper, $12.95
This is a comprehensive, large-format guide to all 250 of California's state park areas. This great resource is very well done and has

good maps, photos, history, camping options, recreation opportunities, and a lot more.

California Whitewater: A Guide to Rivers
by Jim Cassady and Fryar Calhoun, Cassady & Calhoun, 1984, 300 pages, paper, $17.95
This is a good summary, including technical notes, of the many river-running opportunities that exist in California.

Camper's Guide to California Parks, Forests, Trails, and Rivers, Volume 1: Northern California
by Mickey Little, Gulf Publishing, 1988, 176 pages, paper, $12.95
Camper's Guide to California Parks, Forests, Trails, and Rivers, Volume 2: Southern California
by Mickey Little, Gulf Publishing, 1988, 176 pages, paper, $12.95
These two large-format titles are part of the Gulf Camping Guide series, which is reviewed in more detail under "Series Reviews."

Carson-Iceberg Wilderness: A Guide to the High Sierra Between Yosemite and Tahoe
by Jeffrey Schaffer, Wilderness Press, 1987, 182 pages, paper, $12.95
The beautiful wilderness area of southern Alpine County, California's least-populated county, just south of Lake Tahoe, is described in this excllent book. Part of the Wilderness Press Hiking Guide series, which is reviewed in more detail under "Series Reviews," this book includes a separate topographical map.

Combing the Coast: Highway One from San Francisco to San Luis Obispo
by Ruth Jackson, Chronicle Books, 1985, 213 pages, paper, $10.95
Highway One is a wonderful place for tourists and natives alike to explore. It is a beautiful journey filled with interesting things to see and do. Jackson has done a fine job detailing the many wonderful spots along this famous highway, including ideas on places to eat and stay as well as recreational and sightseeing suggestions. This is an excellent, large-format guide for all to enjoy.

The Complete Guide: California Camping
by Tom Stienstra, Foghorn Press, 1987, 598 pages, paper, $15.00
This is a massive compendium of more than 1500 campsites throughout the state—some well known, some in those nooks and crannies that few people discover. These are all organized sites with at least some measure of facilities. For each camping area, information includes the number of tent sites and/or motor-home sites, what facilities are available (including whether there is a grocery store

nearby), whether a fee or reservations are required, who to contact, location, the months of the year the camp is open, and other special notes.

The Complete Guide to the Golden Gate National Recreation Area
by Karen Liberatore, Chronicle Books, 1982, 120 pages, paper, $7.95

Though certainly in need of revision in spots, this will still prove a helpful guide to one of the largest and certainly most spectacularly scenic urban parks anywhere. The view of the Golden Gate Bridge from this park is unparalleled, especially if there is fog below skirting through "the Gate."

Country Inns, Lodges & Historic Hotels: California, Oregon & Washington
by Anthony Hitchcock and Jean Lindgren, Burt Franklin–Publisher, 1988 (10th ed.), 281 pages, paper, $8.95

This is one of the Compleat Traveler's Companions series, which is reviewed in more detail under "Series Reviews." No fees are accepted for inclusion in this annually updated guide.

Crown Insider's Guide: California
by Jane Lasky and David Reed, Crown Publishers, 1988, 336 pages, paper, $10.95

This is a new addition to the growing Crown Insider's Guide series, which is reviewed in more detail under "Series Reviews." The number of pages is approximate.

Cycling the California Outback
by Chuck "Bodfish" Elliot, Bodfish Books, 1985, 65 pages, paper, $5.50

This is a good, down-home collection of maps and descriptions of off-pavement, fat-tire cycling in the national forests of northern California. Generally the emphasis is on main dirt roads, although plenty of side spurs for the adventurous to explore are mentioned. Transferring the map information to the more detailed forest service maps is recommended. Planning notes and other tips are included.

Cycling San Diego
by Jerry Schad and Don Krupp, Centra Publications, 1986, 128 pages, paper, $8.95

This is a carefully prepared guide to 36 day trips ranging from easy tours of urban parks to mountainous, backcountry "grunts." Each trip is nicely detailed and accompanied by a map, elevation chart, and notes on road conditions, traffic conditions, distance, and difficulty rating. This is a collection of tours of coast, desert, mountain, and city.

Cyclists' Route Atlas: A Guide to the Gold Country and High Sierra/South
by Randall Braun, Heyday Books, 1987, 100 pages, paper, $8.95

Cyclists' Route Atlas: A Guide to Yolo, Solano, Napa and Lake Counties
by Randall Braun, Heyday Books, 1986, 110 pages, paper, $7.95

These are two first-class books on a wide variety of cycling routes in many areas of northern California. Each route averages about 50 miles and is well described, often with an accompanying photo. The exact mileage and elevation gain are noted, and the appendix contains helpful elevation profile charts.

Day Hiker's Guide to Southern California
by John McKinney, Olympus Press, 1987, 263 pages, paper, $10.95

This is a fine guide for interesting day hikes through desert, mountain, or beach terrain. From, easy hikes a few miles in length to adventurous day-long, 15-milers, all are clearly described. A bit of history is sprinkled throughout and the necessary information on distances, terrain, best season to hike, and the "topo" needed are all there.

Deepest Valley: A Guide to Owens Valley, Its Roadsides and Mountain Trails
edited by Genny Smith, Genny Smith Books, 1989, 224 pages, paper, $9.95

After a long hiatus, *Deepest Valley* will return to print in 1989. It is a guide, written in a fashion similar to Smith's other book, *Mammoth Lakes Sierra*, to the wonderful valley that lies beneath Mt. Whitney, the highest peak in the Lower 48, in the towering Eastern Sierra Nevada range. Here is a guide, for day-hiker and car traveler alike, to the roadside stops, interesting side roads, geology, flora, fauna, and history of this important area—including discussion of the ongoing struggles for water rights with the Los Angeles Department of Water and Power. This is a welcome, new guide for the traveler.

Desolation Wilderness and the South Lake Tahoe Basin
by Jeffrey Schaffer, Wilderness Press, 1985 (2nd ed.), 160 pages, paper, $9.95

This book is part of the excellent Wilderness Press Hiking Guide series, which is reviewed in more detail under "Series Reviews." A fold-out map is included.

Dirt & Trail Guide for Southern California

by Joe Cheevers and Neil Kluft, Master Link Publishing, 1986, 160 pages, paper, $12.95

California has always been a mecca for the off-road motorcycle bunch. This spiral-bound guide has information and plenty of photos on 35 legal areas in which to ride. Information is included as to requirements (spark arrester, etc.), fees, camping facilities, even the nearest first aid. Maps provide a reasonable orientation to each area.

Discover Historic California: A Travel Guide to Over 1500 Places You Can See

by George and Jan Roberts, New Fortress Publications, 1986, 330 pages, paper, $8.95

This comprehensive compendium of places of historic importance includes all the state historic landmarks. Every landmark is detailed with a short paragraph on its history, as well as a description of its physical location. Location is further specified on general road maps of 76 different regions of the state.

Diving and Snorkeling Guide to Northern California

by Steve Rosenburg, PBC International, 1987, 96 pages, paper, $9.95

This book is part of the well-done Pisces Diving/Snorkeling Guide series, which is reviewed in more detail under "Series Reviews."

Earl Thollander's San Francisco: Walking Tours from the Embarcadero to the Golden Gate

by Earl Thollander, Crown Publishing, 1987, 128 pages, paper, $8.95

Filled with the whimsical drawings that have made Earl Thollander famous and easy-to-follow, hand-drawn maps, this large-format guide describes 30 fascinating walking tours of the City by the Bay.

Easy Day Hikes in Yosemite

by Deborah Durkee, Yosemite Natural History Association, 1985, 40 pages, paper, $4.50

This book details 20 enjoyable trails to try, some for all the family, some a bit more difficult, all in Yosemite. Included is hiking advice and suggestions for hoofing it with children. A good orientation guide, with lots of cute illustrations the kids will like, this book is available at the park as well as by mail.

Eating Out With the Kids in San Francisco and the Bay Area
by Carol Meyers, Carousel Press, 1985, 193 pages, paper, $7.95
A wealth of information is contained in this wonderful book. Restaurants equipped to handle families, picnic sites, the best places to pick up the picnic goods, and activities (such as a children's theater, museums, seasonal events) are located all over the Bay area. The write-ups of each selection are exceptionally good.

Epicurean Rendezvous: 100 Finest Restaurants in Northern California
edited by Maia Madden, AM/PM Publishing, 1987, 208 pages, paper, $5.00
While there are some ads, the panel of judges that has assembled this guide have judged strictly on merit. No fees are charged nor restaurant advertising accepted. The guide is a slick, color-photo-filled book and comments are more descriptive than review-like. But the panel has used some exacting criteria in choosing the best: outstanding cuisine, elegant ambiance, a knowledgeable, cordial staff, daily presence of owners on the premises, a chef with at least ten years experience, an extensive wine cellar, a safe and convenient location, and having been in business for at least three years. For each selection, menu highlights as well as an interior photograph are included. Prices are not mentioned.

Family Bike Rides: A Guide to Over 40 Specially Selected Bicycle Routes in Northern California
by Milton Grossberg, Chronicle Books, 1981, 112 pages, paper, $7.95
This guide goes a step further than other backroad cycling guides. The emphasis is now on families, so the author has selected rides that are "short, level, scenic, well-removed from busy traffic lanes, and close to parks, picnic sites, beaches, museums, fishing piers, and other on-route recreation facilities..." In short, routes perfect for mom, dad, and the kids. But, since the publication date is 1981, be sure to evaluate what time has done to these well-chosen journeys. The rides are well described and supplemented with clear maps.

Fielding's California: The Mission Trail, San Diego to San Francisco
by Lynn Foster, William Morrow & Co., 1988, 264 pages, paper, $10.95
This book is part of Fielding's Historic Trails Guide series, which is reviewed in more detail under "Series Reviews."

50 Grand Picnics: Menus & Recipes for the Best Picnic Sites Around the Bay Area
by Beverly Levine, Chronicle Books, 1982, 184 pages, paper, $6.95
This fun little book contains useful recipe suggestions and some great picnic spots to consider. Most, but not all, spots are organized picnic areas that provide tables, and usually barbecues, restrooms, water, and such. Some changes in specific information may have occurred since this book's publication.

50 Hiking Trails: Lassen, Tahoe, Carson Pass
by Don and Roberta Lowe, The Touchstone Press, 1987, 128 pages, paper, $9.95
This book is part of the Touchstone Hiking Guide series, which is reviewed in more detail under "Series Reviews."

55 1/2 Running Trails of the San Francisco Bay Area
by Tony Burke, Heyday Books, 1985, 133 pages, paper, $7.95
This great selection of running spots, each with an excellent description and a good map, includes distances, type of terrain, how much shade to expect, and other details runners/joggers long to know. Selections are in San Francisco and the six surrounding counties.

Fisher's World: Los Angeles and Vicinity
edited by Robert Fisher, Fisher's World, Inc., 1988, 104 pages, paper, $10.95
This book is part of the Fisher's World Guide series, which is reviewed in more detail under "Series Reviews."

Flashmaps: Instant Guide to Los Angeles
Random House, 1987, 80 pages, paper, $4.95
Flashmaps: Instant Guide to San Francisco
Random House, 1987, 80 pages, paper, $4.95
These two titles are part of the Flashmaps series, which is reviewed in more detail under "Series Reviews." The series is updated annually.

Fodor's California
Fodor's Travel Publications, 1987, 528 pages, paper, $12.95
This book is part of Fodor's Country/Regional Guide series, which is reviewed in more detail under "Series Reviews." The series is updated annually.

Fodor's Fun in Las Vegas, including Reno and Lake Tahoe
Fodor's Travel Publications, 1988, 160 pages, paper, $6.95

Fodor's Fun in San Francisco
Fodor's Travel Publications, 1987, 128 pages, paper, $6.95
Both of these titles are part of Fodor's Fun Guide series, which is reviewed in more detail under "Series Reviews." The Las Vegas title includes areas of Lake Tahoe located in California. The series is updated annually.

Fodor's Los Angeles
Fodor's Travel Publications, 1987, 320 pages, paper, $8.95
Fodor's San Diego and Nearby Attractions
Fodor's Travel Publications, 1987, 192 pages, paper, $7.95
Fodor's San Francisco
Fodor's Travel Publications, 1987, 224 pages, paper, $7.95
These three titles are part of Fodor's City Guide series, which is reviewed in more detail under "Series Reviews." The series is updated annually.

41 Hiking Trails: Northwest California
by Don and Roberta Lowe, The Touchstone Press, 1981, 96 pages, paper, $7.95
This is one of the Touchstone Hiking Guide series, which is reviewed in more detail under "Series Reviews."

Foraging Along the Pacific Coast
by Peter Howorth, Capra Press, 1986, 213 pages, paper, $9.95
This is a guide to careful, ecologically sensitive foraging for cockles, clams, abalones, sea plants, frogs, scallops, lobsters, crabs, octopi, and fish galore all along the Pacific coast.

Frommer's Dollarwise Guide to California and Las Vegas
by Mary Rakauskas, Prentice Hall Press, 1987, 312 pages, paper, $11.95
This is a particularly engaging volume in the Frommer's Dollarwise Guide series, which is reviewed in more detail under "Series Reviews." This series emphasizes selections in the moderate price range and is updated every two years.

Frommer's Guide to Los Angeles
by Mary Rakauskas, Prentice Hall Press, 1987, 216 pages, paper, $5.95
Frommer's Guide to San Francisco
by Mary Rakauskas, Prentice Hall Press, 1987, 217 pages, paper, $5.95
These two titles are part of the Frommer's City Guide series,

which is reviewed in more detail under "Series Reviews." The series is updated every two years.

Golden Gate Park at Your Feet
by Margot Doss, Presidio Press, 1978 (revised ed.), 173 pages, paper, $4.95

This revised edition needs revision but most of the information about this delightful park is still reasonably current, and the maps are helpful.

The Golden Hills of California: A Descriptive Guide to the Mother Lode Counties of the Southern Mines
by Allen Masri and Peter Abenheim, Western Tanager Press, 1979, 156 pages, paper, $6.95

The Golden Hills of California, Volume Two: A Descriptive Guide to the Mother Lode Counties of the Northern Mines
by Allen Masri, Western Tanager Press, 1983, 131 pages, paper, $7.95

The authors describe some interesting driving tours through the famous California gold country in these two books. Pay attention, though, because some road conditions may have changed a bit since the publication date. Plenty of historical notes are included. The Southern guide includes Mariposa, Tuolumne, Calaveras, and Amador counties. The Northern guide includes Placer, El Dorado, Sacramento, Nevada, Yuba, Sierra, and Plumas counties.

Good Eats: A Design and Food Guide to Bay Area Restaurants, Bars, Delis, Bakeries, Ice Creameries, Wines, Wineries, Cravings
by Herb McLaughlin, Peanut Butter Publishing, 1987, 280 pages, paper, $8.95

Types of restaurant guides vary, but this one is unusual in that it reviews and grades both food and architectural design—giving equal value to both. The writing style is witty and entertaining and the recommendations are clear and opinionated. Every price range is represented in this superbly crafted guide.

Grape Expeditions in California: Bicycle Tours of the Wine Country
by Lena Emmery and Sally Taylor, Sally Taylor & Friends, 1987 (5th ed.), 78 pages, paper, $7.50

This is an excellent guidebook for the cyclist (and not the least bit inappropriate for those traveling by car, either). Here are 15 carefully constructed tours of most of the wine regions of California: North Coast (Napa, Sonoma, and Mendocino counties), south of San Francisco (Santa Cruz, Santa Clara Valley, Livermore Valley, and Monterey), and the Central Coast (Paso Robles, San Luis Obispo,

Santa Ynez Valley). Distances for each tour, the terrain, and information on each winery of interest along the way is provided. Each tour is a day's journey, and directions for linking each tour into a longer expedition are given. Recommended inns and bicycle shops nearby are also mentioned.

Great Piers of California: A Guided Tour
by Jean Femling, Capra Press, 1984, 137 pages, paper, $7.95

California's massive coastline is speckled with beautiful piers of every description. And, although several were lost in severe storms since this book was written, 41 piers are described in word and picture, including plenty of historical notes and location maps, in this interesting book. This book is full of fun ideas for the tourist or the interested Californian.

The Great Towns of California
by David Vokac, West Press, 1986, 304 pages, paper, $8.95

This book is part of the well-done Great Towns Guide series, which is reviewed in more detail under "Series Reviews."

The Guide to Architecture in San Francisco and Northern California
by David Gebhard, *et al.*, Gibbs M. Smith, Inc., 1985, 608 pages, paper, $14.95

This is one of the Gibbs M. Smith Architecture Guide series, which is reviewed in more detail under "Series Reviews."

Guide to Catalina and California's Channel Islands
by Chicki Mallan, Moon Publications, 1988, 200 pages, paper, $8.95

This book is part of the Moon Handbook series, which is reviewed in more detail under "Series Reviews." The series is updated every two years. As it was released after press time, the number of pages is approximate.

Guide to Recommended Country Inns of the West Coast
by Julianne Belote, The Globe Pequot Press, 1986, 394 pages, paper, $10.95

This is one of the excellent Recommended Country Inns series, which is reviewed in more detail under "Series Reviews." The author has visited and evaluated each inn personally; no payment has been accepted for inclusion. The series is updated every two years.

Hidden Coast of California
by Ray Riegert, Ulysses Press, 1988, 458 pages, paper, $12.95

Hidden San Francisco and Northern California
by Ray Riegert, Ulysses Press, 1988 (3rd ed.), 422 pages, paper, $12.95
These two superb guides are part of the Hidden Places Guide series, is reviewed in more detail under "Series Reviews." *Hidden Coast of California* covers cities along the extensive California coastline. The series is updated every two years.

Hike Los Angeles, Volume 1: 49 Coastal, Shoreline, and Cityside Walks
by Dennis Gagnon, Western Tanager Press, 1985, 135 pages, paper, $8.95

Hike Los Angeles, Volume 2: 53 High Country, Foothill, and Cityside Walks
by Dennis Gagnon, Western Tanager Press, 1985, 135 pages, paper, $8.95

Hike the Santa Barbara Backcountry: A Guide to the Trails of the Southern Los Padres National Park
by Dennis Gagnon, Western Tanager Press, 1986, 184 pages, paper, $9.95
These are three excellent hiking guides. The two Los Angeles guides explore the nooks and crannies of Los Angeles in all sorts of terrain—desert, mountain, and beach. The Santa Barbara guide sticks strictly to the backcountry. Plenty of easy day hikes are provided, as well as more arduous fare, each with a clear, well-written description. Driving instructions to the trailhead, as well as notes on distances, difficulty, and topos needed are outlined. The Santa Barbara guide also includes directions to more than 100 backcountry trail camps, generally reachable only on foot or horseback.

The Hiker's Guide to California
by Ron Adkison, Falcon Press, 1986, 260 pages, paper, $9.95
This book is part of the Falcon Press Hiking Guide series, which is reviewed in more detail under "Series Reviews."

The Hiker's Hip Pocket Guide to the Humboldt Coast
by Bob Lorentzen, Bored Feet Publications, 1988, 180 pages, paper, $9.95

The Hiker's Hip Pocket Guide to the Mendocino Coast
by Bob Lorentzen, Bored Feet Publications, 1986, 140 pages, paper, $9.95
The Humboldt Coast volume was released after press time, but the comments on the Mendocino Coast guide will probably be pertinent. *The Hiker's Hip Pocket Guide to the Mendocino Coast* is a great guide to the trails and hidden pleasures of the spectacular

Mendocino coastline. The book itself is cleanly and attractively laid out; the text is enjoyable and clearly written and the hand-drawn maps are more than adequate. The more than 40 trails described range from less than a mile to 44 miles in length. A chart accompanies each trail and details distance, elevation gained and lost, best time to go, directions to the trailhead, where to get more information, and specific warnings. Large, easily understood symbols tell at a glance whether there are good picnic spots, if bikes, dogs, or horses are allowed, and whether water is available. This classic guide should be used as a template on how to prepare a guide of this sort. The price and number of pages for the Humboldt Coast guide are approximate.

Hiking the Bigfoot Country: The Wildlands of Northern California and Southern Oregon
by John Hart, Sierra Club Books, 1975, 398 pages, paper, $8.95
Hiking the Great Basin: The High Desert Country of California, Oregon, Nevada, and Utah
by John Hart, Sierra Club Books, 1981, 369 pages, paper, $9.95
These two excellent guides are part of the Sierra Club Hiking Totebook series, which is reviewed in more detail under "Series Reviews."

Hiking the Big Sur Country: The Ventana Wilderness
by Jeffrey Schaffer, Wilderness Press, 1988, 144 pages, paper, $9.95
This book is part of the excellent Wilderness Press Hiking Guide series, which is reviewed in more detail under "Series Reviews."

Hiking Trails of the Santa Monica Mountains
by Milt McAuley, Canyon Publishing, 1987 (4th ed.), 320 pages, paper, $9.95
The Santa Monica Mountains lie adjacent to west Los Angeles and the populous San Fernando Valley. They offer the opportunity of a wide range of hikes, many of them very short and easily accomplished. McAuley's thorough book details each hike, including a good narrative, rating, length, elevation gain, and other practical points. General maps are provided and the appropriate topographical maps are recommended.

Historic Country Inns of California
by Jim Crain, Chronicle Books, 1984, 167 pages, paper, $8.95
The emphasis in this book is on the inn itself, including a large photograph, some history, and a discussion of its more modern usage. The practical facts on staying at these restored landmarks are also included. Since this guide has historically been updated every three

to four years, a new edition should be published soon. Until then, this book is best combined with another, more up-to-date guidebook.

Historic Houses of California: A Directory of Restored Historic Structures You Can Visit
by Daphne Reece, Chronicle Books, 1983, 123 pages, paper, $7.95

House lovers, history lovers, and lovers of architectural design will all love this compendium of ideas. Call ahead and confirm the hours; this book is too old to be entirely accurate.

Hot Springs of the Eastern Sierra
by George Williams, Tree By The River Publishing, 1988, 72 pages, paper, $5.95

This is a good overview of hot-spring locations and amenities—unimproved, primitive, and commercial—from Bridgeport, California to northwest Nevada. Included are directions and Williams's knowledgeable tips.

How to Get Lost & Found in California and Other Lovely Places
by John McDermott, Orafa Publishing, 1982, 295 pages, paper, $9.95

This book emphasizes California, but it covers places all over North America. It is part of the unique Lost and Found Guide series, which is reviewed in more detail under "Series Reviews." Note that this particular title is not currently distributed by Hunter Publishing as noted for Orafa Publishing in the Travel Book Publisher's appendix.

I Love Los Angeles
edited by Marilyn Appleberg, Macmillan Publishing, 1987, 266 pages, paper, $8.95

This book is part of the widely praised I Love Cities Guide series, which is reviewed in more detail under "Series Reviews."

Insight Guide: Northern California
by Apa Productions, Prentice Hall Press, 1986, 350 pages, paper, $15.95
Insight Guide: Southern California
by Apa Productions, Prentice Hall Press, 1986, 341 pages, paper, $15.95

These two titles are part of the excellent Insight Guide series, which is reviewed in more detail under "Series Reviews."

Interstate Gourmet: California and the Pacific Northwest
by Neal Weiner and David Schwartz, Summit Books, 1986, 222 pages, paper, $6.95

This is one of the highly regarded Interstate Gourmet series, which is reviewed in more detail under "Series Reviews."

Jack Shelton's How to Enjoy 1 to 10 Perfect Days in San Francisco
by Jack Shelton, Shelton Publishing, 1986, 228 pages, paper, $4.95

This famous San Francisco guide, hopefully soon to be revised, is filled with crisply written opinions on food, lodging, and all the day's tourist pleasures. Jack Shelton knows San Francisco.

L.A. Bike Rides: A Guide to 37 Specially Selected Bicycle Routes in Los Angeles County
by Loren MacArthur, Chronicle Books, 1985, 95 pages, paper, $7.95

Los Angeles is a total maze that often proves difficult for the native, let alone the uninitiated. In this book, MacArthur shows cyclists the way to great rides. Good directions and information on how to find the trail (most of these rides are actual bike trails), distances, how to link to other trails where possible, and more is included in this good resource.

LA Man
by Francis Chichester, Warner Books, 1988, 220 pages, cloth, $11.95

This guide for the upper crust is one of the Francis Chichester Guide series, which is reviewed in more detail under "Series Reviews." The series was released after press time.

LA Picnics: 75 Stylish Outings
by Ellen Melinkoff, Chronicle Books, 1985, 148 pages, paper, $7.95

This is a good resource of picnic spots, including those that can be reserved for bigger gatherings. Information on facilities and nearby concessions is included. Almost all the picnic spots are in parks.

LA Woman
by Francis Chichester, Warner Books, 1988, 204 pages, cloth, $11.95

This guide for the upper crust is one of the Francis Chichester Guide series, which is reviewed in more detail under "Series Reviews." The series was released after press time.

Lassen Volcanic National Park
by Jeffrey Schaffer, Wilderness Press, 1986 (2nd ed.), 216 pages,
paper, $12.95
This book is part of the excellent Wilderness Press Hiking Guide
series, which is reviewed in more detail under "Series Reviews." It
includes a separate topographical map.

Los Angeles/Access
by Richard Saul Wurman, Prentice Hall Press, 1987, 192 pages,
paper, $12.95
This wonderful guidebook to a difficult tourist city is part of the
highly regarded Access Guide series, which is reviewed in more
detail under "Series Reviews."

Los Angeles Epicure
Peanut Butter Publishing, 1986, 150 pages, paper, $7.95
This is one of the Epicure Guide series, which is reviewed in more
detail under "Series Reviews." The series is updated frequently.

Los Angeles in Your Pocket
Barron's Educational Series, 1987, 192 pages, paper, $3.95
This small-format, all-purpose guide is part of the In-Your-Pocket
Guide series, which is reviewed in more detail under "Series Re-
views." The series is updated every two years.

Let's Go: California & Hawaii
by Harvard Student Agencies, St. Martin's Press, 1988, 528 pages,
paper, $10.95
This book is part of the excellent, budget-oriented Let's Go Guide
series, which is reviewed in more detail under "Series Reviews."
This title includes Reno, Las Vegas, Lake Tahoe, and Baja California,
and is updated annually.

Making the Most of Marin
by Patricia Arrigoni, Wilderness Press, 1988, 288 pages, paper,
$11.95
Making the Most of the Peninsula
by Lee Foster, Wilderness Press, 1988, 288 pages, paper, $11.95
"Marin" refers to Marin County, just north of the Golden Gate
Bridge from San Francisco. The "Peninsula" is the San Francisco
peninsula, which runs south from San Francisco. Each details the
pleasures of the region—not only hikes, as many Wilderness Press
titles do, but also the history, historical landmarks, recreation spots,
nooks and crannies, and best beaches. Both were released after press
time, so price and number of pages for each are approximate.

Mammoth Lakes Sierra: A Handbook for Roadside and Trail
by Genny Smith, Genny Smith Books, 1979 (4th ed.), 148 pages, paper, $7.95

This is an excellent and popular handbook on the Mammoth Lakes area of the Eastern Sierra. Containing plenty of helpful information for the day-hiker, backpacker, or car tourist, this book suggests all sorts of side-road trips and hikes of every sort (including short, easy ones). Information on geology, climate, flora, and fauna is also included. This is a great guidebook and idea book written with obvious love and care for this wonderful region of America.

Marble Mountain Wilderness
by David Green, Wilderness Press, 1980, 168 pages, paper, $11.95

This book is part of the excellent Wilderness Press Hiking Guide series, which is reviewed in more detail under "Series Reviews." It includes a separate topographical map.

A Marmac Guide to Los Angeles
by Marvey Chapman, Pelican Publishing, 1988, 340 pages, paper, $7.95

This is a quality guide from the Marmac Guide series, which is reviewed in more detail under "Series Reviews." The series is updated every two years.

Michael's Guide: Northern California
by Michael Shichor, Hunter Publishing, 1987, 224 pages, paper, $7.95

Michael's Guide: Southern California
by Michael Shichor, Hunter Publishing, 1987, 224 pages, paper, $7.95

These two titles are part of the Michael's Guide series, which is reviewed in more detail under "Series Reviews."

Mono Lake Guidebook: Self-guided Tour
by David Gaines, The Mono Lake Committee, 1981, 114 pages, paper, $5.95

The Mono Lake Committee has brought this magnificent, ancient lake to national prominence in recent years. It is a truly fascinating place for the traveler to explore. This excellent self-guided tour is packed with all sorts of interesting facts and history—including the lake's uncertain future—and will enable visitors to get much more out of their trip.

Mobil Travel Guide: California and the West
Prentice Hall Press, 1988, 274 pages, paper, $8.95
   This is one of the Mobil Travel Guide series, which is reviewed in more detail under "Series Reviews." The series is updated annually.

Monterey Peninsula Walking Tours
by Pat Carr and Steve Tracy, Hampton-Brown, 1984, 16 pages, paper, $4.95
   This is a handy, compact walking-tour guide to three popular northern California areas—Monterey, Carmel and Pacific Grove. Hand-drawn maps, historical notes, and possible side trips are also included.

Mountain Bicycling in the San Gabriels
by Robert Immler, Wilderness Press, 1987, 134 pages, paper, $8.95
   In this excellent collection of mountain bike rides in the L.A. area, 34 well-conceived, off-road trips in the mountains of Los Angeles are drawn carefully on reproduced "topo" maps and well described, including a good narrative, distance, time needed, difficulty, and elevation gain.

Mt. Tam: A Hiking, Running and Nature Guide
by Don and Kay Martin, Martin Press, 1986, 100 pages, paper, $8.95
   Mt. Tamalpais, the big mountain of Marin County (to the north of San Francisco), offers a wide variety of outdoor pleasures. The Martins have produced a quality guide to 32 trails, each rated for hiking and running along with distances, elevation gains, best time of year to go, and detailed logs. Trails range from less than a mile to nearly seven miles in length. Appendices on geology, climate, history, and natural history add to the enjoyment of this delightful place.

Myrna Oakley's Bed and Breakfast Northwest
by Myrna Oakley, Solstice Press, 1987, 113 pages, paper, $7.95
   This quality book contains some selections in Northern California and is reviewed under "The Pacific Northwest."

Naming the Eastern Sierra: Dirty Sock to Bloody Canyon
by Marguerite Sowaal, Chalfant Press, 1985, 125 pages, paper, $8.95
   This great little guide to the "chronology of exploration" of the Eastern Sierra and the pioneers who named its peaks, lakes, and valleys is a fun companion guide for the interested traveler.

Napa Valley Guide
Vintage Publications, 1987, 120 pages, paper, $3.95
  Although a bit clogged with advertisements, this annual large-format guide offers a complete listing of available lodging of all types, with informative, non-judgmental descriptions and practical information for each. An equally comprehensive list of the many wineries of the area includes an easy-to-read chart on all locations, hours, tours, tasting, sales, and recent wine award recipients. Plenty of information on special events of the year, recreation opportunities, spas, etc. is included. The restaurant section is more concise, although it definitely covers some of the best, and includes good descriptions but no critique. This guide contains a wealth of information. A similar annual guide is done for Sonoma County.

Northern California: A History & Guide
by Eugene Newcombe, Random House, 1986, 208 pages, paper, $9.95
  This book is part of the History & Sightseeing Guide series, which is reviewed in more detail under "Series Reviews."

Northwest Trails: A Hiker's Guide to National Parks and Wilderness Areas
by Ira Spring and Harvey Manning, The Mountaineers, 1982, 192 pages, paper, $9.95
  Including Northern California, this book is part of the Mountaineers Hiking Guide series, which is reviewed in more detail under "Series Reviews."

An Outdoor Guide to the San Francisco Bay Area
by Dorothy Whitnah, Wilderness Press, 1984 (4th ed.), 364 pages, paper, $11.95
  This is an excellent collection of hikes, walks, and bicycle rides— 84 in all—varying in length from one to 12 miles, all within 70 miles of the Golden Gate Bridge. Information on public transportation, facilities available, recommended maps, and the difficulty of each route—and a good description of trails selected and the parks that some of them are located in—is all contained in this wonderful resource.

Pacific Boating Almanac: Northern California & Nevada
Western Marine Enterprises, 1987, 432 pages, paper, $10.95
Pacific Boating Almanac: Southern California, Arizona & Mexico
Western Marine Enterprises, 1987, 432 pages, paper, $10.95
  This book on the how and where of boating is part of the Boating

Almanac series, which is reviewed in more detail under "Series Reviews." The series is updated annually.

Parks of the Pacific Coast
by Doug and Bobbe Tatreau, The Globe Pequot Press, 1985, 160 pages, paper, $10.95
Including California, this book is reviewed under "The Pacific Northwest."

Passport to Los Angeles Restaurants
by John Mariani and Peter Meltzer, Passport Restaurant Guides, 1988, 70 pages, paper, $3.95
This is a new, very small-format companion to the successful *Passport to New York Restaurants*, which is reviewed under "New York." The L.A. guide reviews over 300 restaurants.

The Pelican Guide to Sacramento and the Gold Country
by Faren Bachelis, Pelican Publishing, 1987, 280 pages, paper, $9.95
For an area so full of history, it is amazing that more books are not available. This one, however, is a pleasurable tour through Sacramento and the neighboring foothills made famous by '49er gold—history and sights, as well as the fine wineries of the adjacent countryside. While food and lodging is not the emphasis, the appendix provides a list of dining, B&B choices, nightclubs and numerous useful addresses and phone numbers on culture, transportation, human services, etc.

Peninsula Trails: Outdoor Adventures on the San Francisco Peninsula
by Jean Rusmore and Frances Spangle, Wilderness Press, 1982, 206 pages, paper, $9.95
Structured in much the same way as *An Outdoor Guide to the San Francisco Bay Area*, this guide describes 62 strolls and hikes, from very short ones to a good day's hike, in the parks, preserves, and watershed lands south of San Francisco. Also included is how to get there by car and, where possible, by public transportation. This is another excellent resource from Wilderness Press.

Places to Go With Children in Northern California
by Elizabeth Pomada, Chronicle Books, 1985, 156 pages, paper, $7.95
Places to Go With Children in Southern California
by Stephanie Kegan, Chronicle Books, 1986, 160 pages, paper, $7.95
These two helpful guides are part of the Places to Go With Chil-

dren Guide series, which is reviewed in more detail under "Series Reviews."

Point Reyes: A Guide to the Trails, Roads, Beaches, Campgrounds, Lakes, Trees, Flowers, and Rocks of Point Reyes National Seashore

by Dorothy Whitnah, Wilderness Press, 1985 (2nd ed.), 118 pages, paper, $9.95

The author of this book does a fine job of covering the trails and natural history of this most wonderful national seashore north of San Francisco.

Rand McNally Pocket Guide: California and the Golden West

by Carole Chester, Rand McNally & Co., 1983, 128 pages, paper, $5.95

This book is part of the small-format Rand McNally Pocket Guide series, which is reviewed in more detail under "Series Reviews."

Recreation Lakes of California

Sail Sales Publishing, 1987 (7th ed.), 194+ pages, paper, $10.95

This is a comprehensive, large-format, spiral-bound resource guide to 194 recreational lakes throughout California. Each has a description, map, camping, boating, recreation options, facilities available, and where to call or write for more information.

Restaurants of San Francisco: The Definitive Guide to the Bay Area's Best

by Patricia Unterman and Stan Sesser, Chronicle Books, 1986, 212 pages, paper, $8.95

With timely revisions, this first-rate guide certainly merits the Bay Area restaurant-goer's attention. The authors provide in-depth, extensive, rated reviews of 280 restaurants of San Francisco and neighboring cities. Arranged alphabetically, an index lists each according to cuisine and location. This fantastic collection covers all price ranges.

Roadside Geology of the Eastern Sierra Region

by Geological Society of the Oregon Country, Mono Lake Committee, 1982, 42 pages, paper, $3.50

Geology along the major north-south highway of the Eastern Sierra Nevada range, from Bridgeport to Big Pine, as well as numerous side roads along the primary route, is detailed in this fine resource book. The print is very small, but the information should be interesting to all traveling non-geologists who would like to learn something about the fascinating landscape of the area.

Roadside Geology of Northern California
by David Alt and Donald Hundman, Mountain Press, 1975, 244
pages, paper, $9.95
This book is part of the excellent Roadside Geology Guide series,
which is reviewed in more detail under "Series Reviews."

**Roads to Ride: A Bicyclist's Topographic Guide to Alameda, Contra
Costa, and Marin Counties**
by Grant Peterson and Mary Anderson, Heyday Books, 1984, 142
pages, paper, $6.95
**Roads to Ride, South: A Bicyclist's Topographic Guide to San Mateo,
Santa Clara, and Santa Cruz Counties**
by Grant Peterson and John Kluge, Heyday Books, 1985, 132 pages,
paper, $7.95
These two volumes are an extremely valuable, well organized
assemblage of the best cycling opportunities in the counties of the
greater San Francisco Bay area. Fully 280 roads are described, each
with a clear profile map. A map of each county helps locate the
chosen path.

**Roaming the Back Roads: Day Trips by Car Through Northern
California**
by Peter Browning and Carol Holleuffer, Chronicle Books, 1979,
174 pages, paper, $8.95
This is a book of wonderful backwater rambles that, in spite of
the years since this book was written, have not changed very much.
The pleasure is still there. The maps are good, the descriptions better,
and the photos helpful.

San Bernardino Mountain Trails: 100 Hikes in Southern California
by John Robinson, Wilderness Press, 1986 (4th ed.), 258 pages,
paper, $11.95
The author of the very popular Los Angeles area hiking bible,
Trails of the Angeles, does an equally fine job with the mountains
to the east of Los Angeles. A separate "topo" map is included. This
book is part of the Wilderness Press Hiking Guide series, which is
reviewed in more detail under "Series Reviews."

San Diego and the Southland—Just the Facts: A Guide to Sightseeing
by Joan Tucker, Rand Editions, 1984, 160 pages, paper, $7.95
San Diego is filled with great sightseeing areas—Balboa Park, Mission Bay, La Jolla, and Old Town, to name a few—and Tucker has
done a solid job in covering the salient points and information travelers will need to enjoy them. The emphasis is on San Diego, including the north county area, but additional notes on Orange

County (Disneyland, etc.), Los Angeles, Palm Springs, and the areas in between are included.

San Diego...City & County
written and published by Carol Mendel, 1987 (6th ed.), 95 pages, paper, $4.95

Good descriptions, a bit of history, a variety of recommended tours for bicycle or car, well-done maps, and an informed narrative make this a good choice for exploring the most interesting sights of central and coastal San Diego and the many interesting towns and areas throughout the county. This book is concise, compact, and very well done.

San Diego Epicure
Peanut Butter Publishing, 1986, 150 pages, paper, $7.95

This book is part of the Epicure Guide series, which is reviewed in more detail under "Series Reviews." The series is updated frequently.

San Diego On Foot
written and published by Carol Mendel, 1987 (7th ed.), 96 pages, paper, $4.95

Mendel does an excellent job of showing this lovely city with more than 20 easy-to-do walks through 10 major areas of the city and its surroundings. An interesting discussion of each area is followed by a good map and a well-written description of the various planned walks and the sights along the way. Walks vary from 0.5 to 3 miles in length.

San Diego's Scenic Drive
by Leslie Bergstrom, Talk of the Town, 1987, 68 pages, paper, $4.50

The author's interesting commentary and clear maps will guide travelers through the history and sights of the "Scenic Drive," which includes Old Town, Balboa Park, Downtown, Point Loma, Mission Bay, Pacific Beach, Mission Beach, and La Jolla.

San Francisco/Access
by Richard Saul Wurman, Prentice Hall Press, 1987, 192 pages, paper, $12.95

This book is part of the highly regarded Access Guide series, which is reviewed in more detail under "Series Reviews."

San Francisco Epicure
Peanut Butter Publishing, 1986, 150 pages, paper, $7.95
　　This book is part of the Epicure Guide series, which is reviewed in more detail under "Series Reviews." The series is updated frequently.

San Francisco in Your Pocket
Barron's Educational Series, 1987, 112 pages, paper, $3.95
　　This small-format, all-purpose guide is part of the In-Your-Pocket Guide series, which is reviewed in more detail under "Series Reviews." The series is updated every two years.

San Francisco on a Shoestring
by Louis Madison, A. M. Zimmerman & Co., 1987, 153 pages, paper, $5.95
　　This book is perfect for travelers on a tight budget. This edition has added some "splurge" restaurants and hotels to broaden the range of choices. In all, prices listed here range from $6 to $50 per person for lodging and from less than $5 to more than $30 per person for restaurant meals (each grouped by price range). The emphasis is clearly economy, for Madison even includes a list of 17 bars in which free hors d'oeuvres come with price of one drink, including what type of free food to expect. Lots of low-priced entertainment and sightseeing ideas, walking tours, transportation information, and all sorts of practical facts are contained in this well-researched book.

Santa Barbara, El Pueblo Viejo: A Walking Guide to the Historic Districts of Santa Barbara
by Rebecca Conard and Christopher Nelson, Capra Press, 1986, 221 pages, paper, $9.95
　　Santa Barbara was the first American city to set up a Board of Architectural Review. Its interest in maintaining the integrity of the old town, the El Pueblo Viejo Historic District, has continued unabated. The result is a four-star environment for the sightseer. Each walk through the various sections of the district is carefully mapped and each historic structure is detailed by photograph and description. This is a very helpful guide to a visually thrilling place.

The Santa Cruz Mountains Trail Book: San Francisco to Santa Cruz
by Tom Taber, The Oak Valley Press, 1985 (5th ed.), 140 pages, paper, $7.95
　　This is a solidly written, popular guide to trails located in open-space preserves, country parks, state parks, city parks, the Golden Gate National Recreation Area, and several private locations.

Self-Propelled in the Southern Sierra, Vol. 1: The Sierra Crest and the Kern Plateau
by J.C. Jenkins, Wilderness Press, 1982 (2nd ed.), 304 pages, paper, $12.95

Self-Propelled in the Southern Sierra, Vol. 2: The Great Western Divides
by J.C. Jenkins, Wilderness Press, 1984 (2nd ed.), 308 pages, paper, $12.95

Covering hundreds of trails, with topographical maps, in the Sierra closest to Los Angeles, these two titles are part of the Wilderness Press Hiking Guide series, which is reviewed in more detail under "Series Reviews."

The Serious Shopper's Guide to Los Angeles
by Jennifer Merin, Prentice Hall Press, 1987, 384 pages, paper, $14.95

This book is part of the Serious Shopper's Guide series, which is reviewed in more detail under "Series Reviews."

The Sierra Club Guide to the Natural Areas of California
by John and Jane Perry, Sierra Club Books, 1983, 352 pages, paper, $9.95

This is one of the Sierra Club Natural Areas Guide series, which is reviewed in more detail under "Series Reviews."

Sierra North
by Winnett and Winnett, Wilderness Press, 1985 (5th ed.), 296 pages, paper, $11.95

Sierra South
by Winnett and Winnett, Wilderness Press, 1986 (4th ed.), 288 pages, paper, $11.95

Both of these titles are part of the excellent Wilderness Press Hiking Guide series, which is reviewed in more detail under "Series Reviews." Each includes a four-color fold-out map. The Southern edition covers Mono Creek to the backcountry east of Mineral King. The Northern edition covers Mono Creek to Carson Pass.

Ski Touring in California
by David Beck, Wilderness Press, 1980, 222 pages, paper, $9.95

In this book, a well-done section on equipment, technique, and issues such as avalanche dangers is followed by 35 well-described, suggested tours, each with a reproduced topographical map to clearly mark the way. Distances, difficulty rating, elevation gain, and the best season to go are also included.

Ski Tours in the Sierra Nevada, Vol. 1: Lake Tahoe
by Marcus Libkind, Wilderness Press, 1985, 176 pages, paper, $11.95
Ski Tours in the Sierra Nevada, Vol. 2: Carson Pass, Bear Valley and Pinecrest
by Marcus Libkind, Wilderness Press, 1985, 132 pages, paper, $9.95
Ski Tours in the Sierra Nevada, Vol. 3: Yosemite, Huntington and Shaver Lakes, Kings Canyon and Sequoia
by Marcus Libkind, Wilderness Press, 1985, 136 pages, paper, $9.95
Ski Tours in the Sierra Nevada, Vol. 4: East of the Sierra Crest
by Marcus Libkind, Wilderness Press, 1986, 184 pages, paper, $11.95

This is the most comprehensive series to all of the Sierra Nevada's ski touring opportunities. Easy meadow skis or advanced backcountry adventures are all contained in these books. Each tour is evaluated by length, difficulty, elevation change, etc. Good route descriptions are cross-referenced to an adjacent map. A high-quality topographical map is also provided.

Small Hotels of California: The Best of California's Charming Small Hotels and Inns
by Bill Gleeson, Chronicle Books, 1984, 134 pages, paper, $7.95

While everyone else is concentrating on B&Bs, Gleeson has chosen 55 small hotels sprinkled over the entire state. Each selection is given a full two pages, with a photo and an excellent description including historical notes, how to get there, and some of things to do in the area. These first-class selections are priced from moderate to very expensive. As it has not been revised, this book is best used as a supplement to a more up-to-date guide.

Smoke-free Lodging in California
edited by Rene Felciano, Pinerolo Publishing, 1986, 92 pages, paper, $11.95

Leave it to California to lead the way in letting the traveler know about smoke-free lodging options. And there are a lot of them—350 when this helpful compendium was printed, and no doubt even more today. This is the book non-smokers who hate the smell of stale smoke have been waiting for. Pinerolo Press also has a bi-monthly newsletter with information on travel, recreation, and dining for "people who like fresh air wherever they go" (see Travel Newsletters and Magazines appendix).

Sonoma County Bike Trails
by Phyllis Neumann, Sonoma County Bike Trails, 1987, 106 pages, paper, $7.95

Sonoma County, in the heart of the northern California wine country, is a great place to bicycle. Here is a well-done collection that focuses on the casual cyclist who is looking for some cycling fun. Trips included range from five to 26 miles in length and from easy to strenuous in difficulty. A good mountain-bike area is also described. Each route is well described, with a map and profile chart provided, and tips on a good picnic lunch location or a little sightseeing included.

Sonoma County Guide
Vintage Publications, 1987, 136 pages, paper, $3.95

This annual, large-format guide is done in an identical manner to the *Napa County Guide* reviewed above.

South Bay Hot Plates
by Joseph Izzo, Jr., JK West Publications, 1987, 329 pages, paper, $9.95

Izzo, restaurant critic for the *San Jose Mercury News*, details his choices for restaurants located less than an hour south of San Francisco. Each of these 180 restaurants, representing a wide range of cuisine and prices, is given a well-written evaluation. This is a helpful culinary guide to the south end of the San Francisco peninsula.

South Bay Trails: Outdoor Adventures Around the Santa Clara Valley
by Frances Spangle and Jean Rusmore, Wilderness Press, 1984, 297 pages, paper, $11.95

Covering hundreds of miles of trails at the south end of the San Francisco Bay, this book is part of the excellent Wilderness Press Hiking Guide series, which is reviewed in more detail under "Series Reviews."

Special Places for the Discerning Traveler in Oregon, Washington, Idaho, Montana, British Columbia, California Wine Country
by Fred and Mardi Nystrom, Graphics Arts Center Publishing, 1986, 216 pages, paper, $13.95

See "The Pacific Northwest."

Stairway Walks in San Francisco
by Adah Bakalinsky, Lexikos Publishing, 1984, 111 pages, paper, $6.95

Even San Franciscans have no idea how many "stairway streets" exist in their hilly city. The author has woven these delightful by-ways into 26 guided neighborhood walks. Excellent maps and an interesting commentary on the sights make this guide a real must for walkers visiting San Francisco.

Starr's Guide to the John Muir Trail and the High Sierra Region
by Walter Starr, Sierra Club Books, 1974 (12th revised ed.), 224 pages, paper, $8.95
One of the most famous hiking guides anywhere, this book is part of the Sierra Club Hiking Totebook series, which is reviewed in more detail under "Series Reviews."

Sunset: California Freeway Exit Guide
Lane Publishing, 1986, 352 pages, paper, $9.95
This is a large-format reference guide to gas, food, lodging, and other facilities at more than 2800 exits on interstate, U.S., and state highways.

Sunset: California Travel Guide
Lane Publishing, 1986, 264 pages, paper, $12.95
Sunset: Gold Rush Country
Lane Publishing, 1972, 128 pages, paper, $7.95
Sunset: Northern California Travel Guide
Lane Publishing, 1980, 128 pages, paper, $7.95
Sunset: Southern California Travel Guide
Lane Publishing, 1984, 128 pages, paper, $7.95
These four titles are part of the Sunset Travel Guide series, which is reviewed in more detail under "Series Review."

Sunset: Wine Country California
Lane Publishing, 1987, 176 pages, paper, $9.95
In this quick but informative rundown of nearly 500 large and small wineries through the state are good detail maps and other travel tips.

The Tahoe Sierra: A Natural History Guide to 106 Hikes in the Northern Sierra
by Jeffrey Schaffer, Wilderness Press, 1987 (3rd ed.), 309 pages, paper, $15.95
This is another quality member of the Wilderness Press Hiking Guide series, which is reviewed in more detail under "Series Reviews." This one, however, includes well-written chapters on lakes, fish, geology, botany, and zoology to assist the natural history hound.

The Tastes of California Wine Country, Napa/Sonoma
by Sonnie Imes, Tastes of Tahoe, 1986, 340 pages, paper, $9.95
The Tastes of California Wine Country, North Coast
by Sonnie Imes, Tastes of Tahoe, 1987, 391 pages, paper, $9.95
The Tastes of Tahoe III
by Sonnie Imes, Tastes of Tahoe, 1985, 213 pages, paper, $8.95
   This interesting series of books is designed to introduce quality
restaurants, and sometimes bed and breakfasts, via their recipes. A
good description of each establishment and the necessary particulars
are inlcuded, but the main focus is on recipes that allow the traveler
to pick and choose.

There, There: East San Francisco Bay At Your Feet
by Margot Doss, Presidio Press, 1978, 304 pages, paper, $6.95
   This is a great little walker's guide to the East Bay. Maps, directions, historical notes are all included. No doubt times have changed
some of realities of these walks, but *There, There* is still an interesting guide.

**The Thrifty Gourmet: 250 Great Dinners in the Bay Area for $6.95 or
Less**
by Sharon Silva and Frank Viviano, Chronicle Books, 1987, 176
pages, paper, $4.95
   This book presents a diversity of cuisines—Chinese, Cuban, Ja-
maican, Nicaraguan, Greek, Indian, and Italian. Each is described
with a solid paragraph of evaluation, which contains all the pertinent
facts.

Timberline Country: The Sierra High Route
by Steve Roper, Sierra Club Books, 1982, 320 pages, paper, $9.95
**To Walk with a Quiet Mind: Hikes in the Woodlands, Parks, and
Beaches of the San Francisco Bay Area**
by Nancy Olmsted, Sierra Club Books, 1975, 256 pages, paper,
$8.95
   These two quality guides are members of the Sierra Club Hiking
Totebook series, which is reviewed in more detail under "Series
Reviews."

Trails of the Angeles: 100 Hikes in the San Gabriels
by John Robinson, Wilderness Press, 1984 (5th ed.), 232 pages,
paper, $11.95
The Trinity Alps
by Luther Linkhart, Wilderness Press, 1986 (2nd ed.), 192 pages,
paper, $14.95
   These two books are part of the excellent Wilderness Press Hiking

Guide series, which is reviewed in more detail under "Series Reviews." Each includes a separate topographical map. *Trails of the Angeles* describes short and long hikes in the mountains nearest Los Angeles. *The Trinity Alps* concentrates on longer, more rugged treks befitting this spectacular area of northern California.

22 Days in California: The Itinerary Planner

by Roger Rapaport, John Muir Publications, 1988, 136 pages, paper, $6.95

This is one of the Itinerary Planner series, which is reviewed in more detail under "Series Reviews." Note that the title has recently been changed and this book may be found under *California in 22 Days.*

The Unofficial Guide to Disneyland

by Bob Sehlinger, Prentice Hall Press, 1987 (revised ed.), 143 pages, paper, $6.95

This great little guide rates different attractions for different age groups. The author has created various touring strategies for groups with members of varying ages—adults only, with young kids, with older kids, with grandparents. Information on the duration of each ride and the amount of time it will take to get to the front of the line from about 100 back will help save *lots* of time—especially on busy days. Plenty of other information on special events, live entertainment, restaurants, shopping, and other touring tips is also provided. The guide is "unofficial" because it is in no way linked to the business it evaluates and thus, the author maintains, can be more honestly critical where appropriate. In other words, this guide represents one person: the consumer. This book is updated every two years.

Walking from Inn to Inn: The San Francisco Bay Area

by Jacqueline Kudler and Arlene Stark, The Globe Pequot Press, 1986, 288 pages, paper, $8.95

Here is a book focused on walking the European way—from inn to inn. Each walk winds through some interesting part of the San Francisco area and offers suggestions on interesting lodging, directions on how to reach the start of each walk, and how to get back to the starting point either on foot or by public transportation. Walks are often of very reasonable length (two to five miles). Those who have used the book indicate that the directions are sometimes incomplete but that the book works well overall. For longer walks, there are suggestions on how to string different walks together. Good hand-drawn maps are included.

Walks of California

by Gary Ferguson, Prentice Hall Press, 1987, 278 pages, paper, $11.95

This is a fine compendium of 80 day-walks through every sort of terrain—desert, coastline and beaches, forests, and mountains. Along the way, Ferguson provides interesting cultural and natural history notes. The maps provided are probably adequate for the task but are not topographical.

Webster's Wine Tours: California, Oregon and Washington

by Bob Thompson, Prentice Hall Press, 1987, 200 pages, cloth (flexible), $15.95

This book is part of the rapidly growing Webster's Wine Tours series, which is reviewed in more detail under "Series Reviews."

Weekend Adventures for City-Weary People: Overnight Trips in Northern California

by Carole Meyers, Carousel Press, 1984 (3rd ed.), 230 pages, paper, $7.95

This is a quality collection of weekend journeys that includes where to stay and eat, what to see and do, and a little background on each place to visit. Historically, this useful guide has been updated every three to four years, so a new one is due.

Where Shall We Eat in Marin?: A Restaurant Finder

edited by Susan Shaffer, Meadowsweet Press, 1987, 253 pages, paper, $6.95

Travelers to San Francisco should visit beautiful Marin County, which lies across the Golden Gate Bridge. This book will make eating there easier. It is an impartial, comprehensive directory to eating options throughout the county, complete with location maps, directions, type of cuisine, typical menu items, average cost, and short descriptions for each restaurant. No ratings are included but this is still a very useful resource guide.

Winter Recreation in California

Sail Sales Publishing, 1987, 160 pages, paper, $10.95

This large-format, spiral-bound book covers downhill and cross-country ski areas and snowmobile trails throughout California. Included are general maps of trails and ski runs, prices, services and facilities available, and other pertinent information. This is a handy, quick reference guide.

Yosemite National Park
   by Jeffrey Schaffer, Wilderness Press, 1986 (revised 2d ed.), 274
   pages, paper, $14.95
      This is an excellent title in the Wilderness Press Hiking Guide
   series, which is reviewed in more detail under "Series Reviews." It
   contains a well-written overview of the park and information on
   landscape, climate, flora, and fauna. Every trail in the park is carefully described and plotted on a separate, special topographical map
   marked from the author's own hiking experience.

Yosemite Road Guide: Keyed to Roadside Markers
   by Richard Ditton and Donald McHenry, Yosemite National
   History Association, undated, 80 pages, paper, $2.95
      This book details a fascinating tour of the park, its history, its
   giant sequoia groves, its meadows and lakes, all by way of the roadside marker system keyed to the book.

Zagat Los Angeles Restaurant Survey
   Zagat Survey, 1987, 139 pages, paper, $8.95
Zagat San Francisco Restaurant Survey
   Zagat Survey, 1987, 107 pages, paper, $8.95
      These two excellent guides are part of the Zagat Survey series,
   which is reviewed in more detail under "Series Reviews." The series
   is updated annually.

COLORADO ───────────────────────────────────────
See also "The Rocky Mountain/Great Basin States" and "United States
as a Whole."

Atlas of Colorado Ghost Towns: Vol. 1
   by Leanne Boyd and H. Glenn Carson, Carson Enterprises, 1984,
   134 pages, paper, $12.95
Atlas of Colorado Ghost Towns: Vol. 2
   by Leanne Boyd and H. Glenn Carson, Carson Enterprises, 1985,
   183 pages, paper, $15.95
      These two large-format catalogs list hundreds of historic sites,
   ghost and otherwise, arranged by county. Sites are plotted on a map
   of each county and are very briefly described in an alphabetical
   listing.

Bed and Breakfast: Colorado and the Rocky Mountain West
   by Buddy Mays, Chronicle Books, 1985, 110 pages, paper, $7.95
      While other appendices list B&Bs in other Rocky Mountain states,
   all the focus of this title is on Colorado bed and breakfasts. Excellent

reviews are accompanied by something of the history of each selected place. A new edition is needed, however.

Best Choices in Colorado
by Pepper Witteborg, Gable & Gray, 1987, 688 pages, paper, $12.95
This book is part of the Gable & Gray Best Choices Guide series, which is reviewed in more detail under "Series Reviews."

Colorado Accommodations Guide
by D. O'Neill, Falcon Press, 1986, 274 pages, paper, $7.95
Strictly an information resource, this guide gives a comprehensive list of lodging options without opinion or review. Inventories on such things as camping sites, ski resorts, hot springs, and guest ranches are included.

Colorado High Routes
by Louis Dawson, The Mountaineers, 1986, 224 pages, paper, $9.95
Containing information on ski tours for all levels of skill in the Aspen-Vail-Crested Butte area, this book is part of the Mountaineers Cross-Country Skiing Guide series, which is reviewed in more detail under "Series Reviews."

Colorado Off the Beaten Path: A Guide to Unique Places
by Curtis Casewit, The Globe Pequot Press, 1987, 175 pages, paper, $7.95
This book is part of the first-rate Off the Beaten Path Guides series, which is reviewed in more detail under "Series Reviews."

Colorado Scenic Guide: Northern Region
by Lee Gregory, Johnson Books, 1983, 240 pages, paper, $9.95
Colorado Scenic Guide: Southern Region
by Lee Gregory, Johnson Books, 1984, 240 pages, paper, $9.95
These two great books, which fit into the glove compartment, explore every region of Colorado on paved roads, dirt roads, and four-wheel drive roads. Each journey is clearly described with good maps and helpful photographs.

Denver Epicure
Peanut Butter Publishing, 1986, 150 pages, paper, $7.95
This book is part of the Epicure Guides series, which is reviewed in more detail under "Series Reviews." The series is updated frequently.

Floater's Guide to Colorado

by Doug Wheat, Falcon Press, 1983, 296 pages, paper, $9.95

This popular, well-reviewed guide contains information on river adventures for every level of skill, including notes on rapids, hazards, water levels, campgrounds, side hikes, and more.

Fodor's Colorado

Fodor's Travel Publications, 1987, 208 pages, paper, $8.95

One of the better Fodor's Guides, this book is part of Fodor's Country/Regional Guides series, which is reviewed in more detail under "Series Reviews." The series is updated annually.

Four Historic Walking Tours of Pueblo, Colorado

by Ray Bryan, Pueblo County Historical Society, 1983 (2nd ed.), 32 pages, paper, $2.00

If Pueblo is on the itinerary, pick up this handy walking tour booklet from the local historical society and learn something of the history of Pueblo, a town of the old west.

Ghost Towns of the Colorado Rockies

by Robert Brown, Caxton Publishers, 1968, 401 pages, cloth, $12.95

This popular reference book has gone through multiple printings since its first appearance. While there are a few new roads traversing the Rockies now, the directions are still clear, the historical discussions fascinating and detailed, and its collection of historic photos is excellent. Ghost town explorers will find this hardback a fine resource.

Golf Courses of Colorado: A Guide to Public and Resort Courses

by Don and Jim Gallup, Colorado Leisure, 1984, 328 pages, paper, $8.95

This is a handy guide to golfing options throughout Colorado.

A Guide to the Cripple Creek–Victor Mining District

by Brian Levine, Century One Press, 1987, 64 pages, paper, $4.95

Contained herein is the information needed to enjoy the historic Cripple Creek area of the Rockies. Clear maps provide self-guided car or walking tours. The narrative is informative and accompanied by plenty of interesting photos from yesteryear.

A Guide to the Mines of the Cripple Creek District

by Bill Mann, Century One Press, 1984, 72 pages, paper, $6.95

Tourists will find this guide a helpful way to identify the primary mines of this famous area and to learn something of their colorful past.

Hiker's Guide: Pikes Peak & South Park Region

by Zoltan Malocsay, Century One Press, 1983, 197 pages, paper, $7.95

This book contains a wide array of hiking trails, briefly described, as well as a large number of reproduced topographical maps (black-and-white).

The Hiker's Guide to Colorado

by Caryn and Peter Boddie, Falcon Press, 1984, 210 pages, paper, $8.95

This book is part of the Falcon Press Hiking Guide series, which is reviewed in more detail under "Series Reviews."

Jeep Trails to Colorado Ghost Towns

by Robert Brown, Caxton Publishers, 1963, 245 pages, paper, $9.95

This is a popular companion volume to Brown's *Ghost Towns of the Colorado Rockies*. As with his other book, plenty of interesting history and old photographs, as well as directions on how to get to these towns, are included. A few highway designations may need to be adapted to modern realities, but for the most part this book remains up-to-date.

The Pocket Guide to Colorado

Colorado Express, 1985 (2nd ed.), 176 pages, paper, $6.95

This compact, small-format guide is jam-packed with information on just about everything. Write-ups are short and the print can be very small, but there is plenty of value here on lodging, restaurants, recreation, nightlife, shopping, and a whole lot more.

River Runners' Guide to Utah and Adjacent Areas

by Gary Nichols, University of Utah Press, 1986, 168 pages, paper, $14.95

Including Colorado, this book is reviewed under "Utah."

Roadside Geology of Colorado

by Halka Chronic, Mountain Press, 1980, 322 pages, paper, $9.95

This is an excellent member of the highly regarded Roadside Geology Guide series, which is reviewed in more detail under "Series Reviews."

Roadside History of Colorado
by James McTighe, Johnson Books, 1984, 354 pages, paper, $9.95
This motorist's companion to the history of Colorado is a great way to make any trip a bit more interesting. Even long-time natives will find vast amounts of new facts and anecdotes they never knew before.

Rocky Mountain National Park Hiking Trails
by Kent and Donna Dannen, The Globe Pequot Press, 1985 (6th ed.), 288 pages, paper, $8.95
This very popular guide to the spectacular terrain of Rocky Mountain National Park is part of the Globe Pequot Hiking Guide series, which is reviewed in more detail under "Series Reviews."

Short Hikes in Rocky Mountain National Park
by Kent and Donna Dannen, Tundra Publications, 1986, 64 pages, paper, $3.95
The primary focus of this fine booklet is five nicely described nature walks in beautiful sections of this most magnificent park. The walks, while challenging, are appropriate for families with children. Each description is laced with interesting notes on the flora and fauna of the area.

The Sierra Club Guide to the Natural Areas of Colorado and Utah
by John and Jane Perry, Sierra Club Books, 1985, 416 pages, paper, $9.95
This book is part of the Sierra Club Natural Areas Guide series, which is reviewed in more detail under "Series Reviews."

Trips on Twos: 15 Walking Tours of the Pikes Peak Region
by Leslie and Kim Bergstrom, Talk of the Town, 1987 (4th ed.), 72 pages, paper, $4.50
Walks in Old Colorado City, Colorado Springs, Manitou Springs, Broadmoor, nearby parks, and the Air Force Academy (a very beautiful place in its own right) are contained in this first-rate, well-written guide with good maps.

Trips on Wheels: 15 Driving Tours from the Front Range
by Leslie Bergstrom, Talk of the Town, 1985, 128 pages, paper, $7.95
This book is full of thoughtfully arranged, enjoyably written tours by car of the beautiful, historic towns and terrain of the Front Range, the eastern border of Colorado's Rocky Mountains.

Uphill Both Ways: Hiking Colorado's High Country

by Robert Brown, Caxton Publishers, 1976, 232 pages, paper, $5.95

This is an interesting collection of easy and difficult hikes for both summer and winter. The maps are very primitive, though; the appropriate "topo" will be needed.

CONNECTICUT ———————————————————————

See also "New England" and "United States as a Whole."

Appalachian Trail Guide: Massachusetts/Connecticut

Appalachian Trail Conference, 1985 (6th ed.), 145 pages, paper, $8.45

This book is part of the Appalachian Trail Guide series, which is described in more detail under "Series Reviews."

Canoeing Massachusetts, Rhode Island and Connecticut

by Ken Weber, Backcountry Publications, 1986, 160 pages, paper, $7.95

This book is part of the Backcountry Canoeing Guide series, which is reviewed in more detail under "Series Reviews."

Complete Boating Guide to the Connecticut River

edited by Mark Borton, Backcountry Publications, 1986, 244 pages, paper, $9.95

Covering all sorts of boating activities, this is one of the Backcountry Canoeing Guide series, which is reviewed in more detail under "Series Reviews." This guide was produced by the Connecticut River Watershed Council and includes marinas and access areas as well as mile-by-mile descriptions of the river itself.

Country Walks in Connecticut: A Guide to the Nature Conservancy Preserves

by Susan Cooley, Appalachian Mountain Club Books, 1982, 214 pages, paper, $7.95

This book is part of the AMC Walks series, which is reviewed in more detail under "Series Reviews." This particular guide focuses exclusively on the preserves of the Nature Conservancy.

Covered Bridges of Connecticut: A Guide

by Andrew Howard, The Village Press, 1985, 41 pages, paper, $3.95

This book is part of the well-done Covered Bridges Guide series, which is reviewed in more detail under "Series Reviews."

Fifty Hikes in Connecticut: A Guide to Short Walks and Day Hikes in the Nutmeg State
by Gerry and Sue Hardy, Backcountry Publications, 1984 (2nd ed.), 192 pages, paper, $8.95
    This book is part of the Backcountry Fifty Hikes series, which is reviewed in more detail under "Series Reviews."

New York Walk Book
N.Y.-N.J. Trail Conference, Doubleday & Co., 1984 (5th ed.), 393 pages, paper, $15.00
    Including some hikes in Connecticut, this book is reviewed under "New York."

Short Bike Rides in Connecticut
by Edwin Mullen and Jane Griffith, The Globe Pequot Press, 1983, (2nd ed.), 128 pages, paper, $5.95
    Containing 30 rides for every skill in every corner of the state, this book is part of the Globe Pequot Bike Rides series, which is reviewed in more detail under "Series Reviews."

60 Selected Short Walks in Connecticut
by Eugene Keyarts, The Globe Pequot Press, 1988 (2nd ed.), 160 pages, paper, $6.95
    This fine collection of walks is part of the Globe Pequot Walks series, which is reviewed in more detail under "Series Reviews."

Where to Eat in Connecticut: The Very Best Meals and the Very Best Deals
by Jane and Michael Stern, The Globe Pequot Press, 1985, 190 pages, paper, $8.95
    This is a simply wonderful (though dated) assessment of 84 of the best restaurants in the state. And the Sterns do it right—they dine anonymously, they pay for their own meals, and they sample each restaurant at least twice. Selections cover every taste and pocketbook.

DELAWARE ———————————————————————
See also "The Mid-Atlantic States" and "United States as a Whole."

Walks and Rambles on the Delmarva Peninsula: A Guide for Hikers and Naturalists
by Jay Abercrombie, Backcountry Publications, 1985, 195 pages, paper, $8.95
    Including Delaware, this book is reviewed under "The Mid-Atlantic States."

DISTRICT OF COLUMBIA ————————————————————

See also "The Mid-Atlantic States" (which includes the District of Columbia) and "United States as a Whole."

The American Express Pocket Guide to Washington, D.C.
by Christopher McIntosh, Prentice Hall Press, 1987, 160 pages, cloth, $8.95

This is one of the excellent American Express Pocket Guides series, which is reviewed in more detail under "Series Reviews."

Away for the Weekend, Washington, D.C.: 52 Great Getaways Within 200 Miles of Washington D.C.
by Eleanor Berman, Crown Publishers, 1987, 288 pages, paper, $11.95

This is one of the Away for the Weekend Guide series, which is reviewed in more detail under "Series Reviews."

The Best of Washington, D.C.
by Henri Gault and Christian Millau, Prentice Hall Press, 1988, 352 pages, paper, $14.95

Although this book is part of the Gault/Millau 'Best Of' Guide series, which is reviewed in more detail under "Series Reviews," its initial reviews have not been good.

The Complete Capital Runner's Guide
by Kasia Taylor and Kim Diffendal, Diffendal & Johnson, 1985, 99 pages, paper, $7.95

Every city should be so lucky as to have such a fine, spiral-bound guidebook available. Each run is clearly described, including distance (two to 10 miles), surface conditions, terrain, directions on how to get there, and other important notes. An accompanying map is clearly drawn and points out not only the path to take, but also metro stops, parking areas, drinking fountains, and restrooms.

Country Walks Near Washington
by Alan Fisher, Rambler Books, 1984, 210 pages, paper, $7.95

This book is part of the excellent Rambler Walks series, which is reviewed in more detail under "Series Reviews."

Flashmaps: Instant Guide to Washington, D.C.
Random House, 1988, 80 pages, paper, $4.95

This book is part of the Flashmaps series, which is reviewed in more detail under "Series Reviews." The series is updated annually.

Fodor's Washington, D.C.

Fodor's Travel Publications, 1987, 224 pages, paper, $7.95

This book is part of Fodor's City Guide series, which is reviewed in more detail under "Series Reviews." The series is updated annually.

Frommer's Guide to Washington, D.C.

by Rena Bulkin and Faye Hammel, Prentice Hall Press, 1987, 250 pages, paper, $5.95

This book is part of the Frommer's City Guide series, which is reviewed in more detail under "Series Reviews." The series is updated every two years.

Frommer's Washington, D.C. and Historic Virginia on $40 a Day

by Rena Bulkin and Faye Hammel, Prentice Hall Press, 1987, 250 pages, paper, $11.95

This book is part of the budget-oriented Frommer's Dollar-a-Day Guide series, which is reviewed in more detail under "Series Reviews." The series is updated every two years.

Going Places With Children in Washington

edited by Salley Shannon and Ruth Ann Phang, Green Acres School, 1985 (11th ed.), 247 pages, paper, $5.95

This classic Washington guidebook has sold 160,000 copies since its mimeographed origins in 1958. The parents of the Green Acres School kids have explored and evaluated all the places listed. Time-tested, this is a great guide for families. Included are museums, memorials, historic sites, farms, interpretive centers, parks, even shopping and restaurants—all with the kids in mind. Selections cover D.C. and nearby Maryland and Virginia.

Hikes in the Washington Area: Part C: District of Columbia and Prince George's, Charles, and Calvert Counties in Maryland

Potomac Appalachian Trail Club, 1986, 110 pages, paper, $5.00

This is one of the first-rate, small-format Potomac Hiking Guide series, which is reviewed in more detail under "Series Reviews."

I Love Washington Guide

edited by Marilyn Appleberg, Macmillan Publishing, 1987, 205 pages, paper, $9.95

This is a highly regarded member of the I Love Cities Guide series, which is reviewed in more detail under "Series Reviews."

Michelin Green Guide: Washington, D.C.

Michelin Guides and Maps, 1989, 200 pages, paper, $10.95

This is an anticipated addition to the premier sightseeing series, the Michelin Green Guides, which is reviewed in more detail under "Series Reviews." The number of pages is approximate.

More Country Walks Near Washington

by Alan Fisher, Rambler Books, 1985, 219 pages, paper, $7.95

This is one of the excellent Rambler Walks series, which is reviewed in more detail under "Series Reviews."

A Museum Guide to Washington, D.C.

by Betty Ross, Americana Press, 1988, 243 pages, paper, $12.95

This book is a well-written tour of 50 Washington museums, historic houses, libraries and other significant places. Historic notes and other anecdotes, an excellent overview of each collection, practical facts on admission charges (many are free), access for the disabled, the nearest metro stop, additional art galleries in the metropolitan area, and more are all included in this excellent guide. Price and number of pages are approximate for the new edition.

One-Day Trips Through History: 200 Excursions Within 150 Miles of Washington, D.C.

by Jane Smith, EPM Publications, 1982, 334 pages, paper, $9.95

This book is part of the One-Day Trip Books series, which is reviewed in more detail under "Series Reviews."

The Outdoor Sculpture of Washington, D.C.: A Comprehensive Historical Guide

by James Goode, Smithsonian Institution Press, 1974, 528 pages, paper, $13.95

This is the only specialty guide of this type for the capital city. It is thoroughly out-of-date, but still helpful, at least in part. Perhaps the Smithsonian will soon recognize the need of an update.

Trips to Beauty & Bounty: 150 Natural Attractions In and Around Washington, D.C.

by Jane Smith, EPM Publications, 1983, 262 pages, paper, $8.95

This book is part of the One-Day Trip Books series, which is reviewed in more detail under "Series Reviews."

The Walker Washington Guide

by John and Katherine Walker, EPM Publications, 1987, 317 pages, paper, $6.95

With more than 300,000 copies sold since it was first introduced in 1963, this is one of the very best guides to Washington. More than a sightseeing guide, it also covers hotels, restaurants, shopping, museums, parks, how to get around, metro stops, children's activities, and more. The *New York Times Book Review* called it "remarkably comprehensive." For a standard-sized paperback it really packs a wallop.

Walking Tours of Old Washington and Alexandria
by Paul Hogarth, EPM Publications, 1985, 144 pages, paper, $24.95

This is a large-format, beautifully illustrated book with seven walks through the White House neighborhood, downtown D.C., Capitol Hill, the mansions of Massachusetts Ave., Georgetown, Old Alexandria, and Mount Vernon. A delightfully written narrative, filled with history and anecdotes, accompany this well-known British illustrator's renderings of the famous sights.

Washington/Access
by Richard Saul Wurman, Prentice Hall Press, 1988, 200 pages, paper, $11.95

This book is part of the highly regarded Access Guide series, which is reviewed in more detail under "Series Review." This edition was released after press time so the number of pages is approximate.

Washington, D.C. Epicure
Peanut Butter Publishing, 1986, 150 pages, paper, $7.95

This book is part of the Epicure Guide series, which is reviewed in more detail under "Series Reviews." The series is updated frequently.

Washington D.C. in Your Pocket
Barron's Educational Series, 1987, 184 pages, paper, $3.95

This book is part of the small-format In Your Pocket Guide series, which is reviewed in more detail under "Series Reviews." The series is updated every two years.

Washington, D.C. Sightseers' Guide
by Anthony Pitch, Mino Publications, 1987, 127 pages, paper, $3.95

This small-format guide is a real bargain. Washington is a sightseers' paradise and Pitch's book is chock-full of useful practical facts and history on the best sights to see. A map of central D.C. on the outside of the back cover makes it easier to use.

Washington, D.C.: The Complete Guide
by Judy Duffield, William Kramer and Cynthia Sheppard, Random House, 1987, 366 pages, paper, $8.95

This is an excellent, all-purpose guide to what to see and do, hotels and restaurants in every price range, shopping, entertainment, even ideas for picnics and hikes.

Washington Itself: An Informal Guide to the Capital of the United States
by E. J. Applewhite, Alfred Knopf, Inc., 1987, 350 pages, paper, $8.95

This is a fascinating book for those intrigued by architecture and history. Applewhite gives "fresh descriptions of the buildings, museums, and monuments...each presented in the context of what goes on inside the building itself." This unique book is thoroughly delightful.

Washington On Foot: 24 Walking Tours of Washington, D.C., Old Alexandria, Historic Annapolis
edited by John Protopappas and Lin Brown, Smithsonian Institution Press, 1984 (3rd ed.), 222 pages, paper, $5.95

This is a fantastic book for a fantastic price. Included are 22 carefully planned guided tours of this history-packed city, with additional tours of Alexandria, Virginia, and historic Annapolis, Maryland. Well-written and with good maps, this guide is packed with fascinating facts and anecdotes. Each tour is described as to its distance, the time it will generally take, and what metro stops to use.

The Washington One-Day Trip Book: 101 Offbeat Excursions In and Around the Nation's Capital
by Jane Smith, EPM Publications, 1984 (3rd ed.), 228 pages, paper, $7.95

This book is part of the One-Day Trip Books series, which is reviewed in more detail under "Series Reviews."

Washington Past and Present: A Guide to the Nation's Capital
The U. S. Capitol Historical Society, 1983, 144 pages, paper, $6.00

Full of history and color photos, this book will function well as a supplemental companion guide to a more standard travel guide. The index is comprehensive and an excellent several-page color map at the back locates clearly all the buildings of interest.

Zagat Washington, D.C. Restaurant Survey
Zagat Survey, 1987, 123 pages, paper, $8.95
This very popular restaurant guide is based on feedback from thousands of restaurant users like yourself. It is part of the Zagat Survey series, which is reviewed in more detail under "Series Reviews" and updated annually.

FLORIDA —————————————————————————
See also "The South" and "United States as a Whole."

Berlitz: Florida
Macmillan Publishing, 1981, 128 pages, paper, $6.95
Berlitz: Greater Miami and the Beaches
Macmillan Publishing, 1987, 128 pages, paper, $6.95
These books are part of the small-format Berlitz Guides series, which is reviewed in more detail under "Series Reviews."

Best Choices in Tampa Bay Area
by Myles Montgomery, Gable & Gray, 1988, 345 pages, paper, $12.95
This book is part of the Gable & Gray Best Choices Guide series, which is reviewed in more detail under "Series Reviews." As it was released after press time, the number of pages is approximate.

Camper's Guide to Florida Parks, Trails, Rivers, and Beaches
by Mickey Little, Gulf Publishing, 1987, 156 pages, paper, $12.95
This is one of the Gulf Camping Guide series, which is reviewed in more detail under "Series Reviews."

Canoeing and Kayaking Guide to the Streams of Florida, Volume I: North Florida
by Elizabeth Carter and John Pearce, Menasha Ridge Press, 1985, 190 pages, paper, $12.95
Canoeing and Kayaking Guide to the Streams of Florida, Volume II: Central and South Florida
by Lou Glaros and Doug Sphar, Menasha Ridge Press, 1987, 150 pages, paper, $12.95
Both of these titles are part of the Canoeing and Kayaking Guide series, which is reviewed in more detail under "Series Reviews."

Cruising Guide to the Florida Keys
by Frank Papy, The Great Outdoors Publishing, 1986 (5th ed.), 240 pages, paper, $14.95
Though a bit cluttered with ads, this book contains a lot of information on places to go, things to see, weather, marinas, and more,

as well as several aerial satellite photos. Numerous charts (an "artist's sketch, not for navigation") are provided to orient travelers. The book is updated every two to three years.

Diver's Guide to Florida and the Florida Keys
by Jim Stachowicz, Windward Publishing, 1985, 64 pages, paper, $4.50

This is a very useful collection of the best diving and snorkeling spots along the Florida coast, complete with charts, rules and laws to consider, and a review of hazardous marine life to keep an eye on.

Diving and Snorkeling Guide to Florida's East Coast
by Greg Johnston, PBC International, 1987, 96 pages, paper, $9.95

This book is part of the Pisces Diving/Snorkeling Guide series, which is reviewed in more detail under "Series Reviews."

Florida: A Guide to the Best Restaurants, Resorts, and Hotels
by Robert Tolf and Russel Buchan, Crown Publishing, 1988, 320 pages, paper, $9.95

The successful author and publisher of the *Florida Restaurant Guides* have now stepped up to national distribution with this new guide for Crown Publishing. Although this book was released after press time, if it is similar to their earlier guides, travelers can expect that this critical assessment of 248 restaurants and 115 hotels and resorts will be great. Their selections cover every price range, even the most modest, and every geographic corner of the state, including the Florida Keys and, of course, Disney World.

Florida Island Exploring: 57 Tropic Islands and the Keys
by Joan Scalpone, The Great Outdoors Publishing, 1987, 64 pages, paper, $4.95

This book contains myriad day-trip ideas along the lines of Scalpone's *Let's Go Somewhere* booklets described below.

Florida Keys: A History & Guide
by Joy Williams, Random House, 1987, 226 pages, paper, $9.95

This book is part of the History & Sightseeing Guide series, which is reviewed in more detail under "Series Reviews."

Florida Off the Beaten Path: A Guide to Unique Places
by Bill and Diana Gleasner, The Globe Pequot Press, 1985, 157 pages, paper, $7.95

Full of unusual and delightful things to see and do, this book is part of the Off the Beaten Path Guide series, which is reviewed in more detail under "Series Reviews."

The Florida One-Day Trip Book: 52 Offbeat Excursions in and Around Orlando
by Edward Hayes, EPM Publications, 1985, 143 pages, paper, $5.95
    This book is part of the One-Day Trip Books series, which is reviewed in more detail under "Series Reviews."

Florida Parks: A Guide to Camping in Nature
by Gerald Grow, Long Leaf Publications, 1987 (3rd ed.), 255 pages, paper, $11.50
    This is a really excellent guide to the vast selection of parks in Florida. It is arranged regionally, with each park nicely described and camping options and other important facts discussed. The latest updates are added to the back of each regional section. A clear emphasis on the environment and man's impact on it make this a particularly good guide for natives and visitors alike.

Florida Restaurant Guide: Broward/Palm Beach Edition
by Robert Tolf, Buchan Publications, 1986, 224 pages, paper, $4.95
    In this book, a popular restaurant critic shares his picks of over 400 establishments. Each is given a crisp, opinionated half-page review and rated from 0 to 3 stars. A separate chapter details the very few that are really worth a trip. This is a helpful assemblage of the best places to eat for every pocketbook. However, the author's new book, *Florida: A Guide to the Best Restaurants, Resorts, and Hotels* (see above), contains the most current reviews.

Florida's Historic Restaurants and Their Recipes
by Dawn O'Brien and Becky Matkov, John F. Blair–Publisher, 1987, 204 pages, cloth, $12.95
    This is one of the excellent Historic Restaurants & Recipes series, which is reviewed in more detail under "Series Reviews."

Florida's Sandy Beaches: An Access Guide
University Presses of Florida, 1985, 218 pages, paper, $9.50
    The options of where to go to the beach in Florida are many, and this is just the guide to help travelers decide. A large-format book, it gives a bit of history for each coastal county, as well as interesting anecdotes from the past. However, it mainly provides a comprehensive listing of beaches, location maps, and descriptions on how to get there and what to expect. This is a superb resource to the land where the beach is king, but bear in mind that severe weather and other realities can change a beach location in various ways.

Fodor's Florida
Fodor's Travel Publications, 1987, 336 pages, paper, $10.95

This book is part of Fodor's Country/Regional Guide series, which is reviewed in more detail under "Series Reviews." The series is updated annually.

Fodor's Fun in Disney World and the Orlando Area
Fodor's Travel Publications, 1987, 128 pages, paper, $6.95

This book is part of Fodor's Fun Guide series, which is reviewed in more detail under "Series Reviews." The series is updated annually.

Fodor's Greater Miami and the Gold Coast
Fodor's Travel Publications, 1987, 128 pages, paper, $5.95

This is one of Fodor's City Guide series, which is reviewed in more detail under "Series Reviews." The series is updated annually.

Frommer's Orlando, Disney World, & Epcot
by Marilyn Springer, Prentice Hall Press, 1987, 215 pages, paper, $5.95

This book is part of the Frommer's City Guide series, which is reviewed in more detail under "Series Reviews." The series is updated every two years.

Guide to Florida Campgrounds
by Jim Stachowicz, Windward Publishing, 1987, 80 pages, paper, $4.95

This is a good rundown of camping options throughout the state, complete with maps and color photographs.

Guide to the Small and Historic Lodging of Florida
by Herbert Hiller, Pineapple Press, 1986, 268 pages, paper, $12.95

Detailed, exceptionally good descriptions/reviews of 92 historic inns and hotels along Florida's back roads or renovated old downtown areas are provided in this book. The practical information is there, too, including an appendix of important addresses. This is a fantastic selection of very special places to stay.

A Gunkholer's Cruising Guide to Florida's West Coast
by Tom Lenfestey, The Great Outdoors Publishing, 1986 (5th ed.), 148 pages, paper, $9.95

This excellent, large-format book covers in great detail all the specifics of sailing/cruising the waters of Florida's west coast from the Everglades to Pensacola. The charts are exact and usable for navigational purposes. The manuscript is specific as to routes, anchorages, fuel, food, and every other need. This title is updated every one to two years.

Insight Guide: Florida
by Apa Productions, Prentice Hall Press, 1986, 410 pages, paper, $15.95

Ths book is part of the excellent Insight Guide series, which is reviewed in more detail under "Series Reviews."

Let's Go Somewhere: 150 Day Trips, South West Florida
by Joan Scalpone, The Great Outdoors Publishing, 1984, 64 pages, paper, $4.95

Let's Go Somewhere: 150 Day Trips, Tampa to Big Bend, Florida
by Joan Scalpone, The Great Outdoors Publishing, 1986, 72 pages, paper, $4.95

Mini Day Trips: 150 Day Trips, North East Florida
by Joan Scalpone, The Great Outdoors Publishing, 1987, 64 pages, paper, $4.95

These three small booklets offer a wide array of day-trip ideas, from scenic drives and bubbling springs to festivals and flea markets.

Miami Epicure
Peanut Butter Publishing, 1986, 150 pages, paper, $7.95

This book is part of the Epicure Guide series, which is reviewed in more detail under "Series Reviews." The series is updated frequently.

Steve Birnbaum's Walt Disney World/Epcot Center
edited by Stephen Birnbaum, Houghton Mifflin, 1987, 212 pages, paper, $8.95

This is the official guide to Disney World, and the emphasis is on information rather than a more critical appraisal of each ride and attraction. Copious information is provided in this easy-to-read, large-format book. The sheer volume of up-to-date information on every nook and cranny of this delightful place makes this guide well worth the price, even though ratings of many attractions are unclear. The maps are excellent in this annually updated guide.

A Trailer Boat Launching and Cruising Guide for Mid-Florida
by Ernest Miller, The Great Outdoors Publishing, 1984, 66 pages, paper, $5.95

This guide to launching sites—coastal, lake, and river—in the Tampa and Orlando areas and throughout mid-Florida includes plenty of detail maps and facility information.

The Unofficial Guide to Walt Disney World & Epcot
by Bob Sehlinger and John Finley, Prentice Hall Press, 1987, 184 pages, paper, 6.95

Because this guide is unofficial, the authors are not tied in any way to Disney World and therefore can be more opinionated and critical where appropriate. As in the companion volume to California's Disneyland, the authors tell what things they feel are worth the time, what are not, and how long the wait will be. They rate each ride or event for every age group and have put together itineraries for groups with young kids, older ones, or none at all. Plenty of touring tips, including where to eat and what not to miss, are included in this great guide to getting the most out of a trip to Disney. This guide is updated every two years.

A Visitor's Guide to the Everglades
by Jeff Weber, The Great Outdoors Publishing, 1986, 64 pages, paper, $3.95

This is a helpful booklet to a most magnificent park, with ideas on where to go, what to see, and what to do, a few restaurant picks along the way, and information on the flora and fauna of this unique spot.

GEORGIA ───────────────────────────

See also "The South" and "United States as a Whole."

Appalachian Trail Guide to North Carolina/Georgia
Appalachian Trail Conference, 1986 (8th ed.), 172 pages, paper, $14.50

This book is part of the Appalachian Trail Guide series, which is reviewed in more detail under "Series Reviews."

Atlanta Restaurant Guide
by William Cutler and Christiane Lauterbach, Pelican Publishing, 1988, 272 pages, paper, $5.95

The authors of this guide are experienced restaurant reviewers. Both are editors of *Knife & Fork*, an Atlanta monthly newsletter that reviews dining establishments, as well as columnists for *Atlanta Monthly* (Lauterbach) and *Georgia Trends* (Cutler). Now they have pooled their considerable knowledge into these detailed reviews of over 200 area restaurants. The emphasis of the book is on those establishments that highlight some feature of the unique Atlanta culinary scene. As it was released after press time, the price and number of pages are approximate.

Atlanta's Urban Trails, Volume 1: City Trails
by Ren and Helen Davis, Susan Hunter Publishing, 1988, 156 pages, paper, $6.95
   This helpful book contains 25 suggested tours of Atlanta's neighborhoods, historic sites, campuses, and parks. It offers interesting details on history, architecture, and where to park, with a helpful trail map including the points of interest not to miss.

Blue Ridge Mountain Pleasures: An A-Z Guide to North Georgia, Western North Carolina and the Upcountry of South Carolina
by Donald Wenberg, The Globe Pequot Press, 1988 (2nd ed.), 288 pages, paper, $9.95
   See "The South."

Brown's Guide to the Georgia Outdoors: Biking, Hiking and Canoeing Trips
edited by John English, Cherokee Publishing, 1986, 272 pages, paper, $14.95
   This wonderful, large-format book is a collection of the best articles on the Georgia outdoors from the famous but now defunct recreational magazine, *Brown's Guide*. It contains a wide array of well-written articles detailing cycling, hiking, and canoeing trips. This is a fine tribute to a superb magazine.

Georgia's Historic Restaurants and their Recipes
by Dawn O'Brien and Jean Spaugh, John F. Blair-Publisher, 1987, 204 pages, cloth, $12.95
   This book is part of the Historic Restaurants & Recipes series, which is reviewed in more detail under "Series Reviews." Besides the recipes, it contains plenty of useful information on each restaurant selected.

The Hiking Trails of North Georgia
by Tim Homan, Peachtree Publishers, 1987, 293 pages, paper, $8.95
   This is an excellently prepared guide to 92 trails covering 438 miles of scenic northern Georgia. The directions are clear and the trail descriptions very well done. Each hike is rated; distances include easy, short walks, day hikes and strenuous treks. A summary at the back gives an easy-to-read review of ratings, distances, features, the nearest city, and the appropriate maps for each hike.

A Marmac Guide to Atlanta
by William Schemmel and Marge McDonald, Pelican Publishing, 1987, 269 pages, paper, $7.95

This book is part of the Marmac Guides series, which is reviewed in more detail under "Series Reviews." The series is updated every two years.

Mountain Getaways in Georgia, North Carolina and Tennessee
by Rusty Hoffland, On the Road Publishing, 1988, 160 pages, paper, $5.95

See "The South."

Where Atlantans Dine
edited by Barbara Robinson, Susan Hunter Publishing, 1988, 96 pages, paper, $4.95

More than 15,000 customers of over 200 Atlantan restaurants are surveyed each year to produce this popular, annually updated booklet. The compilation of these surveys produces a letter grade (A+ to C-) for quality of food, service, decor, value for the dollar, and an overall grade. The short narratives are informative and include "Best Bite" tips. Symbols tell if there is a non-smoking section, whether low-fat or low-salt menu selections are available, whether there is valet parking, and whether reservations are advised. This is a thoroughly excellent food guide.

HAWAII

See also "United States as a Whole."

Arthur's Guide to Hawaii
by Brian and Pat Arthur, Aptos Publishing, 1987, 300 pages, paper, $9.95

Arthur's Guide to Maui, including Molokai and Lanai
by Brian and Pat Arthur, Aptos Publishing, 1987, 127 pages, paper, $5.95

Arthur's Guide to Waikiki
by Brian and Pat Arthur, Aptos Publishing, 1987, 117 pages, paper, $5.95

The Arthurs have introduced these three self-published works into the crowded Hawaiian travel guide market, and their hard work has certainly produced a solid result, covering practical information on lodging and restaurants in all price ranges, sightseeing, entertainment, sporting activities such as snorkeling and golf, and some of Hawaii's history. Although the competition is stiff, with several classic guides available on the islands, the Arthurs' work is certainly deserves consideration.

Beaches of Maui County
by John Clark, University of Hawaii Press, 1980, 172 pages, paper, $9.95

Beaches of O'ahu
by John Clark, University of Hawaii Press, 1977, 210 pages, paper, $5.95

Beaches of the Big Island
by John Clark, University of Hawaii Press, 1985, 204 pages, paper, $12.95

These are three very useful guides to virtually every beach of interest, complete with comprehensive site descriptions, photographs, detailed maps, and a great deal of the history and lore associated with each location. Available facilities are listed (though some information may be dated) and recreational activities recommended.

Bed and Breakfast Goes Hawaiian
by Evie Warner and Al Davis, Island Bed and Breakfast, 1986, 215 pages, paper, $8.95

This is a informative rundown of the 125 host homes (not inns) available through this group. Included are brief evaluations of nearby restaurants, beaches, and activities. This is a moderately priced, even inexpensive, way to stay in the islands. This book is updated every two years.

Berlitz: Hawaii
Macmillan Publishing, 1980, 128 pages, paper, $6.95

This book is part of the small-format Berlitz Guide series, which is reviewed in more detail under "Series Reviews."

The Best of Hawaii
by Jocelyn Fujii, Crown Publishers, 1987, 448 pages, paper, $13.95

Fujii is a native Hawaiian and one of Hawaii's leading travel writers. In this book, she has assembled her choices of the very best the islands have to offer in a wide range of categories of interest to the tourist.

The Best Places to Stay in Hawaii
by Bill and Cheryl Alters Jamison, The Harvard Common Press, 1988, 400 pages, paper, $10.95

This is an addition to the excellent Best Places to Stay Guide series, which is reviewed in more detail under "Series Reviews." No fees have been accepted for inclusion.

Birnbaum's Hawaii
edited by Stephen Birnbaum, Houghton Mifflin, 1987, 452 pages, paper, $12.95

This is one of the excellent Birnbaum's Guide series, which is reviewed in more detail under "Series Reviews." The series is updated annually.

Condo Lux Vacationer's Guide to Condominium Rentals in the Southwest and Hawaii
by Jill Little, Random House, 1986, 330 pages, paper, $9.95

This is one of the Condo Lux Guide series, which is reviewed in more detail under "Series Reviews."

Diving and Snorkeling Guide to the Hawaiian Islands
by Doug Wallin, PBC International, 1984, 95 pages, paper, $9.95

This book is part of the highly regarded Pisces Diving/Snorkeling Guide series, which is reviewed in more detail under "Series Reviews."

The Essential Guide to Hawaii, the Big Island
Island Heritage, 1988, 175 pages, paper, $9.95
The Essential Guide to Kaua'i
Island Heritage, 1988, 150 pages, paper, $9.95
The Essential Guide to Maui
Island Heritage, 1988, 200 pages, paper, $9.95
The Essential Guide to O'ahu
Island Heritage, 1988, 224 pages, paper, $9.95

There are so many wonderful travel opportunities in the Hawaiian islands that no single guidebook can cover them all. The wise traveler buys two, three, perhaps even four guides and pools their information. If headed to one island in the archipelago, getting a guidebook that focuses on just that island is a particularly good idea. One of the Island Heritage series is a fine choice as part of that strategy. Written with the help of many locals, these guides are particularly wonderful in their consistent emphasis on history and culture, regardless of the particular topic, and for their use of diacritical markings to help visitors learn and appreciate the correct pronunciation of Hawaiian words. A well-chosen array of restaurants, hotels, and entertainment spots in most every price range and the shopping and "exploring" sections on sightseeing and beaches are particularly excellent. Nicely laid out, well-organized, and easy to read and use, the Island Heritage guides are a fine addition to the already top-notch field of guidebooks on Hawaii. These comments are based on a review of the O'ahu volume. The other three titles were released after press time, so their price and number of pages are approximate.

Fisher's World: Hawaii
by Jeri Bostwick, Fisher's World, Inc., 1988, 235 pages, paper, $14.95
This is one of the titles in the Fisher's World series, which is reviewed in more detail under "Series Reviews." The series is updated annually.

Fodor's Fun in Maui
Fodor's Travel Publications, 1986, 128 pages, paper, $6.95
Fodor's Fun in Waikiki
Fodor's Travel Publications, 1987, 128 pages, paper, $6.95
These two titles are part of Fodor's Fun Guide series, which is reviewed in more detail under "Series Reviews." The series is updated annually.

Fodor's Great Travel Values: Hawaii
Fodor's Travel Publications, 1987, 112 pages, paper, $5.95
This is one of the budget-oriented titles in Fodor's Great Travel Values Guide series, which is reviewed in more detail under "Series Reviews." The series is updated annually.

Fodor's Hawaii
Fodor's Travel Publications, 1987, 292 pages, paper, $11.95
This book is part of Fodor's Country/Regional Guide series, which is reviewed in more detail under "Series Reviews." The series is updated annually.

Frommer's Guide to Hawaii
by Faye Hammel, Prentice Hall Press, 1987, 233 pages, paper, $5.95
Hawaii certainly isn't a city, but the islands are small enough that this guide is part of Frommer's City Guide series, which is reviewed in more detail under "Series Reviews." The series is updated every two years.

Frommer's Hawaii on $50 a Day
by Faye Hammel and Sylvan Levey, Prentice Hall Press, 1988, 398 pages, paper, $11.95
This is one of the budget-oriented Frommer's Dollar-a-Day Guide series, which is reviewed in more detail under "Series Reviews." The series is updated every two years.

Great American Runner's Guide: Western States Edition
by Edward Moore, Beaufort Books, 1985, 141 pages, paper, $6.95
Including Hawaii, this book is reviewed under "The Rocky Mountain/Great Basin States."

Hawaii/Access

by Richard Saul Wurman, Prentice Hall Press, 1988, 200 pages,
paper, $12.95

This is one of the unique Access Guide series, which is reviewed
in more detail under "Series Reviews." This edition was released
after press time, so the number of pages is approximate.

Hawaii At Its Best

by Robert Kane, Passport Books, 1985, 220 pages, paper, $9.95

This book is part of the award-winning At Its Best Guide series,
which is reviewed in more detail under "Series Reviews."

Hawaii Handbook

by J. D. Bisignani, Moon Publications, 1987, 788 pages, paper,
$14.95

This is one of the superb Moon Handbook series, which is reviewed in more detail under "Series Reviews." The series is updated
every two years.

Hawaii in 22 Days

See *22 Days in Hawaii* below.

Hawaii's Best Hiking Trails

by Robert Smith, Wilderness Press, 1985 (2nd ed.), 220 pages,
paper, $10.95

Hiking Hawaii

by Robert Smith, Wilderness Press, 1980 (2nd ed.), 116 pages,
paper, $7.95

Hiking Kauai

by Robert Smith, Wilderness Press, 1983 (3rd ed.), 120 pages, paper,
$7.95

Hiking Maui

by Robert Smith, Wilderness Press, 1984 (3rd ed.), 144 pages,
$7.95

Hiking Oahu

by Robert Smith, Wilderness Press, 1983 (3rd ed.), 124 pages, paper,
$7.95

The first title, *Hawaii's Best Hiking Trails,* is a compilation of
what the author considers the best trips described in the other four
books. This is the choice for travelers heading for several islands.
Otherwise, pick up a single-island guide. Each is well written, with
helpful charts to rate potential hikes side by side. Easy family day
hikes, ones for hardy family outings, and others, up to the 18.9-mile
(one way) "grunt" to the top of Mauna Loa—an elevation gain of
over 7000 feet—are included. Good descriptions, with hand-drawn

maps to locate trailheads, as well as public transportation information for the islands of Hawaii and Oahu (the only two with bus systems reliable enough to trust, according to the author) are provided in this great set.

Hawaii's Super Shopper
by Kathleen Wolgemuth and Milly Singletary, Pacific Trade Group, 1986, 141 pages, paper, $4.95
This book contains shopping tips galore for any budget.

Hidden Hawaii: The Adventurer's Guide
by Ray Riegert, Ulysses Press, 1987 (4th ed.), 370 pages, paper, $12.95
This is the excellent, near-classic guidebook that spawned the Hidden Places Guide series, which is reviewed in more detail under "Series Reviews." *Hidden Hawaii* recently won the prestigious Lowell Thomas Award for best travel book. It is updated every two years.

Honolulu Epicure
Peanut Butter Publishing, 1986, 150 pages, paper, $7.95
This book is part of the Epicure Guide series, which is reviewed in more detail under "Series Reviews." The series is updated frequently.

How to Get Lost and Found in Our Hawaii
by John and Bobbye McDermott, Orafa Publishing, 1985, 276 pages, paper, $9.95
This is one title in the highly regarded Lost and Found Guide series, which is reviewed in more detail under "Series Reviews."

The Insider's Guide to Hawaii
Hunter Publishing, 1987, 224 pages, paper, $12.95
This book is part of the Hunter Insider's Guide series, which is reviewed in more detail under "Series Reviews." A large fold-out map is included with this guide.

Insight Guide: Hawaii
by Apa Productions, Prentice Hall Press, 1986, 371 pages, paper, $15.95
This book is part of the excellent Insight Guide series, which is reviewed in more detail under "Series Reviews."

Kauai: A Paradise Guide
by Don and Bea Donohugh, Paradise Publications, 1988, 224 pages, paper, $9.95

This is a new guide, released after press time, from the publishers of the excellent *Maui: A Paradise Guide*. The Donohughs have done a spendid job of covering all the travel bases. Information on lodging of every sort (hotels, condominiums, B&Bs), restaurants, nightlife, what to see, and what to do is all provided. The reviews of restaurants are especially informative. The what-to-see section is very well organized and includes numerous planned tours of the island. The what-to-do section covers a wide variety of options—beaches, shopping, bicycling, snorkeling, boating, horseback riding, etc. Well-conceived and easy to use, this new guide is expected to be updated every two years. A quarterly *Kauai Newsletter* was started in summer 1988 (see the Travel Newsletters and Magazines appendix) to keep readers up-to-date ($5 per year).

Let's Go: California & Hawaii
by Harvard Student Agencies, St. Martin's Press, 1988, 528 pages, paper, $10.95

This is one of the excellent, budget-oriented Let's Go Guide series, which is reviewed in more detail under "Series Reviews." The series is updated annually.

Maui: A Paradise Guide
by Greg and Christie Stilson, Paradise Publications, 1988 (3rd ed.), 224 pages, paper, $8.95

This is a very well-done, often-praised guide to one of the most popular of the Hawaiian islands. The Stilsons' careful research yields helpful tips and assessments of lodging, restaurants, shopping, sightseeing, and special events in every price category. They also offer a rundown of their "personal bests"—best hotel value, best breakfast buffet, best sunset with cocktails, best snorkeling, best beaches, and more. This is a first-class book and, by subscribing to the author's quarterly *Maui Newsletter* ($5 per year—see Travel Newsletters and Magazines appendix), travelers can be sure of having the latest tips. This title is updated every two years.

Maui Handbook
by J. D. Bisignani, Moon Publications, 1986, 235 pages, paper, $7.95

This is one of the superb Moon Handbook series, which is reviewed in more detail under "Series Reviews." The series is updated every two years.

Maui's Hana Highway: A Visitor's Guide
by Angela Kepler, Pacific Trade Group, 1987, 80 pages, paper, $5.95
Plenty of photos and a well-written text highlight this fine guide to the spectacularly scenic Hana Highway.

The Maverick Guide to Hawaii
by Robert Bone, Pelican Pubishing, 1988, 450 pages, paper, $11.95
Robert Bone really knows how to cover the territory. Even Stephen Birnbaum, who edits his own guide to the islands, calls this an "invaluable book." This is the classic guidebook that made the Maverick Guide series famous. The series is reviewed in more detail under "Series Reviews." This guide is updated annually.

Molokai, The Friendly Isle
by Marlene Freedman, distributed by Jane Lael, 1977, unnumbered, paper, $3.95
This nicely done booklet gives a good overview of this often neglected island in the Hawaiian chain. With color photos and text, the author provides a glimpse of what Molokai has to offer. There's no specific information here, just an overview.

The New Holiday Guide to Hawaii
M. Evans & Co., 1988 (10th ed.), 160 pages, paper, $4.95
This book is part of the Holiday Guide series, which is reviewed in more detail under "Series Reviews."

The Sierra Club Guide to the National Parks of the Pacific Southwest and Hawaii
Sierra Club Books, 1984, 261 pages, cloth, $14.95
This is one of the Sierra Club National Parks Guide series, which is reviewed in more detail under "Series Reviews."

South Pacific Handbook
by David Stanley, Moon Publications, 1986, 578 pages, paper, $13.95
This classic guide includes Hawaii and is part of the superb Moon Handbook series, which is reviewed in more detail under "Series Reviews." The series is updated every two years.

Sunset: Hawaii, A Guide to the Islands
Lane Publishing, 1984, 176 pages, paper, $9.95
Sunset: Maui Travel Guide
Lane Publishing, 1987, 64 pages, paper, $6.95
These two titles are part of the large-format Sunset Travel Guide series, which is reviewed in more detail under "Series Reviews."

22 Days in Hawaii: The Itinerary Planner
    by Arnold Schuchter, John Muir Publications, 1988, 136 pages,
    paper, $6.95
        This is one of the Itinerary Planner series, which is reviewed in
    more detail under "Series Reviews." Note that the title has recently
    changed and this book may be found under *Hawaii in 22 Days.*

The Underground Guide to Kauai
    by Lenore Horowitz, Papaloa Press, 1987 (8th ed.), 128 pages,
    paper, $5.95
        This annually updated "family project" consistently receives rave
    reviews and is yet another Hawaiian guidebook approaching classic
    status. It covers the best beaches, restaurants, sightseeing, and ex-
    ploring options. The restaurant write-ups are particularly well done
    and very detailed; the authors are more than willing to call a spade
    a spade—comments are not always complimentary. Exploring op-
    tions include information on hiking, camping, horseback riding, run-
    ning, shopping, museums, special tours, and activities the kids will
    enjoy. For things like riding and hiking, their effort is to orient
    travelers, offer a few tips, and point in the right direction with
    information on other individuals or services to contact. Hotel infor-
    mation is not included in this compact and most helpful book.

IDAHO ————————————————————————————
See also "The Rocky Mountain/Great Basin States" and "United States
as a Whole."

Frommer's Dollarwise Guide to the Northwest
    by Marilyn Springer and Don Schultz, Prentice Hall Press, 1987,
    408 pages, paper, $11.95
        Including Sun Valley, Idaho, this book is part of the Frommer's
    Dollarwise Guide series, which is reviewed in more detail under
    "Series Reviews." The series is updated every two years.

Going Places: Family Getaways in the Pacific Northwest
    by John Biegelow and Breck Longstreth, Seattle's Child
    Publications, 1985, 139 pages, paper, $7.95
        Including Idaho destinations, this book is reviewed under "The
    Pacific Northwest."

The Hiker's Guide to Idaho
    by Jackie Maughan and Ralph Maughan, Falcon Press, 1984, 264
    pages, paper, $8.95
        This book is part of the Falcon Press Hiking Guide series, which
    is reviewed in more detail under "Series Reviews."

Hiking Trails of Southern Idaho

by S. R. Bluestein, Caxton Publishers, 1981, 195 pages, paper, $7.95

This book provides a good rundown of hiking options, including a number of short, easy ones. Good directions, ratings, best season to go, maps to get, and distances are all included. Actual hike descriptions are informative, and various possible extensions to the primary hike are often suggested. But be aware of changes that may have occurred to the trail or road since publication date.

Idaho for the Curious: A Guide

by Cort Conley, Backeddy Books, 1982, 704 pages, paper, $14.95

This massive work is not as out-of-date as it might be. It is a comprehensive tour guide following state and U.S. highways and, while there may have been some changes to the highway system since this was written, the information it offers on history, geology, sightseeing, archaeology, hot springs, parks, etc. is substantially correct. This is a very useful guide for the visitor.

Northwest Wine Country

by Ronald and Glenda Holden, Holden Pacific, 1986, 282 pages, paper, $12.95

Including Idaho wine country, this book is reviewed under "The Pacific Northwest."

River Runners' Guide to Utah and Adjacent Areas

by Gary Nichols, University of Utah Press, 1986, 168 pages, paper, $14.95

Including Idaho, this book is reviewed under "Utah."

Roadside Geology of Idaho

Mountain Press, 1988, 250 pages, paper, $9.95

This is an anticipated addition to the excellent Roadside Geology Guide series, which is reviewed in more detail under "Series Reviews." As it was released after press time, the number of pages is approximate.

Sawtooth National Recreation Area

by Luther Linkhart, Wilderness Press, 1987 (2nd ed.), 222 pages, paper, $12.95

This is another quality member of Wilderness Press Hiking Guides series, which is reviewed in more detail under "Series Reviews." A fold-out map is included.

The Sierra Club Guide to Natural Areas of Idaho, Montana, and Wyoming
by John and Jane Perry, Sierra Club Books, 1988, 416 pages, paper, $10.95
  This is one of the Sierra Club Natural Areas Guide series, which is reviewed in more detail under "Series Reviews."

Southern Idaho Ghost Towns
by Wayne Sparling, Caxton Publishers, 1974, 135 pages, paper, $5.95
  Ghost towns abound in southern Idaho—an ideal place for the history buff. Sparling offers plenty of fascinating information on each town, accompanied by interesting photographs. General location maps are included, but directions are none too specific. Locating some of these sites will require some motivation.

Special Places for the Discerning Traveler in Oregon, Washington, Idaho, Montana, British Columbia, California Wine Country
by Fred and Mardi Nystrom, Graphic Arts Center Publishing, 1986, 216 pages, paper, $13.95
  See "The Pacific Northwest."

Visiting Boise: A Personal Guide
by Dwight Jensen, Caxton Publishers, 1981, 145 pages, paper, $7.95
  Its age makes this primarily a guide for history and a sightseeing, topics that were always the strong points of the book in any case. Otherwise, the specifics on eating, lodging, shopping, and such are thoroughly out-of-date.

Yellowstone National Park
While a small amount of the park is in Idaho, all titles are listed under "Wyoming."

ILLINOIS ——————————————————————————
See also "The Midwest" and "United States as a Whole."

Chicago and Beyond: 26 Bike Tours
by Linda and Steve Nash, Follett Publishing, 1981, 220 pages, paper, $6.95
  This is a well-done collection of cycling trips with a good narrative description, including the sights along the route as well as other practical facts.

Chicago, City of Neighborhoods: Histories & Tours

by Dominic Pacyga and Ellen Skerrett, Loyola University Press, 1986, 582 pages, paper, $19.95

Due to its size, this weighty, large-format book is perfect for driving tours. (Actually, only one of the 15 tours is a walk.) In all, this great book has everything, including a classic collection of photographs and exceptionally clear maps and directions. Incredibly comprehensive and just brimming with historical notes, this is all that a tour book should be.

Chicago Epicure

Peanut Butter Publishing, 1986, 150 pages, paper, $7.95

This book is part of the Epicure Guides series, which is reviewed in more detail under "Series Reviews." The series is updated frequently.

Chicago's Food Favorites: A Guide to Over 450 Favorite Eating Spots

by Pat Bruno, Contemporary Books, 1986, 412 pages, paper, $9.95

This is actually a book on junk food—barbecue ribs, submarines, hot dogs, deep-dish pizza, thin-crust pizza, stuffed pizza, fried chicken, chili, cannoli, Italian beef, steak, Caesar salad, corned beef, hamburgers, soul food, tacos, bakeries, and breakfast. Pat Bruno, restaurant critic for the *Chicago Sun-Times*, supplies some great choices—including sharp, capsule reviews and comments from satisfied customers—for each of these gourmet headings.

Chicago in Your Pocket

Barron's Educational Series, 1987, 112 pages, paper, $3.95

This book is part of the small-format In Your Pocket Guide series, which is reviewed in more detail under "Series Reviews." The series is updated every two years.

Chicago Magazine's Guide to Chicago

edited by Allen Kelson, Contemporary Books, 1983, 437 pages, paper, $12.95

This comprehensive guide is absolutely crammed with information on architecture, history, sightseeing, museums, galleries, dining, entertainment, sports, theater, and a whole lot more. Its only problem is its age; many time-dated specifics have long since changed.

Chicago's Museums: A Complete Guide to the City's Cutural Attractions

by Victor Danilov, Chicago Review Press, 1987, 252 pages, paper, $9.95

This is a compendium of museums, galleries, arboretums, historic houses, nature centers, planetariums, observatories, aquariums, and zoos for young and old alike—144 in all. Each is given a short but informative description. Practical information on admission, hours, address, and phone number are included. This is an excellent resource guide to this very cultural city.

Chicago On Foot: Walking Tours of Chicago's Architecture

by Ira Bach and Susan Wolfson, Chicago Review Press, 1987 (4th ed.), 450 pages, paper, $14.95

The focus of these 31 walks is architecture, and this recent update of this popular guide is superb. The maps and directions are clear, and the history and description of local architectural landmarks is always interesting. This is definitely a top-quality book, although it is fairly large, and heavy for carrying.

Country Walks Near Chicago

by Alan Fisher, Rambler Books, 1987, 208 pages, paper, $8.95

This is a top-notch title in the Rambler Walks series, which is described in more detail under "Series Reviews."

Covered Bridges in Illinois, Iowa and Wisconsin

by Leslie Swanson, Swanson Publishing, 1970, 48 pages, paper, $3.00

This is a great little booklet on the many covered bridges remaining in these Midwestern states.

Flashmaps: Instant Guide to Chicago

Random House, 1987, 80 pages, paper, $4.95

This is one of the titles in the Flashmaps series, which is reviewed in more detail under "Series Reviews." The series is updated annually.

Fodor's Chicago

Fodor's Travel Publications, 1987, 160 pages, paper, $6.95

This book is part of Fodor's City Guide series, which is reviewed in more detail under "Series Reviews." The series is updated annually.

The Great Chicago Bar & Saloon Guide

by Dennis McCarthy, Chicago Review Press, 1985 (2nd ed.), 188 pages, paper, $3.95

This guide is full of McCarthy's refreshing reviews of 200 of Chicago's best.

Hands On Chicago

by Kenan Heise and Mark Frazel, Bonus Books, 1987, 275 pages, paper, $7.95

This entertaining and well-written account of Chicago's history, characters, architecture, and places is arranged alphabetically and will prove a helpful companion book to a more standard guidebook.

Hot Dog Chicago: A Native's Dining Guide

by Rich Bowen and Dick Fay, Chicago Review Press, 1983, 180 pages, paper, $3.95

Inveterate hot dog lovers will love this book, but, alas, it is getting rather old. Double-check the facts first, but by all means check them out, because Chicago is one of the few "hot dog heavens" around.

Illinois Off the Beaten Path: A Guide to Unique Places

by Rod and Julie Fensom, The Globe Pequot Press, 1987, 176 pages, paper, $7.95

This is one of the excellent Off the Beaten Path Guide series, which is reviewed in more detail under "Series Reviews."

I Love Chicago Guide

edited by Marilyn Appleberg, Macmillan Publishing, 1988, 200 pages, paper, $8.95

This book is part of the I Love Cities Guide series, which is reviewed in more detail under "Series Reviews."

Natural Chicago

by Bill and Phyllis Thomas, Henry Holt & Co., 1986, 224 pages, paper, $12.95

This is a guide to good times in the outdoors in parks, gardens, hiking and bicycle trails—all within 50 miles of Chicago. Moderate-sized write-ups lend reasonable detail to a wide range of entertaining choices. Maps give general locations, though clear, detailed directions are lacking. This is a good resource guide for fresh ideas.

Norman Mark's Chicago: Walking, Bicycling and Driving Tours of the City

by Norman Mark, Chicago Review Press, 1987 (3rd ed.), 286 pages, paper, $8.95

This guide contains directions, distances, excellent descriptions with a bit of history, and some welcome stops for food or drink. Each of Mark's 24 guided tours has a hand-drawn map and information on public transportation. His several pub crawls could take all night and he recommends a cab for these. This excellent book is wonderfully entertaining.

Paul Camp's Chicago Tribune Restaurant Guide

by Paul Camp, Academy Chicago Publishers, 1986, 359 pages, paper, $5.95

Paul Camp is a professional eater by trade for the *Chicago Tribune*. He dines anonymously, with one or more friends to add to the feedback, at least twice at each location before writing his critiques. His comments are well written and very informative. Each restaurant is rated from 0 to 4 stars; price ranges cover the gamut, but most are moderate and higher. Lots of good ideas are here.

Sweet Home Chicago: The Real City Guide

by Sherry Kent and Mary Szpur, Chicago Review Press, 1987 (3rd ed.), 370 pages, paper, $8.95

This comprehensive book is so full of facts and fun that they had to make the print extra small just to fit it all in. Chicago natives share the inside lowdown on what they see as the real city, not just the latest trend. They offer their opinions on food, entertainment, arts, and culture, to name a few topics. This is a fantastic resource, although a visitor could only hope to scratch the surface of the options presented here.

What's "In" Chicago: A Guide to Unique Shops & Entertainment

by Marifran Carlson and Anne Trompeter, Academy Chicago Publishers, 1986, 208 pages, paper, $4.95

This is a great guide to a wide range of shops and clubs where travelers can find most any type of clothing or listen to jazz, blues, or rock, or even get up and dance the polka. This book covers the best places for new and used clothing and some of the charming places to show them off.

Where to Find Everything for Practically Nothing in Chicagoland: A Bargain-Hunters Guide to Resale & Thrift Shops

by Trudy Miller, Second Thoughts Publishing, 1987, 170 pages, paper, $6.95

Truly a plus for the shoestring traveler, this is a thorough look at what Chicago and the surrounding towns offer the shopper. The stores are arranged by location and a helpful paragraph is dedicated to describing each thrift shop and resale store.

Zagat Chicago Restaurant Survey

Zagat Survey, 1987, 125 pages, paper, $8.95

The popular guide is one of the excellent Zagat Survey series, which is reviewed in more detail under "Series Reviews." The series is updated annually.

INDIANA ————————————————————————————

See also "The Midwest" and "United States as a Whole."

Indiana Off the Beaten Path: A Guide to Unique Places

by Bill and Phyllis Thomas, The Globe Pequot Press, 1988, 168 pages, paper, $7.95

This book is part of the excellent Off the Beaten Path Guide series, which is reviewed in more detail under "Series Reviews." The 1988 edition was released after press time; the price and number of pages are approximate.

Indianapolis Dining

by Reid Duffy, Chicago Review Press, 1987, 343 pages, paper, $4.95

This is truly a dining guide for Indianapolis. Reid Duffy, a long-time reporter for a local TV station, proves that there are enough restaurants to warrant a guide here. Duffy's goal was an informational guide rather than a critical one, but his descriptions are useful. This is a good resource to have in purse or pocket.

Indianapolis Dining Guide

Shepard Poorman Communications, 1986, 220 pages, paper, $7.95

This large-format guide includes reproductions of menus from the editors' choice of the best full-service restaurants in the city. No fees were paid nor free meals given for inclusion. While each restaurant must meet a certain standard for inclusion, no review is done; only the menus are included. Necessary practical information on hours, dress, credit cards accepted, etc. is provided. This is a good guide for those who would prefer to make their own evaluations.

IOWA ————————————————————————————————

See also "The Midwest" and "United States as a Whole."

Covered Bridges in Illinois, Iowa and Wisconsin

by Leslie Swanson, Swanson Publishing, 1970, 48 pages, paper, $3.00

This is a great little booklet on the many covered bridges remaining in these Midwestern states.

Iowa Historical Tour Guide

by D. Ray Wilson, Crossroads Communications, 1986, 297 pages, paper, $9.95

One of the Historical Tour Guide series, which has greatly helped to fill the travel guide void in this and several other Midwestern states. This series is reviewed in more detail under "Series Reviews."

KANSAS

See also "The Midwest" and "United States as a Whole."

Kansas Historical Tour Guide

by D. Ray Wilson, Crossroads Communications, 1987, 341 pages, paper, $9.95

This book is part of the well-done Historical Touring Guide series, which is reviewed in more detail under "Series Reviews."

Roadside Kansas: A Traveler's Guide to Its Geology and Landmarks

by Rex Buchanan and James McCauley, University Press of Kansas, 1987, 365 pages, paper, $9.95

This fascinating and informative book shows a different sort of Kansas. There is no need to drive straight through; take some time out and explore.

KENTUCKY

See also "The South" and "United States as a Whole."

The Complete Guide to Kentucky Horse Country: Where to Go, What to See, How to Enjoy It

Classic Publishers, 1981, 115 pages, paper, $4.95

Kentucky is a horse-lover's paradise and this little guide gives the information needed on horse farms (over 200 open to visitors), public riding, horse museums, steeplechase and fox-hunting events, horse sales, thoroughbred racing, and polo. In spite of its age, this is still a helpful resource guide.

Canoeing and Kayaking Guide to the Streams of Kentucky

by Bob Sehlinger, Menasha Ridge Press, 1978, 336 pages, paper, $12.95

This is one of the Canoeing and Kayaking Guide series, which is reviewed in more detail under "Series Reviews."

Dining in Historic Kentucky: A Restaurant Guide with Recipes

by Marty Godbey, McClanahan Publishing, 1985, 208 pages, cloth, $12.95

This book details over 40 buildings where history was made and food is now served. Each is captured by attractive line drawings, some of its history revealed, and the restaurant and its evolution described. In addition, two or three recipes from each are included. These restaurants range from casual and family-oriented to dressy, dinner-only affairs. Prices range accordingly and all the practical facts are included, although some may be dated.

The Interstate Gourmet: Midwest
by Neal Weiner and David Schwartz, Summit Books, 1986, 287 pages, paper, $6.95
Including Kentucky, this is one of the excellent Interstate Gourmet Guide series, which is reviewed in more detail under "Series Reviews."

Sample West Kentucky: A Restaurant Guide with Menus and Recipes
edited by Paula Cunningham, McClanahan Publishing, 1985, 108 pages, paper, $7.95
This large-format guide describes some of western Kentucky's best restaurants and reproduces their menus (and even some of their recipes).

LOUISIANA

See also "The South" and "United States as a Whole."

Fodor's Fun in New Orleans
Fodor's Travel Publications, 1986, 128 pages, paper, $5.95
This is one of Fodor's Fun Guide series, which is reviewed in more detail under "Series Reviews." The series is updated annually.

Fodor's New Orleans
Fodor's Travel Publications, 1987, 224 pages, paper, $7.95
This book is part of Fodor's City Guide series, which is reviewed in more detail under "Series Reviews." The series is updated annually.

Frommer's Dollarwise Guide to the Southeast and New Orleans
by Susan Poole, Prentice Hall Press, 1987, 396 pages, pages, $11.95
This is one of the Frommer's Dollarwise Guide series, which is reviewed in more detail under "Series Reviews." The series emphasizes selections in the moderate price range and is updated every two years.

Frommer's Guide to New Orleans
by Susan Poole, Prentice Hall Press, 1987, 200 pages, paper, $5.95
This book is part of the Frommer's City Guide series, which is reviewed in more detail under "Series Reviews." The series is updated every two years.

A Marmac Guide to New Orleans
by Beth Cary and Liz McCarthy, Pelican Publishing, 1988, 266 pages, paper, $7.95
This book is part of the Marmac Guide series, which is reviewed

in more detail under "Series Reviews." The series is updated every two years.

The New Orleans Bicycle Book

by Louis Alvarez, Little Nemo Press, 1984, 167 pages, paper, $5.95

This book contains 56 cycling tours, complete with excellent maps and a brief orientation. These are combined with historical notes on each of the neighborhoods and some of the sights.

New Orleans Epicure

Peanut Butter Publishing, 1986, 150 pages, paper, $7.95

This book is part of the Epicure Guide series, which is reviewed in more detail under "Series Reviews." The series is updated frequently.

New Orleans My Darling: A Selective Budget Guide for the Young and Intrepid

by Barbara and Sandra Heller, Lost Roads Publishers, 1984, 118 pages, paper, $4.95

Travelers on a shoestring can survive in New Orleans with this handy little guide covering all the bases from rooms to laundromats—even a walking tour and some entertainment ideas. A new edition is definitely in order.

New Orleans on the Half Shell: A Native's Guide to the Crescent City

by James Taylor and Alan Graham, Pelican Publishing, 1983, 110 pages, paper, $3.95

This is an informal, insider's guide that shows what the city the locals know and visitors rarely see. This is a survival manual for getting the most from New Orleans—where to go, what to see, how to do it.

New Orleans Yesterday and Today: A Guide to the City

by Walter Cowan, *et al.*, Louisiana State University Press, 1983, 282 pages, paper, $6.95

This comprehensive, scholarly work makes an excellent companion guide to the Crescent City. Travelers will learn a great deal about the rich history of New Orleans, the history that has been preserved, and of its "well-earned reputation for excess and folly, good food and elegant society."

The Pelican Guide to Gardens of Louisiana

by Joyce LeBlanc, Pelican Publishing, 1973, 64 pages, paper, $2.95

This book contains detailed information on all the major gardens—including maps of particularly interesting attractions as well as shorter notes on additional gardens that may be of interest. Note the older publication date, however.

The Pelican Guide to New Orleans

by Tommy Griffin, Pelican Publishing, 1988 (7th ed.), 160 pages, paper, $4.95

This is a block-by-block tour of everything worth seeing in the famous Crescent City, led by a native and veteran newspaperman who really knows his beat. Besides the sights and sounds, there is a special Mardi Gras chapter, and a suggested itinerary for a typical five-day stay. This is a valuable guide to a fascinating city.

The Pelican Guide to Plantation Homes of Louisiana

edited by Nancy and James Calhoun, Pelican Publishing, 1972 (6th ed.), 128 pages, paper, $4.95

This popular guide is thoroughly illustrated and provides 19 easy-to-follow tours of more than 240 architecturally and historically significant homes.

The Pelican Guide to the Louisiana Capitol

by Ellen Jolly and James Calhoun, Pelican Publishing, 1980, 128 pages, paper, $4.95

This little guide will help travelers understand and appreciate Louisiana's famous capitol, its impressive art deco architecture, and Huey Long, once Louisiana's powerful and charismatic governor, who made it all happen. The focus is on history, art, and architecture; the results are thoroughly intriguing.

Zagat New Orleans Restaurant Survey

Zagat Survey, 1988, 110 pages, paper, $8.95

This book is part of the excellent Zagat Survey series, which is described in more detail under "Series Reviews." This edition was released after press time so the number of pages is approximate. The series is updated annually.

MAINE

See also "New England" and "United States as a Whole."

AMC Maine Mountain Guide
Appalachian Mountain Club Books, 1988 (6th ed.), 320 pages, paper, $10.95
    This book is part of the AMC Hiking Guide series, which is reviewed in more detail under "Series Reviews."

Appalachian Trail Guide to Maine
Appalachian Trail Conference, 1983 (10th ed.), 82 pages, paper, $14.50
    This is one of the Appalachian Trail Guide series, which is reviewed in more detail under "Series Reviews."

Covered Bridges of Maine: A Guide
by Andrew Howard, The Village Press, 1982, 43 pages, paper, $2.95
    This is an excellent title in the Covered Bridge Guide series, which is reviewed in more detail under "Series Reviews."

Cruising Guide to Maine, Volume I: Kittery to Rockland
by Don Johnson, Westcott Cove Publishing, 1986, 164 pages, paper, $24.95
Cruising Guide to Maine, Volume II: Rockport to Eastport
by Don Johnson, Westcott Cove Publishing, 1987, 216 pages, paper, $29.95
    These two large-format, spiral-bound books on the how and where of boating are part of the Cruising Guide series, which is reviewed in more detail under "Series Reviews."

Discovering Acadia National Park and Mount Desert Island, Maine
by Albert and Miriam d'Amato, Professional Editorial Services, 1984, 141 pages, paper, $5.95
    This is a useful rundown of various points of interest in the park, with information on accessibility, facilities, short hikes, parking, and things of particular interest to children.

Fifty Hikes in Maine: Day Hikes and Backpacking Trips from the Coast to Katahdin
by John Gibson, Backcountry Publications, 1983 (2nd ed.), 192 pages, paper, $8.95
    This is one of the Backcountry Fifty Hikes series, which is reviewed in more detail under "Series Reviews."

Glaciers & Granite: A Guide to Maine's Landscape & Geology
by David Kendall, Down East Books, 1987, 208 pages, paper, $12.95
    In this fascinatingly written handbook to Maine's varied and in-

triguing geologic past, Kendall covers all the bases, including what to look for and how to find it.

Islands Down East: A Visitor's Guide
by Charlotte Fardelmann, Down East Books, 1984, 135 pages, paper, $8.95
Fardelmann explores 25 of the most interesting and accessible coastal islands of Maine and New Hampshire in this fine book. Included is information relevant to both sailors and non-sailors on food, lodging, camping, picnic areas, docking facilities, etc. Some facts may be out-of-date, but this is a very helpful guide nonetheless.

Katahdin: A Guide to Baxter State Park & Katahdin
by Stephen Clark, Thorndike Press, 1985, 211 pages, paper, $8.95
This is a thoroughly excellent guide to the trails and campgrounds of this unique state park. Its fascinating history is well described, myriad trails are carefully detailed (including distances and other pertinent data), winter uses discussed, and the regulations of the park carefully laid out. All the information is here, along with a large, separate topographical map.

Maine: An Explorer's Guide
by Christina Tree and Mimi Steadman, The Countryman Press, 1987 (3rd ed.), 293 pages, paper, $13.95
This is an excellent volume in the highly regarded Countryman Explorer's Guide series, which is reviewed in more detail under "Series Reviews." The series is updated every two to three years.

The Maine Coast: A Nature Lover's Guide
by Dorcas Miller, The Globe Pequot Press, 1979, 188 pages, paper, $8.95
Published in cooperation with the Maine Audubon Society, *The Maine Coast* is the handbook for understanding more of the natural forces at work in this dynamic state. Covering the issues of climate, geology, botany, and zoology, this is an excellent book for the naturalist.

Maine Geographic: Bicycling
DeLorme Publishing, 1985, unnumbered, paper, $2.95
This is a booklet of good color maps covering the entire coast from New Hampshire to Canada, as well as six inland areas. On each map are clearly marked bicycle tours. The details of each tour are squeezed into the corners of the maps: distance, points of interest, picnic stops, towns where to get refreshments or some help, and campgrounds. This is a compact, useful collection.

Maine Geographic, Canoeing, Volume 1: Coastal and Eastern Rivers
by Zip Kellogg, DeLorme Publishing, 1985, 48 pages, paper, $2.95
Maine Geographic, Canoeing, Volume 2: Western Rivers
by Zip Kellogg, DeLorme Publishing, 1985, 48 pages, paper, $2.95
Maine Geographic, Canoeing, Volume 3: Northern Rivers
by Zip Kellogg, DeLorme Publishing, 1985, 48 pages, paper, $2.95
    These three fine booklets offer a considerable number of canoeing
options, each described (thanks to some very small print) in considerable detail and accompanied by numerous excellent DeLorme
maps.

**Maine Geographic, Coastal Islands: A Guide to Exploring Maine's
Offshore Isles**
by Bernie Monegain, DeLorme Publishing, 1985, 48 pages, paper,
$2.95
    This little guide gives a good orientation to the main islands: their
history, how to reach them, where to stay, places to eat, and things
to see and do. Only the major islands are included here, but it is a
good overview.

Maine Geographic: Day Trips With Children
by Barbara Feller-Roth, DeLorme Publishing, 1987, 48 pages, paper,
$2.95
    This book is filled with dozens of great ideas for day trips with
the kids: a trip to a fish hatchery, panning for gold, the Children's
Museum of Maine, a living history center, an oceanarium, and lots
more.

Maine Geographic, Hiking, Volume 1: Coastal & Eastern Region
DeLorme Publishing, 1985, 48 pages, paper, $2.95
Maine Geographic, Hiking, Volume 2: Western Region
DeLorme Publishing, 1985, 48 pages, paper, $2.95
Maine Geographic, Hiking, Volume 3: Northern Region
DeLorme Publishing, 1985, 48 pages, paper, $2.95
    These small booklets contain good hiking descriptions, nicely
done color maps, and facts and figures on each hike. Handy and well
done, these hiking guides include plenty of easy, short walk/hikes
for every age group.

**Maine Geographic, Historic Sites: A Guide to Maine's Museums,
Period Homes and Forts**
by Bernie Monegain, DeLorme Publishing, 1987, 48 pages, paper,
$2.95
    This is an excellent, compact compendium of historic sites, both
well known and out-of-the-way. Each site is described briefly, with

interesting historical notes. Locations, hours, admission charges (if any) are noted.

Maine Geographic: Lighthouses
by Barbara Feller-Roth, DeLorme Publishing, 1985, 48 pages, paper, $2.95

Maine's rugged coastline has many of these famous sentinels to warn away the ships. This interesting booklet describes 39 lighthouses, as well as a bit of their history and location.

Maine Itineraries: Discovering the Down East Region
by Albert and Miriam d'Amato, Professional Editorial Services, 1987, 60 pages, paper, $3.50

This book contains some suggested driving routes along Route 1 between Ellsworth and Calais which concentrate on the scenic, historical, and cultural sites.

Pocket Guide to the Maine Outdoors
by Eben Thomas, Thorndike Press, 1985, 242 pages, paper, $9.95

If it happens outdoors, this directory will have the facts. From river trips to cross-country ski resorts, hiking trails to wilderness camps, charter boats to moose-watching sites, an amazing amount of practical information on all types of outdoor activities is provided here.

Tides of Change: A Guide to the Harraseeket District of Freeport, Maine
by Bruce Jacobson, *et al.*, Freeport Historical Society, 1985, 82 pages, paper, $6.95

This is a beautifully done guide to this very special area. It includes information on history and other background notes, walks to do and trails to explore (nicely drawn maps included), facts and figures on populations of old and local flora and fauna. There are even profiles on the soft shell crab and the mackerel as well as some famous local folks.

25 Bicycle Tours of Maine: Coastal and Inland Rides from Kittery to Caribou
by Howard Stone, Backcountry Publications, 1984, 176 pages, paper, $8.95

This is one of the Backcountry Bicycle Tours series, which is reviewed in more detail under "Series Reviews."

25 Ski Tours in Maine
by Karl Beiser, Backcountry Publications, 1979, 128 pages, paper, $5.95
   This is part of the Backcountry Ski Tours series, which is reviewed in more detail under "Series Reviews."

Walking the Maine Coast
by John Gibson, Down East Books, 1977, 109 pages, paper, $4.50
   Gibson's great little book contains 25 walking tours from Kittery to Mount Desert Island. Each walk has a small map sufficient to the task, interesting notes on history and the things to see, and directions.

The Wildest Country: A Guide to Thoreau's Maine
by J. Parker Huber, Appalachian Mountain Club Books, 1982, 198 pages, paper, $11.95
   This book is part of the AMC Hiking Guide series, which is reviewed in more detail under "Series Reviews."

MARYLAND

See also "Mid-Atlantic States" and "United States as a Whole."

Appalachian Trail Guide to Maryland/North Virginia
Potomac Appalachian Trail Club, 1986 (12th ed.), 172 pages, paper, $15.25
   This book is part of the Appalachian Trail Guide series, which is reviewed in more detail under "Series Reviews."

Baltimore Epicure
Peanut Butter Publishing, 1986, 150 pages, paper, $7.95
   This book is part of the Epicure Guide series, which is reviewed in more detail under "Series Reviews." The series is updated frequently.

Circuit Hikes in Virginia, West Virginia, Maryland, and Pennsylvania
Potomac Appalachian Trail Club, 1986 (4th ed.), 88 pages, paper, $5.00
   This fine hiking guide is part of the Circuit Hikes Guide series, which is reviewed in more detail under "Series Reviews."

Country Walks Near Baltimore
by Alan Fisher, Appalachian Mountain Club Books, 1988 (2nd ed.), 220 pages, paper, $7.95
   This is one of the AMC Walks series, which is reviewed in more

detail under "Series Reviews." It is also available in the "Rambler Walks" series.

Elegant Lodging: A Guide to Country Mansions & Manor Houses in Virginia, Maryland & Pennsylvania
by Caroline Lancaster and Candyce Stapen, Washington Book Trading Co., 1985, 157 pages, paper, $5.95
See "The Mid-Atlantic States."

Fifty Hikes in West Virginia: Short Walks, Day Hikes and Overnights in the Mountain State and Western Maryland
by Ann and Jim McGraw, Backcountry Publications, 1986, 208 pages, paper, $9.95
This book is part of the Backcountry Fifty Hikes series, which is reviewed in more detail under "Series Reviews."

A Guide to Baltimore Architecture
by John Dorsey and James Dilts, Tidewater Publishers, 1981 (2nd ed.), 327 pages, paper, $4.95
This is a well-done series of planned tours with good descriptions and photographs tied to detailed maps.

Hikes in the Washington Area, Part A: Montgomery, Frederick, and Carroll Counties in Maryland
Potomac Appalachian Trail Club, 1986, 106 pages, paper, $5.00
Hikes in the Washington Area, Part C: District of Columbia and Prince George's, Charles, and Calvert Counties in Maryland
Potomac Appalachian Trail Club, 1986, 110 pages, paper, $5.00
These two titles are part of the first-rate, small-format Potomac Hiking Guide series, which is reviewed in more detail under "Series Reviews."

Maryland's Historic Restaurants and Recipes
by Dawn O'Brien and Rebecca Schenck, John F. Blair–Publisher, 1985, 204 pages, cloth, $12.95
This is one of the Historic Restaurants & Recipes series, which is reviewed in more detail under "Series Reviews."

Maryland One-Day Trip Book
EPM Publications, 1988, 250 pages, paper, $8.95
This is an anticipated addition to the One-Day Trip Books series, which is reviewed in more detail under "Series Reviews." As it was released after press time, the price and number of pages are approximate.

The Pelican Guide to Maryland

by Victor and Tom Block, Pelican Publishing, 1987, 205 pages, paper, $9.95

This is a good sightseeing guide with historical background notes and up-to-date descriptions of numerous places of interest organized in a county-by-county format. Included are directions to each site and other particulars. Separate chapters cover the Chesapeake Bay, the Chesapeake and Ohio Canal, the National Road, and the Mason-Dixon Line in detail.

Shifra Stein's Day Trips from Baltimore: Getaways Less Than 2 Hours Away

by Gwyn Willis, The Globe Pequot Press, 1985, 160 pages, paper, $7.95

This book is part of the Shifra Stein's Day Trips series, which is reviewed in more detail under "Series Reviews."

Walks and Rambles on the Delmarva Peninsula: A Guide for Hikers and Naturalists

by Jay Abercrombie, Backcountry Publications, 1985, 195 pages, paper, $8.95

Including portions of Maryland, this book is reviewed under "The Mid-Atlantic States."

Washington On Foot: 24 Walking Tours of Washington, D.C., Old Alexandria, Historic Annapolis

edited by John Protopappas and Lin Brown, Smithsonian Institution Press, 1984 (3rd ed.), 222 pages, paper, $5.95

See "District of Columbia."

MASSACHUSETTS

See also "New England" and "United States as a Whole."

A.I.A. Guide to Boston

by Susan and Michael Southworth, The Globe Pequot Press, 1984, 396 pages, paper, $14.95

A.I.A. stands for the American Institute of Architects. The book, produced by the Boston Society of Architects, is an extensive architectural review of Boston using numerous, well-described tours to bring the city to life. Photographs are extensively used and the maps are very clear.

AMC Massachusetts-Rhode Island Trail Guide
Appalachian Mountain Club Books, 1988 (6th ed.), 256 pages,
paper, $12.95
    This book is part of the AMC Hiking Guide series, which is
reviewed in more detail under "Series Reviews."

Appalachian Trail Guide to Massachusetts/Connecticut
Appalachian Trail Conference, 1985 (6th ed.), 145 pages, paper,
$8.45
    This book is part of the Appalachian Trail Guide series, which is
reviewed in more detail under "Series Reviews."

The Art Museums of New England: Massachusetts
by S. Lane Faison, Jr., David R. Godine–Publisher, 1982, 251 pages,
paper, $9.95
    This is one of three paperbacks that have been drawn from the
superb, hardbound *Art Museums of New England*, which is reviewed
under "New England."

Beacon Hill: A Walking Tour
by A. McIntyre, Little, Brown & Co., 1975, 118 pages, paper, $8.95
    This exceptionally well written architectural and historical guide
to this most famous Boston area includes numerous photographs and
a helpful architectural glossary providing not only the definitions of
architectural terms but line drawings as well, to illustrate important
structural details. This is definitely a guide to help travelers enjoy
this extraordinarily historic area much, much more.

The Berkshire Book: A Complete Guide
by Jonathan Sternfield, Berkshire House, 1986, 345 pages, paper,
$14.95
    This is the most popular guidebook solely on the Berkshires, the
popular counties that make up far western Massachusetts. The coverage is extensive—restaurant reviews are particularly excellent.
Well-written chapters on transportation, lodging, food, culture, recreation, shopping, and history are included, plus a separate, helpful
chapter on other practical matters.

Blue Guide: Boston and Cambridge
by Jim Freely, W. W. Norton & Co., 1984, 400 pages, paper, $15.95
    This is one of the highly respected Blue Guide series, which is
reviewed in more detail under "Series Reviews."

Boston Best Guide: An Official Guide to Boston
M. Kennedy Publishing, 1988, 64 pages, paper, $2.50
This is a handy quarterly guide to a bit of everything: restaurants, lodging, places of interest, transportation, nightlife, and more.

Boston Epicure
Peanut Butter Publishing, 1986, 150 pages, paper, $7.95
This book is part of the Epicure Guide series, which is reviewed in more detail under "Series Reviews." The series is updated frequently.

The Boston Globe Historic Walks in Cambridge (including Harvard, Radcliffe, and M.I.T.)
by John Harris, The Globe Pequot Press, 1986, 388 pages, paper, $10.95
The Boston Globe's Historic Walks in Old Boston
by John Harris, The Globe Pequot Press, 1982, 352 pages, paper, $9.95
These are two first-class, very comprehensive guides to walking tours through the history of Boston and Cambridge. Clear maps and an excellent narrative make both of these books a good choice for travelers who like to stretch their legs and explore.

Boston in Your Pocket
Barron's Educational Series, 1987, 144 pages, paper, $3.95
This is one of the small-format In Your Pocket Guides series, which is reviewed in more detail under "Series Reviews." The series is updated every two years.

Boston's Best Restaurants
Steve Raichlen, Yankee Books, 1988, 144 pages, paper, $9.95
Raichlen, food critic for *Boston* magazine, has compiled this collection of more than 100 of the best places to eat within a 60-mile radius of Boston. This title was released after press time so the number of pages is approximate.

Canoeing Massachusetts, Rhode Island and Connecticut
by Ken Weber, Backcountry Publications, 1986, 160 pages, paper, $7.95
This is one of the Backcountry Canoeing Guide series, which is reviewed in more detail under "Series Reviews."

Cape Cod Fact and Folklore
by Paul Giambarba, The Scrimshaw Press, 1985, unnumbered, paper, $2.95
This is an amusing collection of anecdotes and entertaining illustrations that take you from Bourne to Provincetown.

Car-Free in Boston: The Guide to Public Transit in Greater Boston & New England
Association for Public Transportation, 1987 (5th ed.), 160 pages, paper, $3.95
Travelers who have ever driven in Boston know why this book was written. Leave the headaches to someone else—let this comprehensive, annual guide get you there safely and sanely.

The Complete Guide to Boston's Freedom Trail
by Charles Bahne, Newtowne Publishing, 1985, 64 pages, paper, $3.95
This is a thorough, well-researched, step-by-step guide to a famous walk through history. Following the trail is easy—it is marked with a red line on the sidewalk or red bricks in the sidewalk pavement. This comprehensive booklet covers a great deal about the origins of an independent America along the course of this historic path. A clearly drawn map is also included.

Country Walks Near Boston
by Alan Fisher, Appalachian Mountain Club Books, 1986 (2nd ed.), 175 pages, paper, $7.95
All the walks in this book are within reach of public transportation. This book is part of the AMC Walks series, which is reviewed in more detail under "Series Reviews," and is also available in the Rambler Walks series.

Covered Bridges of Massachusetts: A Guide
by Andrew Howard, The Village Press, 1978, 46 pages, paper, $2.95
This book is part of the very well done Covered Bridge Guides series, which is reviewed in more detail under "Series Reviews."

Exploring Coastal Massachusetts: New Bedford to Salem
by Barbara Clayton and Kathleen Whitley, Dodd, Mead & Co., 1983, 437 pages, paper, $14.95
This book contains reviews and well-written guided tours of 21 coastal towns and areas. History abounds in places like Plymouth, Salem, Cape Cod, and Boston. An introductory chapter on architectural styles will help travelers appreciate even more of what they see.

Exploring the Berkshires
by Herbert Whitman, Hippocrene Books, 1988, 240 pages, paper, $9.95
> This new title was released after press time.

Fifty Hikes in Massachusetts: Hikes and Walks from the Top of the Berkshires to the Tip of Cape Cod
by John Brady and Brian White, Backcountry Publications, 1983, 224 pages, paper, $9.95
> This is one of the Backcountry Fifty Hikes series, which is reviewed in more detail under "Series Reviews."

Flashmaps Instant Guide to Boston
Random House, 1987, 80 pages, paper, $4.95
> This book is part of the Flashmaps series, which is reviewed in more detail under "Series Reviews." The series is updated annually.

Fodor's Boston
Fodor's Travel Publications, 1987, 224 pages, paper, $7.95
> This book is part of Fodor's City Guide series, which is reviewed in more detail under "Series Reviews." The series is updated annually.

Fodor's Cape Cod
Fodor's Travel Publications, 1987, 256 pages, paper, $8.95
> This is one of Fodor's Country/Regional Guide series, which is reviewed in more detail under "Series Reviews." The series is updated annually.

Frommer's Guide to Boston
Prentice Hall Press, 1987, 200 pages, paper, $5.95
> This is one of Frommer's City Guide series, which is reviewed in more detail under "Series Reviews." The series is updated every two years.

Greater Boston Park and Recreation Guide
by Mark Primack, The Globe Pequot Press, 1983, 338 pages, paper, $9.95
> This comprehensive reference book on public parks, beaches, gardens, wildlife refuges, and state parks contains a lot of information, but be sure to double-check the specifics unless a new edition becomes available.

Guide to Cape Cod
   by Frederick Pratson, The Globe Pequot Press, 1988, 208 pages,
   paper, $9.95
Guide to Martha's Vineyard
   by Polly Burroughs, The Globe Pequot Press, 1988 (4th ed.), 208
   pages, paper, $9.95
Guide to Nantucket
   by Polly Burroughs, The Globe Pequot Press, 1988 (4th ed.), 208
   pages, paper, $9.95
   Two superb, sensitively written guides from Polly Burroughs are
   joined by another excellent and much-needed addition to Globe
   Pequot's guide book series on Massachusetts, the *Guide to Cape
   Cod*, written by the veteran author Frederick Pratson. All three
   guides give clear, helpful information on how to get there, what to
   see, where to stay, where to eat, and activities. Burroughs's books
   include some excellent guided tours and interesting historical notes
   and are updated every two years.

**A Guide to Public Art in Greater Boston: From Newburyport to
Marshfield**
   by Marty Carlock, The Harvard Common Press, 1988, 160 pages,
   paper, $8.95
   This new title uncovers the mysteries behind over 300 murals,
   statues, and abstract works in Boston's public spaces. Filled with
   interesting anecdotes and accurate information, Carlock's work is
   for both the wandering tourist and the serious art student.

Hassle-free Boston: A Manual for Women
   by Mary Maynard and Mary-Lou Dow, The Stephen Greene Press,
   1984, 212 pages, paper, $7.95
   Keyed to the woman traveler, this book contains chapters on hotels
   and restaurants chosen for their service to women, shopping tips,
   cultural activities, traveling in the city safely, networking with wom-
   en's organizations, and more. This is definitely a helpful guide for
   women planning to travel alone. Some specifics may be a little out-
   of-date, however, unless a new edition is released.

I Love Boston Guide
   edited by Marilyn Appleberg, Macmillan Publishing, 1987, 180
   pages, paper, $8.95
   This book is part of the I Love Cities Guide series, which is
   reviewed in more detail under "Series Reviews."

In and Out of Boston With (or Without) Children

by Bernice Chesler, The Globe Pequot Press, 1982 (4th ed.), 327 pages, paper, $9.95

This very popular guide sets the standard. The focus is on fun and exploration, although sections on food and lodging are included. Chapters on animals (zoos, duck-feeding, fish), the arts, day trips, tours, exploring, historic sites, museums, and a vast array of recreational opportunities—as well as a separate list of 151 things to do and see for free—are provided. A fifth edition should not be long in coming.

Inside Guide to Springfield and The Pioneer Valley

by James O'Connell, Western Mass. Publishers, 1986, 179 pages, paper, $9.95

This excellent guide for both visitors and residents of the area contains well-written interpretations of the region's history and culture, a guide to the historic sites, and a very extensive listing of restaurants, delis, diners, inns, and ethnic food of every sort.

The Insider's Guide to Cape Cod and the Islands

edited by Greg O'Brien, Stephen Greene Press, 1988, 320 pages, paper, $10.95

O'Brien, from the *Cape Codder* newspaper, has penned this new title, which was released after press time. It includes separate sections on Upper Cape, Mid-Cape, Outer Cape, Provincetown, and the Islands.

Irish Pubs of Boston

by Richard Wesson, Boardworks Publishing, 1986, 134 pages, paper, $7.95

This is a good resource guide to 50 area pubs—what food they serve, what beers are on tap, and when to expect the entertainment to begin. The words to many Irish songs accompany helpful descriptions.

The Other Massachusetts, Beyond Boston and Cape Cod: An Explorer's Guide

by Christina Tree, The Countryman Press, 1987, 355 pages, paper, $12.95

This book is part of the Countryman Explorer's Guide series, which is reviewed in more detail under "Series Reviews." The series is updated every two to three years.

Short Bike Rides in Greater Boston and Central Massachusetts
by Howard Stone, The Globe Pequot Press, 1988 (2nd ed.), 592 pages, paper, $10.95

Short Bike Rides on Cape Cod, Nantucket & the Vineyard
by Edwin Mullen and Jane Griffith, The Globe Pequot Press, 1988 (3rd ed.), 160 pages, paper, $7.95

These two great titles are part of the Globe Pequot Bike Rides series, which is reviewed in more detail under "Series Reviews." A specially sewn binding will help keep the larger volume on the Boston area intact for years to come.

Short Walks on Cape Cod and the Vineyard
by Hugh and Heather Sadlier, The Globe Pequot Press, 1983 (2nd ed.), 117 pages, paper, $5.95

Containing information on 26 leisurely walks, this book is part of the Globe Pequot Walks series, which is reviewed in more detail under "Series Reviews."

25 Ski Tours in Eastern Massachusetts: Cross-Country Trails from the Quabbin Reservoir to Cape Cod
by Irwin Grossman and Ron Wolanin, Backcountry Publications, 1982, 144 pages, paper, $6.95

This book is part of the Backcountry Ski Tours series, which is reviewed in more detail under "Series Reviews."

Uncommon Boston: A Guide to Hidden Spaces and Special Places
by Susan Berk and Jill Bloom, Addison-Wesley Publishing, 1986, 242 pages, paper, $7.95

Susan Berk has made her living leading tours of Boston, and in this finely done guide she shares the unexpected pleasures she has found—both off the beaten path and in the travel mainstream. History and culture abound, along with favorite pubs and taverns, "chocowalks" for candy lovers, ice cream dreams, a fine review of "booklover's Boston," and an excellent children's chapter divided into sections for ages 5 to 8 and 9 to 13. This is a great complement to more standard guides.

Zagat Boston Restaurant Survey
Zagat Survey, 1988, 120 pages, paper, $8.95

This book is part of the excellent Zagat Survey series, which is reviewed in more detail under "Series Reviews." This edition was released after press time; the number of pages is approximate. The series is updated annually.

MICHIGAN

See also "The Midwest" and "United States as a Whole."

Backpacking in Michigan

by Pat Allen and Gerald DeRuiter, The University of Michigan Press, 1982, 149 pages, paper, $8.95

This is a first-class guide to 20 of Michigan's best hiking trails. Each is nicely reviewed with all the salient facts at hand. A handy chart compares each of the trails for difficulty, length, time needed, best season to go, whether permits are needed, etc. A large collection of maps, while not detailed topographical maps, gives a reasonable orientation to each hike.

Bed and Breakfast in Michigan and Surrounding Areas

by Norma Buzan and Bert Howell, Betsy Ross Publications, 1985, 120 pages, paper, $8.25

See "The Midwest."

Biking the Great Lake Islands

by Kathleen and Lawrence Abrams, Entwood Publishing, 1985, 164 pages, paper, $8.95

This is an excellent guide to cycling on seven islands of the Great Lakes: three islands are part of the state of Michigan (in Lakes Huron and Michigan), two are part of Wisconsin (Lakes Superior and Michigan), and another two are Canadian (Lake Huron). Great descriptions of each ride, with distances, road conditions, a general rating of each route, and information on how to reach each island, are included. Enjoy a cycling paradise, cycle the Great Lakes Islands.

Canoeing Michigan Rivers

by Jerry Dennis and Craig Date, Friede Publications, 1986, 152 pages, paper, $12.95

This is a comprehensive guide to the many canoeing opportunities on Michigan rivers.

Detroit Epicure

Peanut Butter Publishing, 1986, 150 pages, paper, $7.95

This book is part of the Epicure Guide series, which is reviewed in more detail under "Series Reviews." The series is updated frequently.

Isle Royale National Park: Foot Trails & Water Routes
by Jim DuFresne, The Mountaineers, 1984, 136 pages, paper, $8.95
   This is a quality title in the Mountaineers National Park Guide series, which is reviewed in more detail under "Series Reviews."

The Long Blue Edge of Summer: A Vacation Guide to the Shorelines of Michigan
by Doris Scharfenberg, William B. Eerdmans Publishing, 1982, 217 pages, paper, $9.95
   Although some details may have changed since its printing, this is a fine resource to the vast number of vacation possibilities along Michigan's 3000-mile coastline. Information on cities, beaches, sand dunes, wildlife sanctuaries, even ghost towns, is included.

Michigan Off the Beaten Path: A Guide to Unique Places
by Jim DuFresne, The Globe Pequot Press, 1988, 176 pages, paper, $8.95
   This is a new addition to the Off the Beaten Path Guide series, which is reviewed in more detail under "Series Reviews."

Michigan's Town & Country Inns
by Susan and Stephen Pyle, The University of Michigan Press, 1987 (2nd ed.), 232 pages, paper, $12.95
   This is a quality guide to more than 75 inns, B&Bs, and historic hotels on both the Upper and Lower peninsulas of Michigan. Each lodging selection is carefully reviewed and often has two photographs—one inside and one outside—to assist travelers in choosing their lodging for the night. This is a beautiful job which has been updated on an annual basis.

The Sierra Club Naturalist's Guide to the North Woods of Michigan, Wisconsin, Minnesota, and Southern Ontario
by Glenda Daniel and Jerry Sullivan, Sierra Club Books, 1981, 384 pages, paper, $10.95
   See "The Midwest."

Ski Minnesota: A Cross Country Skiers Guide to Minnesota, Northern Wisconsin and Michigan's Upper Peninsula
by Elizabeth and Gary Noren, Nodin Press, 1985, 424 pages, paper, $11.95
   Including Michigan's Upper Peninsula, this book is reviewed under "Minnesota."

MINNESOTA ─────────────────────────────────
See also "The Midwest" and "United States as a Whole."

All Season Guide to Minnesota's Parks: Canoe Routes and Trails
by Jim Umhoefer, Northword, 1984, 104 pages, paper, $9.95
Discover Minnesota's state parks—all 100 of them. Umhoefer provides a good rundown on each, including hiking trails and other activities. No specific hiking trail maps are provided in this large-format booklet, nor are there detailed notes on each trail, rather there is a good orientation to each of the many possibilities that await travelers.

Boundary Waters Canoe Area, Volume 1: The Western Region
by Robert Beymer, Wilderness Press, 1988 (4th ed.), 173 pages, paper, $10.95
Boundary Waters Canoe Area, Volume 2: The Eastern Region
by Robert Beymer, Wilderness Press, 1986 (2nd ed.), 160 pages, paper, $10.95
The Boundary Waters Canoe Area comprises a million acres of lakes, rivers, and forest in northeastern Minnesota. Within this incredible wilderness are 1200 miles of canoe routes. These two guidebooks recommend some of the best, beginning from 47 entry points. All the details for each route are included with typical Wilderness Press thoroughness—length of time needed, distance traveled, total number of lakes on the route, rivers and portages encountered, difficulty rating, and other recommended maps. Each book also includes a large, fold-out color map on which the various routes have been plotted.

Exploring the Twin Cities With Children
by Elizabeth French, Nodin Press, 1986 (4th ed.), 76 pages, paper, $4.95
This spiral-bound little book will prove that there is a lot to do with the kids in Minneapolis/St. Paul—from arboretums and nature centers to parks and model railroads—even a tour of the Children's Hospital to familiarize the children with this sometimes frightening place. This is an excellent resource.

Famous Minneapolis Restaurants and Recipes
by Sue Schildge, Schildge Publishing, 1986, 190 pages, paper, $10.00
This book is part of the Famous Restaurants & Recipes series, which is reviewed in more detail under "Series Reviews."

Frommer's Guide to Minneapolis-Saint Paul
by Lucille Stelling, Prentice Hall Press, 1988, 208 pages, paper, $5.95
This is a new title in Frommer's City Guide series, which is

reviewed in more detail under "Series Reviews." The series is up-dated every two years.

Minneapolis/St. Paul Epicure
Peanut Butter Publishing, 1986, 150 pages, paper, $7.95
This book is part of the Epicure Guide series, which is reviewed in more detail under "Series Reviews." The series is updated frequently.

Minnesota Walk Book, Volume I: A Guide to Backpacking and Hiking in the Arrowhead and Isle Royale
by James Buchanan, Nodin Press, 1974, 108 pages, paper, $4.50
Minnesota Walk Book, Volume II: A Guide to Hiking and Cross-Country Skiing in the Heartland
by James Buchanan, Nodin Press, 1985, 120 pages, paper, $4.50
Minnesota Walk Book, Volume III: A Guide to Hiking in the Hiawathaland Area
by James Buchanan, Nodin Press, 1978, 100 pages, paper, $4.50
Minnesota Walk Book, Volume IV: A Guide to Hiking and Cross-Country Skiing in the Metroland Area
by James Buchanan, Nodin Press, 1978, 104 pages, paper, $4.50
Minnesota Walk Book, Volume V: A Guide to Hiking and Cross-Country Skiing in the Pioneer Region
by James Buchanan, Nodin Press, 1979, 60 pages, paper, $4.50
Minnesota Walk Book, Volume VI: A Guide to Hiking and Cross-Country Skiing in the Vikingland Region
by James Buchanan, Nodin Press, 1982, 64 pages, paper, $4.50
This handsomely prepared series was first introduced in 1974 and now comprises the best collection of the Minnesota hiking and cross-country ski trails, a true encyclopedia of what this region has to offer. Included are walks, hikes, and ski routes of every difficulty, and plenty of practical information, too.

Room at the Inn: Guide to Historic B&Bs, Hotels and Country Inns in Minnesota
by Laura Zahn, Down to Earth Publications, 1988 (revised ed.), 128 pages, paper, $7.95
This new edition, due out in late 1988 or early 1989, will expand its coverage to include the entire state. The previous edition covered only those B&Bs "close to the Twin Cities." The price and number of pages are from the first edition; both may actually increase. The book is done much like Zahn's *Room at the Inn Wisconsin* title and, while expanded to include the entire state, will still have at least fifty inns within easy driving distance of the Twin Cities. Please read the Wisconsin review for more information.

The Sierra Club Naturalist's Guide to the North Woods of Michigan, Wisconsin, Minnesota, and Southern Ontario
by Glenda Daniel and Jerry Sullivan, Sierra Club Books, 1981, 384 pages, paper, $10.95
See "The Midwest."

Ski Minnesota: A Cross-Country Skier's Guide to Minnesota, Northern Wisconsin and Michigan's Upper Peninsula
by Elizabeth and Gary Noren, Nodin Press, 1985, 424 pages, paper, $11.95
The emphasis is on Minnesota but *Ski Minnesota* includes regions of Wisconsin and Michigan, too. It is a truly comprehensive compendium of cross-country touring options with ratings, descriptions, and a multitude of maps. Numerous selections are included for every level of skill.

Tourist and Hiking Guide for Minnesota's North Shore
by Roger Blakely, New Rivers Press, 1981, 36 pages, paper, $2.50
This tiny booklet gives some good hiking suggestions along the North Shore. What maps there are are very primitive; purchasing additional topographical maps is certainly in order, and the author includes general information on these as well.

Voyageurs National Park: Water Routes, Foot Paths & Ski Trails
by Jim DuFresne, The Mountaineers, 1986, 176 pages, paper, $8.95
This is a quality title in the Mountaineers National Park Guide series, which is reviewed in more detail under "Series Reviews."

MISSISSIPPI ————————————————————————————
See also "The South" and "United States as a Whole."

The Pelican Guide to Old Homes of Mississippi, Volume I: Natchez and the South
by Helen Kempe, Pelican Publishing, 1977, 158 pages, paper, $4.95
The Pelican Guide to Old Homes of Mississippi, Volume II: Columbus and the North
by Helen Kempe, Pelican Publishing, 1982, 154 pages, paper, $4.95
This book contains maps, photographs, and helpful information for sightseers of the historic and architecturally significant homes of Mississippi.

Travel Guide to the Natchez Trace Parkway Between Natchez, Mississippi and Nashville, Tennessee
Natchez Trace Parkway Association, 1984, 100 pages, paper, $7.95
The Natchez Trace Parkway is predominantly in Mississippi, although it also nips Alabama before crossing Tennessee to Nashville.

This large-format guide provides notes on the history of the parkway and the many historic sites along "the Trace." It is an interesting resource that will add pleasure to any ride through this beautiful area, complete with many photographs.

MISSOURI

See also "Midwest" and "United States as a Whole."

The Greatest Ozark Guidebook
by Harry and Phyl Dark, Greatest Graphics, 1980 (2nd ed.), 240 pages, paper, $7.95

Only a true Ozarker could write a book with such a depth of pride and understanding of this unique and somewhat mysterious region of middle America. An interesting dollop of history is found here, in addition to a great many suggestions of things to do and see—special ways to enjoy and appreciate this fascinating area. The Ozarks are located in Missouri and Arkansas, and, although there are technically extensions of it reaching into several other neighboring states, this great little book limits its focus to the two. This second edition is still quite useful; a third edition would be even better.

Kansas City Epicure
Peanut Butter Publishing, 1986, 150 pages, paper, $7.95

This book is part of the Epicure Guide series, which is reviewed in more detail under "Series Reviews." The series is updated frequently.

The Pelican Guide to the Ozarks
by Bet Hampel, Pelican Publishing, 1982, 160 pages, paper, $4.95

Divided into tours of 11 different areas within the Ozarks, this useful little guide gives some hints on what to see and how to get there, special events and annual fairs, and recommends numerous places in which to experience the best of the culture and food of this unique area. This is another aging but still-useful guide, so be sure to confirm all time-dated details first.

Shifra Stein's Day Trips: Gas-Saving Getaways Less Than Two Hours From Greater Kansas City
by Shifra Stein, Shifra Stein Productions, 1986, 103 pages, paper, $5.95

This the only title of Shifra Stein's Day Trip Guide series still published by Shifra Stein Productions. The other titles are now published by Globe Pequot Press. The series is reviewed in more detail under "Series Reviews."

Shifra Stein's Kansas City: A Unique Guide to the Metro Area
by Shifra Stein, Shifra Stein Productions, 1986, 64 pages, paper, $9.95

This large-format book provides an overview of points of interest, activities, and the neighborhoods of K.C.—complete with numerous color photographs. This is definitely a overview—each item is discussed only briefly. But there are a lot of suggestions, including restaurants, shopping, kids' stuff, transportation, and more.

St. Louis Epicure
Peanut Butter Publishing, 1986, 150 pages, paper, $7.95

This book is part of the Epicure Guide series, which is reviewed in more detail under "Series Reviews." The series is updated frequently.

MONTANA

See also "The Rocky Mountain/Great Basin States" and "United States as a Whole."

Bitterroot to Beartooth: Hiking Southwest Montana
by Ruth Rudner, Sierra Club Books, 1985, 288 pages, paper, $10.95

This is one of the well-done Sierra Club Hiking Totebook series, which is reviewed in more detail under "Series Reviews."

Glacier-Waterton Explorer's Guide
by Carl Schreier, Homestead Publishing, 1983, 48 pages, paper, $4.95

This book is part of the Park Explorer's Guide series, which is reviewed in more detail under "Series Reviews."

The Hiker's Guide to Montana
by Bill Schneider, Falcon Press, 1983, 247 pages, paper, $8.95

This book is part of the Falcon Press Hiking Guide series, which is reviewed in more detail under "Series Reviews."

Roadside Geology of Montana
by David Alt and Donald Hyndman, Mountain Press, 1986, 427 pages, paper, $12.95

This book is part of the excellent Roadside Geology Guide series, which is reviewed in more detail under "Series Reviews."

The Sierra Club Guide to the Natural Areas of Idaho, Montana and Wyoming
by John and Jane Perry, Sierra Club Books, 1988, 416 pages, paper, $10.95
This is one of the Sierra Club Natural Areas Guide series, which is reviewed in more detail under "Series Reviews."

Special Places for the Discerning Traveler in Oregon, Washington, Idaho, Montana, British Columbia, California Wine Country
by Fred and Mardi Nystrom, Graphic Arts Center Publishing, 1986, 216 pages, paper, $13.95
See "The Pacific Northwest."

A Traveler's Companion to Montana History
by Carroll Van West, Montana Historical Society Press, 1986, 240 pages, paper, $9.95
Road by road, Van West pours forth historical facts and figures intermingled with interesting anecdotes. The result is a finely tuned historical text that will add considerable pleasure to traveling. If only every state had such a wonderful book to answer the inevitable question of the passing traveler: "I wonder what that is?" (Also distributed by Falcon Press.)

Yellowstone National Park
A small portion of the park is in Montana. All books on the subject are listed under "Wyoming."

NEBRASKA ———————————————————————————
See also "The Midwest" and "United States as a Whole."

Nebraska Historical Tour Guide
by D. Ray Wilson, Crossroads Communications, 1983, 340 pages, paper, $9.95
This comprehensive guide to the history of Nebraska helps fill the void in travel books on this area. It is part of the well-done Historical Tour Guide series, which is reviewed in more detail under "Series Reviews."

NEVADA ———————————————————————————
See also "The Rocky Mountain/Great Basin States" and "United States as a Whole."

Best Cat Houses of Nevada
by J. R. Schwartz, Straight Arrow Publishing, 1987, 170 pages,
paper, $5.95
If the infamous legal brothels of Nevada are on the travel agenda,
Schwartz's guide tells about all of them. Included are directions, a
bit of history, "menus," and, well, reviews of a sort. Actually, the
book is quite well done.

The Compleat Traveler: A Guide to the State
by David Toll, Gold Hill Publishing, 1985, 192 pages, paper, $7.95
This is a good overview of many of Nevada's towns—historic and
modern-day—with a brief listing of services available to the traveler.

Fodor's Fun in Las Vegas, including Reno and Lake Tahoe
Fodor's Travel Publications, 1988, 160 pages, paper, $6.95
This book is part of Fodor's Fun Guide series, which is reviewed
in more detail under "Series Reviews."

Frommer's Dollarwise Guide to California and Las Vegas
by Mary Rakauskas, Prentice Hall Press, 1987, 312 pages, paper,
$11.95
This is an excellent volume in Frommer's Dollarwise Guide series,
which is reviewed in more detail under "Series Reviews." The series
emphasizes selections in the moderate price range and is updated
every two years.

Frommer's Guide to Las Vegas
by Mary Rakauskas, Prentice Hall Press, 1987, 200 pages, paper,
$5.95
This book is part of Frommer's City Guide series, which is reviewed in more detail under "Series Reviews." The series is updated
every two years.

**Hiking the Great Basin: The High Desert Country of California,
Oregon, Nevada, and Utah**
by John Hart, Sierra Club Books, 1981, 369 pages, paper, $9.95
This is one of the Sierra Club Hiking Totebook series, which is
reviewed in more detail under "Series Reviews."

Hot Springs and Hot Pools of the Southwest
by Jayson Loam and Gary Sohler, Wilderness Press, 1985 (2nd ed.),
192 pages, paper, $12.95
Including Nevada, this book is reviewed under "The Southwest."

Hot Springs of the Eastern Sierra
by George Williams, Tree By The River Publishing, 1988, 72 pages, paper, $5.95
See "California."

Las Vegas/Access
by Richard Saul Wurman, Prentice Hall Press, 1985, 72 pages, paper, $7.95
This book is part of the Access Guide series, which is reviewed in more detail under "Series Reviews."

Let's Go: California & Hawaii
by Harvard Student Agencies, St. Martin's Press, 1988, 528 pages, paper, $10.95
Including Reno, Las Vegas, and the Lake Tahoe area, this book is part of the excellent, budget-oriented Let's Go Guide series, which is reviewed in more detail under "Series Reviews."

Pacific Boating Almanac: Northern California & Nevada
Western Marine Enterprises, 1987, 432 pages, paper, $10.95
This book is part of the Boating Almanac series, which is reviewed in more detail under "Series Reviews."

The Sierra Club Guide to the Natural Areas of New Mexico, Arizona, and Nevada
by John and Jane Perry, Sierra Club Books, 1985, 412 pages, paper, $10.95
This is one of the Sierra Club Natural Areas Guide series, which is reviewed in more detail under "Series Reviews."

The Tahoe Sierra: A Natural History Guide to 106 Hikes in the Northern Sierra
by Jeffrey Schaffer, Wilderness Press, 1987 (3rd ed.), 309 pages, paper, $15.95
Including Nevada hikes, this title has plenty of natural history notes on fish, botany, zoology, and geology. It is part of the Wilderness Press Hiking Guide series, which is reviewed in more detail under "Series Reviews."

Touring Nevada: A Historic and Scenic Guide
by Mary Ellen and Al Glass, University of Nevada Press, 1983, 253 pages, paper, $8.95
Nevada is a lot more than bombing ranges, endless desert, the green-felt jungle of the gambling meccas, and red-light districts. There are in fact hundreds of fascinating and beautiful nooks and

crannies to explore, as this excellent guide will prove. The book provides well-described tours of each distinctive regions of the Silver State, each accompanied by clear maps and helpful photographs.

NEW HAMPSHIRE

See also "New England" and "United States as a Whole."

AMC Guide to Mt. Washington and the Presidential Range
Appalachian Mountain Club Books, 1988 (4th ed.), 256 pages, paper, $7.95
This book is part of the AMC Hiking Guide series, which is reviewed in more detail under "Series Reviews."

Appalachian Trail Guide to New Hampshire/Vermont
Appalachian Trail Conference, 1985 (4th ed.), 302 pages, paper, $15.95
This is one of the Appalachian Trail Guide series, which is reviewed in more detail under "Series Reviews."

Canoe Camping Vermont & New Hampshire Rivers
by Roioli Schweiker, Backcountry Publications, 1985 (2nd ed.), 128 pages, paper, $6.95
This is one of the Backcountry Canoeing Guide series, which is reviewed in more detail under "Series Reviews."

Fifty Hikes in the White Mountains: Hikes and Backpacking Trips in the High Peak Region of New Hampshire
by Heather and Hugh Sadlier, Backcountry Publications, 1986 (3rd ed.), 206 pages, paper, $9.95
Fifty More Hikes in New Hampshire: Day Hikes and Backpacking Trips from the Coast to Coos County
by Daniel Doan, Backcountry Publications, 1986 (2nd ed.), 208 pages, paper, $9.95
These two titles are part of the Backcountry Fifty Hikes series, which is reviewed in more detail under "Series Reviews."

Roadside Geology of Vermont and New Hampshire
by Bradford Van Diver, Mountain Press, 1987, 230 pages, paper, $9.95
This book is part of the Roadside Geology Guide series, which is reviewed in more detail under "Series Reviews."

25 Bicycle Tours in New Hampshire: A Guide to Selected Backcountry Roads throughout the Granite State
by Tom and Susan Heavey, Backcountry Publications, 1985 (revised ed.), 144 pages, paper, $6.95
    This is one of the Backcountry Bicycle Tours series, which is reviewed in more detail under "Series Reviews."

25 Ski Tours in the White Mountains: A Cross-Country Skier's Guide to New Hampshire's Backcountry Trails
by Salley and Daniel Ford, Backcountry Publications, 1983 (2nd ed.), 128 pages, paper, $5.95
    This book is part of the Backcountry Ski Tours series, which is reviewed in more detail under "Series Reviews."

NEW JERSEY ───────────────────────────────────
See also "The Mid-Atlantic States" and "United States as a Whole."

Appalachian Trail Guide to New York/New Jersey
Appalachian Trail Conference, 1986 (10th ed.), 175 pages, paper, $8.95
    This is one of the Appalachian Trail Guide series, which is reviewed in more detail under "Series Reviews."

Canoeing the Jersey Pine Barrens
by Robert Parnes, The Globe Pequot Press, 1981, 288 pages, paper, $8.95
    History, canoeing lore, river maps, campgrounds, and plenty of practical information are all included in this revised edition.

Circuit Hikes in Northern New Jersey
by Bruce Scofield, N.Y.-N.J. Trail Conference, 1986 (2d ed.), 80 pages, paper, $5.95
    New Jersey is kind of a sleeper. It is the most densely populated state, yet contains the largest wilderness area east of the Mississippi. This excellent volume is part of the Circuit Hikes Guide series, which is reviewed in more detail under "Series Reviews."

Day Walker: 28 Hikes in the New York Metropolitan Area
by the N.Y.-N.J. Trail Conference, Doubleday & Co., 1983, 223 pages, paper, $7.95
    Including New Jersey hikes, this book is reviewed under "New York."

Ed Hitzel's South Jersey Dining Guide
by Ed Hitzel, South Jersey Publishing, 1987, 96 pages, paper, $4.95
This great small-format book fits easily into a pocket and provides informative capsule reviews of more than 175 restaurants, buffets, and brunches in Atlantic City, Cape May, Ocean City, Long Beach Island, and Vineland. Price ranges run the gamut.

Fodor's Atlantic City and the New Jersey Shore
Fodor's Travel Publications, 1986, 160 pages, paper, $7.95
This book is part of Fodor's City Guide series, which is reviewed in more detail under "Series Reviews."

Frommer's Guide to Atlantic City & Cape May
by Gloria McDarrah, Prentice Hall Press, 1987, 213 pages, paper, $5.95
This book is part of Frommer's City Guide series, which is reviewed in more detail under "Series Reviews." The series is updated every two years.

Guide to Ski Touring in New York and New Jersey
N.Y.-N.J. Trail Conference, 1979, 64 pages, paper, $4.95
This is a small, handy guide to suggested touring areas: where to go, how to get there, the difficulty of the route, the facilities available, and helpful maps.

The Jersey Shore: A Travel and Pleasure Guide
by Robert Santelli, The Globe Pequot Press, 1986, 216 pages, paper, $8.95
This is a very well done, comprehensive guide to the many things to do along the 127 miles of Jersey shore. Also included are restaurant recommendations and lodging tips. Interspersed throughout are anecdotes and snippets of history, highlighted from the primary text, which will lend an added measure of pleasure to a vacation.

New Jersey: A Guide to the State
by Barbara Westergaard, Rutgers University Press, 1987, 407 pages, paper, $12.95
This is a wonderful guidebook to several hundred of New Jersey's towns and parks, arranged alphabetically as well as generally located on a map of the state. For each town, some history, suggestions on things to do and see, where to find a walking tour brochure if such exists, other helpful comments, and more than 50 well-drawn maps for areas where the author felt them necessary to avoid confusion are included.

New Jersey Day Trips: A Guide to Outings in New Jersey, New York, Pennsylvania, & Delaware
by Barbara Hudgins, The Woodmont Press, 1986 (3rd ed.), 244 pages, paper, $7.95
   The emphasis is on New Jersey, but many states are covered in this quality book, which is reviewed under "The Mid-Atlantic States."

New Jersey Off the Beaten Path: A Guide to Unique Places
by William Scheller, The Globe Pequot Press, 1988, 176 pages, paper, $8.95
   This is a new title in the well-done Off the Beaten Path Guide series, which is reviewed in more detail under "Series Reviews."

New York Walk Book
by the N.Y.-N.J. Trail Conference, Doubleday & Co., 1984 (5th ed.), 393 pages, paper, $15.00
   Including lots of New Jersey destinations, this book is reviewed under "New York."

Self-Guided Architectural Tours: Cape May, N.J.
by Marsha Cudworth, Bric-a-Brac Bookworks, 1985, 82 pages, paper, $7.95
   Cape May, a fantastically beautiful national landmark town, is well worth exploring, especially for its wonderful Victorian architecture. In this book are various tours, for both walking and driving, of Cape May's architectural pleasures. Each is well described, including good drawings of many of the structures along the way.

Short Bike Rides in New Jersey
by Robert Santelli, The Globe Pequot Press, 1988, 160 pages, paper, $7.95
   This is the newest title in the Globe Pequot Bike Rides series, which is reviewed in more detail under "Series Reviews."

NEW MEXICO ———————————————————————
See also "The Southwest" and "United States as a Whole."

Children's Guide to Santa Fe
by Anne Hillerman, Sunstone Press, 1984, 32 pages, paper, $4.95
   This booklet is filled with lots of good ideas for things to do with the kids. In spite of the publication date, most of this information should still be reasonably up-to-date, but do double-check where appropriate.

Escortguide: The People's Connection to New Mexico
by Joan Adams, Escortguide, 1986 (3rd ed.), 249 pages, paper, $7.95
   Here is a different sort of book, a directory of all sorts of services, professional guides, bicycling or horseback excursions, unusual sightseeing ideas, lesser known inns, ranches and haciendas, and a whole lot more. Some of this information is more for the resident of New Mexico, but a great deal will be of benefit to the traveler. This is an excellent resource of information.

Fodor's New Mexico: Santa Fe, Taos and Albuquerque
Fodor's Travel Publications, 1987, 213 pages, paper, $7.95
   This book is part of Fodor's Country/Regional Guide series, which is reviewed in more detail under "Series Reviews."

Guide to New Mexico's Popular Rivers and Lakes
by Stephen Maurer, Heritage Associates, 1983, 53 pages, paper, $4.95
   This book provides a run-down of New Mexico's eleven largest lakes, including maps and a description of available facilities. In addition, there are river profiles for rafting enthusiasts. Some information may be dated.

Guide to the Recommended Country Inns of Arizona, New Mexico, and Texas
by Eleanor Morris, The Globe Pequot Press, 1987, 290 pages, paper, $9.95
   This is one of the excellent Recommended Country Inns series, which is reviewed in more detail under "Series Reviews." The author has visited and reviewed each inn personally; no payments have been accepted for inclusion. The series is updated every two years.

Hikers and Climbers Guide to the Sandias
by Mike Hill, University of New Mexico Press, 1983 (2nd ed.), 234 pages, paper, $9.95
   This is a first-class guide to the beautiful Sandias, which lie east of Albuquerque. Good sections on weather, plant life, and geology, and important notes on hiking and climbing in these rugged mountains are included. The trails described are numerous and vary from very short, easy walk/hikes to strenuous back-breakers. A separate, fold-out topographical map is included.

How to See La Villa Real de Santa Fe: Walking Tour of Historic S.F.
by Lou Ann Jordan, Sunstone Press, 1986, 32 pages, paper, $4.95
   This is an interesting, large-format walking tour booklet done entirely by hand, with illustrations and hand-lettered narrative of the historic sites.

Insider's Guide to Santa Fe
by Bill Jamison, The Harvard Common Press, 1987, 150 pages,
paper, $8.95
Bill Jamison, a freelance journalist living in Santa Fe, has created
a fine, well-researched book covering every need of the traveler to
this spectacular city. His book is divided into three parts. Part One
is an excellent chapter on Santa Fe's heritage—the pueblos, the early
Spanish settlers, the coming of the American armies in the early
nineteenth century, and the Santa Fe art colony that has since
evolved. Part Two explores the living museum that is Santa Fe—the
plaza, the museums, the fiestas, the mountain trails, and more. Part
Three is a great rundown of the "Best Places" to stay, eat, and shop.
This is a a superb job; perhaps the best guide to Santa Fe available.

New Mexico: A New Guide to the Colorful State
by Lance Chilton, *et al.*, University of New Mexico Press, 1984,
640 pages, paper, $17.50
Six excellent authors have teamed up to create this massive, large-
format guidebook as a tribute to the famous 1940 Federal WPA
(Works Progress Administration) publication of similar title. Here
are finely crafted essays on everything from history and politics to
arts and literature. The bulk of the book is 18 well-conceived, driving
tours to every corner of the state. The maps are clear and the amount
of interesting and useful information crammed into the descriptions
of each tour is truly remarkable. A helpful section of special events
arranged in a month-by-month format is also included. This is truly
a classic guidebook.

New Mexico's Best Ghost Towns: A Practical Guide
by Phillip Varney, University of New Mexico Press, 1981, 190
pages, paper, $13.95
This is an excellent large-format guide to the many ghost towns
of New Mexico. Varney has put together a great collection of photographs and a fine narrative that is sure to tweak travelers' interest.
Included are good directions, some location maps, specific topographical maps available for each area, and comments on how important such maps are to safe exploration of these ghosts of history.

Roadside Geology of New Mexico
by Halka Chronic, Mountain Press, 1987, 255 pages, paper, $9.95
This book is part of the excellent Roadside Geology Guide series,
which is reviewed in more detail under "Series Reviews."

The Santa Fe Guide
by Waite Thompson and Richard Gottlieb, Sunstone Press, 1986 (revised ed.), 64 pages, paper, $5.95

This tiny guidebook gives a solid overview of history, culture, things to see and do, weather information, and transportation. There is also a list of suggested restaurants, although it notes only type of food without further comment.

Santa Fe On Foot: Walking, Running and Bicycling Routes in the City Different
by Elaine Pinkerton, Juniper Junction, 1986, 125 pages, paper, $7.50

This is a wonderful book on interesting routes to walk, run, or bicycle. The fine text will not only provide route information and plenty of background historical material but a pleasurable reading experience as well.

Santa Fe Then and Now
by Sheila Morand, Sunstone Press, 1984, 96 pages, paper, $14.95

This is an interesting book for those who would like to know how the sights they are seeing now looked 100 years ago. The author has lined up old and new photos side by side and located each place on a street map to show travelers firsthand.

The Sierra Club Guide to the Natural Areas of New Mexico, Arizona, and Nevada
by John and Jane Perry, Sierra Club Books, 1985, 412 pages, paper, $10.95

This is one of the Sierra Club Natural Areas Guide series, which is reviewed in more detail under "Series Reviews."

6 One-Day Walks in the Pecos Wilderness
by Carl Overhage, Sunstone Press, 1984 (revised ed.), 60 pages, paper, $4.95

This is a convenient-sized booklet that carefully describes six strenuous hikes (from 11 to 21 miles) for the experienced hiker. Each has a fold-out, hand-drawn map and an elevation chart. Appropriate topographical maps are recommended and instructions on how to reach each area are included.

The State Parks of New Mexico
by John Young, University of New Mexico Press, 1984, 160 pages, paper, $11.95

This is a good overview of New Mexico's many state parks. Included are many black-and-white photographs, a few historical notes, and information on some of the unique qualities of each park.

Summer People, Winter People: A Guide to Pueblos in the Santa Fe Area
by Sandra Edelman, Sunstone Press, 1986 (revised ed.), 32 pages, paper, $4.95
   This is a helpful brochure with overviews of the various pueblos near Santa Fe. Included are the dates of special fiestas, dances, and ceremonies.

The Taos Guide
by Kathryn Johnson, Sunstone Press, 1983, 64 pages, paper, $5.95
   Although its food-and-lodging information is much too old, this tiny pocket-sized guide still has some good sections on history, geology, and points of interest, and a car tour of the area.

Tours For All Seasons: 50 Car Tours of New Mexico
by Howard Bryan, Heritage Associates, 1986, 120 pages, paper, $4.95
   A veteran reporter and writer of a weekly column for the *Albuquerque Tribune* on New Mexico lore shares his best automobile tours in this great book. The dozens of possibilities are grouped by the season in which they are best to do. There is an additional section of trips to do anytime. A great many good ideas to consider are contained in this compact guidebook. Simple orientation road maps are included, although travelers will certainly want to have better ones at hand.

NEW YORK
See also "The Mid-Atlantic States" and "United States as a Whole."

Adirondack Canoe Waters: North Flow
by Paul Jamieson, Adirondack Mountain Club, 1988 (3rd ed.), 284 pages, paper, $10.95
Adirondack Canoe Waters: South and West Flow
by Alec Proskine, Adirondack Mountain Club, 1984, 137 pages, paper, $10.95
   These are two superb guides to canoeing in the Adirondack region. Well-organized, well-written, and with numerous maps (although U.S.G.S. maps are a necessity and are definitely recommended), these guides make fascinating reading and offer tremendous detail on each canoeing opportunity—distances, put-ins, long-distance trips, etc. Jamieson's work is considered a classic in its field. It is good literature, not merely a collection of practical facts. The third edition was

released after press time so the price and number of pages are approximate.

An Adirondack Sampler: Day Hikes for All Seasons
by Bruce Wadsworth, Adirondack Mountain Club, 1986, 124 pages, paper, $5.95
An Adirondack Sampler II: Backpacking Trips
by Bruce Wadsworth, Adirondack Mountain Club, 1981, 122 pages, paper, $6.95
    This is a two-volume introduction to the trails of the Adirondack Park. Included are easy, moderate, and difficult hikes for all levels of skill. Each is clearly described with the necessary practical points: distance, time needed, elevation change, highest elevation on the hike, and the best quadrangle map to obtain. This is an excellent selection from the myriad choices in the 2,000,000-acre park.

The American Express Pocket Guide to New York
by Herbert Livesey, Prentice Hall Press, 1986, 208 pages, cloth, $8.95
    This quality guide to New York City is part of the American Express Pocket Guide series, which is reviewed in more detail under "Series Reviews."

Appalachian Trail Guide to New York/New Jersey
Appalachian Trail Conference, 1986 (10th ed.), 175 pages, paper, $8.95
    This is one of the Appalachian Trail Guide series, which is reviewed in more detail under "Series Reviews."

Appalachian Whitewater, Volume III: The Northern Mountains
by John Connelly and John Porterfield, Menasha Ridge Press, 1987, 140 pages, paper, $13.95
    Including canoeing and kayaking streams in New York as well as the New England states, this book is part of the Appalachian Whitewater Guide series, which is reviewed in more detail under "Series Reviews."

The Art Commission and the Municipal Art Society Guide to Manhattan's Outdoor Public Sculpture
by Margot Gayle and Michele Cohen, Prentice Hall Press, 1988, 352 pages, paper, $15.95
    This is a new guide to outdoor art in the Big Apple described in 11 "easy-to-walk neighborhoods." More than 400 sculptures and monuments are included.

Away for the Weekend: New York: Great Getaways Less Than 200 Miles from New York City for Every Season of the Year
by Eleanor Berman, Crown Publishers, 1988 (2nd ed.), 256 pages, paper, $11.95
   This book is part of the Away for the Weekend Guide series, which is reviewed in more detail under "Series Reviews."

Baedeker's New York
Prentice Hall Press, 1987, 176 pages, paper, $10.95
   This guide to New York City is one of the Baedeker's City Guide series, which is reviewed in more detail under "Series Reviews."

Berlitz: New York
Macmillan Publishing, 1978, 128 pages, paper, $6.95
   This guide to New York City is part of the small-format Berlitz Guide series, which is reviewed in more detail under "Series Reviews."

The Best of Daytripping & Dining in Southern New England and Nearby New York
by Betsy Wittemann and Nancy Webster, Wood Pond Press, 1985, 186 pages, paper, $7.95
   See "New England."

The Best of New York
by Henri Gault and Christian Millau, Prentice Hall Press, 1988, 400 pages, paper, $14.95
   This is a guide to New York City. Unfortunately, if the Washington, D.C. guide is any indication, the famous duo has turned most of the writing chores over to others. This is one of the Gault/Millau 'Best of' Guide series, which is reviewed in more detail under "Series Reviews."

The Best Places to Kiss in New York
by Paula Begoun, Beginning Press, 1988, 80 pages, paper, $7.95
   This guide to New York City is a new title in the Romantic Travel Guide series, which is reviewed in more detail under "Series Reviews." As it was released after press time, the number of pages is approximate.

Blue Guide: Museums and Galleries of New York
W. W. Norton & Co., 1988, 300 pages, paper, $19.95
Blue Guide: New York
by Carol Wright, W. W. Norton & Co., 1983, 623 pages, paper, $14.95

Both of these titles are part of the highly regarded Blue Guide series, which is reviewed in more detail under "Series Reviews." The Museums and Galleries volume is a new, anticipated title. The New York guide focuses on New York City. The Museums and Galleries title was released after press time so the price and number of pages are approximate.

Born to Shop: New York

by Suzy Gershman and Judith Thomas, Bantam Books, 1987, 317 pages, paper, $8.95

This book is part of the Born to Shop Guide series, which is reviewed in more detail under "Series Reviews."

The Candy Apple: New York for Kids

by Bubbles Fisher, Prentice Hall Press, 1987, 365 pages, paper, $11.95

This is a first-rate guide to New York City for resident and visitor alike that addresses the issues of how to prepare for visiting New York with a child, how to cope with the big city, how to find out what's happening of interest to kids, with lots of specific information on holiday parades, street fairs, special events, museums, shopping, and, of course, eating. Bus and subway information are also included in this great source of information.

Canoeing Central New York

by William Ehling, Backcountry Publications, 1982, 176 pages, paper, $9.95

This is one of the Backcountry Canoeing Guide series, which is reviewed in more detail under "Series Reviews."

The Carefree Getaway Guide for New Yorkers: Day and Weekend Trips Without a Car

by Theodore Scull, The Harvard Common Press, 1988 (revised ed.), 258 pages, paper, $9.95

Those who have lived in New York City know that using public transportation is definitely the way to go. Scull offers detailed information on all sorts of interesting trips by bus, train, or boat. This is an excellent collection of well-researched itineraries.

The Companion Guide to New York

by Michael Leapman, Prentice Hall Press, 1983, 337 pages, paper, $7.95

This guide to New York City is part of the excellent Companion Guide series, which is reviewed in more detail under "Series Reviews."

Country Inns of America: New York & Mid-Atlantic
Henry Holt & Co., 1986, 96 pages, paper, $11.95
This is one of the Country Inns of America series, which is reviewed in more detail under "Series Reviews."

Country Walks Near New York
by William Scheller, Appalachian Mountain Club, 1986 (2nd ed.), 200 pages, paper, $7.95
Covering walks near the Big Apple, this book is part of the AMC Walks series, which is reviewed in more detail under "Series Reviews."

Crown Insider's Guide: New York City & State
by Patricia and Lester Brooks, Crown Publishers, 1988, 336 pages, paper, $10.95
This is a new title in the expanding Crown Insider's Guide series, which is reviewed in more detail under "Series Reviews."

Day Walker: 28 Hikes in the New York Metropolitan Area
by the N.Y.-N.J. Trail Conference, Doubleday & Co., 1983, 223 pages, paper, $7.95
This is an excellent source of walks and hikes in the metropolitan area of New York. Each is easily reached by public transportation, and some are appropriate for seniors or families with children. All include detailed descriptions, along with as notes on local history, geology, flora and fauna. Good detail maps are included as well.

Discover the Adirondacks 2: Walks, Waterways and Winter Treks in the Southern Adirondacks
by Barbara McMartin, *et al.*, Backcountry Publications, 1980, 224 pages, paper, $7.95
Discover the Central Adirondacks: Four-Season Adventures in the Heart of the North Woods
by Barbara McMartin, *et al.*, Backcountry Publications, 1986, 160 pages, paper, $8.95
Discover the Eastern Adirondacks: Four-Season Adventures near Lake George, Pharaoh Lake and Beyond
by Barbara McMartin, *et al.*, Backcountry Publications, 1987, 224 pages, paper, $9.95
Discover the Northeastern Adirondacks: Four-Season Adventures from Lake Champlain to the Rock-Crowned Eastern Slopes
by Barbara McMartin, *et al.*, Backcountry Publications, 1987, 176 pages, paper, $8.95

Discover the South Central Adirondacks: Including the Siamese Ponds Wilderness Area
by Barbara McMartin, *et al.*, Backcountry Publications, 1986, 192 pages, paper, $8.95

Discover the Southeastern Adirondacks: Four-Season Adventures on Old Roads and Open Peaks
by Barbara McMartin, *et al.*, Backcountry Publications, 1986, 144 pages, paper, $8.95

Discover the Southwestern Adirondacks: Four-Season Adventures in the Wild-Forested Foothills
by Barbara McMartin, *et al.*, Backcountry Publications, 1987, 208 pages, paper, $9.95

This large series will soon encompass the entire, massive Adirondack Park. Three similarly titled books on the Northern, West Central, and Southern Adirondacks are due out in late 1988. Two additional titles should be released in 1989: Northern Adirondacks and Adirondack High Peaks. Each is much more than a simple trail guide, including bushwacking excursions and just about anything travelers might want to do in the park. Interesting background information on geology, flora, fauna, even picnic spots, is sprinkled throughout the text.

The Dover New York Walking Guide: From The Battery to Wall Street
by Mary Shapiro, Dover Publications, 1982, 46 pages, paper, $2.50

The Dover New York Walking Guide: From Wall Street to Chambers Street
by Mary Shapiro, Dover Publications, 1982, 64 pages, paper, $2.50

The Dover New York Walking Guide: Greenwich Village
by Mary Shapiro, Dover Publications, 1985, 64 pages, paper, $2.50

These handy, lightweight booklets detail three explorations of the downtown New York area. Each walk has nice descriptions. The maps, however, while seemingly clear, are a bit oversimplified (not all streets are drawn in), which can cause a few orientation problems at times.

East Hampton: A History & Guide
by Jason Epstein and Elizabeth Barlow, Random House, 1985 (3rd ed.), 304 pages, paper, $8.95

This is one title in the History & Sightseeing Guide series, which is reviewed in more detail under "Series Reviews."

Famous Adirondack Restaurants & Recipes
by Sue Schildge, Schildge Publishing, 1986, 213 pages, paper,
$12.95
This book is part of the Famous Restaurants and Recipes series,
which is reviewed in more detail under "Series Reviews."

Favorite Short Trips in New York State
by Harriet Webster, Yankee Books, 1986, 176 pages, paper, $8.95
This is a fine collection of possible trips in every corner of the
state. The well-written text includes things to do as well as where
to catch a bite to eat. Good directions to each recommended attraction and interesting photographs are also included.

**Fifty Hikes in Central New York: Hikes and Backpacking Trips from
the Western Adirondacks to the Finger Lakes**
by William Ehling, Backcountry Publications, 1984, 206 pages,
paper, $8.95
**Fifty Hikes in the Adirondacks: Short Trips, Day Trips, and
Backpacks Throughout the Park**
by Barbara McMartin, Backcountry Publications, 1980, 250 pages,
paper, $9.95
**Fifty Hikes in the Hudson Valley: From the Catskills East to the
Taconics, and from the Ramapos North to the Helderbergs**
by Barbara McMartin and Peter Kick, Backcountry Publications,
1985, 221 pages, paper, $9.95
These three titles are part of the comprehensive Backcountry Fifty
Hikes series, which is reviewed in more detail under "Series Reviews."

Fisher's World: New York City
by J. P. MacBean, Fisher's World, Inc., 1988, 352 pages, paper,
$14.95
This is one of the Fisher's World Guide series, which is reviewed
in more detail under "Series Reviews."

Flashmaps: Instant Guide to New York
Random House, 1987, 88 pages, paper, $4.95
This guide to New York City is part of the Flashmaps series, which
is reviewed in more detail under "Series Reviews."

Fodor's Fun in New York City
Fodor's Travel Publications, 1987, 144 pages, paper, $5.95
This is one of Fodor's Fun Guide series, which is reviewed in more
detail under "Series Reviews."

Fodor's New York City

Fodor's Travel Publications, 1987, 320 pages, paper, $8.95
This book is part of Fodor's City Guide series, which is reviewed in more detail under "Series Reviews."

Fodor's New York State

Fodor's Travel Publications, 1987, 320 pages, paper, $9.95
This book is part of Fodor's Country/Regional Guide series, which is reviewed in more detail under "Series Reviews."

The Food Lover's Guide to the Real New York: 5 Boroughs of Ethnic Restaurants, Markets, and Shops

by Myra Alperson and Mark Clifford, Prentice Hall Press, 1987, 276 pages, paper, $12.95
Alperson and Clifford have shared their personal choices in this warmly written and very appealing guide to the best of ethnic foods, markets, and shops in every nook and cranny of New York City. Included are directions by bicycle, car, or subway, as well as interesting walks to enjoy.

Frommer's Dollarwise Guide to New York State

by John Foreman, Prentice Hall Press, 1987, 360 pages, paper, $12.95
Including a complete section on New York City, this book is part of Frommer's Dollarwise Guide series, which is reviewed in more detail under "Series Reviews." The series is updated every two years.

Frommer's Guide to New York

by Faye Hammel, Prentice Hall Press, 1987, 248 pages, paper, $5.95
This guide to New York City is part of Frommer's City Guide series, which is reviewed in more detail under "Series Reviews." The series is updated every two years.

Frommer's New York on $50 a Day

by Joan Hamburg and Norma Ketay, Prentice Hall Press, 1988, 350 pages, paper, $10.95
This guide to New York City is one title in Frommer's Dollar-a-Day Guide series, which is reviewed in more detail under "Series Reviews." The series is updated every two years.

Gerry Frank's Where to Find It, Buy It, Eat It in New York

by Gerry Frank, Gerry's Frankly Speaking, 1987 (5th ed.), 673 pages, paper, $11.95
Gerry Frank is from Oregon and works in Washington, D.C. It is thus a little strange that she should have written one of the best

guidebooks to New York City. But she has, and there is more here than the average guidebook contains. Along with informative restaurant and hotel reviews in various price ranges and good lists of fun things to do and see are extensive listings of shops of every kind (candy, cheese, fruit, nuts, pickles, appliances, clothing, china, luggage, to name a few) as well as just about any service travelers might possibly require (animal services, babysitters, fur rentals, cars for hire, furniture rental, even pen and lighter repairs). This is truly a comprehensive work that will save tourist and resident alike a lot of big-city headaches. This title is updated every two years.

Great New York Restaurants: A Photographic Guide
by Gayle Gleason, Prince Street Editions, 1986, 84 pages, paper, $11.95
  Spectacularly beautiful color photography is the focal point of this guide to some of New York City's finest places to dine. Brief descriptions, menu notes, and practical details are also included.

Guide to Adirondack Trails, Volume I: High Peaks Region
Adirondack Mountain Club, 1985, 304 pages, paper, $10.95
Guide to Adirondack Trails, Volume II: Northern Region
Adirondack Mountain Club, 1986, 164 pages, paper, $10.95
Guide to Adirondack Trails, Volume III: Central Region
Adirondack Mountain Club, 1986, 207 pages, paper, $10.95
Guide to Adirondack Trails, Volume IV: Northville-Placid Trail
Adirondack Mountain Club, 1986, 169 pages, paper, $10.95
Guide to Adirondack Trails, Volume V: West-Central Region
Adirondack Mountain Club, 1987, 250 pages, paper, $10.95
Guide to Adirondack Trails, Volume VI: Eastern Region
Adirondack Mountain Club, 1987, 250 pages, paper, $10.95
  This is an excellent series of trail guides to the massive Adirondack Park, each with a topographical map, directions to trailheads, historical anecdotes and other bits of history, as well as points of interest along each trail. Volume VII (Southern Region) is due in late 1988 and Volume VIII (Catskill Trails) sometime in 1989.

A Guide to New York City Museums
by Cultural Assistance Center, Dover Publications, 1981, unnumbered, paper, $1.50
  This compact but unfortunately aging booklet provides a quick rundown on 157 of the city's museums, zoos, botanic gardens, and historic houses, with information on how to get to each on public transportation.

Guide to Ski Touring in New York and New Jersey

N.Y.-N.J. Trail Conference, 1979, 64 pages, paper, $4.95

This is a small, handy guide to suggested touring areas: where to go, how to get there, the difficulty of the route, the facilities available, and helpful maps. Some specifics on facilities may have changed with the years, however.

Guide to the Catskills with Trail Guide and Maps

by Arthur Adams, *et al.*, Walking News, Inc., 1975, 440 pages, paper, $9.95

This is a well-known, highly regarded guide to the trails, history, legends, and other aspects of this interesting area. Trails are detailed on black-and-white maps that are probably sufficient for most purposes, but not of the quality of full-color topographical quadrangles. Campground information is also included, but is probably quite dated.

Guide to the Long Path

N.Y.-N.J. Trail Conference, 1987 (2nd ed.), 55 pages, paper, $6.95

The Long Path runs from New York City (starting actually on the western side of the George Washington Bridge) and continues, along primarily wooded trailways, (and occasionally paved roads, where no other option exists) all the way to the Adirondacks 200 miles away. This book divides this trail into day hikes with information on parking, food, water, and such for each portion of the hike. Hikes are carefully described, and there is a large, fold-out map included.

Historic & Famous Albany and Saratoga Restaurants & Recipes

by Sue and Christopher Schildge, Schildge Publishing, 1986, 212 pages, paper, $12.95

This book is part of the Famous Restaurants and Recipes series, which is reviewed in more detail under "Series Reviews."

The Hudson River Valley: A History & Guide

by Tim Mulligan, Random House, 1985, 205 pages, paper, $8.95

This is one title in the History & Sightseeing Guide series, which is reviewed in more detail under "Series Reviews."

The Hudson Valley and Catskill Mountains

by Joanne Michaels and Mary Barile, Crown Publishers, 1988, 320 pages, paper, $10.95

Released after press time, this book, written by two local residents, is an interesting-sounding guide to the inns, B&Bs, restaurants, country auctions, antique shops, historic sites, pick-your-own farms, museums, state parks, ski centers, fishing, hiking, walking tours, and country fairs in the 10-county area of the picturesque Hudson Valley and Catskill Mountains.

I Love New York Guide
by Marilyn Appleberg, Macmillan Publishing, 1988, 249 pages, paper, $8.95
This guide to New York City is part of the I Love Cities Guide series, which is reviewed in more detail under "Series Reviews."

In & Around Albany, Schenectady & Troy
by Susanne Dumbleton and Anne Older, Washington Park Press, 1985, 301 pages, paper, $7.95
This is really an expansion of the author's first guidebook effort, *In & Around Albany*. It goes without saying that there is a whole lot more to New York than the Big Apple, a whole other world quite distinct from the metropolis to the south. And, it is quality books such as this one that will help travelers share some of the pleasures of upstate New York. Included in this helpful guide are all the major topics of interest: lodging and restaurants (in various price ranges), shopping, nightlife, cultural opportunities, recreation, transportation, and more. This is a great travel guide for the Capital Region.

Insight Guide: New York State
by Apa Productions, Prentice Hall Press, 1985, 344 pages, paper, $15.95
This is one of the excellent Insight Guide series, which is reviewed in more detail under "Series Reviews."

Let's Go See by Bicycle: Long Island and New York City Metropolitan Area
written and published by Henry Molinoff, 1983 (2nd ed.), 120 pages, paper, $8.95
In this large-format book, Henry Molinoff shares his cycling information with others. Clear maps and directions are included, along with a spot of history here and there. Lots of photographs give some good ideas on how to spend a day or a weekend. These are not difficult routes, but pleasant sojourns through the cities and countryside of Long Island, as well as New York City proper.

Long Island: A Guide to New York's Suffolk and Nassau Counties
by Raymond, Judith, and Kathryn Spinzia, Hippocrene Books, 1988, 284 pages, paper, $14.95
The family Spinzia has written this new guide, released after press time, on the counties lying just east of New York City and comprising the beautiful and sometimes quite rural world of Long Island.

Manhattan Epicure
Peanut Butter Publishing, 1986, 150 pages, paper, $7.95
This book is part of the Epicure Guide series, which is reviewed in more detail under "Series Reviews." The series is updated frequently.

Michael's Guide: New York City
by Michael Shichor, Hunter Publishing, 1987, 224 pages, paper, $7.95
This is one of the Michael's Guide series, which is reviewed in more detail under "Series Reviews."

Michelin Green Guide: New York City
Michelin Guides and Maps, 1986 (8th ed.), 170 pages, paper, $10.95
This is a well-done title in the premier sightseeing guide series, the Michelin Green Guides. The series is reviewed in more detail under "Series Reviews."

Natural New York
by Bill and Phyllis Thomas, Henry Holt & Co., 1983, 278 pages, paper, $10.95
This title is not as old as the publication date would indicate, since it is a guide to hiking and cycling trails, parks, botanic gardens, zoos, nature centers, museums, flora and fauna, forests, working farms, wildlife sanctuaries, and other wild places within a 50-mile radius of New York City. Some admission costs or hours open to the public may have changed, but, in general, this guide is still a good resource.

New York/Access
by Richard Saul Wurman, Prentice Hall Press, 1988, 250 pages, paper, $14.95
This guide to New York City is part of the well-known Access Guide series, which is reviewed in more detail under "Series Reviews." This edition was released after press time so the number of pages is approximate.

New York Art Guide
by Deborah Gardner, Robert Silver Associates, 1986 (2nd ed.), 194 pages, paper, $10.95
This guide to New York City is part of the Robert Silver Art Guide series, which is reviewed in more detail under "Series Reviews."

The New York Bicycle Touring Guide
produced and published by William Hoffman, 1983, unnumbered, paper $9.95

This book details four cross-state bicycle touring routes that connect the major cities but emphasize the more lightly traveled, scenic secondary roads. This is a collection of small tour map strips. Each of the four routes can be purchased separately.

The New York City Wildlife Guide
by Edward Ricciuti, Nick Lyons Books, 1984, 216 pages, paper, $9.95

In this pleasing, sensitively written pocket guide, Ricciuti, former curator at the New York Zoological Society, tells all about the wild mammals, birds, amphibians, reptiles, fish, and other water creatures that call New York City home. He also tells about the best places to view each of them.

New York for the Independent Traveler
by Ruth Humleker, MarLor Press, 1988, 210 pages, paper, $9.95

This is a new title, released after press time, from the author of *London for the Independent Traveler* (see "England").

New York in Your Pocket
Barron's Educational Series, 1987, 144 pages, paper, $3.95

This guide to New York City is part of the small-format In-Your-Pocket Guide series, which is reviewed in more detail under "Series Reviews." The series is updated every two years.

New York Man
by Francis Chichester, Warner Books, 1988, 220 pages, cloth, $11.95

This guide for the upper crust is one of the new Francis Chichester Guide series, which was released after press time. For more details see "Series Reviews." Price and number of pages are approximate.

New York Off the Beaten Path: A Guide to Unique Places
by William Scheller, The Globe Pequot Press, 1987, 158 pages, paper, $7.95

This book is part of the excellent Off the Beaten Path Guide series, which is reviewed under "Series Reviews."

New York: The Best Places
by David Yeadon, *et al.*, Harper & Row, 1987, 200 pages, paper, $4.95

David Yeadon has made his reputation creating well-conceived, well-researched guidebooks. This is his latest effort in concert with the "Best Places team." The result is a compendium of their choices of the best of everything—from delis to children's playgrounds, pizza parlors to health clubs, record stores to picnic spots. Each chosen "best" is briefly but informatively described and located on a map always placed on the adjacent page for easy use. It is difficult to choose the best in a city with so much to offer, but this is a fine effort. Additional titles are expected out for Boston, Chicago, Los Angeles, San Francisco, London, and Paris.

The New York Times Guide to Restaurants in New York City
by Bryan Miller, Times Books, 1987, 396 pages, paper, $12.95

Miller, a food critic for the *New York Times*, shares his reviews of 250 Big Apple restaurants. His reviews are sharp, to the point, and critical where need be. Very few earn a four-star rating, but when they do they deserve it. Price ranges run the gamut and an excellent chapter adds Miller's picks of "Best Dishes" from many of the restaurants reviewed. In addition, a chapter on New York City wine bars is included. There are several excellent, opinionated guides to the city; this is one of them.

New York: 20 Walking Tours of Architecture and History
by Gerald Wolfe, McGraw Hill, 1988 (revised ed.), 300 pages, paper, $14.95

A new edition is expected of this quality guide to the Big Apple's architecture and its fascinating history. The price and number of pages are approximate.

New York Walk Book
by the N.Y.-N.J. Trail Conference, Doubleday & Co., 1984 (5th ed.), 393 pages, paper, $15.00

The New York-New Jersey Trail Conference is a volunteer organization maintaining over 700 miles of trails in the New York City area. This is their most well-known and comprehensive title. Jam-packed with possible hikes in nearby New York state, New Jersey, and Connecticut, it includes very short, easy hikes and long, strenuous ones in its selection. A great many color topographical maps are included in the back of the book as well.

New York Wine Country: A Tour Guide
by Joe Chilberg and Bob Baber, North Country Books, 1986, 172 pages, paper, $7.95

Although not as famous as France or California, New York state has a large and interesting wine country of its own. Dozens of wineries are situated in beautiful districts of the Hudson River Valley, the Finger Lakes, the Chautauqua-Erie area, Long Island, and even one in Niagara. This well-done guidebook gives both a history of the evolution of wine growing industry in New York and a rundown of the origins and present accomplishments of each of the 55 wineries discussed.

New York Woman
by Francis Chichester, Warner Books, 1988, 204 pages, cloth, $11.95

This guide for the upper crust is one of the new Francis Chichester Guide series, which was released after press time. For more details see "Series Reviews." Price and number of pages are approximate.

New York's Great Art Museums: A Guide
by Robert Garrett, Chelsea Green Publishing, 1988, 240 pages, paper, $15.95

Detailed notes and floor plans to seven world class-art museums are the focus of this new book from Chelsea Green. The Metropolitan, Frick, Cloisters, Modern, Brooklyn, Guggenheim, and Whitney are thoroughly covered and discussed by way of 18 separate walking tours, each lasting about one hour.

New York's Nooks and Crannies: Unusual Walking Tours in All Five Boroughs
by David Yeadon, Charles Scribner's Sons, 1986, 352 pages, paper, $11.95

David Yeadon has written a considerable number of travel books. Each bears his own unique mark, a little offbeat and always entertaining. Each is well researched and well written. *New York's Nooks and Crannies* is no exception. These are interesting tours including helpful tips on public transportation to and from, shopping and nibbling along the way, and special markets and annual events.

Old Brooklyn Heights: New York's First Suburb
by Clay Lancaster, Dover Publications, 1979, 218 pages, paper, $5.95

This is a detailed analysis of 619 century-old houses in charming Brooklyn Heights. With copious notes and photographs, Lancaster crisply covers the architectural detail of each. The various streets of the subdivision are discussed in turn, making this a helpful guide for those who would like to construct a walking tour from it.

One-Day Adventures by Car: A Guide to Day Trips from New York City

by Lida Newberry and Joy Johannessen, Hastings House, 1986 (5th ed.), 348 pages, paper, $10.95

This popular work has been helping travelers discover what to do outside New York City since 1971. While its original author has unfortunately passed away, Joy Johannessen has done a fine job with this fifth edition. Most of the day trips lie within a 100-mile radius of the Big Apple and describe all sorts of scenic, historical, and recreational adventures in New York State, Pennsylvania, New Jersey, Connecticut, and Massachusetts. The multitude of possibilities can be arranged into trips that lead to several destinations and include copious directions for the driver.

Oscar Israelowitz's Guide to Jewish New York City

Oscar Israelowitz, Talman Co., 1984, 199 pages, paper, $7.95

This book contains lots of touring tips, walking tours, driving tours, kosher restaurants and eateries, synagogues, and Jewish entertainment throughout the five boroughs of New York City. Although most of the information here is still current, be sure to double-check any time-dated material.

Passport to New York Restaurants

by John Mariani and Peter Meltzer, Passport Restaurant Guides, 1988, 74 pages, paper, $3.95

This excellent book and its new companion, *Passport to Los Angeles Restaurants*, are tiny guidebooks. Inexpensive, they are true pocket guides that pack in an amazing amount of information for their size. The New York City guide reviews over 340 eateries and reevaluates them continually. There is a significant turnover from year to year (there were 72 new listings, 35 deletions, and 100 rewrites this year, for example). The authors are both respected restaurant reviewers (Mariani edited *Mariani's Coast-to-Coast Dining Guide*, reviewed under "United States as a Whole") and the short paragraph on each restaurant is crisp and meaningful. Each selection is also carefully rated up to five stars and every price range is represented. Arranged by district, additional charts at the back group restaurants by cuisine, late nights, Sunday brunch, etc.

Permanent New Yorkers: A Biographical Guide to the Cemeteries of New York

by Judi Culbertson and Tom Randall, Chelsea Green Publishing, 1987, 405 pages, paper, $16.95

Permanent New Yorkers not only makes fascinating reading, it will lead travelers on numerous explorations, including history and anecdotes, of the final resting places of both the famous and the obscure. This guidebook to the Big Apple will truly liven up a holiday.

The Penguin Guide to New York City
edited by Alan Tucker, Viking Penguin, 1988, 224-448 pages, paper, $9.95-12.95

This is one of the first eight volumes in the Penguin Travel Guide series, released after press time. For more details see "Series Reviews." Note that only the price and page-count ranges for the entire series were available at press time.

The Pine Barrens of Ronkonkoma: A Guide for the Hiker to the Long Island Pine Barrens
N.Y.-N.J. Trail Conference, 1986 (2nd ed.), 26 pages, paper, $3.95

This very useful booklet describes the access to and enjoyment of the trails that exist through this fascinating and generally undiscovered area. Maps include trails, parking areas, viewpoints, ponds, public land boundaries, even the location of public telephones.

Rand McNally: New York City
Rand McNally & Co., 1987, 128 pages, paper, $5.95

This is one of the Rand McNally Pocket Guide series, which is reviewed in more detail under "Series Reviews."

The Restaurants of New York
by Seymour Britchky, Simon & Schuster, 1987, 365 pages, paper, $10.95

Very opinionated and "courageously critical," Britchky's reviews of New York City restaurants clearly represent one man's opinion. This *very* popular book, updated annually since 1974, provides evaluations with a considerable amount of useful information. His selections are never very cheap. Even the few "inexpensive" selections will appear moderate to most pocketbooks.

Roadside Geology of New York
by Bradford Van Diver, Mountain Press, 1985, 397 pages, paper, $12.95

This book is part of the excellent Roadside Geology Guide series, which is reviewed in more detail under "Series Reviews."

The Rough Guide to New York
by Jack Holland and Martin Dunford, Routledge & Kegan Paul, 1987, 240 pages, paper, $9.95

This book is part of the excellent Rough Guide series, which is reviewed in more detail under "Series Reviews." Focusing primarily on New York City, with some additional sections on the state, this book is updated every two to three years.

Short Bike Rides on Long Island
by Phil Angelillo, The Globe Pequot Press, 1984 (2nd ed.), 160 pages, paper, $6.95

This is a quality title in the Globe Pequot Bike Rides series, which is reviewed in more detail under "Series Reviews."

Short Walks on Long Island
by Rodney and Priscilla Albright, The Globe Pequot Press, 1983 (2nd ed.), 131 pages, paper, $5.95

This is an excellent title in the Globe Pequot Walks series, which is reviewed in more detail under "Series Reviews."

State Parks and Campgrounds in Northern New York
by John Scheib, Backcountry Books, 1987, 214 pages, paper, $9.95

This is a thoroughly comprehensive work detailing the numerous services and activities of more than 60 state parks and campgrounds of northern New York. A list of other local attractions and a good chapter on the history of each area are also included in this excellent directory.

Tastes of the Adirondack Restaurants!
by Sue Schildge, Schildge Publishing, 1985, 236 pages, paper, $12.95

This book is part of the Famous Restaurants and Recipes series, which is reviewed in more detail under "Series Reviews."

20 Bicycle Tours in and Around New York City
by Dan Carlinsky and David Heim, Backcountry Publications, 1986, 134 pages, paper, $6.95

20 Bicycle Tours in the Finger Lakes: Scenic Routes to Central New York's Best Waterfalls, Wineries, Beaches, and Parks
by Mark Roth and Sally Walters, Backcountry Publications, 1987 (2nd ed.), 160 pages, paper, $7.95

These two titles are part of the highly regarded Backcountry Bicycle Tours series, which is reviewed in more detail under "Series Reviews."

25 Ski Tours in Central New York: The Best Cross-Country Skiing Through the Tug Hill Region, the Eastern Ontario Lowlands & the Appalachian Highlands
by William Ehling, Backcountry Publications, 1987, 144 pages, paper, $7.95

25 Ski Tours in the Adirondacks: Cross-Country Skiing Adventures in the Southern Adirondacks, the Capital District & Tug Hill
by Almy and Anne Coggeshall, Backcountry Publications, 1979, 144 pages, paper, $5.95

These two titles are part of the Backcountry Ski Tours series, which is reviewed in more detail under "Series Reviews."

The Village Voice Guide to Manhattan's Hottest Shopping Neighborhoods
edited by Mary Peacock, Ballantine Books, 1987, 364 pages, paper, $10.95

This is a very comprehensive overview of "the best fashion and best deals" the city has to offer. The authors concentrate on what each store does best, pointing out, where appropriate, what to avoid as well. The reviews are meaty and revealing. Editor Mary Peacock explains how this book fits in: "Pretend you have a best friend in Manhattan who loves to shop . . . This person has just agreed to tell you everything. This book is that friend." And it succeeds admirably. Along the way the authors give a walking tour of each shopping district and interesting notes on history, point out some of the landmarks, and introduce the best spots to get a bite to eat.

Virgin Guide to New York
Pantheon/Random House, 1986, 300 pages, paper, $7.95

The creators of the popular *Virgin Guide to London* turn their attention to the Big Apple and apply the same critical, highly selective approach, avoiding what they consider to be an excess of history, churches, museums, statues, and such, in favor of much smaller, more manageable groupings of sights, restaurants, and other tips to make any vacation in this world-class city more memorable.

Walks and Rambles in Westchester and Fairfield Counties: A Nature Lover's Guide to Thirty Parks and Sanctuaries
by Katherine Anderson, Backcountry Publications, 1986, 144 pages, paper, $7.95

Audubon naturalist Kaye Anderson describes the parks and sanctuaries of which she has long been a part. Nature lovers of most every age will enjoy her work.

Walks in the Catskills
by John Bennet and Seth Masia, The Globe Pequot Press, 1974, 203 pages, paper, $7.95

This guide has received consistent praise for its careful planning and has endured well in spite of its years. Among the hikes suggested are long and short, easy and difficult. This book is part of the Globe Pequot Hiking Guide series, which is reviewed in more detail under "Series Reviews."

Zagat New York City Restaurant Survey
Zagat Survey, 1987, 156 pages, paper, $8.95

This book is part of the highly regarded Zagat Survey series, which is reviewed in more detail under "Series Reviews."

NORTH CAROLINA

See also "The South" and "United States as a Whole."

Appalachian Trail Guide to North Carolina/Georgia
Appalachian Trail Conference, 1985 (7th ed.), 172 pages, paper, $10.95

Appalachian Trail Guide to Tennessee/North Carolina
Appalachian Trail Conference, 1986 (8th ed.), 252 pages, paper, $14.50

These two titles are part of the Appalachian Trail Guide series, which is reviewed in more detail under "Series Reviews."

Backroads of the Carolinas
by Earl Thollander, Crown Publishing, 1985, 192 pages, paper, $12.95

This is one of Earl Thollander's Back Roads series, which is reviewed in more detail under "Series Reviews."

Blue Ridge Mountain Pleasures: An A-Z Guide to North Georgia, Western North Carolina and the Upcountry of South Carolina
by Donald Wenberg, The Globe Pequot Press, 1988 (2nd ed.), 288 pages, paper, $9.95

See "The South."

Carolina Curiosities: Jerry Bledsoe's Outlandish Guide to the Dadblamedest Things to See and Do in North Carolina
by Jerry Bledsoe, The Globe Pequot Press, 1984, 224 pages, paper, $7.95

The author of this book has assembled quite a fascinating list of things to see and do: a restaurant specializing in rabbit dishes, a house made of bottles, the world's largest collection of running

Edsels, the National Hollerin' Contest, wooly worm races, etc. This title is full of some thoroughly wild and wonderful ideas.

The Insider's Guide to Asheville and Western North Carolina
by Carol Costenbader, Aerial Photography Services, 1986, 58 pages, paper, $3.00
This nicely done booklet is arranged into carefully planned itineraries of the best to see and do, a good selection of restaurants recommended "with enthusiasm," some unique and charming places to stay, and a section on interesting side trips. This is definitely a very helpful guide to the area.

Insider's Guide to Charlotte, North Carolina
by Bea Quirk and Carol Timblin, Storie/McOwen Publishing, 1987, 700 pages, paper, $8.95
Insider's Guide to the Outer Banks of North Carolina
by Monty Joynes and Dave Poyer, Storie/McOwen Publishing, 1987, 460 pages, paper, $6.95
Insider's Guide to the Triangle of North Carolina: Raleigh, Cary, Durham, Chapel Hill
by Dee Reid and J. Barlow Herget, Storie/McOwen Publishing, 1987, 712 pages, paper, $8.95
These three guides are part of the Storie/McOwen Insider's Guide series, which is reviewed in more detail under "Series Reviews."

Mountain Getaways in Georgia, North Carolina and Tennessee
by Rusty Hoffland, On the Road Publishing, 1988, 160 pages, paper, $5.95
See "The South."

A Naturalist's Blue Ridge Parkway
by David Catlin, The University of Tennessee Press, 1984, 208 pages, paper, $7.95
The Blue Ridge Parkway is a magnificent highway stretching between the Shenandoah and Great Smoky Mountains National Park of Virginia and North Carolina. The area is a naturalist's dream and Catlin's book has made it possible to enjoy a good deal more of the breathtaking sights. Extensive sections cover geology and the vast array of flora and fauna present along the parkway.

North Carolina Hiking Trails
by Allen DeHart, Appalachian Mountain Club, 1988 (2nd ed.), 352 pages, paper, $14.95
This book is part of the AMC Hiking Guides series, which is reviewed in more detail under "Series Reviews."

North Carolina's Historic Restaurants and Their Recipes
by Dawn O'Brien, John F. Blair–Publisher, 1983, 204 pages, cloth, $12.95

This is an early title in the Historic Restaurants & Recipes series, which is reviewed in more detail under "Series Reviews." The recipes are still good, but this older title is too dated to be much help with restaurant specifics. Watch for a second edition.

Old South: A Traveler's Guide to Virginia, North Carolina and South Carolina
by Dana Facaros and Michael Pauls, Hippocrene Books, 1987 (revised ed.), 124 pages, paper, $5.95

See "The South."

Weekenders' Guide to the Four Seasons
by Robert Shosteck, Pelican Publishing, 1986 (7th ed.), 490 pages, paper, $7.95

Including North Carolina, this book is reviewed under "The Mid-Atlantic States."

NORTH DAKOTA ――――――――――――――――――――

See "The Midwest" and "United States as a Whole."

OHIO ―――――――――――――――――――――――――

See also "The Midwest" and "United States as a Whole."

Backroads of Northeast Ohio
by David Gerrick, Dayton Lab, 1975, 50 pages, paper, $5.95

This is a homemade, spiral-bound little guide to the lesser-used roads of this area, with accompanying descriptions of the various locations noted on the primitive but useful maps. No doubt some revisions should be made, but backroads have a way of changing slowly, so some good ideas should still be here.

Canoeing and Kayaking Guide to the Streams of Ohio, Volume I
by Richard Combs and Stephen Gillen, Menasha Ridge Press, 1983, 160 pages, paper, $9.95

Canoeing and Kayaking Guide to the Streams of Ohio, Volume II
by Richard Combs and Stephen Gillen, Menasha Ridge Press, 1983, 160 pages, paper, $9.95

These two titles are part of the Canoeing and Kayaking Guide series, which is reviewed in more detail under "Series Reviews."

Cleveland Menu Directory: A Guide to the Top Restaurants in the Northeast Ohio Area
Sound Approach, Inc., 1987, 192 pages, paper, $5.95
This large-format guide, sponsored by WDOK, an area FM station, makes no judgments, but rather provides a two-page layout on each of the restaurants generally judged to be the best and most popular in the area. Each two-page section gives a reproduction of the menu, a description, and the practical details. Additional indices break down the listing into regions, types of cuisine, and features such as late-night dining, children's menu, dancing, entertainment, outdoor dining, scenic view, Sunday brunch, and take-out service. This is a good resource guide.

Dining in Historic Ohio: A Restaurant Guide with Recipes
by Marty Godbey, McClanahan Publishing, 1987, 207 pages, cloth, $14.00
This book contains good descriptions, including a bit of the history, of 47 charming, historic sites now used as restaurants. The selections run from casual, family affairs to dressy, reservations-only dinners. Each restaurant has contributed some favorite recipes to aid in selection, and all the practical facts are included.

Life in the Slow Lane: Backroad Tours of Central Ohio for Sunday Drivers, Bicyclists, and Other Explorers
by Jeff and Nadean Traylor, Backroad Chronicles, 1987 (revised ed.), unnumbered, paper, $9.95
Life in the Slow Lane: Backroad Tours of Southwest Ohio for Sunday Drivers, Bicyclists, and Other Explorers
by Jeff and Nadean Traylor, Backroad Chronicles, 1987, unnumbered, paper, $9.95
These two excellent tour guides each consist of moderately sized fold-out maps of planned loop-route tours of 14 interesting areas. The maps are first-class and each loop route is accompanied by information on length, terrain, some history, and points of interest. A chart at the front of each book compares the various routes—distances, the types of sights, and whether swimming, picnic tables, hiking/walking trails, and/or camping are available.

Ohio Off the Beaten Path: A Guide to Unique Places
by George Zimmerman, The Globe Pequot Press, 1988 (3rd ed.), 176 pages, paper, $8.95
This book is part of the highly regarded Off the Beaten Path Guide series, which is reviewed in more detail under "Series Reviews."

Shifra Stein's Day Trips from Cincinnati
by Gwyn Willis, The Globe Pequot Press, 1984, 160 pages, paper, $7.95

This book is part of the well-done Shifra Stein's Day Trips series, which is reviewed in more detail under "Series Reviews."

OKLAHOMA

See also "The Southwest" and "United States as a Whole."

Guide to Oklahoma Museums
by David Hunt, University of Oklahoma Press, 1981, 147 pages, paper, $9.95

This is a comprehensive guide to the museums of Oklahoma, as well as the state's important historic sites and zoological parks. In all, nearly 150 places are described, including some most unusual museums, including oil museums, doll museums, and three national halls of fame: softball, wrestling, and cowboy. This is a fine but aging directory, so be sure to confirm all time-dated facts.

Outdoor and Trail Guide to the Wichita Mountains of Southwest Oklahoma
by Edward Ellenbrook, In-the-Valley-of-the-Wichitas House, 1984, 108 pages, paper, $6.50

This helpful guide to the Wichita Mountains was prepared with obvious love for and interest in this southwest corner of Oklahoma. The guide offers a little history, a large selection of places to go (and how to get there), listings of numerous trails and walks both long and short, guided tours of the Valley of the Wichitas, Red Rock Canyon, and the Rock of Ages, and other helpful facts on outdoor fun, including hunting and fishing.

OREGON

See also "The Pacific Northwest" and "United States as a Whole."

Best Choices in Central and Eastern Oregon
by William Faubion, Gable & Gray, 1987, 239 pages, paper, $9.95
Best Choices in Portland and the North Willamette Valley
by William Faubion, Gable & Gray, 1987, 416 pages, paper, $9.95
Best Choices Off Oregon's Interstates
by William Faubion, Gable & Gray, 1986, 389 pages, paper, $9.95
Best Choices On the Oregon Coast
by William Faubion, Gable & Gray, 1986, 303 pages, paper, $9.95

These four titles are part of the Gable & Gray Best Choices series, which is reviewed in more detail under "Series Reviews."

Back Roads of Oregon
by Earl Thollander, Crown Publishing, 1979, 208 pages, paper, $10.95

This is one of Earl Thollander's Back Roads series, which is reviewed in more detail under "Series Reviews."

Bed and Breakfast Homes Directory: California, Oregon, Washington
by Diane Knight, Knighttime Publications, 1986 (4th ed.), 230 pages, paper, $8.95

See "The Pacific Northwest."

Bicycling the Backroads of Northwest Oregon
by Philip Jones, The Mountaineers, 1984, 192 pages, paper, $9.95

This book is part of the well-done Bicycling the Backroad Guide series, which is reviewed in more detail under "Series Reviews."

Canoe Routes, Northwest Oregon
by Phil Jones, The Mountaineers, 1982, 160 pages, paper, $8.95

Complete with all the necessary details and maps, this book contains 50 one-day flatwater trips for all levels of skill.

Country Inns, Lodges & Historic Hotels: California, Oregon & Washington
by Anthony Hitchcock and Jean Lindgren, Burt Franklin–Publisher, 1988 (10th ed.), 281 pages, paper, $8.95

This book is part of the Compleat Traveler's Companions series, which is reviewed in more detail under "Series Reviews." No fees are accepted for inclusion in this annually updated title.

Crater Lake National Park and Vicinity
by Jeffrey Schaffer, Wilderness Press, 1983, 160 pages, paper, $11.95

This is another fine title in the Wilderness Press Hiking Guide series, which is reviewed in more detail under "Series Reviews." This book contains a 1986 supplement and numerous topographical maps to the many trails described.

Cross-Country Ski Routes of Oregon's Cascades
by Klindt Vielbig, The Mountaineers, 1984, 255 pages, paper, $9.95

This book is part of the well-done Mountaineers Cross-Country Skiing Guide series, which is reviewed in more detail under "Series Reviews."

Exploring the Oregon Coast by Car
by Marje Blood, Image Imprints, 1986 (2nd ed.), 203 pages, paper, $9.95

   This is a finely written guide to a wide range of special places to see and things to do. Travelers will find themselves caught up in Marje Blood's enthusiasm for Oregon's classic coastline and will learn about the historical facts that affect this magnificent coast. This enjoyable book to just sit and read will also direct many a memorable outing.

50 Hiking Trails: Portland & Northwest Oregon
by Don & Roberta Lowe, The Touchstone Press, 1986, 128 pages, paper, $9.95

   This is one of the Touchstone Hiking Guide series, which is reviewed in more detail under "Series Reviews."

Hiking the Bigfoot Country: The Wildlands of Northern California and Southern Oregon
by John Hart, Sierra Club Books, 1975, 398 pages, paper, $8.95
Hiking the Great Basin: The High Desert Country of California, Oregon, Nevada and Utah
by John Hart, Sierra Club Books, 1981, 320 pages, paper, $9.95

   These two titles are part of the well-done Sierra Club Hiking Totebook series, which is reviewed in more detail under "Series Reviews."

Offbeat Oregon: A Connoisseur's Collection of Travel Discovery in Oregon
by Mimi Bell, Chronicle Books, 1983, 129 pages, paper, $6.95

   This is a good collection of lesser-known sightseeing ideas for those prone to wander off the beaten path and explore a bit. Most of these suggestions will still be substantially up-to-date in spite of the publication date.

Oregon Coast Hikes
by Paul Williams, The Mountaineers, 1985, 206 pages, paper, $9.95

   Detailing 60 hikes, from easy day trips on sandy beaches to full-scale backpacks, including six along the Rogue River, this book is part of the Mountaineers Hiking Guides series, which is reviewed in more detail under "Series Reviews."

Oregon for the Curious
by Ralph Friedman, Caxton Publishers, 1972 (3rd ed.), 246 pages, paper, $5.95

   This book is old now but it still contains some interesting historical tours with good driving directions, although the directions may need to be adapted to include the newer roads that have inevitably appeared.

Oregon Free: A Guide to the Best of the State's Cost Free Attractions

by Kiki Canniff, KI-2 Enterprises, 1986 (3rd ed.), 386 pages, paper, $9.95

This book contains something for everyone—hiking trails, historic sites, museums, covered bridges, waterfalls, wildlife refuges, caves, art galleries, tours, ghost towns, rockhounding areas, hot springs, and more. Arranged by geographic section, each attraction is briefly described. Large, eye-catching symbols are also used to highlight items of interest. This is a fine resource to a spectacular state.

Oregon Geographic Names

by Lewis McArthur, Oregon Historical Society, 1982 (5th ed.), 839 pages, paper, $14.95

This is a hefty, comprehensive guide to the stories behind the names for Oregon's towns, cities, valleys, creeks, and rivers. A very popular book, it makes for fascinating reading and will prove a great companion guide.

Portland: An Informal History & Guide

by Terence O'Donnell, Oregon Historical Society, 1984, 212 pages, paper, $6.95

Including an excellent history section for visitor and native alike, this book details three walking tours of downtown, old town, and new town, three driving tours of the areas immediately around Portland, and three additional one-day tour suggestions to the mountains, the sea coast, and through the Willamette Valley. The tours in and around Portland are very well described, with excellent maps, historical notes, distances, and touring time needed.

Portland's Public Art: A Guide and History

by Norma Gleason and Chet Orloff, Oregon Historical Society, 1983, 70 pages, paper, $4.95

This is a useful guide to the public art of Portland in place prior to 1983. Plenty of historical notes, good photographs, and a number of maps are included.

Portland: Rainy Day Guide

by Katlin Smith, Chronicle Books, 1983, 127 pages, paper, $6.95

This somewhat dated, but still useful guide is part of the Rainy Day Guides series, which is reviewed in more detail under "Series Reviews."

Roadside Geology of Oregon
by David Alt and Donald Hundman, Mountain Press, 1978, 272 pages, paper, $9.95
This book is part of the excellent Roadside Geology Guide series, which is reviewed in more detail under "Series Reviews."

The Sierra Club Guide to the Natural Areas of Oregon and Washington
by John and Jean Perry, Sierra Club Books, 1983, 360 pages, paper, $9.95
This is one of the Sierra Club Natural Areas Guide series, which is reviewed in more detail under "Series Reviews."

60 Hiking Trails: Central Oregon Cascades
by Don & Roberta Lowe, The Touchstone Press, 1979, 128 pages, paper, $9.95
62 Hiking Trails: Northern Oregon Cascades
by Don & Roberta Lowe, The Touchstone Press, 1979, 128 pages, paper, $9.95
These two titles are part of the Touchstone Hiking Guide series, which is reviewed in more detail under "Series Reviews."

Southern Oregon: Short Trips into History
by Marjorie O'Harra, Southern Oregon Historical Society, 1985, 200 pages, paper, $11.95
This is a well-written companion guide to the lesser-known roads and the history of which they were a part. Clear maps and directions will point the way to each of these intriguing trips into Oregon's past.

Special Places for the Discerning Traveler in Oregon, Washington, Idaho, Montana, British Columbia, California Wine Country
by Fred and Mardi Nystrom, Graphic Arts Center Publishing, 1986, 216 pages, paper, $13.95
See "The Pacific Northwest."

Sunset Oregon Travel Guide
Lane Publishing, 1987, 128 pages, paper, $8.95
This large-format book is part of the Sunset Travel Guide series, which is reviewed in more detail under "Series Reviews."

Webster's Wine Tours: California, Oregon and Washington
by Bob Thompson, Prentice Hall Press, 1987, 200 pages, cloth
(flexible), $15.95
  This book is part of the Webster's Wine Tours series, which is
reviewed in more detail under "Series Reviews."

Where to Find the Oregon in Oregon
by Bridget McCarthy, Where to Find the Oregon in Oregon, 1987,
126 pages, paper, $5.95
  This all-purpose guide is arranged regionally, with a clear emphasis
on shopping, particularly handicrafts and art. Inns and restaurants
and other food sources are mentioned only if they are particularly
quaint and interesting. Well-written, this guide uses symbols to
facilitate use.

PENNSYLVANIA ─────────────────────────────────

See also "The Mid-Atlantic States" and "United States as a Whole."

Appalachian Trail Guide to Pennsylvania
Appalachian Trail Conference, 1985 (6th ed.), 148 pages, paper,
$14.50
  This book is one of the Appalachian Trail Guide series, which is
reviewed in more detail under "Series Reviews."

Circuit Hikes in Virginia, West Virginia, Maryland, and Pennsylvania
Potomac Appalachian Trail Club, 1986 (4th ed.), 88 pages, paper,
$5.00
  This book is part of the Circuit Hikes Guide series, which is
reviewed in more detail under "Series Reviews."

Country Walks Near Philadelphia
by Alan Fisher, Rambler Books, 1983, 211 pages, paper, $7.95
  This book is part of the excellent Rambler Walks series, which is
reviewed in more detail under "Series Reviews."

**Elegant Lodging: A Guide to Country Mansions & Manor Houses in
Virginia, Maryland & Pennsylvania**
by Caroline Lancaster and Candyce Stapen, Washington Book
Trading Co., 1985, 157 pages, paper, $5.95
  See "The Mid-Atlantic States."

**Fifty Hikes in Central Pennsylvania: Day Hikes and Backpacking
Trips in the Heart of the Keystone State**
by Tom Thwaites, Backcountry Publications, 1985, 200 pages,
paper, $9.95

Fifty Hikes in Eastern Pennsylvania: Day Hikes and Backpacks from the Susquehanna to the Poconos
by Carolyn Hoffman, Backcountry Publications, 1982, 224 pages, paper, $9.95

Fifty Hikes in Western Pennsylvania: Walks/Day Hikes from the Laurel Highlands to Lake Erie
by Tom Thwaites, Backcountry Publications, 1983, 208 pages, paper, $9.95

These three titles are part of the Backcountry Fifty Hikes series, which is reviewed in more detail under "Series Reviews."

Flashmaps: Instant Guide to Philadelphia
Random House, 1987, 80 pages, paper, $4.95

This is one of the Flashmaps series, which is reviewed in more detail under "Series Reviews." The series is updated annually.

Fodor's Philadelphia
Fodor's Travel Publications, 1987, 208 pages, paper, $7.95

This book is part of Fodor's City Guide series, which is reviewed in more detail under "Series Reviews." The series is updated annually.

Frommer's Guide to Philadelphia
by Jay Golan, Prentice Hall Press, 1987, 218 pages, paper, $5.95

This book is part of Frommer's City Guide series, which is reviewed in more detail under "Series Reviews". The series is updated every two years.

A Guide's Guide to Philadelphia
by Julie Curson, Curson House, 1986 (5th ed.), 493 pages, paper, $8.95

This is a quality guide to Philadelphia in which Curson, a professional guide in the City of Brotherly Love, shares her considerable knowledge. The book is comprehensive, covering all the categories of importance with warmth and clarity. No doubt even long-time residents will discover all sorts of interesting things they didn't know before. The author, who makes a point of saying she is not a great believer in reviews, provides an extensive list of restaurants and hotels of every description with notes on menu, ambiance, unique features, and general price range. Also included are special sections on Philadelphia for children, the elderly, and the handicapped. This excellent guide has only been updated every three to four years on average, which represents its only minus.

A Marmac Guide to Philadelphia
by Janet Fallow, Pelican Publishing, 1988, 278 pages, paper, $7.95
    This book is part of the well-done Marmac Guides series, which is reviewed in more detail under "Series Reviews." The series is updated every two years.

Pennsylvania's Historic Restaurants and Their Recipes
by Dawn O'Brien and Claire Walter, John F. Blair–Publisher, 1986, 204 pages, cloth, $12.95
    This is one of the Historic Restaurants & Recipes series, which is reviewed in more detail under "Series Reviews."

The Philadelphia One-Day Trip Book
by Jane Smith, EPM Publications, 1985, 222 pages, paper, $8.95
    This book is part of the One-Day Trip Book series, which is reviewed in more detail under "Series Reviews."

Philadelphia's Outdoor Art: A Walking Tour
by Roslyn Brenner, Camino Books, 1987, 111 pages, paper, $8.95
    This book contains well-organized walking tours accompanied by clear maps and the interesting history and anecdotes behind each of the pieces of public art described. A photograph of each work of art is included.

Rich/Poor Man's Guide to Pittsburgh: Hidden Secrets of the City
by Dorothy Miller, New Pittsburgh Publications, 1986, 150 pages, paper, $7.50
    This is the guide for the hungry person visiting Pittsburgh. It contains extensive reviews of restaurants of every price and category, with special sections on business/executive dining and a "Rich Man's Guide" where money is no object. In addition, plenty of information on Pittsburgh after dark, the best Sunday brunches, outdoor dining, gourmet food to go, budget food, and best restaurants in the suburbs is included. The choices are incredible; this town really likes to eat! After 144 pages of food, fun, and more food is a listing of 50 romantic and unusual things to do, as well as a pull-out sightseeing guide with accompanying map. This great gastronomic resource is updated every two to three years.

25 Bicycle Tours in Eastern Pennsylvania
by Dale Adams and Dale Speicher, Backcountry Publications, 1984, 168 pages, paper, $7.95
    This book is part of the Backcountry Bicycle Tours series, which is reviewed in more detail under "Series Reviews."

RHODE ISLAND

See also "New England" and "United States as a Whole."

AMC Massachusetts-Rhode Island Trail Guide

Appalachian Mountain Club Books, 1988 (6th ed.), 256 pages, paper, $12.95

This book is part of the AMC Hiking Guide series, which is reviewed in more detail under "Series Reviews."

Canoeing Massachusetts, Rhode Island and Connecticut

by Ken Weber, Backcountry Publications, 1986, 160 pages, paper, $7.95

This is one of the Backcountry Canoeing Guide series, which is reviewed in more detail under "Series Reviews."

Exploring Rhode Island: A Visitor's Guide to the Ocean State

by Phyllis Meras, The Providence Journal Co., 1984, 82 pages, paper, $4.95

This book highlights Rhode Island, with history, sightseeing tips, and walking tours of various towns, including clear directions to each starting point.

Newport: A Tour Guide

by Anne Randall and Robert Foley, Peregrine Press, 1983, 144 pages, paper, $6.95

This book contains practical, house-to-house architectural walking tours, including photographs and architectural notes on each structure discussed.

Short Bike Rides in Rhode Island

by Howard Stone, The Globe Pequot Press, 1988 (3rd ed.), 256 pages, paper, $8.95

This is a fine title in the excellent Globe Pequot Bike Rides series, which is reviewed in more detail under "Series Reviews."

Walks and Rambles in Rhode Island: A Guide to the Natural and Historic Wonders of the Ocean State

by Ken Weber, Backcountry Publications, 1986, 176 pages, paper, $8.95

This is a well-done guide to 40 carefully described walks in every corner of the state. Explore the beaches, woods, rocky ravines, and waterfalls hidden from the highway's view.

SOUTH CAROLINA

See also "The South" and "United States as a Whole."

Back Roads of the Carolinas
by Earl Thollander, Crown Publishing, 1985, 192 pages, paper, $12.95

This is one of Earl Thollander's Back Roads series, which is reviewed in more detail under "Series Reviews."

Blue Ridge Mountain Pleasures: An A-Z Guide to North Georgia, Western North Carolina and the Upcountry of South Carolina
by Donald Wenberg, The Globe Pequot Press, 1988 (2nd ed.), 288 pages, paper, $9.95

See "The South."

The Grand Strand: An Uncommon Guide to Myrtle Beach and its Surroundings
by Nancy Rhyne, The Globe Pequot Press, 1985, 124 pages, paper, $5.95

Rhyne's book gives a rundown of the things to do and see along this 60-mile section of beautiful coastal beaches. She shares the history, legends, and facts and figures of this interesting corner of the world.

Old South: A Traveler's Guide to Virginia, North Carolina and South Carolina
by Dana Facaros and Michael Pauls, Hippocrene Books, 1987 (revised ed.), 124 pages, paper, $5.95

See "The South."

South Carolina Hiking Trails
by Allen de Hart, The Globe Pequot Press, 1984, 288 pages, paper, $8.95

This book is part of the Globe Pequot Hiking Guides series, which is reviewed in more detail under "Series Reviews".

South Carolina Historic Restaurants and Their Recipes
by Dawn O'Brien and Karen Mulford, John F. Blair–Publisher, 1984, 204 pages, cloth, $12.95

This is one of the Historic Restaurants & Recipes series, which is reviewed in more detail under "Series Reviews." The recipes are still great, but be sure to confirm the present status of the restaurants. Watch for a second edition.

SOUTH DAKOTA ──────────────
See also "The Midwest" and "United States as a Whole."

South Dakota Recreation Guide
by Barbara McCaig and Lynn Soli, Melius & Peterson Publishing, 1985, 82 pages, paper, $9.95

The authors of this book cover a wide variety of recreational opportunities in five regional sections. These include state parks and recreation areas, national parks and monuments, national forests, the Missouri River system and South Dakota golf courses. Large maps locate the places discussed and detailed charts will give a quick summary of what each place has to offer.

TENNESSEE ──────────────
See also "The South" and "United States as a Whole."

Appalachian Trail Guide to Tennessee/North Carolina
Appalachian Trail Conference, 1986 (8th ed.), 252 pages, paper, $14.50

This is one of the Appalachian Trail Guide series, which is reviewed in more detail under "Series Reviews."

Canoeing and Kayaking Guide to the Streams of Tennessee, Volume 1
by Bob Sehlinger, Menasha Ridge Press, 1983, 220 pages, paper, $10.95
Canoeing and Kayaking Guide to the Streams of Tennessee, Volume II
by Bob Sehlinger, Menasha Ridge Press, 1983, 220 pages, paper, $10.95

These books are part of the Canoeing and Kayaking Guide series, which is reviewed in more detail under "Series Reviews."

Mountain Getaways in Georgia, North Carolina and Tennessee
by Rusty Hoffland, On the Road Publishing, 1988, 160 pages, paper, $5.95
See "The South."

Tennessee Hiking Guide: Sierra Club, Tennessee Chapter
edited by Robert Brandt, The University of Tennessee Press, 1982, 30 pages, paper, $1.95

This is a handy guide to a variety of short, easy day hikes and longer backpacks throughout the state. Each hike is given a brief description and directions are given to the trailhead. Additional information is also provided on maps.

Tennessee Trails
by Evan Means, The Globe Pequot Press, 1988 (3rd ed.), 208 pages, paper, $8.95
This excellent guide, containing more than 100 hiking and backpacking trails, is part of the Globe Pequot Hiking Guide series, which is reviewed in more detail under "Series Reviews."

Travel Guide to the Natchez Trace Parkway Between Natchez, Mississippi and Nashville, Tennessee
Natchez Trace Parkway, 1984, 100 pages, paper, $7.95
See "Mississippi."

TEXAS
See also "The Southwest" and "United States as a Whole."

The Alamo and Other Texas Missions to Remember
by Nancy Foster, Gulf Publishing, 1984, 88 pages, paper, $9.95
This large-format book tells a good deal about the history and architecture of Texas, as well as the many tours available at the various missions in the state. Notes on the special events that are held each year are also provided. In addition, this helpful guide to Texas's fascinating history contains clear locator maps and nicely chosen photographs.

Amazing Texas Monuments & Museums: From the Enchanting to the Bizarre
by Ann Ruff, Gulf Publishing, 1984, 104 pages, paper, $9.95
This is a guide to unusual sights—monuments erected to the strawberry, pecan, roadrunner, mosquito, and jackrabbit, and museums featuring things like 10,000 bird's eggs or Lee Harvey Oswald's can opener. Many tombstones are also included in this guide to sightseeing fun.

Austin: The Complete Guide to Texas's Capital City
by Richard Zelade, Texas Monthly Press, 1988 (2nd ed.), 272 pages, paper, $9.95
This book is part of the Texas Monthly Guide series, which is reviewed in more detail under "Series Reviews."

Authentic Texas Cafes
by Susan and Ed Kennard, Texas Monthly Press, 1986, 202 pages, paper, $8.95
This is a good rundown on the Kennards' pick of the top 100 cafés in the state that are located in or near 87 different towns. As the authors state, these are places "where good food is still more important than speed or gimmicks."

Backroads of Texas
by Ed Syers, Gulf Publishing, 1988 (2nd ed.), 176 pages, paper, $12.95
Syers's 62 tours of the backcountry are well planned, well written, and just plain fun. It's time to explore the ghost towns, boom towns, farm towns, cow towns, and all those places of interest in between. This guide is comprehensive, compact, and definitely first-class.

Beachcomber's Guide to Gulf Coast Marine Life
by Nick Fotheringham, Gulf Publishing, 1980, 124 pages, paper, $9.95
See "The South."

Bed and Breakfasts of the Deep South
by Sarah-Margaret Brown and Ruth Bruns, Variety House, 1985, 86 pages, paper, $6.70
Including Texas, this book is reviewed under "The South."

The Best Country Cafés in Texas: The East
by John Forsyth and Meg Tynan, Texas Geographic Interests, 1983, 146 pages, paper, $7.95
The Best Country Cafés in Texas: The West
by John Forsyth and Meg Tynan, Texas Geographic Interests, 1984, 128 pages, paper, $6.95
Forsyth and Tynan really have a knack for capturing the flavor of a place—gastronomic and otherwise. Their superb compilation of the hundreds of country cafés throughout the state has been a real service to the traveler, and they have tried to keep their information fairly up-to-date by including a list of those cafés that have bitten their final bullet and closed their doors. Since 1985 they have written a weekly restaurant review column for the *Houston Chronicle* and so, armed with all these new ideas, have stated that a single-volume update is in the works. Watch for it.

**The Best of Texas Festivals: Your Guide to Rootin' Tootin'
Downhome Texas Good Times!**
by Ann Ruff, Gulf Publishing, 1986, 100 pages, paper, $9.95
This is just the ticket—a single resource, arranged in a month-to-month format, giving the inside scoop on 60 good-time Texas festivals: a citrus fiesta, a peach jamboree, the fiddler's festival, and the Hushpuppy Olympics, for example. All the needed information along with addresses and phone numbers for further details, is included.

**Camper's Guide to Texas: Parks, Lakes, and Forests—Where to Go
and How to Get There**
by Mickey Little, Gulf Publishing, 1983, 148 pages, paper, $9.95
This is one of the Gulf Camping Guide series, which is reviewed in more detail under "Series Reviews."

Country Inns, Lodges, & Historic Hotels: The South
by Anthony Hitchcock and Jean Lindgren, Burt Franklin–Publisher, 1988 (10th ed.), 283 pages, paper, $8.95
This is one of the Compleat Traveler's Companion series, which is reviewed in more detail under "Series Reviews." No fees have been accepted for inclusion in this annually updated guide.

Dallas Epicure
Peanut Butter Publishing, 1986, 160 pages, paper, $7.95
This book is part of the Epicure Guide series, which is reviewed in more detail under "Series Reviews." The series is updated frequently.

**The Dallas Morning News Guide to Dallas Restaurants: The
Definitive Guide to the 150 Best**
Chronicle Books, 1986, 160 pages, paper, $7.95
There are plenty of places to eat in Dallas and this book tells about some of the best, of every type and in every price range. A helpful section on the foods of Texas and a rundown on the 16 wineries that were in business in the Lone Star state in 1986 are included, as well as brief touring information and phone numbers in case a tasting tour is on the agenda. Restaurant reviews are well done and all the necessary information is provided.

Dallas: Your Complete Guide to a Vibrant Texas City
by Ellen Gunter, Texas Monthly Press, 1987, 265 pages, paper, $9.95
This book is part of the Texas Monthly Guide series, which is reviewed in more detail under "Series Reviews."

Eyes of Texas Travel Guide: Dallas/East Texas
by Ray Miller, Gulf Publishing, 1988 (2nd ed.), 224 pages, paper, $10.95

Eyes of Texas Travel Guide: Fort Worth/Brazos Valley
by Ray Miller, Gulf Publishing, 1981, 200 pages, paper, $9.95

Eyes of Texas Travel Guide: Hill Country/Permian Basin
by Ray Miller, Gulf Publishing, 1982, 200 pages, paper, $9.95

Eyes of Texas Travel Guide: Houston/Gulf Coast
by Ray Miller, Gulf Publishing, 1987 (2nd ed.), 224 pages, paper, $10.95

Eyes of Texas Travel Guide: Panhandle/Plains
by Ray Miller, Gulf Publishing, 1982, 200 pages, paper, $9.95

Eyes of Texas Travel Guide: San Antonio/Border
by Ray Miller, Gulf Publishing, 1979, 250 pages, paper, $9.95

This well-known series, listed above in its entirety, combines Miller's penchant for history with the facts and figures of modern Texas. Packed with photographs, these regional guides make great companion guides, excellent supplements to more standard travel guides.

Flashmaps: Instant Guide to Dallas/Ft. Worth
Random House, 1987, 72 pages, paper, $4.95

This is one of the Flashmaps series, which is reviewed in more detail under "Series Reviews." The series is updated annually.

Fodor's Dallas-Fort Worth
Fodor's Travel Publications, 1987, 128 pages, paper, $5.95

Fodor's Houston and Galveston
Fodor's Travel Publications, 1987, 128 pages, paper, $5.95

These two titles are part of Fodor's City Guide series, which is reviewed in more detail under "Series Reviews." The series is updated annually.

Fodor's Texas
Fodor's Travel Publications, 1988, 368 pages, paper, $8.95

This book is part of Fodor's Country/Regional Guide series, which is reviewed in more detail under "Series Reviews." The series is updated annually.

Fort Worth & Tarrant County: A Historical Guide
edited by Ruby Schmidt, Texas Christian University Press, 1984, 101 pages, paper, $5.95

This is a very well done assemblage of the history behind a vast array of historical buildings, homes, churches, cemeteries, schools, etc. in the Fort Worth area. Entries are arranged alphabetically. Those located in Fort Worth proper are accompanied by several hand-drawn maps. Nonetheless, an additional map of the surrounding area is recommended. Most sites will have a historical marker. However, the historical notes in this guidebook go well beyond those included on the marker itself. The index also clearly references all the pages for cemeteries, churches, etc., which is helpful for travelers particularly interested in one type of historic site.

Frommer's Dollarwise Guide to Texas
by Rena Bulkin, Prentice Hall Press, 1986, 300 pages, paper, $11.95
This book is part of Frommer's Dollarwise Guide series, which is reviewed in more detail under "Series Reviews." This series is updated every two years.

Frontier Forts of Texas
by Charles Robinson, Gulf Publishing, 1986, 86 pages, paper, $9.95
This is a large-format travel guide that delivers the practical facts along with fascinating accounts of those adventurous events of yesteryear. The stories cover the more than two dozen forts that have survived the years, as well as those that were destroyed. Travel information covers visitor facilities and local events at each of the still-existent forts.

A Guide to Bicycling in Texas: Tours, Tips, and More
by George Sevra, Gulf Publishing, 1985, 96 pages, paper, $9.95
This is a great collection of tours—one-day, inter-city, and more lengthy routes—spanning the entire state, which will prove that Texas is not just flat and empty. Helpful lists of bicycle shops, sources of maps (though some good-sized detail maps are included in this large-format book), and local Chambers of Commerce are provided.

A Guide to Historic Texas Inns and Hotels
by Ann Ruff, Gulf Publishing, 1985 (2nd ed.), 132 pages, paper, $9.95
A popular guide from an equally popular writer, this large-format book offers excellent descriptions of the best of the historic lodging spots. The practical facts are listed separately in the margin for easy access, and each selection is accompanied by a line drawing or, sometimes, a photograph.

Guide to Recommended Country Inns of Arizona, New Mexico, and Texas
by Eleanor Morris, The Globe Pequot Press, 1987, 290 pages, paper, $9.95
This is one of the excellent Recommended Country Inns series,

which is reviewed in more detail under "Series Reviews." The author has visited and reviewed each inn personally; no payments have been accepted for inclusion. The series is updated every two years.

A Guide to Texas Rivers and Streams
by Gene Kirkley, Gulf Publishing, 1983, 120 pages, paper, $9.95
   This is a large-format guide to whitewater canoeing and kayaking, float trips, fishing, or just plain fun along Texas's many waterways.

Great Hometown Restaurants of Texas
by Mary Beverley, Gulf Publishing, 1984, 150 pages, paper, $9.95
   This large-format guide is a lot of fun, with great write-ups on all sorts of intriguing spots where home-style cooking is the rule. It includes all the practical data, but be aware of the publication date.

Hiking and Backpacking Trails of Texas
by Mildred Little, Gulf Publishing, 1985 (2nd ed.), 148 pages, paper, $9.95
   This book contains notes on the beautiful countryside in Texas. This large-format book divides the state into four regions. In each region trails are clearly located, adequate trail notes and distances included, and maps, sometimes topographical ones, are provided as well.

Hill Country: Discover the Secrets of the Texas Hill Country
by Richard Zelade, Texas Monthly Press, 1987 (2nd ed.), 509 pages, paper, $9.95
   This superb book, while part of the Texas Monthly series, is structured differently. Here are 10 driving tours through the hills of central Texas—including areas near Austin and San Antonio. Each tour can be done in a day, although they are up to several hundred miles in length and dawdling is encouraged. History of the area and points of interest, both on and off the beaten track, are included. You'll learn the best spots to stop at when it's chow time and get some tips on lodging along the way. Good directions, clear maps, and tips on restaurants and lodging make this a wonderful guidebook.

Historic Homes of Texas: Across the Thresholds of Yesterday
by Ann Ruff and Henri Farmer, Gulf Publishing, 1987, 130 pages, paper, $18.95
   Take a look at the homes built by the cattle and oil barons and the genteel women who came west in times gone by. Each is recognized by the Texas Historical Commission, many are on the National Register of Historic Places, and all are open to the public. Included is all the information on finding and enjoying each historic

site. Also included are details for tours of other homes not normally open to the public.

Historic Texas Hotels & Country Inns

by Linda Johnson and Sally Ross, Eakins Press, 1982, 230 pages, paper, $8.95

Photographs, historical notes, and nice descriptions of each hotel or inn are the strong point of this book. The historical significance of each selected spot is certainly obvious, but visitors should check on the current status of each. A new edition would certainly be in order.

Houston Epicure

Peanut Butter Publishing, 1986, 160 pages, paper, $7.95

This is one of the Epicure Guide series, which is reviewed in more detail under "Series Reviews." The series is updated frequently.

Houston: Your Complete Guide to Texas' Largest City

by John Davenport, Texas Monthly Press, 1985 (4th ed.), 175 pages, paper, $9.95

This book is part of the Texas Monthly Guide series, which is reviewed in more detail under "Series Review."

Insight Guide: Texas

by Apa Productions, Prentice Hall Press, 1985, 384 pages, paper, $15.95

This book is part of the highly regarded Insight Guide series, which is reviewed in more detail under "Series Reviews."

Interstate Gourmet: Texas and the Southwest

by Barbara Rodriguez and Tom Miller, Summit Books, 1986, 232 pages, paper, $6.95

This is one of the excellent Interstate Gourmet series, which is reviewed in more detail under "Series Reviews."

A Marmac Guide to Houston and Galveston

by Dale Young, Pelican Publishing, 1988, 270 pages, paper, $7.95

This book is part of the Marmac Guide series, which is reviewed in more detail under "Series Reviews." The series is updated every two years.

Places to Go With Children in Dallas & Fort Worth

by Joan Jackson and Glenna Whitley, Chronicle Books, 1987, 144 pages, paper, $7.95

This book is part of the Places to Go With Children Guide series, which is reviewed in more detail under "Series Reviews."

Ray Miller's Texas Forts: A History and Guide

by Ray Miller, Gulf Publishing, 1985, 223 pages, paper, $13.95

Miller presents a lively history of the many forts, including the famous Alamo, that sprung up during the 19th century and were the focal points of many battles during the Mexican War, the Indian wars, and the Civil War. This title includes many interesting photographs.

Ray Miller's Texas Parks: A History and Guide

by Ray Miller, Gulf Publishing, 1984, 232 pages, paper, $13.95

This book contains the practical information on the numerous parks in the state system and a large measure of the history behind the sights. Some specifics about each park may be dated—call ahead to see—but this an excellent resource nonetheless.

San Antonio: An Indispensable Guide to One of Texas's Favorite Cities

by Ben Fairbank, Jr. and Nancy Foster, Texas Monthly Press, 1988 (2nd ed.), 224 pages, paper, $9.95

This book is part of the Texas Monthly Guide series, which is reviewed in more detail under "Series Reviews."

Shifra Stein's Day Trips From Houston

by Carol Barrington, The Globe Pequot Press, 1988 (3rd ed.) 180 pages, paper, $7.95

This book is part of the well-done Shifra Stein's Day Trip Guide series, which is reviewed in more detail under "Series Reviews." This third edition was due out in late 1988; price and number of pages are tentative.

6 Central Texas Auto Tours

by Myra McIlvain, Eakins Press, 1980, 220 pages, paper, $9.95

This is a book of driving tours, filled with historical notes and anecdotes, in the central Texas area around Austin. Some of the roadways in the area may have changed since this book was published, but most of the copious detail should still be valid.

Texas Bed & Breakfast: Your Complete Guide to Bed and Breakfast Inns in More Than 35 Texas Cities
by Ann Ruff, *et al.*, Texas Monthly Press, 1985, 250 pages, paper, $9.95
Bed and breakfast hit Texas in the 1980s and this guide is full of helpful descriptions and fairly current practical information on all the best.

Texas Coast: Discover Delights Along the Gulf Coast of Texas
by Robert Rafferty, Texas Monthly Press, 1986, 289 pages, paper, $9.95
This book is part of the Texas Monthly Guides series, which is reviewed in more detail under "Series Reviews." The emphasis in this book is the long Texas beachfront from Port Arthur to Brownsville and the "boating, fishing, fiestas, seafood, shopping, history and hilarity" found in the different spots.

Texas—Family Style: Parent's Guide to Hassle-free, Fun Travel With the Kids
by Ruth Wolverton, Gulf Publishing, 1981, 120 pages, paper, $7.95
Although it is getting older now, this large-format guide is still a source of lots of good ideas for what to do with the entire family.

Texas Golf: The Comprehensive Guide to Golf Courses and Resorts of the Lone Star State
by Frank Hermes, Taylor Publishing, 1987, 192 pages, paper, $7.95
This is a best-bet compendium of golfing information in Texas.

Texas Parks and Campgrounds: Central, South, and West Texas
by George Miller and Delena Tull, Texas Monthly Press, 1984, 141 pages, paper, $7.95
Texas Parks and Campgrounds: North, East, and Coastal Texas
by George Miller and Delena Tull, Texas Monthly Press, 1984, 127 pages, paper, $7.95
These two titles give a good rundown of the many state parks and campgrounds, including good notes of the attractions of the area, its ecology, facilities, fees (if any), and some succinct comments on hiking options as well. Call ahead to determine up-to-date information.

Texas Restaurant Guide
by Pat Pugh, Pelican Publishing, 1987, 243 pages, paper, $4.95
In this book, Pugh provides information and opinion on more than 450 restaurants in the big cities and cow towns alike. Both budget

and high-price selections are included along with all the necessary practical facts.

Texas: The Newest, the Biggest, the Most Complete Guide to All of Texas

by Patricia Sharpe and Robert Weddle, Texas Monthly Press, 1982, 724 pages, paper, $13.95

This Texas-sized guidebook is no longer quite so new, but the word from the publisher is that they will probably update this popular guide in the fall of 1988—or in any case sometime soon. If that is so, travelers will find that a combination of this guide and one of the other regional guides will work well. This is part of the Texas Monthly Guide series, which is reviewed in more detail under "Series Reviews."

Tour Guide to North Texas

by Catherine Gonzalez, Eakin Press, 1982, 224 pages, paper, $8.95

Here are seven well-conceived driving tours of north Texas complete with good driving instructions, historical notes and anecdotes, and a variety of interesting photographs. Included are the Dallas area and the Red River country—north Texas, "a land, of lakes, pines, and history."

Traveling Texas Borders: A Guide to the Best of Both Sides

by Ann Ruff, Gulf Publishing, 1983, 119 pages, paper, $9.95

This guide gives a good detailing of the many things to do and see along Texas's vast border. Included are activities in Arkansas, Louisiana, Mexico, New Mexico, and Oklahoma. This large-format guide offers plenty of interesting suggestions.

Why Stop? A Guide to Texas Historical Roadside Markers

by Claude and Betty Dooley, Gulf Publishing, 1985 (2nd ed.), 560 pages, paper, $14.95

There are more than 2600 roadside markers in Texas with historical notes on all sorts of interesting subjects. Now, with this guide, travelers can read the markers without necessarily even stopping the car. This is a handy resource guide to keep on the back seat.

UTAH

See also "The Rocky Mountain/Great Basin States" and "United States as a Whole."

The Hiker's Guide to Utah
by Dave Hall, Falcon Press, 1982, 209 pages, paper, $8.95
This book is part of the Falcon Press Hiking Guide series, which is reviewed in more detail under "Series Reviews."

Hiking in the Great Basin: The High Desert Country of California, Oregon, Nevada, and Utah
by John Hart, Sierra Club Books, 1981, 369 pages, paper, $9.95
This is one of the Sierra Club Hiking Totebook series, which is reviewed in more detail under "Series Reviews."

The Historical Guide to Utah Ghost Towns
by Stephen Carr, Wasatch Publishers, 1972, 174 pages, paper, $9.95
Utah is loaded with fascinating ghost towns, and this large-format book explores them. Location maps point the way and excellent, extensive commentaries on each, accompanied by some fine old photos, help capture the history and charm of these once-bustling places. This is a great guide for the history hound.

River Runners' Guide to Utah and Adjacent Areas
by Gary Nichols, University of Utah Press, 1986, 168 pages, paper, $14.95
This is a fine guide to over 90 river trips for rafts, kayaks, and canoes. For each there is a good overview map, description, and rating. The rating includes not only the standard International Scale of Difficulty classification, but information on gradients and flow levels. Nichols also notes the best time of year to run the river, access points, number of river miles, and topographical maps to obtain. Most of the runs are in Utah, but nearby runs in Wyoming, Colorado, Idaho, and Arizona are also included. Color and black-and-white photographs highlight the scenic pleasures that await you.

The Sierra Club Guide to the Natural Areas of Colorado and Utah
by John and Jane Perry, Sierra Club Books, 1985, 416 pages, paper, $9.95
This is one of the Sierra Club Natural Areas Guide series, which is reviewed in more detail under "Series Reviews."

Utah! A Family Travel Guide
by Tom Wharton, Wasatch Publishers, 1987, 224 pages, paper, $8.50
Utah is a great place for families—especially those who like to camp, go for a hike, eat lunch in the great outdoors, ski down a hill, or just learn about the great outdoors. Such is the emphasis of this excellent guide. The choices are extensive, the scenery magnificent,

the fun overflowing, and Wharton has done a fine job detailing all the many opportunities for family enjoyment in Utah's five national parks, 46 state parks, and two national recreation areas, not to mention national forests, extensive BLM (Bureau of Land Management) land, and numerous national monuments. In addition, excellent appendices tell where to get more information.

Utah: A Guide to the State

by Ward Roylance, Wasatch Publishers, 1982, 779 pages, paper, $8.95

In a project sponsored by the Utah Arts Council, the touring portion of the old, classic WPA guide first published in 1941 was revised and updated. Practically, this new version is only based on the older text, since it has been thoroughly reconstructed into modern-day driving tours of the eleven acknowledged travel regions of the state. And less history and anecdote are left from the earlier edition, because of size limitations. Nonetheless, this is a massive work, by travel book standards, and contains plenty of information and history on all the sights.

Utah Handbook

by Bill Weir, Moon Publications, 1988, 400 pages, paper, $10.95

This is a new title in the superb Moon Handbook series, which is reviewed in more detail under "Series Reviews." The series is updated every two years.

Utah Ski Country

by Brooke Williams, Falcon Press, 1986, 128 pages, paper, $15.95

The emphasis in this book is on beautifully reproduced color photography, but plenty of information on Utah's spectacular ski country is included as well. This is a fine introduction to Utah's ski country.

VERMONT ———————————————————————————

See also "New England" and "United States as a Whole."

Appalachian Trail Guide to New Hampshire/Vermont

Appalachian Trail Conference, 1985 (4th ed.), 302 pages, paper, $15.95

This is one of the Appalachian Trail Guide series, which is reviewed in more detail under "Series Reviews."

Canoe Camping Vermont & New Hampshire Rivers
by Roioli Schweiker, Backcountry Publications, 1985, 128 pages, paper, $6.95
   This book is part of the Backcountry Canoeing Guide series, which is reviewed in more detail under "Series Reviews."

Day Hiker's Guide to Vermont
The Green Mountain Club, 1987 (3rd ed.), 184 pages, paper, $7.50
   This great little book will easily slide into a pocket. Containing detailed information on each hiking trail, including very clear topographical maps onto which each trail is plotted, this book packs an amazing amount of information in a small space. The print is a little smaller than that of larger guides but it is clearly produced, with good use of boldface type, and sturdily bound.

Famous Vermont Restaurants & Recipes
by Sue Schildge, Schildge Publishing, 1987, 211 pages, paper, $12.95
   This is one of the Famous Restaurants & Recipes series, which is reviewed in more detail under "Series Reviews."

Fifty Hikes in Vermont: Walks, Day Hikes, and Backpacking Trips in the Green Mountains
by Heather and Hugh Sadlier, Backcountry Publications, 1985, 184 pages, paper, $8.95
   This book is part of the comprehensive Backcountry Fifty Hikes series, which is reviewed in more detail under "Series Reviews."

Guide Book of the Long Trail
Green Mountain Club, 1987 (23rd ed.), 175 pages, paper, $8.50
   This famous Long Trail runs north-to-south the full distance of Vermont. It is basically a ridgetop trail, although it often descends into the valleys between. Along the way this great little pocket-sized guide covers more than 40 of the highest peaks in the state. A fold-out orientation map, another fold-out topographical map, and small topographical maps throughout the text are provided. The write-ups are clear and accurate—born of years of careful revision to this popular guide.

Roadside Geology of Vermont and New Hampshire
by Bradford Van Diver, Mountain Press, 1987, 230 pages, paper, $9.95
   This book is part of the excellent Roadside Geology Guide series, which is reviewed in more detail under "Series Reviews."

Sentinels of Time: Vermont's Covered Bridges

by Phil Ziegler, Down East Books, 1983, 133 pages, paper, $8.95

Beautiful drawings of 117 covered bridges, including both those travelers can still seek out and admire and those that have long since succumbed to the pressures of time. The bridges are arranged by county and, where appropriate, their location is noted. Maps are not provided. A brief discussion of types of trusses and portals is also included in this sensitive and thought-provoking book.

25 Bicycle Tours in Vermont: 950 Miles of Sights, Delights and Special Events

by John Freidin, Backcountry Publications, 1984, 176 pages, paper, $7.95

This book is part of the well-done Backcountry Bicycle Tours series, which is reviewed in more detail under "Series Reviews."

Vermont: An Explorer's Guide

by Christina Tree and Peter Jennison, The Countryman Press, 1988 (3rd ed.), 322 pages, paper, $11.95

This is one of the excellent Countryman Explorer's Guide series, which is reviewed in more detail under "Series Reviews." The series is updated every two to three years.

Vermont Golf Courses: A Player's Guide

by Bob Labbance and David Cornwell, The New England Press, 1987, 144 pages, paper, $12.95

This book contains helpful information on all 50 golf courses open to the public in Vermont. Each is given a good overview, including a drawing of the course layout as well as information on fees, the season each course is usually open, and directions to the clubhouse. This is a handy summary for the golfer looking for a place to tee off.

Vermont on $500 a Day (More or Less)

by Peter Jennison, The Countryman Press, 1987, 119 pages, paper, $10.00

Jennison has compiled the very best places to stay, dine, play, and shop in the Green Mountain State. Travelers lucky enough to have a substantial travel budget, should take advantage of these fantastic, wonderfully described hotels, restaurants, and shops.

VIRGINIA ────────────────────────────

See also "The Mid-Atlantic States" and "United States as a Whole."

All About Alexandria: A Visitor's Guide

by Nicholas Bailey, Cole House, 1985, 62 pages, paper, $5.95

This is a helpful, compact guide to Alexandria. Included are notes on history, a walking tour, shopping tips, an informative (hopefully not too dated) paragraph on selected places to stay, and restaurant picks.

Appalachian Trail Guide to Central and Southern Virginia

Appalachian Trail Conference, 1986 (9th ed.), 290 pages, paper, $14.50

Appalachian Trail Guide to Maryland and Northern Virginia

Potomac Appalachian Trail Club, 1986 (12th ed.), 172 pages, paper, $15.25

Appalachian Trail Guide to Shenandoah National Park

Potomac Appalachian Trail Club, 1986 (9th ed.), 275 pages, paper, $16.00

These three titles are part of the Appalachian Trail Guides series, which is reviewed in more detail under "Series Reviews."

Arlington National Cemetery: Shrine to America's Heroes

Woodbine House, 1986, 335 pages, paper, $9.95

This is a guide to the points of interest at our national cemetery. The book includes biographies of 100 the most famous heroes buried at Arlington.

Circuit Hikes in Shenandoah National Park

Potomac Appalachian Trail Club, 1986 (12th ed.), 86 pages, paper, $5.00

Circuit Hikes in Virginia, West Virginia, Maryland, and Pennsylvania

Potomac Appalachian Trail Club, 1986 (4th ed.), 88 pages, paper, $5.00

Both of these titles are fine pocket guides in the Circuit Hikes Guide series, which is reviewed in more detail under "Series Reviews."

Civil War Sites in Virginia: A Tour Guide

by James Robertson, Jr., The University Press of Virginia, 1982, 102 pages, paper, $5.95

The most exposed of the states that seceded from the Union, Virginia became the major battleground of the war. More than 100 years later, the fascination with the war between the states lives on here. Robertson has divided the state into six regions and, first marking each important site on a regional map, discusses in an informative paragraph the important aspects of that site. Civil war buffs should be sure to take this helpful guide along.

Elegant Lodging: A Guide to Country Mansions & Manor Houses in Virginia, Maryland & Pennsylvania
by Caroline Lancaster and Candyce Stapen, Washington Book Trading Co., 1985, 157 pages, paper, $5.95
See "The Mid-Atlantic States."

Fodor's South
Fodor's Travel Publications, 1987, 448 pages, paper, $12.95
Fodor's Virginia
Fodor's Travel Publications, 1987, 176 pages, paper, $7.95
These two titles are part of Fodor's Country/Regional Guide series, which is reviewed in more detail under "Series Reviews." The series is updated annually.

Fodor's Williamsburg, Jamestown and Yorktown
Fodor's Travel Publications, 1986, 160 pages, paper, $7.95
This book is part of Fodor's City Guide series, which is reviewed in more detail under "Series Reviews."

Frommer's Washington, D.C. and Historic Virginia on $40 a Day
edited by Arthur Frommer, Prentice Hall Press, 1988, 325 pages, paper, $11.95
This book is part of Frommer's Dollar-a-Day Guide series, which is reviewed in more detail under "Series Reviews." The series is updated every two years.

A Guidebook to Virginia's Historical Markers
compiled by Margaret Peters, The University Press of Virginia, 1985, 273 pages, paper, $9.95
This very handy guidebook is perfect for the glove compartment. Assembled here in logical order is the text of all the historical markers located throughout Virginia. With this book in hand, travelers will not only be able to read the marker more easily but also be able to recall for later discussion what each marker actually said.

Guide to Skyline Drive and Shenandoah National Park
by Henry Heatwole, Shenandoah Natural History Association, 1985 (3rd ed.), 226 pages, paper, $4.50
This is a comprehensive source of practical information and trail hikes of all types. Numerous maps detailing the beautiful Skyline Drive, as fine a car tour as exists anywhere, are provided. Trail maps are included, but are fairly general in format. This is a well-done resource guide.

Hikes in the Washington Area, Part B: Arlington, Fairfax, Loudoun, and Prince William Counties in Virginia
Potamac Appalachian Trail Club, 1986, 110 pages, paper, $5.00
This is one of the excellent, small-format Potomac Hiking Guide series, which is reviewed in more detail under "Series Reviews."

Hiking the Old Dominion: The Trails of Virginia
by Allen de Hart, Sierra Club Books, 1984, 480 pages, paper, $10.95
This fine, small-format book is part of the Sierra Club Hiking Totebook series, which is reviewed in more detail under "Series Reviews."

Insider's Guide to Southside Hampton Roads, Virginia
by Nancy Venable and Sam Martinette, Storie/McOwen Publishing, 1987, 700 pages, paper, $8.95
Insider's Guide to Williamsburg, Virginia
by Susan Bruno and Donna Quaresima, Storie/McOwen Publishing, 1987, 256 pages, paper, $5.95
These two titles are part of the Storie McOwen Insider's Guide series, which is reviewed in more detail under "Series Reviews."

A Naturalist's Blue Ridge Parkway
by David Catlin, The University of Tennessee Press, 1984, 208 pages, paper, $7.95
See "North Carolina".

Off 13: The Eastern Shore of Virginia Guidebook
by Kirk Mariner, The Book Bin, Inc., 1987, 172 pages, paper, $7.95
Head for the ocean with this nicely done guide, logically arranged for the tourist, to the pleasures of the the coast. Mariner has provided walking tours, car tours, historical notes on the sights, tips on architecture, and selected and briefly described restaurants and lodging.

Old South: A Traveler's Guide to Virginia, North Carolina and South Carolina
by Dana Facaros and Michael Pauls, Hippocrene Books, 1987 (revised ed.), 124 pages, paper, $5.95
See "The South."

The Pelican Guide to Virginia
by Shirley Morris, Penguin Publishing, 1981, 160 pages, paper, $4.95
This is primarily a sightseeing guide and, while it is certainly a

little old and out-of-date on some details, the vast majority of its information is still quite helpful.

The Pelican Guide to the Shenandoah

by Regina Pierce and Sharon Yackso, Pelican Publishing, 1987, 128 pages, paper, $7.95

This is an all-purpose guide, arranged geographically and highlighting history, recreational opportunities, shopping, lodging, dining, seasonal events, and more, for tourists working their way up the Shenandoah Valley. Included are visits to Winchester, Front Royal, Luray, Staunton, and Charlottesville as well as such historic sites as The National Road, Harpers Ferry National Historic Park, and the Blue Ridge Parkway.

Roadside Geology of Virginia

by Keith Frye, Mountain Press, 1986, 278 pages, paper, $9.95

This book is part of the excellent Roadside Geology Guide series, which is reviewed in more detail under "Series Reviews."

The Southern Bed & Breakfast Book

by Corinne Ross, The Globe Pequot Press, 1986, 192 pages, paper, $8.95

This is one of the Bed & Breakfast Book series, which is reviewed in more detail under "Series Reviews."

Virginia: A History & Guide

by Tim Mulligan, Random House, 1986, 285 pages, paper, $9.95

This book is part of the History & Sightseeing Guide series, which is reviewed in more detail under "Series Reviews."

Virginia Off the Beaten Path: A Guide to Unique Places

by Judy and Ed Colbert, The Globe Pequot Press, 1986, 176 pages, paper, $7.95

This book is part of the well-done Off the Beaten Path Guide series, which is reviewed in more detail under "Series Reviews."

The Virginia One-Day Trip Book

by Jane Smith, EPM Publications, 1986, 221 pages, paper, $8.95

This book is part of the One-Day Trip Book series, which is reviewed in more detail under "Series Reviews."

Virginia's Historic Restaurants and Their Recipes
by Dawn O'Brien, John F. Blair–Publisher, 1988, 205 pages, cloth, $12.95
 This is one of the Historic Restaurants & Recipes series, which is reviewed in more detail under "Series Reviews."

Walking Tours of Old Washington and Alexandria
by Paul Hogarth, EPM Publications, 1985, 144 pages, paper, $24.95
 Including Alexandria, Virginia, this book is reviewed under "District of Columbia."

Walks and Rambles on the Delmarva Peninsula: A Guide for Hikers and Naturalists
by Jay Abercrombie, Backcountry Publications, 1985, 195 pages, paper, $8.95
 Including portions of Virginia, this book is reviewed under "The Mid-Atlantic States."

Washington On Foot: 24 Walking Tours of Washington, D.C., Old Alexandria, Historic Annapolis
edited by John Protopappas and Lin Brown, Smithsonian Institution Press, 1984 (3rd ed.), 222 pages, paper, $5.95
 See "District of Columbia."

WASHINGTON ———————————————————
See also "The Pacific Northwest" and "United States as a Whole."

Backcountry Skiing in Washington's Cascades
by Rainer Burgdorfer, The Mountaineers, 1986, 232 pages, paper, $9.95
 This excellent, detailed guide to 78 backcountry tours for intermediate and advanced ski-mountaineers is part of the Mountaineers Cross-Country Skiing Guide series, which is reviewed in more detail under "Series Reviews."

Back Roads of Washington
by Earl Thollander, Crown Publishing, 1981, 208 pages, paper, $9.95
 This is one of Earl Thollander's Back Roads series, which is reviewed in more detail under "Series Reviews."

Bed and Breakfast Homes Directory: California, Oregon, Washington
by Diane Knight, Knighttime Publications, 1986 (4th ed.), 230 pages, paper, $8.95
 See "The Pacific Northwest."

Best Choices in Western Washington
> by Eric Larson, Gable & Gray, 1987, 648 pages, paper, $12.95
> This is one of the Gable & Gray Guide series, which is reviewed in more detail under "Series Reviews."

Bicycling the Backroads Around Puget Sound
> by Erin and Bill Woods, The Mountaineers, 1981, 224 pages, paper, $9.95

Bicycling the Backroads of Northwest Washington
> by Erin and Bill Woods, The Mountaineers, 1984, 208 pages, paper, $9.95
> These two titles, covering a total of 93 tours replete with details, maps, and mileage logs, are part of the Bicycling the Backroads Guide series, which is reviewed in more detail under "Series Reviews."

City of Dreams: A Guide to Port Townsend
> edited by Peter Simpson, Bay Press, 1986, 330 pages, paper, $10.95
> This is a superb companion guide to picturesque, historic Port Townsend, including history and background information on topics of every sort. This well-done guide will make a wonderful complement to a more traditional guidebook.

Cross-Country Ski Trails of Washington's Cascades and Olympics
> by Tom Kirkendall and Vicky Spring, The Mountaineers, 1983, 208 pages, paper, $9.95
> Detailing 80 trips from easy to advanced, this book is part of the Mountaineers Cross-Country Skiing Guide series, which is reviewed in more detail under "Series Reviews."

Discover Seattle With Kids: Where to Go and What to Do in the Puget Sound Area
> by Rosanne Cohn, JASI/Discover Books, 1987 (5th ed.), 224 pages, paper, $8.95
> Cohn's well-written, frequently updated book is popular among Seattle residents. Visitors to the area will find it the most timely source of "to do and see" ideas for the whole family, including special places to eat with the kids and the best take-out spots to gather the goods for a memorable picnic. All sorts of possibilities—museums, events, farms, nature centers, and lots more.

Exploring Washington's Smaller Cities
> by Clifford Burke, Quartzite Books, 1987, 260 pages, paper, $10.95
> This is a comprehensive look at Port Angeles, Vancouver (Washington, that is), Olympia, Anacortes, Wenatchee, Yakima, Walla Walla, Pullman, Ellensburg, and Spokane. Included is information

on dining, lodging, shopping, parks, events, entertainment, and sightseeing.

50 Hikes in Mt. Rainier National Park

by Ira Spring and Harvey Manning, The Mountaineers, 1978, 136 pages, paper, $8.95

This is one of the excellent Mountaineers Hiking Guide series, which is reviewed in more detail under "Series Reviews."

Footsore 1—Seattle to Issaquah Alps: Walks and Hikes Around the Puget Sound

by Harvcy Manning, The Mountaineers, 1988 (2nd ed.), 220 pages, paper, $9.95

Footsore 2—Snoqualmie to Skykomish: Walks and Hikes Around the Puget Sound

by Harvey Manning, The Mountaineers, 1987 (2nd ed.), 216 pages, paper, $9.95

Footsore 3—Everett to Bellingham: Walks and Hikes Around the Puget Sound

by Harvey Manning, The Mountaineers, 1983, 220 pages, paper, $9.95

Footsore 4—Puyallup, Nisqually, Kitsap: Walks and Hikes Around the Puget Sound

by Harvey Manning, The Mountaineers, 1983, 220 pages, paper, $9.95

The fact that there are four volumes detailing the many walks and hikes possible around the Puget Sound certainly hints at the rich and varied outdoor adventure possibilities in the area. This is a fantastic place and Manning has done a great job organizing the many ideas for easy walks and more strenuous hikes into four manageable packages. Distances, elevation gain, the best season to go, and the directions to the trailhead (including possible public transportation where available) are noted for each walk or hike. These four excellent resource guides will fill many weekends with pleasure.

Hiking the North Cascades

by Fred Darvill, Jr., Sierra Club Books, 1982, 384 pages, paper, $10.95

This book is part of the Sierra Club Hiking Totebook series, which is reviewed in more detail under "Series Reviews."

Mt. St. Helen's National Volcanic Monument: A Pocket Guide for Hikers, Viewers and Skiers
by Chuck Williams, The Mountaineers, 1988, 112 pages, paper, $4.95
Released after press time, this new title details the post-eruption realities of the area.

Nature Walks in & Around Seattle
by Stephen Whitney, The Mountaineers, 1987, 240 pages, paper, $9.95
This first-class book details 25 easy, enjoyable strolls through the picturesque greater Seattle area, most of which are less than a mile in length. Nicely described with plenty of nature notes, each walk includes a detail map, instructions on how to reach it by car or public transportation, the best season to do it, some nice photographs, and other highlights.

Olympic Mountains Trail Guide: National Park & National Forest
by Robert Wood, The Mountaineers, 1984, 303 pages, paper, $10.95
After a good introduction to the pleasures and dangers of hiking in the Olympic range, Wood carefully describes the numerous hiking trails available. This book is part of the Mountaineers Hiking Guide series, which is reviewed in more detail under "Series Reviews."

Olympic National Park & the Olympic Peninsula: A Traveler's Companion
by Robert Steelquist, Woodlands Press, 1985, 72 pages, paper, $6.95
This is a fine orientation to this spectacular area—the history, the towns, the parks, and the people. Included are beautiful color photographs: A good companion guide to a more traditional guidebook.

100 Hikes in the Alpine Lakes
by Vicky Spring, *et al.*, The Mountaineers, 1985, 240 pages, paper, $9.95
100 Hikes in the Inland Northwest
by Rich Landers and Ida Rowe Dolphin, The Mountaineers, 1987, 224 pages, paper, $9.95
100 Hikes in the North Cascades
by Ira Spring and Harvey Manning, The Mountaineers, 1985, 240 pages, paper, $9.95
100 Hikes in the South Cascades and Olympics
by Ira Spring and Harvey Manning, The Mountaineers, 1985, 240 pages, paper, $9.95
These four titles are part of the excellent Mountaineers Hiking

Guide series, which is reviewed in more detail under "Series Reviews."

Places to Go With Children Around Puget Sound

by Elton Welke, Chronicle Books, 1986, 104 pages, paper, $7.95

This book is part of the Places to Go With Children Guide series, which is reviewed in more detail under "Series Reviews."

Poorman's Gourmet Guide to Seattle Restaurants

by Bob Chieger, Homestead Publishing, 1986, 115 pages, paper, $4.95

Good food for a cheap price—that's the focus of this tiny, backpocket guidebook. Good write-ups and all the practical information are included.

Roadside Geology of Washington

by David Alt and Donald Hyndman, Mountain Press, 1984, 320 pages, paper, $9.95

This book is part of the excellent Roadside Geology Guide series, which is reviewed in more detail under "Series Reviews."

The San Juan Islands Afoot & Afloat

by Marge Mueller, The Mountaineers, 1986, 224 pages, paper, $9.95

This is an excellent, detailed recreation guide to the nooks and crannies of these most popular islands—their history, parks, and facilities, and suggested tours, hikes, and other explorations. Included are good detail maps, revealing photos, and information on how to reach the islands by ferry, car, boat, or air.

Seattle Best Places

by David Brewster, Sasquatch Books, 1988 (4th ed.), 309 pages, paper, $10.95

This is the top-notch companion volume to the near-classic *Northwest Best Places*. Restaurant and lodging reviews are handled the same way in both volumes (please read the review under "The Pacific Northwest"), but *Seattle Best Places* covers much more, particularly other kinds of establishments and activities that deserve the rating "best": shops, entertainment, the arts, outings, nightlife, sightseeing, etc. The recommendations in all categories are sharp and decisive; the numbers of options so great that travelers will never run out of places to eat or sleep, or things to do. The detail maps are excellent and a separate fold-out map of the downtown area has traditionally been included. This title is updated every two years.

Seattle Cheap Eats: 230 Terrific Bargain Eateries
by Kathryn Robinson, Sasquatch Books, 1988 (3rd ed.), 144 pages, paper, $7.95

The publishers of the excellent *Northwest Best Places* and *Seattle Best Places* have concentrated on food in this superb, informative guide to Seattle. The reviews are extremely well done. Very useful indices group restaurants by neighborhood, cuisine, and other features. *Seattle Cheap Eats* is simply wonderful. The book will be updated every two years.

Seattle Epicure
Peanut Butter Publishing, 1986, 160 pages, paper, $7.95

This is one of the Epicure Guide series, which is reviewed in more detail under "Series Reviews." The series is updated frequently.

Seattle Guidebook
by Archie Satterfield, The Globe Pequot Press, 1987 (6th ed.), 240 pages, paper, $9.95

This is a richly detailed guide to just about everything in the Seattle area, including history, sightseeing, walks, art in public places, sports, recreation, transportation, shopping, museums, entertainment, lodging, restaurants, and a whole lot more. This is an excellent, popular resource for both residents and visitors alike.

Seattle Rainy Day Guide
by Clifford Burke, Chronicle Books, 1983, 125 pages, paper, $6.95

This great, but unfortunately somewhat dated, resource guide is part of the Rainy Day Guide series, which is reviewed in more detail under "Series Reviews."

The Sierra Club Guide to the Natural Areas of Oregon and Washington
by John and Jean Perry, Sierra Club Books, 1983, 360 pages, paper, $9.95

This is one of the Sierra Club Natural Areas Guide series, which is reviewed in more detail under "Series Reviews."

South Puget Sound Afoot & Afloat
by Marge and Ted Mueller, The Mountaineers, 1983, 224 pages, paper, $8.95

The Muellers have assembled myriad ideas for fun in or on the multitude of tiny waterways around the South Puget Sound, whether approached on foot, bicycle, or boat. Enjoy the quiet backroads, coves and inlets, explore historic sites and marine life, or hike in organized park facilities. The choices are many and well detailed, although some specifics may have changed since 1983.

Special Places for the Discerning Traveler in Oregon, Washington, Idaho, Montana, British Columbia, California Wine Country
by Fred and Mardi Nystrom, Graphic Arts Center Publishing, 1986, 216 pages, paper, $13.95
    See "The Pacific Northwest."

Sunset Washington Travel Guide
Lane Publishing, 1987, 128 pages, paper, $8.95
    This large-format guide is part of the Sunset Travel Guide series, which is reviewed in more detail under "Series Reviews."

33 Hiking Trails: Southern Washington Cascades
by Don and Roberta Lowe, The Touchstone Press, 1985, 80 pages, paper, $7.95
    This book is part of the Touchstone Hiking Guide series, which is reviewed in more detail under "Series Reviews."

Trips and Trails: Family Camps, Short Hikes, & View Roads Around the North Cascades
by E. M. Sterling, The Mountaineers, 1986 (3rd ed.), 228 pages, paper, $9.95
Trips and Trails: Family Camps, Short Hikes, & View Roads Around the Olympics, Mt. Rainer and South Cascades
by E. M. Sterling, The Mountaineers, 1983, 228 pages, paper, $9.95
    Washington is full of great family camping sites, hikes appropriate to groups of all ages, and spectacular scenery. Sterling has put together a fantastic collection of the best that the state has to offer in these two volumes. Good descriptions, clear maps (no topographical maps, though), and helpful photographs make for two excellent resource guides.

Washington Free: A Guide to the Best of the State's Cost Free Attractions
by Kiki Canniff, KI-2 Enterprises, 1984, 316 pages, paper, $9.95
    Here are a wide variety of things to do and see that are admission-free (or at least were in 1984). Arranged regionally, this book contains many ideas.

Washington in Your Pocket

by Kiki Canniff, KI-2 Enterprises, 1986, 80 pages, paper, $4.95

This is a handy collection of excursion ideas in the northwest corner of the state written at the time of Expo '86 for visitors coming from the Vancouver area.

Washington Public Shore Guide

by Marine Waters, University of Washington Press, 1986, 348 pages, paper, $14.95

This is a comprehensive compilation of the vast number of beach and shoreline locations available to the public throughout the Puget Sound, including the many islands of the area and the Pacific Ocean coastline. With narrative, detail maps, and helpful charts, travelers can discover where each location is situated, how large it is, and what facilities, activities, and types of shoreline are available (rock beach, sand beach, mud beach, sand dunes, tidepools, wetlands, bluffs). Copious resource information is also included on wildlife refuges, beach hiking, tides, etc. This is a fantastic resource to this complex and sometimes confusing area. From time to time, to keep information up-to-date between printings, supplements are included with the book.

Washington Whitewater, 2: A Guide to Seventeen of Washington's Lesser-Known Whitewater Trips

by Douglass North, The Mountaineers, 1987, 176 pages, paper, $9.95

This is a fine, carefully prepared guide. Included are mile-by-mile river maps, water-level curves, access points, car-shuttle points, rapids, landmarks, hazards, campsites, etc.

Webster's Wine Tours: California, Oregon and Washington

by Bob Thompson, Prentice Hall Press, 1987, 200 pages, cloth (flexible), $15.95

This book is part of the Webster's Wine Tours series, which is reviewed in more detail under "Series Reviews."

WASHINGTON, D.C.

See "District of Columbia."

WEST VIRGINIA

See also "The Mid-Atlantic States" and "United States as a Whole."

Circuit Hikes in Virginia, West Virginia, Maryland, and Pennsylvania
Potomac Appalachian Trail Club, 1986 (4th ed.), 88 pages, paper, $5.00

This fine pocket guide to hiking fun is part of the Circuit Hikes Guide series, which is reviewed in more detail under "Series Reviews."

Fifty Hikes in West Virginia: Short Walks, Day Hikes and Overnights in the Mountain State and Western Maryland
by Ann and Jim McGraw, Backcountry Publications, 1986, 208 pages, paper, $9.95

This book is part of the Backcountry Fifty Hikes series, which is reviewed in more detail under "Series Reviews."

Hiking the Mountain State: The Trails of West Virginia
by Allen de Hart, Appalachian Mountain Club, 1986, 340 pages, paper, $12.95

This book is part of the AMC Hiking Guide series, which is reviewed in more detail under "Series Reviews."

A Walker's Guide to Harpers Ferry, West Virginia
by Dave Gilbert, Pictorial Histories Publishing, 1983, 74 pages, paper, $4.95

This is a good walking guide through this historic spot, with plenty of information and separate historical pieces interspersed throughout.

WISCONSIN
See also "The Midwest" and "United States as a Whole."

All Season Guide to Wisconsin's Parks: Forests, Recreation Areas & Trails
by Jim Umhoefer, Northword, Inc., 1982, 80 pages, paper, $8.95

This is a large-format compendium of Wisconsin parks—their location, highlights, facilities, and recreational opportunities. Most of this information should still be useful in spite of the publication date.

Best Canoe Trails of Southern Wisconsin
by Michael Duncanson, Wisconsin Trails, 1974, 68 pages, paper, $9.95

This is a large-format book covering 16 rivers with maps, descriptions, access points, and other details.

Best Wisconsin Bike Trips: 30 Best One-Day Tours for Young and Old

by Phil Van Valkenberg, Wisconsin Trails, 1985, 80 pages, paper, $9.95

This is a large-format book with excellent, easy-to-read maps and well-written trip notes, including interesting places to visit along the route. Routes for both mountain bikes and on-road bikes are included. Parks, camping, swimming, even 24-hour traffic volumes on various highways are noted on each map—a real help in planning. An excellent resource for day-trip riding fun.

Biking the Great Lake Islands

by Kathleen and Lawrence Abrams, Entwood Publishing, 1985, 164 pages, paper, $8.95

Including several islands that are part of Wisconsin, this book is reviewed under "Michigan."

Covered Bridges in Illinois, Iowa and Wisconsin

by Leslie Swanson, Swanson Publishing, 1970, 48 pages, paper, $3.00

This is a great little booklet on the many covered bridges remaining in these Midwestern states.

Milwaukee Dining

by Willard Romantini, Chicago Review Press, 1987, 206 pages, paper, $9.95

This is a first-class guide to Milwaukee and its surrounding suburbs. Written by knowledgable *Milwaukee Magazine* restaurant critic Willard Romantini, it provides native and visitor alike with a diverse selection of eateries that have met his criteria for quality—a stamp of approval long recognized for its accuracy. The cuisines represented go far beyond the expected meat-and-potatoes variety, and the price ranges run the gamut in this excellent review of over 160 exciting spots to dine. All the practical facts are there, too, including information on access for the handicapped.

Room at the Inn Wisconsin: Guide to Wisconsin's Historic B&Bs and Country Inns

by Laura Zahn, Down to Earth Publications, 1987, 224 pages, paper, $9.95

This is a delightfully written guide to 86 inns and bed and breakfasts in every corner of the state. Included are a nice photograph, the necessary practical data, and driving times from Chicago, Madison, Milwaukee, and the Twin Cities. The author has personally visited each selection and has accepted no fee for inclusion in this book.

The Sierra Club Naturalist's Guide to the North Woods of Michigan, Wisconsin, Minnesota, and Southern Ontario
by Glenda Daniel and Jerry Sullivan, Sierra Club Books, 1981, 384 pages, paper, $10.95
This book is part of the Sierra Club Naturalist's Guide series, which is reviewed in more detail under "Series Reviews."

Ski Minnesota: A Cross-Country Skier's Guide to Minnesota, Northern Wisconsin and Michigan's Upper Peninsula
by Elizabeth and Gary Noren, Nodin Press, 1985, 424 pages, paper, $11.95
See "Minnesota."

WYOMING ———————————————————————————————

See also "The Rocky Mountain/Great Basin States" and "United States as a Whole."

Climbing and Hiking the Wind River Mountains
by Joe Kelsey, Sierra Club Books, 1980, 400 pages, paper, $9.95
This is one of the Sierra Club Hiking Totebook series, which is reviewed in more detail under "Series Reviews."

A Field Guide to Yellowstone's Geysers, Hot Springs and Fumaroles
by Carl Schreier, Homestead Publishing, 1987, 96 pages, paper, $9.95
This is an excellent, compact guide filled with beautiful color photographs of the many pools, geysers, and fumaroles (holes in volcanic regions through which gases and vapor escape). Good descriptions of each location and clear maps help travelers locate each one throughout the park.

Grand Teton Explorer's Guide
by Carl Schreier, Homestead Publishing, 1982, 48 pages, paper, $4.95
This book is part of the Park Explorer's Guide series, which is reviewed in more detail under "Series Reviews."

Grand Teton National Park: Guide and Reference Book
by Cliff McAdams, Caxton Publishers, 1983, 86 pages, paper, $7.95
This is a good overview of geology, flora, fauna, places to see, things to do, and hiking opportunities. A single contour map locates various trails which are briefly commented on.

Hiking the Teton Backcountry
by Paul Lawrence, Sierra Club Books, 1973, 160 pages, paper, $6.95

Hiking the Yellowstone Backcountry
by Orville Bach, Jr., Sierra Club Books, 1973, 240 pages, paper, $8.95

Both of these titles are part of the Sierra Club Hiking Totebook series, which is reviewed in more detail under "Series Reviews."

The Lakes of Yellowstone: A Guide for Hiking, Fishing, & Exploring
by Steve Pierce, The Mountaineers, 1987, 200 pages, paper, $9.95

This is a superbly done guide to the many lakes in our first national park. Detail maps to each region of the park show the locations of trails near the various lakes. Each lake is described, along with its various access routes, appropriate topographical maps, types of fish, size, depth, and elevation noted.

Roadside Geology of Wyoming
Mountain Press, 1988, 250 pages, paper, $9.95
Roadside Geology of Yellowstone Country
by William Fritz, Mountain Press, 1985, 160 pages, paper, $8.95

These two titles are part of the excellent Roadside Geology Guide series, which is reviewed in more detail under "Series Reviews." *Roadside Geology of Wyoming* was released after press time so the price and number of pages are approximate.

The Sierra Club Guide to the Natural Areas of Idaho, Montana and Wyoming
by John and Jane Perry, Sierra Club Books, 1988, 416 pages, paper, $10.95

This is one of the Sierra Club Natural Areas Guide series, which is reviewed in more detail under "Series Reviews."

Wyoming Historical Tour Guide
by D. Ray Wilson, Crossroads Communications, 1984, 264 pages, paper, $9.95

This book is part of the Historical Tour Guide series, which is reviewed in more detail under "Series Reviews."

Yellowstone Explorer's Guide
by Carl Schreier, Homestead Publishing, 1983, 52 pages, paper, $4.95

This book is part of the Park Explorer's Guide series, which is reviewed in more detail under "Series Reviews."

Oceania

OCEANIA AS A WHOLE

See also "The World." Comprising New Zealand and the islands of the South Pacific. Australia is listed separately.

Adventuring in the Pacific: The Sierra Club Travel Guide to the Islands of Polynesia, Melanesia, and Micronesia
by Susanna Margolis, Sierra Club Books, 1988, 400 pages, paper, $12.95
  This is a new addition to the Sierra Club Adventure Travel Guide series, which is reviewed in more detail under "Series Reviews." It includes information on history and natural history, cultural profiles, and recreation opportunities for each of 15 island nations.

Fisher's World: Australia, New Zealand, and the South Pacific
by John McLeod, Fisher's World, Inc., 1988, 336 pages, paper, $14.95
  Including, Fiji, the Samoas, and French Polynesia, this book is part of the Fisher's World Guide series, which is reviewed in more detail under "Series Reviews." The series is updated annually.

Fodor's Australia, New Zealand & the South Pacific
Fodor's Travel Publications, 1987, 628 pages, paper, $15.95
Fodor's South Pacific
Fodor's Travel Publications, 1988, 192 pages, paper, $7.95
  These two titles are part of Fodor's Country/Regional Guide series, which is reviewed in more detail under "Series Reviews." The series is updated annually.

Frommer's Dollarwise Guide to the South Pacific
by W. P. Goodwin, Jr., Prentice Hall Press, 1987, 275 pages, paper, $12.95
This book is part of Frommer's Dollarwise Guide series, which is reviewed in more detail under "Series Reviews." These guides emphasize selections in the moderate price category and are updated every two years.

Shopping in the Exotic South Pacific: Your Passport to Exciting Australia, New Zealand, Papua New Guinea, Tonga, Fiji, Tahiti, and the Solomon Islands
by Ronald Krannich, *et al.*, Impact Publications, 1989, 450 pages, paper, $13.95
This is an anticipated, new title in the excellent Shopping in Exotic Places series, which is reviewed in more detail under "Series Reviews." The series is updated every two years. Price and number of pages are approximate.

South Pacific Handbook
by David Stanley, Moon Publications, 1986, 578 pages, paper, $13.95
One of the great travel guides anywhere, this is part of the superb Moon Handbook series, which is reviewed in more detail under "Series Reviews." This series is updated every two years.

Sunset: Islands of the South Pacific
Lane Publishing, 1979, 128 pages, paper, $7.95
Sunset: South Pacific Travel Guide
Lane Publishing, 1986, 384 pages, paper, $14.95
These two titles are best for orientation and planning, and are part of the Sunset Travel Guide series, which is reviewed in more detail under "Series Reviews."

COUNTRIES OF OCEANIA

THE COOK ISLANDS

See also "Oceania as a Whole."

How to Get Lost & Found in the Cook Islands
by John and Bobbye McDermott, Hunter Publishing, 1986 (2nd ed.), 212 pages, paper, $9.95
This book is part of the delightfully different Lost & Found Guide series, which is reviewed in more detail under "Series Reviews."

Rarotonga & the Cook Islands: A Travel Survival Kit
by Tony Wheeler, Lonely Planet Publications, 1986, 113 pages, paper, $7.95

This book is part of the popular Travel Survival Kit series, which is reviewed in more detail under "Series Reviews." The series is updated every two to three years.

FIJI
See also "Oceania as a Whole."

Fiji: A Travel Survival Kit
by Rob Kay, Lonely Planet Publications, 1986, 192 pages, paper, $7.95

Another quality guide from the author of the highly praised *Tahiti & French Polynesia: A Travel Survival Kit*, this book is part of the popular Travel Survival Kit series, which is reviewed in more detail under "Series Reviews." The series is updated every two to three years.

Finding Fiji
by David Stanley, Moon Publications, 1986, 123 pages, paper, $6.95

The author of the classic *South Pacific Handbook* develops his substantial section on Fiji still further in this separate book. This book title is different, but the format and content fit clearly into the excellent Moon Handbook series, which is reviewed in more detail under "Series Reviews." This series is updated every two years.

How to Get Lost & Found in Fiji
by John McDermott, Hunter Publishing, 1984 (4th ed.), 195 pages, paper, $9.95

This book is part of the Lost & Found Guide series, which is reviewed in more detail under "Series Reviews."

MICRONESIA
See also "Oceania as a Whole." Comprising the Caroline Islands, Kiribati Islands, Mariana Islands, Marshall Islands, Palau Islands, and Senyavin Islands.

Guide to the National Park Areas: Western States
by David and Kay Scott, The Globe Pequot Press, 1987, 272 pages, paper, $9.95

Including Guam, one of the Mariana Islands, this book is reviewed under "The Southwest" (U.S.A.).

Micronesia: A Travel Survival Kit

by Glenda Bendure and Ned Friary, Lonely Planet Publications, 1988, 190 pages, paper, $8.95

This is one of the popular Travel Survival Kit series, which is reviewed in more detail under "Series Reviews." As it was released after press time, the number of pages is approximate. This book is updated every two to three years.

Micronesia Handbook

by David Stanley, Moon Publications, 1985, 238 pages, paper, $7.95

This book is part of the uniformly superb Moon Handbook series, which is reviewed in more detail under "Series Reviews." Moon's new policy is to update every two years, but a new edition of this title has not been announced.

NEW ZEALAND

See also "Oceania as a Whole."

ABC Air Asia, Australia & New Zealand

ABC International, monthly editions, 250 pages, paper, $7.00

This is the book of schedules for travelers needing to make many connections and having to be their own travel agent.

Bed & Breakfast New Zealand

by Elizabeth Hansen, Chronicle Books, 1987, 230 pages, paper, $8.95

This is an excellent guide to the best lodging at B&B inns, country lodges, historic hotels, private homes and even farms on both the North and South Islands in various price ranges.

Berlitz: New Zealand

Macmillan Publishing, 1984, 128 pages, paper, $6.95

This book is one of the small-format Berlitz Guide series, which is reviewed in greater detail under "Series Reviews."

Fisher's World: Australia, New Zealand, and the South Pacific

by John McLeod, Fisher's World, Inc., 1988, 336 pages, paper, $14.95

This book is part of the Fisher's World Guide series, which is reviewed in more detail under "Series Reviews." The series is updated annually.

Fodor's New Zealand
 Fodor's Travel Publications, 1987, 128 pages, paper, $7.95
 This book is part of Fodor's Country/Regional Guide series, which is reviewed in more detail under "Series Reviews." The series is updated annually.

Frommer's New Zealand on $40 a Day
 by Susan Poole, Prentice Hall Press, 1988, 240 pages, paper, $11.95
 This book is part of the budget-oriented Frommer's Dollar-a-Day Guide series, which is reviewed in more detail under "Series Reviews." The series is updated every two years.

Golf Courses of Auckland
 ISBS, 1984, 47 pages, paper, $4.95
Golf Courses of Canterbury
 ISBS, 1984, 48 pages, paper, $4.95
Golf Courses of Marlborough, Nelson & Wesland
 ISBS, 1984, 31 pages, paper, $4.95
Golf Courses of Otago
 ISBS, 1984, 44 pages, paper, $4.95
Golf Courses of South Canterbury
 ISBS, 1984, 34 pages, paper, $4.95
Golf Courses of Southland and Fiordland
 ISBS, 1984, 32 pages, paper, $4.95
Golf Courses of Wellington
 ISBS, 1984, 47 pages, paper, $4.95
 This series of booklets covering the golf courses of New Zealand includes a course description, a general course layout map, and information on how to get there.

Hildebrand's Travel Guide: New Zealand
 Hunter Publishing, 1987, 192 pages, paper, $10.95
 This is one of the Hildebrand's Guide series, which is reviewed in more detail under "Series Reviews."

How to Get Lost & Found in Upgraded New Zealand
 by John and Bobbye McDermott, Hunter Publishing, 1986 (2nd ed.), 335 pages, paper, $9.95
 This book, a sequel to the widely acclaimed first edition, is part of the delightfully different Lost & Found Guide series, which is reviewed in more detail under "Series Reviews."

Insight Guide: New Zealand

by Apa Productions, Prentice Hall Press, 1986, 339 pages, paper,
$16.95

This is one of the highly regarded Insight Guide series, which is
reviewed in more detail under "Series Reviews."

The Maverick Guide to New Zealand

by Robert Bone, Pelican Publishing, 1987 (5th ed.), 308 pages,
paper, $11.95

This is one of the excellent Maverick Guide series, which is reviewed in more detail under "Series Reviews." This guide is updated
every two years.

Mobil New Zealand Travel Guide: North Island

by Diana and Jeremy Pope, Hunter Publishing, 1987, 327 pages,
paper, $14.95

Mobil New Zealand Travel Guide: South Island, Stewart Island and the Chatham Islands

by Diana and Jeremy Pope, Hunter Publishing, 1987, 423 pages,
paper, $14.95

When these quality books first came out, they had no American
distributor. Now, however, they are available through Hunter Publishing and are much more accessible. Up-to-date and very detailed,
these two guides are packed with information on what to see and
do in the big cities, tiny towns, and mountain and coastal playgrounds. They also include plenty of history, natural history, geology,
and folklore—all supplemented with lots of town and regional maps.

New Zealand: A Travel Survival Kit

by Tony Wheeler, Lonely Planet Publications, 1985, 246 pages,
paper, $7.95

This book is part of the popular Travel Survival Kit series, which
is reviewed in more detail under "Series Reviews." These guides are
generally updated every two to three years.

New Zealand Handbook

by Jane King, Moon Publications, 1987, 512 pages, paper, $13.95

This book is a wonderful new addition to the always superb Moon
Handbook series, which is reviewed in more detail under "Series
Reviews." The series is updated every two years.

New Zealand in 22 Days

See *22 Days in New Zealand* below.

A Personal Kiwi-Yankee Dictionary for the New Zealand Traveler
by Louis Leland, Pelican Publishing, 1984, 115 pages, paper, $4.95
This is the perfect book for travelers hoping to fit in with the natives by speaking their language—it is the alternative to the blank stare.

Sunset: New Zealand Travel Guide
Lane Publishing, 1984, 128 pages, paper, $9.95
Basically an orientation and planning book, this book is part of the Sunset Travel Guide series, which is reviewed in more detail under "Series Reviews."

A Tramper's Guide to New Zealand's National Parks
by R. Burton and M. Atkinson, Hunter Publishing, 1987, 243 pages, paper, $12.95
These walks are in all twelve national parks of New Zealand—from the easiest strolls to serious backpacks. Each hike or walk is rated and described in detail. Several color maps accompany the text in this useful resource book.

Tramping in New Zealand
by Jim DuFresne, Lonely Planet Publications, 1982, 168 pages, paper, $6.95
This quality guide to backpacking all over New Zealand provides the information needed to enjoy all sorts of hikes of varied length and difficulty.

The Traveler's Guide to Asian Customs and Manners
by Elizabeth Devine and Nancy Braganti, St. Martin's Press, 1986, 315 pages, paper, $9.95
Including New Zealand, this book is reviewed under "Asia as a Whole."

The Travellers' Guide to Pubs of the North Island
by Ian Jenkins, ISBS, 1984, 228 pages, paper, $9.95
This book, organized by region, reviews a wide array of places to drink, to eat, and to sleep. A bit dated, it will nonetheless be a great help to the North Island traveler.

22 Days in New Zealand: The Itinerary Planner
by Arnold Schuchter, John Muir Publications, 1988, 136 pages, paper, $6.95
This is a new title in the Itinerary Planner series, which is reviewed in more detail under "Series Reviews." The title has recently changed and this book may be found under *New Zealand in 22 Days.*

The Walking Tracks of New Zealand's National Parks

by John Cobb, ISBS, 1987, 208 pages, cloth, $34.95

This hardback book is not the kind to carry along with on a hike, but it contains some great ideas for walks and short hikes throughout the national parks of New Zealand. No detailed maps are included, but the starting point of each walk/hike is described, as are as some of the points along the way. Numerous color photos are provided.

The Woman's Travel Guide to New Zealand

by Elizabeth Hansen, ISBS, 1984, 159 pages, paper, $9.95

This book covers every topic—hotels, restaurants, sightseeing and more—from a woman's point of view. Unfortunately, some specifics will be out-of-date, but the well-organized book should still prove useful.

TAHITI AND FRENCH POLYNESIA

See also "Oceania as a Whole."

Cruising Guide to Tahiti and the French Society Islands

by Marcia Davock, Wescott Cove Publishing, 1985, 272 pages, paper, $29.95

This large-format, spiral-bound guide is part of the Cruising Guide series, which is reviewed in more detail under "Series Reviews."

How to Get Lost & Found in Tahiti

by John McDermott, Hunter Publishing, 1986 (2nd ed.), 247 pages, paper, $9.95

This book is part of the Lost & Found Guide series, which is reviewed in more detail under "Series Reviews."

Tahiti: A Complete Travel Guide to All of the Islands

by Vicki Poggioli, Hippocrene Books, 1987, 142 pages, paper, $9.95

This book is a solid, moderately detailed, all-purpose guide to Tahiti, Moorea, Bora Bora, and other islands. The restaurants and hotels selected have good descriptions and are in various price categories.

Tahiti & French Polynesia: A Travel Survival Kit

by Robert Kay, Lonely Planet Publications, 1985, 136 pages, paper, $7.95

This is a widely praised title in the well-known Travel Survival Kit series, which is reviewed in more detail under "Series Reviews." This series is expected to be updated every two to three years.

South America

SOUTH AMERICA AS A WHOLE

See also "The World." Guidebooks to "South America as a Whole" include all nations unless otherwise noted. Any of the islands of South America included are specifically noted.

Birnbaum's South America
by Stephen Birnbaum, Houghton Mifflin, 1987, 800 pages, paper, $12.95
This is one of the excellent Birnbaum's Guide series, which is reviewed in more detail under "Series Reviews." This book includes Easter Island, the Galapagos Islands, the Falkland Islands, and the Juan Fernandez Islands. The series is updated annually.

Fodor's South America
Fodor's Travel Guides, 1987, 640 pages, paper, $14.95
This is part of Fodor's Country/Regional Guide series, which is reviewed in more detail under "Series Reviews." This includes Easter Island and the Galapagos Islands. The series is updated annually.

Frommer's South America on $30 a Day
by Arnold and Harriet Greenberg, Prentice Hall Press, 1987, 432 pages, paper, $10.95
This is a particularly good title in the budget-oriented Frommer's Dollar-a-Day Guide series, which is reviewed in more detail under "Series Reviews." Including Easter Island and the Galapagos Islands, this guide is updated every two years.

Latin America on Bicycle
by J. P. Panet, Passport Press, 1987, 156 pages, paper, $12.95
This fine little guide for cycling adventurers is reviewed under "Central America as a Whole."

South America On a Shoestring
by Geoff Crowther, Lonely Planet Publications, 1986 (2nd ed.), 734 pages, paper, $14.95

While many of the Lonely Planet titles receive consistent praise, this one has received more than its share of criticism from travelers reporting back to their local travel bookstore. Since Lonely Planet prides itself in being responsive to its readers—their quarterly *Lonely Planet Update* highlights reader comments (see "Series Review" for details)—it seems strange that there should be so many complaints. In any case, they are most likely working hard to rectify the situation in the next edition. This title is one of the On a Shoestring Guide series, which is reviewed in more detail under "Series Reviews." This title includes Easter Island and the Galapagos Islands, and excludes Suriname and French Guiana. The series is updated every two to three years.

The South American Handbook (including Caribbean, Mexico, and Central America)
edited by John Brooks, Rand McNally & Co., 1988 (64th ed.), 1341 pages, cloth, $28.95

This famous, annual guide, the product of British ingenuity and know-how, has long been considered the definitive work on South America. The print is small, the number of pages formidable, the amount of information staggering (over a million words on more than 2000 cities in 32 countries), yet this remarkable hardback is amazingly compact and portable. It covers all the primary tourist bases well: hotels, restaurants, excursions, transportation, places of interest, health hints, and excellent tips and hints specific to each area. This book includes the Caribbean, Mexico, Central America, the Bahamas, and Bermuda. One of a kind, it is thoroughly updated each year.

Staying Healthy in Asia, Africa, and Latin America
by Dirk Schroeder, Volunteers in Asia, 1988, 168 pages, paper, $8.95

This excellent third world health guide is reviewed under "Africa as a Whole."

COUNTRIES OF SOUTH AMERICA

ARGENTINA

See also "South America as a Whole."

Buenos Aires Alive
by Arnold and Harriet Greenberg, Alive Publications, 1988, 300 pages, paper, $10.95

The authors of *Frommer's South America, Brazil On Your Own,* and *Israel On Your Own* are reviving their excellent, self-published "Alive Guide" series in 1988 with three initial titles. The series is reviewed in more detail under "Series Reviews." As it was released after press time, the number of pages is approximate.

Michael's Guide: Argentina, Chile, Paraguay, & Uruguay
by Michael Shichor, Hunter Publishing, 1987, 222 pages, paper, $7.95

This book is part of the Michael's Guide series, which is reviewed in more detail under "Series Reviews."

BOLIVIA

See also "South America as a Whole."

Adventuring in the Andes: The Sierra Club Travel Guide to Ecuador, Peru, Bolivia, the Amazon Basin, and the Galapagos Islands
by Charles Frazier, Sierra Club Books, 1986, 278 pages, paper, $10.95

This book is part of the Sierra Club Adventure Travel Guide series, which is reviewed in more detail under "Series Reviews."

Backpacking and Trekking in Peru and Bolivia
by Hilary Bradt, Hunter Publishing, 1987, 150 pages, paper, $11.95

This is one of the Hunter Walking/Hiking Guide series, which is reviewed in more detail under "Series Reviews."

Michael's Guide: Bolivia, Peru
by Michael Shichor, Hunter Publishing, 1987, 222 pages, paper, $7.95

This is part of Michael's Guide series, which is reviewed in more detail under "Series Reviews."

Nagel's Bolivia
Passport Books, 1980, 239 pages, cloth, $39.95

This classic, cultural guide is part of the Nagel's Guide series, which is reviewed in more detail under "Series Reviews."

A Traveler's Guide to El Dorado and the Inca Empire

by Lynn Meisch, Viking Penguin, 1984 (revised ed.), 448 pages, paper, $14.95

This excellent guide includes Bolivia and is reviewed under "Peru."

BRAZIL

See also "South America as a Whole."

Adventuring in the Andes: The Sierra Club Travel Guide to Ecuador, Peru, Bolivia, the Amazon Basin, and the Galapagos Islands

by Charles Frazier, Sierra Club Books, 1986, 278 pages, paper, $10.95

This book is part of the Sierra Club Adventure Travel Guide series, which is reviewed in more detail under "Series Reviews."

Berlitz: Rio de Janeiro

Macmillan Publishing, 1981, 128 pages, paper, $6.95

This is one of the small-format Berlitz Guide series, which is reviewed in more detail under "Series Reviews."

Brazil On Your Own

by Arnold Greenberg, Passport Books, 1988, 480 pages, paper, $12.95

This is the second of the On Your Own Guide series to be released. The focus of this series is on independent, adventurous travelers of any age, looking for for a guidebook that will take them to destinations and points of interest less frequented by mainstream travelers. To facilitate this, a major emphasis is placed on orientation—both to the realities of today and to a more historical perspective. Coverage runs the gamut, with a wide selection of hotels and restaurants in most price categories (for hotels, "inexpensive" translates to under $60 double, so this is hardly for true budget travelers). Included are shopping tips, excursions, walks, sightseeing, nightlife, and those don't-miss special events. Notes on history, culture, folklore, and a general orientation are provided for most of the cities covered—Rio de Janeiro, Salvador, Manaus, Brasilia, Iguacu Falls, Sao Paulo, Recife, Curitiba, Pantanal, and Porto Alegre. The text is enjoyable, informative, and easy to use.

Fodor's Brazil

Fodor's Travel Publications, 1987, 208 pages, paper, $13.95

This book is part of Fodor's Country/Regional Guide series, which is reviewed in more detail under "Series Reviews." The series is updated annually.

Fodor's Fun in Rio
Fodor's Travel Publications, 1987, 160 pages, paper, $6.95
This book is part of Fodor's Fun Guide series, which is reviewed in more detail under "Series Reviews." The series is updated annually.

The Insider's Guide to Rio de Janeiro
by Christopher Pickard, Luso-Brazilian Books, 1987, numbered by section, paper, $12.95
Begun in 1984, this guide is written and published in Rio de Janeiro and updated annually. It is arranged by section—facts, hotels, eating out, sports, shopping, places of interest, history, day trips and walks, transportation—with each section numbered separately. The reviews are informative and hotels and eating spots in all price ranges are carefully rated. The maps are complete and quite detailed.

Michael's Guide: Brazil
by Michael Shichor, Hunter Publishing, 1987, 192 pages, paper, $8.95
This is one of the Michael's Guide series, which is reviewed in more detail under "Series Reviews."

Nagel's Brazil
Passport Books, 1980, 479 pages, cloth, $39.95
This classic, cultural guide is part of the Nagel's Guide series, which is reviewed in more detail under "Series Reviews."

Rio Alive
by Arnold and Harriet Greenberg, Alive Publications, 1988, 396 pages, paper, $10.95
This is one of three initial titles in the recently revived Alive Guide series, written by the respected authors of *Frommer's South America* and other titles, which is reviewed in more detail under "Series Reviews."

CHILE
See also "South America as a Whole."

Chile & Easter Island: A Travel Survival Kit
by Alan Samagalski, Lonely Planet Publications, 1987, 277 pages, paper, $8.95
This is one of the newer additions to the popular Travel Survival Kit series, which is reviewed in more detail under "Series Reviews." The series is updated every two to three years.

Michael's Guide: Argentina, Chile, Paraguay & Uruguay
by Michael Shichor, Hunter Publishing, 1987, 222 pages, paper, $7.95

This is part of the Michael's Guide series, which is reviewed in more detail under "Series Reviews."

COLOMBIA
See also "South America as a Whole."

Birnbaum's Caribbean, Bermuda & the Bahamas
edited by Stephen Birnbaum, Houghton Mifflin, 1987, 786 pages, paper, $12.95

Including Colombia's Caribbean coast, this book is part of the excellent Birnbaum's Guide series, which is reviewed in more detail under "Series Reviews." The series is updated annually.

Michael's Guide: Ecuador, Colombia, Venezuela
by Michael Shichor, Hunter Publishing, 1987, 236 pages, paper, $7.95

This is one of the Michael's Guide series, which is reviewed in more detail under "Series Reviews."

A Traveler's Guide to El Dorado and the Inca Empire
by Lynn Meisch, Viking Penguin, 1984 (revised ed.), 448 pages, paper, $14.95

This excellent guide includes Colombia and is reviewed under "Peru."

Easter Island: See "Islands of South America" below.

ECUADOR
See also "South America as a Whole."

Adventuring in the Andes: The Sierra Club Travel Guide to Ecuador, Peru, Bolivia, the Amazon Basin, and the Galapagos Islands
by Charles Frazier, Sierra Club Books, 1986, 278 pages, paper, $10.95

This book is part of the Sierra Club Adventure Travel Guide series, which is reviewed in more detail under "Series Reviews."

Climbing and Hiking in Ecuador

by Rob Rachowiecki, Hunter Publishing, 1987, 160 pages, paper, $11.95

This book is part of the Hunter Walking/Hiking Guide series, which is reviewed in more detail under "Series Reviews."

Ecuador & the Galapagos Islands: A Travel Survival Kit

by Rob Rachowiecki, Lonely Planet Publications, 1986, 240 pages, paper, $7.95

This book is part of the well-known Travel Survival Kit series, which is reviewed in more detail under "Series Reviews." The series is updated every two to three years.

Michael's Guide: Ecuador, Colombia, Venezuela

by Michael Shichor, Hunter Publishing, 1987, 236 pages, paper, $7.95

This is one of the Michael's Guide series, which is reviewed in more detail under "Series Reviews."

A Traveler's Guide to El Dorado and the Inca Empire

by Lynn Meisch, Viking Penguin, 1984 (revised ed.), 448 pages, paper, $14.95

This excellent guide includes Ecuador and is reviewed under "Peru."

French Guiana: See "South America as a Whole."
Guyana: See "South America as a Whole."

ISLANDS OF SOUTH AMERICA

See also "South America as a Whole." Books on Easter Island and the Galapagos Islands are listed below. The Falkland Islands and Juan Fernandez Islands are included in several titles under "South America as a Whole."

Adventuring in the Andes: The Sierra Club Travel Guide to Ecuador, Peru, Bolivia, the Amazon Basin, and the Galapagos Islands

by Charles Frazier, Sierra Club Books, 1986, 278 pages, paper, $10.95

This book is part of the Sierra Club Adventure Travel Guide series, which is reviewed in more detail under "Series Reviews."

Chile & Easter Island: A Travel Survival Kit

by Alan Samagalski, Lonely Planet Publications, 1987, 277 pages, paper $8.95

Ecuador & the Galapagos Islands: A Travel Survival Kit
by Rob Rachowiecki, Lonely Planet Publications, 1986, 240 pages,
paper, $7.95
These books are part of the well-known Travel Survival Kit series,
which is reviewed in more detail under "Series Reviews." The series
is updated every two to three years.

Falkland Islands: See "South America as a Whole."
Galapagos Islands: See "Islands of South America."
Juan Fernandez Islands: See "South America as a Whole."

PARAGUAY

See also "South America as a Whole."

Michael's Guide: Argentina, Colombia, Paraguay & Uruguay
by Michael Shichor, Hunter Publishing, 1987, 222 pages, paper,
$7.95
This is one of the Michael's Guide series, which is reviewed in
more detail under "Series Reviews."

PERU

See also "South America as a Whole."

**Adventuring in the Andes: The Sierra Club Travel Guide to Ecuador,
Peru, Bolivia, the Amazon Basin, and the Galapagos Islands**
by Charles Frazier, Sierra Club Books, 1986, 278 pages, paper,
$10.95
This book is part of the Sierra Club Adventure Travel Guide series,
which is reviewed in more detail under "Series Reviews."

Apus & Incas: A Cultural Walking & Trekking Guide to Cuzco, Peru
written and published by Charles Brod, 1986, 147 pages, paper,
$9.95
After a good orientation to the area, including the types of foods
available, problems that can be encountered, and the best maps to
obtain, Brod offers a variety of walks and treks ranging from four to
five hours and 8 km to a major trek of seven to eight days and 160
km. Six of the walks are one day or less. Each choice is nicely
described (as is the quickest way to get to the starting point) and
total elevation lost and gained is noted. *Apus & Incas* will help bring
this ancient Inca capital alive.

Backpacking and Trekking in Peru and Bolivia
by Hilary Bradt, Hunter Publishing, 1987, 150 pages, paper, $11.95
This is one of the Hunter Walking/Hiking Guide series, which is
reviewed in more detail under "Series Reviews."

Michael's Guide: Bolivia, Peru
by Michael Shichor, Hunter Publishing, 1987, 222 pages, paper, $7.95
This book is part of the Michael's Guide series, which is reviewed in more detail under "Series Reviews."

Nagel's Peru
Passport Books, 1978, 250 pages, cloth, $39.95
This classic, cultural guide is one of the Nagel's Guide series, which is reviewed in more detail under "Series Reviews."

Peru: A Travel Survival Kit
by Rob Rachowiecki, Lonely Planet Publications, 1987, 378 pages, paper, $12.95
This book is a newer addition to the popular Travel Survival Kit series, which is reviewed in more detail under "Series Reviews." The series is updated every two to three years.

The Rough Guide to Peru
by Dilwyn Jenkins, Routledge & Kegan Paul, 1986, 264 pages, paper, $10.95
This book is part of the excellent Rough Guide series, which is reviewed in more detail under "Series Reviews." The series is updated every two to three years.

A Traveler's Guide to El Dorado and the Inca Empire
by Lynn Meisch, Viking Penguin, 1984 (revised ed.), 448 pages, paper, $14.95
Called by the *New York Times* "a superbly practical guide," this well-done book tells how to get there, how to fit in, how to cut the red tape, how to stay comfortable and healthy, and how to experience and enjoy the rich native cultures of the Andes. Restaurants and hotels are dealt with more generally: how to get lodging and what foods to be sure to try. This is a well-organized, well-written, excellent guide. This revised edition came out three years after the first edition, so another update is a definite possibility.

Suriname: See "South America as a Whole."

URUGUAY

See also "South America as a Whole."

Michael's Guide: Argentina, Colombia, Paraguay & Uruguay
by Michael Shichor, Hunter Publishing, 1987, 222 pages, paper,
$7.95
    This is one of the Michael's Guide series, which is reviewed in
more detail under "Series Reviews."

VENEZUELA

See also "South America as a Whole."

Birnbaum's Caribbean, Bermuda & the Bahamas
edited by Stephen Birnbaum, Houghton Mifflin, 1987, 786 pages,
paper, $12.95
    Including Venezuela's Caribbean coast, this book is part of the
excellent Birnbaum's Guide series, which is reviewed in more detail
under "Series Reviews." The series is updated annually.

Michael's Guide: Ecuador, Colombia, Venezuela
by Michael Shichor, Hunter Publishing, 1987, 236 pages, paper,
$7.95
    This book is part of the Michael's Guide series, which is reviewed
in more detail under "Series Reviews."

West Indies and Bermuda
(including the Caribbean and Bahamas)

See also "The World." The islands of the West Indies include: the Bahamas; the Greater Antilles, consisting of Cuba, Hispaniola (the island comprising Haiti and the Dominican Republic), Jamaica, and Puerto Rico; and the Lesser Antilles, consisting of Trinidad, Barbados, Tobago, the Leeward Islands, the Windward Islands, and the islands to the north of Venezuela. Bermuda, lying far to the north, is not part of the West Indies, but is included in this section both for clarity and convenience.

REGIONS OF THE WEST INDIES

THE CARIBBEAN

The Caribbean includes all the islands of the West Indies except the Bahamas. Individual titles may or may not cover all the islands and do not, except where noted, include Cuba.

Baedeker's Caribbean
> Prentice Hall Press, undated, 250 pages, paper, $14.95
> This book is part of the Baedeker's Country/Regional Guide series, which is reviewed in more detail under "Series Reviews."

Bed and Breakfast in the Caribbean
> by Kathy Strong, The Globe Pequot Press, 1987 (2nd ed.), 278 pages, paper, $9.95
> This book has been given a new title with this edition, but is still part of the Bed and Breakfast Book series, which is reviewed in more detail under "Series Reviews." The series is updated every two years.

Berlitz Cruise Guide: Caribbean
Macmillan Publishing, 1986, 352 pages, paper, $8.95
This book is a good, solid overview of cruising options and ports of call throughout the Caribbean.

Berlitz: Southern Caribbean
Macmillan Publishing, 1981, 128 pages, paper, $6.95
This book is part of the small-format Berlitz Guide series, which is reviewed in more detail under "Series Reviews."

Best Places to Stay in the Caribbean
by Bill and Cheryl Jamison, The Harvard Common Press, 1989, 400 pages, paper, $14.95
An anticipated, 1989 addition to the Best Places to Stay Guide series, which is reviewed in more detail under "Series Reviews." The price and number of pages are approximate. No fees have been accepted for inclusion.

Birnbaum's Caribbean, Bermuda & the Bahamas
edited by Stephen Birnbaum, Houghton Mifflin, 1987, 786 pages, paper, $12.95
This book is part of the excellent Birnbaum's Guide series, which is reviewed in more detail under "Series Reviews." Note that this book also includes Cuba and the Caribbean coastal areas of Mexico, Colombia, and Venezuela. The series is updated annually.

Cadogan Guides: The Caribbean
by Frank Bellamy, The Globe Pequot Press, 1987, 358 pages, paper, $12.95
This book, once called *Caribbean Island Hopping* and part of the Island Hopping series, is a guide that has been thoroughly updated and made part of the respected Cadogan Guide series, which is reviewed in more detail under "Series Reviews." Bellamy's work, while certainly competent, is somewhat dry, but does include Cuba. The series is updated every two years.

Caribbean Ports of Call: A Guide for Today's Cruise Passenger
by Kay Showker, The Globe Pequot Press, 1987, 504 pages, paper, $14.95
This book is excellent for the cruise ship traveler to the Caribbean. It is a great help in planning and selecting the best cruise but also provides plenty of specifics on how to make the most of stays in ports of call. Each port of call section includes an overview, some quick facts, lists of attractions, a walking tour, shopping guides, and dining recommendations.

The Condo Lux Vacationer's Guide to Condominium Rentals in the Bahamas and the Caribbean Islands
by Jill Little, Random House, 1986, 303 pages, paper, $9.95
   This is one of the Condo Lux Guide series, which is reviewed in more detail under "Series Reviews."

Crown Insider's Guide: The Caribbean
by Virginia Puzzo, Crown Publishers, 1988, 336 pages, paper, $10.95
   This book is part of the Crown Insider's Guide series, which is reviewed in more detail under "Series Reviews."

Fielding's Caribbean
by Margaret Zellers, William Morrow & Co., 1988, 780 pages, paper, $12.95
   This book is for the traveler with at least a moderately sized travel budget. It has long been considered the best, most comprehensive guide to the area and is certainly the best guide in the Fielding Travel Guide series, which is reviewed in more detail under "Series Reviews." Zellers's stimulating and thoroughly researched guide also includes useful, up-to-date information on the political and social climates of each country. Purchasers of the book can also avail themselves of her quarterly newsletter to stay even more on top of things. This superb travel guide is updated annually.

Fisher's World: Caribbean
by Sandra Hart, Fisher's World, Inc., 1988, 329 pages, paper, $14.95
   This is one of the Fisher's World Guide series, which is reviewed in more detail under "Series Reviews." The series is updated annually.

Fodor's Caribbean
by Fodor's Travel Publications, 1987, 531 pages, paper, $13.95
   This book is part of Fodor's Country/Regional Guide series, which is reviewed in more detail under "Series Reviews." The series is updated annually.

Fodor's Great Travel Values: Caribbean
Fodor's Travel Publications, 1987, 256 pages, paper, $6.95
   This is one of the budget-oriented Fodor's Great Travel Values Guide series, which is reviewed in more detail under "Series Reviews." The series is updated annually.

Frommer's Dollarwise Guide to the Caribbean
by Darwin Porter, Prentice Hall Press, 1988, 683 pages, paper, $13.95
This book is part of Frommer's Dollarwise Guide series, which is reviewed in more detail under "Series Reviews." This series emphasizes selections in the moderate price range and is updated every two years.

Frommer's Shopper's Guide to the Caribbean
by Jeanne and Harry Harman, Prentice Hall Press, 1987, 558 pages, paper, $12.95
These 20-year residents of the Caribbean, experts on shopping, share their intimate knowledge of the best places to shop for every Caribbean specialty, including art, foods, and yes, of course, rum. Including street maps,they cover more than 2000 stores on over 30 islands.

Ian Keown's Caribbean Hideaways
by Ian Keown, Crown Publishers, 1988, 320 pages, paper, $12.95
This is an update of a great little guide to more than 100 of the most romantic inns, hotels, and resorts throughout the Caribbean. Keown is known for his "refreshingly frank and discriminating critiques," which, combined with good taste, make for an excellent guidebook.

The New Holiday Guide to the Caribbean and the Bahamas
M. Evans & Co., 1988 (10th ed.), 160 pages, paper, $4.95
This is part of the Holiday Guide series, which is reviewed in more detail under "Series Reviews."

The Penguin Guide to the Caribbean
edited by Alan Tucker, Viking Penguin, 1988, 224-448 pages, paper, $9.95-12.95
This is one of the initial eight titles in the new Penguin Travel Guide series, which is reviewed in more detail under "Series Reviews." Only price and page-count ranges for the entire series were available at press time.

Rum and Reggae: What's Hot and What's Not in the Caribbean
by Jonathan Runge, St. Martin's Press, 1988, 227 pages, paper, $9.95
Billed as the hip alternative to other Caribbean guides, *Rum and Reggae* is divided into chapters that focus on a particular activity or non-activity. The categories are scuba, hedonism (carnival time), cruising, cerebral (the Rastaman-reggae experience), golf, outdoors,

windsurfing, and hip (just hanging out at those really cool spots). For each orientation, specific destinations are suggested. After a revealing discussion of the ins and outs of the island, Runge lays out some good selections of hotels, restaurants, photo safaris, walks, etc. His evaluations are sharp, to the point, and fun to read. This is a fine guide for those who are looking for something a bit different.

The South American Handbook (including Caribbean, Mexico and Central America)
edited by John Brooks, Rand McNally & Co., 1988, 1341 pages, cloth, $28.95

This definitive single-volume guide to South America, covering the Caribbean and Cuba as well, is reviewed under "South America as a Whole." This book is updated annually.

Undiscovered Islands of the Caribbean
by Burl Willes, John Muir Publications, 1988, 209 pages, paper, $12.95

This interesting title, released after press time, covers 38 little-known islands off the Bahamas and Antilles, and the coasts of the Yucatan, Puerto Rico, Central America, and Venezuela that offer "undiscovered fishing villages, colorful marketplaces, friendly local people, and not a condo in sight."

A Walking Guide to the Caribbean: From the Virgin Islands to Martinique
by Leonard Adkins, Johnson Books, 1987, 172 pages, paper, $7.95

This excellent book has practical information for those who like to walk. Included are walks and hikes ranging from the short and easy to rugged efforts over every sort of Caribbean terrain. Plenty of natural history notes and the best beaches and swimming spots along the way are provided. A wide array of islands are included, both large and small.

FRENCH WEST INDIES

See also "The Caribbean." The French West Indies comprise Guadeloupe, Martinique, Desirade, Les Saintes, Marie Galante, St. Barthelemy, and part of St. Martin.

Berlitz: French West Indies
Macmillan Publishing, 1978, 128 pages, paper, $6.95

This book is part of the small-format Berlitz Guide series, which is reviewed in more detail under "Series Reviews."

Collier World Traveler Series: Mexico, Belize, Guatemala & the French Antilles
edited by Philippe Gloaguen and Pierre Josse, Macmillan Publishing, 1985, 192 pages, paper, $6.95
This book is part of the Collier World Traveler Guide series, which is reviewed in more detail under "Series Reviews."

Fodor's Fun in St. Martin/Sint Maarten
Fodor's Travel Publications, 1987, 96 pages, paper, $5.95
This is one of Fodor's Fun Guide series, which is reviewed in more detail under "Series Reviews." The series is updated annually.

LEEWARD ISLANDS AND WINDWARD ISLANDS

See also "The Caribbean." The Leeward Islands are those islands extending from the Virgin Islands on the north to Dominica on the south, and including Antigua, Anguilla, Montserrat, and Guadeloupe. The Windward Islands comprise those islands of the Lesser Antilles extending south from Martinique, excluding Barbados, Tobago, and Trinidad. These include Grenada, St. Lucia, and St. Vincent.

22 Days in the West Indies: The Itinerary Planner
by Cyndy & Sam Morreale, John Muir Publications, 1987, 132 pages, paper, $6.95
This book, focusing on the lesser-traveled locations in the Windward and Leeward Islands of the West Indies, is part of the Itinerary Planner series, which is reviewed in more detail under "Series Reviews." Note that this is a new title for this book and it may also be found under *West Indies in 22 Days.*

Yachtsman's Guide to the Windward Islands
by Julius Wilensky, Wescott Cove Publishing, 1978, 176 pages, paper, $19.95
The Grenadines, part of the Windward Islands, are classic yachters' territory. This aging but still helpful book on the where and how of boating in that region is part of the Cruising Guide series, which is reviewed in more detail under "Series Reviews."

COUNTRIES OF THE WEST INDIES

ARUBA

See also "The Caribbean." Aruba is part of the Netherlands Antilles, just off the coast of Venezuela.

Diving and Snorkeling Guide to Bonaire and Curacao

by George Lewbel, PBC International, 1984, 96 pages, paper, $9.95

This guide, containing information on snorkeling and diving in Aruba, is part of the Pisces Diving/Snorkeling Guide series, which is reviewed in more detail under "Series Reviews."

BAHAMAS

Berlitz: Bahamas

Macmillan Publishing, 1980, 128 pages, paper, $6.95

This is one of the small-format Berlitz Guide series, which is reviewed in more detail under "Series Reviews."

Birnbaum's Caribbean, Bermuda & the Bahamas

edited by Stephen Birnbaum, Houghton Mifflin, 1987, 786 pages, paper, $12.95

This is one of the excellent Birnbaum's Guide series, which is reviewed in more detail under "Series Reviews." The series is updated annually.

The Compleat Guide to Nassau

by Steve Dodge, White Sound Press, 1987, 116 pages, paper, $4.95

This delightful book details an interesting walking tour of Old Nassau, includes notes on the history of Nassau and the Bahamas, and provides a selective restaurant list emphasizing native food served in the ethnic "Over-the-Hill" area. Transportation information, guides to Paradise Island, activities throughout New Providence Island, and more are included in this nicely done guide complete with beautiful line drawings.

The Condo Lux Vacationer's Guide to Condominium Rentals in the Bahamas and the Caribbean Islands

by Jill Little, Random House, 1986, 303 pages, paper, $9.95

This is one of the Condo Lux Guide series, which is reviewed in more detail under "Series Reviews."

Cruising Guide to the Abacos and the Northern Bahamas

by Julius Wilensky, Westcott Cove Publishing, 1980, 220 pages, paper, $24.95

This guide to the when and where of boating is part of the Cruising Guide series, which is reviewed in more detail under "Series Reviews."

Diving and Snorkeling Guide to the Bahamas, Nassau, and New Providence Island
by Steve Blount, PBC International, 1985, 64 pages, paper, $9.95
This book is part of the Pisces Diving/Snorkeling Guide series, which is reviewed in more detail under "Series Reviews."

Fielding's Bermuda and the Bahamas
by Rachel and Walter Christmas, William Morrow & Co., 1988, 250 pages, paper, $7.50
This book is part of the Fielding's Travel Guide series, which is reviewed in more detail under "Series Reviews." The series is updated annually.

Fisher's World: Bahamas
by Diane Lawes, Fisher's World, Inc., 1988, 172 pages, paper, $14.95
This is one of the Fisher's World Guide series, which is reviewed in more detail under "Series Reviews." The series is updated annually.

Fodor's Bahamas
Fodor's Travel Publications, 1987, 176 pages, paper, $7.95
This book is part of Fodor's Country/Regional Guide series, which is reviewed in more detail under "Series Reviews." The series is updated annually.

Fodor's Fun in the Bahamas
Fodor's Travel Publications, 1987, 128 pages, paper, $5.95
This book is one of Fodor's Fun Guide series, which is reviewed in more detail under "Series Reviews." The series is updated annually.

Frommer's Dollarwise Guide to Bermuda and the Bahamas
by Darwin Porter, Prentice Hall Press, 1987, 371 pages, paper, $11.95
This book is part of the Frommer's Dollarwise Guide series, which is reviewed in more detail under "Series Reviews." This series emphasizes selections in the moderate range, and is updated every two years.

A Guide and History of Hope Town
by Steve Dodge and Vernon Malone, White Sound Press, 1985, 48 pages, paper, $4.00
This delightful little booklet provides an enjoyable, informative

walking tour through Hope Town, followed by a history of this quiet, charming village.

Insight Guide: Bahamas

by Apa Productions, Prentice Hall Press, 1986, 337 pages, paper, $16.95

This is one of the acclaimed Insight Guide series, which is reviewed in more detail under "Series Reviews."

The New Holiday Guide to the Caribbean and the Bahamas

M. Evans & Co., 1988 (10th ed.), 160 pages, paper, $4.95

This book is part of the Holiday Guide series, which is reviewed in more detail under "Series Reviews."

The Pelican Guide to the Bahamas

by James Moore, Pelican Publishing, 1988 (2nd ed.), 353 pages, paper, $11.95

This is an excellent, up-to-date, comprehensive guide which covers the full range of interests from budget to deluxe: guided tours, night life, water sports, hotels, restaurants, transportation, and more. The emphasis is on the middle-of-the-road traveler. Evaluations are extensive and well-written. This is definitely a solidly researched, quality book.

The South American Handbook (including Caribbean, Mexico, and Central America)

edited by John Brooks, Rand McNally & Co., 1988 (64th ed.), 1341 pages, cloth, $28.95

The definitive single-volume work on South America covers the Bahamas as well and is reviewed under "South America as a Whole." This book is updated annually.

BARBADOS

See also "The Caribbean."

Fodor's Fun in Barbados

Fodor's Travel Publications, 1987, 118 pages, paper, $6.95

This book is part of Fodor's Fun Guide series, which is reviewed in more detail under "Series Reviews." The series is updated annually.

Insight Guide: Barbados
by Apa Productions, Prentice Hall Press, 1986, 315 pages, paper, $16.95

This is one of the acclaimed Insight Guide series, which is reviewed in more detail under "Series Reviews."

BERMUDA

The Bed and Breakfast Guide
by Phyllis Featherton and Barbara Ostler, Talman Co., 1987 (3rd ed.), 457 pages, paper, $11.95

This book describes only members of the National Bed & Breakfast Association and includes several association members in Bermuda.

Berlitz: Bermuda
Macmillan Publishing, 1982, 128 pages, paper, $6.95

This book is part of the small-format Berlitz Guide series, which is reviewed in more detail under "Series Reviews."

The Bermuda Handbook
by Brigitte Geh, Hunter Publishing, 1988, 228 pages, paper, $13.95

This interesting-sounding title, released after press time, covers information on numerous recreational possibilities (golf, sailing, scuba, best places to swim), as well as profiles of recommended hotels and restaurants. Hundreds of color photos are included.

Birnbaum's Caribbean, Bermuda & the Bahamas
edited by Stephen Birnbaum, Houghton Mifflin, 1987, 786 pages, paper, $12.95

This book is part of the excellent Birnbaum's Guide series, which is reviewed in more detail under "Series Reviews." The series is updated annually.

Fielding's Bermuda and the Bahamas
by Rachel and Walter Christmas, William Morrow & Co., 1988, 250 pages, paper, $7.95

This is one of the Fielding's Travel Guide series, which is reviewed in more detail under "Series Reviews." The series is updated annually.

Fisher's World: Bermuda
by Susan Irwin-Wiener, Fisher's World, Inc., 1988, 101 pages, paper, $10.95

This book is part of the Fisher's World Guide series, which is reviewed in more detail under "Series Reviews." The series is updated annually.

Fodor's Bermuda
Fodor's Travel Publications, 1987, 176 pages, paper, $8.95
This is one of Fodor's Country/Regional Guide series, which is reviewed in more detail under "Series Reviews." The series is updated annually.

Frommer's Dollarwise Guide to Bermuda and the Bahamas
by Darwin Porter, Prentice Hall Press, 1987, 371 pages, paper, $11.95
This book is part of Frommer's Dollarwise Guide series, which is reviewed in more detail under "Series Reviews." The series emphasizes selections in the moderate price range. The series is updated every two years.

Frommer's Guide to Honeymoon Destinations
by Risa Weinreh, Prentice Hall Press, 1988, 628 pages, paper, $12.95
Including Bermuda, this book is reviewed under "North America as a Whole."

The South American Handbook (including Caribbean, Mexico, and Central America)
edited by John Brooks, Rand McNally & Co., 1988 (64th ed.), 1341 pages, cloth, $28.95
This definitive single-volume on South America covers Bermuda as well and is reviewed under "South America as a Whole." This book is updated annually.

BONAIRE

See also "The Caribbean." Bonaire is part of the Netherlands Antilles, just off the coast of Venezuela.

Diving and Snorkeling Guide to Bonaire and Curacao
by George Lewbel, PBC International, 1984, 96 pages, paper, $9.95
This book is part of the Pisces Diving/Snorkeling Guide series, which is reviewed in more detail under "Series Reviews."

CAYMAN ISLANDS

See also "The Caribbean." The Cayman Islands is a small island group northwest of Jamaica and directly south of Cuba.

Diving and Snorkeling Guide to Grand Cayman Island Including Little Cayman and Cayman Brac
   by Carl Roessler, PBC International, 1984, 96 pages, paper, $9.95
   This is book is part of the Pisces Diving/Snorkeling Guide series, which is reviewed in more detail under "Series Reviews."

CUBA

See also "The Caribbean."

The Complete Travel Guide to Cuba
   by Paula DiPerna, St. Martin's Press, 1979, 274 pages, paper, $4.95
   This comprehensive guide no doubt needs some updating, but it will answer a lot of questions on visiting Cuba, including customs, art, currency, transportation, major cities, and some of the out-of-the-way places not to miss.

Hildebrand's Travel Guide: Cuba
   Hippocrene Books, 1985, 176 pages, paper, $8.95
   This title, part of the Hildebrand's Guide series, which is reviewed in more detail under "Series Reviews," was not picked up by Hunter Publishing and will, hopefully, continue to be available through Hippocrene Books. If not, try the nearest travel bookstore.

CURACAO

See also "The Caribbean." Curacao is part of the Netherlands Antilles, just off the coast of Venezuela.

Diving and Snorkeling Guide to Bonaire and Curacao
   by George Lewbel, PBC International, 1984, 96 pages, paper, $9.95
   This book is part of the Pisces Diving/Snorkeling Guide series, which is reviewed in more detail under "Series Reviews."

DOMINICAN REPUBLIC

See also "The Caribbean."

Guide to Puerto Rico and the Virgin Islands (including the Dominican Republic)
   by Harry Pariser, Moon Publications, 1986, 174 pages, paper, $6.95
   This fantastic guide to the area, is more geared to the young and adventurous, but is still helpful to any traveler. Although the title is different, the similarity of format and type of content make this book part of the superb Moon Handbook series, which is reviewed in more detail under "Series Reviews." The series is updated every two years.

Hildebrand's Travel Guide: Hispaniola
Hunter Publishing, 1987, 143 pages, paper, $9.95
This book is part of the Hildebrand's Guide series, which is reviewed in more detail under "Series Reviews."

Latin America on a Bicycle
by J. P. Panet, Passport Press, 1987, 156 pages, paper, $12.95
Including the Dominican Republic, this book is reviewed under "Central America as a Whole."

HAITI

See also "The Caribbean."

Guide to Jamaica (including Haiti)
by Harry Pariser, Moon Publications, 1986, 174 pages, paper, $6.95
This is an excellently prepared guide, especially geared to the young and adventurous, but very helpful for any traveler. Because of its similar focus, it is part of the always first-class Moon Handbook series, which is reviewed in more detail under "Series Reviews." The series is updated every two years.

Hildebrand's Travel Guide: Hispaniola
Hunter Publishing, 1987, 143 pages, paper, $9.95
This book is part of the Hildebrand's Guide series, which is reviewed in more detail under "Series Reviews."

JAMAICA

See also "The Caribbean."

The Adventure Guide to Jamaica
Hunter Publishing, 1988, 288 pages, paper, $12.95
This book is part of the new Hunter Adventure Guide series, which is reviewed in more detail under "Series Reviews."

Berlitz: Jamaica
Macmillan Publishing, 1981, 128 pages, paper, $6.95
This is one of the small-format Berlitz Guide series, which is reviewed in more detail under "Series Reviews."

Fodor's Fun in Jamaica
Fodor's Travel Publications, 987, 128 pages, paper, $6.95
This book is part of Fodor's Fun Guide series, which is reviewed in more detail under "Series Reviews."

Guide to Jamaica (including Haiti)
by Harry Pariser, Moon Publications, 1986, 174 pages, paper, $6.95

This excellently prepared guide is especially geared to the young and adventurous, but very helpful for any traveler. Because of its similar focus, it is part of the always first-class Moon Handbook series, which is reviewed in more detail under "Series Reviews." The series is updated every two years.

Hildebrand's Travel Guide: Jamaica
Hunter Publishing, 1985, 128 pages, paper, $8.95

This is one of the Hildebrand's Guide series, which is reviewed in more detail under "Series Reviews."

Insight Guide: Jamaica
by Apa Productions, Prentice Hall Press, 1987, 319 pages, paper, $16.95

This book is part of the acclaimed Insight Guide series, which is reviewed in more detail under "Series Reviews."

PUERTO RICO
See also "The Caribbean."

America's Wonderful Little Hotels and Inns: Eastern Edition
edited by Sandra Soule, St. Martin's Press, 1988, 512 pages, paper, $13.95

Including Puerto Rico, this book is reviewed under "New England" (U.S.A.).

The Bed and Breakfast Guide
by Phyllis Featherton and Barbara Ostler, Talman Co., 1987 (3rd ed.), 457 pages, paper, $11.95

Describing only members of the National Bed & Breakfast Association, this book includes one association member in Puerto Rico.

Berlitz: Puerto Rico
Macmillan Publishing, 1977, 128 pages, paper, $6.95

This is one of the small-format Berlitz Guide series, which is reviewed in more detail under "Series Reviews."

Bob Damron's Address Book
Bob Damron Enterprises, 1988, 413 pages, paper, $12.00

This annually updated book on services and entertainment for the gay man includes Puerto Rico, the Virgin Islands, the United States, Canada, and Mexico.

Fodor's Fun in Puerto Rico

Fodor's Travel Publications, 1987, 128 pages, paper, $5.95

This book is part of Fodor's Fun Guide series, which is reviewed in more detail under "Series Reviews." The series is updated annually.

Guide to National Park Areas: Eastern States

by David and Kay Scott, The Globe Pequot Press, 1987 (2nd ed.), 272 pages, paper, $10.95

Including Puerto Rico, this book is reviewed under "The South" (U.S.A.).

Guide to Puerto Rico and the Virgin Islands (including the Dominican Republic)

by Harry Pariser, Moon Publications, 1986, 174 pages, paper, $6.95

This is a fantastic guide to the area, more geared to the young and adventurous, but very helpful to any traveler. Although the title is different, the similarity of format and type of content make it part of the superb Moon Handbook series, which is reviewed in more detail under "Series Reviews." The series is updated every two years.

Insight Guide: Puerto Rico

by Apa Productions, Prentice Hall Press, 1987, 295 pages, paper, $16.95

This book is part of the acclaimed Insight Guide series, which is reviewed in more detail under "Series Reviews."

The Other Puerto Rico

by Kathryn Robinson, Hunter Publishing, 1988 (3rd ed.), 160 pages, paper, $11.95

The strong point of this book, published in Puerto Rico, is its ability to introduce places of interest that might not be mentioned elsewhere. Each chapter describes separate adventure hikes to semi-secret beaches, unspoiled valleys, jungles, and mountains. Directions are included, along with some history notes and color photos. This is a nicely written and most enjoyable source of good ideas.

Puerto Rico and St. Thomas Travel Guide

by Antonio Villa, Modern Guides Co., 1987, 190 pages, paper, $5.95

This little guidebook is published in Puerto Rico. The suggested tours, restaurants, sights to see, history, secluded country inns, sports, shopping, and nightlife are all chosen by a Spanish tourist executive.

ST. MARTIN/SINT MAARTEN

See also "The Caribbean" and "Leeward Islands and Windward Islands." Divided into two distinct regions, St. Martin is a possession of France and Sint Maarten is a possession of the Netherlands.

Fodor's Fun in St. Martin/Sint Maarten
Fodor's Travel Publications, 1987, 96 pages, paper, $6.95
This book is one of Fodor's Fun Guide series, which is reviewed in more detail under "Series Reviews." The series is updated annually.

TRINIDAD & TOBAGO

See also "The Caribbean."

Insight Guide: Trinidad and Tobago
by Apa Productions, Prentice Hall Press, 1987, 287 pages, paper, $16.95
This book is one of the acclaimed Insight Guide series, which is reviewed in more detail under "Series Reviews."

VIRGIN ISLANDS (U.S. & BRITISH)

See also "The Caribbean" and the "Leeward Islands and Windward Islands."

The Bed and Breakfast Guide
by Phyllis Featherton and Barbara Ostler, Talman Co., 1987 (3rd ed.), 457 pages, paper, $11.95
Describing only members of the National Bed & Breakfast Association, this book includes association members in the Virgin Islands.

Berlitz: Virgin Islands
Macmillan Publishing, 1977, 128 pages, paper, $6.95
This book is one of the small-format Berlitz Guide series, which is reviewed in more detail under "Series Reviews."

Bob Damron's Address Book
Bob Damron Enterprises, 1988, 413 pages, paper, $12.00
This book details services and entertainment for the gay man. Including Puerto Rico, the Virgin Islands, the United States, Canada, and Mexico, this book is updated annually.

Diving and Snorkeling Guide to the Virgin Islands

by George Lewbel, PBC International, 1984, 96 pages, paper, $9.95

This book is part of the Pisces Diving/Snorkeling Guide series, which is reviewed in more detail under "Series Reviews."

Fodor's Virgin Islands (U.S. & British)

Fodor's Travel Publications, 1987, 160 pages, paper, $8.95

This is one of Fodor's Country/Regional Guide series, which is reviewed in more detail under "Series Reviews." The series is updated annually.

Guide to Puerto Rico and the Virgin Islands (including the Dominican Republic)

by Harry Pariser, Moon Publications, 1986, 174 pages, paper, $6.95

This fantastic guide to the area is more geared to the young and adventurous, but very helpful to any traveler. Although the title is different, the similarity of format and type of content make it part of the superb Moon Handbook series, which is reviewed in more detail under "Series Reviews." The series is updated every two years.

Appendixes

PHRASE BOOKS

The amount of information on languages available to the traveler is extremely large. This subject has not been addressed in the body of this text, but below is a quick summary of the major phrase book series. Phrase books are useful because, short of actually learning the language, which is unrealistic for most visitors to a foreign country, or studying tapes on how to pronounce new words, the best single language aid is a phrasebook. While some of the phrase books below include a dictionary, travelers are cautioned to use dictionaries with care. Dictionaries tend to confuse as much as they help if relied upon solely to build usable sentences in a new language. A phrase book, on the other hand, offers practical, short statements of need or interest. Phrase books provide visual as well as oral methods of communication because they allow travelers in need to show the page to someone if they cannot pronounce the phrase themselves. Phrase books are practical, eminently useful and recommended baggage. Note that the following is a summary of the major phrase book series only and is not meant to be an exhaustive compilation of all phrase books in print.

American Express Phrase Books and Dictionaries
Prentice Hall Press

The largest of the phrase books listed here, the American Express series has semi-hardback yet flexible covers. The books will still slide into a pocket, but they are quite tall. These are combination phrase book/dictionaries. The added dictionaries are quite extensive, covering about 10,000 words, and make for a much larger book. Nonetheless, the phrase book section is well done, easy to use, and covers all the pertinent topics.

Languages available: French, German, Italian, Spanish, all priced at $6.95

At A Glance Phrase Books
Barron's Educational Series
The At A Glance series is quite popular with knowledgeable travelers. One of its big pluses, given that phrase books are really very
similar in substance, is its durable, plastic cover. The books are
pocket-sized and include about 1500 phrases grouped by topic, as
well as a dictionary of more than 2000 essential words. Maps, travel
tips, shopping and restaurant guides are also included.
Languages available: Arabic ($5.95), Chinese ($5.95), French
($4.95), German ($4.95), Italian ($4.95), Japanese ($5.95), Spanish
($4.95), The Traveler's Phrase Book (single volume covering French,
German, Italian, and Spanish, $6.95)

Berlitz Phrase Books
Macmillan Publishing
The distinct feature of the Berlitz series is its color coding. The
edges of the pages are distinctly colored, allowing travelers to flip
quickly to the needed category. Categories include hotel service,
eating out, traveling around, shopping, etc. More than 1000 useful
phrases are covered.
Languages available: Arabic, Chinese, Danish, Dutch, Finnish,
French, German, Greek, Hebrew, Hungarian, Italian, Japanese, Korean, Norwegian, Polish, Portuguese, Russian, Serbo-Croatian, Spanish, Spanish (Latin America), Swahili, Swedish, Turkish, all priced
at $4.95

Collins Phrase Books
Prima Publishing
This English series with a thick, flexible cover, just barely rates
the label "pocket-sized." It is well organized into major sections on
pronunciation, transportation, enjoying a stay (hotels, food, sightseeing, menu guide), shopping, health, and practical facts—everything
is included here.
Languages available: French, German, Greek, Italian, Spanish, all
priced at $4.95

Hugo Phrase Books
Hunter Publishing
These are solid phrase books covering all the topics of concern
(hotels, restaurants, shopping, travel, health, etc.), plus an extensive
menu guide (some 600 entries) and a mini-dictionary of about 1800
words. The books are average size in the pocket-sized division.
Languages available: Dutch, French, German, Greek, Italian, Japanese, Portuguese, Spanish, Turkish, all priced at $3.25

Jiffy Phrase Books
Langenscheidt Publishers
Medium sized with a sturdy plastic cover, these excellent phrase books are well organized. They contain more than 1000 phrases as well as a 4000 word dictionary.
Languages available: French, German, Italian, Spanish, all priced at $4.95.

Just Enough Phrase Books
Passport Books
These books contains hundreds of useful phrases on a wide variety of important travel topics, including shopping, food, accommodations, transportation, etc. Inexpensive and pocket-sized, they are somewhat larger than most phrase books.
Languages available: Dutch, French, German, Greek, Italian, Japanese, Portuguese, Serbo-Croat, Spanish, all for $3.95. In addition, Scandinavian (single volume on Danish, Norwegian, Swedish, $5.95) and Multilingual Phrase Book (single volume covering Spanish, French, Dutch, Portuguese, German, Italian, Serbo-Croat, Greek, $6.95)

Lonely Planet Phrase Books
Lonely Planet Publications
The tiniest of the pocket-sized phrase books, the Lonely Planet guides primarily cover languages not available elsewhere. All the key topics are covered—lodging, food, transportation, health, etc.— in these practical and compact books.
Languages available: Bahasa (Indonesia, $2.95), Burmese ($2.95), Mandarin (China, $2.95), Hindi/Urdu ($2.95), Korean ($2.95), Nepali ($2.95), Pidgin (Papua New Guinea, $2.95), Sinhala (Sri Lanka, $2.95), Swahili ($2.95), Tibetan (2.95), Thai ($3.95)

Say It Phrase Books
Dover Publications
These tiny books cover 1000 or more phrases and have the added benefit of a sewn binding, which will keep pages secure for a long time. The organization takes a little time to get used to—there is no table of contents, only an index—but these are definitely a handy choice once you get used to the unique numbering system used for each phrase.
Languages available: Arabic ($2.75), Mandarin (China, $3.00), Czech ($3.50), Danish ($2.50), Dutch ($2.95), Finnish ($3.50), French ($2.50), German ($2.50), Greek ($2.75), Hebrew ($2.95), Hindi ($3.50), Hungarian ($3.50), Indonesian ($3.50), Italian ($2.50), Japanese ($3.00), Norwegian ($2.50), Polish ($2.95), Portuguese (Brazilian,

$2.50), Portuguese (Continental, $2.75), Russian ($2.95), Spanish (Latin American, $2.50), Swahili ($2.95), Swedish ($2.95), Turkish ($2.50), Yiddish ($2.95)

TRAVEL BOOKSTORES AND MAIL ORDER

We have endeavored, through a variety of sources, to compile as complete a list as possible of travel bookstores, travel book mail order businesses, and those general bookstores of which we are aware that emphasize travel and/or have staff specializing in travel books. If you know of other stores that should be included, we would appreciate hearing from you. Each travel bookstore has a slightly different orientation in terms of the type of books it stocks. We suggest, if several are within traveling distance, that you explore each of them. Travel bookstores are a lot of fun. It should go without saying that we are not familiar with all of these stores firsthand. Those we have worked with on this project we can certainly recommend (see "Acknowledgements" at the front of the book). As for the rest, you alone will have to be the judge. We would suggest that if you find that a particular employee of a store is not well versed in the subject you are interested in that you ask whether it would be more appropriate to speak to some other staff member. If there is no one to meet your needs, don't hesitate to seek out a different travel bookstore. There are stores that will have the answers you seek.

Barry's Bookstore
11701 Wilshire Blvd.
Los Angeles, CA 90025
213-820-7771
Travel Bookstore

Beaucoup Books
5414 Magazine St.
New Orleans, LA 70115
504-895-2663
General Bookstore with
  emphasis on travel

Book Passage
51 Tamal Vista
Corte Madera, CA
  94925
800-321-9785
415-927-0960 (CA)
Retail Travel Section,

Travel Book Mail
Order

Bookworks
4022 Rio Grande Blvd,
  NW
Albuquerque, NM
  87107
505-344-8139
Travel Bookstore

British Travel Bookshop
40 W. 57th St.
New York, NY 10019
212-765-0898
Travel Bookstore

Carousel Press
Family Travel Guides
P. O. Box 6061
Albany, CA 94706

415-527-5849
Travel Book Mail Order
(Specializing in
Family Travel
Guides)

Complete Traveller
199 Madison Ave.
New York, NY 10016
212-685-9007
Travel Bookstore and
Travel Book Mail
Order

Dial-A-Book
512 South Baldwin Ave.
Marion, IN 46953
317-662-0403
800-448-2665
General Bookstore
Specializing in Travel

Easy Going
Shattuck Commons
1400 Shattuck Ave.
Berkeley, CA 94109
415-843-3533
Travel Bookstore and
Travel Book Mail
Order

Easy Going
1617 Locust St.
Walnut Creek, CA
94596
415-947-6660
Travel Bookstore and
Travel Book Mail
Order

Forsyth Travel Library
P. O. Box 2975
9154 West 57th St.
Shawnee Mission, KS
66201
800-367-7984
816-384-3440

Travel Bookstore and
Travel Book Mail
Order

Geographia Map &
Travel Book Store
4000 Riverside Dr.
Burbank, CA 91505
818-848-1414
Travel Bookstore

Geostat Map & Travel
Center
Wick Shopping Plaza
U.S. Highway 1 and
Plainfield Ave.
Edison, NJ 08817
201-985-1555
Travel Bookstore

Geostat Map & Travel
Center
910 N. Route 73
Marlton, NJ 08053
609-983-3600
Travel Bookstore

Geostat Map & Travel
Center
Caldor Shopping Center
Routes 10 and 202
Morris Plains, NJ 07950
201-538-7707
Travel Bookstore

Geostat Map & Travel
Center
Routes 206 and 518
Skillman, NJ 08558
609-924-2121
Travel Bookstore

Geostat Map & Travel
Center
125 S. 18th St.
Philadelphia, PA 19103
215-564-4700
Travel Bookstore

Globe Corner Bookstore
1 School St.
Boston, MA 02108
617-523-6658
Travel Bookstore

Globe Corner Bookstore
40 Brattle St.
Cambridge, MA 02138
617-497-6277
Travel Bookstore

Globe Corner Bookstore
Settlers' Green, Route
16
North Conway, NH
03860
603-356-7063
Travel Bookstore

Gourmet Guides
1767 Stockton St.
San Francisco, CA
94133
415-391-5903
Travel Bookstore and
Travel Book Mail
Order

Gulliver's Travel
Bookshop
609 Bloor St., West
Toronto, Ontario,
Canada M6G 1K5
416-537-7700
Travel Bookstore

Hagstrom's Map and
Travel Center
57 W. 43rd St.
New York, NY 10036
212-398-1222
Travel Bookstore

Harvard Coop
1400 Massachusetts
Ave.
Cambridge, MA 02138

617-492-1000
General Bookstore
Specializing in Travel

Home, Garden and
Travel Bookstore
2476 Bolsover St.
Houston, TX 77005
713-527-0619
Travel Bookstore

Home, Garden and
Travel Bookstore
5868 Westheimer St.
Houston, TX 77057
713-789-2269
Travel Bookstore

John Cole's Book Shop
780 Prospect St.
La Jolla, CA 92037
619-454-4766
General Bookstore
Specializing in Travel

Latitudes
4400 Ashford
Dunwoody Rd.
Atlanta, GA 30346
404-394-2772
Travel Bookstore

Latitudes
3349 Peachtree Rd., NE
Atlanta, GA 30326
404-237-6144
Travel Bookstore

Latitudes
3801 Grand Ave., S.
Minneapolis, MN
55409
612-823-3742
Travel Bookstore

Le Travel Store
295 Horton Plaza
San Diego, CA 92101

619-544-0005
Travel Bookstore

The Literate Traveller
8306 Wilshire Blvd.,
    Suite 591
Beverly Hills, CA 90211
213-934-7280

Lloyd Books, Ltd.
3145 Dumbarton St.,
    N.W.
Washington, D.C.
    20007
202-333-8989
Travel Bookstore

The Map & Globe Store
1120 East Colonial Dr.
Orlando, FL 32803
800-227-7538
305-425-0185
Travel Bookstore

The Map & Globe Store
2328 Apalachee
    Parkway, Suite 6
Tallahassee, FL 32301
904-656-7723
Travel Bookstore

The Map & Globe Store
1606 East Michigan
    Ave.
Lansing, MI 48912
517-484-1978
Travel Bookstore

The Map Center
2440 Bancroft Way
Berkeley, CA 94704
415-841-6277
Specializing in Travel
    Books for the "Self-
    Propelled" (Hiking,
    Cycling, River Sports,
    etc.)

Map Centre, Inc.
2611 University Ave.
San Diego, CA 92104
619-291-3830
Travel Bookstore

The Map Store
348 North Robert St.
St. Paul, MN 55101
612-227-1328
Travel Bookstore

The Map Store
First Bank Place West
    211 Skyway
120 South Sixth St.
Minneapolis, MN
    55402
612-339-4117
Travel Bookstore

The Map Store, Inc.
Farragut Square
1636 Eye St., N.W.
Washington, D.C.
    20006
202-628-2608
Travel Bookstore

Marketplace Books
296 East Fifth Ave.
Eugene, OR 97401
505-343-5614
General Bookstore
    Specializing in Travel

Metsker Maps of
    Seattle
702 First Ave.
Seattle, WA 98104
206-623-8747
Travel Bookstore

Michael Chessler Books
P. O. Box 2436
Evergreen, CO 80439
800-654-8502
303-670-0093

Travel Book Mail Order
(Specializing in
Adventure Travel
Books)

Nomadic Books
401 NE 45th St.
Seattle, WA 98105
206-634-3453
Travel Book Mail order
(Specializing in
Budget and
Adventure Travel
Books)

Open Air Books &
Maps
25 Toronto St.
Toronto, Ontario,
Canada M5C 2R1
416-363-0719
Travel Bookstore

Pacific Travelers Supply
529 State St.
Santa Barbara, CA
93101
805-963-4438
Travel Bookstore

Passenger Stop
732 Dulaney Valley
Court
Towson, MD 21204
301-821-5888
Travel Bookstore

Phileas Fogg's Books
and Maps for the
Traveler
87 Stanford Shopping
Center
Palo Alto, CA 94304
800-533-3644
800-233-3644 (CA)
415-327-1754
Travel Bookstore

Pioneer Maps
14125 N.E. 20th St.
Bellevue, WA 98007
206-746-3200
Travel Bookstore

Places & People
2623 N. Campbell Ave.
Tucson, AZ 85719
602-577-9620
Travel Bookstore

Plan-It Travel Store
777 S. Main St.
Orange, CA 92668
714-973-8979
Travel Bookstore

Powell's Travel Store
Pioneer Courthouse
Square
701 S.W. Sixth Ave.
Portland, OR 97204
503-228-1108
Travel Bookstore

Quo Vadis
427 Grand Ave.
Carlsbad, CA 92008
619-434-4301
Travel Bookstore

Rand McNally Map
Store
23 East Madison
Chicago, IL 60602
312-332-4627
Travel Bookstore

Rand McNally Map
Store
595 Market St.
San Francisco, CA
94105
415-777-3131
Travel Bookstore

Sandmeyer's Bookstore
714 South Dearborn St.

Chicago, IL 60605
312-922-2104
Travel Bookstore

Savvy Traveller
50 E. Washington St.
Chicago, IL 60602
312-263-2100
Travel Bookstore

Sierra Club Books
San Francisco Bay
  Chapter
6014 College Ave.
Oakland, CA 94618
415-658-7470
Good Source of Sierra
  Club Travel Titles

Tattered Cover
  Bookstore
2930 East Second Ave.
Denver, CO 80206
303-322-7727
General Bookstore with
  Staff Specialized in
  Travel

Thomas Bros. Maps and
  Books
603 W. Seventh St.
Los Angeles, CA 90017
213-627-4018
Travel Bookstore

Thomas Bros. Maps and
  Books
550 Jackson St.
San Francisco, CA
  94133
415-981-7520
Travel Bookstore

Thomas Bros. Maps and
  Books
17731 Cowan
Irvine, CA 92714
714-863-1984
Travel Bookstore

Travel & Things
5940 College Ave.
Oakland, CA 94618
415-547-6560
Travel Agency and
  Bookstore

Travel Book Center
719 E Street
San Diego, CA 92101
619-234-6355
Travel Bookstore

Travel Books Unlimited
4931 Cordell Ave.
Bethesda, MD 20814
301-951-8533
Travel Bookstore and
  Travel Book Mail
  Order

The Travel Bookstore
1514 Hillhurst Ave.
Los Angeles, CA 90027
213-660-2101
Travel Bookstore

Travel Bound Bookstore
815 S. Aiken Ave.
Pittsburgh, PA 15232
412-681-4100
Travel Bookstore

Travel Collection
8235 Shoal Creek Blvd.
Austin, TX 78758
512-454-7151
Travel Bookstore

Travel Depot
1539 Garnat Ave.
San Diego, CA 92109
619-483-1421
Travel Bookstore

Travel Experience
111 South Bemiston
  Ave.
St. Louis, MO 63105

314-862-2222
Travel Bookstore

Travel Experience
11431 Concord Village
  Ave.
St. Louis, MO 63123
314-849-5255
Travel Bookstore

The Travel Gallery
1007 Manhattan Ave.
Manhattan Beach, CA
  90266
213-379-9199
Travel Bookstore

Travel Genie Map and
  Book Store
113 Colorado Ave.
Ames, IA 50010
515-292-1070
Travel Bookstore

Travel Market
Golden Gateway
  Commons
130 Pacific Avenue
  Mall
San Francisco, CA
  94111
415-421-4080
Travel Bookstore

Travel Merchandise
  Mart
1425 K St., N.W.
Washington, D.C.
  20005
202-371-6656
Travel Bookstore

Travel Plus
420 East Sahara Ave.
Las Vegas, NV 89104
702-369-2555
Travel Agency and
  Bookstore

Travel Store
56-1/2 N. Santa Cruz
  Ave.
Los Gatos, CA 95030
408-354-9909
Travel Bookstore

Travel Suppliers
727 N. Placentia Ave.
Fullerton, CA 92631
714-528-2502
Travel Bookstore

Traveller's Bookstore
75 Rockefeller Plaza
22 W. 52nd St.
New York, NY 10019
212-664-0995
Travel Bookstore and
  Travel Book Mail
  Order

TraveLore Books
2 Elm St.
Huntington Village, NY
  11743
516-673-6066
Travel Bookstore

Travelshelf
2834 South Sherwood
  Forest Blvd.
Baton Rouge, LA 70816
504-293-0900
Travel Bookstore

Ulysses Bookstore
1208 St-Denis
Montreal, Quebec,
  Canada H2X 3J5
514-843-7135
Travel Bookstore

Voyager Travel Books
724 Ridge Dr.
McLean, VA 22101
703-847-2900
Travel Bookstore

Vroman's
694 East Colorado Blvd.
Pasadena, CA 91101
818-449-5320
General Bookstore with
    Staff Specialized in
    Travel

Wayfarer Books
P. O. Box 1121
Davenport, IA 52805
319-355-3902
Travel Book Mail order

Whole Earth Provision
    Co.
8868 Research Blvd.
Austin, TX 78758
512-458-6333
Travel Bookstore

Whole Earth Provision
    Co.
2934 South Shepard St.
Houston, TX 77098
713-526-5226
Travel Bookstore

Whole Earth Provision
    Co.
2410 San Antonio St.
Austin, TX 78705
512-478-1577
Travel Bookstore

Whole Earth Provision
    Co.
4006 South Lamar Blvd.
Austin, TX 78704
512-444-9974
Travel Bookstore

Wide World Books and
    Maps
401 N.E. 45th St.
Seattle, WA 98105
206-634-3453
Travel Bookstore

Wide World of Maps
2626 West Indian
    School Rd.
Phoenix, AZ 85017
602-279-2323
Travel Bookstore

Wide World of Maps
1526 North Scottsdale
    Rd.
Tempe, AZ 85281
602-949-1012
Travel Bookstore

Wide World of Maps
1440 South Country
    Club Dr.
Mesa, AZ 85202
602-844-1134
Travel Bookstore

Word Journeys Travel
    Bookshop
Lomas Santa Fe Plaza
971-C Lomas Santa Fe
    Dr.
Solana Beach, CA
    92075
619-481-4158
Travel Bookstore

World Wide Books &
    Maps
949 Granville St.
Vancouver, B.C.,
    Canada V6Z 1G3
604-687-3320
Travel Bookstore

Yamhill Books
818 S.W. First
Portland, OR 97204
503-242-0047
General Bookstore with
    Staff Specialized in
    Travel

TRAVEL BOOK PUBLISHERS

The following list includes all publishers or American distributors of foreign books referenced in *Going Places*. American publishers who have indicated a particular distributor(s) for ordering have been included as well. If you cannot, for some reason, order a particular book through your travel bookstore or other bookstore, it is possible to order it on your own. In doing so, be sure to contact the distributor first if one is listed. Distributor addresses and phone numbers are listed alphabetically along with publisher information. Bear in mind that ordering on your own should only be done when there is no other option. The book will cost you more than in a retail store, not less. You will pay full cost, plus shipping and handling. Contact the publisher or distributor for these added costs before ordering. If you cannot, $2.00 will almost always cover these added expenses.

ABC International
131 Clarendon St.
Boston, MA 02116
617-262-5000

Academy Chicago
    Publishers
425 North Michigan
    Ave.
Chicago, IL 60611
312-644-1723

Accel Distributing
P. O. Box 854
Seal Beach, CA 90740
213-430-2311

Acropolis Books
2400 17th St., N.W.
Washington, DC 20009
800-451-7771
202-387-6805

Adama Books
306 West 38th St.
New York, NY 10018
212-594-5770
Distributed by:
    Franklin Watts

Addison-Wesley
1 Jacob Way

Reading, MA 01867
800-447-2226
617-944-3700

Adirondack Mountain
    Club, Inc.
174 Glen St.
Glens Falls, NY 12801
518-793-7737

A. D. M. Co., Inc.
P. O. Box 10462
Phoenix, AZ 85016
602-279-2070

Adventure Productions,
    Inc.
1401 Duff Dr., Suite
    600
Fort Collins, CO 80524
303-493-8776

Aerial Photography
    Services, Inc.
2511 South Tryon St.
Charlotte, NC 28203
704-333-5143
Distributed by: Baker &
    Taylor (Midwest)

Affordable Adventures,
    Inc.

924 West Eula Court
Glendale, WI 53209
414-964-3753

Alaska Natural History
Assn.
2525 Gambell St.
Anchorage, AK 99503
907-274-8440

Alaska Northwest
Publishing Co.
130 Second Ave., South
Edmonds, WA 98020
206-774-4111

Alive Publications, Ltd.
11 Park Place
New York, NY 10007
212-962-0316
Distributed by: Hunter
Publishing

Altarinda Books
13 Estates Drive
Orinda, CA 94563
415-254-3830

Americana Press
3516 Albemerle St.,
N.W.
Washington, DC 20008
202-362-8538

AM/PM Publishing
2293 Filbert St.
San Francisco, CA
94123
415-921-2676

Anchor Books
see Doubleday & Co.

And Books
702 South Michigan,
Suite 836
South Bend, IN 46618
219-232-3134
Distributed by:
Distributors

Appalachian Mountain
Club Books
5 Joy Street
Boston, MA 02108
617-523-0636

Appalachian Trail
Conference
P. O. Box 807
Harpers Ferry, WV
25425

Applewood Books
P. O. Box 2870
Cambridge, MA 02139
617-350-0311

Apollo Books
5 Schoolhouse Lane
Poughkeepsie, NY
12603
800-431-5003
800-942-8222 (NY)

Aptos Publishing Co.
P. O. Box 2278
Aptos, CA 95001
408-688-0280
Distributed by:
Publisher Marketing

ARA Books &
Magazines
16150 West Lincoln
Ave.
New Berlin, WI 53214
414-786-5650

Arbor House
105 Madison Ave.
New York, NY 10016
212-481-0350
Distributed by: William
Morrow

Ariel Publishing
14417 SE 19th Place
Bellevue, WA 98007

206-641-0518
Distributed by:
  Bookpeople

Arizona Highways
2039 West Lewis Ave.
Phoenix, AZ 85009
602-258-6641

Association for Public
  Transportation
P. O. Box 192
Cambridge, MA 02238

Association of
  American Historic
  Inns
P. O. Box 336
Dana Point, CA 92629
714-496-6953

Atheneum/Charles
  Scribner's Sons
115 Fifth Ave.
New York, NY 10003
800-257-5755
212-614-1300

Backcountry
  Publications
P. O. Box 175
Woodstock VT 05091
800-635-5009
802-457-1049

Backeddy Books
Box 301
Cambridge, ID 83610

Backroad Chronicles
12 Westerville Square
Westerville, OH 43081

Baja Trail Publications
P. O. Box 6088
Huntington Beach, CA
  92615
714-969-2252

Baker & Taylor,
  Midwest Division
501 Gladiolus St.
Momence, IL 60954
815-472-2444

Baker & Taylor, Eastern
  Division
50 Kirby Ave.
Somerville, NJ 08876
201-722-8000

Baker & Taylor,
  Southeast Division
Mt. Olive Rd.
Commerce, GA 30529
404-335-5000

Baker & Taylor,
  Western Division
380 Edison Way
Reno, NV 89564
800-648-3450
702-786-6700

Ballantine Books
see Random House

Bantam Books, Inc.
666 Fifth Ave.
New York, NY 10103
800-323-9872
212-765-6500

Barron's Educational
  Series, Inc.
113 Crossways Park Dr.
Woodbury, NY 11797
800-645-3476
800-257-5729 (NY)
516-921-8750

Bay Press
914 Alaskan Way
Seattle, WA 98104
206-447-1871

BDIT, Inc.
P. O. Box 7708
Flushing, NY 11352

Beaufort Books,
  Publishers
9 East 40th St.
New York, NY 10016
Distributed by:
  Kampmann & Co.

Beginning Press
5418 South Brandon
Seattle, WA 98118
206-723-6300
Distributed by: Pacific
  Pipeline, Publishers
  Group West

Berkley Publishing
  Group
200 Madison Ave.
New York, NY 10016
800-223-0510
212-686-9820

Berkshire House
P. O. Box 28
Great Barrington, MA
  01230
413-528-3156
Distributed by:
  Countryman Press

Betsy Ross Publications
3057 Betsy Ross Dr.
Bloomfield Hills, MI
  48013
313-646-5357

Betterway Publications
White Hall, VA 22987
804-823-5661

Basil Blackwell, Inc.
432 Park Ave. South,
  Suite 1503
New York, NY 10016
212-684-2890
Distributed by: Harper
  & Row

John F. Blair, Publisher
1406 Plaza Dr.
Winston-Salem, NC
  27103
800-222-9796
919-768-1374

Suzanne Blair
P. O. Box 339, Collins
  St.
Melbourne, 3000
Australia

Bloch Publishing Co.
37 West 26th St.
New York, NY 10010
212-532-3977

Boardworks Publishing
P. O. Box 1241
Jamaica Plain, MA
  02130
617-325-7722

Bodfish Books
P. O. Box 69
Chester, CA 96020
916-342-1055

Boerum Hill Books
Box 286
Brooklyn, NY 11217
718-624-4000

Bonus Books, Inc.
160 East Illinois St.
Chicago, IL 60611
800-225-3775
312-467-0580

The Book Bin, Inc.
Four Corners Plaza
Onley, VA 23418

Book Dynamics
836 Broadway
New York, NY 10003
212-254-7798

Bookmen, Inc.
525 N. Third St.
Minneapolis, MN
  55401
800-328-8411
612-341-3333

Bookpeople
2929 Fifth St.
Berkeley, CA 94710
800-227-1516
800-624-4466 (CA)
415-549-3030

Bookslinger
213 East Fourth St.
St. Paul, MN 55101
612-221-0429

Bored Feet Publications
P. O. Box 1832
Mendicino, CA 95460
707-964-6629

Bric-A-Brac Bookworks
Box 887
Forked River, NJ 08731
609-693-4053

Broadman Press
127 Ninth Ave., North
Nashville, TN 37234
800-251-3225
615-251-2544

Charles Brod
3749 Willamette Dr.
Portland, OR 97267

Buchan Publications
P. O. Box 7218
St. Petersburg, FL 33734
813-526-9121

Ed Buryn, Publisher
Box 31123
San Francisco, CA
  94131
415-824-8938

Distributed by:
  Bookpeople
Pacific Pipeline
Distributors
Book Dynamics

Cambridge University
  Press
32 E. 57th St.
New York, NY 10022
800-872-7423
212-688-8888

Camino Books
P. O. Box 59026
Philadelphia, PA 19102
215-732-2491

Canyon Publishing Co.
8561 Eatough Ave.
Canoga Park, CA 91304
818-702-0171

Capra Press
P. O. Box 2068
Santa Barbara, CA
  93120
805-966-4590

Caroline House, Inc.
250 Frontenac Rd.
Naperville, IL 60540
800-245-2665
312-983-6400

Carousel Press
P. O. Box 6061
Albany, CA 94706
415-527-5849

Carson Enterprises
Drawer 71
Deming, NM 88031
505-546-3252

Cassady & Calhoun
P. O. Box 3580
Berkeley, CA 94703
415-540-0800

Caxton Printers, Ltd.
P. O. Box 700
Caldwell, ID 83605
208-459-7421
800-451-8791 (ID)

Centra Publications
4705 Laurel St.
San Diego, CA 92105
619-263-7942
Distributed by: Sunbelt
Publications

Century One Press
2325 East Platte Ave.
Colorado Springs, CO
80909
303-471-1322

Chalfant Press, Inc.
P. O. Box 787
Bishop, CA 93514
619-873-3535

Chatham Press
P. O. Box A
Old Greenwich, CT
06870
203-531-7755

Chelsea Green
Publishing Co.
P. O. Box 283
Chelsea, VT 05038
802-685-3108

Cherokee Publishing
Co.
P. O. Box 1523
Marietta, GA 30061
404-424-6210

Chicago Review Press,
Inc.
814 North Franklin St.
Chicago, IL 60610
312-337-0747

China Books &
Periodicals Inc.

2929 24th St.
San Francisco, CA
94110
415-282-2994

Chronicle Books
One Hallidie Plaza,
Suite 806
San Francisco, CA
94102
800-722-6657
800-445-7577 (CA)
415-777-7240

Classic Publishers
1008 Kent Rd.
Prospect, KY 40059
502-228-4446

Cobble & Mickle Books
P. O. Box 3521
San Diego, CA 92103
619-231-1586

Cole House, Inc.
P. O. Box 19526
Alexandria, VA 22320
703-780-7222

William Collins
8 Grafton St.
London W1X 3LA
England

Colorado Express
18214 Capitol Hill
Station
Denver, CO 80218

Colorado Leisure Sports
P.O. Box 1953
Estes Park, CO 80517
303-586-6846

Columbia University
Press
562 West 113th St.
New York, NY 10025
212-316-7100
914-591-9111

Congdon & Weed
298 Fifth Ave., 7th
 Floor
New York, NY 10001
800-221-7945
212-736-4813
Distributed by:
 Contemporary Books

Consumer Reports
 Books
110 East 42nd St., No.
 1301
New York, NY 10017
212-682-9280

Contemporary Books,
 Inc.
180 North Michigan
 Ave.
Chicago, IL 60601
312-782-9181

Costano Books
P. O. Box 355
Petaluma, CA 94953
707-762-4848

Countryman Press, Inc.
P. O. Box 175
Woodstock, VT 05091
800-635-5009
802-457-1049

Crossroads
 Communications
P. O. Box 7
Carpentersville, IL
 60110
312-587-1658

Crown Publishers, Inc.
225 Park Avenue, South
New York, NY 10003
800-526-4264
212-254-1600

Curson House Inc.,
 Publishers

250 South 18th St.
Philadelphia, PA 19103
215-732-7111

Bob Damron
 Enterprises
P. O. Box 11270
San Francisco, CA
 94101
415-864-5040

David and Charles, Inc.
P. O. Box 257
North Pomfret, VT
 05053
800-423-4525
802-457-1911

Dayton Laboratories
3235 Dayton Ave.
Lorain, OH 44055
216-246-1397

De Lorme Publishing
 Co.
P. O. Box 298
Freeport, ME 04032
800-227-1656
207-865-4171

Delta Dragon Books
6th Flr., Sun Ping Bldg.,
 916 Cheung Sha Wan
 Rd.
Cheung Sha Wan,
 Kowloon, Hong Kong

Dialogue Publications,
 Inc.
3100 South Oak Park
 Ave.
Berwyn, IL 60402
312-749-1908

Diffendal & Johnson
P. O. Box 76985
Washington, DC 20013
202-546-4103
202-543-8145

Distributors
702 South Michigan
South Bend, IN 46618
800-348-5200
219-232-8500

Dodd, Mead & Co.
71 Fifth Ave.
New York, NY 10003
800-237-3255
212-627-8444

Doubleday & Co., Inc.
245 Park Ave.
New York, NY 10017
800-457-7605
800-645-6156
212-984-7561

Dover Publications, Inc.
180 Varick St.
New York, NY 10014
800-223-3130
516-294-7000

Down East Books
P. O. Box 679
Camden, ME 04843
207-594-9544
800-432-1670 (ME)

Down to Earth
   Publications
1426 Sheldon
St. Paul, MN 55108
612-644-3047

E. P. Dutton
2 Park Ave.
New York, NY 10016
212-725-1818

Eakins Publications,
   Inc.
P. O. Box 23066
Austin, TX 78735
512-288-1771

William B. Eerdmans
   Publishing Co.

255 Jefferson Ave., SE
Grand Rapids, MI
   49503
800-253-7521

Eldan Press
1259 El Camino, No.
   288
Menlo Park, CA 94025
415-322-8777
Distributed by:
   Publishers Group
   West

Emerald City Press
P. O. Box 21066
Little Rock, AR 72212
501-224-3897

Empire State Railway
   Museum, Inc.
P. O. Box 666
Middletown, NY 10940
914-343-4219

Enchiridion
   International
Box 2589
Cullowhee, NC 28723
704-255-0408

Entwood Publishing Co.
P. O. Box 268
Wausau, WI 54402
715-842-7250
Distributed by:
   Caroline House

EPM Publications
1003 Turkey Run Rd.
McLean, VA 22101
703-442-7810

Escortguide
535 Cordova Rd., Suite
   125
Santa Fe, NM 87501
505-988-7099

Eurail Guide Annual
27540 Pacific Coast
  Hwy.
Malibu, CA 90265
213-457-7286

Eurasia Press
168 State St.
Teaneck, NJ 07666
800-242-7737
212-564-4099
Distributed by:
  Houghton Mifflin

M. Evans & Co., Inc.
216 E. 49th St.
New York, NY 10017
212-688-2810
Distributed by: Henry
  Holt & Co.

Excogitations
P. O. Box 6260
Pasadena, TX 77506
713-476-1767

Faber and Faber, Inc.
50 Cross St.
Winchester, MA 01890
617-721-1427
Distributed by: Harper
  & Row

Facts on File, Inc.
460 Park Ave., South
New York, NY 10016
800-322-8785
212-683-2244

Fair Oaks Publishing
941 Populus Pl.
Sunnyvale, CA 94086
408-732-1078

Falcon Press Publishing
  Co, Inc.
P. O. Box 731
Helena, MT 59624
800-582-2665

800-592-2665 (MT)
406-442-6597

Far West Book Service
3515 N.E. Hassalo
Portland, OR 97232
503-234-7664

Farm/Ranch Vacations
36 East 57th St.
New York, NY 10022
212-355-6334

Farrar, Straus & Giroux,
  Inc.
19 Union Square, West
New York, NY 10003
800-242-7737
212-741-6900

Fawcett Book Group
see Random House

Ferrari Publications
P. O. Box 35575
Phoenix, AZ 85069
602-863-2408
Distributed by:
  Bookpeople
Inland Book Co.

Fisher's World, Inc.
Nutmeg Farm
Laporte, PA 18626
800-777-0400

Fleet Press Corp.
160 Fifth Ave.
New York, NY 10010
212-243-6100

Focal Press
80 Montvale Ave.
Stoneham, MA 02180
800-544-1013
617-438-8464

Fodor's Travel
  Publications
201 East 50th St.

New York, NY 10022
212-872-8254
Distributed by: Random
House

Foghorn Press
2687 45th Ave.
San Francisco, CA
94116
415-564-4918
Distributed by:
Bookpeople
Publishers Group West

Follett Publishing Co.
1000 W. Washington
Blvd.
Chicago, IL 60607

Fords Travel Guides
19448 Londelius St.
Northridge, CA 91324
818-701-7414

Burt Franklin, Publisher
P. O. Box 856
New York, NY 10014
800-223-0766
212-627-0027

Freeport Historical
Society
P. O. Box 358
Freeport, ME 04032

Friede Publications
2339 Venezia Dr.
Davidson, MI 48423
313-658-1955

Gable & Gray
1307 West Main
Medford, OR 97501
800-522-7753
800-622-7753 (OR)

Garrett Park Press
P. O. Box 190 E

Garrett Park, MD
20896
301-946-2553

Gem Guides Book Co.
3677 San Gabriel
Parkway
Pico Rivera, CA 90660

Gerry's Frankly
Speaking
P. O. Box 2225
Salem, OR 97308
503-585-8411

Glastonbury Press
12816 E. Rose Dr.
Whittier, CA 90601
213-698-4243
Distributed by:
Publishers Group
West
Gem Guides Book Co.

Global Travel
Publishers
P. O. Box 2567
Pompano Beach, FL
33072

The Globe Pequot Press
10 Denlar Dr.
P.O. Box Q
Chester, CT 06412
800-243-0495
800-962-0973 (CT)
203-526-9571

David R. Godine,
Publishers, Inc.
300 Massachusetts Ave.
Boston, MA 02115
617-536-0761
Distributed by: Harper
& Row

Gold Hill Publishing
Co., Inc.

Drawer F
Virginia City, NV
 89440
702-847-0222

Golden West Publishing
4113 N. Longview
Phoenix, AZ 85014
602-265-4392

Gower Publishing Co.
Old Post Road
Brookfield, VT 05036
802-276-3162

Graphic Arts Center
 Publishing Co.
P. O. Box 10306
Portland, OR 97210
800-452-3032
503-226-2402

Grastorf, Lang & Co.,
 Inc.
142 W. 24th St.
New York, NY 10011
212-255-5693

Great Outdoors
 Publishing Co.
4747 28th St., North
St. Petersburg, FL 33714
813-525-6609
800-433-5560 (FL)

Greatest Graphics, Inc.
P. O. Box 4467
Springfield, MO 65804
417-862-6500

Green Acres School
11701 Danville Dr.
Rockville, MD 20852
301-881-4100

Green Mountain Club,
 The
P. O. Box 889
Montpelier, VT 05602
802-223-3463

Stephen Greene Press
15 Muzzey St.
Lexington, MA 02173
617-861-0170
Distributed by: Viking
 Penguin

Grove Press
920 Broadway
New York, NY 10010
800-521-0178
212-207-6900
Distributed by: Random
 House

Gulf Publishing Co.
P. O. Box 2608
Houston, TX 77252
713-529-4301

Robert Hale Co.
1840 130th Ave., NE,
 Suite 10
Bellevue, WA 98005
206-881-5212

G. K. Hall & Co.
70 Lincoln St.
Boston, MA 02111
800-343-2806
617-423-3990

Hampton-Brown Co.
200 Clock Tower, Suite
 201-A
Carmel, CA 93923
408-625-3666

Hancock House
 Publishers
1431 Harrison Ave.
Blaine, WA 98230
604-538-1114

Harbour Publishing
P. O. Box 219, Madeira
 Park,
B.C., Canada, V0N2H0
Distributed by:

Publishers Group
West

Harper & Row
10 E. 53rd St.
New York, NY 10022
800-242-7737
212-207-7000

The Harvard Common
Press
535 Albany St.
Boston, MA 02118
617-423-5803
Distributed by:
Kampmann & Co.

Hastings House,
Publishers
260 Fifth Ave.
New York, NY 10001
Distributed by:
Kampmann & Co.

Haynes Publications,
Inc.
861 Lawrence Dr.
Newbury Park, CA
91320
818-889-5400
805-498-6703

Hearst Publications
105 Madison Ave.
New York, NY 10016
212-481-0355

W. S. Heinman
Imported Books
1780 Broadway, Suite
1004
New York, NY 10019
212-757-7628

Herald Press
616 Walnut Ave.
Scottdale, PA 15683
800-245-7894
412-887-8500

Heritage Associates,
Inc.
P. O. Box 6291
Albuquerque, NM
87197
505-268-0155

Heyday Books
P. O. Box 9145
Berkeley, CA 94709
415-549-3564

Hideaways
International
P. O. Box 1270
Littleton, MA 01460
800-843-4433
617-486-8955

Hippocrene Books, Inc.
171 Madison Ave.
New York, NY 10016
212-685-4371

Ed Hitzel
300 Grace Ave.
Mays Landing, NJ
08330

William N. Hoffman
53 Claire Ave.
New Rochelle, NY
10804
914-636-7597

Holden Pacific
814-35th Ave.
Seattle, WA 98122
206-325-4324

Henry Holt & Co.
521 Fifth Ave.
New York, NY 10175
212-599-7600

Homestead Publishing
Box 193
Moose, WY 83012

Houghton Mifflin Co.
1 Beacon St.
Boston, MA 02108
800-225-3362
617-272-1500

HP Books
P. O. Box 5367
Tucson, AZ 85703
800-528-4923
602-888-2150

Hunter Publishing, Inc.
300 Raritan Center
    Parkway
Edison, NJ 08818
201-225-1900

Susan Hunter
    Publishing
1447 Peachtree St., NE,
    #807
Atlanta, GA 30309
404-874-5473

IIAS (Intl. Inst. for
    Advanced Studies)
8000 Bonhomme Ave.,
    Suite 403
Clayton, MO 63105

Image Imprints
P. O. Box 2764
Eugene, OR 97402
503-998-2612
Distributed by: Far
    West Book Service

Impact Publications
10655 Big Oak Circle
Manassas, VA 22111
703-361-7300

Imported Publications,
    Inc.
320 W. Ohio St.
Chicago, IL 60610
800-345-2665
312-787-9017

In-the-Valley-of-the-
    Wichitas House
P. O. Box 6741
Lawton, OK 73506
405-536-7118

Incline Press
456 Columbia Ave.
Merced, CA 95340
209-723-3667

Indiana Periodicals
2120 South Meridian
    St.
Indianapolis, IN 46225
317-786-1488

Ingram Book Co.
347 Reedwood Dr.
Nashville, TN 37217
800-251-5900
615-361-5000

Inland Book Co.
22 Hemingway Ave.
East Haven, CT 06512
800-243-0138
203-467-4527

Inns-Piration Guide
    Publishing Co.
P. O. Box 404
Newark, NY 14513
315-331-3904
Distributed by:
    Distributors
Quality Books
North Country Books

Inter-Ski Services
Box 3635, Georgetown
    Station
Washington, D.C.
    20007
202-342-0886

International Intertrade
P. O. Box 636, Federal
    Square

Newark, NJ 07101
201-686-2382

International Marine
Publishing Co.
21 Elm St.
Camden, ME 04843
800-328-0059
800-637-9240
207-236-4342

Irish Books & Media
2115 Summit Ave., Box
5026
St. Paul, MN 55105
612-647-5678

ISBS (Intl. Specialized
Book Services)
5602 NE Hassalo St.
Portland, OR 97213
800-547-7734
503-287-3093

Island Bed & Breakfast
Hawaii, Inc.
P. O. Box 449
Kapaa, HI 96746
805-822-7771
Distributed by: Pacific
Trade Group
Pacific Pipeline
Bookpeople

Island Heritage
1819 Kahai St.
Honolulu, HI 96819
808-847-5566

Island Press
175 Bahia Via
Fort Myers Beach, FL
33931
813-463-9482

Jadetree Press, Inc.
P. O. Box 11130
Arlington, VA 22210
703-522-9550

JASI/Discover Bks
c/o P. Johnson
P. O. Box 19786
Seattle, WA 98109

JK West Publications
P. O. Box 18758
San Jose, CA 95158

Johnson Books
P. O. Box 990
Boulder, CO 80301
303-443-1576

Joy Publishing Co.
P. O. Box 2532
Boca Raton, FL 33427
305-276-5879

Juniper Junction
899 Zia Road
Santa Fe, NM 87505

Kampmann & Co., Inc.
226 W. 26th St.
New York, NY 10001
800-526-7626
212-727-0190

William Kaufman, Inc.
P. O. Box 504901
Palo Alto, CA 94303
415-945-4081

M. Kennedy Publishing
Co.
310 Franklin St., No.
285
Boston, MA 02110

KI-2 Enterprises
P. O. Box 13322
Portland, OR 97213
502-256-3486
Distributed by: Pacific
Pipeline
Publishers Group West

Knighttime
Publications

890 Calabasas Road
Watsonville, CA 95076
408-684-0528
Distributed by:
  Publishers Group
  West
Quality Books

Alfred Knopf Inc.,
  Random House
201 E. 50th St.
New York, NY 10022
800-638-6460

Kodansha International
see Harper & Row

Jane Lael
P. O. Box 701
Kapaau, HI 96755

Lane Publishing Co.
80 Willow Rd.
Menlo Park, CA 94025
800-227-7346
415-321-3600

Langenscheidt
  Publishers, Inc.
46-35 54th Rd.
Maspeth, NY 11378
718-784-0055

Lexikos Publishing
4079 19th Ave.
San Francisco, CA
  94132
415-584-1085

Little, Brown & Co.
34 Beacon St.
Boston, MA 02108
800-343-9204
617-227-0730

Little Nemo Press
198 E. Seventh St., No.
  12
New York, NY 10009
212-254-4779

Lonely Planet
  Publications
112 Linden St.
Oakland, CA 94607
415-893-8555

Longleaf Publications
P. O. Box 4282
Tallahassee, FL 32315
904-385-0383

Longwood Publishing
  Group, Inc.
27 S. Main St.
Wolfeboro, NH 03894
800-343-9444
603-569-4576

Lost Roads, Publishers
Box 5848, Weybosset
  Hill Sta.
Providence, RI 02903
401-941-4188
Distributed by: Inland
  Book
Small Press
Bookslinger

Louisiana State
  University Press
Highland Road
Baton Rouge, LA 70893
504-388-6666

Loyola University Press
3441 North Ashland
  Ave.
Chicago, IL 60657
800-621-1008
312-281-1818

Luso-Brazilian Books
Times Plaza Sta., Box
  286
Brooklyn, NY 11213

Nick Lyons Books
see Doubleday & Co.

Macmillan Publishing
Co., Inc.
866 Third Ave.
New York, NY 10022
800-257-5755
212-702-2000
609-461-6500

Marcor Publishing
P. O. Box 1072
Port Hueneme, CA
93041

MarLor Press
4304 Brigadoon Dr.
St. Paul, MN 55126
612-483-1588
Distributed by:
Contemporary Books

Martin Press
P. O. Box 2109
San Anselmo, CA
94960
415-454-7985
Distributed by:
Bookpeople
Publishers Group West

Master Link Publishing
Co.
P. O. Box 30520
Long Beach, CA 90853
213-438-3185
Distributed by: Accel
Distributing

Maverick Publications
Drawer 5007
Bend, OR 97708
503-382-6978

McClanahan Publishing
House, Inc.
Rte 2, Box 32
Kuttawa, KY 42055
502-388-9388

McDonald & Woodward
Publishing Co.
P. O. Box 10308
Blacksburg, VA 24060
703-639-5632

McGraw-Hill Book Co.
1221 Ave. of the
Americas
New York, NY 10020
212-512-2000
609-426-5254
415-898-5598

Douglas McIntyre, Ltd.
1615 Venables St.
Vancouver, B.C.,
V5L2HI, Canada

Meadowbrook, Inc.
18318 Minnetonka
Blvd.
Deephaven, MN 55391
800-338-2232
612-473-5400
Distributed by: Simon
& Schuster

Meadowsweet Press
P. O. Box 295
Corte Madera, CA
94925
415-924-1310
Distributed by:
Bookpeople

Melius & Peterson
Publishing Co.
P. O. Box 925
Aberdeen, SD 57401
605-226-0488
Distributed by: Slawson
Comm.

Menasha Ridge Press,
Inc.
P. O. Box 59257

Birmingham, AL 35259
205-991-0373

Carol Mendel
P. O. Box 6022
San Diego, CA 92106
619-226-1406

Meru Publishing
P. O. Box 1278
Captain Cook, HI
  96704
808-328-9656
Distributed by: Pacific
  Trade Group
Publishers Group West
Pacific Pipeline

Methuen, Inc.
29 West 35th St.
New York, NY 10001
212-244-3336

Metropolitan Press
228 Fourth St.
Del Mar, CA 92014

Michelin Guides &
  Maps
P. O. Box 3305
Spartanburg, SC 29304
803-599-0850

Mino Publications
9009 Paddock Lane
Potomac, MD 20854
301-294-9514

Modern Guides Co.
P. O. Box 1340
Old San Juan, PR 00902
809-723-9105

Henry C. Molinoff
234 Edgewood Ave.
Smithtown, NY 11787
516-265-1051

The Mono Lake
  Committee

Box 29
Lee Vining, CA 93541
619-647-6386
Distributed by:
  Bookpeople
Publishers Group West

Montana Historical
  Society Press
225 N. Roberts St.
Helena, MT 59620
406-444-4708
Distributed by: Univ. of
  Washington Press

Moon Publications
722 Wall St.
Chico, CA 95928
916-345-5473
Distributed by:
  Bookpeople
Publishers Group West
Quality Books

William Morrow & Co.
105 Madison Ave.
New York, NY 10016
212-889-3050
201-227-7200

Mountain Press
  Publishing Co.
P. O. Box 2399
Missoula, MT 59806
800-732-3669
406-728-1900

Mountaineers Books
306 Second Ave., West
Seattle, WA 98119
800-553-4453
206-285-2665

John Muir Publications
P. O. Box 613
Santa Fe, NM 87504
505-982-4078
Distributed by: W. W.
  Norton & Co.

Murphy & Broad
 Publishing Co.
P. O. Box 1639
Newport Beach, CA
 92663
714-673-3348
Distributed by:
 Publishers Group
 West
Baker & Taylor

Mustang Publishing
P. O. Box 9327
New Haven, CT 06533
203-624-5485
Distributed by:
 Kampmann & Co.

N. Y.-N. J. Trail
 Conference
232 Madison Ave.
New York, NY 10016
212-696-6800

Natchez Trace Parkway
 Assn.
P. O. Drawer A
Tupelo, MS 38802

National Bestseller
 Corp.
955 American Lane
Schaumburg, IL 60173
312-240-7720

National Textbook Co.
4255 W. Touhy Ave.
Lincolnwood, IL 60646
800-323-4900
312-679-5500

New England Press, Inc.
P. O. Box 575
Shelburne, VT 05482
802-863-2520

New Fortress
 Publications

2332 S. Peck Rd., Suite
 268
Whittier, CA 90601
213-699-3443

New Pittsburgh
 Publications
P. O. Box 81875
Pittsburgh, PA 15217
412-681-8528

New Rivers Press
1602 Selby Ave.
St. Paul, MN 55104
612-645-6324
Distributed by:
 Bookslinger
Small Press

New York Zoetrope
838 Broadway
New York, NY 10003
800-242-7546
212-420-0590

Newtowne Publishing
P. O. Box 1882
Cambridge, MA 02138
617-354-0539

Nodin Press,
 c/o The Bookmen,
 Inc.
525 N. Third St.
Minneapolis, MN
 55401
612-333-6300

Nor'Westing Inc.
P. O. Box 375
Edmonds, WA 98020
206-776-3138

North Country Book
 Express
P. O. Box 9223
Moscow, ID 83843
208-882-0888

North Country Books
18 Irving Place
Utica, NY 13501
315-735-4877

Northland Press
P. O. Box N
Flagstaff, AZ 86002
800-346-3257
602-774-5251

Northword
P. O. Box 128
Ashland, WI 54806
800-336-5666
715-682-9418
Distributed by:
 Bookmen, Inc.
Portland News
Baker & Taylor

W. W Norton & Co.,
 Inc.
500 Fifth Ave.
New York, NY 10110
800-233-4830
800-223-2588
212-354-5500

Oak Valley Press
228 Virginia Ave.
San Mateo, CA 94402
415-341-2991

Oakton Hill
 Publications
P. O. Box 557
Oakton, VA 22124
703-255-1270

Ocean Publications
34 Buckingham Palace
 Rd.
London
SW1 England

Olivia & Hill Press, Inc.
P. O. Box 7396

Ann Arbor, MI 48107
313-663-0235

Olympus Press
P. O. Box 2397
Santa Barbara, CA
 93120
805-965-7200

On Our Way, Inc.
P. O. Box 1972
Sedona, AZ 86336
602-282-5427

On the Road Publishing
2870-1 Twin Brooks
 Rd., NE
Atlanta, GA 30319
404-261-8396
Distributed by:
 Cherokee Publishing

Orafa Publishing Co.,
 Inc.
3055 La Pietra Circle
Honolulu, HI 96815
808-922-5177
Distributed by: Hunter
 Publishing

Oregon Historical
 Society
1230 S.W. Park Ave.
Portland, OR 97205
503-222-1741

Our Sunday Visitor,
 Publishing Div.
200 Noll Plaza
Huntington, IN 46750
800-348-2440
219-356-8400

Oxford University
 Press, Inc.
200 Madison Ave.
New York, NY 10016
212-679-7300
201-796-8000

Pacific Pipeline
19215 66th Ave., South
Kent, WA 98032
800-426-4727
206-872-5523

Pacific Trade Group
P. O. Box 668
Pearl City, HI 96782
808-671-6735

Paige Publications
P. O. Box 1384
Rancho Mirage, CA
  92270
619-328-7898

Pantheon
see Random House

Papaloa Press
362 Selby Lane
Atherton, CA 94025
415-369-9994
Distributed by:
  Bookpeople
Pacific Pipeline
Baker & Taylor (east)

Paradise Publications
8110 S.W. Wareham
  Circle
Portland, OR 97223
503-246-1555

Passport Books
see National Textbook
  Co.

Passport Press
Box 1346
Champlain, NY 12919
514-937-8155

Passport Restaurant
  Guides
843 Lexington Ave.,
  Suite 115
New York, NY 10021
212-772-3942

PBC International, Inc.
One School St.
Glen Cove, NY 11542
516-676-2727
Distributed by: Rizzoli
  International
Hearst Publications

Peachtree Publishers
494 Armour Circle, NE
Atlanta, GA 30324
800-241-0113
800-282-0225 (GA)
404-876-8761

Peanut Butter
  Publishing
329 Second Avenue,
  West
Seattle, WA 98119
206-281-5965

Pelican Publishing Co.
P. O. Box 189
Gretna, LA 70053
800-843-1724
800-843-4558 (LA)
504-368-1175

Penguin Books
see Viking Penguin

Pepper Publishing
2901 E. Mabel
Tucson, AZ 85716
602-881-0783

Peregrine Press
Box 751
Old Saybrook, CT
  06475
203-388-0285

Pergamon Press
Maxwell House,
  Fairview Park
Elmsford, NY 10523
914-592-7700

Pergot Press
1001-J Bridgeway, Suite
227E
Sausalito, CA 94965
415-332-0279
Distributed by:
Bookpeople
Distributors
Quality Books

Perkins Publishing Co.
(summer)
Box 129
Mineral, CA 96063
916-565-3260

Perkins Publishing Co.
(winter)
Box 910
South Lake Tahoe, CA
95705
916-544-2100

Peterson's Guides
P. O. Box 2123
Priceton, NJ 08543
800-225-0261
609-924-5338

Pictorial Histories
Publishing
713 South Third
Missoula, MT 59801
406-549-8488

Pilot Books
103 Cooper St.
Babylon, NY 11702
516-422-2225

Pin Prick Press
2664 S. Green Rd.
Shaker Heights, OH
44122
216-932-2173

Pine Cone Press
587 Europa Ct.

Walnut Creek, CA
94598
415-945-6774

Pineapple Press, Inc.
P. O. Box 314
Englewood, FL 33533
813-475-2238

Pinerolo Publishing Co.
1275 Fourth St., # 203
Santa Rosa, CA 95404
707-578-8890

Portland News
P. O. Box 1728
South Portland, ME
04104
207-774-2633

Potomac Appalachian
Trail Club
1718 N St., NW
Washington, DC 20036
202-638-5307

Potomac Area Council/
AYH Inc.
P. O. Box 28607,
Central Sta.
Washington, DC 20038
202-783-4943

Prentice Hall Press
1 Gulf & Western Plaza
New York, NY 10023
800-223-2336
212-373-8500

Preservation Press
1785 Massachusetts
Ave., NW
Washington, DC 20036
202-673-4058

Presidio Press
31 Pamaron Way
Novato, CA 94947
415-883-1373

Prima Publishing &
  Communication
P. O. Box 1260
Rocklin, CA 95677
916-624-5718
Distributed by: St.
  Martin's Press

Prince Street Editions
8 Prince St.
New York, NY 10012
212-226-7086

Professional Editorial
  Service
62 Floyd St.
Winthrop, MA 02152
617-846-5639

Providence Journal Co.
75 Fountain St.
Providence, RI 02902
401-277-7461

Pruett Publishing Co.
2928 Pearl St.
Boulder, CO 80301
800-247-8224
303-449-4919

Publications in English
Apdo. 7-1230
1000 San Jose,
Costa Rica

Publisher Marketing
  Services
11661 San Vincente Bl.,
  # 206
Los Angeles, CA 90049
213-820-8672

Publishers Group West
5855 Beaudry St.
Emeryville, CA 94608
800-982-8319
415-658-3453

Pueblo County
  Historical Society

33550 Highway 96E,
  No. 190
Pueblo, CO 81001
303-948-3290
303-545-4272

Quality Books, Inc.
918 Sherwood Dr.
Lake Bluff, IL 60044
800-323-4241
312-498-4000

Quartzite Books
P. O. Box 1931
Mt. Vernon, WA 98273

Rambler Books
1430 Park Ave.
Baltimore, MD 21217
301-669-6694

Rand Editions/Tofua
  Press
P. O. Box 2610
Leucadia, CA 92024
619-753-2500

Rand McNally & Co.
P. O. Box 7600
Chicago, IL 60680
800-323-4070
312-673-9100

Random House, Inc.
201 E. 50th St.
New York, NY 10022
800-638-6460
301-848-1900
212-751-2600

Reader's Digest Assn.,
  Inc.
260 Madison Ave.
New York, NY 10016
212-850-7007
914-769-7000
Distributed by: Random
  House

Renaissance House
Box 292, Village Station
New York, NY 10014
212-674-0120

Rhode Island
Publications Society
189 Wickenden St.
Providence, RI 02903
401-272-1776

Riverdale Co., Inc.
5506 Kenilworth Ave.,
No. 102
Riverdale, MD 20737
301-864-2029

Rizzoli International
Publications
597 Fifth Ave.
New York, NY 10017
800-433-1238
212-223-0100

Rocky Mountain
Nature Assn.
Rocky Mountain
National Park
Estes Park, CO 80517
303-586-2371

Routledge & Kegan
Paul/Methuen, Inc.
29 W. 35th St.
New York, NY 10001
212-244-3336

RSG Publishing
P. O. Box 28083
Detroit, MI 48228
313-582-8860

Running Press Book
Publishers
125 S. 22nd St.
Philadelphia, PA 19103
800-428-1111
215-567-5080

Rutgers University
Press
109 Church St.
New Brunswick, NJ
08901
201-932-7764
301-338-6947

Sail Sale Publishing
P. O. Box 1028
Aptos, CA 95001
408-662-2456
Distributed by:
Publishers Group
West
Bookpeople

Salem House Publishers
462 Boston St.
Topsfield, MA 01983
800-624-8947
508-887-8199

Sandlapper Publishing
Co., Inc.
P. O. Box 1932
Orangeburg, SC 29116
803-531-1658

Sasquatch Publishing
Co.
1931 Second Ave.
Seattle, WA 98101
206-441-5555
Distributed by: Pacific
Pipeline

Schildge Publishing Co.
RD 2, Box 336
Plattsburgh, NY 10901
518-561-4752
Distributed by: North
Country Books
Bookmen, Inc.

Scott, Foresman & Co.
1900 E. Lake Ave.
Glenview, IL 60065
312-729-3000

Charles Scribner's Sons
866 Third Ave.
New York, NY 10022
800-257-5755
212-702-2000

Scrimshaw Press
P. O. Box 10
Centerville, MA 02632
508-775-7745

Seattle's Child
  Publishing
P. O. Box 22578
Seattle, WA 98122
206-322-2594
Distributed by: Pacific
  Pipeline

Second Thoughts
  Publishing
153 Halsted
Chicago Heights, IL
  60411
312-756-7500

Sepher-Hermon Press,
  Inc.
1265 46th St.
Brooklyn, NY 11219
718-972-9010

Seven Hills Books
49 Central Ave., Suite
  300
Cincinnati, OH 45202
513-381-3881

Seven Seas Press
524 Thames St.
Newport, RI 02840
Distributed by: Simon
  & Schuster

Shameless Hussy Press
Box 5540
Berkeley, CA 94705

Shelter Publications,
  Inc.

P. O. Box 279
Bolinas, CA 94924
415-868-0280
Distributed by: Random
  House
HP Books

Shelton Publications
P. O. Box 391
Sausalito, CA 94966
415-332-1165
Distributed by:
  Publishers Group
  West
Bookpeople

Shenandoah Natural
  History Assn.
Rt. 4, Box 209
Luray, VA 22835
703-999-2243

Shepard Poorman
  Communications
P. O. Box 68110
Indianapolis, IN 46268
317-293-1500
Distributed by: Indiana
  Periodicals

Sheridan House, Inc.
145 Palisade St.
Dobbs Ferry, NY 10522
914-693-2410

Shore/Campbell
  Publishing
1437 Lucille Ave.
Los Angeles, CA 90026
213-666-6967

Sierra Club Books
730 Polk St.
San Francisco, CA
  94109
415-923-5603
Distributed by: Random
  House

Robert Silver Associates
307 E. 37th St.
New York, NY 10016
212-686-5630

Simon & Schuster
1230 Avenue of the
  Americas
New York, NY 10020
800-223-2348
800-223-2336
212-698-7000

Slawson
  Communications
3719 Sixth Ave.
San Diego, CA 92103
619-291-9126

Small Press
  Distribution
1814 San Pablo Ave.
Berkeley, CA 94702
415-549-3336

Genny Smith Books
1304 Pitman Ave.
Palo Alto, CA 94301
415-321-7247
619-934-6185

Gibbs M. Smith, Inc.
P. O. Box 667
Layton, UT 84041
800-421-8714
801-554-9800

Smithsonian Institution
  Press
955 L'Enfant Plaza,
  Suite 2100
Washington, DC 20560
202-287-3765
Distributed by: Tab
  Books

Solstice Press
see North Country
  Book Express

Sonoma County Bike
  Trials
50 Crest Way
Penngrove, CA 94951
707-795-8911

Sound Approach, Inc.
109 Caernarvon Ct.
Exton, PA 19341
215-363-2900

South Jersey Publishing
300 Grace Ave.
Mays Landing, NJ
  08330
609-625-7433
800-582-7055 (NJ)

South Oregon
  Historical Society
P. O. Box 480
Jacksonville, OR 97530
503-899-1847

St. Martin's Press
175 Fifth Ave.
New York, NY 10010
800-221-7945
212-674-5151

Stacey International
128 Kensington Church
  St.
London
W8 4BH England

State Mutual Book
  Service
521 Fifth Ave., 17th
  Floor
New York, NY 10175
212-682-5844

Shifra Stein Productions
P. O. Box 5862
Kansas City, MO 64111

Sterling Publishing Co.,
  Inc.

2 Park Ave.
New York, NY 10016
800-367-9692
212-532-7160

Stewart, Tabori &
  Chang, Publishers
740 Broadway
New York, NY 10003
212-460-5000
Distributed by:
  Workman Publishing
Random House

Storey
  Communications,
  Inc.
Schoolhouse Road
Pownal, VT 05261
800-441-5700
Harper & Row

Storie/McOwen
  Publishing, Inc.
P. O. Box 308
Manteo, NC 27954
800-832-7773
800-443-5879 (NC)
919-473-5881

Straight Arrow
  Publishing
Box 1236
Los Altos, CA 94023

Summit Books
1230 Ave. of the
  Americas
New York, NY 10020
212-698-7501
Distributed by: Simon
  & Schuster

Sunbelt Publications
8858 Dallas St.
La Mesa, CA 92041
619-697-4811

Sunstone Press
P. O. Box 2321
Santa Fe, NM 87504
505-988-4418

Surface Travel
  Publications, Co.
P. O. Box 714
Woodbury, NJ 08096
609-853-7940

Swanson Publishing Co.
P. O. Box 334
Moline, IL 61265

Tab Books, Inc.
13347 Blue Ridge Ave.
Blue Summit, PA 17214
717-794-2148

Talk of the Town
1313 Sunset Rd.
Colorado Springs, CO
  80909
303-633-2724

Talman Co.
150 Fifth Ave.
New York, NY 15011
212-620-3182

Tastes of Tahoe
P. O. Box 6114
Incline Village, NV
  89450
702-831-5182

Sally Taylor & Friends
1442 Willard St.
San Francisco, CA
  94117
415-824-1563
Distributed by:
  Bookpeople
Pubisher's Group West

Taylor Publishing Co.
1550 Mockingbird Lane
Dallas, TX 75235
214-637-2800

Teak Wood Press
160 Fiesta Dr.
Kissimmee, FL 32743
305-348-7330

Teal Publishing
P. O. Box 69421
Seattle, WA 98168

Texas Christian Univ.
  Press
Box 30783
Fort Worth, TX 76129
817-921-7822
409-845-1436

Texas Geographic
  Interests
P. O. Box 9932
Austin, TX 78766
512-453-1885

Texas Monthly Press
P. O. Box 1569
Austin, TX 78767
512-476-7085
800-252-4437 (TX)

Thorndike Press
P. O. Box 157
Thorndike, ME 04986
800-223-6121
207-948-2962

Tidewater Publishers
P. O. Box 456
Centerville, MD 21617
800-638-7641
301-758-1075

Timber Press
9999 S.W. Wilshire
Portland, OR 97225
503-292-0745

Times Books
see Random House

Timetable Publishing
P. O. Box 36

Peterborough
TE3 6SB England

Tioga Publishing Co.
P. O. Box 98
Palo Alto, CA 94302
415-854-2445
Distributed by: William
  Kaufman
Publishers Group West

Title Books, Inc.
P. O. Box 31170
Birmingham, AL 35233
205-324-2596

Touchstone Press
P. O. Box 81
Beaverton, OR 97075
503-646-8081

Trafton Publishing
Evelyn Way
Cobham, Surrey
KT11 2SJ England

Travel Interludes
P. O. Box 4276
Carmel, CA 93921
408-624-0928

Travel Keys Books
P. O. Box 160691
Sacramento, CA 95816
916-452-5200
Distributed by: St.
  Martin's Press

Travel Press
P. O. Box 70
San Mateo, CA 94401
415-342-9117
Distributed by: Warner
  Books

Traveler's Library
20 N. Wacker Dr.
Chicago, IL 60606
312-332-3571

Tree By The River
  Publishing
Box 463-H
Bridgeport, CA 93517
619-932-7590

Tundra Publications
Moraine Route
Estes Park, CO 80517
303-586-5794

Turnagain Products
13201 Ridgeway Circle
Anchorage, AL 99516

Charles E. Tuttle Co.,
  Inc.
P. O. Box 410
Rutland, VT 05701
802-773-8930

Twin Peaks Press
P. O. Box 8097
Portland, OR 97207
206-256-1670

U. S. Capitol Historical
  Society
200 Maryland Ave., NE
Washington, DC 20002
202-543-8919

U. S. Information
  Moscow
3220 Sacramento St.
San Francisco, CA
  94115
415-922-2422

Ulysses Press
Box 4000 H
Berkeley, CA 94704
415-644-0915
Distributed by:
  Publishers Group
  West

University of California
  Press

2120 Berkeley Way
Berkeley, CA 94720
800-822-6657
415-642-6683

University of Hawaii
  Press
2840 Kolowalu St.
Honolulu, HI 96822
808-948-8697

University of Michigan
  Press
P. O. Box 1104
Ann Arbor, MI 48106
313-764-4330
313-764-4392

University of Nebraska
  Press
901 N. 17th St.
Lincoln, NE 68508
402-472-3581

University of Nevada
  Press
Reno, NV 89557
702-784-6573

University of New
  Mexico Press
Journalism Bldg, Rm.
  220
Albuquerque, NM
  87131
505-277-2346

University of
  Oklahoma Press
100 Asp Ave.
Norman, OK 73019
800-638-3030
405-325-5711
Distributed by: Harper
  & Row

University of Tennessee
  Press

293 Communications
Bldg.
Knoxville, TN 37996
615-974-3321
607-277-2211

University of Texas
Press
Box 7819
Austin, TX 78713
800-252-3206
512-471-7233

University of Toronto
Press
340 Nagel Dr.
Cheektowaga, NY
14225
716-683-4547

University of Utah
Press
101 University Services
Bldg.
Salt Lake City, UT
84112
800-662-0062
801-581-6771

University of
Washington Press
P. O. Box 50096
Seattle, WA 98145
800-441-4115
206-543-4050

University Press of
Kansas
329 Carruth
Lawrence, KS 66045
913-864-4154

University Press of
Virginia
P. O. Box 3608,
University Sta.
Charlottesville, VA
22903
804-924-3468

University Presses of
Florida
15 NW 15th St.
Gainesville, FL 32603
904-392-1351

Van Nostrand Reinhold,
Co.
115 Fifth Ave.
New York, NY 10003
212-254-3232
606-525-6600

Arthur Vanous Co.
P. O. Box 650279
Vero Beach, FL 32965
305-562-9186

Variety House
P. O. Box 8128
New Orleans, LA 70182
504-822-5046

Vendome Press
515 Madison Ave.
New York, NY 10022
Distributed by: Rizzoli
International

Viking Penguin, Inc.
40 W. 23rd St.
New York, NY 10010
800-631-3577
212-337-5200
201-933-1460

Viking Productions
P. O. Box 8097
Longmont, CO 80501
303-776-6775

Village Press
P. O. Box 174
Unionville, CT 06085
203-673-9827

Vintage Publications
1207 Fourth St.
Santa Rosa, CA 95404
707-539-1699

VLE Ltd.
P. O. Box 547
Tenafly, NJ 07670
201-567-5536

Volunteers In Asia, Inc.
P. O. Box 4543
Stanford, CA 94305
415-723-3228

Walking News, Inc.
P. O. Box 352, Canal St.
  Station
New York, NY 10013
212-925-2632

Wandering You Press
P. O. Box 20
Lodi, NJ 07644
201-772-1052

Warner Books
666 Fifth Ave.
New York, NY 10103
800-638-6460
212-484-2900
Distributed by:
  Ballantine Books

Wasatch Publishers,
  Inc.
4647 Idlewild Rd.
Salt Lake City, UT
  84124
801-278-3174

Washington Book
  Trading Co.
P. O. Box 1676
Arlington, VA 22210
703-525-6873

Washington Park Press
7 Englewood Pl.
Albany, NY 12203
518-465-0169

Franklin Watts, Inc.
387 Park Ave., South

New York, NY 10016
800-672-6672
212-686-7070

Wayfinder Press
Box 1877
Ouray, CO 81427
303-325-4797
Distributed by: Johnson
  Books

Wescott Cove
  Publishing Co.
Box 130
Stamford, CT 06904
203-322-0998

West Press
P. O. Box 99717
San Diego, CA 92109
619-270-9096

Western Marine
  Enterprises, Inc.
Box Q
Ventura, CA 93002
805-644-6043

Western Massachusetts
  Publishers
101 Caseland St.
Springfield, MA 01107
413-732-3321

Western Tanager Press
1111 Pacific Ave.
Santa Cruz, CA 95060
408-425-1111

WestPark Books
717 Baca
Santa Fe, NM 87501
505-982-0283
Distributed by: Quality
  Books

Westwater Books
P. O. Box 365
Boulder City, NV 89005
702-293-1406

Where to Find the
Oregon in Oregon
7277 S. W. Barnes Rd.
Portland, OR 97225

White Sound Press
1615 W. Harrison Ave.
Decatur, IL 62526
217-423-0511

Wide World Publishing/
Tetra
P. O. Box 476
San Carlos, CA 94070
415-593-2839
Distributed by:
Bookpeople
Publishers Group West
Quality Books

Wilderness Press
2440 Bancroft Way
Berkeley, CA 94704
415-843-8080

John Wiley & Sons, Inc.
605 Third Ave.
New York, NY 10158
212-850-6418
201-469-4400
801-972-5828

William Street Press
53 William St.
Stratford, Ontario
N5A 4X9 Canada

H. J. Williams
P. O. Box 203
Sausalito, CA 94966
415-332-8635
Distributed by:
Publisher's Group
West

Williamson Publishing
Co.
P. O. Box 185
Charlotte, VT 05445
802-425-2102

Windham Bay Press
P. O. Box 34283
Juneau, AK 99803
907-789-4362
Distributed by:
Bookpeople
Publishers Group West

Windward Publishing
Co.
P. O. Box 371005
Miami, FL 33137
305-576-6232

Charles R. Winkler,
Ltd.
7222 W. Cermak Rd.
North Riverside, IL
60546
312-447-3800
Distributed by:
Dialogue Publications

Winterbourne Press
1407 Gilman St.
Berkeley, CA 94706
415-527-9885

Wisconsin Books
2769 Marshall Parkway
Madison, WI 53713
608-257-4126

Wisconsin Trails
P. O. Box 5650
Madison, WI 53705

Wood Pond Press
365 Ridgewood Rd.
West Hartford, CT
06107
203-521-0389

Woodall Publishing Co.
11 N. Skokie Hwy.,
Suite 205
Lake Bluff, IL 60044
312-295-7799
Distributed by: Simon
& Schuster

Woodbine House
10400 Connecticut,
  Suite 512
Kensington, MD 20895
800-843-7323
301-949-3590

Woodlands Press
79 San Marino Dr.
San Rafael, CA 94901
415-258-0729

Woodmont Press
P. O. Box 108
Green Village, NJ 07935
201-377-6243

Workman Publishing
  Co., Inc.
1 W. 39th St.
New York, NY 10018
800-722-7202
212-398-9160

World Leisure Corp.
177 Paris St.
Boston, MA 02128
617-569-1966
Distributed by:
  Kampmann & Co.

Writer's Digest Books
1507 Dana Ave.
Cincinnati, OH 45207
800-543-4644

800-543-8677 (OH)
513-531-2222

Yankee Books
Depot Square
Peterborough, NH
  03458
800-423-2271

Yes! Inc.
1035 31st St., NW
Washington, DC 20007
800-252-3433
202-338-6969

Yosemite Association
P. O. Box 230
El Portal, CA 95318
209-379-2648

Zagat Survey
45 W. 45th St., Suite
  609
New York, NY 10036
212-302-0505

A. M. Zimmerman &
  Co.
2210 Jackson St., Suite
  404
San Francisco, CA
  94115
415-929-7577
Distributed by:
  Publishers Group
  West
Bookpeople

TRAVEL NEWSLETTERS AND MAGAZINES

Note: For those publications we are familiar with, we have provided short comments as to their orientation. In every case, however, we suggest you write the publisher (some of the more popular magazines may be on your neighborhood newstand) for more information and current subscription prices. In some cases, you can receive a sample issue. Others will send information only.

Adirondack Life
Route 86, Box 97
Jay, NY 12941
A bimonthly magazine
on outdoor recreation
in the Adirondacks.

Adventure Magazine
American Adventure
12910 Totem Lake
Blvd.
Kirkland, WA 98034
A monthly magazine on
camping and RV
travel.

Adventure Travel
1515 Broadway, 11th
Floor
New York, NY 10036
A quarterly magazine
on a wide variety of
adventurous
vacations, such as
cycling in France,
sailing in Ireland,
glacier skiing in
Canada, or rafting for
the gourmet, along
with travel tips,
photography, and
more.

Africa Update
c/o Legesse Travel/Tour
516 Fifth Ave., Suite
205
New York, NY 10036
A bimonthly magazine
on business and
travel on the African
continent.

Alabama Tourist Guide
Bureau of Tourism and
Travel
532 South Perry St.
Montgomery, AL 36104

A quarterly magazine
for the tourist.

America
Whittle
Communications
505 Market St.
Knoxville, TN 37902
A quarterly student
travel publication.

American in Britain
Whitehall Overseas
Publishing
230 Vauxhall Bridge Rd.
London SW 1, England
A bimonthly
publication for the
American traveler in
Britain.

*Andrew Harper's
Hideaway Report*
Harper Associates, Inc.
Box 300
Whitefish, MT 59937
An highly regarded,
exclusive monthly
newsletter. The
"connoisseur's guide
to peaceful and
unspoiled places."

Appalachian Journal
Appalachian Mountain
Club
5 Joy St.
Boston, MA 02108
A semi-annual hiking
publication.

Arizona Highways
2039 West Lewis Ave.
Phoenix, AZ 85009
A monthly magazine
focused on
automobile touring
and emphasizing

history, nature, sightseeing, art, and crafts.

Atterbury Letter
P. O. Box 926
Tiburon, CA 94920
A newsletter published eight times a year and emphasizing in-depth coverage of a few specific selections on the topics of wine, dining, and travel (cruises, tours, etc.)

Australian Caravan World and Outdoor Life
New Press, Ltd.
603-611 Little Londale St.
Melbourne, Victoria, 3000, Australia
Published 13 times a year.

Backpacker
Ziff-Davis
1 Park Ave.
New York, NY 10016
A bimonthly magazine on the places to go, with practical information for the hiking traveler.

Bed & Breakfast Update
Rock Point Press
Box 4814
North Hollywood, CA 91607
A bimonthly newsletter for B&B travelers.

Berkshire Restaurant and Entertainment Guide
Ski America Enterprise, Inc.
Riverside Rd.
Box 737
Lenox, MA 01240
A semi-annual publication.

Best of London Eating Out
Where Publications
35-57 Great Marlborough St.
London W1V 1DD, England
A quarterly publication.

Bikereport
Bikecentennial, Inc.
The Bicycle Travel Association
Box 8308
Missoula, MT 59807
A bimonthly magazine on all aspects of cycle touring.

The Camper Times
Royal Productions, Inc.
Box 6294
Richmond, VA 23230
A bimonthly tabloid on outdoor activities related to camping and RV use.

Camperways
1108 North Bethlehem Pike
Box 460
Spring House, PA 19477
A tabloid, published ten times a year, emphasizing

recreational vehicle camping and travel.

Camping Canada
CRV Publishing
  Canada, Ltd.
2077 Dundas St., East
Suite 202
Mississauga, Ontario,
  Canada L4X 1M2
Published seven times a
  year with a focus on
  camping and RV's.

Camping Magazine
American Camping
  Association
Bradford Woods
Martinsville, IN 46151
Published seven times a
  year.

Camping Today
T-A-W Publishing Co.
9425 South Greenville
  Rd.
Greenville, MI 48838
A monthly magazine,
  the official
  publication of the
  National Campers
  and Hikers
  Association (the
  largest non-profit
  camping organization
  in U.S. and Canada),
  on the full array of
  camping and hiking
  issues.

Cape Cod Guide
MPG Communications
Box 959
Long Pond Rd.
Plymouth, MA 02360
Published 30 times a
  year.

Caribbean Newsletter
c/o GeoMedia #316
1771 Post Road East
Westport, CT 06880
A quarterly newsletter
  available to those
  who purchase
  Fielding's Caribbean,
  the top-rated travel
  guide by Margaret
  Zellers. It features
  several islands in
  each issue, plus
  special events coming
  up.

*Caribbean Travel &
  Life*
606 North Washington
  St., Suite 400
Alexandria, VA 22314
A quarterly magazine
  on the Caribbean,
  the Bahamas and
  Bermuda. Topics
  include shopping,
  restaurants,
  particularly great
  finds in travel,
  culture, and special
  attractions.

Caribbean Treasures
Close Communications
Box 466
Keene, NH 03431
A bimonthly newsletter
  highlighting "island
  discoveries for
  discriminating
  travelers."

Cascades East
716 NE 4th St.
Box 5784
Bend, OR 97708
A quarterly magazine

on outdoor recreation in Central Oregon.

Chevy Outdoors, A Celebration of American Recreation and Leisure
Ceco Communications, Inc.
30400 Van Dyke
Warren, MI 48093
A quarterly magazine on outdoor recreation.

Coast Magazine, The Weekly Vacationer's Guide
Resort Publications, Ltd.
500 North Kings Highway
Box 2448
Myrtle Beach, SC 29577
Published 38 times a year, this magazine features a wide array of vacation articles, emphasizing the coastal areas of North and South Carolina.

Colorado Outdoor Journal
Continental Divide Publishing, Inc.
Box 432
Florence, CO 81226
A bimonthly magazine on hunting, fishing, and camping in Colorado and portions of adjacent states.

Compass
Dept. of Leisure Sport and Tourism

Shell House
140 Phillip St.
Sydney, N.S.W., 2000, Australia
A monthly publication.

Condé Nast's Traveler
360 Madison Ave.
New York, NY 10017
A monthly magazine for sophisticated travelers. Each issue features numerous destination articles throughout the world, as well as tips, reader feedback, and more.

Condo Lux Newsletter
4207 Taylor Rd.
Jamesville, NY 13078
A monthly newsletter focusing on condominium rentals as well as activities, dining selections, and other tips for each area.

Connecticut Trails
Totoket Communications, Inc.
245 College St.
New Haven, CT 06510
A monthly publication.

Connoisseur
The Hearst Corporation
959 Eighth Ave.
New York, NY 10019
A monthly magazine for affluent, sophisticated readers that always features a travel column and other travel and dining articles.

Consumer Reports Travel Letter
Consumer Union of U.S., Inc.
256 Washington St.
Mount Vernon, NY 10553
A monthly newsletter from the famous representative of the common man and publisher of *Consumer Reports.* Each issue covers a wide variety of topics from bargain travel ideas to no-holds-barred ratings of travel guides.

Country Inns/Bed & Breakfast
Country Inn Publications, Inc.
Box 182
South Orange, NJ 07079
A very popular quarterly publication on inns and B&B's.

Cross-Country Ski Areas of America Newsletter
RD 2, Boston Rd.
Winchester, NH 03457
A bimonthly newsletter.

Cruising World
524 Thames St.
Newport, RI 02840
A monthly magazine featuring worldwide destination articles for those who enjoy traveling the world by private boat.

Cycletouring
Cyclist's Touring Club
69 Meadrow
Godalming, Surrey, England
A bimonthly publication.

Cyprus Time Out
Comarts
P. O. Box 3697
Nicosia, Cyprus
A monthly tourist and shopping guide.

The Discerning Traveler
P. O. Box 2999
Princeton, NJ 08543
A newsletter published eight times a year which focuses on "the Northeast's most memorable, delightful and delicious destinations."

Diversion
60 East 42nd St.
New York, NY 10165
A monthly magazine to leisure pleasures for physicians (but anyone can subscribe).

Eastern Seasons
Image Design, Ltd.
P. O. Box 102
St. Johns, Newfoundland, Canada A1C 5N5
A quarterly magazine on the Canadian outdoors.

Egypt Travel Magazine
Ministry of Tourism
5 Sh. Adly
Cairo, Egypt
A quarterly magazine.

Endless Vacation
Endless Vacation
  Publications, Inc.
Box 80260
Indianapolis, IN 46280
A bimonthly magazine
  for "upper end"
  travelers seeking
  variety and quality in
  their vacation. Each
  issue includes
  destination articles,
  book excerpts, how-to
  articles, and more.

Entree
1470 East Valley Rd.
P. O. Box 5184
Santa Barbara, CA
  93150
A monthly newsletter
  covering the best
  buys for the well-
  heeled and well-
  traveled, an insider's
  look at hotels,
  restaurants, and
  travel throughout the
  world. Subscribers
  also have access to a
  24-hour hotline.

Epicurean Review
4619 Nigel Ave.
Sarasota, FL 34242
A monthly newsletter.

Equinox
Equinox Publishing,
  Ltd.
7 Queen Victoria Rd.

Camden East, Ontario,
  Canada K0K 1J0
A bimonthly "magazine
  of Canadian
  discovery."

Europe for Travelers!
Europe Incorporated
408 Main St.
Nashua, NH 03060
A semi-annual
  magazine providing a
  detailed look at the
  seasonal picks,
  including a calendar
  of events for all the
  special festivals and
  activities coming up
  in the months ahead.
  Plenty of tips,
  information on tours,
  and guidebook picks.

European Travel & Life
122 East 42nd St.
New York, NY 10168
A high-class magazine,
  published ten times a
  year, focusing on the
  very best of
  everything. Definitely
  la creme de la creme,
  but a lot of good
  ideas can also be
  gleaned for more
  moderate budgets.

Executive Travel
ABC Travel
  Publications, Ltd.
242 Vauxhall Bridge Rd.
London, WC2, England
A monthly publication.

Explore
Explore Publishing, Ltd.
550 Bronte Rd.

Oakville, Ontario,
 Canada L6J 4Z3
A bimonthly magazine
 on the Canadian
 outdoors

Family Motor Coaching
8291 Clough Pike
Cincinnati, OH 45244
A monthly magazine on
 all aspects of motor-
 home travel.

Family Travel Times
Travel With Your
 Children
80 Eighth Ave.
New York, NY 10011
A monthly newsletter
 which addresses, as
 its name points out,
 where and how to
 travel with your kids.
 Each issue includes
 comments on
 destinations,
 guidebooks, and
 more.

Far East Traveler
Far East Reporters, Inc.
1-4-28 Moto Azabu
Minato-ku, Tokyo,
 Japan
A monthly publication.

Fine Dining
Connell Publications,
 Inc.
1897 N.E. 164th St.
North Miami, FL 33162
A bimonthly magazine,
 which focuses on the
 New York, Florida,
 Philadelphia, and
 Washington, D.C.
 area, and includes

restaurant reviews,
 hotels, country inns,
 and special travel
 activities
 emphasizing fine
 cuisine.

Finigan Wine Letter
Counterpoint
 Publishing, Inc.
101 Fifth Ave.
New York, NY 10003
A monthly newsletter
 which emphasizes
 wine but usually
 includes a few dining
 and lodging tips in
 one wine region or
 another.

First Class Confidential
824 East Baltimore St.
Baltimore, MD 21202
A monthly newsletter
 focusing on the best
 food, lodging, and
 activities each
 destination has to
 offer. Destinations are
 worldwide in their
 scope.

Food & Wine
Food & Wine
 Associates
1120 Avenue of the
 Americas
New York, NY 10036
A monthly magazine
 for upscale,
 sophisticated readers,
 which includes
 plenty of information
 of use to travelers on
 food and wine
 worldwide.

Footloose
Kelthorn, Ltd.
26 Commercial
   Buildings
Dunston, Tyne & Wear,
   NE11 9AA, England
A monthly publication.

France Today
FrancePress, Inc.
1051 Divisadero St.
San Francisco, CA
   94115
A monthly newsletter
   on a wide variety of
   issues concerning
   France, some travel
   oriented, some news
   and analysis.
   FrancePress also
   publishes a French
   language newsletter
   for Americans.

*Gallup Monthly Report
   on Eating Out*
Gallup Organization
53 Bank St.
Princeton, NJ 08542
A expensive, monthly
   assessment of
   restaurants from the
   famous poll-taking
   organization.

Globehopper Magazine
57 Berkeley St.
Toronto, Ontario,
   Canada M5A 2W5
A bimonthly magazine.

*Go: The Authentic
   Guide to Atlanta*
Go Magazine, Inc.
541 Julie St.
New Orleans, LA 70130
A monthly publication.

*Go: The Authentic
   Guide to Dallas*
Go Magazine, Inc.
541 Julie St.
New Orleans, LA 70130
A monthly publication.

*Go: The Authentic
   Guide to the Nation's
   Capitol*
Go Magazine, Inc.
541 Julie St.
New Orleans, LA 70130
A monthly publication.

*Go: The Authentic
   Guide to New
   Orleans*
Go Magazine, Inc.
541 Julie St.
New Orleans, LA 70130
A monthly publication.

*Go: The Authentic
   Guide to San
   Antonio*
Go Magazine, Inc.
541 Julie St.
New Orleans, LA 70130
A monthly publication.

*Going Places: The
   Newsletter of
   International Travel*
Signature Publications
2020 Dempster
Evanston, IL 60202
A monthly publication.

Gourmet
560 Lexington Ave.
New York, NY 10022
A monthly magazine
   for moneyed,
   traveled, food-wise
   people. Included are
   articles on festivals,
   famous chefs, and

hotel and restaurant recommendations throughout the world.

Great Expeditions, Canada's Adventure and Travel Magazine
Box 46499
Station G
Vancouver, B.C.,
  Canada V6R 4G7
A bimonthly magazine, described as a "how-to National Geographic," featuring fascinating adventure and travel ideas both in Canada and throughout the world.

Great Lakes Travel & Living
Great Lakes Publishing Co.
108 West Perry St.
Port Clinton, OH 43452
A monthly magazine on events, restaurants, specialty shops, travel and living in all the Great Lakes states and southern Ontario.

Hideaways Newsletter
Hideaways International
P. O. Box 1270
Littleton, MA 01460
A bimonthly newsletter for members of Hideaways International. While you can purchase the *Hideaways Guide* (see "The World") without becoming a

member, membership does have its privileges. The newsletter details cruises, adventure vacations, places to stay, activities, practical tips, and more.

Holiday Time in Thailand
Tourism Authority of Thailand
4 Rachadamneon Nok Ave.
Bangkok, 1, Thailand
A quarterly publication.

Holiday Which?
Consumers Association
14 Buckingham St.
London WC2N 6DS, England
A quarterly publication from the sister organization of the publisher of America's *Consumer Reports* and the *Consumer Reports Travel Letter*.

Holidays in Romania
(English Edition)
Rompresfilatelia
P. O. B. 12-201
Calea Grvitei nr., 64-66, Romania
A monthly publication.

Hong Kong Travel Bulletin
Hong Kong Tourist Association
Box 2597
Hong Kong, Hong Kong
A monthly publication.

Hosteler's Knapsack
American Youth
   Hostels
Box 37613
Washington, DC 20013
A quarterly magazine
   featuring articles on
   general interest
   topics, hosteling, and
   travel.

*Humm's Guide to the
   Florida Keys*
Crain Communications,
   Inc.
Box 330712
Miami, FL 33133
A quarterly publication
   featuring articles on
   travel, history, and
   general interests, plus
   columns on fishing
   and diving—all in the
   Florida Keys.

*Ian Keown's Very
   Special Places*
280 Midland Ave.
Saddle Brook, NJ 07662
A newsletter published
   eight times a year
   which details this
   popular writer's
   special reports on
   inns, resorts, hotels,
   and hideaways
   throughout the world.

*In Touch, The
   International Tours
   Travel Magazine*
Go, Inc.
110 Broad St.
Boston, MA 02110
A bimonthly magazine
   promoting single,
   couple, and family

travel to easily
   bookable
   destinations.

Inn Review
P. O. Box 1789
Kankakee, IL 60901
A newsletter published
   ten times a year. Each
   issue reviews
   numerous country
   inns, small hotels and
   bed & breakfasts
   located throughout
   the country.

Inside America
Travel Guide Inc.
414 East Market St.
Charlottesville, VA
   22901
A monthly newsletter
   for the sophisticated
   traveler on lodging,
   dining, and travel tips
   from the publishers
   of *La Belle France*. A
   special New York
   City section is
   included with each
   issue.

International Living
Agora Publishing
824 East Baltimore St.
Baltimore, MD 21202
A monthly newsletter
   for both the affluent
   and not-so-affluent,
   who dream of living
   overseas.

*International Travel
   News*
1779 Tribute Rd.,
   Suite L
Sacramento, CA 95815
A large, monthly

newsletter usually numbering 60 pages or more. The focus is on detailed travel information for the "high-frequency international traveler." Plenty of inside tips and information, with a strong emphasis on tours of every sort.

Ireland of the Welcomes
Irish Tourist Board
Baggot St. Bridge
Dublin 2, Ireland
A bimonthly publication.

Islands, An International Magazine
3886 State St.
Santa Barbara, CA 93105
A sophisticated bimonthly magazine to travel adventures on islands in every corner of the world. Included are feature articles, travel tips, and more.

Istanbul, Handbook for Tourists
Turk Turing Turizm Isletmeciligi
Sisli Meydani
364, Istanbul, Turkey
A quarterly publication.

Italia Turistica
I.T.U.R.I.
Via P. Metatasio 2

Casella Postale 1060/8
35100, Padua, Italy
A bimonthly cultural and tourism guide written in English, German, and Italian.

Itinerary, The Magazine for Travelers with Physical Disabilities
Box 1084
Bayonne, NJ 07002
A bimonthly publication.

Jim Dine's San Francisco Letter
P. O. Box 837
Belvedere, CA 94920
A monthly newsletter for the sophisticated traveler. The topics may concern San Francisco—there always seem to be a San Francisco restaurant of the month—but will just as likely present vacation hideaways in the four corners of the world.

Jungle
Wildlife Camp
A-268-Defence Colony
New Delhi 3, India
A bimonthly journal for the promotion of tourism and nature study.

Karen Brown's European Country Inns Newsletter
Travel Press
P. O. Box 70

San Mateo, CA 94401
The publishers of the
wonderful Karen
Brown's Country Inns
series also make
available a seasonally
published newsletter
that will help you
update their travel
guides with the latest
information.

The Kauai Update
Paradise Publications
8110 S.W. Wareham
Portland, OR 97223
A new quarterly
newsletter. The
publishers of the
*Kauai: A Paradise
Guide* (as well as the
very popular *Maui: A
Paradise Guide*)
make available this
update on lodging,
restaurants, and
activities to
supplement their
book.

Key Travel Guide
Key Travel Publications
6 Kriezotou St.
Gr-016
71, Athens, Greece
A monthly publication.

*La Belle France: The
Sophisticated Guide
to France*
Travel Guide Inc.
414 East Market St.
Charlottesville, VA
22901
A monthly newsletter
for the discriminating
traveler, the true

Francophile, on
dining, lodging,
itinerary suggestions,
shopping, and travel
tips. Each issue
includes a special
Paris section.

London Outlook
Janic Productions, Inc.
P. O. Box 498
Millwood, NY 10546
A newsletter published
ten times a years.
The focus is London
and everything about
it: walks, art, hotels,
shops, etc. Very
detailed.

*London Restaurant
Guide*
Where Publications
55-57 Great
Marlborough St.
London W1V 1DD,
England
A quarterly publication.

London Travel Letter
Siewert Publications,
Ltd.
Box 662
London W10 6EW,
England
A detailed, monthly
newsletter from
England covering all
topics of interest:
transportation, hotels,
day trips, beer,
restaurants, nightlife,
etc.

Long Trail News
Green Mountain Club
P. O. Box 889
Montpelier, VT 05602

A quarterly hiking publication.

Look at Finland
Finnish Tourist Board
Box 53
00521 Helsinki, Finland
A quarterly publication.

LTD Travel
931 Shoreline Dr.
San Mateo, CA 94404
A quarterly newsletter "for able and disabled travelers." Addresses important information for the disabled, hearing impaired, and others on travel, destinations, guidebooks, and more. Each issue focuses on a particular itinerary, plus book reviews.

The Maui Update
Paradise Publications
8110 S.W. Wareham
Portland, OR 97223
A quarterly newsletter. The publishers of the popular *Maui: A Paradise Guide* make available this update on lodging, restaurants, and activities to supplement their book. Each issue contains plenty of good tips, whether you use their guidebook or not.

Midwest Outdoors
111 Shore Dr.

Hinsdale, IL 60521
A monthly publication.

Military Travel Times
Box 9
Oakton, VA 22124
A bimonthly newsletter providing low-cost travel information to the U. S. military family—officer, enlisted, active, retired, and reserve—throughout the world.

Montana Outdoors
Dept. of Fish, Wildlife and Parks
1420 East Sixth
Helena, MT 59620

Motel/Hotel Insider Newsletter
ATCOM, Inc.
2315 Broadway
New York, NY 10024
A weekly newsletter.

Motorhome
29901 Agoura Rd.
Agoura, CA 91301
A monthly magazine for motorhome owners, which includes articles on places to travel and things to do when you get there.

National Geographic Traveler
National Geographic Society
17th and M St., SW
Washington, DC 20036
A quarterly magazine highlighting primarily United States and

Canadian travel spots, along with some destination pieces on Europe, Mexico, the Caribbean, and, occasionally, the Pacific.

New England Getaways
New England Publishing Group, Inc.
21 Pocahontas Dr.
Peabody, MA 01960
A monthly magazine featuring special events and other travel pieces on the Northeast.

New Mexico Magazine
1100 St. Francis Dr.
Santa Fe, NM 87503
A monthly magazine with a strong emphasis on New Mexico subjects of interest, for the more sophisticated, college-educated traveler.

New Mexico Vacation Guide
New Mexico Magazine
1100 St. Francis Dr.
Santa Fe, NM 87503
A well-done, annual guide from the New Mexico Tourism and Travel Division on all sorts of attractions and activities within the state.

New York's Nightlife &
Long Island Nightlife
MJC Publications, Inc.

1770 Deer Park Ave.
Deer Park, NY 11729
A monthly entertainment magazine.

Northeast Outdoors
Box 2180
Waterbury, CT 06722
A monthly tabloid on outdoor activities, especially family camping and recreational vehicle travel, throughout the Northeast.

Odyssey
H. M. Gousha Publications
Box 6227
San Jose, CA 95150
A quarterly magazine devoted to travel and leisure, with national and international coverage. Each issue contains destination articles, notes on what to see and do, and practical travel issues.

Oklahoma Today
Oklahoma Dept. of Tourism and Recreation
Box 53384
Oklahoma City, OK 73152
A bimonthly magazine covering travel and recreation in the state.

Oregon Outdoors
Oregon Trails Publications, Inc.

Box 644
Hillsboro, OR 97123
Published ten times a
    year.

Outdoor Alberta
Saffron, the Investment
    Group, Ltd.
12514-124th St.
Edmonton, Alberta,
    Canada T5L 0N5
A quarterly publication.

Outside
Mariah Publication
    Corp.
1165 North Clark St.
Chicago, IL 60610
Published ten times a
    year, this magazine
    addresses a wide
    array of outdoor
    activities, including
    outdoor adventure
    and sports, as well as
    travel topics—
    especially those on
    exotic and rarely
    visited cultures.

Ozark Mountaineer
Rt. 3, Box 868
Branson, MO 65616
A bimonthly
    publication.

Pacific Island Monthly
Pacific Publications
Box 3408 GPO
Sydney, N.S.W., 2001,
    Australia
A monthly publication.

*Palm Springs Life
    Desert Guide*
Desert Publications,
    Inc.
303 N. Indian Ave.

Palm Springs, CA
    92262
A monthly publication.

*Panorama, Boston's
    Official Guide
    Magazine*
Jerome Press
263 Summer St.
Boston, MA 02210
A biweekly magazine.

Passport
20 Wacker Dr.
Chicago, IL 60606
An exclusive monthly
    newsletter for the
    sophisticated traveler
    on hotels, dining,
    excursions, and
    activities throughout
    the world. Each issue
    contains all sorts of
    inside tips to keep
    you "ahead of the
    guidebooks."

Pathfinder
Canadian Youth Hostel
    Association
10922 88th Ave.
Edmonton, Alberta,
    Canada T6G 0Z1
Published three times a
    year.

Pennsylvania Outdoors
Great Lakes Sportsman
    Group
2665 Oregon St.
Oshkosh, WI 54901
Published seven times a
    year.

*Pocket Guide to the
    Bahamas*
Cartwright Publications
Box N494

Nassau, Bahamas
A semi-annual
   publication.

Potomac Appalachian
Potomac Appalachian
   Trail Club
1718 N St., NW
Washington, DC 20036
A monthly hiking
   publication.

The Privileged Traveler
42 Usonia Rd.
Pleasantville, NY 10570
A bimonthly newsletter
   for the well-traveled
   and well-heeled on
   destinations
   throughout the world.
   Included are tips on
   travel, hotels,
   activities, food, etc.

Recreation Canada
Canadian Parks
   Recreation
   Association
333 River Rd.
Ottawa, Ontario,
   Canada K1L 8H9
Published nine times a
   year.

*Recreation, Sports and
   Leisure*
Lakewood Publications,
   Inc.
50 South 9th St.
Minneapolis, MN
   55402
A tabloid published
   nine times a year.

*The Restaurant
   Reporter*
Bower Publishing Co.,
   Inc.

71 Vanderbilt Ave.,
   Room 320
New York, NY 10169
A newsletter published
   16 times a year on
   the restaurants of
   New York. Reviews
   are quite extensive.

Road Rider
Fancy Publications, Inc.
Box 6050
Mission Viejo, CA
   92690
A monthly magazine
   for motorcycle
   touring.

*Seymour Britchky's
   Restaurant Letter*
15 East 10th Street
New York, NY 10003
A monthly newsletter
   by the author of the
   highly respected
   *Restaurants of New
   York*. Each issue will
   keep the
   sophisticated New
   York City restaurant
   connoisseur in the
   know and up-to-date.

*Signpost for Northwest
   Trails*
Washington Trails
   Association
16812 36th Ave., West
Lynwood, WA 98037
A monthly publication.

The Smoke-Free Press
Pinerolo Publishing,
   Co.
1275 Fourth St., #203
Santa Rosa, CA 95404
Bimonthly newsletter
   on travel, recreation

and dining in a smoke-free atmosphere.

South American Explorer
South American Explorer Club
2239 East Colfax Ave.
Denver, CO 80206
A quarterly publication.

Southern Outdoors
BASS Publications
1 Bell Rd.
Box 17915
Montgomery, AL 36141
Published nine times a year.

Southern Travel
5520 Park Ave.
Box 395
Trumbull, CT 06611
A quarterly magazine which covers numerous travel opportunities in the South and helps you get the most for your travel dollar.

Sri Lanka Official Tourist Handbook
Ceylon Tourist Board
Box 1504
Colombo, Sri Lanka
A semi-annual publication.

The State, Down Home in North Carolina
Box 2169
Raleigh, NC 27602
A monthly magazine emphasizing, among other topics, travel in North Carolina

(resorts, dining, destinations).

Texas Highway Magazine
State Dept. of Highways and Public Transportation
11th and Brazos
Austin, TX 78701
A monthly magazine, of particular interest to the automobile traveler, emphasizing sightseeing, history, and destination topics.

Thunder Bay Destinations
North Superior Publishing, Inc.
1081 Barton St.
Thunder Bay, Ontario, Canada P7B 5N3
A bimonthly publication.

Thunder Bay Guest
Algoma Publishers, Ltd.
1126 Roland St.
Thunder Bay, Ontario, Canada P7B 5M4
A monthly visitor's magazine.

Toronto Life Epicure
59 Front St., East
Toronto, Ontario, Canada M5E 1B3
A quarterly publication.

Touch of Paris
Publi Regies
65 rue de Sevres
92100, Boulogne, France
A bimonthly publication.

Tourism and Wildlife
G. C. Verma
24 Gola Market
Netaji Subash Marg
New Delhi 110002,
    India
A quarterly publication.

Tours & Resorts, The
    World-Wide Vacation
    Magazine
World Publishing Co.
990 Grove St.
Evanston, IL 60201
A bimonthly magazine
    focuses, as the title
    indicates, on
    organized vacation
    tours as well as
    interesting resort
    destinations.

Trail Walker
N.Y.-N.J. Trail
    Conference
232 Madison Ave.
New York, NY 10016
A bimonthly
    publication on hiking
    and conservation.

Trailer Life
29901 Agoura Rd.
Agoura, CA 90301
A monthly magazine
    for owners of trailers,
    campers, and motor
    homes. Included are
    articles on travel,
    hikes, fishing,
    boating, as well as
    practical how-to tips.

Trails-A-Way
9425 South Greenville
    Rd.
Greenville, MI 48838

A newsletter, published
    eleven times a year,
    on RVs and camping
    in Michigan, Ohio,
    and Indiana.

Transitions Abroad
18 Hulst Rd.
Box 344
Amherst, MA 01004
Published periodically
    as a resource guide to
    work, study, and
    special-interest travel
    overseas for travelers
    on a low budget.

Travel & Leisure
American Express
    Publishing Corp.
1120 Avenue of the
    Americas
New York, NY 10036
An in-depth, monthly
    magazine for the
    "American Express
    Card set" with
    excellent information
    on fascinating
    destinations, tours,
    health, photography,
    weather, expenses,
    and the "inside
    stuff "—the latest
    travel tips.

Travel-Holiday
Travel Building
51 Atlantic Ave.
Floral Park, NY 11001
The oldest of the travel
    magazines, published
    monthly, and
    featuring fairly
    middle-of-the-road
    looks at 9 or 10
    interesting vacation

destinations per issue, plus practical advice on the latest in transporation options, travel do's and don'ts, etc.

Travel Smart
Communications House, Inc.
40 Beechdale Rd.
Dobbs Ferry, NY 10522
A monthly newsletter on travel information such as discount air travel, unusual travel ideas, inside tips, travel and the tax laws, etc.

Travel Utah
Utah Holiday Publishing Co.
419 East 100 S.
Salt Lake City, UT 84111
A monthly publication.

Travelwriter Marketletter
c/o Robert Scott Milne
Room 1723, Plaza Hotel
New York, NY 10019
A monthly publication for travel writers.

Traveling Times
MAI Enterprises, Inc.
23929 West Valencia Blvd., 3rd Floor
Valencia, CA 91355
A quarterly tabloid for upscale readers on leisure travel, travel tips, cruises, travel bargains, and more.

The Travelore Report
1512 Spruce St.
Philadelphia, PA 19102
A monthly newsletter focusing on travel bargains of every sort—airfares, destinations, hotels, restaurants—throughout the world.

TravLtips
163-07 Depot Rd.
Flushing, NY 11358
A bimonthly tabloid.

Unique & Exotic Travel Reporter
P. O. Box 98833
Tacoma, WA 98499
A monthly newsletter providing information on unusual and intriguing trips, dining, activities, and retreats. Worldwide in scope.

Victor Emanuel Nature Tours Newsletter
P. O. Box 33008
Austin, TX 78764
A quarterly newsletter covering a wide variety of planned nature tours throughout the world.

The Villa Report
P. O. Box 4690
Greenwich, CT 06830
A quarterly newsletter providing "a connoisseur's guide to vacation homes" in every corner of the globe.

Vintage, The Magazine of Food, Wine and Gracious Living
Wine News, Inc.
370 East 76th St., Suite 370
New York, NY 10021
A monthly magazine which includes travel articles on interesting destinations—always with a wine focus, of course.

Voyager International
Argonaut Enterprises, Inc.
P. O. Box 2777
Westport, CT 06880
A monthly newsletter which covers worldwide destinations—where to stay, where to go, practical tips on weather, what to see. Quite detailed.

Walking Tours of San Juan
Caribbean World Communications, Inc.
First Federal Building, Office 301
Santurce, PR 00909
A semi-annual magazine on history, Spanish colonial culture, art, architecture, etc. of interest to those planning vacation walks through beautiful San Juan, Puerto Rico.

Western Canada Outdoors
McIntosh Publishing Co., Ltd.
1132-98th St.
Box 430
Brattleford, Saskatchewan, Canada S9A 2Y5
A bimonthly tabloid on outdoor activities, especially wildlife and fishing, in Western Canada.

Western Outdoors
3197 East Airport Loop Dr.
Costa Mesa, CA 92626
Published ten times a year.

Western RV Traveler
Recreation Publications
2019 Clement Ave.
Alameda, CA 94501
A monthly magazine for the western RV user, including travel topics.

What's On and Where to Go
182 Pentonville Rd.
London N1 9LB, England
A weekly publication.

Where to Eat in London
Where? Publications
55-57 Great Marlborough St.
London W1V 1DD, England
A quarterly publication.

Where, When, How
Peruvian Times

Apdo 2484
Lima, Peru
A monthly publication.

*Wilderness Arts and
   Recreation*
Big Bear Wilderness
   Services
Box 2640
Edson, Alberta, Canada
   T0E 0P0
A bimonthly
   publication.

*The Wine Spectator
Wine Maps: The
Complete Guide to
Wineries,
Restaurants, Lodging
in California Wine
Country*
Wine Maps Order
   Department
The Wine Spectator
Opera Plaza, Suite 2040
601 Van Ness Ave.
San Francisco, CA
   94102
An annual magazine
   focusing on more
   than 500 wineries in
   nine different wine-
   producing regions in
   California and abroad.

Wine Tidings
Kylix Media, Inc.
5165 Sherbrooke St.,
   West
Montreal, Quebec,
   Canada H4A 1T6
Published eight times a
   year, this magazine
   includes travel
   articles on vacations
   to wine-producing
   countries worldwide.

Wining and Dining
HS Publishing
16 Ennismore Ave.
Chiswick, London W4,
   England
A monthly publication.

*Winston's Travel
   Discoveries*
P. O. Box C
Sausalito, CA 95966
A bimonthly newsletter
   for the sophistcated
   traveler seeking an
   "exclusive guide to
   hotels, inns, resorts,
   and restaurants
   worldwide." Done in
   considerable detail.

Wisconsin Trails
Box 5650
Madison, WI 53705
A bimonthly magazine
   which includes
   "active articles about
   people, places, events,
   and outdoor
   adventures in
   Wisconsin."

Women Outdoors
474 Boston Ave.
Boston, MA 02155
A quarterly publication.

*Women's Travel
   Connections*
Travel Trend
   Publishing, Inc.
Box 6117
New York, NY 10150
A monthly publication.

World Traveling
Midwest News Service,
   Inc.
30943 Club House Lane

Farmington Hills, MI
48018
A bimonthly magazine
on many travel
issues: adventure
travel, restaurant
reviews, travel tips,
etc.

*World Wide Travel
Planner*
Wineberg Publications
7842 North Lincoln
Ave.
Skokie, IL 60077
A bimonthly
publication.

Yacht Vacations
P. O. Box 755
Jensen Beach, FL 34958
This magazine,
published ten times a
year, focuses totally
on yacht charter
vacations.

*Yankee Magazine's
Travel Guide to New
England & Its
Neighbors*
Yankee Magazine
Depot Square
Peterborourgh, NH
03458
A large, annual
magazine on a vast
array of inns,
restaurants, shops,
tours, festivals,
sightseeing, camping,
and other activities in
the New England
states, New York
state, and Eastern
Canada.

Subject Index

In order to make sorting through the many titles in this book easier, those travel guides that are solely or primarily focused on one, two, or perhaps three travel subjects have been indexed. With the exception of budget travel guides, all-purpose guidebooks that cover dozens of subjects of importance to the traveler under a single cover are not included. The subject index is the best means of locating specialized travel books that will be useful supplements to the more traditional, all-purpose titles. Note that there is considerable overlap between some subjects. Be sure always to check the other recommended headings. For accommodations, be aware that "Lodging" has been the general category, which includes books covering a variety of hotels, inns, and/or bed and breakfasts. For titles exclusively on one of these types of lodging, see "Hotels," "Inns," and "Bed and Breakfast." Finally, when the title does not clearly indicate where a particular book is reviewed, the location has been indicated in parentheses.

Air Travel
ABC Air Asia, Australia & New Zealand, 108
ABC Air Europe, Middle East & North Africa, 172
Fly There For Less (General Travel), 73
Fly/Ride Europe (Europe as a Whole), 182
How to Get From the Airport to the City (The World), 88
Money Saving Secrets of Smart Airline Travelers (General Travel), 75
Round the World Air Guide, 90
Things That Go Bump in the Flight (General Travel), 77

Amusement (see Entertainment)

Antiques (see Shopping)

Archaeology (see Cultural Guides)

Architecture (see also Cultural Guides, Walks)
A.I.A. Guide to Boston (Massachusetts), 548
Alec Clifton-Taylor's Buildings of Delight (England), 256
Architecture in Los Angeles (California), 468
Atlas of European Architecture (Europe as a Whole), 173
Beacon Hill: A Walking Tour (Massachusetts), 549

Blue Guide: Victorian Architecture in England, 258
Chicago On Foot: Walking Tours of Chicago's Architecture (Illinois), 534
Great American Bridges and Dams (United States as a Whole), 388
Great American Movie Theatres (United States as a Whole), 388
Guide to Architecture in San Francisco (California), 482
Guide to Baltimore Architecture (Maryland), 547
Guide to the Architecture of Metro Phoenix (Arizona), 463
Leningrad: Art and Architecture (Soviet Union), 323
New York: 20 Walking Tours, 586
Newport: A Tour Guide (Rhode Island), 604
Old Brooklyn Heights: New York's First Suburb, 587
Pelican Guide to Plantation Homes of Louisiana, 541
Pelican Guide to the Louisiana Capitol, 541
Phaidon Art & Architecture Guides (Series Reviews), 54
Poland, 315
Self-Guided Architecture Tours: Cape May, New Jersey, 569
South Clyde Estuary (Scotland), 276
Washington Itself (District of Columbia), 514

Art (see also Cultural Guides, Museums)
Art Commission Guide to Manhattan's Outdoor Public Sculpture (New York), 574
Blue Guides: Museums and Galleries of London (England), 258
Guide to Public Art in Greater Boston (Massachusetts), 553
Knopf Guides to Art (Series Reviews), 41
Leningrad: Art and Architecture (Soviet Union), 323
Outdoor Sculpture of Washington, D.C. (District of Columbia), 512
Phaidon Art & Architecture Guides (Series Reviews), 54
Philadelphia's Outdoor Art (Pennsylvania), 603
Portland's Public Art (Oregon), 599
Robert Silver Art Guides (Series Reviews), 57
Traveler's Guide to the Great Art Treasures of Europe (Europe as a Whole), 193

Auto Travel (see also Day Trips, Itineraries, Sightseeing, Rural Travel)
AA Regional Touring Guides (Series Reviews), 2
AA 250 Tours of Britain, 235
Adventures on & off Interstate 80 (California), 467
Britain Off the Motorway (Great Britain), 239
Chicago, City of Neighborhoods (Illinois), 533
Drive Around Denmark, 206
Drive Around Sweden, 334
Europe Free! (Europe as a Whole), 179
Explore Australia, 161
Exploring the Oregon Coast by Car, 598
Fielding's Motoring and Camping Europe (Europe as a Whole), 181
Fodor's Interstate Guides (Series Reviews), 28
France on Backroads, 216
Going Places: Motor Touring Guide to Wales, 278
Hill Country (Texas), 612
Interstate Gourmet Guides (Series Reviews), 39
Just Off the Autoroute (France), 220

Louis Motorist's Guide to the Soviet Union (Soviet Union), 323
Maine Intineraries, 545
Motoring in Norway, 314
Motoring Mexico, 377
Motorist's Guide to the Soviet Union, 323
Oregon for the Curious, 598
Pelican Guide to Plantation Homes of Louisiana, 541
Peter Brereton's Touring Guide to English Villages, 268
Roadside History of Colorado, 507
Scotland for the Motorist, 275
Signposts: French, 227
Signposts: German (West Germany), 343
6 Central Texas Auto Tours, 614
Sunset Highway Services Exit by Exit (The Southwest, U.S.A.), 446
Touring Nevada, 565
Tours For All Seasons (New Mexico), 573
Travel Arizona, 466
Travel Guide to the Natchez Trace Parkway (Mississippi), 560
Trips on Wheels: 15 Driving Tours (Colorado), 507

Back Roads (see Rural Travel)

Backpacking (see Hikes)

Bars (see Pubs)

Beaches (see also Nature, Recreation)
Beaches of Maui, O'ahu, the Big Island (Hawaii), 523
California Coastal Access Guide, 473
Florida's Sandy Beaches: An Access Guide, 517
Great Piers of California, 482
National Seashores (United States as a Whole), 390
Washington Public Shore Guide (Washington), 632
World Guide to Nude Beaches, 95

Bed and Breakfast (see also Lodging)
AA Bed and Breakfast (Great Britain), 230
AA Bed and Breakfast in Europe (Europe as a Whole), 171
Affordable Bed and Breakfast (North America as a Whole), 347
Bed & Breakfast American Style (North America as a Whole), 348
Bed & Breakfast Coast to Coast (North America as a Whole), 348
Bed & Breakfast Directory (North America as a Whole), 348
Bed & Breakfast Guide, East Coast (New England), 395
Bed & Breakfast Guide, West Coast (The Pacific Northwest, U.S.A.), 447
Bed & Breakfast New Zealand, 640
Bed & Breakfast: North America (North America as a Whole), 348
Bed & Breakfast of the Deep South (The South, U.S.A.), 418
Bed & Breakfast U.S.A. (North America as a Whole), 349
Bed and Breakfast Books (Series Reviews), 8
Bed and Breakfast Cookbook (United States as a Whole), 382
Bed and Breakfast Goes Hawaiian (Hawaii), 523
Bed and Breakfast Guide (Great Britain), 236

Bed and Breakfast Homes Directory (The Pacific Northwest, U.S.A.), 448
Bed and Breakfast in Michigan and Surrounding Areas (The Midwest, U.S.A.), 425
Bed and Breakfast in New England, 395
Bed and Breakfast in the Mid-Atlantic States (U.S.A.), 409
Bed and Breakfast Inns of New England (U.S.A.), 396
Bed and Breakfast Traveler (Canada), 358
Bed and Breakfast: California, 470
Bed and Breakfast: Colorado, 503
Best Bed & Breakfast in the World (Great Britain), 237
Canadian Bed & Breakfast Book, 360
Canadian Bed and Breakfast Guide (Canada), 360
Complete Guide to American Bed and Breakfast (United States as a Whole), 384
Complete Guide to Bed and Breakfast (North America as a Whole), 350
Farm Holiday Bureau B&B and Self-Catering Holidays (Great Britain), 243
Fodor's Bed & Breakfast Guide (North America as a Whole), 351
French Country Welcome (France), 216
Frommer's Bed & Breakfast (North America as a Whole), 352
Myrna Oakley's Bed and Breakfast (The Pacific Northwest, U.S.A.), 453
Official Guide to America's Historic Bed and Breakfast Inns and Guesthouses
    (United States as a Whole), 390
Scotland, Where to Stay, Bed and Breakfast, 275
Texas Bed and Breakfast, 615
Wales: Bed and Breakfast, 278

Bicycling (see Cycling)

Boats (see also Canals, Cruises)
ABC Passenger Shipping Guide (The World), 83
Alaska's Southeast: Touring the Inside Passage, 457
Boating Almanacs (Series Reviews), 12
Cruising French Canals and Rivers, 213
Cruising Guide to the Chesapeake (Mid-Atlantic States, U.S.A.), 410
Cruising Guide to the Florida Keys, 515
Cruising Guides (Series Reviews), 19
Ferries of America (United States as a Whole), 386
Ferryliner Vacations in North America (North America as a Whole), 351
Gunkholer's Cruising Guide to Florida's West Coast, 518
How to Cruise to Alaska Without Rocking the Boat Too Much, 459
Ocean Ferryliners of Europe (Europe as a Whole), 189
Trailer Boat Launching and Cruising Guide for Mid-Florida, 519
Watertrips: A Guide to East Coast Cruise Ships, Ferryboats (Mid-Atlantic States
    U.S.A.), 416

**Budget Travel (see also Air Travel, Auto Travel, Buses, Camping, Planning, Senior
    Citizens, Train Travel)**
AA Best Value (Great Britain), 231
AA Britain for Free (Great Britain), 231
Affordable Travel (General Travel), 71
Asia Through the Back Door (Asia as a Whole), 109
Australia For Free, 160

Best Low Cost Things to See and Do (North America as a Whole), 349
Budget Dining & Lodging in New England, 396
Budget Vacationers Guidebook, Western U.S. (Rocky Mountain States), 431
Cheap Eats in Paris (France), 211
Cheap Sleeps in Paris (France), 211
Cheap/Smart Travel (General Travel), 71
Cheap/Smart Weekends (North America as a Whole), 350
Day Trips and Budget Vacations in New England, 398
Daytrips, Getaway Weekends, and Budget Vacations (Mid-Atlantic States, U.S.A.), 410
Directory of Low Cost Vacations (The World), 85
Eating Cheap in Japan, 132
Egon Ronay's Just a Bite (Great Britain), 243
Europe For Free (Europe as a Whole), 178
Europe Through the Back Door (Europe as a Whole), 179
European Country Inns (Europe as a Whole), 180
Fielding's Economy Europe (Europe as a Whole), 180
Fodor's Great Travel Values Guides (Series Reviews), 27
Frommer's Beat the High Cost of Travel (General Travel), 73
Frommer's Dollar-a-Day Guides (Series Reviews), 29
Frommer's Where to Stay (United States as a Whole), 387
Good Value Britain (Great Britain), 245
Good Value France, 218
Good Value Guide to Paris (France), 219
Guide to Budget Motels (North America as a Whole), 353
Guide to Free Attractions (United States as a Whole), 388
Guide to Free USA Campgrounds (United States as a Whole), 388
Hitchhiker's Guide to Africa and Arabia (Africa as a Whole), 97
Hitchhiker's Guide to Europe (Europe as a Whole), 185
Hosteling USA (United States as a Whole), 389
How to Camp Europe by Train (Europe as a Whole), 185
How to Go Around the World Overland, 88
Let's Go Guides (Series Reviews), 42
Malaysia, Singapore, Brunei Traveller's Handbook (Malaysia), 140
Mobil Lodging for Less (Series Reviews), 47
National Directory of Budget Motels (North America as a Whole), 353
National Directory of Free Tourist Attractions (United States as a Whole), 390
New Orleans My Darling (Louisiana), 540
On A Shoestring Guides (Series Reviews), 51
Oregon Free, 599
Pauper's Paris (France), 225
People's Guide to Mexico, 378
Rough Guides (Series Reviews), 58
San Francisco on a Shoestring (California), 495
Senior Citizen's Guide to Budget Travel (Europe as a Whole), 191
Senior Citizen's Guide to Budget Travel (North America as a Whole), 355
South-East Asia Handbook, 112
Thrifty Gourmet: 250 Great Dinners in the Bay Area (California), 500
Touring Guide to Europe (Europe as a Whole), 192

Travel & Vacation Discount Guide (General Travel), 78
Travel Survival Kits (Series Reviews), 65
Vagabond Globetrotting (General Travel), 81
Vagabonding in the USA (United States as a Whole), 393
You Can Travel Free (General Travel), 82

Buses
Bus Traveler's Guide to USA (United States as a Whole), 384
Car-Free in Boston (Massachusetts), 551
England by Bus and Coach, 260
Nicholson: London by Bus and Tube (England), 267
USA by Bus and Train (United States as a Whole), 392

Business Travel
Berlitz Business Travel Guide to Europe (Europe as a Whole), 173
Birnbaum's Europe for Business Travelers (Europe as a Whole), 175
Birnbaum's USA for Business Travelers (United States as a Whole), 384
China Business Handbook, 116
Economist Business Traveller's Guides (Series Reviews), 21
International Herald Tribune Guide (Asia as a Whole), 109
International Herald Tribune Guide to Business Travel (Europe as a Whole), 186
Passport's Guide to Business Capitals (The World), 89
Scandinavian Guide (Scandinavia), 197
World Class Executive (The World), 94

Camping (see also Budget Travel)
AA Camping and Caravaning (Great Britain), 232
AA Camping and Caravaning in Europe (Europe as a Whole), 171
Alan Rogers's Selected Sites (Europe as a Whole), 172
Camper's Companion (Europe as a Whole), 175
Colorado Accommodations Guide, 504
Complete Guide: California Camping, 474
Farm Holiday Guide to Holidays (Great Britain), 244
Fielding's Motoring and Camping Europe (Europe as a Whole), 181
Guide to Florida Campgrounds, 518
Gulf Camping Guides (Series Reviews), 34
Outdoors in Arizona: A Guide to Camping, 464
Rand McNally RV Park & Campground Directory (North America as a Whole),
    355
Scotland: Camping and Caravan Parks, 275
State Parks and Campgrounds in Northern New York, 590
Texas Parks and Campgrounds, 615
Trips and Trails (Washington), 631
Woodall's California/Nevada/Mexico Campground Directory (The Southwest,
    USA), 447
Woodall's Campground Directory (North America as a Whole), 357
Woodall's Tenting Directory: Western Edition (The Midwest, U.S.A.), 429
Woodall's Western Campground Directory (Rocky Mountain States, U.S.A.), 439

Canals (see also Boats)
Canals of Mid-America (The Midwest, U.S.A.), 425

Cruising French Canals and Rivers, 213
Exploring England by Canal, 260
Shell Book of Inland Waterways (Great Britain), 252

Canoeing (see River Sports)

Castles (see also Cultural Guides, Inns, Sightseeing)
AA Castles in Wales, 277
Chambers Guide to the Castles of Scotland, 273

Children (see Family Travel)

Churches (see also Architecture, Cultural Guides, Religion)
Blue Guide: Cathedrals and Abbeys (Great Britain), 238
Collins Guide to Cathedrals, Abbeys, and Priories of England and Wales (Great
    Britain), 241
London Churches Step by Step (England), 264
New Bell's Cathedral Guides (England), 266
Nicholson: Guide to English Churches, 266

Cross-Country Skiing (see Skiing)

Cruises (see also Boats)
ABC Passenger Shipping Guide (The World), 83
Alaska's Southeast: Touring the Inside Passage, 457
Berlitz Complete Guide to Cruising (The World), 84
Berlitz Cruise Guide: Alaska, 458
Bon Voyage! (General Travel), 71
Caribbean Ports of Call, 656
Fielding's Worldwide Cruises, 86
Ford's Freighter Travel Guide (The World), 86
Ford's International Cruise Guide (The World), 86
Frommer's Dollarwise Guide to Cruises (The World), 87
Steam Ship Passenger Directory (United States as a Whole), 392
Stern's Guide to the Cruise Vacation (The World), 92
Total Traveler By Ship (The World), 93
Watertrips: A Guide to East Coast Cruise Ships, Ferryboats (Mid-Atlantic States,
    U.S.A.), 416

Cultural Guides (see also Architecture, Art, Literature, Museums, Religion)
Americans in Paris (France), 209
Apple's Europe (Europe as a Whole), 172
Arlington National Cemetery (Virginia), 621
Asia 101 (Asia as a Whole), 108
Blue Guides (Series Reviews), 11
Blue Plaque Guide to London (England), 258
Britain Before the Conquest Guides (Series Reviews), 13
Bulgaria: A Guide, 203
Carta's Official Guide to Israel, 128
Companion Guides (Series Reviews), 15
Coptic Egypt, 100
Culturgrams (The World), 85
Discovering Cultural Japan, 132

Discovering Moscow (Soviet Union), 321
DuMont Guides (Series Reviews), 19
Europe 101 (Europe as a Whole), 179
Eyes of Texas Guide, 610
Fort Worth & Tarrant County: A Historical Guide (Texas), 610
Guide to Ancient Maya Ruins (Mexico), 375
Guide to Ancient Sites (Great Britain), 245
Guide to Central Europe (Europe as a Whole), 184
Guide to the Dordogne (France), 219
Guide to Tuscany (Italy), 300
Guides from Russia (Series Reviews), 33
Hands On Chicago (Illinois), 535
Here's England (England), 262
Historic Houses of California, 485
Intelligent Traveller's Guide to Historic Britain (Great Britain), 247
Intelligent Traveller's Guide to Historic Scotland, 274
Lost & Found Guides (Series Reviews), 43
Magnificent China, 118
Nagel's Guides (Series Reviews), 50
Old Kyoto (Japan), 137
Pelican Guide to the Louisiana Capitol, 541
Penguin Guide to France, 225
Penguin Guide to Medieval Europe (Europe as a Whole), 190
Permanent New Yorkers, 588
Permanent Parisians (France), 226
Ray Miller's Texas Forts, 614
Santa Fe Then and Now (New Mexico), 572
Shell Guide to Northern Scotland and the Islands, 276
Sophisticated Traveler Guides (Series Reviews), 62
Strolling Through Istanbul (Turkey), 158
Third World Guide (The World), 92
Time Travel in the Malay Crescent (Malaysia), 141
Traveler's Companion to Montana History, 563
Traveler's Key Guides (Series Reviews), 65
Treasures of Yugoslavia, 346
Venice for Pleasure (Italy), 305
Visitor's Guide to the Dingle Peninsula (Ireland), 292
Washington Itself (District of Columbia), 514

Customs/Duty (see Planning)

Customs of Different Cultures
Dining Customs Around the World, 85
Do's and Taboos Around the World (General Travel), 72
Japan Today!, 136
Traveler's Guide to Asian Customs (Asia as a Whole), 110
Traveler's Guide to European Customs (Europe as a Whole), 193

Cycling (see also Recreation)
Backcountry Bicycle Tours (Series Reviews), 6
Best Wisconsin Bike Trips, 634

Bicycle Touring in Europe (Europe as a Whole), 174
Bicycle Touring in the Western United States (Rocky Mountain States), 431
Bicycling Across America (United States as a Whole), 383
Bicycling Country Roads (California), 472
Bicycling the Pacific Coast (The Pacific Northwest, U.S.A.), 448
Bicyclist's Guide to Bay Area History (California), 472
Biking the Great Lake Islands (Michigan), 556
Biking Through Europe (Europe as a Whole), 174
Chicago and Beyond: 26 Bike Tours (Illinois), 532
Complete Guide to Bicycling in Canada, 360
CTC Route Guide to Cycling in Britain and Ireland (Great Britain), 241
Cycling in Europe (Europe as a Whole), 177
Cycling San Diego, 475
Cycling the California Outback, 475
Cyclist's Britain (Great Britain), 242
Cyclist's Guide (New England), 398
Cyclist's Route Atlas (California), 476
Europe By Bike (Europe as a Whole), 177
Family Bike Rides (California), 478
Globe Pequot Bike Rides (Series Reviews), 31
Grape Expeditions in California, 481
Grape Expeditions in France, 219
Greater Washington Area Bicycle Atlas (Mid-Atlantic States, U.S.A.), 412
Guide to Bicycling in Texas, 611
L.A. Bike Rides (California), 486
Latin America on Bicycle (Central America as a Whole), 166
Let's Go See by Bicycle: Long Island and New York City, 583
Maine Geographic: Bicycling, 543
Mountain Bicycling in the San Gabriels (California), 489
Natural Chicago (Illinois), 535
Natural New York, 584
New Orleans Bicycle Book (Louisiana), 540
New York Bicycle Touring Guide, 585
Roads to Ride (California), 493
Sonoma County Bike Trails (California), 498

Day Hikes (see Hikes)

Day Trips (see also Itineraries)
AA Day Trips: North West England, 254
AA Day Trips: West Midlands (England), 254
AA The Second Touring Guide (Great Britain), 234
AA Touring Book (Great Britain), 234
Best of Daytripping & Dining (New England), 396
Carefree Getaway Guide for New Yorkers, 576
Coastal Daytrips in New England, 397
Day Trips and Budget Vacations in New England, 398
Days Out: In and Around London (England), 260
Daytrips, Getaway Weekends, and Budget Vacations (Mid-Atlantic States, U.S.A.), 410

Earl Steinbicker's Day Trips (Series Reviews), 20
Favorite Daytrips in New England, 399
50 Grand Picnics, San Francisco Bay Area (California), 479
Florida Island Exploring, 516
LA Picnics (California), 486
Let's Go Somewhere (Florida), 519
Maine Geographic: Day Trips With Children, 544
New England's Special Places, 405
One-Day Adventures by Car (New York), 588
One-Day Trip Books (Series Reviews), 52
Roaming the Back Roads (California), 493
Shifra Stein's Day Trips (Series Reviews), 59

Disabled
AA Touring Guide for the Disabled (Europe as a Whole), 172
AA Traveler's Guide for the Disabled (Great Britain), 234
Access to the World, 83
Travel for the Disabled (General Travel), 78
Traveling Like Everybody Else (General Travel), 80

Discounts (see Budget Travel, Planning, Senior Citizens)

Diving
Baja California Diver's Guide (Mexico), 372
Diver's Guide to Florida and the Florida Keys, 516
Diver's Guide to Underwater Mexico, 373
Pisces Diving/Snorkeling Guides (Series Reviews), 54

Educational Travel
Peterson's Learning Vacations (The World), 90
Volunteer Vacations (The World), 94
Work, Study, Travel Abroad (The World), 94

Entertainment (see also Budget Travel, Music, Wine Tours)
Bangkok's Back Streets (Thailand), 153
Best Cat Houses of Nevada, 564
Best of Texas Festivals, 609
Birnbaum's Disneyland (California), 473
Blue Ridge Mountain Pleasures (The South, U.S.A.), 418
Celebrations: America's Best Festivals (North America as a Whole), 350
Complete Guide to Kentucky Horse Country, 538
Europe Off the Wall (Europe as a Whole), 179
Europe: Where the Fun Is (Europe as a Whole), 179
Festivals U.S.A. (United States as a Whole), 386
Japan at Night, 135
Joy in the Mountains (The South, U.S.A.), 421
Nino LoBello's Guide to Offbeat Europe (Europe as a Whole), 189
Steve Birnbaum's Walt Disney World/Epcot Center (Florida), 519
Unofficial Guide to Disneyland (California), 501
Unofficial Guide to Walt Disney World & Epcot (Florida), 520
What's "In" Chicago (Illinois), 536

Family Travel (see also Entertainment)
AA Family Days Out (Great Britain), 232
Baby Travel (The World), 83
Candy Apple: New York for Kids, 576
Children's Guide to London (England), 259
Children's Guide to Santa Fe (New Mexico), 569
Children's Treasure Hunt Guides (Series Reviews), 14
Discover Seattle With Kids (Washington), 626
Eating Out With the Kids in San Francisco (California), 478
Exploring the Twin Cities With Children (Minnesota), 558
Fielding's Europe with Children (Europe as a Whole), 181
Fielding's Family Vacations (United States as a Whole), 386
Going Places: Family Getaways in the Pacific Northwest (U.S.A.), 451
Going Places With Children in Washington (District of Columbia), 511
Great Family Trips in New England, 400
Great Vacations With Your Kids (United States as a Whole), 389
How to Take Great Trips With Your Kids (General Travel), 74
In and Out of Boston With (or Without) Children (Massachusetts), 554
Kid's London (England), 263
Kids and Cars (General Travel), 75
Maine Geographic: Day Trips With Children, 544
Places to Go With Children Guides (Series Reviews), 55
Texas—Family Style, 615
Travel With Children (Asia as a Whole), 110
Trips and Trails (Washington), 631
Utah! A Family Travel Guide, 617
What to Do With the Kids This Year (North America as a Whole), 356

Ferries (see Boats)

Festivals (see Entertainment)

Flea Markets (see Shopping)

Food (see also Restaurants)
Eating Your Way Through Baja (Mexico), 373
Food Lover's Guide to France, 215
Food Lover's Guide to Paris (France), 215
Food Lover's Guide to the Real New York, 580
Guide to Food Buying in Japan, 134
On-Your-Own Guides (Series Reviews), 52
Patty's On-the-Road Gourmet (Europe as a Whole), 190

Gardens (see also Sightseeing)
American Garden Guidebook (New England), 393
Collins Book of British Gardens (Great Britain), 241
Gardens of North America and Hawaii (North America as a Whole), 352
New England Gardens Open to the Public, 404
Rose Gardens of England, 269

Gay Travel
Bob Damron's Address Book (North America as a Whole), 350
Gayellow Pages (North America as a Whole), 353

Places for Men (North America as a Whole), 354
Places of Interest (North America as a Whole), 354
Places of Interest to Women (North America as a Whole), 355
Spartacus Guide (The World), 91

Geology
Earth Treasures (Series Reviews), 20
Glaciers and Granite (Maine), 542
Roadside Geology Guides (Series Reviews), 57
Roadside Geology of the Eastern Sierra Region (California), 492
Roadside Kansas, 538

Ghost Towns
Atlas of Colorado Ghost Towns, 503
Ghost Towns of the Colorado Rockies, 505
Ghost Towns of the Northwest (The Pacific Northwest, U.S.A.), 450
Historical Guide to Utah Ghost Towns, 617
Jeep Trails to Colorado Ghost Towns, 506
New Mexico's Best Ghost Towns, 571
Southern Idaho Ghost Towns, 532

Golf (see also Recreation)
AA Guide to Golf (Great Britain), 232
Golf Courses of Colorado, 505
Golf Courses of New Zealand, 641
Golfer's Travel Guide: Great Lakes Edition (The Midwest, U.S.A.), 427
Good Golf Guide (Scotland), 274
Northwest Golfer (The Pacific Northwest, U.S.A.), 453
Play the Best Courses (Great Britain), 251
Scotland: Home of Golf, 275
Texas Golf, 615
Vermont Golf Courses, 620

Health (see also Spas)
Fitness on the Road (North America as a Whole), 351
Overcoming Jet Lag (General Travel), 76
Passport's Health Guide for International Travelers (General Travel), 76
Pocket Doctor (General Travel), 77
Staying Healthy in Asia, Africa, and Latin America (Africa as a Whole), 97
Travel Well (General Travel), 79
Traveler's Medical Manual (General Travel), 80

Hikes (see also Parks, Recreation, Walks)
Adirondack Sampler (New York), 574
Afoot and Afield in Orange County (California), 468
Afoot and Afield in San Diego County (California), 468
All Season Guide to Minnesota's Parks, 558
All Season Guide to Wisconsin's Parks, 633
AMC Hiking Guides (Series Reviews), 3
Anza-Borrego Desert Region (California), 468
Appalachian Trail Guides (Series Reviews), 4

Apus & Incas: A Cultural Walking & Trekking Guide to Cuzco, Peru, 652
Atlanta's Urban Trails (Georgia), 521
Backcountry Fifty Hikes (Series Reviews), 7
Backpacking and Camping in the Developing World (The World), 84
Backpacking in Michigan, 556
Bushwalking in Australia, 161
Bushwalking in Papua New Guinea (Asia), 144
Circuit Hikes Guides (Series Reviews), 14
Classic Walks (Series Reviews), 15
Day Hiker's Guide to Southern California, 476
Day Hiker's Guide to Vermont, 619
Day Walker: 28 Hikes in the New York Metropolitan Area, 577
Deepest Valley: A Guide to Owens Valley (California), 476
Discover the Adirondacks (New York), 577
Easy Day Hikes in Yosemite (California), 477
Falcon Press Hiking Guides (Series Reviews), 23
Footsore Guides (Washington), 627
Globe Pequot Hiking Guides (Series Reviews), 32
Greece On Foot, 282
Guide Book of the Long Trail (Vermont), 619
Guide to Adirondack Trails (New York), 581
Guide to Skyline Drive and Shenandoah National Park (Virginia), 622
Guide to the Catskills (New York), 582
Guide to the Long Path (New York), 582
Guide to Trekking in Nepal, 141
Hawaii's Best Hiking Trails, 526
Hike Los Angeles (California), 483
Hike Santa Barbara (California), 483
Hiker's Guide: Pikes Peak & South Park Region (Colorado), 506
Hiker's Hip Pocket Guide to the Humboldt Coast (California), 483
Hiker's Hip Pocket Guide to the Mendocino Coast (California), 483
Hikers and Climbers Guide to the Sandias (New Mexico), 570
Hiking and Backpacking Trails of Texas, 612
Hiking and Walking Guide to Europe (Europe as a Whole), 184
Hiking from Inn to Inn, Maine to Virginia (New England), 402
Hiking Trails of North Georgia, 521
Hiking Trails of Southern Idaho, 531
Hiking Trails of the Santa Monica Mountains (California), 484
Hunter Mountain Walks (Series Reviews), 37
Hunter Walking/Hiking Guides (Series Reviews), 37
Hunter Walks (Series Reviews), 38
Lakes of Yellowstone (Wyoming), 636
Long Walks in France, 221
Maine Geographic Hiking Guides (Maine), 544
Mammoth Lakes Sierra (California), 488
Minnesota Walk Book, 559
Mono Lakes Guidebook (California), 488
Mt. Tam: A Hiking, Running, Nature Guide (California), 489
National Trust Book of Long Walks (Great Britain), 250

Natural New York, 584
New York Walk Book, 586
Northwest Trails (The Pacific Northwest, U.S.A.), 454
Olympic Mountains Trail Guide (Washington), 628
On Foot in the Grand Canyon (Arizona), 464
Outdoor and Trail Guide to the Wichita Mountains (Oklahoma), 596
Outdoors in Arizona: A Guide to Hiking and Backpacking, 464
Peninsula Trails (California), 491
Pine Barrens of Ronkonkoma (New York), 589
Point Reyes: A Guide (California), 492
Rocky Mountain National Park Hiking Trails (Colorado), 507
San Bernadino Mountain Trails (California), 493
Santa Cruz Mountains Trail Book (California), 495
Scotland: Walks and Trails, 275
Senior Guide: Day Hiking in the Southwestern National Parks (U.S.A.), 445
Short Hikes in Rocky Mountain National Park (Colorado), 507
Sierra Club Hiking Totebooks (Series Reviews), 60
6 One-Day Walks in the Pecos Wilderness (New Mexico), 572
Tennessee Hiking Guide, 606
Touchstone Hiking Guides (Series Reviews), 64
Tourist and Hiking Guide for Minnesota's North Shore, 560
Tramper's Guide to New Zealand's National Parks, 643
Tramping in New Zealand, 643
Tramping Through Europe (Europe as a Whole), 192
Trekker's Guide to the Himalaya (Nepal), 142
Trekking in the Indian Himalaya (India), 125
Trekking in the Nepal Himalaya, 143
Trips and Trails (Washington), 631
Uphill Both Ways (Colorado), 508
Wales: Walking, 278
Walker's Britain (Great Britain), 253
Walking Ancient Trackways (Great Britain), 253
Walking Europe From Top to Bottom (Europe as a Whole), 194
Walking From Inn to Inn: The San Francisco Area (California), 501
Walking Guide to the Caribbean (West Indies), 659
Walking in France, 229
Walking Switzerland—the Swiss Way, 338
Walking the Maine Coast, 546
Walking Through Britain Guides (Series Reviews), 67
Walking Tracks of New Zealand's National Parks, 644
Walks and Rambles in Rhode Island, 604
Walks and Rambles in Westchester and Fairfield Counties (New York), 591
Walks and Rambles on the Delmarva Peninsula (Mid-Atlantic States, U.S.A.), 416
Walks of California, 502
Walks in the Catskills (New York), 592
Western Trips & Trails (Rocky Mountain States, U.S.A.), 438
Wilderness Press Hiking Guides (Series Reviews), 68
Woodland Walks (Great Britain), 253
Woodland Walks (Series Reviews), 69

History (see Cultural Guides)

Hot Springs (see Spas)

Hotels (see also Budget Travel, Lodging)
AA Hotels and Restaurants (Great Britain), 233
AA Traveler's Guide to France, 208
Ackerman Guide (Great Britain), 235
All-Suite Hotel Guide (United States as a Whole), 381
America's Grand Resort Hotels (North America as a Whole), 347
Ashley Courtenay's Hotel Guide (Great Britain), 236
British Selection (Great Britain), 239
Charming Small Hotel Guide: Italy, Sicily & Sardinia (Italy), 298
Charming Small Hotel Guide: Britain & Ireland (Great Britain), 240
Derek Johansen's Recommended Hotels (Great Britain), 242
Egon Ronay's Hotels and Restaurants-Great Britain & Ireland (Great Britain), 242
Elegant Small Hotels (United States as a Whole), 385
Florida: A Guide to the Best Restaurants, Resorts, and Hotels, 516
Fodor's Selected Hotels of Europe (Europe as a Whole), 182
Fodor's Selected Resorts and Hotels (United States as a Whole), 387
French Selection, 217
French Way: An Insider's Guide, 218
Guide to Greater London (England), 262
Guide to Scotland and the Lake District (Great Britain), 246
Historic Country Hotels of England, 262
Historic Country House Hotels (Great Britain), 246
Historic Hotels of London (England), 262
Hotels & Restaurants of Britain (Great Britain), 247
Michelin Red Guides (Series Reviews), 46
Mobil Travel Guides (Series Reviews), 47
Northwest Best Places (Pacific Northwest, USA), 453
Premier Hotels of Great Britain (Great Britain), 251
RAC Continental Hotel Guide (Europe as a Whole), 187
RAC Hotel Guide (Great Britain), 251
Recommended Country Hotels (Great Britain), 251
Romantik Hotels and Restaurants (Europe as a Whole), 191
Scotland, Where to Stay, Hotels and Guesthouses, 275
300 Best Hotels in the World (The World), 92

Inns (includes Castles, Lodges, etc. See also Budget Travel, Lodging)
Country Inns of America Guides (Series Reviews), 17
Elegant Lodging (Mid-Atlantic States, U.S.A.), 411
European Country Cuisine (Europe as a Whole), 180
Guide Relais & Châteaux (France), 219
Historic Country Inns of California, 484
Inns of the Southern Mountains (The South, U.S.A.), 421
INNSpiration Northeast (New England), 402
Karen Brown's Country Inns (Series Reviews), 41
Recommended Wayside Inns (Great Britain), 251
Romantic Inns of Mexico, 379
Walking Switzerland—the Swiss Way, 338

Itineraries (see also Auto Travel, Cycling)
Away for the Weekend Guides (Series Reviews), 6
Carefree Getaway Guide for New Yorkers, 576
Day Trips and Budget Vacations (New England, U.S.A.), 398
Day Trips, Getaways and Budget Vacations (Mid-Atlantic States, U.S.A.), 410
Favorite Weekends in New England, 399
Fielding's Literary Africa, 97
Getaways for Gourmets in the Northeast (New England), 400
Great European Itineraries (Europe as a Whole), 183
Great Weekend Escape Book from Virginia to Vermont (New England), 400
Guide to Aegean and Mediterranean Turkey, 157
Guide to Eastern Turkey and the Black Sea Coast, 157
Guide to North Yemen, 143
Itinerary Planners (Series Reviews), 40
Karen Brown's Country Inns (Series Reviews), 41
Marilyn Wood's Wonderful Weekends (New England, U.S.A.), 403
Mountain Getaways (The South, U.S.A.), 422
Paradores of Spain, 331
Pousadas of Portugal, 318
Romantik Hotels and Restaurants (Europe as a Whole), 191
Touring Guide to Europe (Europe as a Whole), 192
Traveller's Portugal, 318
Travels in Provence (France), 228
Unforgettable British Weekends (Great Britain), 253

Jet Lag (see Health)

Jobs (see also Educational Travel)
Student's Guide to the Best Summer Jobs in Alaska, 461
Work Your Way Around the World (General Travel), 81
Work, Study, Travel Abroad (The World), 94

Jogging (see also Recreation)
Complete Capital Runner's Guide (District of Columbia), 510
55½ Running Trails of the San Francisco Bay Area (California), 479
Fitness on the Road (North America as a Whole), 351
Great American Runner's Guide (Rocky Mountain States), 433
Mt. Tam: A Hiking, Running, Nature Guide (California), 489

Kayaking (see River Sports)

Literature (see also Cultural Guides)
Blue Guide: Literary Britain and Ireland (Great Britain), 238
Fielding's Literary Africa (Africa as a Whole), 97
Guide to Writer's Homes in New England, 401
Joyce's Dublin: A Walking Tour to Ulysses (Ireland), 290
Literary Britain (Great Britain), 248
Oxford Literary Guide (Great Britain), 250
Paris, A Literary Companion (France), 224

Lodges (see Inns)

Lodging (see also Bed and Breakfast, Budget Travel, Hotels, Inns, Rentals)
AA Seaside Accommodations (Great Britain), 233
AAA Europe Lodging Guide (Europe as a Whole), 171
America's Wonderful Little Hotels and Inns, Eastern Edition (New England), 394
America's Wonderful Little Hotels and Inns, Western Edition (Rocky Mountain States), 430
Best Places to Stay Guides (Series Reviews), 10
Colorado Accommodations Guide, 504
Compleat Traveler's Companions (Series Reviews), 15
Country Hotels and Inns (France), 212
Country Inns and Back Roads (Series Reviews), 16
Europe's Wonderful Little Hotels and Inns (Europe as a Whole), 180
Farm Holiday Guide to Holidays (Great Britain), 244
Fielding's Havens and Hideaways (United States as a Whole), 386
Guide to Historic Texas Inns and Hotels, 611
Guide to Recommended Castle & Palace Hotels (Europe as a Whole), 184
Guide to the Small and Historic Lodging of Florida, 518
Historic Texas Hotels & Country Inns, 613
Ian Keown's Caribbean Hideaways (West Indies), 658
Ian Keown's European Hideaways (Europe as a Whole), 185
Michigan's Town and Country Inns, 557
Mobil Travel Guides (Series Reviews), 47
Most Romantic Hotels and Inns (Great Britain), 249
Northwest Best Places (The Pacific Northwest, U.S.A.), 452
Paradores of Spain, 331
Passport to Europe's Small Hotels and Inns (Europe as a Whole), 190
Pousadas of Portugal, 318
Room at the Inn (Minnesota), 559
Room at the Inn Wisconsin, 634
Small Hotels of California, 497
Smoke-free Lodging in California, 497
Staying Off the Beaten Path (England), 270
Wales: Where to Stay, 278

Medical (see Health)

Motorcycles
Complete Guide for Motorcycle Travelers (General Travel), 72
Dirt & Trail Guide for Southern California, 477
Motorcycle Touring in Europe (Europe as a Whole), 188

Museums (see also Architecture, Art, Cultural Guides)
Amazing Texas Monuments & Museums, 607
America On Display (North America as a Whole), 347
Art Museums of New England, 394
Blue Guide: Museums and Galleries in New York, 575
Blue Guide: Museums and Galleries of London (England), 258
Cambridge Guide to the Museums of Great Britain and Ireland (Great Britain), 240
Chicago's Museums (Illinois), 533
Eldan Museum Guides (Series Reviews), 21
Experiencing America's Past (United States as a Whole), 385

Guide to Art Museums: Midwest Edition (U.S.A.), 427
Guide to New York City Museums, 581
Guide to Oklahoma Museums, 596
Hermitage: An Illustrated Guide (Soviet Union), 322
Irish Museums Guide, 290
Knopf Guides to Art (Series Reviews), 41
Maine Geographic: Historic Sites, 544
Mona Winks: A Guide to Enjoying Europe's Top Museums (Europe as a Whole), 188
Museum Guide to Washington, D.C. (District of Columbia), 512
Museums & Galleries in Great Britain and Ireland (Great Britain), 249
Museums in and Around Moscow (Soviet Union), 324
New York's Great Art Museums, 587
132 Unusual Museums (Europe as a Whole), 189
Quilt Collections (North America as a Whole), 355
Russian Museum: A Guide (Soviet Union), 324
Special Museums of the Northeast (New England), 406
Wings of History: The Air Museums of Europe (Europe as a Whole), 194

Music (see also Entertainment)
Best of Texas Festivals, 609
Book of British Music Festivals (Great Britain), 238
Celebrations: America's Best Festivals (North America as a Whole), 350
Festivals U.S.A. (United States as a Whole), 386
Music Lover's Europe (Europe as a Whole), 188

Native Americans
Guide to America's Indians (United States as a Whole), 388
Indian Mounds of the Atlantic Coast (Mid-Atlantic States, U.S.A.), 413
Indian Mounds of the Middle Ohio Valley (The Midwest, U.S.A.), 428
Indian Villages of the Southwest (The Southwest, U.S.A.), 443
North American Indian Travel Guide (North America as a Whole), 354
Summer People, Winter People (New Mexico), 573

Nature (see also Recreation)
Arizona Outdoor Adventure, 462
Beachcomber's Guide to Gulf Coast Marine Life (The South, U.S.A.), 418
Birding Around the World, 84
Birdwatcher's Britain (Great Britain), 237
Birdwatcher's Guide to Japan, 132
Deepest Valley: A Guide to Owens Valley (California), 476
Foraging Along the Pacific Coast (California), 480
Grand Teton National Park (Wyoming), 635
Guide to New England's Landscape (U.S.A.), 400
Handbook for Beach Strollers from Maine to Cape Hatteras (New England), 401
Land's Edge: Barrier Beaches from Maine to North Carolina (New England), 403
Maine Coast: A Nature Lover's Guide, 543
Mammoth Lakes Sierra (California), 488
Mono Lake Guidebook (California), 488
Natural Attractions: A Select Guide to Experiencing North America's Unique Wildlife (North America as a Whole), 353

Natural Chicago (Illinois), 535
Natural New York, 584
Naturalist's Blue Ridge Parkway (North Carolina), 593
Nature Observer's Handbook (General Travel), 76
New York City Wildlife Guide, 585
Point Reyes: A Guide (California), 492
Sierra Club Naturalist's Guides (Series Reviews), 61
Tides of Change: Freeport, Maine, 545
Tour of British Bird Preserves (Great Britain), 252
Where to Watch Birds (Europe as a Whole), 194

Packing (see Planning)

Parks (see also Hikes, Nature, Walks)
Adirondack Sampler (New York), 574
Alaska's Parklands, 457
All Season Guide to Minnesota's Parks, 558
All Season Guide to Wisconsin's Parks, 633
California State Parks, 473
California State Parks Guide, 473
Canada's National Parks, 359
Circuit Hikes in Shenandoah National Park (Virginia), 621
Complete Guide to Cabins & Lodges (United States as a Whole), 385
Complete Guide to the Golden Gate National Recreation Area (California), 475
Crater Lake National Park (Oregon), 597
Discover the Adirondacks (New York), 577
Discovering Acadia National Park (Maine), 542
Exploring Manning Park (Canada), 361
Exploring Our National Parks (United States as a Whole), 385
Field Guide to Yellowstone's Geysers, Hot Springs and Fumaroles (Wyoming), 635
Florida Parks: A Guide to Camping in Nature, 517
Golden Gate Park at Your Feet (California), 481
Grand Teton National Park (Wyoming), 635
Greater Boston Park and Recreation Guide (Massachusetts), 552
Guide to Skyline Drive and Shenandoah National Park (Virginia), 622
Guide to the Catskills (New York), 582
Guide to the National Park Areas: Eastern States (The South, U.S.A.), 420
Guide to the National Park Areas: Western States (The Southwest, U.S.A.), 443
Katahdin: A Guide to Baxter State Park (Maine), 543
Lakes of Yellowstone (Wyoming), 636
Mountaineers National Park Guides (Series Reviews), 49
Mt. St. Helen's National Volcanic Monument (Washington), 628
National Parks of Japan, 136
National Parks of the Rocky Mountains (U.S.A.), 436
Olympic Mountains Trail Guide (Washington), 628
Olympic National Park & the Olympic Peninsula (Washington), 628
Park Explorer's Guides (Series Reviews), 52
Parks of the Pacific Coast (The Pacific Northwest, U.S.A.), 454
Rand McNally National Park Guide (United States as a Whole), 391
Ray Miller's Texas Parks, 614

Rocky Mountain National Park Hiking Trails (Colorado), 507
Santa Cruz Mountain Trail Book (California), 495
Sawtooth National Recreation Area (Idaho), 531
Senior Guide: Day Hiking in the Southwestern National Parks (U.S.A.), 445
Short Hikes in Rocky Mountain National Park (Colorado), 507
Sierra Club National Parks Guides (Series Reviews), 60
Sierra Club Natural Areas Guides (Series Reviews), 61
State and National Parks: Lodges and Cabins (United States as a Whole), 392
State Parks and Campgrounds in Northern New York, 590
State Parks of Arizona, 466
State Parks of New Mexico, 572
Texas Parks and Campgrounds, 615
Tourist Guide to Mount McKinley (Alaska), 461
Tramper's Guide to New Zealand's National Parks, 643
Visiting Our Western National Parks (Rocky Mountain States, U.S.A.), 438
Visitor's Guide to the Everglades (Florida), 520
Walking Tracks of New Zealand's National Parks, 644
Walks and Rambles in Westchester and Fairfield Counties (New York), 591
Walks in the Catskills (New York), 592
Yosemite National Park (California), 503
Yosemite Road Guide (California), 503

Pets (see Planning)

Photography
Fieldbook of Nature Photography (General Travel), 73
Fielding's Travel Photography Handbook (General Travel), 73
Photographer's Guide to London (England), 269
Travel Photography (General Travel), 78

Planning (see also Disabled, Health, Transportation, Safety)
Best European Travel Tips (Europe as a Whole), 174
Best Mexican Travel Tips, 372
Carol Haber's Discriminating Traveler (The World), 84
Directory of Free Vacation & Travel Information (North America as a Whole), 351
Escortguide (New Mexico), 570
Guide to the Best Buys in Package Tours (General Travel), 74
How to Pack a Suitcase (General Travel), 74
Insider's Guide to the Travel Game (General Travel), 74
Liberated Traveller's Guide to Europe (Europe as a Whole), 187
Manston's Before You Leave on Your Vacation (General Travel), 75
New World of Travel (General Travel), 76
New York Times Practical Traveler (General Travel), 76
Portable Pet (General Travel), 77
Rand McNally Vacation Places Rated (United States as a Whole), 391
Tips for the Savvy Traveler (General Travel), 77
Travel Wise, Smart & Light (General Travel), 79
Tropical Traveller (General Travel), 81
Where to Go Guides (Series Reviews), 68
World of Travel Tips (General Travel), 81

Pubs

Best Pubs of Great Britain (Great Britain), 237
Egon Ronay's Pubs & Bar Food (Great Britain), 243
Good Pub Guide (Great Britain), 245
Great Chicago Bar & Saloon Guide (Illinois), 534
Guide to Greater London (England), 262
Guide to Scotland and the Lake District (Great Britain), 246
Ireland's Pubs, 290
Irish Pubs of Boston (Massachusetts), 554
Nicholson: London Pub Guide (England), 267
Traveller's Guide to Pubs of the North Island (New Zealand), 643

Rafting (see River Sports)

Rail Travel (see Train Travel)

Recreation (see also Beaches, Cycling, Diving, Golf, Hikes, River Sports, Skiing, Spas, Walks)

Adventure Vacations in Five Mid-Atlantic States (U.S.A.), 407
Alaska Adventure Book, 457
Anza-Borrego Desert Region (California), 468
Baja Adventure Book (Mexico), 371
Bermuda Handbook, 664
Brown's Guide to the Georgia Outdoors, 521
Explorer's Guide: British Columbia (Canada), 361
Field Guide to U.S. National Forests (United States as a Whole), 368
Greater Boston Park and Recreation Guide (Massachusetts), 552
Guide to New Mexico's Popular Rivers and Lakes, 570
Hunter Adventure Guides (Series Reviews), 37
Natural Chicago (Illinois), 535
Norman Mark's Chicago (Illinois), 535
Outdoor Guide to the San Francisco Bay Area (California), 490
Outdoor Traveler's Guide (Australia), 164
Pat Dickerman's Adventure Travel (North America as a Whole), 354
Pat Dickerman's Adventure Travel Abroad (The World), 90
Pocket Guide to the Maine Outdoors, 545
Recreation Lakes of California, 492
Santa Fe on Foot: Walking, Running, Bicycling Routes (New Mexico), 572
Sierra Club Adventure Travel Guides (Series Reviews), 60
Sobek's Adventure Vacations (The World), 91
South Dakota Recreation Guide, 606
Winter Recreation in California, 502

Religion (see also Churches, Cutural Guides)

Catholic Shrines of Europe (Europe as a Whole), 175
Evangelical's Guide to the Holy Land (Israel), 128
Guide to Christian Europe (Europe as a Whole), 184
Guide to Jewish Amsterdam (Netherlands), 311
Guide to Jewish Europe (Europe as a Whole), 184
Holy Places in Jersusalem (Israel), 129
Jewish Travel Guide (The World), 89

Jewish Traveler (The World), 89
Mennonite Tourguide (Europe as a Whole), 187
New Testament Guide to the Holy Land (Israel), 131
Nino LoBello's Guide to the Vatican (Italy), 303
Oscar Israelowitz's Guide to Jewish New York City, 588
Oscar Israelowitz's Guide to Jewish U.S.A., Northeast (New England, U.S.A.), 405
Pilgrimages to Rome and Beyond (Greece), 284
Pilgrimages: A Guide to the Holy Places of Europe (Europe as a Whole), 190
Six New Testament Walks in Jerusalem (Israel), 131
Traveler's Guide to Jewish Landmarks (Europe as a Whole), 193
Traveling Jewish in America (United States as a Whole), 392
World Guide for the Jewish Traveler, 94

Rentals (see also Lodging)
AA Holiday Homes, Cottages and Apartments (Great Britain), 333
Condo Lux Guides (Series Reviews), 16
Farm Holiday Bureau B&B and Self-Catering Holidays (Great Britain), 243
French Farm and Village Holiday Guide, 217
Frommer's Swap & Go (General Travel), 73
Hideaway Guide (The World), 88
Home Exchanging (General Travel), 74

Restaurants (see also Budget Travel, Food)
AA Hotels and Restaurants (Great Britain), 233
Ackerman Guide (Great Britain), 235
Atlanta Restaurant Guide (Georgia), 520
Authentic Texas Cafes, 608
Benenson Restaurant Guide (North America as a Whole), 349
Berlitz European Menu for Travellers (Europe as a Whole), 174
Best Country Cafes in Texas, 608
Best Places to Eat in America (North America as a Whole), 349
Boston's Best Restaurants (Massachusetts), 550
Chicago's Food Favorites (Illinois), 533
Classic Diners of the Northeast (New England, U.S.A.), 396
Cleveland Menu Directory (Ohio), 595
Dallas Morning News Guide to Dallas Restaurants (Texas), 609
Dining in Historic Kentucky, 538
Dining in Historic Ohio, 595
Eating Cheap in Japan, 132
Eating Out: A Guide to European Dishes (Europe as a Whole), 177
Eating Your Way Through Baja (Mexico), 373
Ed Hitzel's South Jersey Dining Guide (New Jersey), 568
Egon Ronay's Guide (Europe as a Whole), 177
Egon Ronay's Guide to Healthy Eating Out (Great Britain), 242
Egon Ronay's Hotels and Restaurants-Great Britain & Ireland (Great Britain), 242
Epicure Guides (Series Reviews), 21
Epicurean Rendezvous (California), 478
Famous Restaurants & Recipes (Series Reviews), 23
Florida: A Guide to the Best Restaurants, Resorts, and Hotels, 516
Florida Restaurant Guide, 517

Fodor's Views to Dine By Around the World, 86
Food Lover's Guide to France, 215
Food Lover's Guide to Paris (France), 215
Food Lover's Guide to the Real New York, 580
French Way: An Insider's Guide, 218
Good Eats: A Design and Food Guide to the Bay Area (California), 481
Good Food Guide (Great Britain), 245
Good Tokyo Restaurants (Japan), 134
Great Hometown Restaurants of Texas, 612
Great New York Restaurants, 581
Guide to Greater London (England), 262
Guide to Japanese Food and Restaurants, 134
Guide to Scotland and the Lake District (Great Britain), 246
Guide to the Restaurants of New England, 401
Guide to Vancouver's Chinese Restaurants (Canada), 364
Healthiest Dining in America (United States as a Whole), 389
Historic Restaurants & Recipes (Series Reviews), 35
Hot Dog Chicago (Illinois), 535
Hotels & Restaurants of Britain (Great Britain), 247
Indianapolis Dining (Indiana), 537
Indianapolis Dining Guide (Indiana), 537
Interstate Gourmet Guides (Series Reviews), 39
James Barber's Personal Guide to the Best Eating in Vancouver (Canada), 365
La Creme de la Creme (France), 221
Mariani's Coast-to-Coast Dining Guide (United States as a Whole), 389
Marling Menu-Masters (Series Reviews), 44
Michelin Red Guides (Series Reviews), 46
Milwaukee Dining (Wisconsin), 634
New York Times Guide to Restaurants in New York City, 586
Northwest Best Places (The Pacific Northwest, U.S.A.), 453
100 Best Restaurants in Arizona, 464
Paris Rendez-Vous (France), 225
Passport to Los Angeles Restaurants (California), 491
Passport to New York Restaurants, 588
Paul Camp's Chicago Tribune Restaurant Guide (Illinois), 536
Pleasures of Paris (France), 226
Poorman's Gourmet Guide to Seattle Restaurants (Washington), 629
Restaurants of New York, 582
Restaurants of San Francisco (California), 492
Rich/Poor Man's Guide to Pittsburgh (Pennsylvania), 603
Roadfood and Goodfood (United States as a Whole), 391
Romantik Hotels and Restaurants (Europe as a Whole), 191
Sample West Kentucky, 539
Seattle Cheap Eats (Washington), 630
South Bay Hot Plates (California), 498
Tastes of Tahoe (California), 500
Texas Restaurant Guide, 615
Thrifty Gourmet (California), 500
Toronto Underground Restaurant Book (Canada), 368

What's What in Japanese Restaurants (Japan), 138
Where Atlantans Dine (Georgia), 522
Where Shall We Eat in Marin (California), 502
Where to Eat in Connecticut, 509
Zagat Survey (Series Reviews), 69

River Sports (see also Parks, Recreation)
Adirondack Canoe Waters (New York), 573
All Season Guide to Minnesota's Parks, 558
Appalachian Whitewater (Series Reviews), 5
Backcountry Canoeing Guides (Series Reviews), 6
Best Canoe Trails of Southern Wisconsin, 633
Boundary Waters Canoe Area (Minnesota), 558
California White Water, 474
Canoe Routes: Northwest Oregon, 597
Canoeing and Kayaking Guides (Series Reviews), 13
Canoeing Michigan Rivers, 556
Canoeing the Delaware (Mid-Atlantic States, U.S.A.), 409
Canoeing the Jersey Pine Barrens (New Jersey), 567
Coastal Kayaker (Canada), 360
Floater's Guide to Colorado, 505
Grand Canyon River Guide (Arizona), 463
Guide to New Mexico's Popular Rivers and Lakes, 570
Guide to Texas Rivers, 612
Maine Geographic Canoeing Guides (Maine), 544
Rafting in British Columbia (Canada), 367
River Runner's Guide to the History of the Grand Canyon (Arizona), 465
River Runner's Guide to Utah, 617
Washington Whitewater (Washington), 632
Whitewater Home Companion (The South, U.S.A.), 424

Rural Travel (see also Auto Travel)
AA Where to Go in the British Countryside (Great Britain), 235
Alaska Wilderness Milepost, 457
Arizona Off the Beaten Path, 462
Backcountry Mexico, 371
Backroads of Northeast Ohio, 594
Backroads of Southern Europe (Europe as a Whole), 173
Backroads of Texas, 608
Colorado Scenic Guide, 504
Countryside Guides (Series Reviews), 18
Earl Thollander's Back Roads (Series Reviews), 20
Explorer's Handbook (General Travel), 72
Exploring Rural Europe Guides (Series Reviews), 22
Fielding's Discover Europe Off the Beaten Path (Europe as a Whole), 180
Life in the Slow Lane (Ohio), 595
Off the Beaten Path Guides (Series Reviews), 51
Other Puerto Rico, 669
Places In Between (Italy), 304
Reader's Digest: Off the Beaten Path (United States as a Whole), 391

Southwest China Off the Beaten Path, 119
Through Britain on Country Roads (Great Britain), 252

Safety (see also Planning)
International Safe Travel Guide (General Travel), 75
International Traveler's Security Handbook (The World), 88
Pocket Guide to Safe Travel (General Travel), 77
Travel Safety (General Travel), 79

Senior Citizens
Discount Guide for Travelers Over 55 (General Travel), 72
Senior Citizen's Guide to Budget Travel (Europe as a Whole), 191
Senior Citizen's Guide to Budget Travel (North America as a Whole), 355
Senior Guide: Day Hiking in the Southwestern National Parks (U.S.A.), 445
Travel Easy (General Travel), 78
Trips for Those Over 50 (New England, U.S.A.), 406

Shopping
Antiques: A Buyer's Guide to London (England), 257
Born to Shop Guides (Series Reviews), 12
Complete Guide to Hong Kong Factory Bargains, 121
Factory Store Guide to All New England (U.S.A.), 398
Fielding's Select Shopping Guide (Europe as a Whole), 181
Frommer's Shopper's Guide to the Caribbean, 658
Guide to Antique Shops (Great Britain), 246
Hawaii Super Shopper, 527
Inside Outlets (New England, U.S.A.), 402
Keep One Suitcase Empty (Europe as a Whole), 186
Keep One Suitcase Empty (Great Britain), 248
Luxury Shopping Guide to London (England), 265
Nicholson: London Shopping Guide (England), 267
Serious Shopper's Guides (Series Reviews), 58
Shopping in China, 119
Shopping in Exotic Places (Series Reviews), 59
Shopwalks (Series Reviews), 59
Top Shopping in Japan, 138
Travel Key Guides (Series Reviews), 65
Vancouver Super Shopper (Canada), 369
Village Voice Guide to Manhattan's Hottest Shopping Neighborhoods (New York),
    591
What's "In" Chicago (Illinois), 536
Where to Find Everything for Practically Nothing in Chicagoland (Illinois), 536

**Sightseeing (see also Architecture, Art, Auto Travel, Churches, Cutural Guides,
    Gardens, Literature, Museums, Rural Travel, Walks)**
AA Book of British Villages, 231
AA Discovering Britain (Great Britain), 232
AA Illustrated Guide to Country Towns and Villages of Britain (Great Britain), 233
AA Illustrated Guide to Britain (Great Britain), 233
AA Illustrated Guide to Britain's Coast (Great Britain), 233
AA Scotland: Where to Go, What to Do, 272

AA Secret Britain (Great Britain), 233
AA Stately Homes, Museums, Castles, and Gardens (Great Britain), 234
AA Treasures of Britain (Great Britain), 234
AA Where to Go (Great Britain), 235
Alamo and Other Texas Missions to Remember, 607
America's Historic Battlefields (United States as a Whole), 382
American's Guide to Britain (Great Britain), 236
Ancient Cities of the Southwest (The Southwest, U.S.A.), 440
Baedeker's City Guides (Series Reviews), 7
Baedeker's Country/Regional Guides (Series Reviews), 8
Budapest: A Complete Guide (Hungary), 285
Canada, 359
Chicago, City of Neighborhoods (Illinois), 533
Civil War Sites in Virginia, 621
Covered Bridges Guides (Series Reviews), 18
Discover Historic California, 477
Explore Arizona, 463
Explore Australia, 161
Exploring Britain (Great Britain), 243
Exploring Coastal Massachusetts, 551
Exploring Rhode Island, 604
Exploring the A.C.T. and Southeast N.S.W. (Australia), 162
Exploring the Hunter Region (Australia), 162
Frontier Forts of Texas, 611
Golden Hills of California, 481
Great Lakes Guidebook (The Midwest, U.S.A.), 427
Guide to the Cripple Creek–Victor Mining District (Colorado), 505
Guide's Guide to Philadelphia (Pennsylvania), 602
Historic Homes of Texas, 612
Historic Houses, Castles and Gardens (France), 220
Historic Houses, Castles, & Gardens (Great Britain), 247
Historical Tour Guides (Series Reviews), 36
Hume: Australia's Highway of History (Australia), 163
Hungary: A Complete Guide, 286
Journey to the High Southwest (Rocky Mountain States, U.S.A.), 435
Landmarks of the West (Rocky Mountain States, U.S.A.), 435
Maine Geographic: Lighthouses, 545
Maui's Hana Highway (Hawaii), 529
Maya Sites of the Yucatan (Mexico), 377
Michelin Green Guides (Series Reviews), 46
National Trust Atlas (Great Britain), 249
New Visitor's Guides (Series Reviews), 50
Next Time You Go to Russia (Soviet Union), 324
Nicholson Guides (Series Reviews), 51
Nino LoBello's Guide to the Vatican (Italy), 303
Offbeat Oregon, 598
Palace Under the Alps (Europe as a Whole), 189
Pelican Guide to Maryland, 548
Poland, 315

Portland: An Informal History & Guide (Oregon), 599
Reader's Digest: Off the Beaten Path (United States as a Whole), 391
San Diego and the Southland (California), 493
San Diego...City & County (California), 494
San Diego's Scenic Drive (California), 494
Scotland: 1001 Things to See, 275
Sentinels of Time: Vermont's Covered Bridges, 620
Sydney by Ferry & Foot (Australia), 165
Three Rivers of France, 227
Touring Nevada, 565
Tourist Guide (Wales), 278
Visitor's Guides (Series Reviews), 66
Washington, D.C. Sightseers' Guide (District of Columbia), 513
What to Do In and Around Dublin (Ireland), 292
World of Tikal, Guatemala, 170

Skiing
Audi Ski Guide (Europe as a Whole), 173
Backcountry Ski Tours (Series Reviews), 7
Best Ski Touring in America (North America as a Whole), 349
Budget Skiers Guidebook, Western U.S. (Rocky Mountain States, U.S.A.), 431
California Downhill, 431
Colorado High Routes, 504
Complete Guide to Cross-Country Skiing in Canada, 360
Critical Guide to Cross-Country Ski Areas (New England, U.S.A.), 398
Cross Country Ski Inns of Eastern U.S. (New England, U.S.A.), 398
Fodor's Ski Resorts (North America as a Whole), 352
Frommer's Dollarwise Guide to Skiing in Europe (Europe as a Whole), 179
Frommer's Dollarwise Guide to Skiing USA East (New England, U.S.A.), 399
Frommer's Dollarwise Guide to Skiing USA West (Rocky Mountain States, U.S.A.), 433
Good Skiing Guide (Europe as a Whole), 183
Guide to Cross-Country Skiing in New England (U.S.A.), 400
Guide to Ski Touring in New York and New Jersey, 582
Minnesota Walk Book, 559
Ski Europe (Europe as a Whole), 191
Ski Minnesota, 560
Ski Touring Arizona, 465
Ski Touring in California, 496
Ski Tours in the Sierra Nevada (California), 497
Utah Ski Country, 618
White Book of Ski Areas (North America as a Whole), 356

Snorkeling (see Diving)

Solo Travel
China Solo, 117
Europe for One (Europe as a Whole), 178
Japan Solo, 135

Spas (see also Health, Recreation)
Great Hot Springs of the West (Rocky Mountain States, U.S.A.), 434
Guide to Health Spas Around the World, 87
Hot Springs and Hot Pools of the Northwest (The Pacific Northwest, U.S.A.), 452
Hot Springs and Hot Pools of the Southwest (The Southwest, U.S.A.), 443
Hot Springs of the Eastern Sierra (California), 485
1988 Spas (The World), 89

Sports (see Recreation)

Train Travel (see also Budget Travel)
ABC Rail Guide (Great Britain), 235
Baedeker's Rail Europe (Europe as a Whole), 173
Bernina Express (Switzerland), 335
Britain by Britrail (Great Britain), 239
Britain by Train (Great Britain), 239
British Railway Journeys (Great Britain), 239
Eurail Guide (The World), 85
Europe by Eurail (Europe as a Whole), 177
Europe by Rail (Europe as a Whole), 178
Europe by Train (Europe as a Whole), 178
Famous Glacier Express (Switzerland), 335
From Moscow to Vladivostok (Soviet Union), 322
Rail Ventures (North America as a Whole), 355
Ride Guide to the Historic Alaska Railroad, 461
See Ireland by Train, 292
Steam Passenger Service Directory (United States as a Whole), 392
Thomas Cook European Timetable (Europe as a Whole), 192
Thomas Cook Overseas Timetable (The World), 92
Train Trips (North America as a Whole), 356
Trans-Siberian Rail Guide (Soviet Union), 325
USA by Bus and Train (United States as a Whole), 392

Transportation (see Air Travel, Auto Travel, Boats, Budget Travel, Buses, Cruises, Motorcycles, Train Travel)

Travel Tips (see Planning)

Travel Writing
Travel Writer's Handbook (General Travel), 79
Travel Writer's Markets (General Travel), 79
Writer's Market (General Travel), 82

Traveling Alone (see Solo Travel)

Walks (see also Architecture, Hikes, Recreation, Parks, Sightseeing)
AA Book of Country Walks (Great Britain), 231
AMC Walks (Series Reviews), 3
America's Greatest Walks (United States as a Whole), 382
Atlanta's Urban Trails (Georgia), 521
Beach Towns: Walker's Guide to L.A.'s Beach Communities (California), 469
Beacon Hill: A Walking Tour (Massachusetts), 549
Boston Globe Historic Walks (Massachusetts), 550

Chicago On Foot (Illinois), 534
Citywalks (Series Reviews), 14
Complete Guide to Boston's Freedom Trail (Massachusetts), 551
Dover New York Walking Guide, 578
Earl Thollander's San Francisco (California), 477
Four Historic Walking Tours of Pueblo, Colorado, 505
Globe Pequot Walks (Series Reviews), 32
Guide and History of Hope Town (Bahamas), 662
Guide to Jewish Amsterdam (Netherlands), 311
Historic Walks in London, Bath, Oxford, and Edinburgh (Great Britain), 247
Holiday Which? Good Walks Guide (Great Britain), 247
How to See La Villa Real de Santa Fe (New Mexico), 570
Hunter Walks (Series Reviews), 38
In Our Grandmothers' Footsteps: A Walking Tour of London (England), 263
Kyoto: Seven Paths to the Heart of the City (Japan), 136
London Walkabouts With Kate Lucas (England), 264
Monterey Peninsula Walking Tours (California), 489
Mystery Reader's Walking Guide (England), 265
New York's Nooks and Crannies, 587
Peninsula Trails (California), 491
Permanent New Yorkers, 588
Permanent Parisians (France), 226
San Diego on Foot (California), 494
Santa Barbara, El Pueblo Viejo (California), 495
Scotland: Walks and Trails, 275
Shell Book of British Walks (Great Britain), 252
Short Walks in English Towns (England), 269
Six New Testament Walks in Jerusalem (Israel), 131
Stairway Walks in San Francisco (California), 498
Step-by-Step Guides (Series Reviews), 62
There, There: East San Francisco Bay At Your Feet (California), 500
Tides of Change: Freeport, Maine, 545
Trips on Twos: 15 Walking Tours of the Pikes Peak Region (Colorado), 507
Turn Left at the Pub (England), 270
Turn Right at the Fountain (Europe as a Whole), 193
Venice for Pleasure (Italy), 305
Walker's Guide to Harpers Ferry, West Virginia, 633
Walking Guide to the Caribbean (West Indies), 659
Walking Tours of Old Washington and Alexandria (District of Columbia), 513
Walks and Rambles in Rhode Island, 604
Walks and Rambles in Westchester and Fairfield Counties (New York), 591
Walks and Rambles on the Delmarva Peninsula (Mid-Atlantic States, U.S.A.), 416
Walks of California, 502
Walks in the Catskills (New York), 592
Washington On Foot (District of Columbia), 514
Way-Ahead Guides (Series Reviews), 67

Weather
Times Books World Weather Guide, 93
Travelers Almanac (North America as a Whole), 356

Wine Tours
Alexis Lichine's Guide (France), 208
Art of the Winemaker (The World), 83
Backroad Wineries of California, 469
Eperon's French Wine Tour, 214
Grape Expeditions in California, 481
Grape Expeditions in France, 219
Napa Valley Guide (California), 490
New York Wine Country, 586
Northwest Wine Country (The Pacific Northwest, U.S.A.), 454
Sonoma County Guide (California), 498
Sunset: Wine Country California, 499
Webster's Wine Tours (Series Reviews), 68
Wine Lover's Guide (France), 230
Wine Roads of Europe (Europe as a Whole), 194

Women (see also Planning, Solo Travel)
Going Alone (The World), 87
Half the Earth (The World), 88
Hassle-Free Boston (Massachusetts), 553
In Our Grandmothers' Footsteps: A Walking Tour of London (England), 263
Places of Interest to Women (North America as a Whole), 355
Survival Manual for the Independent Woman Traveler (General Travel), 77
Wandering Woman's Phrasebook (General Travel), 81
Woman's Travel Guide (United States as a Whole), 393
Woman's Travel Guide to New Zealand, 644

Work (see Educational Travel, Jobs)

Geographical Index

Acapulco (see Mexico)
Afghanistan (see the Middle East)
Africa, 96
Africa as a Whole, 96
Alabama, 456
Alaska, 456
Albania, 197
Albuquerque (see New Mexico)
Alexandria (see Egypt)
Alexandria (see Virginia)
Algeria (see Northern Africa)
American Samoa (see Oceania as a
    Whole)
Amsterdam (see Netherlands)
Anchorage (see Alaska)
Andorra, 197
Angola (see Southern Africa)
Anguilla (see the Caribbean and
    Leeward Islands)
Antarctica, 107
Antigua (see the Leeward Islands)
Antilles (see West Indies for specific
    islands)
Argentina, 646
Arizona, 462
Arkansas, 466
Aruba, 660
Asia, 108
Asia as a Whole, 108
Athens (see Greece)
Atlanta (see Georgia)
Auckland (see New Zealand)
Austin (see Texas)
Australia, 160
Austria, 198
Azores (see Islands of the Eastern and
    Northern Atlantic Ocean)

Bahamas, 661
Bahrain, 114
Bali (see Indonesia)
Baltimore (see Maryland)
Bangkok (see Thailand)
Bangladesh, 113

Barbados, 663
Barcelona (see Spain)
Belfast (see Northern Ireland)
Belgium, 201
Belize, 167
Benin (see Western Africa)
Berlin (see West Germany and East
    Germany)
Bermuda, 664
Bhutan, 114
Bogata (see Colombia)
Bolivia, 647
Bombay (see India)
Bonaire, 665
Bora Bora (see Tahiti and French
    Polynesia)
Boston (see Massachusetts)
Botswana (see Southern Africa)
Brazil, 648
British Columbia (see Canada)
British West Indies (see Bahamas,
    Cayman Islands, Jamaica,
    Leeward Islands, Trinidad and
    Tobago, Virgin Islands, Windward
    Islands)
Brunei, 114
Brussels (see Belgium)
Budapest (see Hungary)
Buenos Aires (see Argentina)
Bulgaria, 203
Burkina Faso (see Western Africa)
Burma, 114
Burundi (see Central Africa)

Cairo (see Egypt)
Calcutta (see India)
California, 467
Cameroon (see Western Africa)
Canada, 357
Canary Islands (See Islands of the
    Eastern and Northern Atlantic
    Ocean)
Canton (see China)
Cape Cod (see Massachusetts)

Cape Verde (see Islands of the Eastern and Northern Atlantic Ocean)
Capetown (see South Africa)
Caracas (see Venezuela)
Caribbean, 655
Caroline Islands (see Micronesia)
Catalina Island (see California)
Cayman Islands, 665
Celebes (see Indonesia)
Central Africa, 97
Central African Republic (see Central Africa)
Central America, 166
Central America as a Whole, 166
Chad (see Western Africa)
Chaing Mai (see Thailand)
Channel Islands (see California)
Channel Islands (see England)
Chicago (see Illinois)
Chile, 649
China, 115
Cincinnati (see Ohio)
Cleveland (see Ohio)
Colombia, 650
Colorado, 503
Comoro Islands (see Islands of the Western Indian Ocean)
Congo (see Central Africa)
Connecticut, 508
Cook Islands, 638
Copenhagen (see Denmark)
Corsica (see France)
Costa Rica, 168
Crete (see Greece)
Cuba, 666
Curacao, 666
Cyprus, 204
Czechoslovakia, 205

Dallas (see Texas)
Damascus (see Syria)
Danish West Indies (see the Virgin Islands)
Delaware, 509
Denmark, 205
Denver (see Colorado)
Desirade (see French West Indies)
Detroit (see Michigan)
District of Columbia, 510
Djibouti (see Eastern Africa)
Dominica (see the Leeward Islands)
Dominican Republic, 666
Dublin (see Ireland)

East Germany (German Democratic Republic), 206

Easter Island (see Islands of South America)
Eastern Africa, 98
Eastern Europe, 195
Ecuador, 650
Edinburgh (see Scotland)
Egypt, 100
El Salvador (see Central America as a Whole)
England, 254
Equatorial Guinea (see Western Africa)
Ethiopia (see Eastern Africa)
Europe, 171
Europe as a Whole, 171

Falkland Islands (see South America as a Whole)
Faroe Islands (see Scandinavia)
Federal Republic of Germany (see West Germany)
Fiji, 639
Finland, 207
Florence (see Italy)
Florida, 515
Florida Keys (see Florida)
Fort Worth (see Texas)
France, 208
French Guiana (see South America as a Whole)
French Polynesia (see Tahiti and French Polynesia)
French West Indies, 659

Gabon (see Western Africa)
Galapagos Islands (see Islands of South America)
Gambia (see Western Africa)
Geneva (see Switzerland)
Georgia, 520
German Democratic Republic (see East Germany)
Germany (see East Germany and West Germany)
Ghana (see Western Africa)
Gibraltar (see Europe as a Whole)
Glasgow (see Scotland)
Great Basin States (U.S.A.; see Rocky Mountain/Great Basin States)
Great Britain, 230
Great Lakes (see Midwest, U.S.A.)
Great Plains States (U.S.A.; see the Midwest)
Greater Antilles (see West Indies for specific islands)
Greece, 279

Greenland (see Islands of the Eastern and Northern Atlantic Ocean)
Grenada (see the Windward Islands)
Grenadines (see the Windward Islands)
Guadeloupe (see French West Indies and the Leeward Islands)
Guam (see Micronesia)
Guatemala, 169
Guinea (see Western Africa)
Guinea-Bissau (see Western Africa)
Guyana (see South America as a Whole)

Hague, The (see Netherlands)
Haiti, 667
Hawaii, 522
Helsinki (see Finland)
Holland (see Netherlands)
Honduras, 170
Hong Kong, 120
Honolulu (see Hawaii)
Houston (see Texas)
Hungary, 285

Iceland (see Islands of the Eastern and Northern Atlantic Ocean)
Idaho, 530
Illinois, 532
India, 123
Indiana, 537
Indianapolis (see Indiana)
Indonesia, 126
Iowa, 537
Iran, 127
Iraq (see the Middle East)
Ireland, 286
Islands of South America, 651
Islands of the Eastern and Northern Atlantic Ocean, 293
Islands of the Western Indian Ocean, 102
Israel, 127
Istanbul (see Turkey)
Italy, 295
Ivory Coast (see Western Africa)

Jakarta (see Indonesia)
Jamaica, 667
Japan, 131
Java (see Indonesia)
Jerusalem (see Israel)
Johannesburg (see South Africa)
Jordan, 138
Juan Fernandez Islands (see South America as a Whole)

Juneau (see Alaska)

Kampuchea (see Southeast Asia)
Kansas, 538
Kansas City (see Missouri)
Katmandu (see Nepal)
Kentucky, 538
Kenya, 103
Key West (see Florida)
Khartoum (see Sudan)
Kiribati Islands (see Micronesia)
Korea (see North Korea and South Korea)
Kuwait (see the Middle East)
Kyoto (see Japan)

Lake Tahoe (see California and Nevada)
Laos (see Southeast Asia)
Las Vegas (see Nevada)
Lebanon (see the Middle East)
Leeward Islands, 660
Leningrad (see Soviet Union)
Les Saintes (see French West Indies)
Lesotho (see Southern Africa)
Lesser Antilles (see West Indies for specific islands)
Liberia (see Western Africa)
Libya (see Northern Africa)
Liechtenstein, 306
Line Islands (see Oceania as a Whole)
Lisbon (see Portugal)
London (see England)
Los Angeles (see California)
Louisiana, 539
Luxembourg, 307

Macau, 139
Madagascar (see Islands of the Western Indian Ocean)
Madeira (see Islands of the Eastern and Northern Atlantic Ocean)
Madras (see India)
Madrid (see Spain)
Maine, 541
Malawi (see Southern Africa)
Malaysia, 140
Maldives (see Islands of the Western Indian Ocean)
Mali (see Western Africa)
Malta, 308
Manila (see Philippines)
Mariana Islands (see Micronesia)
Marie Galante (see French West Indies)
Marrakech (see Morocco)

Marshall Islands (see Micronesia)
Martha's Vineyard (see
    Massachusetts)
Martinique (see French West Indies
    and the Windward Islands)
Maryland, 546
Massachusetts, 548
Mauritania (see Northern Africa)
Mauritius (see Islands of the Western
    Indian Ocean)
Mazatlan (see Mexico)
Melanesia (see Oceania as a Whole)
Melbourne (see Australia)
Mexico, 370
Mexico City (see Mexico)
Miami (see Florida)
Michigan, 556
Micronesia, 639
Mid-Atlantic States (U.S.A.), 407
Middle East, 111
Midwest (U.S.A.), 424
Milan (see Italy)
Milwaukee (see Wisconsin)
Minneapolis (see Minnesota)
Minnesota, 557
Mississippi, 560
Missouri, 561
Monaco, 309
Montana, 562
Montevideo (see Uruguay)
Montreal (see Canada)
Montserrat (see the Leeward Islands)
Moorea (see Tahiti and French
    Polynesia)
Morocco, 104
Moscow (see Soviet Union)
Mozambique (see Southern Africa)

Nairobi (see Kenya)
Namibia (see Southern Africa)
Nantucket (see Massachusetts)
Nassau (see Bahamas)
Nebraska, 563
Nepal, 141
Netherlands, 309
Netherlands Antilles (see Aruba,
    Bonaire, Curacao, St. Martin, and
    the Caribbean)
Nevada, 563
New Caledonia (see Oceania as a
    Whole)
New England (U.S.A.), 393
New Hampshire, 566
New Jersey, 567
New Mexico, 569

New Orleans (see Louisiana)
New York, 573
New Zealand, 640
Nicaragua (see Central America as a
    Whole)
Niger (see Western Africa)
Nigeria (see Western Africa)
North America, 347
North America as a Whole, 347
North Carolina, 592
North Dakota (see Midwest, U.S.A.)
North Korea, 143
Northern Africa, 98
Northern Ireland, 313
Northern Mariana Islands (see
    Micronesia)
Northern Yemen, 143
Northwest (U.S.A., see Pacific
    Northwest)
Norway, 314

Oceania, 637
Oceania as a Whole, 637
Ohio, 594
Oklahoma, 596
Oman, 144
Ontario (see Canada)
Oregon, 596
Orlando (see Florida)
Oslo (see Norway)

Pacific Northwest (U.S.A.), 447
Pakistan, 144
Palau Islands (see Micronesia)
Panama, 170
Papua New Guinea, 144
Paraguay, 652
Paris (see France)
Peking (see China)
Pennsylvania, 601
People's Democratic Republic of
    Yemen (see Southern Yemen)
People's Republic of China (see
    China)
Peru, 652
Philadelphia (see Pennsylvania)
Philippines, 145
Phoenix (see Arizona)
Phoenix Islands (see Oceania as a
    Whole)
Pittsburgh (see Pennsylvania)
Poland, 314
Ponape (see Oceania as a Whole)
Port-au-Prince (see Haiti)
Portland (see Oregon)

Portugal, 315
Prague (see Czechoslovakia)
Puerto Rico, 668

Qatar, 145
Quebec (see Canada)
Queen Charlotte Islands (see Canada)

Rangoon (see Burma)
Rarotonga (see Cook Islands)
Reunion (see Islands of the Western Indian Ocean)
Reykjavik (see Iceland under Islands of the Eastern and Northern Atlantic Ocean)
Rhode Island, 604
Rio de Janeiro (see Brazil)
Rocky Mountain/Great Basin States (U.S.A.), 430
Romania, 319
Rome (see Italy)
Russia (see Soviet Union)
Rwanda (see Central Africa)

Saba (see the Leeward Islands)
Salt Lake City (see Utah)
Samoa, American (see Oceania as a Whole)
Samoan Islands (see Oceania as a Whole)
San Antonio (see Texas)
San Diego (see California)
San Francisco (see California)
San Juan (see Puerto Rico)
San Marino (see Europe as a Whole)
Santa Fe (see New Mexico)
Santiago (see Chile)
Santo Domingo (see Dominican Republic)
Sao Tome (see Western Africa)
Sardinia (see Italy)
Saudi Arabia, 146
Scandinavia, 195
Scotland, 272
Seattle (see Washington)
Senegal (see Western Africa)
Senyavin Islands (see Micronesia)
Seoul (see South Korea)
Seychelles (see Islands of the Western Indian Ocean)
Shanghai (see China)
Sierra Leone (see Western Africa)
Singapore, 146
Sint Maarten (see St. Martin)

Society Islands (see Tahiti and French Polynesia)
Sofia (see Bulgaria)
Solomon Islands (see Oceania as a Whole)
Somalia (see Eastern Africa)
Sophia (see Bulgaria)
South (U.S.A.), 416
South Africa, 105
South America, 645
South America as a Whole, 645
South Carolina, 605
South Dakota, 606
South Korea, 147
Southeast Asia, 112
Southern Africa, 99
Southern Yemen, 150
Southwest (U.S.A.), 439
Soviet Union, 319
Spain, 326
Sri Lanka, 150
St. Barthelemy (see French West Indies)
St. Eustatius (see the Caribbean)
St. Louis (see Missouri)
St. Lucia (see the Windward Islands)
St. Martin, 670
St. Vincent (see the Windward Islands)
Stockholm (see Sweden)
Sudan, 106
Sumatra (see Indonesia)
Suriname (see South America as a Whole)
Swaziland (see Southern Africa)
Sweden, 333
Switzerland, 334
Sydney (see Australia)
Syria, 152

Tahiti and French Polynesia, 644
Taipei (see Taiwan)
Taiwan, 152
Tampa (see Florida)
Tanzania (see Eastern Africa)
Taos (see New Mexico)
Tazmania (see Australia)
Tennessee, 606
Texas, 607
Thailand, 153
Tobago (see Trinidad and Tobago)
Togo (see Western Africa)
Tokelau Islands (see Oceania as a Whole)
Tokyo (see Japan)

Tonga (see Oceania as a Whole)
Toronto (see Canada)
Trinidad and Tobago, 670
Truk Islands (see Oceania as a Whole)
Tucson (see Arizona)
Tunis (see Tunisia)
Tunisia, 106
Turkey, 156
Tuvalu (see Oceania as a Whole)

U.S.S.R. (see Soviet Union)
Uganda (see Eastern Africa)
United Arab Emirates, 158
United Kingdom (see Great Britain
    and Northern Ireland)
United States, 381
United States as a Whole, 381
Upper Volta (see Western Africa)
Uruguay, 653
Utah, 616

Vancouver (see Canada)
Vanuatu (see Oceania as a Whole)
Venezuela, 654
Venice (see Italy)
Vermont, 618
Vienna (see Austria)
Vietnam (see Southeast Asia)
Virgin Islands, 670
Virginia, 620

Waikiki (see Hawaii)
Wales, 277
Wallis and Futuna Islands (see
    Oceania as a Whole)
Warsaw (see Poland)
Washington, 625
Washington, D.C. (see District of
    Columbia)
West Germany, 339
West Indies, 655
West Virginia, 632
Western Africa, 99
Western Sahara (see Northern Africa)
Windward Islands, 660
Wisconsin, 633
World (Travel Books on the World), 83
Wyoming, 635

Yap (see Oceania as a Whole)
Yemen (see Southern Yemen and
    Northern Yemen)
Yemen Arab Republic (See Northern
    Yemen)
Yugoslavia, 344
Yukon (see Canada)

Zaire (see Central Africa)
Zambia (see Southern Africa)
Zimbabwe (see Southern Africa)
Zurich (see Switzerland)

Form for Reader's Suggestions and Comments

We would like to hear from you. If you have comments on guides we have included in our book or suggestions of ones we did not, please let us know. Thank you for your help in sharing information with your fellow travelers. (You need only note the title of any book already a part of *Going Places*.)

Title: _____

Author(s): _____

Publisher/Distributor: _____

Publisher/Distributor address, if noted: _____
_____

Publication Date: _____

Paperback or Cloth (Hardback)? _____

Your Comments (include both positive and negative): _____
_____
_____
_____

Other Suggestions: _____
_____
_____
_____

Send your comments to: Greg Hayes and Joan Wright
P. O. Box 3626
Carson City, NV 89702

Form for Reader's Suggestions and Comments

We would like to hear from you. If you have comments on guides we have included in our book or suggestions of ones we did not, please let us know. Thank you for your help in sharing information with your fellow travelers. (You need only note the title of any book already a part of *Going Places*.)

Title: _____

Author(s): _____

Publisher/Distributor: _____

Publisher/Distributor address, if noted: _____

_____

Publication Date: _____

Paperback or Cloth (Hardback)? _____

Your Comments (include both positive and negative): _____

_____

_____

_____

Other Suggestions: _____

_____

_____

_____

Send your comments to: Greg Hayes and Joan Wright
P. O. Box 3626
Carson City, NV 89702

Don't Lose Touch

Although Greg Hayes and Joan Wright have finished writing their book, they haven't stopped gathering information. In order to keep you abreast of the latest additions to the travel guide field, they have created *Going Places: The Guide to Travel Guides* newsletter: a newsletter devoted solely to travel guidebooks.

Your first issue of the newsletter is *free*. To receive your copy please write to:

> The Harvard Common Press
> 535 Albany Street
> Boston, Massachusetts 02118

Also . . .

The Harvard Common Press publishes a variety of travel guides, including the Best Places to Stay series. If you would like a copy of our complete catalogue, please write to us at the above address.